Towards Competition in Network Industries

Telecommunications, Energy and Transportation in Europe and Russia

Springer
Berlin
Heidelberg
New York
Barcelona
Hong Kong
London
Milan
Paris
Singapore
Tokyo

Further Publications by *Paul J. J. Welfens*

P. J. J. Welfens
Market-oriented Systemic Transformations in Eastern Europe
Problems, Theoretical Issues, and Policy Options
1992. XII, 261 pp. 20 figs., 29 tabs., Hardcover, ISBN 3-540-55793-8

M. W. Klein, P. J. J. Welfens
Multinationals in the New Europe and Global Trade
1992. XV, 281 pp. 24 figs., 75 tabs., Hardcover, ISBN 3-540-54634-0

R. Tilly, P. J. J. Welfens
European Economic Integration as a Challenge to Industry and Government
Contemporary and Historical Perspectives on International Economic Dynamics
1996. X, 558 pp. 43 figs., Hardcover, ISBN 3-540-60431-6

P. J. J. Welfens
European Monetary Integration
EMS Developments and International Post-Maastricht Perspectives
3rd revised and enlarged edition
1996. XVIII, 384 pp. 14 figs., 26 tabs., Hardcover, ISBN 3-540-60260-7

P. J. J. Welfens
European Monetary Union
Transition, International Impact and Policy Options
1997. X, 467 pp. 50 figs., 31 tabs., Hardcover, ISBN 3-540-63309-7

P. J. J. Welfens, G. Yarrow
Telecommunications and Energy in Systemic Transformation
International Dynamics, Deregulation and Adjustment in Network Industries
1997. XII, 501 pp. 39 figs., Hardcover, ISBN 3-540-61586-5

P. J. J. Welfens, H. C. Wolf
Banking, International Capital Flows and Growth in Europe
Financial Markets, Savings and Monetary Integration in a World with Uncertain Convergence
1997. XIV, 458 pp. 22 figs., 63 tabs., Hardcover, ISBN 3-540-63192-5

P. J. J. Welfens
Economic Aspects of German Unification
Expectations, Transition Dynamics and International Perspectives
2nd revised and enlarged edition
1996. XV, 527 pp. 34 figs., 110 tabs., Hardcover, ISBN 3-540-60261-5

P. J. J. Welfens, D. Audretsch, J. T. Addison and H. Grupp
Technological Competition, Employment and Innovation Policies in OECD Countries
1998. VI, 231 pp. 16 figs., 20 tabs., Hardcover, ISBN 3-540-63439-8

J. T. Addison, P. J. J. Welfens
Labor Markets and Social Security
Wage Costs, Social Security Financing and Labor Market Reforms in Europe
1998. IX, 404 pp. 39 figs., 40 tabs., Hardcover, ISBN 3-540-63784-2

P. J. J. Welfens
EU Eastern Enlargement and the Russian Transformation Crisis
1999. X, 151 pp. 12 figs., 25 tabs., Hardcover, ISBN 3-540-65862-9

P. J. J. Welfens
Globalization of the Economy, Unemployment and Innovation
1999. VI, 255 pp. 11 figs., 31 tabs., Hardcover, ISBN 3-540-65250-7

P. J. J. Welfens, G. Yarrow, R. Grinberg, C. Graack
Towards Competition in Network Industries
Telecommunications, Energy and Transportation in Europe and Russia
1999. XXII, 570 pp. 63 figs., 63 tabs., Hardcover, ISBN 3-540-65859-9

P. J. J. Welfens, J. T. Addison, D. B. Audretsch, T. Gries, H. Grupp
Globalization, Economic Growth and Innovation Dynamics
1999. X, 160 pp. 15 figs., 15 tabs., Hardcover, ISBN 3-540-65858-0

Paul J. J. Welfens · George Yarrow
Ruslan Grinberg · Cornelius Graack
Editors

Towards Competition in Network Industries

Telecommunications, Energy and Transportation in Europe and Russia

With 63 Figures
and 63 Tables

Springer

Prof. Dr. Paul J. J. Welfens
University of Potsdam
European Institute for International Economic Relations
August-Bebel-Str. 89
14482 Potsdam
Germany
http://www.euroeiiw.de

Prof. George Yarrow
Oxford University
Regulatory Policy Research Centre
Hertford College
Oxford OX 13 BW
Great Britain

Prof. Dr. Ruslan Grinberg
Russian Academy of Sciences
Institute for International Economic & Political Studies
Novocheryomushkinskaya 46
117418 Moscow
Russia

Dipl.-Vw. Cornelius Graack
University of Potsdam
European Institute for International Economic Relations
August-Bebel-Str. 89
14482 Potsdam
Germany

ISBN 3-540-65859-9 Springer-Verlag Berlin Heidelberg New York

Library of Congress Cataloging-in-Publication Data
Die Deutsche Bibliothek – CIP-Einheitsaufnahme
Towards competition in network industries: telecommunications, energy and transportation in Europe and Russia: with 63 tables / Paul J. J. Welfens, Cornelius Graack, Ruslan Grinberg, George Yarrow (eds). – Berlin; Heidelberg; New York; Barcelona; Hong Kong; London; Milan; Paris; Singapore; Tokyo: Springer, 1999
ISBN 3-540-65859-9

Printed in Germany

Hardcover-Design: Erich Kirchner, Heidelberg

SPIN 10724753 43/2202-5 4 3 2 1 0 – Printed on acid-free paper

TABLE OF CONTENT

II. Liberalizing the Energy Sector

III. Changes in the Transportation Sector

LIST OF FIGURES

Contribution A

Contribution C

Contribution D

Contribution H

Contribution I

Contribution M

Contribution O

Contribution P

Contribution Q

Contribution T

Contribution U

LIST OF TABLES

Contribution A

Contribution C

Contribution F

Contribution G

Contribution H

Contribution I

Contribution J

Contribution K

Contribution M

Contribution N

Contribution O

Contribution P

Contribution T

Contribution U

Introduction

The dynamic telecommunications sector has dominated the liberalization of network industries during the 1990s. This dominance of telecoms is not only because telecoms is an important sector in its own right, but also because newcomers from the energy sector and the railway systems intend to enter and - have already done so - the strongly growing telecommunications markets. This, however, is only one of the links between the three sectors.

Network industries such as telecommunications, energy and transportation make up the core of a market economy´s infrastructure and have some special characteristics such as high capital intensity, declining marginal costs – over some output range – and in the network expansion stage so-called network externalities. The latter means that the marginal utility of the first groups of users will be raised by other users with whom communication or joint production can be set up more easily than with few users. This quasi-externality on the demand side has long been neglected while it should have been emphasized in industries in which a natural monopoly problem exists only as long as demand is not growing sufficiently rapidly – so that at some point marginal costs start increasing and the potential problem of ruinous competition becomes irrelevant. This is not to deny that natural monopoly problems could constitute an important problem for economic policy. From a dynamic perspective the natural monopoly problem can and has been affected by technological change: for example modern mobile telephony is less characterized by declining marginal costs than fixed-line networks. Another example is digitization which reinforces substitution competition – at least with respect to basic services - between satellite transmission, cable TV transmission (broadband), fixed line networks and mobile telecommunications networks. Technology could also reduce competition intensity, namely in those cases where higher sunk costs (R&D expenditures, marketing expenses, certain investment costs) are incurred under the modern technology than under the traditional one.

Modern network industries in EU countries and post-socialist ex-CMEA countries are important for economic growth and for international integration, both in the field of trade and in foreign direct investment. The European Commission has given strong impulses for liberalizing both the telecommunications and the energy sector at the turn of the century, while the developments in railway transportation – and in transports in general – were more hesitant.

A major pitfall for regulators of natural monopolies has been the tendency to allow a state-owned or private monopoly with declining marginal costs to expand into areas with increasing marginal costs under the cover of "monopoly enlargement". For example, directory assistance in telecommunications has constant or increasing marginal costs and thus should be provided under a fully competitive regime. In the energy sector high sunk costs and falling marginal transmission costs mean that the electricity grid should be considered to be a natural monopoly, but there is no reason to exempt electricity generation from competition – especially if different groups of users require add-on services (e.g. benchmarking data on electricity consumption of all firms of a nationwide chain of hotels or restaurants). The railway network poses a natural monopoly problem plus high sunk costs, but the transportation business itself can be organized as a competitive private franchise. An integrated monopoly will be rather inefficient and non-innovative. Furthermore, it can become ever more dependent on growing government subsidies (e.g. Italy) which initially were meant to cover the difference between average costs and marginal cost pricing but in the long term encourage general inefficiency and squandering of resources.

A natural monopoly must be regulated by government authorities, especially if the government wishes to impose universal services. However, sector-specific regulation imply various regulation problems which create social costs. There is a massive conflict of interest if the natural monopoly is a state-owned firm since the government then plays both the role of a regulator and of an entrepreneur and lacks the discipline provided by the capital market. This was the exact problem encountered in most EU countries and in transforming Russia. In Russia there also exist, of course, specific problems related to systemic transformation at where the first attempt at transformation has largely failed for various reasons. Failure to restructure and privatize the energy sector played a role in this failure, and it is indeed noteworthy that government revenues from privatizating the energy sector amounted to some $ 80 bill. in the UK while the Russian government collected less then 5 bill. from the privatization of the Russian energy sector. As regards the Russain transformation crisis the interested reader is referred to the analysis under http://www.euroeiiw.de

The papers presented in this book grew out of an TACIS-ACE project – with major research results published in Russian in 1998 – and deal with both theoretical analysis and policy problems. **Paul J.J. Welfens**' contribution discusses the basic theoretical problems of network industries and emphasizes that benefits from privatization will be very limited if it is not combined with competition. Foreign direct investment (FDI) in network industries plays an increasing role in the long run as privatization and the profit motive of private investors drive firms, which (under the new competitive regime) face declining market shares at home, to conquer foreign markets by producing abroad. While two-way foreign direct investment in OECD countries after 1945 has become a standard element of international integration (except in the case of Japan characterized by a very low stock of inward foreign direct investment) foreign direct investment inflows in eastern Europe and Russia are of a more recent date. As regards Russia one cannot overlook the enormous lack of foreign direct investment inflows. In Hungary, Poland and the Czech Republic FDI it has played a gradually increasing role and has been indispensible both for raising the investment-output ratio – after the strong fall in early transformation – and for stimulating the restructuring of industry. The Russian privatization and foreign investment policies were largely a disaster, most obviously in the telecoms sector. Massive foreign investment is urgently needed as a catalyst for restructuring, while privatization from above (concerning existing firms) and from below (the creation of new firms) should have been organized in a different way than that actually chosen by governments which were reluctant to explain the goals, strategic approaches and expected medium term results of economic policies. **Pieter H.M. Ruys** offers his comments to this critical evaluation.

Piotr Jasinski analyzes privatization, competition and regulation in transforming economies with respect to electricity and telecommunications. While the transition problems are considered to be complex there also exist basic rules of wisdom that should be observed in the interest of an efficient allocation of resources. Restructuring must come before privatization – a rule often violated in eastern Europe and Russia where short-term interest in high privatization proceeds are emphasized by a political system which is less interested in the long term growth bonus of restructing cum competition. **Horst Brezinski** in his comments emphasizes some political economy aspects of the transformation process.

The focus of **Cornelius Graack** is on the European telecommunication market which in almost all EU countries has witnessed privatization and which has seen the official introduction of competition at a European level in 1998. Incumbent operators have, of course, anticipated the critical liberalization date which was facilitated by early liberalization in the UK. Within a few years the fixed network segment have started to internationalize and thus are following the international strategies of mobile networks. However, alliances formed by incumbent operators turned out to be rarely stable and there are prospects for more comprehensive merger and acquisition strategies. There is no doubt that liberalization and privatization are to the benefit both of the business community and of residential users. Valuable comments on this paper are beeing presented by **Dieter Elixmann**.

Martin Andersson gives a fascinating account of the Finnish developments, namely full competition in telecommunications. The analysis clearly shows that competiton has brought about enormous benefits which range from falling long-distance and international prices to positive impulses for the mobile telecommunications segment – including the hardware components.

Jacqueline Spindler´s paper gives an overview of the US situation which also is one of full competition. Her focus is both on international liberalization along WTO lines and on US implementation of the new Telecom Act. Interconnection, universal service and access reform are the key areas for regulation.

Günter Knieps analyzes the problem of market entry in the presence of a dominant telecoms operator. He points to oversized regulation and the necessity of a symmetric regulatory approach. An important distinction needs to be made between contestability and monopolistic bottlenecks. Finally, the analysis deals with interconnection problems and some issues of universal service. The arguments show that a refined approach to network competition in telecommunications is highly relevant. **Jürgen Müller**´s comments emphasize various practical problems of efficient regulation and raises doubts that such a regulation can easily be established.

Morten Falch analyzes some important newcomers in the telecommunications business, namely firms from the electricity sector and the railway networks. In his perspective the cost structure of telecommunications is important in assessing the opportunities for newcomers in terms of market entry. Moreover, investment costs and changing demand conditions are also important. In the long term newcomers could play a crucial role for competition in telecommunications. **Oliver Lorz** offers his comments on these new perspectives.

Jerzy Kubasik deals with liberalization of telecommunications in central Europe. Deregulation and liberalization were difficult and time-consuming challenges in Poland where the government issued various local and regional licences for considerably high fees.

The role of telecommunications in Russia is an important subject but, as **Svetlana Petuhova** and **Alexander Vronetz** emphasize, the issues of regulation, foreign investment and competition are rather unsettled in post-socialist Russia. **Wolfgang Pfaffenberger** offers his critical comments on this topic.

Ruslan Grinberg analyzes the Russian economic reforms and the role of foreign direct investment. His assessment shows that there was considerable progress in stabilization – prior to the August 1998 crisis – and that the government had started to nurture foreign direct investment inflows. Given more than seven decades of development without multinational companies it is not surprising that Russia´s policy towards foreign investors is not very consistent. **Herbert Brücker** gives his comments, taking into account the special situation of Russia and the CIS, respectively.

In her paper on the Russian internet **Svetlana Petuhova** shows that the internet is developing rather slowly in Russia but that the development has accelerated in the context of FDI inflows. The internet could be quite important not only for economic opening up of the Russian economy but also as a platform for discussions about the transition process.

The panel discussion on competition in telecommunications and market perspectives in the information society highlighted two key topics: **Dimitri Ypsilanti**´s focus is on the role of competition forces in Europe where EU countries are catching-up with US developments – not least due to the 1998 liberalization date set by the European Commission. **Bert Eichhorn**´s analysis is on copyrights and related rights in the information society, i.e. crucial legal issues for promoting ecommerce and other modern telecommunication services. With so many new technologies and innovations there are many unsettled legal issues which could impair investment in networks and service activities.

A second big topic of liberalization in network industries is the energy sector for which the European Commission has initiated gradual liberalization**. Alison Sinclair**´s analysis is on the electricity supply industry and the links between competition and investment decisions. Her emphasis is on issues of vertical integration, namely both from the perspective of the firm and from the economy as a whole. It is shown that policymakers are not facing easy choices and that restructuring the electricity sector in an efficient way could be difficult to achieve. **Peter Palinkas** offers his critical comments on this topic.

Zdenek Hruby´s analysis is on the electricity sector in CEE transition countries. His contribution takes a view at several countries and identifies problems on both the supply and the demand side in the transition stage. Post-socialist countries show different concepts of privatization policies in this sector on the one hand, while on the other hand the long term capacity adjustments required differ between countries.

Vladimir Voloshin discusses the Russian electricity industry's difficult move towards the market. The structure of the electricity sector is changing only gradually, and the degree of internationalization remains low. While the government apparently is willing to learn from foreign experiences, vested interests in the political system – both at the regional and the national level – render efficient restructuring and privatization as well as opening up for foreign direct investment cumbersome. **Misha Belkinda**´s reflections give some additional insights into major problems of infrastructure modernization in Russia.

José Carbajo and **Steven Fries** give a broad overview of the problems of restructuring infrastructure in transition economies. There indeed are specific problems of transformation with respect to telecommunications, electricity and transportation. Tariff reform – i.e. rebalancing of tariffs – is a crucial element of a rational policy approach which aims at raising productivity and growth. To achieve competition with adequate regulation is a long term strategic challenge in all post-socialist countries. Adequate infrastructure modernization and regulation of infrastructure services will be crucial not only from an east European perspective, it also is important from an EU perspective in the context of an EU eastern enlargement. **Paul J.J. Welfens** in his comments emphasizes that combining privatization and competition is important for efficiency gains in infrastructure services.

Georg Erdmann´s focus is on the interesting post-socialist restructuring of the energy sector in East Germany. He points out that the organizational and property rights changes were comprehensive but that the political pressure to achieve rapid restructuring has impaired prospects for strong competition.

Transportation is the third topic in this book which, however, can cover only selected aspects. The most interesting sector in the medium term is the railways system in Europe, where bold reforms with respect to privatization and dismemberment in the UK stand for a pioneering approach in revitalizing private railway transportation – in the 19th century a key source for positive growth impulses and more spatial competition in increasingly overlapping regional markets. After nationalization in the late 19th century (mainly for military reasons) and the first half of the 20th century the railways system has continuously lost market shares in both freight and passenger transport. Government played both the role of a regulator and of an owner – the benefits of contracts in functional markets were not really exploited in such a framework; cross-border railway freight transportation was particularly slow to adjust to new customer needs in the EU. Moreover, most government owned railway systems in Europe are loss-makers and they are slow to respond to changing customer needs and to launch differentiated and innovative services. Only the recent arrival of high speed trains has stimulated some revival of the railways business. An intiative of the European Commission to open up the EU rail network to fast freight services – to establish trans-European rail freight freeways - failed in late 1998 as individual rail administrations refused to cooperate. The French government and the SNCF are rather unwilling to open up national rail networks to freight operators. Germany and the Deutsche Bundesbahn AG have used high access charges to slow down competition. Between 1970 and 1994 the railway industry lost about 50% of its market share in the EU, the share falling to 16% in 1994. The average speed in international freight transportation is extremely low, namely about 15 km per hour, and British initiatives to set up a fast route between London and Hungary foundered because some railways on the route were refusing to provide prices, were unwilling to hand over responsibility for hiring out their track and wanted excessive charges combined with much bureaucratic documentation. This is another example for how national companies undermine international integration and European-wide prosperity. This creates negative external effects both by indirectly stimulating rising cross-border truck traffic with its high emissions and by undermining EU integration. Moreover, all this points to the benefit of privatization to the extent that it creates an international network of shareholders: International listing on the stock market and adequate regulation can stimulate the management to become more cooperative and innovative – all to the benefit of the capital owners, the users and the taxpayers. The government can still influence the sector by regulation and subsidies for the provision of certain services (at lowest costs within an auction model).

George Yarrow gives an in-depth analysis of the regulation of privatised railways in Britain. His contribution develops a clear picture of the regulatory structure and the problems associated with the interaction between the companies in the restructured industry. Contract management becomes a field of key importance for all companies. While it is too early to evaluate the success of British railway reform the British example can serve as an inspiring role model.

Russia´s railway system needs modernization and commercialization in a broad sense. **Lev Resnikov** describes major problems and recent developments in the Russian railways system. It seems that economic policy has difficulties in adopting an adequate modernization approach.

Andreas Brenck describes the reforms of the German railway system which consisted of several stages, including some regionalization in passenger transportation. As regards improving opportunities for exploiting the rail network intramodel, competition plays a key role but is difficult to introduce as access regulation rarely follows basic economic principles. The revival of the railway systems could be short-lived in Germany (and other EU countries) if efficient regulation cannot be introduced and if ongoing politization of the railway business undermines differentiated tariff schemes and flexible responses to user needs.

A rather different topic is analyzed by **Hartmut Stiller** whose focus is on direct and indirect environmental effects of various modes of transportation: the different material intensities of alternatives mode of transportation have crucial implications for sustainable mobility in Europe. From his results one may draw some conclusions in favor of expanding some forms of waterway transportation on the one hand, while on the other hand rational infrastructure policies should include aspects of material flows during the construction and the operation of new facilities and should also include pricing policies that encourage the optimal use of existing infrastructure. **Rainer Hillebrand**´s comments emphasize that it is necessary to focus on pricing and value-added aspect in addition to physical units of input, material flows and output.

Daniel Höltgen discusses perspectives for European transport networks. Trans-European Networks have been emphasized by the European Commission for years as a vital element of EU infrastructure and growth policies. However, cooperation within a multimodal approach seems to be rather difficult. Claus-Friedrich Laaser offers his comments and argues that efficient solutions are not easily achieved at the supranational level.

The final panel discussion is on selected financing aspects of transportation and electricity networks in Europe and Russia. The views from industry, investment banking and economics are not always convergent as the arguments of **Christoph Schalast**, **Matthias Rußwurm** and **Claus-Friedrich Laaser** show. As regards Europe market-based financing – sometimes with support from the EIB – there are no major problems in financing even very large investment projects, although the experience of the Channel financing was not quite encouraging in the medium run. The situation in Russia is very different since the country has lost access to private capital flows in late 1998 – a problem which could not be anticipated by the panelists. It seems that the Russian government is ill-advised as it failed to understand which harsh consequences the unilateral debt moratorium on the GKO bonds would have, and it could easily have been avoided if the government had sought early talks with Western creditors. Certain superpower attitudes might also impair the willingness of the government to learn and accept basic rules in international transactions. For example, the sale of 2.5% of Gazprom in late 1998 to Ruhrgas AG took place in New York under conditions of transfer uncertainty which never occur in normal international aquisitions. This points, of course, also to the failure of international financial organizations – with a big role in Russian transformation – to implement adequate technical assistence and to convey the basic rules of market economy grammar.

We gratefully acknowledge funding from the European Commission (TACIS ACE Programme 1994) whose focus mainly was on Russia. We are also grateful to the Volkswagen Stiftung for financing the EIIW′s annual 1996 conference during which some of the papers included in this volume were presented in an early draft. Alisan Sinclair deserves high praise for helping with the editing process, Ralf Wiegert and Niels Theis were responsible for the technical preparation of the manuscript. We very much hope that this collection of papers provides useful information about the developments and policy debates while stimulating novel theoretical analysis of network industries which are so crucial for economic growth and international integration in Europe.

Potsdam, December 1998
Paul J. J. Welfens, Coordinator of TACIS project

I. Deregulation and Market Dynamics in Telecommunications

A: Competition, Privatization and Foreign Direct Investment in Network Industries

Paul J.J. Welfens

1. Introduction

Liberalization of network industries, i.e. telecommunications, electricity, railways and air transportation, is making rapid progress in western Europe in the 1990s due mainly to initiatives of the European Commission and the European Court of Justice - in the case of the latter these initiatives have been mainly in the field of transportation policy. In the very different context of systemic transformation, network industries are also being liberalized in eastern Europe and Russia where increasing demand for modern infrastructure puts strains on government budgets. In a European East-West comparison Eastern Europe and Russia suffer from lack of modern infrastructure capable of accomodating the high transportation and telecommunications needs of capitalist growth. At the same time energy intensities in former socialist CMEA countries are much higher than in OECD countries (see appendix).

Major dynamic efficiency gains can be expected from competition and privatization in telecommunications which provides crucial inputs to all sectors but will generate growth momentum in its own right – mainly via the growth of the internet and electronic commerce. It will generate worldwide sales of $45 bill. in 1998 up from $0 in 1993 and $13 bill. in 1997 (ITO, 1997). Economic globalization is strongly linked to economic growth of the internet and global networks.

As modernization of infrastructure is very costly there could be a tendency for myopic governments to provide insufficient infrastructure services. Private organizers of infrastructure provision, however, have in many cases adequate incentives to provide infrastructure in an efficient way. This assumes appropriate regulation which does not impair potential market entry, optimal use of capacity by time-varying user charges, and that there are no major external costs and benefits of the services derived from infrastructure, which certainly is a bold assumption.

Important external effects of infrastructure concern environmental costs. Construction is rather resource intensive, while the use of infrastructure in some cases (e.g. telematics) is environmentally friendly and in others (long-haul transportation, traditional energy generation) polluting and resource-intensive. Bottleneck problems in infrastructure use always imply environmental costs. Congestion costs are crucial for determining optimal investment. Infrastructure networks have some specific characteristics:

1. Networks provide essential services which are used by all sectors, raising the marginal product of capital and labor. To the extent that they are provided for free firms using infrastructure services will record higher profits and tend to invest more than otherwise. With higher local investment government expenditures on infrastructure can be financed from higher future tax receipts based on rising output. However, globalization of industry renders this tax calculus of governments uncertain since mobile investors could use free infrastructure to mainly promote business expansion abroad.
2. Networks cover large areas and allow an extensive allocation across space which is crucial for economic welfare, international competitiveness, spatial trade structures and regional economic prosperity clusters as can be derived from the gravity trade model and the new growth theory, respectively. Benefits of various networks are highest if networks can be interconnected in a seamless way without bottlenecks.
3. Demand for infrastructure strongly varies over time (24 hour cycle, 365 day cycle), implying different opportunity costs for users with different time slots. Differentiated prices and independent network control sytems are potential means for exploiting capacity optimally over time.
4. Infrastructure services were often considered to be of strategic importance so that government either tried to establish state ownership or ensure via adequate regulation that an optimal infrastructure would be provided. Market entry on the user side was restricted in most cases.
5. Infrastructure networks are largely financed and operated by government or by state-owned monopolies or regional private monopolies in Europe. This often made them subject to strong political interference. Only partial or full privatization in combination with competition can impose the discipline of private capital markets on firms.
6. Infrastructure is capital intensive and often characterized by substantial economies of scale (as in the case of telecommunications) or economies of scope so that competition could be impaired. Declining falling average costs seem to constitute a critical natural monopoly problem. However, as modern theoretical analysis shows there is no competition problem as long as sunk costs are rather low so that potential entrants have a disciplining effect on the incumbent's behavior (contestable market theory). Sunk costs are represented by those specific investments or marketing expenditures which cannot be recovered by the incumbent operator when going out of business, and therefore he will disregard such costs in his pricing strategy if an aggressive newcomer is to be fended off. For the newcomer all costs are reversible prior to market entry. Natural monopolies characterized by falling average costs are not a problem for competition policy if sunk costs are low because this makes the market contestable.

7. Networks consist of integrated elements in space so that local bottleneck problems can impair the functioning of the whole network. If overcoming the bottleneck requires dedicated specific investments there will be market entry problems.

The provision of infrastructure traditionally was heavily regulated by governments in Europe. Moreover, foreign investment in network industries was restricted - only recently some liberalization was introduced in telecommunications where public telecoms operators extended their business beyond the home territory in the 1980s. The OECD (1995, p. 5) noted: *Increasingly, the target market for services is expanding beyond those to whom national telecommunications policy is addressed. In the past, both telecommunication policy and services were addressed to national users. Services are being extended to include both national and foreign users in national and foreign markets. A number of policy issues thus arise. Asymmetry in the level of liberalization between OECD countries adds to the economic impact of PTO globalization. Thus national telecommunications policy has broader cross-border implications than was the case in the past.* Since the main newcomers in fixed line telephony will be from the electricity and railway sector, deregulation and internationalization of telecoms will also affect the energy and transportation sector. Moreover, if liberalization of the telecoms sector is useful and feasible why should not similar developments in other network industries be allowed and politically be encouraged? Indeed the European Commission emphasized that liberalized trans-European networks are crucial for growth and prosperity in western Europe. In eastern Europe and Russia lack of public finance has stimulated the search for new ways of organizing and financing infrastructure services.

Functional infrastructure stimulates spatial growth, and it is also important to attract foreign direct investment and to mobilize domestic investment necessary for growth and employment. With the existence of various regional (national) networks interconnection at the national (international) level is important in Europe and Russia. This relates to the topic of interoperability of network segment which involves a technical interface problem typically defined by open network standards in a pro-competitive network. Another important topic is the integration - the linking - of competing network platforms - e.g. in the field of transportation the linking of airports with railway networks or a railway station with a bus system, or in the case of telephony the linking of satellite, mobile and fixed link networks. Here government intervention is required in order to achieve standards for links or to define gateway technology requirements. European-wide integrated networks are necessary to accommodate the quickly rising traffic within the single market as well as the fast expansion of east-west trade in the new Europe. The logic of the gravity approach to explaining trade patterns suggests that effective reduction of transportation time and costs will stimulate market expansion and economic growth.

Competing private operators of infrastructure could cause harmful doubling of infrastructure investment in the field of railways only, while electricity networks - with third party access - and telecoms are unlikely fields of inefficient overinvestment. Large investments require functional capital markets and clear politically independent regulation, including transitory price cap regulation, so that reasonable price expectations can be formed. If government is both owner and regulator of an industry, inconsistent policies are likely. Investors will require adequate rates of return and stable policy approaches. Countries with favorable ratings, i.e. good access to capital markets, could finance the expansion of infrastructure easily and might rely less on foreign investors than otherwise.

Regulatory authorities could be captured by powerful industry thus being manipulated to act not in favor of consumers but in favor of the dominating firm(s). In transforming economies as well as in some EU countries the strong vertical integration of telephony and of electricity implies that powerful industry interests are lobbying against vertical disintegration. Since regulation is costly for society and for the firms concerned, regulations will play only a limited role in an optimal network policy. The main means of controlling powerful firms is competition - the example of IBM in the 1980s showed that even the biggest company in a given sector does not enjoy serious long-term market power as long as market entry is open. If firms A, B, C check other firms a, b and c in a dynamic competitive process so that best-practice technologies diffuse and innovations are stimulated, government can rely on very limited sector-specific regulation or on general competition laws. This is generally a useful approach since natural information asymmetry - concerning costs and technologies - between the regulator and the regulatee implies that the regulatory authority will face serious problems to efficiently control the regulated firm. Finally, it is clear that all regulatory changes affecting the network will indirectly affect the business prospects of related hardware (upstream) and services (downstream) industries. Regulatory authorities certainly should maintain competition, not impair it – e.g. by allowing the dominant telecoms operator to link with alternative network platforms such as railway networks or cable TV firms.

The paper is divided into three sections. In Chapter 2 theoretical aspects of network theory, technological progress and network competition are discussed. This section is followed by a basic analysis of competition and privatization in the three network industries: Telecommunications, Energy and Transportation (Chapter 3). Finally, Chapter 4 deals with foreign direct investment in network industries.

2. Network Theory, Technological Progress and Competition

Infrastructure is important in economic terms for five reasons:

1. positive income and employment effects as the infrastructure is built;
2. increase in the economy's overall fixed capital stock raising the productivity of complementary factors and potential output;
3. the provision of services which are crucial inputs for many sectors;
4. indirect pro-competitive effects as infrastructure expansion increases the size of markets, provided that there is no recurrent congestion;
5. the provision of services by competing service providers requiring control systems necessary for optimal hazard-free capacity utilization - control systems can be organized by the government as in the case of police services in road traffic, by private monopolist as in the case of air transportation or by vertical integration as in telecoms, electricity and railway systems.

Modernizing network industries is necessary to cope with rising trade and traffic in the new Europe and a globalizing economy and hence is crucial for economic prosperity. Since many traditional arguments for exclusive government provision of infrastructure seem no longer valid and as tight government budget constraints in almost all industrialized countries are stimulating the search for new ways to organize network industries, private sector activities have become more important. Competition in network industries can take various forms, ranging from regulated monopoly to competition for the market (network), competition in the net (separation of network and competitive services), and finally full competition of integrated networks (Fig. A1).

Network operation, control and services - emphasized as three distinct layers of infrastructure by KNIEPS (1996) and illustrated in Fig. A2 - can in principle be vertically separated although national monopoly operators tended to organize these activities jointly. Since network industries are highly capital intensive there is a natural interest of the network owner to ensure profitability of investment and provision of profitable services by vertical integration. But this often impairs market access.

Infrastructure networks often are integrated systems which offer commercial services across space. Typically, one may assume some basic public interest in the general availability of such services. This is the universal service problem which implies a basic cross-subsidization problem or an explicit deficit-financing problem. Regulations are imposed that are designed to ensure appropriate public service. However, the positive theory of economic regulation (VON WEIZSÄCKER, 1982; KNIEPS, 1988) argues that the regulatee has an incentive to create a monopoly position and to engage in rent-seeking activities, i.e. lobbying-activities, financed from monopoly profits and designed to maintain the monopoly by comfortable and market-entry impairing regulations. This raises the problem that regulatory institutions should be both independent from industry and the political system.

Another problem concerns market power derived from exclusive control over essential facilities associated with high sunk costs, allowing the incumbent to fend off newcomers with strategic pricing. Problems for newcomers also exist if service quality is impaired by feasible bypass options. A convenient way for preventing market entry is "vicious vertical integration", namely to combine infrastructure operation with an exclusive control system that typically represents high sunk costs and a natural monopoly. Independent integrated European railway and telecommunications control firms - each covering several countries, thus exploiting scale economies - could stimulate competition in both sectors. To illustrate the point simply imagine that in each European country airline traffic control were vertically integrated with the nationally dominant airline. The number of effectively competing airlines at given time intervals would drastically reduce in the long run. This points to the importance of the long-run neglected problems of vertical integration in infrastructure.

Fig. A1: Competition in Network Industries

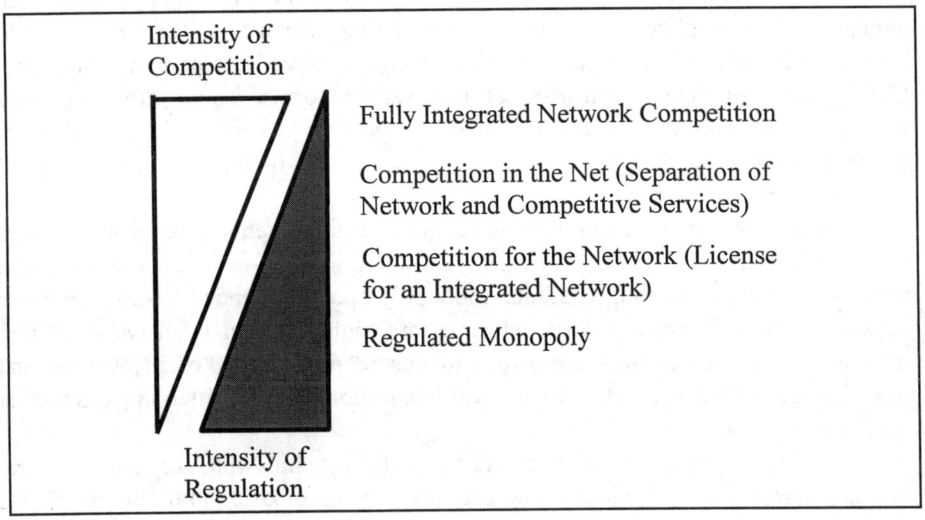

Source: WELFENS/GRAACK (1995).

Network Aspects

Network theory of infrastructure has emphasized mainly two points which complicate the achievement of efficient allocation via the market: (i) positive network externalities on the demand side; and, discussed here at first (ii) capital intensive infrastructure networks which often exhibit economies of scale; thus falling average costs were characteristic implying both a deficit problem at the socially optimal quantity (Fig. A7, appendix) and a problem of ruinuous competition. Government ownership and national or regional monopoly with regulation was the institutional answer to this problem (except for telephony in some countries where individual rental rates combined with capacity pricing avoided the deficit problem - via a two part tariff). This, however, meant to ignore problems identified by public choice, namely the self-interest of bureaucrats in government in the overmanning of public firms and in impairing market access for newcomers. Moreover, the principal agent problem typical for the private firms clearly was even more difficult for state-owned firms where the ultimate owner is the dissipated group of poorly informed taxpayers. The political voting mechanism can be no effective substitute for a functional capital market. Moreover, national ownership reduces options for the internationalization of telecommunications which is a relatively R&D intensive sector and therefore is a candidate for foreign direct investment (as markets for technology are very imperfect).

Fig. A2: Layers of Infrastructure Business Relevant for Competition

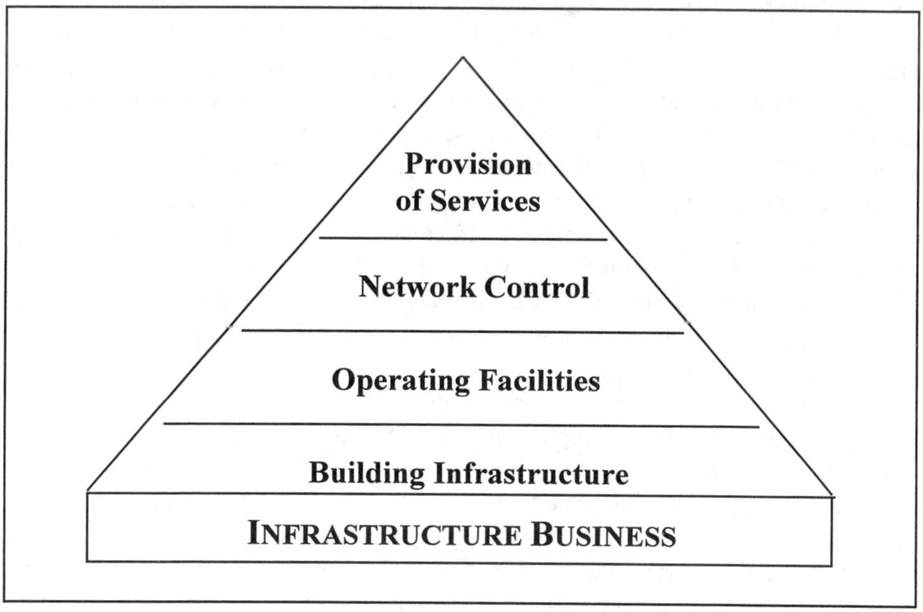

From a theoretical point of view falling costs are no justification for a regulated monopoly. A regulated monopoly for activity A is only appropriate if there are high sunk costs in this activity, e.g. as in the case of the local fixed network or for the rail track in the case of railway companies, and - this may be emphasized additionally - if there are no "superior" by-pass technologies for the respective activity available by newcomers. High sunk costs in combination with falling average costs create the problem of an uncontestable market in infrastructure. Facing potential market entry the incumbant dominant operator could disregard all sunk costs which cannot be recovered when going out of business. Therefore in a strategic pricing battle high sunk costs could lead to a limit pricing strategy which fends off newcomers that are more efficient than the incumbant operator. If the A-firm bundles A-activities with other activities, say B and C, it becomes an integrated monopoly assuming it achieves regulation preventing market entry in the respective activities. In addition to A, activities B and C become monopolized. In historical perspective this problem was worst in telecommunications, where only network operation represents high sunk costs (powerful mobile telephony was not available before the early 1980s).

Sunk costs can not only occur in hardware investment but also in the know-how of its users so that an inferior technological trajectory actually becomes an optimal one as so many users invested in complementary skills (DAVID and BUNN, 1988; BENTAL and SPIEGEL, 1995). Similarly a suboptimal institutional setting could be optimal if path-dependency is ruling in the sense that many firms and individuals invested with high sunk costs into complementary “assets”.

A second aspect concerns positive network externalities which means that with a rising number of network users the marginal utility of network use is increasing; as more and more interesting business or communication partners are connected to the network the number of useful connections is increasing so that the marginal willingness to pay will increase (WELFENS, 1995; see Fig. A8, appendix; HOLLER, 1996); by implication the optimum quantity is much higher than without such network effects - there is a risk of underinvestment. For many isolated network operators it might be difficult to anticipate the respective network effects so that an underdimensioned network will result. By creating a government monopoly it could become easier to anticipate the net social benefits from positive network externalities on the demand side.

If one supports the monopoly solution it should be clear that, strictly speaking, the externality argument justifies only temporary government intervention, including possibly a monopoly, and then full privatization of the network. Alternatively, government could impose an open network provision (plus requiring interconnection) and subsidize investment of each firm in a way that positive external network effects are internalized within a seamless open network. One may indeed argue that network externalities can be internalized by fiscal instruments as an alternative to monopoly. The monopoly solution is inferior because public choice theory suggests that a state bureaucracy with economic monopoly power has no incentive to give this power away. The effective owner of the monopoly - de facto the party or parties of the political system - extracts a political rent from state monopolies, namely options to manipulate the services and options to get rid of political losers who can join the management of state firms. The politicization of infrastructure service and the lack of pressure from capital markets in the case of state-owned firms explains the tendency for overmanning in such companies. Politicization of infrastructure business also explains the massive subsidies which railways obtain in the EU, most heavily in Italy (EUROPEAN COMISSION, 1998; Tab. A6, appendix). It is unclear whether European high speed trains can optimally be built in Europe without strong reliance on capital markets; more willingness to harmonize technical standards (WHITELEGG/HULTEN/FLINK, 1993) is also needed.

Finally, there is the argument that infrastructure is a collective good so that free-rider strategies, i.e. biased revealing of preferences, will impair optimal provision of infrastructure. This argument is correct as long as technologies for the exclusion of free riders are costly (relative to the service provided which for obvious reasons never was a problem in air transportation). With modern telematics and camera technology there should be no problem to organize nationwide toll roads or at least special toll truck highways. Toll truck highways would allow - based on regulated prices (containing an implicit tax to cover external effects) – internalization of the negative external effects of truck transportation and thus create a more level playing field in intermodal competition in transportation. Public infrastructure investment is rather inefficient because it is subject to election cycles and does not take into account the marginal willingness to pay by users nor their interest in product differentiation. At the end of this section one may note that switching from free road transportation to toll systems has social drawbacks as poor people can no longer substitute waiting time for income anymore (the effective price paid for using transport is the ticket fare plus the opportunity costs of total travelling time), and therefore the switch to a toll road system should either involve compensation for poor families or a reasonable allocation of free tickets for such families.

2.1 Technological Progress and Competition

Sunk costs of established technologies play a considerable role in all network industries. Recently, however, new technologies have reinforced options for competition. In telecommunications bypassing fixed networks in the local loop has been facilitated by new wireless technology and, in principle, by satellite options. In electricity markets there are new options for decentralized solar electricity generation as well as new opportunities to transport electricity over longer distances with low loss rates. In the medium term rising use of renewable energies in general and decentralized solar systems in particular could become a big challenge for traditional power plants relying on oil or coal. Modern combined heat and power plants that rely on gas turbines are likely to remain viable alternatives to decentralized electricity generation over a long period because gas is both relatively cheap and environmentally friendly due to low emissions.

Vertical integration plays a role in the telecommunications, railways and energy sectors which are rather capital intensive and require high sunk costs in network construction. Vertical integration as well as product differentiation raises, of course, the problem of cross-subsidization. It is doubtful that simple accounting separation - a potential requirement by the industry regulator - is sufficient to avoid cross-subsidizations and the inefficiencies associated with such practices.

2.2 Problems of Standardization and Interconnection

With different operators of infrastructure in Europe (including the former CIS) it is important to ensure technical compatibility so that an open and seamless network can be created. In the area of road transportation there are minor problems probably because the early internationalization of the motor vehicle industry encouraged common road standards. Interconnection problems within the European railway system such as different standards in signaling and voltage are well-known; the incompatibilities reflect the "nationalism propensity" of national monopoly networks, namely to pamper a national equipment industry which had few incentives to care about international network concepts. Modern electronics help to overcome such problems. More difficult are different tracks used in the United Kingdom, continental Europe and Russia. The introduction of high speed levitation trains could establish a new pan-European standard in a niche segment of transportation after 2000. In the 1990s air transportation in Europe has to cope with deregulation as cabotage impediments are lifted. Concentration in the European airline industry as well as more intensive competition is to be expected. This could stimulate a more flexible allocation of landing slots at EU airports as well as more competition in airport airline services. The European air control system is still rather inefficient because of different national air control standards, allowing EU controllers to handle less than a quarter of planes controlled by US counterparts.

With respect to standardization and interconnection the situation is best in telecommunications because there is a functional European standardization institution (ETSI) and because the Commission has encouraged the adoption of GSM in mobile telephony. As regards global communications the International Telecommunications Union worked rather effectively in the past when there was a limited number of actors and a regime of national telecommunications monopolies. But setting international accounting rates was an area in which the ITU found it difficult to follow technological progress and cost reductions. This reinforced international imbalances in international services accounts of the US, Europe and Japan. Since the US - due to low telephone prices caused by competition (and due to relatively high per capita income) - records much more outgoing calls than Europe there is a large US deficit in network operation. With many private operators in most countries after 1998, the ITU and in fact any government body will find it difficult to impose global standards.

The high speed of technological progress and the internationalization of the telecommunications network, service and hardware industry is likely to encourage autonomous setting of standards by industry itself. The international trade implications of standard setting and of intellectual property rights are very important and were, therefore, part of the Uruguay GATT round. The telecommunications negotiation group of the World Trade Organization was expected to reach an agreement in 1997. Electricity and airline dregulation has largely remained a bilateral issue at the international level, except for EU-internal policy initiatives.

With the coming convergence of the computer (chip), software and telecommunications industry the process of standardization is likely to become similar to the computer and software industry. There will be rivalry in industry standard setting but only a small number of competing technical platforms. Antitrust authorities in major industrial countries will have to make sure that the dominance of some standards do not undermine long-term competition in the respective sector. This policy field will be of growing importance in the future.

The main problem of interconnection is pricing in the presence of a dominant network operator. Newcomers in the telecoms business can rely on building their own network facilities in some regions and for some purposes (they will also use leased lines – the only option for pure resellers) but they will also need access to the final customers. As long as wireless-loop technologies and satellite links are rather expensive, the price at which the dominant operator grants access to the final user will be crucial for competition. Here the regulator is most important. Only a politically independent operator can be expected to come up with efficient pricing decisions.

3. Competition and Privatization

Competition in network operation will reinforce competition in the hardware plus software segment and in the network service industry which will attract more business as network operation costs are falling. Privatization can stimulate competition if vertical disintegration is achieved, thus creating contestable markets. One may notice that taxation of retained versus distributed profits will influence the propensity for vertical (and horizontal) integration. A relatively low tax rate for retained earnings will facilitate the attempts by managers to maintain or restore vertical integration.

Privatization of infrastructure is facilitated by allowing the toll-based use of infrastructure, including road pricing and airport slot pricing. In late autumn 1996 a first private infrastructure investment fund was set up in Australia where government allowed toll roads and privatized ports and airports. Private infrastructure financing was rather common in the 19th century, and there is no reason why governments facing tight budgets should not revitalize private financing schemes. Privatization is rarely organized at the political level in a way which is optimal for long-term factor allocation. The main reason for this is conflicitng interests between short-term revenue and adverse employment effects and positive productivity, competition and internationalization effects (Fig. A3), which favorably emerge only in the long term. Long-term productivity gains associated with modernized network industries - leading also to indirect productivity effects in sectors using better infrastructure services - will raise overall real income and hence tax revenues. Privatized network operators aiming to cut costs will intensify international outsourcing and seek to exploit foreign investment opportunities. Hesitant privatization policies are often observed in less strong systemic competition and in the presence of governments being afraid of unemployment problems and of a partial downward wage pressure in newly privatized firms (rivalry of economic systems in combination with locational competition, i.e. the quest for mobile investors, stimulate international political bandwagon effects). The privatization of British Airways is a good example since BA - gaining in competitive strength as a consequence of more competition - made aggressive inroads in the markets of European rivals. This led to falling profits or even losses of state-owned carriers in the EU and stimulated restructuring of such firms and ultimately privatization as government budget deficits stemming from loss-making state-owned firms became unbearable.

3.1 Telecommunications

Competition in telecommunications can be easily established in principle, namely by organizing dismemberment of the incumbant operator and allowing market entry of newcomers. Except for the US case with its judicial verdict on AT&T in 1982 no OECD country was bold enough to split up its dominant telecoms operator. In Germany government did not even decide that the dominant operator was to hive off its cable TV network which (in western Germany) was almost fully owned by Deutsche Telekom AG. Cable TV generally is a potential alternative telecoms network since telecom signals can be piggy-backed into the cable TV transmission network. Satellite TV, cable TV networks and newcomers from the railway and electricity sector all have a partial overlap with the fixed line telecoms network (Fig. A3). Digitization contributes to convergence of former separated markets – e.g. cable TV and fixed line telephony – and allows the introduction of a hole array of new services and the more efficient use of scarce frequencies and network capacity, respectively. As regards line density, digitization of the telecoms network and the use of the internet, there is a large east-west gap in Europe – with Russia being behind the EU (but with good long-term options for catching up once the right political decisions are adopted).

Fig. A3: Strategic Aspects of Privatization

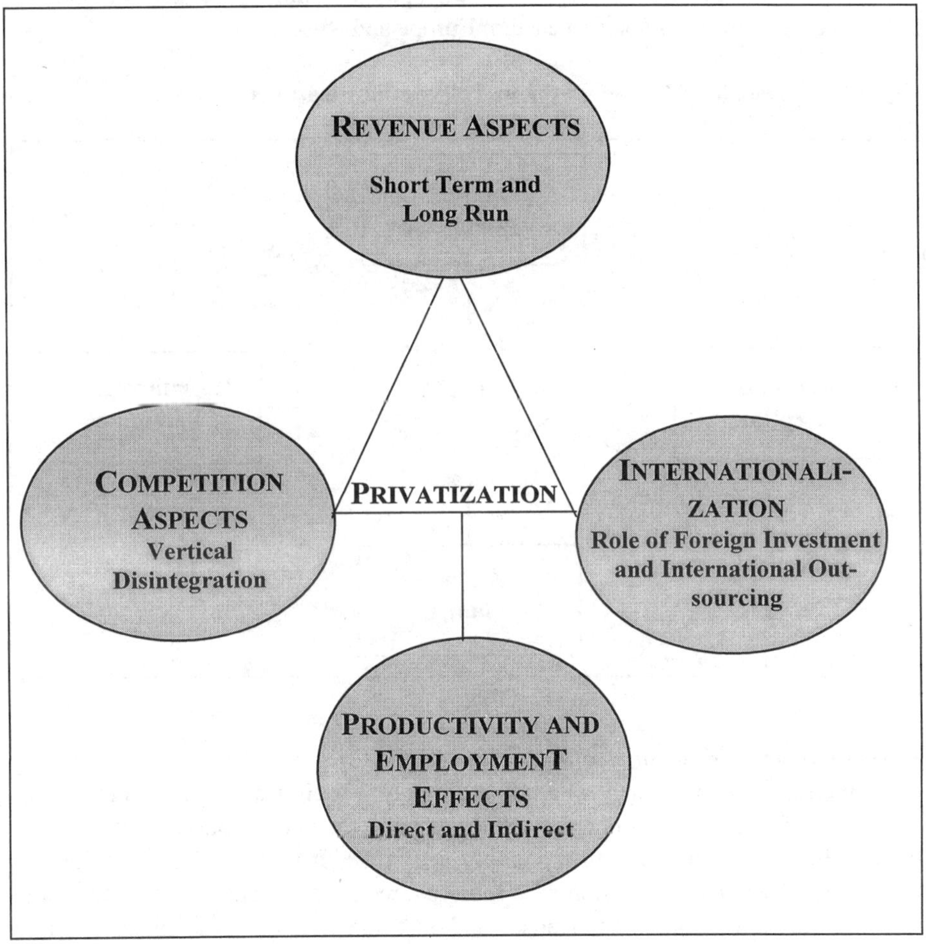

Newcomers in Eastern and Western Europe could not only come from the cable TV business but from electricity companies or railway companies which decide to use - after upgrading and investment - their existing firm internal network for public telephony. Both the railway system and electricity system have the ingredients necessary for successful market entry: an existing customer base; access to capital markets; options for personal recruitment; right of ways; and know-how (Fig. A4). Most difficult for newcomers is securing modern know-how since managing a large public switched network is much more difficult than organizing a firm internal network. However, since overstaffed national operators in western Europe are reducing their staff and since universities constantly generate new engineers and telecom specialists the labor market for newcomers should be rather elastic in the EU. By contrast, the existing excess demand in east European telecoms markets renders massive lay-offs of the incumbant operator unlikely so that newcomers could face recruiting problems in eastern Europe and Russia.

Fig. A4: Basis for Market Entry in Telecommunications

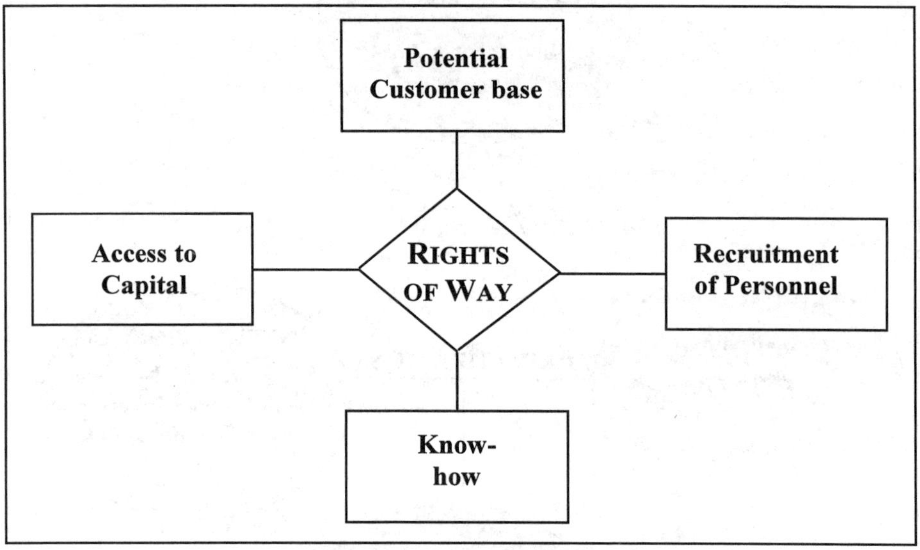

Competition in Telecommunications

Telecommunications is partly a natural monopoly – i.e. it has falling average costs - but this itself is no reason to organize telecoms as a regulated monopoly, where state ownership was combined with monopoly in Europe. It took until 1984 before the Commission developed a vision of a more competitive market, later reinforced by free choice of the telephone handset and liberalization of value-added services; finally, the liberalization date of January 1, 1998 for voice telephony and network operation was adopted (the Commission which had to decide about allowing Spanish Telefonica to join the Unisource consortium, consisting of the Swiss PTT, the Dutch KPN and the Swedish Telia, successfully pressed Spain to forego an extended transition period and match 1998, although only in December). There are various approaches to regulation and privatization in Europe (WELFENS and GRAACK, 1996; WELFENS and YARROW, 1997).

The main historical reason for European telecom monopolies was rather universal service obligation which required allowing the monopoly operator to earn sufficient profits in certain activities so that the political goal of providing telephone services at uniform prices to people in the countryside could be met. It was feared that private companies would give access to telephony for many poor people and for people in the countryside at prohibitive costs or not at all.

Appropriate unbundling of the dominant network operator - namely separation of local network and long distance network - can solve the sunk cost problem in telecommuications in principle; however, mobile network operators using part of fixed line networks as well as long distance operators will all face an interconnection problem which is difficult to solve in the presence of asymmetric partners (big operators vs. small operators). Privatization of national telecoms operators in Western Europe left vertically integrated operators intact, possibly because this is a way for governments to maximize short-term government revenues.

With new wireless bypass technology for the local loop, regulatory authorities might find it appropriate to endorse full network competition and thus to eliminate administrative market demarcations as was done in the US in 1996 (SCHWARTZ, 1996). It is also important that large cable TV networks - facing attacks on its core business from powerful digital satellite technology - stand ready (after some marginal network investments) to enter the local telephony market. Similarly, satellite systems are invaders into cable TV market segments (see Fig A8). Pure resellers which use leased lines are crucial for competition. In 1997/8 there were still large price differences for leased lines within the group of OECD countries.

A newcomer will conquer a market with high sunk costs only if its competitive advantage – e.g. due to innovation - is high enough to overcompensate the sunk costs advantage of the incumbant operator. With every new technology there could be new opportunities for creating competition in the telecommunications market, and therefore regulation should evolve flexibly over time. The only nontechnical regulation problem which will remain in the long term is the extent and financing mode of universal services. An efficient financing scheme would be to give the universal franchise service to the company requiring the lowest subsidy. Price regulation is difficult in the sense that too much pressure on the incumbent operator to lower prices could (i) depress the profitability of the operator so that access to capital markets could be undermined; (ii) denote poor profit prospects which could also undermine newcomer entry.

With a monopoly there is need for regulation which could be a rate of return regulation - known to cause excessive capital spending - or price cap regulation which is incentive-compatible and fostering efficiency: the operator will have to reduce the real price (in growth rates: RPI-X) for a basket of services by a certain percentage point X which is the anticipated rate of technological progress. Regulations can be a means to restrict competition - as was the case in the US in the 1960s and 1970s - or to stimulate the competition process. The latter was the case in the UK in the 1980s when an asymmetric regulatory regime was imposed which gave more freedom to the newcomer MCI than to the dominating BT and, as of 1996, for all other 46 operators which have applied for a telecoms license. The British regulatory regime is politically independent and relies on price caps for some telecom services on the one hand; on the other hand, it makes sure that BT and the newcomers find appropriate interconnection agreements necessary to create seamless networks and to generate a functional mobile telephony system.

Fig. A5: Partial Overlap of Markets Relevant for Telecommunications

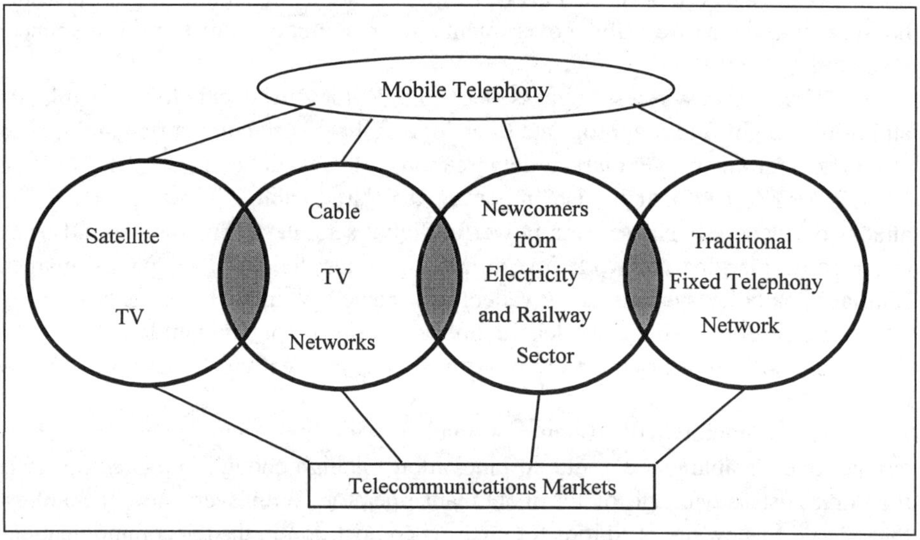

From a theoretical perspective only local telephony networks represent high sunk costs, but this part of the network operation served in Europe as a pretext to organize the whole telecoms network operation and the whole telecoms services as a government monopoly. The first step towards competition in telephony would be to organize a pure network operation company (or several ones) which then sells network capacity to competing telecoms service providers; for technical reasons network management and network operation (and ownership) go together in telecommunications. Vertical integration in network operation beyond this stage is not necessary; it would be efficient only if there were economies of scope.

Moreover, there could indeed be several network operators, including several which purely rely on virtual networks based on leased line capacity which in turn requires allowing resale of leased line capacity; creating a wholesale business in telephony still has to be realized in continental Europe. This would optimize capacity use and thus reduce investment requirements for network capacity which in turn will allow reduced prices for telecommunications services. A major problem occurs, however, if local telephony services are provided for free because this requires that some other activities of an integrated telephone operator have to generate excess profits required for financing internal cross-subsidization of local telephony. Providing free local telephony is a strategic move of integrated telecoms network operators which want to expand into profitable services markets - relying on strong local customer loyality built via the free local phone service.

The US did not adopt an ideal competitive structure in the context of the AT&T antitrust case. But the US was clever enough to split off the local networks from AT&T in 1984, thus creating the so-called baby bell companies. These baby bells became profitable strategic investors in the expanding European mobile telephony business in the early 1990s.

Mobile telephony is, possibly except for advanced DECT concepts, no full alternative to fixed network transmission, especially as regards reliable high quality data transmission which is important for video conferencing and some internet applications. Cable TV networks are a full substitute for all kinds of fixed network telephony, and marginal costs of providing telephony are small as examples from the UK (with many cable TV networks offering telephony), Belgium (Telenet starting trial services in Flanders in 1997) and Australia (newcomer Optus partly relying on a cable TV network) show.

Combined provision of cable TV and telecommunications requires at least accounting separation if markets are not to be distorted massively by cross-subsidization. A similar problem occurs if railway companies and railway networks or electricity companies enter the telecommunications market with an augmented internal communications network which basically means to add fiber optic cables and new computer equipment for network management to the existing internal network. In the EU and the Visegrad countries plus Russia electricity companies certainly will be among the newcomers in the telecommunications markets in the late 1990s.

3.2 Energy

The main interest in this section will be on electricity. However, it is is clear that alternative fuel inputs are affected by changes in the market for electricity. The EU has decided to adopt a gradual liberalization of the electricity sector. Several member countries decided to adopt comprehensive national liberalization as well as privatization. The UK and Scandinavian countries were leading in this field in the early 90s, where the UK and Sweden attracted heavy investment flows into the utility sector.

Privatizing nuclear energy generation is quite difficult as the British example showed. Since operators fear the risks and potential liability claims associated with nuclear power plants, government will always find it difficult to get private investors to acquire nuclear power plants. Insufficient insurance - i.e. liability - coverage typical for most countries amounts to distorting competition in the whole energy sector.

The EU has adopted a gradual liberalization scheme. This scheme foresees (i) the vertical separation of activities in accounting terms, and (ii) the introduction of competition for initially 22.5% of the market, later to be extended to 32%. However, it is left up to the individual member states to choose the method for introducing competition - the choice being between negotiated third party access or the single-buyer model. Furthermore member states still have the option to restrict competition in the name of environmental protection and security of supply. According to pending legislation in Germany exclusive regions for monopoly power producers will no longer hold in the future and third party access will be granted. The very high German electricity prices - compared to other EU countries - are supposed to be reduced as a consequence in the long term.

The Strategic Role of Regulatory Policies

The energy sector has some specific characteristics: it is capital intensive; it is characterized by typical peak-load problems (peak demand at certain intervals); and it is a network industry which means that there are certain technical indivisibilities. In many EU countries government ownership or regulation - i.e. industry-specific competition rules - are means to cope with the specific problems of the energy sector. While private regulated regional monopolies have been and are typical of the US and Germany, many EU countries have relied on state ownership in the energy sector (e.g. the UK until 1990; Italy; Spain; France). Because of falling average costs the energy sector is often considered to be a natural monopoly which does not allow competition or at least will not achieve efficiency via competition. This view favoring a monopoly framework is, if generally applied to the energy sector, seriously flawed. Recently several European countries have successfully launched competition in the electricity sector: Norway, the UK, Sweden and Finland. In 1992 the Finnish state-owned utility IVO separated its production, engineering and transmission into different companies. The Ministry of Trade and Industry emphasizes three challenges for Finland: the need to build new installed capacity; to diversify energy imports; and to open up markets to competition. The liberalization experiences of the UK and Finland are particularly valuable for Eastern Europe.

Similarly the European Commission has launched various initiatives after 1988 to achieve more competition in the energy sector in which national political and economic interests are deeply entrenched and often hostile to more competition. Transforming economies, which all have opportunities to combine privatization with new efficiency-oriented competition rules, can take a fresh look at these issues. Modern economic theory has shown that monopolies can be disciplined by potential competition in cases where there are no sunk costs (case of contestable monopoly), and scientific reasoning argues that unbundling of activities in a way that isolates uncontested natural monopolies is a way to achieve more competition and hence efficiency in a market economy. Specific regulations are necessary only in the case of an uncontestable monopoly. A weak form of disentangling complementary activities, such as generation and distribution of energy, is accounting separation.

Regulations as exemptions from the general competition law are a politico-economic problem in a market economy since the regulatees have an incentive to lobby for rules that protect the industry rather than contribute to competitive efficient outcomes. This is the problem of regulatory capture emphasized by the Chicago school. The sector to be regulated manipulates legislators and authorities in a way which in effect amounts to establishing a privileged protected sector. This problem could be quite relevant in transforming economies which inherited highly concentrated industries capable of launching effective lobbying. At the same time the political systems are not characterized by a strong consensus about the need for competition. The problem of regulatory capture suggests that the regulated area of the energy sector should be kept as small as possible while the regulatory authorities should be transparent, politically independent and accountable to the public.

Regulations should contribute to competition, not impair it. Competition is required for static productive efficiency (producing at minimal costs) and allocative efficiency (equilibrating post-tax marginal products of capital) as well as for dynamic efficiency which is related to the innovativeness of the respective sector. In a competitive market economy only innovation-based divergences between prices and marginal costs are acceptable. Competitive pressure in gas and, above all, in electricity markets will contribute to higher degrees of technological effectiveness in generation and transmission and will save scarce resources for power generation and the network. This is not only part of efficiency improvements but also a contribution to environmental progress. Increasing efficiency in capital intensiveness will reduce environmental damages and resource flows which are causing emissions; a rising capital productivity implies that overall resource flows are reduced. This still leaves open the question of an efficient ecological tax regime.

Regulatory Policies Required for Competition in Electricity

Network industries raise the problem of interconnection and transit. The conditions of interconnection and transit should be non-discriminatory and transparent. In the

EU the entities negotiating a contract must notify the Commission and the national authorities about transition requests (exceeding one year in duration). The Commission and national authorities have to be informed of the conclusion or failure of negotiations. Each negotiating entity may request the European Commission to chair a conciliation body which will also include sectoral representatives. The problems mentioned and the EU procedures used could be useful for Eastern European economies, too. Rather more problematic is the EU approach to third party access (TPA). The Commission favors negotiated TPA - as opposed to full TPA - which would allow electricity producers to sell supplies to large power consumers via negotiated access to their network regarding the transport tariff and other conditions.

The electricity supply industry consists of four main activities: (a) generation; (b) transmission (high voltage grid); (c) distribution; and (d) supply (retail sales). Retail supply means trading, and there is no need for the supplier to be either a transporter of electricity or gas or to be a producer of electricity or gas. Under open access to the transmission and distribution system a supplier may purchase energy from power generators or gas or oil companies, use the transport system of transmission and distribution companies for a fee and sell energy to the final user at the negotiated terms. Efficiency can be established in the energy sector provided that competition is imposed and vertical integration is prohibited.

If the electricity industry is vertically integrated one might consider the industry as a whole as an uncontestable natural monopoly that has to be regulated. However, falling average costs in combination with sunk costs only play a role in the case of the network, i.e. in transmission and distribution. Competition in electricity generation can be organized quickly by privatizing existing generators, removing any existing regional franchise and allowing freedom of establishment for domestic and foreign newcomers. Retail sale (electricity trading) could in principle - assuming open access to the distribution system - be undertaken by new firms which need to be neither a generator nor a transporter of energy. Electricity trade consists then of purchasing electricity from generators and buying transmission capacity, while selling electricity to the final customers at negotiated terms. The final customers' choice of the supplier will influence the competition process. Specialized electricity traders might be useful because they will flexibly bring together specific demand for electricity and related services (e.g. metering every x minutes for the sake of cost control and cost saving) with those generators that supply the desired product and services at low prices. Moreover, some customers might wish to buy (at rather high prices) only energy from environmentally friendly sources which in turn will stimulate competition among generators to introduce more environmentally friendly technologies. All these options are ruled out if the electricity sector is vertically integrated. Any negotiated third party access that would allow a generator to use the network of another integrated generator would be a weak alternative to a full separation of energy generation, transmission and supply. Unbundling of the electricity industry therefore should be part of the privatization of the electricity sector in transforming economies. A weak form of unbundling of activities would be to establish separate accounting for each activity (a-d). However, there are various forms of organizing accounting separating, including forms that will allow cross-subsidization and impair market entry.

Bold Plans in Poland

To date Poland's plans for liberalization are consistent with competition and third-party grid access in the future - representing a possible role model for other transforming countries, too. In March 1996 the Polish government published a White Paper on the energy industry. The pollution-ridden energy sector needs to be modernized. Poland's industry minister is about to privatize the 2740 MW Patnow-Adamov-Konin generating complex (accounting for about 1/10 of Poland's power generation). This is a pilot privatization program along with the sale of two regional distributors (ZE Gliwice in Silesia and ZE Poznan). The general approach to privatization of the energy sector is largely modelled on the UK power sector privatization. The Polish government intends to impose third-party access to the national electricity grid and the network of gas pipelines. Hence all energy producers could use the distribution system without discrimination. However, it is currently still unclear whether TPA - a politically controversial principle - will be included in the new energy law. The Polish Power Grid Company buys power from generators and sells (distributes) it to 33 regional distribution companies. The Polish government envisages an approach under which the grid company - to be privatized soon - will continue to manage the distribution system but give up the wholesale function, which in turn will be assumed by the distributors and newly emerging energy brokers. In its White Paper the government envisages 5-10 groups of power producers to be augmented by smaller local generators from among the 62 existing power and heat plants. These companies will sell power to regional distributors and directly to large customers. The grid company will initially handle imports and exports through Poland's new links to Western Europe established in 1995. TPA is a conflict-prone topic in Poland since the gas lobby fears competition from future supplies of Russian gas.

Regulatory Policies Required for Competition in Gas

Competition in gas is difficult to implement although it clearly is not impossible as the example of the UK demonstrates. British Gas (BG) was a statutory national monopoly until 1982. The Oil and Gas Act nominally opened up access to British Gas's storage and pipeline system to rivals which exceeded a certain threshold (25 000 therms p.a.). The 1986 Gas Act followed the pattern of the earlier flotation of

British Telecom. A new regulatory body, the Office of Gas Supply (Ofgas) and a new regulator (Director General of Gas Supply) were established to monitor and enforce a RPI-X+Y price cap for domestic and smaller commercial companies (JASINSKI et al. 1995). The maximum price increase for a bundle of services is thus determined on a formula basis: retail price inflation (RPI) minus expected productivity growth (X) plus a transition factor (Y). The 1986 privatization failed to be accompanied by policies able to correct the weakness of the 1982 legislation - British Gas still had a set of long-term gas purchase contracts that largely foreclosed the market to new entrants. Naturally monopolistic gas transport (or storage) and potentially competitive gas trading were treated as part of an overall "gas sector", so that there was no accounting, business or regulatory separation between the two activities. There were insufficient impulses to offset the crucial bottleneck facilities, transport and storage system. Competition was only achieved by further actions by the regulator, antitrust authorities and the Secretary of State, where the establishment of a new regulatory body (Ofgas) was decisive. The establishment of Ofgas helped to avoid industry representatives bringing all problems to the political agenda. Moreover, there was a clear-cut division of responsibilities between the industry regulator and the Office of Fair Trading (OFT). Ofgas oversees monopolist activities while the OFT is responsible for the competitive parts of the industry. Recommendations of the Monopolies and Merger Commission were implemented in 1989 and brought new common carriage rates. According to regulations BG was to make a return of 4.5% on the capital assets employed (based on replacement costs). In 1992 a new Act introduced separate regulation for pipelines and storage. There was also a reduced monopoly threshold with the effect of increasing the number of users able to choose their gas supplier. Finally, transportation terms and tariffs for the use of British Gas' network by independent gas traders were published. In 1995 independent traders altogether achieved over 50% of the firm contract market, which testifies to the effectiveness of competition. The European Commission also aims to establish an internal gas market at the European level, but so far liberalization has been very difficult to achieve. Facilitating transit and TPA have been goals of Commission initiatives and directives.

For Eastern Europe and Russia it is obvious that pro-competitive steps in the gas sector should include the following:

- dismemberment of oversized monopolistic firms
- privatizing the gas sector
- setting up a politically independent gas regulatory authority
- applying an appropiate price cap rule
- imposing transparent transit charges that are based on economic principles (marginal cost)

- accounting separation and - as a superior alternative - dismemberment of various activities in the gas sector
- encouraging and developing capital markets

3.3 Transportation

Europe's and Russia's main challenge in the medium term is the railways system. Modern railway technology allows the building of fast networks that could cause not only a revival of the railway for merchandise and passenger transport but also support the expansion of industries related to the railways system. Most railway systems in Europe are characterized by high debt loads and massive subsidies. In the EU subsidies are highest in Italy (see appendix). Overall indebtedness of public railways in the EU reached ECU 112.5 bill. in 1994 which amounted to 1.8% of Community GDP. The top of the league was the Italian railway system which accounted for a debt load equivalent to 5% of the Italian GDP.

In the Visegrad countries there are plans to modernize the railway network segments that are leading to EU countries. In Hungary the government-owned MAV has launched a broad modernisation project whose financing, however, might suffer from strongly declining freight revenues in transportation to Russia (after the August 1998 crises). MAV Rt has also started to diversify into communications by acquiring a minority stake in the newcomer PanTel (which is controlled by the Dutch KPN with its 49% stake). Fiber optic network expansion along the railway track has a high priority for challenging MATAV in the long run.

Creating weak competition is not difficult if government separates network operation and the rolling stock, i.e. network use, and thus creates one or several network operation companies and several train operating firms (competition in the net). This will help to maximize network use since the private network operator has no incentive to impose monopoly prices or to adopt a limit-pricing strategy for potential newcomers in train operation.

For competition it will be crucial how franchises are allocated and what information firms have to provide to customers and the capital market. Governance problems are a cause of many inefficiencies in state-owned railway systems. Privatization of railways could help to restore the healthy historical dynamics of European private railway operators prior to being nationalized in many countries for military reasons in the last quarter of the century.

Transportation Problems from an Intermodal Perspective

Infrastructure can to a large extent be provided by relying on market signals and private investment. An early pioneer in highway traffic modernization in Western Europe was France which lacked an extented network in the 1960s, but the backwardness relative to Germany was erased within two decades by way of new toll-financed highways. In developing countries and in transforming economies new Build-Operate-Transfer (BOT) arrangements were applied which mean that private firms construct infrastructure on the basis of finances raised in capital markets, then recover costs from operation and then transfer at an agreed date the infrastructure to the state (such arrangements also apply to the electricity sector). Government-owned railway systems lost in the intermodal competition in Western Europe in the 1970s and 1980s when private truck operators raised their share of merchandise transports. The historically dominating railway transport system - built up in the 19th century by private entrepreneurs and nationalized for military reasons - was apparently unable to offer what markets wanted - fast, reliable and cheap service for national and international transportation which was supplied by truck transportation. The market share of EU railways in freight (passenger) transportation fell from 32% (10%) in 1970 to 15% (6 %) in 1995 (EUROPEAN COMMISSION, 1995). Had these been a private network with efficient intermodel competition and Pigouvian taxes on truck transport, market shares of railway transport would have remained high. Modern telematics could reinforce the comparative advantage of private truck transportation as transport management is facilitated.

Free trade in services in the EU requires that railway network operation and railway services be separated. Without such a separation - going beyond accounting separation - efficient network use is excluded since the dominant operator has an incentive to set user fees for outsiders above marginal costs in order to maintain its dominant market share. The single market project with the envisaged liberalization of services is incomplete as long as railway networks have not been reorganized in a way which separates network operation and network service business. International network integration on the basis of harmonized technologies in signalling and electricity could yield large economic benefits because transportation would become faster and cheaper. This would help to raise market shares of the railway system in intermodal competition. For undistorted intermodal competition it would, of course, be important that competing transport systems are not directly or indirectly subsidized. According to the international motor vehicle construction association the overall costs of road transportation in western Europe were estimated at ECU 165.1 bill. in 1995. This consists of infrastructure user costs of ECU 64.2 bill. to which costs of accidents and environmental damage of ECU 100.9 bill. are added. Road pricing revenues, gas taxes and car taxes were estimated to have reached ECU 163 bill. so that the costs of car and truck mobility appear to be covered. A recent study at the Wuppertal Institute (WELFENS et al., 1996) which uses a rather conservative approach to estimate the shadow subsidies of automotive mobility suggested for western Germany alone shadow subsidies (in the area of free parking, health insurance costs and tax allowances for car users) in the range of DM 20.8-40.3 bill. in 1991. Assuming for western Germany with 64 million inhabitants a true value of shadow subsidies of DM 30 bill. would suggest for the whole EU shadow subsidies of some ECU 100 bill. This implies that the automotive industry association underestimates mobility costs by more than one-third and that relative prices are biased in favor of road transportation. Moreover, for economic efficiency it is not sufficient that automobile users cover their costs at the aggregate; rather on an individual user basis each vehicle driver has to cover his individual social costs. Otherwise there will be inefficient cross-subsidization, so that policy reforms are urgent (WELFENS/HILLEBRAND, 1998). Implicit subsidies also benefit the railway system because noise-abatement costs by residents close to railway tracks are not covered by national railway operators.

4. Foreign Direct Investment in Network Industries

4.1 Importance of Multinational Companies

Foreign direct investment is a way to organize technological intensive production of goods and services across countries when trade is not optimal for serving markets or when international outsourcing within the multinational company generates competitive advantages in global markets. Market entry of a foreign firm will be only possible if the foreign newcomer has firm-specific competitive advantages in the fields of management and technology which implies that the host country will benefit from foreign investment inflows by adopting more productive technologies. Massive foreign inflows will cause an exchange rate appreciation in the host country such that further capital inflows become less likely. This is the natural economic barrier that saves a country's industry from being fully taken over in the long term. Moreover, if the trade regime in the host country is export promoting, a rising presence of foreign investors will contribute to rising net exports of goods which in turn will also cause an appreciation.

Foreign investment can, of course, only occur in the presence of private firms, but once firms are privatized foreign investment inflows can rapidly occur. This is clearly shown in the case of the privatization and liberalization of the British telecommunication and energy sector in the 1980s and the railway system in 1995/96 as well as in the case of Sweden which recorded record capital inflows in 1995/96 as a consequence of privatizing utilities. Foreign investors can be very useful to jump-start competition provided that the domestic monopoly operator has been dismembered prior to privatization. Telbras – the Brazilian telecoms monopoly - was split up into 12 separate companies (8 regional mobile operators, 3 long distance companies and 1 international operator) first and then privatized in July 1998.

Foreign investment into infrastructure is sometimes problematic because infrastructure which was built with subsidies of national taxpayers is obtained by foreign owners who will appropriate economic rents based on taxpayers' money. The international lease of network capacity - in railways, electricity and telephony - could be a way to cope with the problem. Foreign investment can also be a political and economic problem if the investor's market entry relies upon the supernormal profits realized in dynamic domestic markets. If foreign competition is in the form of a BOT arrangement one may think of a pro-competitive transfer stage, namely one in which the transfer period is linked with a fully pre-determined privatization approach.

It is clear that with respect to prospective host countries foreign investors will require competitive rates of return, possibly including a political risk premium. Hence if political stability can be achieved higher inflows of foreign investment can be expected. With a rising presence of foreign investors in industry, the demand for improving infrastructure will increase. Given the increased flow of foreign direct investment in the 1980s and early 1990s, there is increasing locational competition which will reinforce the pressure to provide functional infrastructure for foreign investors. For most firms paying for infrastructure services will not constitute a problem as they can recover such costs in the market. Free infrastructure services will, however, affect profitability so that affluent and cheap infrastructure services will help to attract high foreign direct investment inflows. New ways of financing infrastructure projects (e.g. BOT) have created new options for cash-strapped governments to finance infrastructure modernization.

Mobile foreign investors are well informed about the level of infrastructure services in most countries of the world so that subsidiaries of multinational companies can be expected to be rather demanding with respect to the quality and reliability of infrastructure services. As regards transportation (except for international air transportation), electricity and telecommunications the latter certainly is the field in which multinational companies will be most pressing by their international service arbitrage. Once one-stop-shopping at a single international telecoms operator (e.g. Concert, Worldcom, Global One) becomes feasible, multinational firms will prefer to deal with only one company which in turn will provide services by combining its own network with foreign network services.

Secondary monopolization

Foreign investment has two pitfalls for competition. If a private or state-owned monopoly is directly sold to a foreign investor, a foreign monopolist is established which will transfer part of its profits abroad so that the currency should depreciate.

Such a strategy might be attractive for some transforming countries in certain cases since this promises a maximum of short-term government proceeds from privatization. Another problematic case is "secondary monopolization" which occurs when foreign investors x_1,x_2, x_n from country X buy various firms z_1, z_2, z_m in country Z while later on the x-firms merge thereby causing an indirect monopolization (Fig. A6b) of the previously competitive Z-market (Fig. A6a). This shows that regulatory policies and competition policy especially in major source countries of foreign direct investment will have international external effects.

Multinationalization of the Energy Sector

According to a report by the US energy department (ENERGY INFORMATION ADMINISTRATION, 1996) restructuring of privatized energy companies and modernization investment will require more than $ 1000 bill. in new investment over the next decade. To finance such huge investments mergers, acquisitions, consolidations and strategic alliances have been established in the industry. "Oil and gas companies have become electricity companies; domestic regional electric utilities have become multinational electricity companies; electricity companies have become generation companies; and generation companies have become distribution and transmission companies". With privatization of energy companies in Scandinavia, the UK, Spain and Portugal in Western Europe and partial privatization of the energy sector in the Visegrad countries and Russia, there is an increasing influence of foreign investors which often are desired as strategic players ensuring efficient governance of firms; in particular the global influence of US multinational energy companies has been strengthened. One may notice that US electricity companies, US railway companies and US telecommunications companies are among the most active investors in the liberalized British electricity markets, railway network operation and telecommunication markets, respectively. It seems obvious that US investors enjoy the benefit of already having experience with competition in the home market so that they are well positioned to acquire newly privatized companies in Europe and Russia.

With decreasing financing from the World Bank and other development agencies private financing for international investment projects is developing. Major sources include natural gas pipeline companies and oil producers but also new players, such as construction firms and power equipment manufacturing companies applying BOT contracts. The coal industry - accounting for about one-fourth of world energy consumption - is also internationalizing since EU multinational conglomerates stepped up their foreign investment in the 1990s as reduced domestic subsidies for coal pits encouraged the search for new foreign business activities. Privatization of utilities in combination with domestic price cap regulation can also stimulate investment abroad as the British example shows. Since privatization and restructuring can raise efficiency and profits only for a limited time international diversification will have to be considered by management, especially if domestic profits are impaired by strict price cap regulation as in the UK.

Fig. A6: Host and Source Countries of FDI

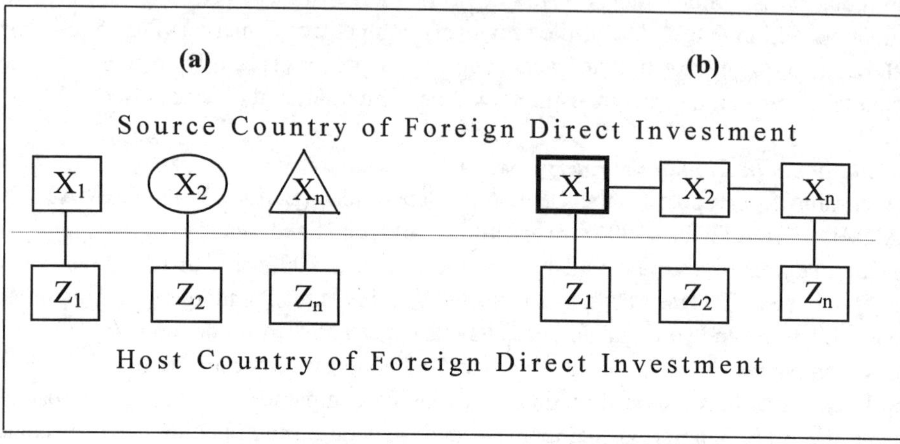

One may assume that gradual opening up of EU electricity markets in combination with domestic price cap regulation will encourage electricity companies to expand abroad which will finally lead to a mutual conquest of assets and markets such that a multinational EU electricity business will emerge. However, foreign investment inflows will not be possible in France as EDF (Electricite de France) is a fully state-owned company. If France is not willing to privatize EDF other EU countries might not accept French foreign investment in their respective electricity sector. With full privatization and increasing multinationalization of electricity companies there should be strong productivity gains and therefore falling electricity prices. The overall resource use of the electricity sector could reduce as new and more efficient power stations are replacing older ones. Since new technologies allow transmission of electricity over more than 1000 km at low loss rates there could be a strong increase in EU electricity trade on the one hand, and, on the other hand, higher trade between Europe and Russia.

Multinationalization of Telecommunications and Transportation

Foreign investment in telecoms networks can occur only after privatization or in newcomer activities, e.g. in mobile telephony. The liberalization of national telecoms markets reduces profitability of domestic telecommunications for the dominant operator which then has an incentive to realize compensating investment opportunities abroad. Since this rationale holds for all telecoms operators in Europe one may expect massive FDI after 1998. Many US and EU operators are likely to increasingly look into the investment opportunities in eastern Europe.

In railway transportation there are only few prospects for internationalization, namely as railway networks open up for external users. By contrast the air transportation industry is quite internationalized and will be increasingly so after 1997 when restrictions with respect to cabotage weree removed. Aggressive foreign investment of British airways (and BT) testifies to the benefits of having been exposed to a competitive home market.

4.2 Foreign Direct Investment in Europe vs. FDI in Transforming Economies

Foreign direct investment in telecommunications and energy will quickly increase in the late 1990s as more and more EU telecoms operators are privatized and private electricity companies face competition. Except for cases of state-ownership there are no principal impediments to foreign investment in the EU.

In transforming eastern Europe western strategic investors were welcome in the mobile and fixed line telephony as well as in electricity companies in the Visegrad countries (except for Slovakia). Hungary found it difficult to accept Gasprom - a monopoly at home - as a foreign investor in its gas sector. Gasprom certainly was eager to invest in downstream markets in order to secure outlets for its gas supply. Russia, however, was reluctant to accept FDI.

Foreign investment in railways is still an exception in all European countries except for the UK. In principle there is no problem to establish multinational consortia that build and operate international - or national - networks. The poor profit record of the Chunnel operator, however, points to problems in establishing viable private railway projects in the presence of strong intermodal competition. Also the UK failed to modernize the rail track to London.

Foreign direct investment in OECD telecommunications may be estimated to have reached about $ 100 bill. in the period 1990-95, while that in eastern Europe was about $ 12 bill. (including foreign investment in the equipment industry). Deutsche Telekom invested within a majority stake approach jointly with Ameritech in the Hungarian MATAV. The Dutch KPN invested within a majority stake approach jointly with Swiss Telecom in the Czech SPT Telekom. Romania's and Bulgaria's telecoms firms are also looking for a strategic foreign investor as is the Polish TPSA. Investment necessary in eastern Europe plus Russia to catch up with western Europe's 1980 figures could reach about $ 100 bill. within a decade. This clearly will be extremely difficult if only domestic savings could be tapped. Prospects to attract high FDI inflows are rather favorable in the Visegrad countries as outgoing international calls are growing at a high rate as a consequence of rapidly increasing trade and a growing presence of multinational companies. In Russia the situation is much more difficult since the envisaged privatization of the second network operator (with STET from Italy as a prospective strategic investor) failed in 1996 – the government then considered merging the two network operators leaving mobile telphony as the only liberalized network segment. Russia has not seriously considered to split up Rostelcom which could be a useful starting point for jump-starting competition and attracting high FDI flows in the telecommunications sector. The modernization of the telecoms sector would also be very useful to raise factor productivity in information intensive sectors and in the overall economy; empirical evidence from western economies clearly show significant productivity and growth effects of the use of information and telecommunications technology (ANTONELLI, 1998; ITU, 1997).

The most active foreign investors in eastern Europe are Deutsche Telekom, France Telekom, the Swedish Telia, KPN, Swisscom and Tele Denmark plus Telecom (see Tab. A1) where a dominant focus is on the Visegrad countries and future EU accession countries, respectively. By contrast, Russia plays only a small role as a host country. Russia fell victim to internal policy pitfalls on the one hand; on the other hand it pursued a very orthodox IMF transition approach which emphasized macroeconomic stabilization, low budget deficits and fixed exchange rates, while an adequate sequence would have started with doing away with government wage arrears – even if higher budget deficits and inflation rates had been the consequence – in order to establish credibility of the government in its role of reshaping institutions and economic policy. A market economy is a contract economy and thus cannot thrive without the rule of law, and government itself must obey the rules of the game if the private sector is to observe the new rules (WELFENS, 1999).

Estonia sold a stake of 51% of its national operator in an initial private offering in 1998; 40% is owned by Baltic Tele (Telia and Telecom Finland). Latvia sold a strategic stake in 1995, while an initial public offering is linked to formation of a joint stock company; TILTS which is composed of Telecom Finland and Cable & Wireless will represent strategic foreign ownership – the deal was made with exclusive fixed voice and data rights until 2013 which is a very late date for a prospective EU accession country, but desired changes in the contract meet resistance of the foreign companies which fear lower profits. In Russia 49% of Rostelcom was sold in 1993 where foreign and domestic investors are the main owners – apart from the goverment with its 51%. Svyazinvest which is a holding company of some 85 local regional telephone firms has some minority foreign ownership, but the Svyazinvest restructuring might be difficult as the purchasing group Onexim-bank plus the George Soros investment group plus Deutsche Morgan Grenfell brings only very modest hands-on telecoms experience. The important role of a strategic foreign investor was clearly brought out by the MATAV case.

Hungary's network size increased from 1.3 mill. to 2.4 mill. in 1998 and the revenue level achieved in 1998 is close to $ 440 million, close to the Spanish figure. MATAV benefits from clear governance structures as a consequence of foreign majority ownership, namely 67.2% for Magyarcom (Ameritech plus Deutsche Telekom). Countries which rely on a minority stake of foreign investors are likely to face governance problems in the incumbant operator and to see less investment from abroad than in the case of majority ownership for the foreign partner. Besides political preferences for minority ownership in many east European countries there is the problem of rebalancing, that is to bring prices in line with marginal costs (e.g. raising local prices and thus removing implicit subsidization of local calls, while reducing overpricing in long distance). Rebalancing issues which are politically sensitive should be settled prior to privatization or searching for a foreign investor. The sequence of reforms in eastern Europe and Russia rarely is adequate; politically independent regulatory authorities and functional court systems which are vital for settling disputes – often between the incumbant and newcomers with own facilities or resellers – also are an exception to the rule. For the prospective EU accession countries there clearly will be pressure to fall in line with standard practices in EU countries.

Tab. A1: CEE Investments by Members of Major West European Telecom Operators

Country / Investor	Company name	Stake (%)	Purchase date	Business operations
Deutsche Telekom				
Hungary	Matáv	29.79%	Dec 1993	**National** operator with monopoly on national and international telephony
Czech Republic	RadioMobil	41.3%	March 1996	**Mobile** operator (GSM)
Poland	Era GSM	24.5%	Feb 1996	**Mobile** operator (GSM)
Ukraine	UTEL	19.5%	March 1993	**Long** distance, international operator
Ukraine	UMC	16.3%	Sept 1992	**Mobile** operator (NMT & GSM)
Russia	MTS	39%	July 1993	**Moscow**-based mobile operator (GSM)
CEE	DeTeSat	100%	-	**Regional** satellite with footprint over

Tab. A1 (cont.)

Telia				
Estonia	Eesti Telefon	24.5%	1991	**Long** distance, international operator
Estonia	Eesti Mobiiltelefon	24.5%	1991	**Mobile** operator (NMT & GSM)
Latvia	LMT	24.5%	1992	**Mobile** operator (NMT & GSM)
Lithuania	Lithuanian Telecom	30%	June 1998	**National** operator with monopoly on national and international telephony
Lithuania	Tietelija	100%	-	**Fixed**-line local telephony
Poland	Netia Telecom	27.8%	1995	**Fixed**-line local telephony
Poland	Netia South	25%	1995	**Fixed**-line local telephony
Russia	St Petersburg	12.5%	Dec 1994	**Mobile** operator (GSM)
KPN				
Czech Republic	SPT Telecom	13.5%	June 1995	**National** operator with monopoly on national and international telephony
Hungary	Pantel	49%	June 1998	**Alternative** operator, specializing in business communications
Hungary	Pannon GSM	23.22%	March 1994	**Mobile** operator (GSM)
Ukraine	UMC	16.33%	1992	**Mobile** operator (NMT & GSM)
Ukraine	UTEL	10%	March 1993	**Long** distance, international operator
Swisscom				
Czech Republic	SPT Telecom	13.5%	June 1995	**National** operator with monopoly on
				national and international telephony
Tele Danmark				
Lithuania	Brité GSM	35.82%	1995	Mobile Operator
	Comliet UAB	24.5%		Mobile Operator
Poland	Polkomtel S.A.	19.25%	October 1996	Mobile Operator
Czech Republic	Radio Ceske Komunikaie	20.8%	Aug. 1997	TV and Telephon Transmission
Hungary	Pannon GSM Rt.	23.21%	1993	Mobile Operator
Ukraine	Ukraine Mobil Communication (UMC)	16.33%	1993	Mobile Operator

Notes: OTE has a stake in Telecom Srbija (Serbia) and Armen Tel (Armenia); joint management of Romanian operator with GTE.

Source: OTE (Greece), ROM TELECOM press articles; PUBLIC NETWORKS EUROPE (1998).

Russian Perspectives

For the international integration and modernization of Russia the telecommunications sector is the most important network industry. However, in telecommunications Russia has pursued a totally inconsistent liberalization and restructuring strategy despite the many opportunities which could have emerged from a situation with a high backlog of unsatified domestic demand and prospects to intensify international communication as part of a general modernization and growth strategy; in international telephony the number of outgoing telephone minutes per subscriber in 1997 was only 1/7 of the Polish figure in 1997 (ITU, 1997), 1/14 of the Mexican (or the German) figure – a special variant of Russia as a still rather closed economy. Given Russia broad technological capabilities and the high expected benefits from a comprehensive economic opening up the poor state of the telecomms sector is surprising. The high failure rate in telephony, high prices for international telecommunications and a very low internet density all reflect inadequate restructuring, privatization and deregulation. Since empirical evidence for Germany (JUNGMITTAG/WELFENS, 1996, see Tab. A 2, appendix) clearly suggests that the use of telecommunications is an important positive growth factor the underdeveloped Russian telecomms sector is equivalent to foregone growth opportunities.

Russia could have followed the very successful Finnish competition strategy which is based on full competition: between the formerly dominant national and international operator, Telecom Finnland, foreign newcomers, and the separate local network operator eager to invade the national and international market. In Russia Rostelecom (long-distance and international carriers) and the regional network Svyainvest with controlling stakes in 88 regional companies - plus foreign newcomers could have launched a broad successful modernization and competition. However, government failed to disintangle the two Russia telecom companies: Svyazinvest has a 38% stake and 51% of the voting rights of Rostelecom, and 25% plus one share of Svyazinvest were sold to the Mustcom investor group in summer 1997. Restructuring should have come before privatization, ie first a full separation of the two fixed network operators, then possibly looking in at least one case for a strategic foreign investor. Instead government ignored the restructuring task, and in early January 1999 the government – desperately looking for revenues to trim the budget deficit - announced plans to sell another 25 percent of Svyazinvest (minus two shares) for at least Rs. 14 billion ($600 million; about 1/3 of the revenue envisaged in October 1998 – but the planned sale was cancelled in the wake of the transformation and devaluation crisis). One mayor problem of IMF programs is that there is no pro-competitive transformation facility which would encourage governments to pursue prudent long term restructuring and privatization strategies, ie less emphasis on short-term revenue from selling a quasi-monopolist and more emphasis on combining restructuring, competition and privatization within a long term growth approach. Actually, an innovative reform of the WTO or the EBRD could provide such crucial financial assistance in the future.

5. Conclusions

Competition in network industries could be achieved in OECD countries and Russia in the long run as the model of telecoms deregulation shows. Competition in electricity requires privatization and deregulation which is difficult to realize as so many resistances in the political area at various layers have to be overcome. Competition for services could be a minimal way to achieve competition in railway transportation, but this will require vertical disintegration (possibly separation of physical infrastructure, network management and railway services). With railway traffic being the slowest way of transporting goods, improved efficiency in railway networks - resulting from privatization, deregulation and foreign investment - should not only lower prices of railway transportation but also induce price reductions of alternatives to this way of transportation; railway prices indeed are a floor price for other modes of transportation. Since railway network and electricity companies are the main newcomers in the liberalized fixed telephony sector deregulation impulses in telcommunications could have spillover effects - stimulating liberalization - in these sectors, too. Telecoms regulation could indeed require that newcomers from the energy and railway sector liberalize their core business so that long-term cross-subsidization is ruled out.

Foreign investment will strongly rise worldwide if FDI restrictions for network industries are removed and if privatization proceeds gain momentum in Europe and Russia. One may anticipate growing mergers & acquisitions in Euroland where rising market transparency, technological progress (including internet telephony) and pressure on former monopoly operators to raise profits by invading foreign markets play a crucial role. The BT-AT&T alliance created in 1998 certainly will impose adjustment requirements on other alliances in Europe and worldwide.

Positive welfare effects can be expected from FDI in the long term, while the short term will be characterized by the pain of restructuring. In a globalizing economy national regulatory policy and competition policy in major FDI source countries will have international external effects as was shown for the case of secondary monopolization. New infrastructure projects in Europe can stimulate economic growth which could be reinforced by emphasis on asset unbundling and vertical disintegration. More private provision of infrastructure could be politically feasible if special income transfers for poor strata of society were granted as a way of compensation. Telecommunications is the most dynamic infrastructure industry in Europe and Russia. Post-socialist countries suffer from a lack of foreign direct investment inflows, most notably in the case of Russia. FDI inflows are crucial for restructuring in infrastructure services – even more so in manufacturing industry – which is hardly politically accepted in Russia. Prudent dismemberment policies are required prior to privatization, and competition policy – conducted by an independent authority – should play a major role in a growth-oriented

stability and functional institutions are the core requirements for reform in Russia and eastern Europe.

Appendix

Fig. A7: Average Costs Pricing as a Problem in Industry with Falling Marginal Costs

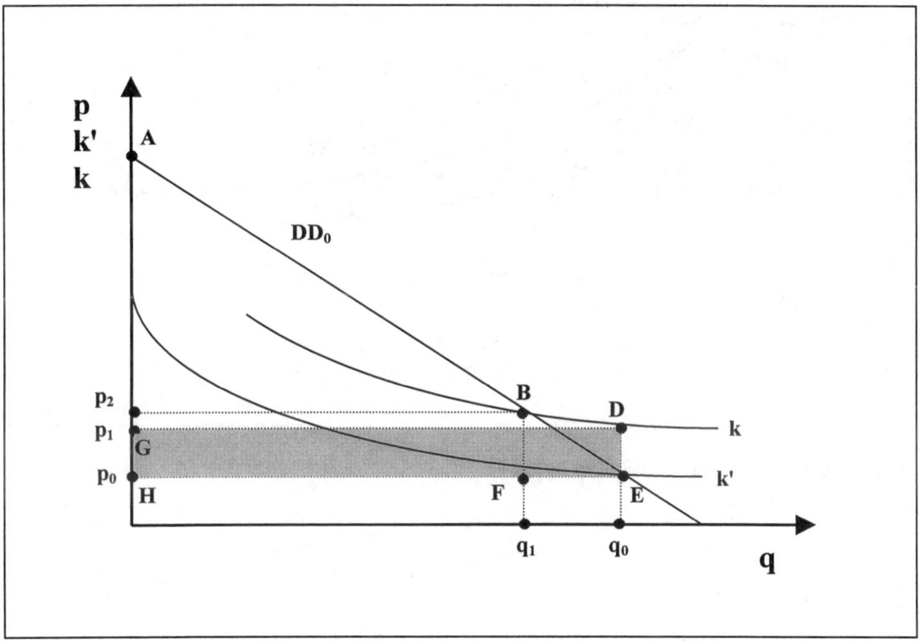

Source: WELFENS/YARROW (1997), p.107.

Fig. A8: Natural Monopoly with Positive External Effects on the Demand Side (Network Effects)

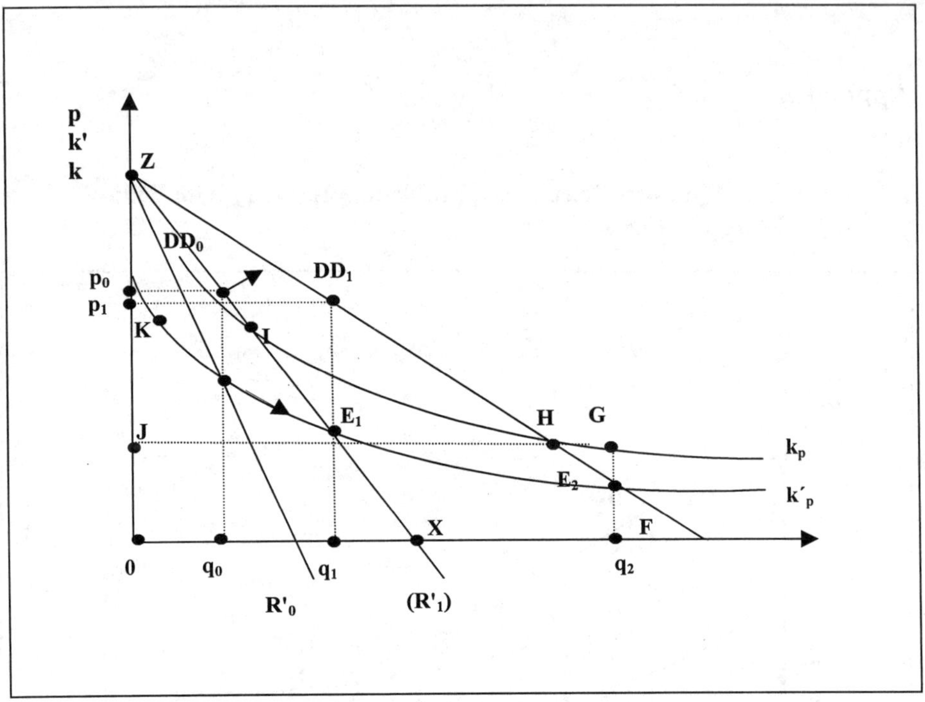

Source: WELFENS/YARROW (1997), p. 111.

Tab. A2: Explaining the Growth of Real Gross Value-Added in the Enterprise Sector in Germany

Source of Growth	Average annual growth rate						
	61 - 90	61 - 65	66 - 70	71 - 75	76 - 80	81 - 85	86 - 90
k_t	1.5	2.5	1.9	1.8	1.1	0.8	1.0
l_t	0.2	0.7	0.1	-0.6	0.5	-0.6	1.1
pat_{t-2}	0.1	0.3	0.2	-0.3	0.2	0.1	0.3
la_t	0.3	0.4	0.3	0.3	0.0	0.0	0.8
tv_t	1.1	1.2	1.7	1.2	1.3	0.7	0.7
Total: Estimated	3.3	5.2	4.3	2.3	3.2	0.9	4.0
Actual	3.3	5.2	4.4	1.7	3.6	1.1	3.8

Note: The sum of the individual growth rate components may diverge from total estimated growth rates due to rounding; k = capital stock, l = labor volume, pat = patents, la = real expenditures on licences, tv = number of telephone calls.

Source: JUNGMITTAG/WELFENS (1996).

Tab. A3: Infrastructure

Economies	Power System losses, 1990 (% of total output)	Paved roads Road density, 1988 (km per million persons)
Lower-middle-income		
• Ukraine	x	x
• Poland	15	617
• Slovak Republic	x	x
• Czech Republic	x	x
• Russian Federation	x	x
Upper-middle-income		
• Hungary	11	5 804
• Slovenia	x	x
• Korea, Rep.	6	236
• Greece	x	x
• Portugal	11	1 740

Tab. A3 (cont.)

High-income		
• Spain	9	x
• Netherlands	4	6 875
• Germany[a)]	5	x
• United States	9	14 172

Note: a) Data refer to the Federal Republic of Germany before unification.

Source: WORLD BANK (1994), p. 225.

Tab. A4: Railway Density in Europe

Country	Length of lines	Country size (km^2)	Net density (m/km^2)
East Germany	14 054	108 267	129.81
Germany	40 833	356 945	114.40
Belgium	3 432	30 519	112.45
West Germany	26 779	248 678	107.69
Luxembourg	275	2 586	106.34
United Kingdom	16 528	242 100	68.27
Austria	5 605	83 858	66.83
Netherlands	2 753	41 861	65.76
France	32 731	543 965	60.17
Denmark	2 306	43 093	53.51
Italy	16 112	301 302	53.47
Portugal	3 062	92 389	33.14
Ireland	1 944	70 284	27.66
Spain	13 041	504 782	25.83
Sweden	9 846	449 964	21.88
Greece	2 484	131 957	18.82
Finland	5 874	338 107	17.37
CSFR	13 099	127 900	102.42
Hungary	7 727	93 033	83.06
Poland	25 254	312 683	80.77
Bulgaria	5 488	110 993	49.44
Rumania	11 430	237 500	48.13

Source: UIC Statistik, 1992 and 93/94, FISCHER WELTALMANACH (1994), own calculations.

Tab. A5: Commercial Energy

Economies	Energy consumption 1980 - 1992 average annual growth rate (%)	Energy use (oil equivalent), 1992 per capita (kg)	GDP output per kg ($)
Lower-middle-income			
• Ukraine	x	3 885	0.5
• Poland	-1.7	2 407	0.9
• Slovak Republic	x	3 202	0.6
• Czech Republic	x	3 873	0.7
• Russian Federation	x	5 665	0.5
Upper-middle-income			
• Hungary	-0.3	2 392	1.4
• Slovenia	x	x	x
• Korea, Rep.	9.2	2 569	2.6
• Greece	3.5	2 173	3.5
• Portugal	4.9	1 816	4.4
High-income			
• Spain	2.9	2 409	6.1
• Netherlands	1.3	4 560	4.6
• Germany	0.2	4 358	5.5

Source: WORLD BANK (1994), p. 71.

Tab. A6: Railway Subsidies in Europe

Country	Total Cost of Railway	Overall Subsidies	Ratio Revenue[a]/Costs(%)
United Kingdom	3591	636	82
France	6201	3194	48
Germany (West)	8763	3611	59
Italy	7226	6059	16
Belgium	1309	761	42
Netherlands	834	377	55

Source: EUROPEAN COMMISSION (1998), p. 51

Tab. A7: Telecom and Internet Densities

Penetration	**No.**	**Main Lines (ML) per 100 Inhabitants**	**Digital ML of ML**	**Mobile Subscribers / Inhab.**	**Internet / Online Users / 100 Inhab.**
1996		%	%	%	%
France	1	56.6	97.6	4.29	11.7
Finland	2	55.8	95.0	29.09	10.2
Sweden	3	68.0	96.2	28.09	7.6
Luxembourg	4	59.5	100.0	10.98	5.4
UK	5	52.3	93.3	11.59	5.1
Switzerland	6	64.4	75.3	9.38	4.6
Netherlands	7	54.0	80.2	6.50	4.3
Western Europe [1]	8	46.9	83.6	8.02	4.0
Norway	9	56.9	92.0	28.66	3.6
Germany	10	53.8	81.5	6.70	3.4
Ireland	11	38.7	83.0	7.38	3.0
Spain	12	39.3	67.4	7.64	2.8
Denmark	13	63.1	84.2	26.56	2.3
Belgium	14	46.7	72.3	4.71	2.3
Austria	15	48.4	72.0	7.42	1.4
Italy	16	44.1	85.1	11.21	1.3
Greece	16	50.8	42.6	4.89	1.3
Portugal	17	38.2	78.6	6.75	0.8
Hungary	18	26.2	71.2	4.56	0.8
Poland	19	16.6	49.4	0.63	0.4
Czech Republic	20	27.1	33.0	1.95	0.2
Romania	21	14.0	25.4	0.08	0.1
Russia	22	12.0	n.a.	0.05	0.1
Bulgaria	23	29.4	6.8	0.42	0.0

Note: 1) Incl. Turkey

Source: EITO (1998), p. 380.

Tab. A8: Prices of Leased Lines [1] 1997

Country	Pound Sterling
Italy	8 664
Netherlands	3 240
France	5 561
Sweden	1 916
Germany	4 155
UK	3 254
USA [2]	1 594

Notes: 1) 300 Km, 2 Mbits/s; 2) 1.5 Mbit/s.

Source: ITU (1997).

References

ANTONELLI, C. (1998), Localized Technological Change, New Information Technology and the Knowledge-based Economy: The European Evidence, Journal of Evolutionary Economics, Vol. 8, pp. 177-198.

BENTAL, B. and M. SPIEGEL (1995), Network Competition, Product Quality, and Market Coverage in the Presence of Network Externalities, Journal of Industrial Economics, Vol. 42, pp. 197-208.

DAVID, P.A. and J. BUNN, (1988), The Economics of Gateway Technologies and Network Evolution: Lessons from Electricity Supply History, Information Economics and Policy, pp.165-202.

EUROPEAN COMMISSION (1995), Vierter Bericht über staatliche Beihilfen, Bruxelles.

ENERGY INFORMATION ADMINISTRATION (1996), Privatization and the Globalization of Energy Markets, Washington DC.

EUROPEAN COMMISSION (1996), Eine Strategie zur Revitalisierung der Eisenbahn in der Gemeinschaft, Brussels.

EUROPEAN COMMISSION (1998), Faire Preis für Infrastrukturbenutzung: Ein abgestuftes Konzept für einen Gemeinschaftsrahmen für Verkehrsinfrastrukturgebühren in der EU, Weißbuch, Brüssel.

EUROPEAN INFORMATION TECHNOLOGY OBSERVER (EITO) (1998), Frankfurt/Main.

EUROPEAN PARLIAMENT (1996), East-West Energy Cooperation, Working Paper, Directorate-General for Research, Luxembourg .

HOLLER, M.J. (1996), Die Modellierung von Netzeffekten und Ansätze industriepolitischer Steuerung, paper presented at the symposium "Neue Politische Ökonomie", Königslutter, October 16-18.

ITU (1997), Challenge to the Network, Geneva.

ITU (1997b) World Telecommunication Development Report 1996/97. Geneva.

JASINSKI, P., T. SKOCZNY and G. YARROW (1995), Competition Rules and Regulation in the Energy Industry, Hertford College/Oxford University, mimeo.

JUNGMITTAG, A. and P.J.J. WELFENS (1996), Telekommunikation, Innovation und die langfristige Produktionsfunktion: Theoretische Aspekte und eine Kointegrationsanalyse für die Bundesrepublik Deutschland, EIIW Discussion Paper No. 20, Potsdam.

KNIEPS, G. (1988), Theorie der Regulierung und Entregulierung, in: HORN, M., G. KNIEPS. and J. MÜLLER, eds., Deregulierungsmaßnahmen in den USA: Schlußfolgerungen für die Bundesrepublik Deutschland, Gutachten des Deutschen Instituts für Wirtschaftsforschung Berlin, Baden-Baden: Nomos, pp. 39-42.

KNIEPS, G. (1996), Möglichkeiten und Grenzen des Aufbaus transeuropäischer Netze, paper presented at the symposium "Neue Politische Ökonomie", Königslutter, October 16-18.

OECD (1995), The Changing Role of Telecommunications in the Economy: Globalization and its Impact on National Telecommunication Policy, Working Paper GD (95) 116, Paris.

OICA (Organisation Internationale des Constructeurs d'Automobiles), ed. (1996), Die externen Kosten des Straßenverkehrs, Köln: Deutscher Institutsverlag.

PUBLIC NETWORKS EUROPE (1998), July/August.

SCHWARTZ, M. (1997), Telecommunications Reform in the United States: Promises and Pitfalls, in: WELFENS, P.J.J. and G. YARROW, eds. (1997), Telecommunications and Energy in Transforming Economies, Heidelberg and New York: Springer.

VON WEIZSÄCKER, C.C. (1982), Staatliche Regulierung - positive und normative Theorie, in: Schweizerische Zeitschrift für Volkswirtschaft und Statistik, Heft 3, 325-242.

WELFENS, M. et al. (1996), Schattensubventionen im motorisierten Individualverkehr, in: KÖHN, J. and M. J. WELFENS, eds. (1996), Neue Ansätze in der Umweltökonomie, Marburg: Metropolis.

WELFENS, P.J.J. (1995), Telecommunications and Transition in Central and Eastern Europe, in: Telecommunications Policy, Vol. 19, No.7, pp.561-577.

WELFENS, P. J. J. (1999), EU Eastern Enlargement and the Russian Transformation Crisis, Heidelberg/New York: Springer.

WELFENS, P.J.J. and GRAACK, C. (1995), Deregulierungspolitik und Wettbewerb in Netzindustrien: Bedeutung und Optionen für osteuropäische Transformationsländer, EIIW Discussion Paper No. 6, Potsdam.

WELFENS, P.J.J. and C. GRAACK (1996), Telekommunikationswirtschaft: Deregulierung, Privatisierung und Internationalisierung, Heidelberg: Springer.

WELFENS, P. J. J. and R. Hillebrand (1998), Environmental Problems in the Single EU Market: Development, Theory and Policy Options, paper presented at the EIIW Annual Conference 1998, Internationalisation of the Economy, Environmental Problems, and New Policy Options.

WELFENS, P.J.J. and G. YARROW, eds. (1997), Telecommunications and Energy in Transforming Economies, Heidelberg and New York: Springer.

WHITELEGG, J., S. HULTEN and T. FLINK, eds. (1993), High Speed Trains: Fast Tracks to the Future, Old Chapel: Leading Edge.

WORLD BANK (1994), World Development Report 1994: Infrastructure for Development, New York.

Comments on: Competition, Privatization and Foreign Direct Investment in Network Industries

Pieter H. M. Ruys

The paper describes an extremely relevant and important subject - the conditions for developing and financing the huge infrastuctural projects in network industries, to be realized in Eastern Europe and Russia. Since domestic public finance opportunities are limited, it is essential to attract foreign investments from the volatile international capital markets. In order to achieve that goal, however, the governance structure of the network industries should be transparent and dependable. Welfens concentrates on the competition and privatization aspects in three network industries: electricity, transport and telecommunications.

His description of the external effects and the characteristics of the various networks is interesting and deserves close reading. My comments, however, are aimed at the governance aspects of these industries. Welfens' policy recommendation is concentrated on fostering competition by means of privatization. He considers various forms of competition in network industries, ranging from a regulated monopoly (without competition) to full competition of integrated networks (see Figure A1 in his paper). He invokes the theory of contestable markets where it has been shown that potential entrants have a disciplining effect on the incumbent's behavior as long as sunk costs are rather low. I think that this is hardly the case for the large infrastructural projects considered, and therefore it is not a safe underpinning of competition in the industry.

A better argument provides vertical de-integration of the heavily integrated industries. Various levels or layers of productive activities may be distinguished in an industry. In transportation distinction can be made between the production of a (rail)road system and the production of transport services using this system. The system in the automotive industry whereby mark-ups on the individual transport services (such as taxes on cars or on gasoline) finance the road system may be generalized to any network industry. Mark-ups on services by using the network may finance the network. When integrated, a huge public transport system would emerge - a natural monopoly without competition. When de-integrated in two levels, the transport system allows for competition on both levels. There is strong competition in the market of private cars, providing for private transport services, and a managed competition in the market of road construction. In case of toll roads there exists also a market for road operators. The point I want to make is that the transport industry has developed and is developing gradually a governance structure that consists of various interdependent markets, each disciplined by competition. It is not the mixture or the integration of products in an industry that makes competition feasible, but it is the separation of these products, each processed in its own - possibly artificially constructed and supported - market. An example of such a constructed market is the spot market for electricity, even if its performance is not flawless. This development of new markets for de-integrated and new products is in line with Welfens' observation that technological progress will support and reinforce options for competition. However, where he states that "privatization of infrastructure is facilitated by allowing the toll-based use of infrastructure, including road pricing and airport slot pricing", I would prefer to substitute the word `privatization' for `private financing'. The infrastructure itself need not be privatized. It even should not be privatized if it cannot be made a marketable commodity, i.e. a commodity for which there exists a market. Other legal titles exist, such as franchise or BOT-contracts and arrangements, or may be developed, which guarantee procurement and take account of the public aspects and responsibilities.

This approach of de-integration or unbundling of production activities may also be applied to the other industries. The main problem in this unbundling will be the definition and the safeguard of property rights. These rights need not to apply on tangible commodities or concrete physical networks. Just as there exist many new financial products that are derivatives of classical stocks and bonds, so new legal contractual schemes may replace the classical property rights. The main virtue of this allotment of property rights is the separation of responsibilities between the various stakeholders in a large infrastructural project. This separation can only enhance the integrity of the governance structure designed and the reputation of the enterprise, which is needed for assessing the risk involved and success of its financing. The non-political institutions involved should be transparent, politically independent and accountable to the public, as modern corporate governance requires.

The development of such a governance structure requires substantial institutional or transaction costs. Governance structures have to be developed and the establishment of institutes such as a regulator may be expensive. Governments don't have much experience with setting up such institutional structures, although the situation improves rapidly. The article by Welfens mentions a lot of examples. More has to be said about the interaction between the roles of the government and the roles of the markets, but given the globalization of the financial markets it is fair to start with this last group.

To conclude, the design of effective governance structures in network industries is a prerequisite for the financing and implementation of infrastructural projects on a European scale in network industries. The paper by Welfens presents this problem in a fascinating way.

B: Privatisation, Competition and Regulation in Transforming Economies: The Cases of the Electricity Supply Industry and Telecommunications

Piotr Jasinski

1. Introduction

My paper is going to be, at least initially, quite philosophical in character, as I am going to begin with discussing rather concepts than real life developments. The latter will, however, eventually receive the attention it deserves. Since our project is supposed to be policy orientated, this seems precisely to be the way to approach the issues we are interested in. Namely, concepts used have to be defined and explained carefully and extensively in order to make clear the essence of changes going on in transforming economies of Central and Easter Europe and of the former Soviet Union. Without having understood these changes correctly all policy recommendation will be hanging in the air.

In what follows I shall discuss such concepts as competition, regulation and privatisation, and their choice is not accidental. Since competition, regulation and ownership are key determinants of economic efficiency, both productive and allocative (YARROW, 1986) the way in which these three issues are solved affects smooth operation of any economy. At the same time, one has to remember that it is precisely the simultaneous changes in these three spheres that constitute so-called systemic transformation, that is the transformation of Soviet-type economies (STEs) into market ones.

I shall start my paper with a few remarks on competition and regulation in the STEs (Section 2). In Section 3 systemic transformation defined as marketisation and liberalisation will be discussed. Regulation sensu largo, i.e. the rule of law and antitrust legislation will by analysed in Section 4. Finally, in Section 5, regulation sensu stricto, i.e. regulation of public utilities will stand in the centre of our attention. These considerations will be applied to the electricity supply industry and telecommunications in Section 6.

2. Competition and Regulation in STEs

Competition understood as rivalry in and for market places not only was all but impossible under the old regime, but was also thought of as highly wasteful and therefore undesirable. This did not mean that state-owned enterprises (SOEs) did not compete with each other. In the world of scarce, administratively allocated resources this was the only way to survive. SOEs had to compete with each other, most often in the process of increasingly multilateral bargaining, to force central planners to give them as much as possible (and demand as little as possible). However, this competition for investment funds, raw materials and other inputs had nothing to do with the competition in and for markets which can be observed in market economies, where it is the most effective mechanism to increase economic efficiency. From this point of view the degree of monopolisation as well as that of openness in STEs did not really matter, and their importance was further diminished by persistent shortages. Freedom of entry was excluded, and the concept of anticompetitive practices (e.g. abuse of market power) was known only from Western economic literature.

The situation did not change much in reformed STEs where one tried to give autonomy to enterprises and to introduce better incentives.[1] These attempts, considered audacious at that time but later on labelled by Kornai as naïve, were called marketisation. But even much bolder liberalisation together with creation of the necessary institutional framework, although a precondition of competition, would have been unable to transform the economic system of an STE. As long as most assets belonged to the state and money played only a passive role, competition in STEs and in market economies were too distant cousins to use the same name. In other words, it is privatisation and monetisation that have to accompany marketisation for the economic system to be transformed and, in consequence, for competition to develop and bring about improvements with respect to economic efficiency.

As far as regulation is concerned, the ubiquitous character of public ownership and the absence of competition, following therefrom, implied that it was regulation that played the decisive role in solving the principal/agent problem. This is hardly surprising, as one could say that central planning was nothing else but an all embracing regulation. However, it went much further than even the most restrictive regulations in market economies, because specific decisions were taken on behalf of or imposed on the regulatees. What is more, in trying to regulate too much, central planners were unable to solve informational and incentive problems unavoidably arising when the agency problem is tackled by regulation alone (JASINSKI, 1993). This was one of the reasons for which STEs could not work and eventually collapsed, the poor state of these economies precipitating such political changes that have made possible systemic transformation.

As far as industry specific regulation in STEs is concerned there are two possible interpretations: either that there was no such regulation or that everything was not only industry but also firm specific. However, one thing is certain: there was no special regulatory agency like, to use telecoms as an example, FCC in the US or OFTEL in the UK and nobody felt any need of them. This state of affairs constitutes yet another challenge in the process of systemic transformation, when it is clear that something has to be done with the way that public utilities are controlled.

Under market socialism the degree of incentive compatibility allegedly improved and the participation constraint was not binding because of the state's monopoly on managerial jobs, but monitoring deteriorated significantly. The existing structure of ownership rights together with diminished political pressure strongly reduced the commitment of principals to improve information flows as well as incentives structure for agents. What is more, although even in Western liberal democracies no general election is fought exclusively on the issue of the performance of public sector enterprises, the complete absence of such an electoral mechanism was yet another negative factor. Therefore, the situation in the reformed STEs may also be interpreted as a continuation of the attempt to solve the agency problem by regulation alone and that by regulation deprived of any independent yardstick. In other words, the efforts of principals, insufficient as they were, could not be supported by the pressure coming from various markets, e.g. from the markets for managers, for property rights, and for goods and services. There was neither threat of bankruptcy nor of hostile takeover, and the banking sector, even if there was more than one bank, was only an element of the all-embracing bureaucratic structure. Knowing the disciplining effect of these institutions on managers, one should not be surprised with what happened under market socialism.

3. Systemic Transformation

The process of systemic transformation, i.e. the passage from a centrally planned STE to a market one or, perhaps better, from (real) socialism to capitalism started, or considerably accelerated, in the Summer and Autumn of 1989, when the Mazowiecki government, the first non-communist dominated government in CEE was formed in Poland. Other Central and East European countries, the Soviet Union including, followed soon, although they differed from each other from the point of view of degree of clarity about what they wanted to achieve. In other words, not every country had its Balcerowicz or Klaus.

Two main characteristics of this unique enterprise have to be stressed, although they are hardly surprising. Firstly, it was a process started by a process: there was no single cause, and no single event can be identified as its beginning or as its exclusively decisive turning point. Thus in the search for relevant factors we have to go back in time perhaps almost as far as the moment of Stalin's death, because, for example, in Poland that proved to be a precondition for the decollectivisation of agriculture and in consequence for an increase in the share of privately owned (productive) assets in the Polish economy.[2]

Secondly, in this process politics is inseparably linked with economics. This characteristic of systemic transformation has its roots in the fact that under the old regime in a sense everything was politics. Equally important, however, was the feedback effect between developments in spheres traditionally understood as either typically economic or political. In the first systemic transformation the economy was transformed for political and/or ideological reasons, but the failure of the new economic system to produce the expected results eventually forced political changes which in turn made retransformation of the economy possible.

Whatever our opinion on whether STEs constituted a separate (meta)economic system, let us repeat that real socialism was, schematically speaking, based on central planning and on public ownership of the means of production. In consequence, systemic transformation has to change both these defining or constitutive characteristics. In the most general terms, therefore, it consists of marketisation and privatisation. Marketisation, in turn, embraces liberalisation, i.e. extending the sphere of economic freedom and reconstruction of the legal and institutional framework (ordo) within which economic agents exchange goods, services, and assets (WELFENS and JASINSKI, 1994).

These two, or rather three, types of actions, i.e. privatisation, liberalisation and, so to say, reinstitutionalisation, differ from each other with respect to their internal dynamics and degree of complexity. It was relatively easy to remove restrictions, but in doing so without putting in place a new, consistent legal framework one risked compromising the whole undertaking. An institutional structure does not consist exclusively of written law, but also of certain behavioural patterns. Both were missing, and developing them had to take time. What is more, the knowledge level of economic agents regarding the operation of market mechanisms was and still is far from sufficient, let alone satisfactory. Political instability and various vested interests, often based on exploiting existing legal gaps, did not encourage farsighted law making, and were instrumental in creating behavioural pattern which sooner or later will have be eradicated. Last but not least, in some STEs - in 1989 it was Poland, later on Romania, and in 1992-93 the republics of the former Soviet Union - systemic transformation had to be accompanied or even preceded by macroeconomic stabilisation policy, with all the undesired and dysfunctional trade-offs that result.

In all of this, ownership changes were always supposed to play a central role and in October 1989, when the Mazowiecki government announced their economic programme, in charge of which was Leszek Balcerowicz, one of the main objectives of this first non-communist dominated government was to set up a market system akin to the one found in the industrially developed countries, to cite the programme announced on 9 October 1989. That is why, the process of systemic transformation, following the framework introduced above, has to be looked at in more detail from two points of view: regulation and competition. Together with ownership they co-determine economic efficiency, both productive and allocative. In the case of post-STEs they are absolutely vital as far as the efficiency of the whole economic system is concerned, and therefore also for the success of privatisation of these economies.

4. Regulation Sensu Largo

Regulation as a determinant of economic efficiency of and within an economic system can be considered at, as it were, three levels: the rule of law, antitrust legislation and regulation sensu stricto. Variously understood, regulation is an integral part of any economy and therefore the main problem of regulating economic activities is not whether it should exist but rather the way in which it is done and the rules which govern it. In industrialised countries their legal systems and their adherence to the rule of law, the importance that they ascribe to promotion and protection of competition, as well as the institutional frameworks within which, just to give one example, their public utilities operate, all exemplify regulation. Their existence is a matter of fact, even if the reasons given to justify it are not always beyond doubt.

It follows that one aspect of economic systemic transformation is the necessity to introduce this kind of regulation that exists in industrialised countries, or rather to change the structure, character and activities of the inherited regulatory institutions. Transformation of the economic system will have to be accompanied by transformation of the political system, in the process of which transformation the rule of law will have to become a real corner stone of the new order. Competition will have to be appreciated, protected and promoted. Perhaps even par excellence regulatory agencies taking care of, for example, public utilities (network industries, natural monopolies) will have to be established and their briefs defined. To these ends the institutional arrangements of market economies of industrialised countries will have to be both imitated and adjusted to local needs.

To change the political system it was apparently enough to call a free general election and let the newly elected MPs to gather together and form a government. To reestablish the rule of law it would then suffice to ask the legislative, executive and judicial branches of government to follow some procedures as well as to consider properly the scope for their activities. But the rules first had to be set up and the laws written, to say the least. In some countries the existence of a pre-communist democratic tradition and the permeation of western culture seemed to be on the side of the newcomers, but there were no political parties to help mediate between voters and candidates and structure political processes. The social groups, the actions of which made the breakthrough possible, perceived the world around them as a black and white cliché of "us" and "them", and it was naïve to expect that forty or so years of propaganda would leave the minds of the public intact. What is more, even in those Central and East European countries where the opposition was best organised, things moved so quickly that programmes had to be written after the new equipe was already in power. On the one hand, the implementation of these programmes had to be entrusted to the old nomenklatura, who were too large a group to be sacked and replaced by new people. On the other, the ideas that some members of the "new nomenklatura" had about what market economies are all about also left much to be desired. In this context a fully fledged, western-style liberal democracy could easily be confused with its external appearances, but its taking root and gaining support from universally acknowledged social values had to take time.

Against this background of political systemic transformation, i.e. of change in the broadly understood regulatory structure of post-STEs, one has to look at more specific problems of the law in force. Whatever one's views on the legitimacy of the old regime and therefore on the legal acts introduced by it, one has to acknowledge that declaring all the inherited laws as null and void has never been a realistic option. From the theoretical point of view it would have been a rather controversial option, and from the practical point of view one that would have been almost impossible to follow. The revolutionary changes of 1989 had their source in a rejection of (a particular form of) communist rule in Central and Eastern Europe, but no revolution is able to break all the links with the past, least of all such a peaceful revolution as the one witnessed by most parts of the former Soviet empire in the late 1980s. Some continuity is unavoidable and the legal systems of these countries is just one example, even though their legislatures have been very busy over the last few years. Eventually any parliament may decide to overturn almost all the laws passed by its predecessors, but this pragmatic attitude consisting in the acceptance of the inherited laws as a departure point for the new ones, was potentially able to undermine the legitimacy of the new regimes, not least because of the limitations of the productive capabilities of any legislature. What ordinary people often saw were often simply old bureaucrats implementing old laws.

But the problem of legitimacy, although important in itself, was not the only one connected with regulation sensu largo. Leaving aside the problem of whether and to what extent the introduction of the rule of law can be simply declared, one could not close one's eyes to the fact that piecemeal reform of the legal system was creating the risk of serious inconsistencies and gaps, regardless of whether or not introduced or overlooked purposefully. This was particularly dangerous in the sphere of what we called above the law of contract, in which sphere the inherited laws were simply incompatible with the newly established. Obviously, (economic) systemic transformation was started and is being brought about above all by changing existing laws and introducing new ones and quite a lot had to be done at the very beginning, as it were, in one go. But reworking the whole of the legal system, however long it was to take, was one thing, and making the new one operational, quite another. And all of this runs against one of the most important requirements with respect to economic laws, namely their stability.

Before we move to the issue of competition, there is one more regulatory problem which has to be mentioned, namely that of regulation sensu stricto. To the extent that post-STEs are going to - ideally not uncritically - imitate the institutional structure of industrialised countries, one may realistically expect that, as we have analysed this above, the new regulatory structures will go beyond the rule of law and promotion and protection of competition, even though this state of affairs does not seem absolutely necessary and alternative solutions are feasible. In other words, although it is easy to agree that there will be regulation in the strict sense of the word, altogether there are more questions than answers. But how should it look like? Should each industry be regulated separately or should there be just one regulatory body, for instance for all subsectors of the energy industry? Should they take the form of a committee or be headed by a director general who on his or her own takes decisions and is responsible for them? What is the best place for regulatory bodies in the government structure and how can such position be squared with their independence and accountability? Who is going to have the final say in conflicts between regulators and regulatees? Is sunshine regulation to be relied upon? What is to be the role of public opinion in the regulatory process? And, going from the general to the more specific, should it be profits or only prices that are regulated? It is certainly true that something simply has to be done about public utilities, once central planning has been abandoned, and one of the decisive factors in shaping institutional choice will be the degree of progress in privatising public utilities in these countries.[3] However, although institutional arrangements existing e.g. in the OECD or, even more relevant, in the EU Member States offer some guidelines, one cannot deduce from them what form should their counterparts takes in transforming economies.

Despite there existing a variety of particular institutional solutions and a pluralism of political traditions, democracy and its corner stone, the rule of law, are both important common denominators among existing country members and necessary requirements for those who want to apply. More specifically, although there are differences as far as the level of enthusiasm and conviction is concerned, all Member States, both separately and in sharing their responsibility for the Single Market, try at least to protect the existing level of competition, and Articles 85 and 86 of the Treaty of Rome are used more and more to this end.

But are these kinds of common denominators sufficient to help post-STEs to make the right decisions? All the choices that have to be made in this transition period are tainted with indeterminacy, because although the direction of necessary changes is clear enough one cannot deduce from it the exact institutional form that the political system including protection and promotion of competition, ought to take, not to mention regulation sensu stricto. The solutions applied elsewhere are a result of more or less smooth evolution of market institutions, with all the limitations involved, and therefore of limited applicability in the countries in which capitalist continuity was interrupted. And there is much more to it than only differences in traditions; evolution of economic institutions means also that there are solutions suitable for the given stage of economic development, which is one more argument against simply copying the laws from elsewhere.

Another context in which the issue of regulation appears but which deserves our attention also on its own is that of competition. In the process of competing with each other, economic agents, so to say, regulate each other's behaviour and at the same time antitrust legislation doubtless belongs to explicit regulatory structures.

In Central and Eastern Europe it was only after the break of 1989 that the possibility - and, as time passes by, the necessity - to compete in and for markets arose; now even casual observation suggests that such competition is a relatively widespread phenomenon in former STEs. What is, however, most important is that, compared with the status quo ante, competition in (post-)STEs changed its nature, methods and objects. Only one thing remained as it had been: success was still necessary to survive.

At the most general level such competition in and for markets, in itself a necessary attribute of any market economy, is a consequence of systemic transformation, i.e. of marketisation and privatisation. Opening the borders, reducing tariffs, demonopolising foreign trade and, last but not least, introducing (internal) convertibility, all these factors played important roles. However when one looks at the behavioural and structural inheritance with which post-STEs started to rely on competition in allocating their resources, there arises a problem of what kinds of measures are necessary to protect what has already been achieved as well as to encourage further development of competition. Equally important is the question regarding more positive actions aiming, for example, at changing the structure of previously monopolised industries.

More or less institutionalised competition policy belongs to the regulatory infrastructure of any market economy. Trying to translate these general remarks and considerations into what is required for post-STEs on their way back to capitalism, one should point out that sooner or later, and rather sooner than later, antitrust laws will have to be passed, specialised institutions created, and practices established. All of this is an integral part of systemic transformation, of creating an institutional structure suitable for market self-coordination of economic activities. Yet the difference between transforming economies and mature market economies consists in that although, as we have said, all economic agents would like to be monopolists, in post-STEs there are many enterprises entering the brave new world as monopolists which never won anything apart from the arbitrary favours of central planners interacting with local party bosses. This makes the dilemma regarding not punishing the most competitive enterprises even more acute, because available criteria are blurred by unreliable data. What is more, the usual conflict between a vocal minority claiming that their industry is special and the silent majority in favour of (the fruits of) competition, i.e. of lower prices and larger variety of goods, is not going to go away, and those trying to solve it in the public interest cannot as yet rely on the support of the public at large.

The relevance of this kind of approach to regulation sensu largo in the process of systemic transformation is additionally strengthened by the desire of all Central and

East European countries to join the European Union, which necessitates some kind of harmonisation of existing legal arrangements and institutional structures.[4]

5. Regulation Sensu Stricto

Western experience suggests that regulatory problems will become particularly urgent when the governments of Central and Eastern Europe are deciding about what - but the "when" and "how" are not less important - should be privatised. Although it is often pointed out that these economies were highly monopolised, most of the industries there are at least potentially competitive, just as in any other market economy, especially if free trade prevails and borders remain relatively open. In consequence, most of privatisation - even though, as in Poland, individual decisions have to be approved by the Antimonopoly Office - will be, so to say, regulation-free. Or perhaps better said, the regulatory aspect of state ownership will disappear in the moment of privatisation; the activities of given enterprises will be subject only to general legal regulation, and no industry specific regulatory structures will be created.

Since we have devoted so much space to the issue of regulation in general and regulation sensu stricto in particular it seems nonetheless appropriate to devote part of this section to the issue of privatisation of network industries (public utilities, natural monopolies). The present speed of privatisation in post-STEs suggests that it will take a long time before all assets in non-public utilities sectors of the economy are transferred to the private sector, which would put them in more or less the same position as the British government was in the early 1980s.[5] But should they wait so long? Should they start with at least potentially competitive industries and proceed to public utilities only when they are done with them? Are not public utilities so important that they should be taken care of as soon as possible? These are by and large rhetorical questions. Since, as noted above, new structures and ways of proceeding have to be created anyway, and since regulation both in theory and in practice works better if it is separated from ownership, it seems that this kind of privatisation-cum-regulation should not be postponed for too long.

It is most likely in this context that Western and in particular British privatisation experiences can be most useful for their Central and East European followers. If these experiences are in any sense relevant, it is because they show how complex privatisation of public utilities is. In consequence, in the case of post-STEs the possibility of having public utilities in the public or private sector does not seem to be an either/or alternative describing the dilemma that politicians have to solve here and now, but rather refers to a sequence of future events. In other words, in the immediate future one can at best expect a mixed ownership structure of public utilities, with two models makings themselves immediately available: either some shares in a monopoly are sold to a foreign investor, like with the Hungarian telecoms company Matav (but this proved to be only the first stage of a far reaching restructuring involving, among other things, vertical separation and prospects for competition), or some assets in the given industry are transferred to the private sector, preferably to different owners. Although complete privatisation could be a better solution, whatever option is chosen, there will appear serious regulatory problems which will have to be solved, which point out yet another relationship between privatisation and regulation. The design of appropriate regulatory agencies, independent, powerful and accountable is in this context of absolutely crucial importance.

6. The ESI and Telecommunications

For these, more or less general considerations, regarding regulation, both sensu stricto and sensu largo, competition and privatisation, to become policy relevant, they have to be applied to some specific situations. As the most appropriate examples I chose the electricity supply industry (ESI) and telecommunications.

6.1 The Electricity Supply Industry

On 1 April 1990 the new structure of the ESI in England and Wales became operational, but six years or so after the Vesting Day the whole transformation process of the ESI in England and Wales has not yet finished. From the formal point of view, this process was supposed to - and certainly will - last eight years, and it will be finished only when the remaining supply monopolies are completely abolished. This is supposed to happen on - or, according to the most recent press speculations, in the quarter following - 1 April 1998. However, the changes since 1990 have gone far beyond the initial restructuring and gradual, prescheduled liberalisation. All the parties involved: the government, the regulator, the antitrust authorities, and the firms, both from the industry and from outside it, both British and foreign, as well as the consumers, all interacted with each other in a sometimes chaotic train of actions and reactions. In other words, both the implemented and planned changes as well as subsequent interventions generated a dynamic, evolutionary process, in which various parties may use their prerogatives and freedoms, but which in its totality is no longer controllable by any single party.

The evolutionary character of changes in the ESI in the UK has, apart from making any assessment and/or evaluation much more difficult, two consequences: the initial arrangements are becoming less and less relevant (and therefore the mistakes, if any, made at the beginning matter less and less), and what really has to be evaluated is the direction of the undergoing changes. For example, it is increasingly important to ask how and to what extent various impatient interventions by the regulator helped - or otherwise - this evolutionary process.

After 6 years of successful functioning of the new structure and arrangements, it is the highest time to stop talking about the experiment (which word was fully justified when Vickers and Yarrow wrote their 1991 Economic Policy paper) and analyse the British experience.[6] With one caveat, however: being specifically British does not exclude its international relevance. Just the opposite. Now that the European Union has reached an agreement on the internal electricity market directive, imperfect as its provisions are (JASINSKI and SKOCZNY, 1996) and some East and Central European and Third World countries are trying hard to learn positive lessons from what happened in England and Wales on 1 April 1990 and has happened since then, it is time for a more balanced and objective interpretation of these experiences. The learners should be helped not with just detailed, competent descriptions of what happened, but also with balanced interpretation, going beyond the noise of daily newspaper stories.

Is the UK experience really applicable to post-STEs (JASINSKI, SZABLEWSKI and YARROW, 1995)? The example of Poland well illustrates most ambiguities involved. According to the letter written by the Polish government to the World Bank, a special agency for the whole of the energy industry was to be created before the end of 1992, but the birth process is still going on, and it is by no means certain whether the looming parliamentary election is going to have any positive effect on the legislative process.

As in all other post-STEs and their public utilities, what was - and, in a sense, still is - needed was indeed a fundamental overhaul of the governance structure of the sector, which meant, among other things, establishing completely new principles governing relationships among government institutions, energy enterprises and customers. This was to be done by implementing the following two guiding rules:

1. that the level of government involvement in the day-to-day management, planning, and staffing decisions of the energy enterprises should be reduced, and in this way the autonomy and accountability of energy enterprises increased; and
2. that the institutional reforms should establish clearly defined, stable, consistent, and transparent sets of rules and procedures, which were to be followed by all actors involved (SZABLEWSKI, 1996).

In practice the task consisted in separating different roles that the government was until then playing in the energy industry: policy maker, owner and regulator. It was argued that the advantage of giving the different roles to separate Government departments is that each has clear responsibilities and accountability. The concept of separation of the Government's roles was accepted by the Polish Government and it agreed that the most important part of the whole concept is the establishment of a separate, independent regulatory agency responsible only for economic regulation of the energy sector.

The delays meant that the opportunities offered by the turbulent character of the first phase of the process of systemic transformation were wasted, and at the same time uncertainty in the industry was unnecessarily prolonged and increased. Nevertheless, the newest draft of the Energy Law, most recently approve by the Parliamentary Select Committee, still provides for such an agency. The Energy Regulatory Agency (Urzad Regulacji Energetyki, URE or "the Authority" in the text of the draft) is to be "a central state administration organ, appropriate in the matter of energy and fuels economy regulation, reporting to the Council of Ministers", although it has not yet been decided whether it should be managed by a president or by the board of five, in both cases appointed and removed by the President of Council of Ministers (Prime Minister). The URE's tasks read as follows:

- issuing, amending and withdrawing licences;
- approval and control of tariffs of energy and fuel (...);
- approval and control of quality customer service standards;
- hearing complaints and resolving disputes within the scope of the Act;
- determination of terms of use and of third party access to the grid, in case it is impossible to reach an agreement for parties concerned;
- imposing fines upon the principles in the Act;
- cooperation with the relevant organs in counteracting the abuse by energy enterprises of a monopolistic or dominant position;
- publishing information with a view to improving efficiency of energy and fuels consumption;
- gathering and processing information relating to energy management.

As one can see, the prerogatives of the URE with respect to the very important issue of energy prices are rather limited, and the way in which the regulator(s)'s independence is guaranteed also leaves quite a lot to be desired.

What is more, if we agree that a sound regulatory system consists in protection against monopoly abuse, encouragement of efficiency and innovation, low burden of regulation in terms of information costs, degree of discretion and implementation, promotion of competition, and regulatory simplicity and predictability (VELJANOVSKI, 1993), it will soon become obvious that the proposed structure and division of tasks does not fully correspond to this ideal. Does this, however, mean that it is unable to deliver what it was created for? Is better to have a regulator like this rather then none? Apart from the unforgivable delay, the problem that I personally have with the regulatory developments in Poland, is that so much is left to be decided by secondary legislation and implementing acts. In addition, many articles of the new Energy Law have, after the committee stage, more than one version. Anything may, therefore, happen and politics may get an upper hand again.

This embarrassingly slow progress in setting up a new legal and regulatory framework stands in sharp contrast with the progress achieved in procompetitive restructuring (POPCZYK, 1996). It is true that the Polish Power Grid Company (PSE S.A.) is at present a monopsony buyer and a monopoly seller of almost all electricity, but the structure of the Polish electricity supply industry is such that once the Pool becomes fully operational - it is already being tried -, third party access introduced (and distribution separated from supply), and some progress with privatisation achieved, Poland could easily have one of the most competitive electricity supply industries in Europe apart from the UK and some Scandinavian countries. What is still missing is an independent regulator, but then what is the use of having an independent regulator, if, as it happened in Hungary earlier this year, the government is able - and did - overrule the price increases, agreed by the regulator and the regulatees?

There exist many opportunities to learn not only from the British experiences but also from one's own mistakes. The former teaches us that there a lot of scope for competition in the public utilities sector, but effective competition requires pro-competitive restructuring which should precede privatisation. Regulators should be independent, and their relationships with the antitrust authorities well defined, in particular as far as appeal procedures are concerned. Radical reforms may help overcome backwardness and create competitive advantage.

6.2 Telecommunications

The growing importance of broadly understood communications in any modern economy and society implies the necessity for a holistic approach. Systemic transformation, i.e. both its economic (privatisation, liberalisation and re-institutionalisation) and political (democratisation) aspects, makes this kind of approach even more necessary. That is so because of the inherited situation as well as because of the challenges specific to such a unique period of time. Therefore one must not concentrate one's attention just on single enterprises, however important they are in the given context, nor on individual services and types of infrastructure. Developments in other countries, and, in particular, in the European Union are important, but one must see - and anticipate - the trends, and not just the variety of still co-existing solutions. Last but not least, one has to ask about what should drive the development strategy for telecommunications and related sectors, the strategy currently being formulated and about to find its expression in the new communications act. In other words, one must not allow the plans for the future to be dominated either by the fiscal interests of the state or by particular sectoral interests. The interests of the economy as a whole and of the consumers in particular have to be brought to the fore.

Looking at the historical developments in this area, one has to notice that although telecommunications organisations were often put together with those responsible for postal services, this sector was always considered as well defined and distinct (DAVIES, 1994). Various telecommunication services, limited as their choice was for a very long time, were also seen as clearly different from each other, but at the same time their joint - and in many instances monopolistic - provision was justified on the grounds of economies of scale and scope. All of this, in turn, was seriously tainted by the considerations of strategic importance

Technological progress accelerated incredibly in the last few decades, and by and large deprived the subdivisions within telecommunications sector of their economic justification. The distinctions between local, long distance and international connections make less and less sense. Similarly, the advent of wireless local loop technology links fixed and mobile networks (cellular phones and pagers), and satellite technology will be another step in this direction. Telecommunications networks gradually loose their naturally monopolistic character, and the distinction between basic and value added services is perhaps the most outdated one (WELFENS and GRAACK, 1996).

It is the highest time for technological progress to have an influence on the structure and organisation of this sector, and in such a way that new technologies are not merely reluctantly accommodated, but really anticipated. There is no end in sight to the R&D results becoming implementable and implemented, and this kind of dynamics implies that open structures and liberalisation are in this context the only ways forward. This in turn calls for effective regulation for competition, possibly exercised by a sector specific, independent authority, either broadly or narrowly defined, and for rethinking the role of the Antimonopoly Office. In Poland the latter will have to take seriously its newly acquired task of consumer protection, but the more the communication markets become similar to other markets, the broader will be the scope for using general antitrust provisions. Counteracting the abuse of dominant position will certainly figure prominently among the AO's tasks.

New technologies not only made obsolete various subdivisions with the telecommunications sectors, but also blurred the borders between telecommunications and broadcasting and multimedia (KPMG, 1996). On the one hand, cable TV, if proper provisions are in place, often offers an opportunity to construct new, much more modern, local loop networks. On the other hand, the existing fixed telephone networks are being tested for interactive services, video on demand included. Telecommunications and broadcasting meet also in the sky, where the use of digital technology in satellites seems to be the way forward. That is why both sectors will possibly have to be liberalised simultaneously.

Obviously, integration within the communications sector, broadly understood, has to be looked at not only from the point of view of making use of the constantly appearing technological opportunities, but also from the point of view of economic efficiency, both of the sector itself and the economy as a whole. A useful way of looking at these issues is from the point of view of the determinants of economic efficiency: competition, regulation and ownership. In the area under consideration, the three of them are particularly interwoven, and demand being dealt with jointly: competition between publicly and privately owned companies, in the situation in which the regulator is also exercising state ownership rights with respect to one (or more) of the parties, will at best be distorted and probably will never become effective. This is why privatisation of TP S.A. (Polish Telecom) is of primary importance, but equally significant is separation and transfer to the private sector of telecommunications businesses of PSE S.A. (Polish Power Grid Company) and PKP (Polish State Railways) (KONTKIEWICZ-CHACHULSKA, 1996). In this way new entrants providing alternative infrastructure will not have to start from scratch, and at the same time will be driven by commercial considerations and free from the temptation of cross-subsidisation. However, transforming a public monopoly into a private one creates more problems than solves: apart from the usual difficulties with the regulation of a monopolist, there also appears the problem of respect for property rights as well as of keeping whatever promises were made in the process of privatisation.

Despite the present multiplicity of regulatory agencies, the present regulatory structure of Polish telecommunications is perhaps its weakest point. Conflict of interest is perhaps the most polite way of describing what is going on. The role of the Antimonopoly Office is under-defined, and its actions constrained by political and policy considerations. Most liberalisation measures remain on paper, and the whole licensing process is marked with huge, international controversy. The prospects for self-sustaining competition are grim. And when one looks at communications, broadly understood, the potential problems (and opportunities), not to mention the possibilities of solving (exploiting) them, are not even noticed (JASINSKI, SKOCZNY and YARROW, 1995).

All of this has from the Polish point of view one more important aspect. Namely, the process of liberalisation of EU telecommunications not only progressed remarkably far since the 1987 Green Paper, but also is close to its practical completion on 1 January 1998 (STEHMAN, 1995). Therefore, what is at stake with respect to the issue of what telecommunications the Poles and other Central and East Europeans need, is not only the future development of this and related sectors as well as of the Polish society and economy and of its competitiveness, but also the much more mundane task of simply having to fulfil certain requirements implied by the desire to become a Member State of the EU, as specified in the May 1995 White Paper.

All in all, the following areas and issues are certainly of key importance:

- integrated, holistic approach to communications sector, broadly understood, and in particular on their importance for the economy as a whole and on the interactions between telecommunications and broadcasting;

- industry specific regulation and the role of competition policy, and in particular on regulation for competition;
- consequences of the EU Association Agreement and future full membership.

Endnotes

[1] For an overview, see BRUS and Laski (1989).

[2] This action constituted a step towards privatisation of the Polish economy but it did not result in a systemic transformation because the coordination mechanisms remained unchanged and no critical mass of privately owned assets was achieved. Paradoxically, so one may reach the conclusion that there is no such a thing as systemic transformation. What we actually observe are market economies returning to their capitalist equilibria after having suffered a prolonged external metaeconomic shock caused by the October Revolution and the Soviet imperialist policy towards Central and Eastern Europe as well as towards the Third World. The cases of socialism in Yugoslavia, China and Cuba, although different in their origins, only confirm this general rule. In other words, the processes of building and dismantling socialism not only immediately followed each other but perhaps even overlapped!

[3] Although the jury still seems to be out on regulation UK-style, this institutional model has to compete with its American counterpart, and attempts to create regulatory offices or agencies face resistance from those who prefer (federal) commissions. The choice is far from being straightforward, but at least two things have be taken into account. Firstly, one similarity between the UK and post-STEs is that, regardless of the speed of privatisation in the latter, sooner or later regulatory agencies will have to deal with industries in which most economic agents recently were or even still are in the public sector. Regulation UK-style was designed for transitional period and therefore most likely can be used in the process of systemic transformation too. Secondly, it seems that British regulatory institutions are more modern than the American ones. Such a statement does not uncritically assume that newer institutions are necessarily better than older ones, but at least in some industries, like for example telecommunications and, perhaps, the ESI, technological progress has to have an effect on regulatory structures. And this is precisely what happened in the UK in the 1980s. Institutions designed for and set up in post-STEs have to be forward- and not backward-looking.

[4] This in itself is an attempt to hit a moving target as the official commencement of the single market has so far had almost no effect such industries as telecommunication and energy.

[5] There is always an odd one out: the budgetary pressures forced the Hungarian government to achieve remarkably much in this area.

[6] For one of the most recent and thorough accounts, see: SURREY (1996), but see also JASINSKI (1996).

References

BRUS, W. and K. LASKI (1989), From Marx to the Market. Socialism in Search of an Economic System, Oxford, Clarendon Press.

DAVIES, A. (1994), Telecommunications and Politics: the Decentralised Alternative, London, Pinter Publishers.

JASINSKI, P., (1993), Financial regulation of state-owned enterprises in Central and Eastern Europe. The soft budget constraint under central planning, market socialism and in the process of systemic transformation, Oxford: Regulatory Policy Institute.

JASINSKI, P. (1996), Review of Surrey (1996), The Journal of Energy Literature, vol. 2 (2), pp. 64-67.

JASINSKI, P. and SKOCZNY, T., eds., (1996), Elektroenergetyka (Studia nad integracja europejska, vol. 1) [The Electricity Supply Industry (European Integration Studies, vol. 1)], Oxford and Warsaw: RPRC and the Centre for Europe.

JASINSKI, P., SKOCZNY, T. and YARROW, G., (1995), Zasady konkurencji i regulacja w telekomunikacji [Competition Rules and Regulation in Telecommunications], Warszawa: Urzad Antymonopolowy.

JASINSKI, P., SZABLEWSKI, A. and YARROW, G., (1995), Konkurencja i regulacja w energetyce: Brytyjskie doswiadczenia a polskie problemy [Competition and regulation in the energy industry: British experiences and Polish problems], Warszawa: INE PAN and Elipsa.

KONTKIEWICZ-CHACHULSKA, H., (1996), The Recent Evolution of Telecommunications in Poland, Discussion Papers No 8, Oxford, RPRC.

KPMG, Public Policy Issues Arising from Telecommunications and Audiovisual Convergence. Summary Report, Brussels: European Commission.

POPCZYK, J., (1996), Polska polityka elektroenergetyczna, in: SZABLEWSKI, A., ed. Mechanizmy rynkowe w energetyce i telekomunikacji [Market mechanisms in the energy industry and telecommunications], Warszawa: INE PAN and Elipsa, pp. 45-74.

STEHMAN, Oliver, (1995), Network Competition for European Telecommunications, Oxford, OUP.

SURREY, J., ed., (1996), The British Electricity Experiment: Privatization: the record, the issues, the lessons, London, Earthscan Publications Ltd.

SZABLEWSKI, A. (1996), Designing a new regulatory regime for the Polish energy sector, Discussion Papers No 8, Oxford, RPRC.

VELJANOVSKI, C. (1993), The Future of Industry Regulation in the UK. A Report of an Independent Inquiry, London: European Policy Forum for British and European Market Studies.

VICKERS, J. and G. YARROW (1991), The British electricity experiment, Economic Policy, 12, pp. 187-232.

WELFENS, P.J.J. and C. GRAACK (1996), Telekommunikationswirtschaft. Deregulierung, Privatisierung and Internationalisierung, Heidelberg, Springer.

WELFENS, P.J.J. and P. JASINSKI (1994), Privatisation and Foreign Direct Investment in Transforming Economies. Theoretical and Policy Issues of Systemic Transformation in an International Perspective, Aldershot, Dartmouth Press.

YARROW, G. (1986), Privatisation in theory and practice, Economic Policy, 2, pp.323-379.

Comments on: Privatisation, Competition and Regulation in Transforming Economies: The Cases of the Electricity Supply Industry and Telecommunications

Horst Brezinski

Piotr Jasinski starts out by claiming that privatisation, competition, and regulation constitute the main elements of systemic transformation because they are „the key determinants of economic efficiency, both productive and allocative". This is more or less true when we consider that the Soviet-type economies failed because they neglected economic efficiency. However, the argumentation has to be seen put in a broader perspective. The experiences made during the transformation process since 1989 and the development of institutional economics as well as of economic analysis of transition indicate that we have to widen our views.

1. Privatisation, competition and regulation are definitively important cornerstones for the functioning of a market economy and may contribute to economic efficiency. They are important elements of a market economy. Yet, as we know from recent experience, the market consists of more than these three elements, because there exist various market configurations with specific institutions because „...the real world is riddled with imperfect and asymmetric information as endowments over which agents have property rights" (VAN BRABANT, 1998, p.110). The gathering and processing of information is costly. Scale economies and externalities exist due to the impossibility to define and to implement specific property rights. Monopolies and oligopolies exist. Thus, corrective action and regulation is needed. Consequently, market institutions, such as legal codes, legal institutions, financial agents and property rights, have to be set up. In addition to this, the workability of all these institutions has to be implemented. The process of implementation is a time-consuming process. The previous Soviet-type economy has left a specific systemic structure which does not vanish overnight. There are many vested interests that impede the implementation of market institutions. Moreover, knowledge and skills are needed in order to understand and to handle market institutions. Of vital importance is an adequate infrastructure of competent skills, partly acquired through education, but organizational capabilities must also be available (VAN BRABANT, 1998, p.488). Consequentely, knowledge and information in designing and implementing transformation policies play an additional and important role. The three policy elements mentioned in the paper, privatisation, competition and regulation, are only instruments that are necessary as a precondition, but they alone do not guarantee a successful transition. Informal

institutions evolving from a certain type of behaviour, in conformity with a market economy, are badly needed.

2. Jasinski mentions that the three elements lead to allocative and productive efficiency. In reality the degree of efficiency is relative. We are looking for improvements compared with the current situation. The Russian example tells us more than clearly that the stress on immediately improving allocative and productive efficiency by introducing pure market elements does not help us achieve the desired goals. Emerging markets sometimes need instruments which are not in conformity with a market environment such as control and restrictions of capital flows.[1] What is needed most in the situation of a transforming country is adaptative efficiency. Adaptative efficiency is concerned with the kind of rules that shape the way an economy evolves through time. „It is also concerned with the willingness of a society to acquire knowledge and learning, to induce innovation, to undertake risk and creative activity of all sorts, as well as to resolve problems and bottlenecks of the society through time" (NORTH, 1990, p.80). According to North „the society that permits the maximum generation of trials will be most likely to solve problems through time. Adaptative efficiency, therefore, provides the incentive to encourage the development of decentralized decision-making processes that will allow societies to maximize the efforts required to explore alternative ways of solving problems." (NORTH 1990, p.81) Allocative efficiency and adaptative efficiency may not always be consistent. It is just in periods of transition that adaptative efficiency is more needed than allocative efficiency because the emerging market economy has to find its own institutional environment. Thus, apart from looking for allocative and productive efficiency which deserves a special notion in market economies (VICKERS/YARROW, 1989), in economies of transition the stress should be laid on adaptative efficiency.

Jasinski correctly points out that regulation in the sense of a market-type system deserves a special notion in economies of transition. The cases of the electricity supply industry and telecommunications demonstrate the difficulties of regulation *sensu stricto* in a transforming economy. Countries such as Poland can learn from the experience in market economies. However, the cases of both industries, especially that of telecommunications, show that economic systems have to be able to evolve through time and be flexible in order to find new solutions. The analysis of the telecommunication industry shows that due to technical changes and innovation telecommunications no longer constitute a natural monopoly except in the case of local networks (FRITSCH/WEIN/EWERS, 1996). Indivisibilities and sunk costs no longer play a major role due to innovation and organizational changes. Therefore, telecommunications largely qualify for an integration into the market mechanism. Due to the current state of technological and organizational change this integration has to take place in several steps. A regulation agency is still needed. The tasks of that agency, however, should be subject to permanent monitoring and lead to changes in the extent and quality of regulation. Consequently, the telecommunication sector - and the same applies to the energy sector (NOWOTNY, 1997), also characterized by innovation and organizational changes - have to be designed in a transforming country according to the present level of technology and organization. The regulation of these sectors has to be flexible and cannot follow a static blueprint taken over from a successfully performing market economy. Given that in some transforming countries these sectors are subject to competition by foreign suppliers the regulation to be implemented requires a restructuring of all national companies before privatization, because otherwise they would not survive in the new regulated market.

Jasinki's contribution thus demonstrates very clearly that privatization and liberalization in former Soviet-type economies are just the first steps towards a market economy. These steps, however, do not guarantee success and improved performance unless they are accompanied by the establishment of new institutions which will have to be shaped according to the national, regional or local conditions. Thus, transition is a much harder and more time consuming task than many politicians as well as economists make the public believe.

Endnotes

[1] Such unconventional proposals are made e.g. by Paul Krugman. See 'Währungspolitik aus dem Giftschrank' in Neue Zürcher Zeitung, 28./29. 8. 1998, p.21.

References

FRITSCH, M., T. WEIN and H. J. EWERS (1996), Marktversagen und Wirtschaftspolitik, 2ed., München: Vahlen.

NORTH, D. C. (1990), Institutions, Institutional change and Economic Performance, Cambridge: Cambridge University Press.

NOWOTNY, K. (1997), Electric Utilities: Through the Looking Glass, paper presented at the Annual Conference of the Association for Evolutionary Economics, New Orleans 3-5 January.

VAN BRABANT, J. M. (1998), The Political Economy of Transition, London: Routledge.

VICKERS, J. and G. YARROW (1989), Privatization - An Economic Analysis, Cambridge, Massachusetts: MIT Press.

C: Deregulation, Privatization and Internationalization of European Telecoms Markets

Cornelius Graack

1. Introduction

Since the beginning of the 1990s, the European telecommunications market is in a phase of transition. Liberalization pressure is coming from liberalized national markets as well as from national and supranational organizations such as the European Commission. The experiences in liberalized telecoms markets such as USA (1983), Great Britain (1984), Japan (1985), Korea (1990), New Zealand (1991), Sweden (1992) and Finland (1994) made it clear that competition leads to higher efficiency of telecoms operators, lower prices, and better quality of services as well as to innovative network systems and value-added services. Reliable and low-priced network services are not only crucial for the efficient functioning of a national economy but are also an important determinant of its international competitiveness. National economies with a liberalized telecoms market therefore have an advantage, that helps them not only to compete in international markets for tradable goods and services but also to attract foreign direct investment.

The strategic role of the telecoms industry has been well acknowledged by the European Commission which gradually harmonized and liberalized the European telecoms sector - despite national efforts to undermine the liberalization process. Since the first liberalization efforts in 1984, beginning with the release of the "Community action program on telecommunications", the progress in liberalization within the European Union became considerable in the early 1990s after the implementation of EC Directives initiated by the 1987 Green Paper on the development of the Common Market for Telecommunications services and equipment (EUROPEAN COMMISSION, 1987). EC Directives are binding for Member States but - in accordance with the principles of subsidiarity - they leave a certain degree of freedom to the national legislature to make national law commensurate with EC legislation. Between 1988 and 1993 the Directives in the area of telecommunications mainly focused on services, open network provision, terminal equipment, standardization, mobile communications and satellite communications. The aim of these Directives was to create a framework for effective competition in selected telecoms segments by harmonization (e.g. adaptation of common standards, reciprocity of licenses) on the one hand and liberalization (e.g. public procurement policy) on the other hand (WELFENS and GRAACK, 1996). Yet, for many years the core fields of national telecoms monopolies, namely voice telephony services and public switched telecommunications networks (PSTN), have not been touched by the above mentioned EC Directives, mainly as a result from opposition at the national level of EU member states (politicians, network operators, trade unions). Revenues from PSTN-services amount to up to 80% of total revenues, making it the key segment that has to be liberalized if effective competition in the telecoms sector is the objective. Therefore, the European Council of 22 July 1993 agreed to proposals by the EU Commission to fully liberalize the telephony services within the Union on 1st January 1998; exceptions are being made for Luxembourg, Greece, Ireland, Portugal and Spain. Furthermore, to support effective competition, the Telecommunication Ministers Council of 17 November 1994 decided to deregulate infrastructure by the same date (EUROPEAN COMMISSION, 1995). However, in addition to this "Full Competition Directive" a second directive came into effect in 1996 that sets the deadline for the liberalization of alternative networks on mid-1996. The directive requires that all restrictions on owners of alternative networks who intend to offer liberalized services or sell capacity to competitive service providers are lifted by 1 July 1996 (Directive 96/19/EC).

The EU liberalization plans have led to a rapid change in the structure of the European telecommunications sector. While at the beginning of the 1980s national EU telecoms markets were characterized by a state-owned monopoly, dominating in all fields of telecoms services (fixed and mobile infrastructure, services and end user equipment), the model of a single state-owned network operator that keeps monopoly rights and focuses - as a result of administrative protection - exclusively on the national market segments is fading out. Today, European telecoms markets are in a process of transformation triggered by deregulation, market entry of newcomers (competition), privatization, cooperation and internationalization (ELIXMANN, 1996; GRAACK, 1997).

This paper focuses on the trends and developments in the European telecommunications sector. In Section 2, recent developments at the national level of EU member states are described. Liberalization not only leads to structural changes at the national level but also affects the international telecoms segment. Internationalization trends, cooperation between EU network operators and their impacts on the telecoms market structure in the European Union are therefore discussed in Section 3. The paper concludes with some final remarks.

2. Developments on the National Level of EU Member States

As a result of EC Directives, several telecoms market segments such as the market for terminal equipment, the market for value-added services and the market for leased lines have been liberalized in all or at least in most EU member states and opened to competition. This does not hold for the infrastructure segment, where market entry of newcomers is still restricted in most European countries. While in the mobile communications sector at least one newcomer is licensed in all Western European countries in 1995 (except Luxembourg), competition in the fixed network segment with network operators offering voice telephony is currently limited to four EU countries: Finland, Great Britain, Sweden and - since 1 July 1996 - Denmark. Competition between different network systems (fixed and mobile) is also limited due to the fact that in all EU countries the mobile segment is dominated by the mobile subsidiary of the incumbent fixed network operator. The only exception is Greece - normally Europe's bad man out - where both national GSM licenses were awarded to private consortia.

Liberalization - defined as a process of opening up markets by removing administrative barriers to entry - does not necessary lead to effective competition. "Effective" competition means that market forces ensure efficient economic output: strategic decisions taken by one competitor with respect to prices, investments, services or quality are evaluated by the other market participants and imitated - if good - or sanctioned - if bad. In other words, there is a check and balance situation between all competitors. Efficient competition depends on the market structure. In network industries, effective competition is most likely in a market characterized by several operators of rather equal strength (market power in terms of main line and bottleneck facilities) that are equally treated by regulatory authorities. Due to an interconnection problem a dominant firm with bottleneck facilities carries the risk of discriminating smaller network operators. Moreover, market entry barriers such as sunk cost could also hamper effective competition.

2.1 Developments in EU Countries Characterized by Competing Fixed Network Operators

In liberalized EU countries, market structures as well as competition intensity are quite heterogeneous as a result of the market structure existing before liberalization, the pursued deregulation strategies and country-specific regulatory frameworks.

The first European country that liberalized the fixed network segment was Great Britain in 1984. Yet, competition was limited to two operators until 1991 (duopoly approach). In Great Britain, the establishment of competition in network operation was very much an experiment and therefore officials had the feeling that some degree of caution was appropriate (CARSBERG, 1991). Even if this argument holds true for the UK, which could not - at that time - resort to liberalization experiences made in other countries except the hardly comparable USA, the strategic decision of a duopoly must also be seen in the context of BT's privatization process. However, the duopoly strategy was planned to be taken under review in 1991.

Mercury, the second network operator besides British Telecom, got a license to build up and operate a fixed network. The market entry of Mercury was flanked and facilitated by so-called asymmetric regulation which consisted of four measures: (1) Prices of the incumbent operator were regulated by a price-cap formula. (2) British Telecom alone was obliged to offer universal service obligations, that is, to offer a selected basket of services to all households and firms on an equal basis. (3) BT had to guarantee Mercury access to its network. (4) Moreover, Mercury was allowed to interconnect with BT's network without making an equivalent contribution to BT's costs resulting from universal service obligation.

As a result of the regulatory framework, Mercury concentrated its activities on the highly profitable national and international long-distance market segment. However, Mercury failed to gain bigger market shares in both segments and neglected the local loop segment (except the profitable area around London). In 1991 Mercury had market shares (in per cent of telephone traffic) of about 6% in national long-distance segment, 11% in the international segment and 30% in the district of London (ATTENBOROUGH, 1993). The figures indicate that OFTEL's aim to promote competition in the British fixed network segment somehow failed: seven years after liberalization the British telecoms market was still characterized by a dominant network operator.

In 1991, as a consequence of weak competition, the duopoly model was replaced by a more liberal approach. Since then, the number of network operators, especially cable network operators, has steadily increased. However, BT was still the dominant player in 1995, although BT's market shares have decreased slowly but steadily to 89% in local and national long-distance calls, 70% in outgoing international calls and 89% in value-added and other systems business calls (OFTEL, 1995). Yet, alternative long-distance operators such as Mercury or Energis, a subsidiary of the National Grid company, are less profitable than one would expect. The permanent decrease in call charges resulting from a price cap regulation imposed on BT has been putting pressure on profit margins. Yet, overall telephone charges are still considerable high (see Tab. C1)

Things might change in the future. In 1995, for the first time since liberalization in 1984, BT felt the pressure of upcoming competition in the local loop by cable-TV-operators. Last year, BT suffered a net loss of about 50.000 subscribers, while mostly American-owned cable network operators could add as much as 50.000 lines a month. In fall 1996, cable-TV-network operators had more than 1.6 million television subscribers and about 2 million phone lines (1.8 million residential subscribers and 200,000 business lines). This trend could likely to be continued in the future. According to cable-TV executives, there could be as many as 6.5 million residential telephone lines and 1 million business lines by 2001 (SNODDY, 1996). Further competitive pressure on BT comes from a merger of Mercury and three cable-TV-operators announced in October 1996. The new company, Cable&Wireless Communications (C&WC), offers telephone services to about 2.5 million customers (1.25 million business lines and 1.29 million residential lines). Yet, the total number of subscribers is only about 1/10 of the number of subscribers connected to the BT network (BRITISH TELECOM, 1996). However, 11 years after the first liberalization efforts and 4 years after the full liberalization of the telecoms sector, market entry of cable-TV-operators in the local loop in cooperation with long-distance network operators is smoothly but steadily intensifying competition in the UK.

Since 1992 the Swedish telecoms market is one of the most liberal markets in the world: the provision of telecommunications services is open to competition without any restrictions, including network operation (SWEDISH MTC, 1994). Consequently, the Swedish market is - together with the British telecoms market - a very important test market for other European countries that intend to liberalize their telecoms markets. However, the Swedish situation in 1992 very much differed from the British one in 1984. While the poor performance of BT - BT's labor productivity was among the lowest in Europe - was one of the arguments in favor of the liberalization process in Britain, Swedish Telia offered one of the most reliable services at low prices, which holds true until today (see Fig. C1).

With a penetration rate of 69% Swedish Telia also kept the top position of the world's leading telecoms operators in 1994. The strong performance of the Swedish network operator makes it extremely difficult for newcomers to get a foothold into the Swedish market. Newcomers such as Tele 2, a joint venture of British Cable&Wireless and the Swedish Kennevik Group which is currently the second important network operator in Sweden, AT&T and Telenordia (a joint venture of BT, Tele Danmark and Norwegian Telenor) are therefore concentrating their forces on gaining market shares in the profitable long-distance market segments. While in 1994, their common market share in outgoing international long-distance calls amounted to approximately 10% (in comparison to 0% in 1993), Telia's share has fallen to around 70% in 1995. This trend does not hold true for the national long-distance or local segment with Telia having a market share of 95% and 100% respectively (SWEDISH MTC, 1996).

Since 1987 the Finnish Ministry of Transports and Communications pursued a liberalization strategy by gradually opening up the market for voice telephony. Under the 1987 Telecommunications Service Act, all established monopoly rights were eliminated and telecommunications activities liberalized subject to license, describing rights and duties of the licensee. Since January 1994, all national telephone services have been exposed to free competition, including international services as of July 1994. Consumers benefit most from liberalization, since competition leads to a wider choice, lower prices and higher quality of services. Compared to the monopoly situation of ten years ago, customers are saving a total of 1.5 billion Finnmarks (around $ 346 million) a year (FINNISH MTC, 1994, 1995).

Fig. C1: Telephone Charges for Business and Residential Customers in Selected European Countries

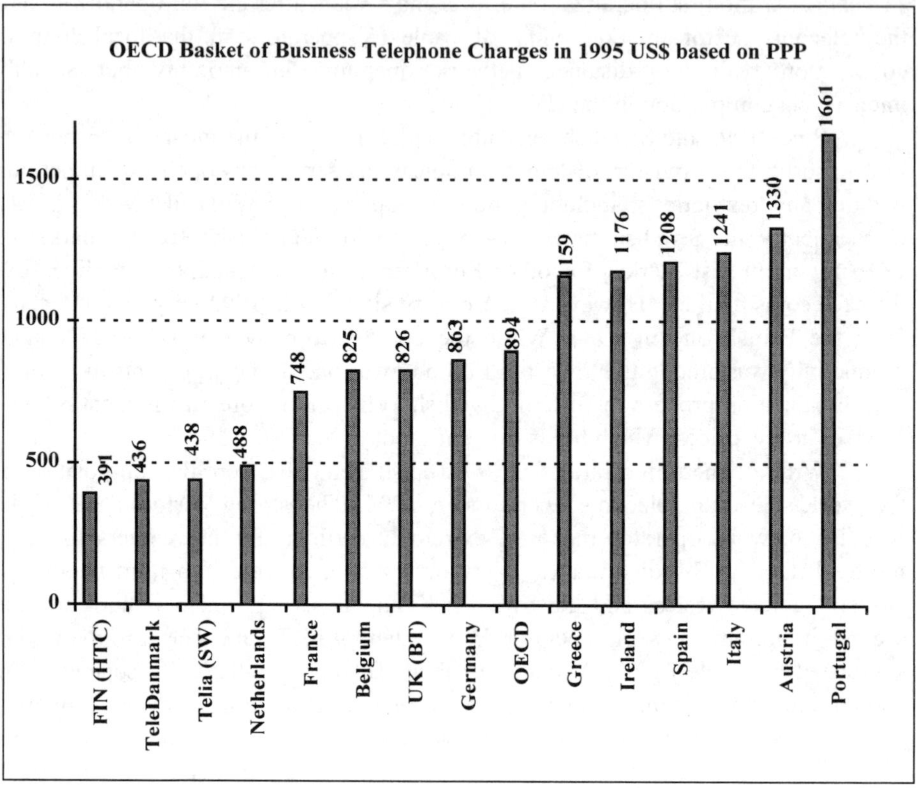

Source: OECD (1996), pp. 119.

The Finnish success story of introducing competition in the fixed network segment results from the special telecoms structure in Finland. Before liberalization, several telecoms operators offered services at the local level, while the national level was served by PT Finland, the state-owned Post and Telecommunications company. In 1994, PT Finland was turned into a state-owned stock company and the various services were separated into four subsidiaries (post, telecoms, data processing and vehicle leasing). Telecom Finland, the subsidiary charged with telecoms services, is by far the largest national player of the 70 Finnish telecoms operators in terms of turnover, expenses or investment. Most of the 48 smaller local operators are owned by the users, which is another characteristic of the Finnish telecoms market.

Fig. C1 (cont.)

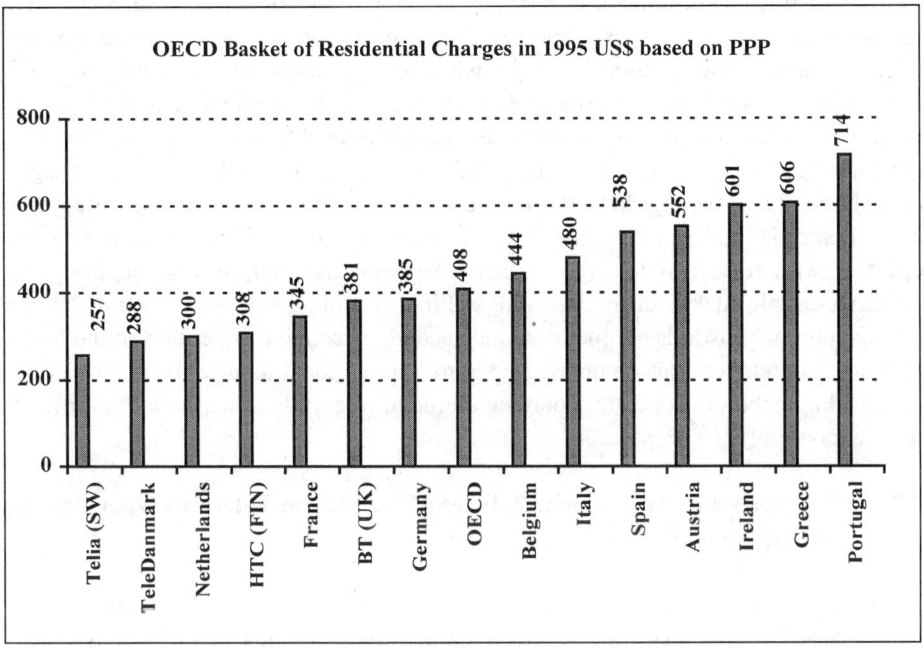

Note: Data as of January1996

Source: OECD (1996), p.119f.

In the aftermath of liberalization, the market shares in the long-distance market segment tremendously changed. Telecom Finland, that kept a market share of 94.5% in the national long-distance and of 99.1% in the international market segment in 1993, faced heavy market losses, especially in the national long-distance segment. Within one year, Kaukoverkko - the second Finnish long-distance network operator owned by Finnet Group, the association of Finnish local telecoms operators - gained a share of 51.6% in the national long-distance segment in terms of long-distance calls leaving Telecom Finland behind. This trend continued in 1995 with Kaukoverkko gaining a market share of 60.1% (Telecom Finnland: 36.5%, others: 3.4%). In the international segment, Telecom Finland's market share losses are less severe: 73% of all outgoing calls were still transmitted by Telecom Finland in 1995 in comparison to 18,3% by Finnet International and 8.7% by others (FINNISH MTC, 1996). Yet, newcomers will have a special stake in entering into the profitable international market segment. Competition is likely to intensify in the years to come.

The experiences made in Finland, Sweden and the UK make it clear that the future structure of the European telecommunications sector is not predictable yet. However, the three countries demonstrate that in the process of liberalization, the telecoms sector will certainly change while the intensity and speed of sectoral change very much depend on the already existing market structure and the starting position of each network provider. The Finnish case shows that the existence of network operators, especially in the local loop, leads to tough competition right after liberalizing the market. By contrast, the Swedish case demonstrates that market entry is the less likely, the better the performance of the incumbent network operator with regard to low (cost-oriented) prices and high service quality. The British example makes clear two things: First, a highly regulated duopoly is the wrong approach towards competition and second, effective competition in the long-distance markets requires competing operators in the local loop. This could best be achieved by cable-TV-operators playing a crucial role in the transformation process from a monopoly to competition.

2.2 Strategies and Adjustment Policies of Incumbent Telecoms Operators in Anticipation of 1998

At present, the structure of the European fixed network segment is still characterized by national monopolies. Competition is limited to Finland, Sweden, the UK and - since mid-1996 - to Denmark. Yet, the liberalization deadline for all EU member states is set by the European Commission leading to a change in all European telecoms sectors in the forefront of liberalization. Two tendencies can be observed in most member states: national monopolies are undertaking necessary reforms in order to adapt to new circumstances while potential newcomers such as national utilities are forming national and international alliances in order to successfully enter the market after liberalization. Concerning the incumbent fixed network operator, besides network modernization (digitization, innovative transmission techniques such as ATM and ADSL, expansion of ISDN networks) two main trends could be observed: restructuring of prices and internal reorganization.

Tab. C1: European Public Switched Telephony Tariffs, (31.01.1996, in $)

Country	Connection charges[1]	Rental per month	Cost of meter unit[2]	Usage per minute in peak hours[3]						
				Local	50 km	100 km	250 km	Adjacent country	USA	Japan
GB-MCL	151.61	16.08	-	-	0.09	0.10	0.10	0.40	0.44	1.16
GB-BT	151.61	17.44	-	0.05	0.11	0.13	0.13	0.46	0.51	1.34
SWE	155.52	17.28	-	0.03	0.07	0.09	0.09	0.35	0.62	1.24
FRAU	45.72	7.92	0.11	0.04	0.15	0.28	0.32	0.56	0.74	1.43
GER	53.57	13.18	0.06	0.04	0.15	0.32	0.34	0.55	0.77	1.29
IRL	179.10	14.93	0.14	0.05	0.13	0.27	0.27	0.44	0.82	1.79
NL	108.02	12.73	0.08	0.03	0.03	0.10	0.10	0.49	0.87	1.80
DK	194.97	12.54	0.05	0.04	0.07	0.09	0.09	0.41	0.89	1.26
BEL	104.60	13.75	0.15	0.04	0.06	0.22	0.22	0,45	0.90	1.49
FIN	4500.00	6.89	0.06	0.05	0.10	0.10	0.10	0.48	0.99	1.74
GRE	206.44	6.81	0.04	0.01	0.29	0.42	0.76	0.33	1.01	2.06[4]
POR	72.60	8.75	0.06	0.02	0.17	0.41	0.41	0.76	1.11	1.69
AUS	105.08	14.01	0.07	0.06	0.35	0.35	0.47	0.70	1.11	1.58
ITL	123.99	10.66	0.08	0.05	0.33	0.39	0.39	0.57	1.13	1.72
LUX	74.72	6.58	0.13	0.03	0.03	0.03	-	0.43	1.30	1.44
SPA	158.58	9.27	0.04	0.03	0.16	0.40	0.40	0.80	1.33	2.52

Notes: The above figures are based on standard rates and exclude all discount schemes. All prices are exclusive of tax.; 1) Some operators charge lower rates where the process involves the takeover of an existing line. The rate shown for Telecom Finland is the "member option", where the subscription involves taking a share in the company and paying a relatively low rental charge. Subscribers can instead choose to pay a lower connection fee and a higher rental charge; 2)These figures represent the price charged for each billing unit by those operators which charge for calls on a per-unit system. Telecom Finland uses per-unit billing only for local calls; other calls are charged on a per-second basis. BT, Mercury and Telia use per-second billing for all calls; 3)The rates for Denmark, Italy, Spain and Sweden include an element of the fixed call set-up charges that are imposed by the operators in these countries. In these cases, one-third of the set-up charges has been added to each per minute rate, on the assumption that on average call lasts for three minutes; 4) This figure does not take account of the recent change in the OTE rate for calls from Greece to Japan.

Source: FINANCIAL TIMES (1996), p.7.

Restructuring of Prices

Traditionally, prices set by national telecommunications monopolies are often distorted. Due to politico-social goals and the principals of average tariffing (uniform tariffing), the prices of basic access are well below their incremental costs, making large cross-subsidies from other telephone services necessary. Yet, internal cross-subsidization only works under a monopoly. Under competition, distorted prices lead to market entry of newcomers in those market segments where prices are above costs. As a result, prices and hence profits will decrease making an internal cross-subsidization impossible. Therefore, incumbent operators have to rebalance their tariff structure in order to become competitive.

Since the beginning of the 1990s European carriers have gone a considerable distance towards rebalancing their call tariffs. In most European countries, basic access charges and local call charges were increased while long-distance charges were lowered (EUROPEAN COMMISSION, 1996). However, as Tab. C1 shows, tariff structures in EU member states still considerably differ from each other indicating that many EU telecoms operators still have a very long way to go before they are ready to face competition.

Price adjustments are most obvious in the international segment where competition arises from call back service providers - independent on a national's regulatory framework. Spain's Telefonica, for example, has drastically reduced its international tariffs to up to 31% as a result of much lower international call charges offered by call back providers such as Atlantic Telecom, Telegroup Inc., Telepassport and USA Global Link (WARDEN, 1996). Even if all European network operators have had to lower their international call charges, prices were slashed extremely in Spain, Italy, Greece and Germany in 1995/96. As indicated in Fig. C2, this trend is likely to continue in the years to come as a result of upcoming competition. Moreover, deregulation in Europe could lead to a reform of the existing charging practices for international telecommunications services where prices (so-called accounting rates) are at present much higher than the actual costs (GRAACK, 1996).

Internal Reorganization, Labor Productivity and Employment

In the absence of effective competition, firms, especially monopolies, tend to become inefficient. Capital and labor productivity decreases while the number of employees increases. In most European countries, especially in Greece, the telecoms operator was seen as a legal instrument of job creation. One example of an extremely inefficient telecoms monopoly was British Telecom. In 1980, labor productivity was as low as 74 main lines per employee, compared with a main line per employee ratio of 99 in France, 105 in Germany, and 125 in Italy. BT's labor productivity only increased slowly between 1980 and 1990, partly due to a lack of competitive pressure from the second network operator and the regulatory body. Since 1990, as a result of intensified competition as well as of shrinking profits resulting from the price cap regulation, BT massively reduced the number of its staff. Between 1989/90 and 1994/95, BT nearly halved the number of its labor force to 137,500, leading to strong productivity gains: 197 main lines per employee in

1996 compared with a ratio of 101 in 1990 (BRITISH TELECOM, 1995). Yet further reductions in the work force are likely to occur, since the productivity is still low compared with that of US Bell companies (above 270 lines per employee).

Similar developments can be observed in other liberalized EU telecoms markets. Between 1990 and 1994, Telecom Finland and the Local Telecom Companies in Finland reduced the number of employees by about 40% and 9% respectively. The same holds for Swedish Telia that employed only two-thirds of the number of employees in 1990. Even if newcomers create new jobs, Tab. C2 shows that the job creation by newcomers cannot offset job losses. While the six main operators in Finland, Sweden and the UK together employed approximately 300,000 people in 1990, the number decreased to about 195,000 in 1994. Even if UK cable TV operators and other fixed network operators in Sweden and Finland are not included in this calculation, the direct net job effect of liberalization is apparently negative. While network operators in liberalized markets massively reduced their number of employees, the reduction of the labor force in European telecoms monopolies seems to be moderate. By contrast, the total number of employees of all 11 telecoms monopolies slightly increased from 686,240 in 1990 to 695,990 in 1994 - although this trend mainly results from an increase in 13.000 employees in Germany due to German unification. Since liberalization in Finland, Sweden and the UK led to a massive reduction in telecoms emloyees, the question arises how the European labor market for telecoms specialists will develop in anticipation of and following market liberalization in 1998. In order to answer this question, one has to take into consideration four employment effects that might result from the liberalization of the telecoms sector: productivity gains, network expansion, job creation in other telecom segments, e.g. mobile communications, and the creation of jobs in the information sector.

Fig. C2: Developments of International Call Charges from Selected European Countries to the US (in $)

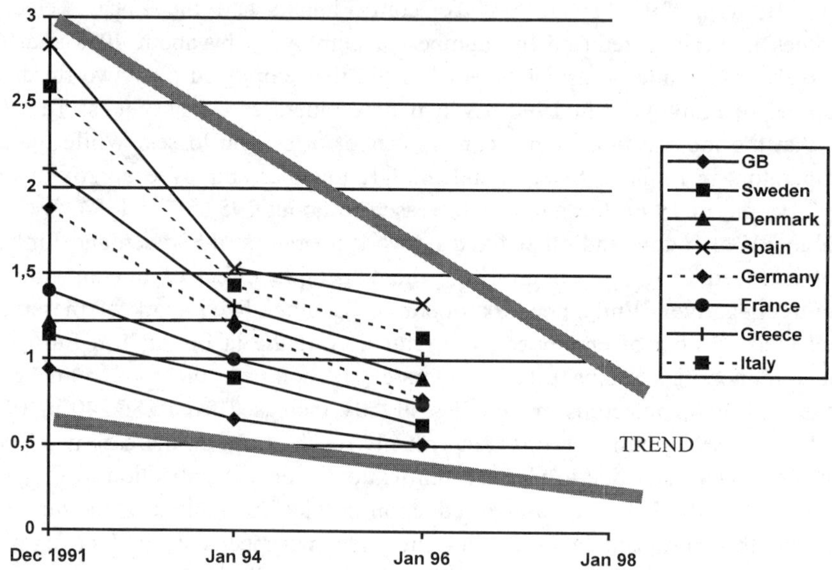

International call charges in US$ per minute, peak rate, excluding tax, based on a four minutes call (1991 and 1994), respectively three minutes call (1996)

Sources: OECD (1993), p. 55; OECD (1995), p. 61; FINANCIAL TIMES (1996), p. 7.

If one assumes that competiton in the telecoms sector does not only lead to productivity gains but also to a higher penetration rate - since network operators are competing for existing as well as potential costumers -, the future number of employees could be calculated as follows. The current population in the European Union is about 372 million inhabitants. Let us assume an average EU penetration rate of 60%, then the number of main lines will approximately amount to 223 million ("Estimation" in Tab. C2). Let us further assume that the average labor productivity will be around 250 main lines per employee, then the total number of main lines requires about 892,000 employees which is approximately the same as in 1994 (Both figures, the penetration rate and the rate of productivity are of cause arbitrary. However, they are not unrealistic although the number of mainlines per employee could be much higher in the long run. Moreover, regional disparities with respect to economies of densities are neglected in this calculation). Although the estimated number of employees corresponds to the actual number, the calculated number for each country differs a lot from the present figure (see last column in Tab. C2). In Germany, for example, the potential number of employees is much lower than the actual (195,600 in comparison to 225,000) while in other countries, indicated by those figures highlighted in Tab. C2, the potential number of employees is above the actual one. If the assumption that liberalization fosters network expansion holds true then liberalization impacts on the labor market are quite different amoung EU countries. In some countries, employment effects in the fixed network segment could even be positive. In other countries, however, liberalization will lead to a massive reduction of employees in the fixed network segment. Deutsche Telekom, for example, has already announced to reduce the number of employees by around 50.000 to 170.000 in the years to come (KRÖSKE, 1996).

Tab. C2: Number of Persons[1] Employed by EU Telecoms Operators (1990-1994, in 1000)

	1990	1991	1992	1993	1994	Estimation[5]
British Telecom[2]	226.90	210.50	170.70	156.00	137.50	139.9
Mercury[2]	5.00[3]	6.37	7.26	9.33	10.07	
Telecom Finland	10.48	9.73	6.95	6.45	6.21	12.24
ATC Finland	9.59	9.35	9.12	8.65	8.28	
Telia	47.97	46.21	41.77	34.09	32.59	24.28[6]
Tele2	--	0.06	0.10	0.14	0.16	
Belgacom	26.30	27.30	27.30	26.70	26.90	24.24
Deutsche Telekom	212.00	229.00	231.00	231.00	225.00	195.60
Eireann	13.54	13.43	13.10	12.82	12.33	8.64
France Télécom	156.10	156.10	155.30	154.60	152.60	139.20
KPN/PTT Telecom	29.26	30.82	32.33	31.98	31.67	36.96
OTE	28.09	27.59	26.72	26.35	26.14	24.96
Portugal Telecom[4]	23.56	23.07	22.64	20.15	19.83	23.76

Tab. C2: (Cont.)

PTT Austria	18.00	18.00	17.90	17.90	17.90	19.20
Tele Danmark	17.70	18.00	17.30	16.80	16.70	12.48
Telecom Italia[4]	85.80	87.60	87.50	86.10	94.90	137.28
Telefonica	75.35	75.50	74.44	74.34	72.21	94.08
EU-14	985.64	988.63	941.43	913.40	890.99	892.00

Notes: 1) Part-time jobs converted to full-time jobs in this calculation; 2) Financial year ends on 1.03; 3) Own estimates; 4) In 1994, Telecom Portugal, Telefones de Lisboa e Porto and Teledifusora Nacional were merged to form Telecom Portugal. Data from different years may therefore not be comparable. The same holds for Telecom Italia which resulted from a merger of 4 Italian telecoms operators; 5) Figures are calculated as follows: Number of employees = (Number of inhabitants • 0.6 ÷ 250); 6) The formula has been changed slightly since actual penetration rate is 69.

Source: National PTO, Annual Reports, various issues; own calculations.

Although the future number of employees could be approximately the same as in 1994, in comparison to 1990 the number of employees has definitely decreased by about 100,000 employees. Yet, one has to take into consideration new job opportunities in the fields of mobile communications and teleworking. According to a study by the German Ministry of Economics (BMWI, 1996) around 20,400 new jobs have been created in the mobile communications sector between 1990 and 1994 (network and service provider: +9,400; production and distribution of equipment: +11,000). Comparing the number of mobile subscribers in Germany (4.15 million at the beginning of 1996) with the total number of subscriber in the EU at the same time (23.39 million) approximately one out of six mobile phones is used in Germany. If the same relation holds true for employment in the European mobile segment, the estimated total number of newly created jobs amounts to 115,000, which is roughly the number of jobs cut in the fixed network segment. In a liberalized telecoms segment, this figure could even be higher since liberalization in the fixed network segment also leads to lower call charges in the mobile communications segment, fostering demand for mobile communications services.

Even if the number of new jobs created in the mobile segment is already impressive, the number of potential teleworkers is even more fascinating. According to the BANGEMANN-REPORT (1994) the aim of the European Commission is to create 10 million teleworking jobs by the year 2000. Even if this target seems to be too optimistic, other studies estimate that the number of teleworkers could be as high as 7 million by the end of the century (see e.g. EITO, 1996). Yet, the number of telejobs depends on the developments in the telecommunications segment. Modern telecommunications networks that offer reliable customs-related services at low costs are seen as a prerequisite for the creation of new telejobs. Modernization-cum-dismantling of X-inefficiencies in the fixed network segment is therefore a necessary step in the right direction. Job losses in the short run could easily be outweighed by job gains in the teleworking segment in the medium and long run.

2.3 Privatization of EU Fixed Network Operators

Network modernization as well as network expansion requires huge amounts of money as demonstrated in the German case. Since German unification in 1990, Telekom has concentrated its financial and human resources on developing an efficient network infrastructure in the new "Länder". More than 5 million new subscribers have been connected in the ex-GDR with the penetration rate rising from 10.1% to 34.0%, compared with a West German penetration rate of 49.9%. Network expansion and network modernization swallowed DM 28 billion (1990-1993); investments of another DM 32 billion have been announced for the period up to the year 2000 (DEUTSCHE TELEKOM, 1994, 1995). Since Telekom is a state-owned company, the possibility of raising additional equity is very limited, especially in periods characterized by high state budget deficits. As a result, investments were mainly covered by loans, leading to a sharp decline in the capital-and-reserve to total-assets ratio from 30.1% in 1990 to 21.5% in 1994 (and even lower under the new accounting rules) (DEUTSCHE TELEKOM, 1992, 1995, 1996). In response to the need for additional capital as well as a greater degree of freedom, which is necessary to conduct domestic and international business activities, the political parties in Germany approved transformation and privatization plans at the end of 1993/beginning of 1994. Deutsche Telekom was transformed into a state-owned joint-stock company, partly sold to the public and quoted on the stock exchange in November 1996.

Yet, Deutsche Telekom is not the only European operator that has already been or should be privatized. Since the beginning of the 1990s, the legal status of most EU telecoms operators has been changed from a public enterprise to a state-owned stock company (formal privatization). Formal privatization is the first step towards selling former public enterprises to the public or, alternatively, to strategic investors (material privatization). At the beginning of 1997, all EU network operators were joint-stock companies. Of the 17 telecoms operators listed in Tab. C3, 13 operators are at least partly privatized. The range of privatization varies between 100% (Finnet Group, Mercury, Tele2, Telefonica and British Telecom, where the state holds a so-called "golden share" in order to keep special veto rights) and 6% (OTE). Yet, only in 6 out of 17 operators state ownership is below 50%. In all other cases, the state keeps the majority of shares and hence could veto unpopular management decisions. However, this situation is likely to change in the future (see comments / prospects in Tab. C3) as governments are in need for additional (privatization) revenues in order to fulfill fiscal constraints imposed by the Maastricht treaty.

Tab. C3: Legal Status of European Network Operators

Operator	Status	Comments / Prospects
Finnet	Privately owned	Smaller operators are most often owned by users
Mercury	Privately owned	C&W (80%), Bell Canada (20%)
Tele 2	Privately owned	Kennevik Group (60,1%), C&W 39,9%)
Telefonica	Privately owned	In 1995, privatization of 12% raised $1.33 billion, last tranche of 21% was sold for $ 4.2 billion in 1997, no strategic investor.
British Telecom	0,5% state-owned	No strategic investor, number of shareholders: 2.5 m
KPN/PTT Telecom	48% state-owned	Privatization revenue: $7.2 billion, another 10-20% to be privatized in 1996/97, no strategic investor
Belgacom	50.1% state-owned	Privatization to a strategic investor (Ameritech, Singapore Telecom, Tele Danmark), revenue $2.46 billion
Tele Danmark	51% state-owned	No strategic investor
Portugal	51% state-owned	49% raised $1.93 billion in 1995/96, no strategic investor yet. A third tranche is expected to be sold to the public or to a strategic investor in 1997. State is going to retain a "golden share" of 25%.
Telecom Italia	64.3% state-owned	Main share holder, state-owned STET, to be privatized in 1996, no strategic investor.
Deutsche Telekom	74% state-owned	26% were sold in 1996, a second tranche is likely to follow in 1998, no strategic investor
Eireann	80% state-owned	20% were sold to a strategic investor (KPN/Telia) for $ 292 million.
OTE	94% state-owned	No strategic investor, 6% were privatized in 1996, a second tranche of 8-10% is expected to be floated in 1997.
Austrian PTA	100% state-owned	Partial privatization in 1998/99

Tab. C3 (cont.)

Telecom Finland	100% state-owned	New law proposal is being prepared, ownership basis will then be examined, date of privatization unknown
Telia	100% state-owned	Privatization plans have been postponed, but are again under consideration
France Télécom	100% state-owned	49% of the company would be offered in two tranches in 1997/98, no strategic investor

Note: All telecoms operators are joint-stock companies. Data as of March 1997.

Source: Own research based on annual reports of PTOs and newspaper articles.

With respect to the ownership of the national fixed network operators, different options are available: (1) fully state-owned, (2) partial privatization to the public and/or to a strategic investor or (3) total privatization to the public and/or to a strategic investor. As indicated in Tab. C3, most of the European fixed network operators have already been or will be privatized in the near future. This does not hold for Swedish Telia that should, in contrast to the announcement of the previous government, continue to be fully state-owned. The Swedish government has obviously chosen the first option aiming at "pursuing a more active ownership role in order to promote development of its companies" (SWEDISH MTC, 1996, 49). In 1997, however, new rumors about future privatization plans for Swedish Telia emerged. In all other cases a clear trend toward privatization is apparent, although different operators are pursuing different strategies. While most of the bigger telecom operators such as Deutsche Telekom, BT or France Télécom as well as internationally competitive smaller fixed network operators such as Dutch KPN/PTT Telecom and Tele Danmark have been or will be privatized through public offering, the question arises for smaller network operators whether to go to the stock markets or to enter a financial partnership with foreign strategic investors. The latter option, partial privatization through strategic partners was chosen by Belgacom and Telecom Eireann. In 1995, the Belgium government agreed to sell 49.9% to an international consortium, consisting of Ameritech, Singapore Telecom and Tele Danmark for $2.46 billion, while in 1996, 20% of Telecom Eireann were sold jointly to Telia and KPN for IR£ 183 ($292 million). By contrast, Telecom Portugal, one of the smallest fixed network operators in the EU, has been partly sold through public offering: 49% of Telecom Portugal was floated during 1995 and 1996. Yet, the Portuguese government intends to sell another 25% of Telecom Portugal. Although the question whether to sell the next tranche to the public or to an international consortium is still open, the management is believed to be in favor of some form of strategic partnership (MANOFF, 1996). While, from the management's point of view, an international strategic partnership carries the risk of loosing autonomy and independence in strategic decisions, this option offers an opportunity of building up strong international links to other network operators in a sector characterized by blurring national boundaries and growing relevant markets. On the one hand, strategic investments are generally associated with inflows of technical and managerial know how (intra-industry tradable goods and firm-specific network management) and, on the other hand, foreign strategic investors consisting of foreign network operators offer an opportunity to smaller national network operators to participate in a European-wide or worldwide strategic alliance without pursing their own, capital-intensive internationalization strategies. In a market that is becoming increasingly international, the latter aspect is of special importance.

2.4 Internationalization Strategies and International Cooperation

During the last decade, a worldwide trend towards the internationalization of economies could be observed. Due to international cooperation and agreements such as GATT (General Agreement on Tariffs and Trade) and GATS (General Agreement on Trade in Services), that reduce import and export barriers to trade and services, international flows of goods, services and capital have increased. Moreover, technological change in telecommunications and new hardware generations are allowing a decentralized production across countries, leading to a more efficient division of labor between nations. International coordination of goods and services makes a sophisticated logistical system even more necessary, requiring efficient national telecommunications networks and international cooperation. Business customers, especially multinationals operating across national frontiers, require telecom services in the form of one-stop-shopping. One-stop-shopping allows enterprises (and other customers) to contact only one telecommunications operator to order and manage all leased international links. "Seamless" global communication, meaning that a customer wants all telecom networks involved to appear to be a single network, is another example for new business requirements. Since national operators are historically restricted to national boundaries, most of the network operators are pursing some sort of internationalization strategy (foreign direct investment, partial privatization to a foreign strategic investor, formation of international strategic alliances) in order to cope with the upcoming competitive pressure in the international as well as national segments and to offer services tailored to specific needs of such profitable customers as multinational companies.

Internationalization Strategies of EU Network Operators

While most national telecoms operators are pursuing a strategy of "going international", the significance of international joint-venture activities is still quite limited but steadily growing. In 1995, only 2% of BT's turnover arose from operations outside the UK. This figure is, however, a bit confusing since Concert, a joint venture of BT and MCI, alone has just completed its first trading year in 1995 and has won $ 1 billion dollars in committed revenue which is equivalent to about 4.5% of BT's turnover (BRITISH TELECOM, 1996). The strategic value of international operations is more apparent in Spain. Telefónica International (TISA), Téléfonica's holding company for its international subsidiaries, contributed to about 16% of Telefónicas consolidated turnover in 1995 (TELEFONICA, 1996). Although all European network operators are mainly engaged in their national home markets, international commitments are gaining importance. As described by Fig.C3, Western European operators are pursuing different strategies under different regulatory frameworks.

- Austrian PTA, Belgacom, Eireann, OTE and Portugal Telecom are focusing solely or mainly on the national market (as a monopoly). Their strategy is to withstand increased pressure from international competition by reinforcing their national position. Yet, in order to strengthen their national and international ability to compete in a changing market, Belgacom and Eireann have been partly sold to an international consortium of internationally active network operators in order to strengthen their strategic position in a globally changing telecoms market. In Portugal, the question whether to sell another 25% of Portugal Telecom to the public or to a foreign strategic investor has not been decided yet.
- The strategy of entering foreign markets while home markets are still protected by regulation is pursued by France Télécom, Deutsche Telekom, Telecom Italia, Telefonica and Dutch Telecom.
- Finnish Telecom, British Telecom and Telia are expanding their activities into foreign markets, aiming to compensate losses in liberalized home markets. Since 1994 Tele Danmark faces competition in the voice telephony segment; the Danish fixed network segment was liberalized in mid-1996.
- Energis, the Finnet Group, Mercury and Tele2 are concentrating on national markets. Yet, Mercury and Tele2 are backed by international consortia, while National Grid is looking for a strategic partner for loss making Energis which could likely be a foreign network operator. The Finnet Group, the association of Finnish local network operators, could gain a market share of 60% in the national long-distance segment within two year resulting from Finnet's strong position in the local loop. With growing market power, it is likely that Finnet will pursue its own internationalization strategies in the future while some of

the bigger local telecom companies are already committed to regional or local investments abroad. Helsinki Telephone, the largest member of the Finnet Group, is engaged in partnerships with new telecoms companies being set up in major German cities (FINNET GROUP, 1996).

Fig. C3: Strategies of European Network Operators under Different Regulatory Regimes

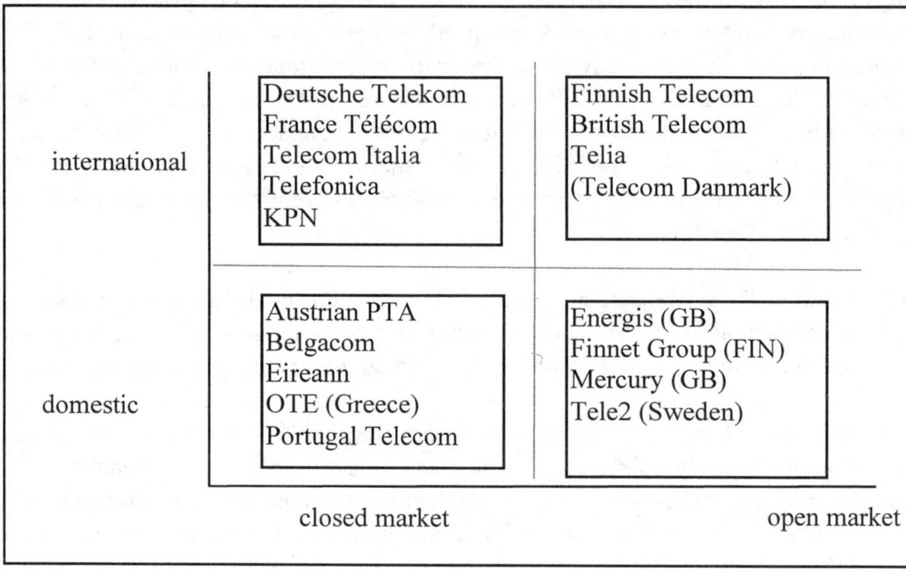

International Cooperation in International and National Markets

Since the beginning of the 1990s, intensified cooperation between network operators on the one hand and foreign network operators and national industries on the other hand can be observed. On the international level, cooperation between network operators is intensifying in the form of international or global alliances as a result of new service requirements of national and multinational enterprises such as one-stop shopping and seamless global communications networks. Among the most significant global players are CONCERT (a joint venture between US American MCI and British Telecom), UNISOURCE (a joint venture of four smaller European network operators: Dutch PTT Telecom, Spanish Telefonica, Swiss PTT and Swedish Telia), GLOBAL ONE (a joint venture between Deutsche Telekom, France Télécom and US American Sprint) and WORLDPARTNERS (an alliance between Japanese KDD, Singapore Telecom, Australian Telstra, Canadian Unitel and US American AT&T). Yet further European-wide or global alliances are currently under discussion, e.g. an alliance between Italian STET and IBM or La

Red Panamericana, an international alliance in South America headed by Telefónica (GRAACK, 1995).

International cooperation between network operators is also visible in the form of bidding consortia for network operators that are being partly privatized. In the case of a partial privatization of an incumbent operator, cooperation between foreign network operators is not only advantageous from a financial point of view but also wise from an investor's point of view: risks can be diversified by cooperation while winning the contract is the more likely. International consortia bidding for national telecoms operators could be seen both in Western Europe (Belgacom, Eireann) and in Eastern Europe (Estonian ETC, MATAV, Czech SPT).

A third group of international cooperation consists of international consortia that aim at penetrating national market segments. Consortia of that sort are most obvious in the mobile communications sector. Yet, in anticipation of 1998 deregulation process, international consortia are also forming in order to enter the still protected national fixed network segment. Most often, these consortia consist of national industries, that offer private telephone networks (corporate networks), rights of ways or financial resources, and foreign network operators with firm specific know-how (experience with building and successfully operating a telecommunications network). At present, alliances of that sort are most obvious in Germany (VIAG-British Telecom, Veba-RWE-Cable & Wireless, Arcor-AT&T-Unisource, Thyssen-Bell South), the Netherlands (railways-British Telecom, cable-TV-operators-energy utilities-US Bell Operating Companies). Yet, alternative network providers backed by foreign telecoms companies are also emerging in most other EU countries, e.g. Belgium (cable-TV-operators-US West) or Italy (Olivetti-Bell Atlantic).

3. Impacts of the Liberalization and Privatization Process on EU Telecoms Market Structures

Due to liberalization efforts initiated at the EU level, the present fixed network market structure will rapidly change within the next years. In mid-1996, the Directive on Alternative Infrastructure came into effect pushing forward the liberalization of the fixed network infrastructure. In most EU countries the directive will be implemented within 1996, while Greece, Ireland, Luxembourg and Portugal requested additional implementation periods. After 1997, the voice telephony segment will also be liberalized in all European countries except those countries where the telephone network is underdeveloped (Greece, Ireland, Portugal and Spain, exemption until 2003) or very small (Luxembourg, 2000). Yet, several countries have already declared that they will deregulate their telecoms markets before the official deadline set by the EU Commission: Denmark (1996), Luxembourg (1998), Spain (1998), Ireland (2000) and Portugal (2000).

Tab. C4: Network Operators and Potential Newcomers at the National Level in EU Countries

Country	Incumbent Operators	Newcomers / Potential alternative network operators
Austria	• Post und Telekom Austria	• Verbundgesellschaft AG (power utilities) • Österreichische Bundesbahn (state-owned railways) • Local cable-TV-companies
Belgium	• Belgacom	• Codenet (subsidiary of the electricity company "Electrabel") • SNCF (state-owned railways) • Telenet Vlaanderen (cable-TV-operators-US West) • Foreign network operators (BT, France Télécom, etc.)
Denmark	• Tele Danmark	• DSB (state-owned railways) • Danish Electricity Companies (Elsam, NVE, NESA, SEAS) • Foreign Network Operators (Telia, France Télécom) • Local cable-TV-operators
Finland	• Telecom Finland • Finnet Group / ATC	• Several other network operators as well as service providers who have no right to construct telecommunications networks outside of the primises in its possession
France	• France Telecom	• SNCF (state-owned railway) • Local transport companies (RATP etc.) • Utility and private motorway companies (EDF, Sanef, etc.) • Cegetel (Compagnie Générale des Eaux-BT) • STET-Bouygues-Veba
Germany	• Deutsche Telekom	• Arcor (Mannesmann-DBKom)-AT&T-Unisource • Vebacom-RWE-Cable & Wireless • Thyssen-Bell South • Viag-Intercom (Viag, BT) • Local utilities

Tab. C4: (cont.)

Greece	• OTE	• none
Ireland	• Telecom Eireann	• Electricity Supply Board (ESB) • National bus and railways operators (CIE)
Italy	• Telecom Italia	• Olivetti (together with US Bell Companies) • RAI (broadcasting) • Albacom (BT, Banco Nacionale de Lavorno) • Foreign network operators (France Télécom etc.)
Luxemburg	• P&T	• none
Netherlands	• PTT Telecom	• Enertel (electricity utilities, cable-TV-operators) • Telfor (railway companies [NS], BT)
Portugal	• Portugal Telecom	• Utility consortium (EdP-Transgas-Gas de Portugal)
Spain	• Telefonica	• Retevision (broadcasting) • Red Electrica (electricity company) • Foreign network operators (BT, C&W, France Télécom, etc.)
Sweden	• Telia	• Tele2 (Kinnevik, Cable & Wireless) • Bahnverket (railway company) • Telenordia (BT, Tele Danmark, Telenor) • Other foreign network operators (France Télécom etc.)
UK	• British Telecom • Mercury • Kingston Telecom	• Energis (Energy Utilities) • Regional Energy Utilities • Association of CATV-operators • Foreign network operators (Telia, US-Sprint, etc.)

Source: Annual reports of national PTOs, own research.

The future telecoms market structure resulting from the liberalization process is not predictable yet. As regards the EU liberalization plans, which are supposed to lead to tougher competition, governmental officials and representatives of national telecoms operators are undertaking the necessary preparations. While national incumbent telecoms operators are restructuring the internal organization, potential newcomers are looking for suitable market entry strategies. Thus, alternative network providers such as railways, electricity companies, water suppliers and cable network operators are looking for suitable partners with a strong financial background or the knowledge of how to run a telecoms network. New alliances are most obvious in Great Britain, that has one of the most liberal telecommunications markets in the world, but also in Germany with one of the worlds most attractive and profitable telecoms market. However, potential competitors, most often international consortia consisting of national industries backed by foreign network operators, are also evident in other EU countries such as Italy, the Netherlands, Spain and - since recently - in France (Tab. C4).

While most of the national and international cooperations and alliances are still at an early stage of formation, their significance will grow in the future but only if they prove to be stable. This holds especially for strategic alliances. An alliances is likely to be stable if all participants pursue the same objectives. Another aspect concerns market power and internal influence of each partner. The more homogenous the group in size and market power, the more likely are stable alliances. While until recently international alliances, so called "Global Alliances" such as Concert, Global One and Unisource seemed to be stable, Telefonica's change from Unisource to Concert, an alliance that could be enlarged by Portugal Telecom and Japanese NTT in the near future, points to the fact that even in the international segment the long-term stability of strategic alliances must be questioned. The same holds for international alliances aiming to enter national markets, which could best be observed in Germany. In Spring 1996, two important alliances have been formed in Germany: (1) RWE-Viag-BT and (2) Veba-Cable&Wireless-Mannesmann. After Mannesmann purchased 49.9% of DBKom, the telecoms subsidiary of German railway Deutsche Bahn AG, in September three major telecom alliances emerged (1) RWE-Viag-BT, (2) Mannesmann, DBKom in cooperation with AT&T and Unisource and (3) Veba-Cable&Wireless-Wintershall-Ruhrgas. However, in fall 1996 RWE changed from the Viag-BT-alliance to the Vebacom alliance while Cable&Wireless has announced to leave the alliance with the aim to join a larger one. The problem with unstable telecoms alliances is that an unsuccessful alliance not only consumes financial and human ressources but also precious time. In Germany as well as in other EU countries it looks like that only a few alternative network operators will be able to offer telecoms services over their own network right after liberalization in 1998. The only market participants that will profit from this situation are incumbent national telecoms operators such as Deutsche Telekom.

The developments in Germany indicate that Europe's alliance merry-go-round is far from over. This holds especially for larger EU countries such as France, Germany, Italy and Spain. Assuming that international and national alliances prove to be stable in the future, their effect on competition at various levels (local, regional, national and international) is difficult to predict. The ITU developed three alternative scenarios (ITU, 1994):

- Through mergers and acquisitions as well as strategic alliances the number of competitors is reduced, so that a handful of global players dominates the international markets while several operators compete at the national level.
- Continuing the status quo with national carriers dominating the national market while forming international alliances. Competition takes place only at the international level or in some national niche markets such as mobile communication.
- The third scenario much depends on customer requirements and technical developments. While existing network operators offer telephone services via fixed networks, real competition will be between alternative technology platforms (copper vs. fiber vs. satellite vs. radio) rather than between network operators using the same technology base. This could lead to a fragmentation of the telecoms sector into technology-specific and regional markets.

The developments in the telecommunications sector much depend on the regulatory framework at the national and international level. The latter holds especially for developments within the European Union. If the 1998 liberalization program becomes reality, scenario 2 is less likely, since foreign operators in connection with national conglomerates are expected to penetrate national markets, as expected in most European telecoms markets. The market structure is more likely to change as described in Fig. C4. On the one hand, liberalization of national markets will lead to an expansion of the relevant market of each national network operator (indicated by the circles for some of the countries) that could result in an intensifying cross-border competition between established network operators. On the other hand, newcomer e.g. national companies (utilities, railways etc.) often backed by foreign network operators will enter the newly liberalized profitable market segment such as national long-distance or niche segments. The latter scenario is a mixture of the above describe scenarios I and III.

However, the competition intensity within the European Union very much depends on the European and national regulatory framework as well as on the internationalization and cooperation strategies pursued by the national operators. At the national level, the regulatory framework has to be set in a non-discriminative way that allows all sort of potential network operators to enter into the targeted market segment. Arbitrary market entry rules as well as monopolistic license fee - as proposed by the German government - have to be rejected from a market-oriented point of view. The German government has unreveiled plans to cover budget deficits, that cannot be financed by additional credits due to rules of the Maastricht treaty, by taxes put on telecom licences. If these plans become reality, one-off license fees could be as high as $ 53 million for a facility-based carrier plus annual renewal fees (BLAU, 1996). Even if licenses should not be granted for free, the German plans violate the EC recommendation that licence fees should be in line with administrative costs. Prohibitive license fees will hamper the market entry of network operators and hence restrict not only the number of national operators but also the number potential strategic partners in the international segment. Yet, the market structure as well as the competition intensity not only depends on the regulatory framework but also on internationalization and cooperation strategies of national incumbent operators and newcomers. Whether international cooperation leads to a higher or lower competition after liberalization in 1998 very much depends on the structure and the aims of international cooperation. International alliances and strategic cooperations between existing and potential European fixed network operators are described in Fig. C5.

Fig. C4: Structural Change in the European Fixed Network Segment

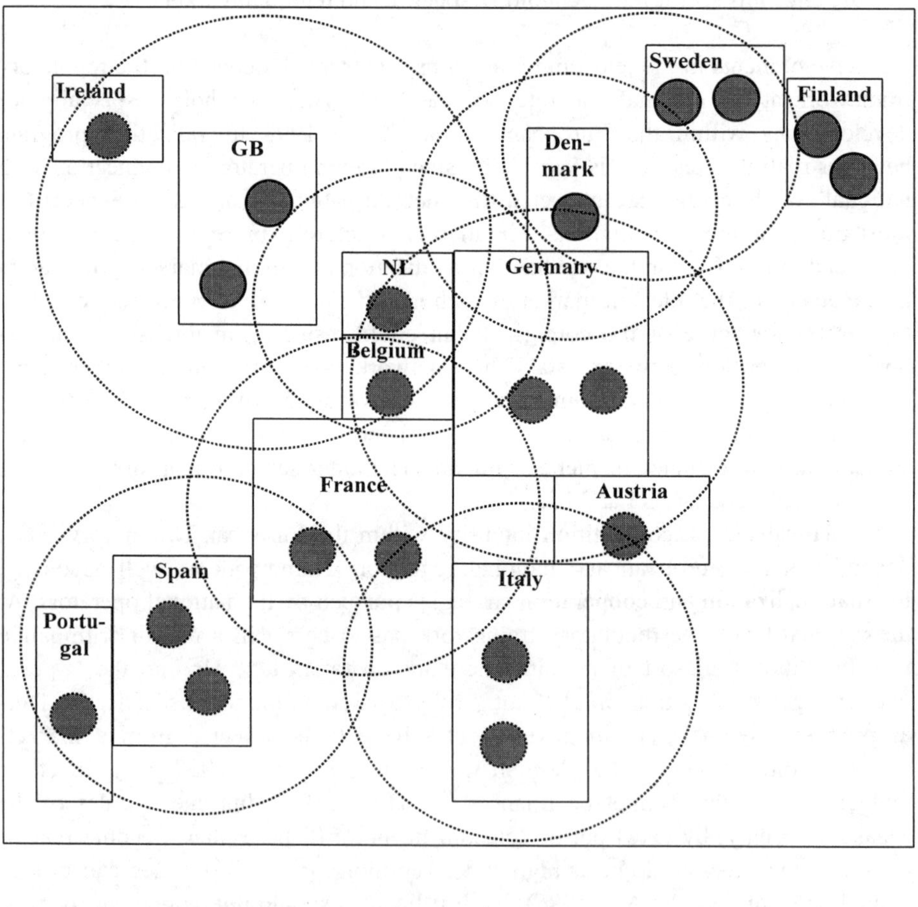

Fig. C5 points to the fact that international cooperation between European network operators is intensifying. Most network operators, with OTE, Portugal Telecom, PTA Austria, Telecom Finland and Finnet Group being an exception, have direct or indirect links to other European network operators. Many newcomers are backed by foreign telecoms operators which could facilitate market entry and intensify competition at the national level. At the European level, however, four main players could be observed: British Telecom, Cable&Wireless, Deutsche Telekom-France Télécom and Unisource. As a general rule, these "European players" are integrated into global alliances such as Concert, C&W Group, Global One or Worldpartners. While competition at the European and international level intensifies through international alliances, cooperation between incumbent network operators carries the risk of weakening cross-border competition and hence competition at the national level. Even if strategic alliances are created by two or several independent companies in order to cooperate only in special market segments while pursing different strategies or competing in other fields of business (BACKHAUS and PILTZ, 1990), it seems less likely that two incumbent network operators say Deutsche Telekom and France Télécom will compete in their home market. Here, a tacit agreement between both operators not to enter the partners home market seems to be more likely.

4. Conclusions

The developments in the national and international telecommunications sectors much depend on the future regulatory framework as well as cooperation strategies pursued by national network operators. The liberalization process within the European telecoms sector is expected to lead to intensified national, cross-border and international competition as demonstrated in liberalized EU countries. However, competitive pressure resulting from a dismantling of administrative market entry barriers could be undermined by strategic alliances or cross-border cooperation between national (incumbent) operators. At present, a tendency towards going international and international cooperation can be observed. Although the future structure of the European telecoms fixed network segment is not fully predictable yet, the paper points to the fact that the first of the ITU scenarios (a handful of global players dominates the international markets while several operators compete at the national level) could become reality. In the European fixed network segment four network operators or strategic alliances can be identified that could play a dominant role in a fully liberalized European telecoms sector: British Telecom, Cable&Wireless, Deutsche Telekom-France Télécom and Unisource.

Fig. C5: International Alliances and Cooperation between EU Network Operators

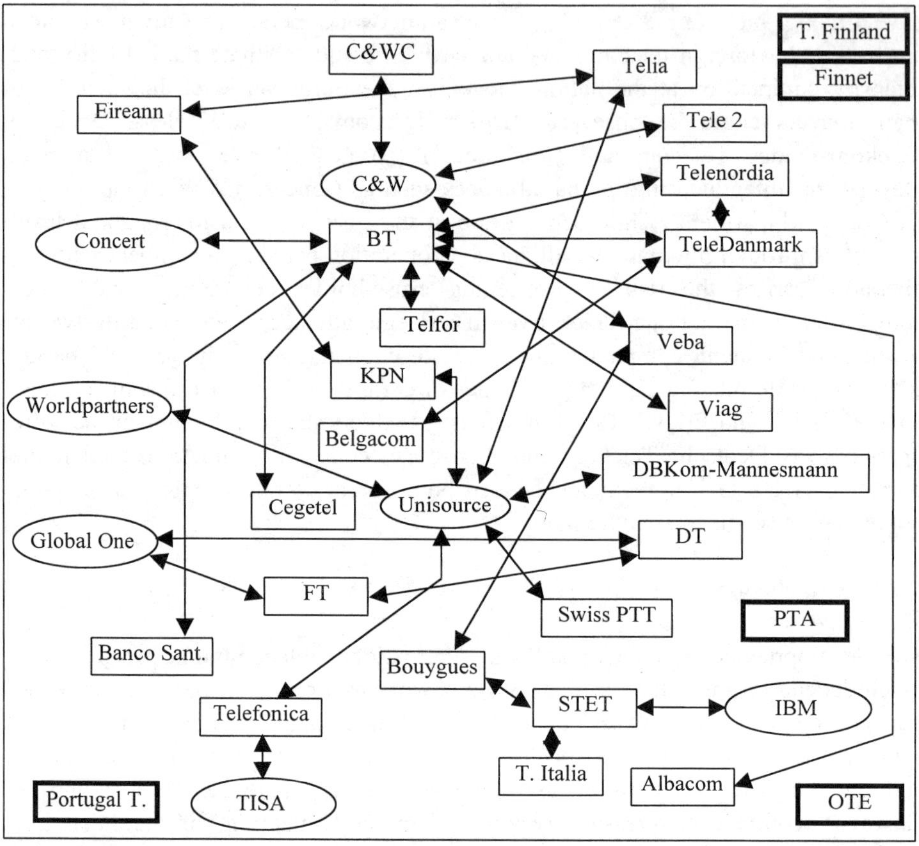

The competition effects of these dominant players on the national, European and international segment is not predictable yet. While national newcomers backed by foreign network operators - with BT being one of most active strategic partners for national newcomers - are expected to intensify competition at the national level, cross-border cooperation between incumbent network operators, e.g. Deutsche Telekom-France Télécom - could reduce competitive pressure at the national level since tacit agreements between incumbent operators not to enter in their home markets seems to be likely. However, since Europe's alliance merry-go-round is far from over, the future situation might well change in one or the other direction.

References

ATTENBOROUGH, N. (1993), Regulation of Competitive Telecommunications Markets, nera-topics no.12, London.

BACKHAUS, K. and K. PILTZ (1990), Strategische Allianzen - eine neue Form kooperativen Wettbewerbs?, in: Schmalenbachs Zeitschrift für betriebswirtschaftliche Forschung (zfbf), Sonderheft 27, pp. 1-10.

BANGEMANN-REPORT / MEMBER OF THE HIGH-LEVEL GROUP ON THE INFORMATION SOCIETY (1994), Europe and the global information society, Recommendations to the European Council, Brussels.

BLAU, J. (1996), German tax may cripple competition, in: Communications Week International, no. 174, p.7.

BMWI (1996), Info 2000, Bonn.

BRITISH TELECOM (1995), Annual Report 1994/95, London.

BRITISH TELECOM (1996), Annual Report 1995/96, London.

CARSBERG, B. (1991), OFTEL: Competition and the Duopoly Review, in: VELJANIOVSKI, C. (Ed.). Regulators in the Market, An Assessment of the Growth of Regulation in the UK, London: IEA,

DEUTSCHE TELEKOM (1994), Aufbauprogramm von Telekom in den neuen Bundesländern und Ostberlin, Bonn.

DEUTSCHE TELEKOM (1995), Das Geschäftsjahr 1994, Bonn.

DEUTSCHE TELEKOM (1996), Das Geschäftsjahr 1995, Bonn.

EITO (1996), European Information Technology Observatory, Frankfurt/M.

ELIXMANN, D. (1996), Internationale Konsortien als neue Spieler in einem liberalisierten Telekommunikationsmarkt, in: KUBICEK, H. et al. (Eds.), Jahrbuch Telekommunikation und Gesellschaft 1996 - Öffnung der Telekommunikation: Neue Spieler - Neue Regeln, Heidelberg: Decker.

EUROPEAN COMMISSION (1987), Green Paper on the development of the Common Market for Telecommunications services and equipment (COM(87)290, 30,06,87), Brussels,

EUROPEAN COMMISSION (1995), The Community Telecommunications Policy, Brussels.

EUROPEAN COMMISSION (1996), Universal Service for Telecommunications in the Perspective of a Fully Liberalised Environment, Brussels.

FINANCIAL TIMES (1996), Telecom Markets, 01.02.1996, p. 7

FINNET GROUP (1996), From local expertise to global coverage, Helsinki.

FINNISH MTC (1994), Telecommunications in Finland, Helsinki: Finnish Ministry of Transport and Communications.

FINNISH MTC (1995), Visions of Communications by a Finnish Expert, Press release, 9 March 1995, Helsinki: Finnish Ministry of Transport and Communications.

FINNISH MTC (1996), Telecommunications Statistics, Helsinki: Finnish Ministry of Transport and Communications.

GRAACK, C. (1995), EU-Telecom Markets and International Network Alliances: Developments, Strategies and Policy Implications, Discussion paper No. 8, European Institute for International Economic Relations, Potsdam.

GRAACK, C. (1996), Internationale Aspekte der Telekommunikationswirtschaft: Liberalisierung, internationale Tarifmechanismen und Wohlfahrtseffekte, Discussion paper No. 19, European Institute for International Economic Relations, Potsdam.

GRAACK, C. (1997), Telekommunikationswirtschaft in der Europäischen Union: Innovationsdynamik, Regulierungspolitik und Internationalisierungsprozesse, Heidelberg, Physica.

ITU (1994), World Telecommunication Development Report 1994, Geneva.

KRÖSKE, J. (1996), Rede anläßlich der Bilanz-Pressekonferenz 1996 am 04.06.1996, Bonn.

MANOFF, G. (1996), Small telcos, privatization and the pleasures of partnership, in: Communications Week International, no. 173, p.9.

OECD (1993), Communications Outlook 1993, Paris.

OECD (1995), Communications Outlook 1995, Paris.

OECD (1995), Communications Outlook 1996, draft version, Paris.

OFTEL (1995), Pricing of Telecommunications Services from 1997, London, OFTEL.

SNODDY, R. (1996), Calling C&W number one, in: Financial Times, 23.10.1996, p. 16.

SWEDISH MTC (1994), Telecommunications in Sweden, Stockholm, Ministry of Transport and Communications.

SWEDISH MTC (1996), Modern Telecommunications for Everybody, Stockholm, Ministry of Transport and Communications.

TELEFONICA (1996), Annual Report 1995, Madrid.

WARDEN, R. (1996), Telefonica responds to pressure from rivals, in: Communications Week International, No. 157, p.4.

WELFENS, P.J.J. and GRAACK, C. (1996), Telekommunikationswirtschaft: Deregulierung, Privatisierung und Internationalisierung, Heidelberg, Springer.

Comments on: Deregulation, Privatization and Internationalization of European Telecoms Markets

Dieter Elixmann

I would like to concentrate my discussion on four main elements: the issues raised in the paper, the methodology applied, the main messages which can be derived, and some further personnel comments on Cornelius' analysis.

Issues

As far as I can see the paper focuses on three main issues:

1. What is the experience of competition in the European fixed network segment so far?
2. How do European incumbent telecommunications (telecomms) companies behave in anticipation of 1998?
3. What is the impact of liberalization, privatization and internationalization on the future EU telecoms market structure?

Methodology

Cornelius' argumentation rests on an in-depth investigation of actual developments in the telecomms markets of 15 EU countries where he concentrates primarily on the 1990s. His research guidelines are the regulatory environment, the scope of market entry, and the business strategies of incumbent companies and entrants. He has enriched his analysis with interesting and detailed empirical data. The paper mirrors a competent understanding and description of the situation in different European countries.

The Main Points

As to the preceding issues, the paper yields the following observations.

Firstly, from developments in liberalized EU countries, one can infer that competition brings about significant changes. Yet, the intensity and speed of sectoral change very much depends on the existing market structure before liberalization, especially with regard to the starting position of each network operator, and the country-specific regulatory frameworks.

Secondly, there are five main trends observable as regards incumbent fixed network operators in anticipation of 1998: network modernization, rebalancing of prices, internal reorganization (including employment adaptations), privatization and internationalization (FDI, strategic alliances).

Thirdly, the future market structure is not predictable yet. However, some stylized facts characterizing future development can be observed. While most of the national and international corporations and alliances are still at an early stage of formation, they will become increasingly significant.. A crucial issue is, however, the stability of these alliances ("Europe's alliance merry-go-round is far from over").

A likely scenario for the future market structure could be a handful of global players dominating international markets, while several operators compete at national level. Yet, the competitive intensity within the EU very much depends on the European and national regulatory framework, as well as on the strategies for internationalization and cooperation pursued by the national operators. Whether international cooperation leads to a higher or lower level of competition after liberalization in 1998 depends very much on the structure and the objectives of international cooperation.

Further comments

In my view, Cornelius' paper allows one to draw at least four lessons from trends and developments in the European fixed-link telco market. I shall deliberately outline these in a rather simplistic way:

1. Liberalizing a market does not necessarily bring about immediate benefits of competition. One reason for this is that bottleneck facilities owned by the incumbents are not offered under favourable conditions for market entrants. Another reason is the ability of dominant incumbent companies to rebalance their prices, i.e. bring them more into line with costs. Provided the absence of predatory pricing, this in turn makes market entry viable only if the entrant is at least as efficient as the incumbent.
2. Privatization is inevitable. However, there are different modes and different speeds of reducing State activity in the telco sector.
3. Different European operators pursue different internationalization strategies. The stragegy is dependent on the focus of internationalization in the service sector, the geographical region, and also the organizational mode of governing activities abroad.
4. In a liberalized national telco market, entry from abroad is inevitable. These players often have deep pockets and much expertise regarding technical issues and marketing.
5. However, in order to be able to assess the upcoming market structure in the domain of fixed-link services, especially if we concentrate on the intensity of competition, we have to understand in more detail and also explain the factors driving the strategy of the telco services companies in Europe as well as the inherent market conditions in the telco services market and how they evolve over time.

Yet, in my view a couple of basic issues require further discussion, therefore I shall leave aside day-to-day regulatory topics such as interconnection, universal service obligations and modes of price regulation.

Firstly, there is a potential for substitution of fixed-link by (cellular) mobile services. Even if a decrease in access line development has so far not taken place, many carriers worldwide are predicting likely decreases in fixed-link traffic growth. For example U.S.forecasts claim that 90% of fixed-link traffic will be substituted by mobile traffic by 2005 due to the rapid penetration of PCS services.

Secondly, foreseeable technological developments may bring about massive incentives for a re-orientation of the business strategies of traditional telco (common) carriers. Examples are Internet telephony and upcoming bearer services. The latter may be conceived as a technology independent transportation infrastructure allowing the provision of a variety of communications services. Thus, links between production and distribution (marketing) of services may alter fundamentally.

Thirdly, we need a better understanding of the driving forces and limits of competition in the telecommunications sector, even if competition is introduced. What constitutes barriers to entry into the telco market in the mid and long term perspective? Is it true, that effective competition in long distance markets requires competing operators in the local loop? Cornelius makes this claim in his paper and concludes that this could best be achieved by cable TV operators. However, we have to assess the future role of wireless local loop technologies (DECT, PHS) and of city carriers. In addition it already seems obvious today that the future market structure in the long-distance and international segments in European countries will be an oligopoly. In my view, there will be a strong push for a concentration process among entrants into the EU telco markets and it would not be surprising if two big (facilities based) players (i.e. a duopoly) are the ultimate outcome. Another facet which has to be investigated further is the incentive for a concentration process among European incumbent carriers due to forces released by the European monetary union. It is highly likely that a politically united Europe with a single currency will bring about the environment for the realization of economies of scale and scope. In my view these forces will be stronger than the traditionally minded 'one country, one carrier' doctrine.

D: Full Competition in Telecommunications: The Experience of Finland

Martin Andersson

In giving my account on the status of telecommunications in Finland, I shall start with a few facts about my country. The land area of Finland is over 300 000 sq. km in size, and its population stands at over 5 million. Finland is the most sparsely populated country in the European Union. There are vast areas, where population density is very low. In terms of telecommunication this means long transmission lines and few opportunities for traffic concentration.

Telecommunications in Finland began in 1855 with the construction of the first telegraph line between St. Petersburg and Helsinki. The first telephone line was constructed in 1877 and the first telephone company was established in 1882. Finland and Russia share this early history because at that time the country was a Grand Duchy under Russian rule. Licences for telephone operations were granted only to local undertakings which were beyond Russian administrative powers. For this reason a lot of small local telephone companies were established in Finland and the multi-operator environment was born. The number of local telephone companies, peaked in 1933, with a total of 809. Today that figure has decreased to 46.

The telegraph services and State telephone services were annexed administratively to the postal services in 1927. The State entered the field by purchasing several local companies and a long distance company in the 1930s continued to make further acquisitions from then on. The state-owned telecommunications enterprise is now known as Telecom Finland Ltd.

Liberalization in Finnish telecommunications began with the adoption of the Telecommunications Act in 1987. The basic objective of the Act was to guarantee a diversified supply of up-to-date telecommunication services and to make possible the development of different forms of telecommunication. This legislative work was achieved before the country had any European Union Directives to follow. Due to the unique historical background in Finland it was quite natural to continue to maintain the multi-operator environment which had been in existence for the previous 100 years. With the 1987 Act, the element of competition was introduced by the establishment of a telecommunications licensing system.

The Telecommunications Act has been updated several times since then, most recently in August this year, to further liberalise the sector and to meet the challenges of development. This amendment made market entry easier. Nowadays only the construction of public telecommunications and mobile networks require a licence. The provision of public telephone services, the construction of public data communications networks and the activities of Closed User Groups (CUGs) operate under a notification procedure. All other types of telecommunications, for instance data communications services and value added telecommunications services, need no authorisation.

Finland has pursued a consistent policy of telecommunications liberalization for over a decade. Competition in telecommunication is realized on a large scale, in both services and networks. Competition has existed in the field of data communications since 1985. In 1988 telecommunications in business networks were partially freed for competition. Mobile telecommunications were opened to competition in 1990 and finally voice telephony was fully opened to competition in 1994. At present there are over 80 telecommunications operators in Finland of which 57 are operating public networks.

Finland has a good history of competition which has reduced tariffs and improved the provision of services. The users have clearly been the winners in the liberalization of the telecommunications market. In national long-distance and international telephone calls in particular, remarkable price reductions have taken place.

The results of scompetition have not only brought benefits to both business and the public in the form of better and cheaper services, it has also made telecommunications operators more competitive. Early established competition has also benefited the Finnish telecommunications equipment industry. Due to the multi-operator environment, Nokia has faced competition from the beginning from other companies, like Ericsson and Siemens. This has helped these companies to be more competitive abroad.

In Finland we find an over-emphasis on the issue of universal service in a competitive environment. Our experiences of competition show no evidence of a threat to the provision of services. The provision of telephone services still remains profitable for the operators in spite of competition. Services are provided on a high level throughout the entire country and prices are reasonable. The operators set their own prices and there are regional differences. However, it might be useful to have some form of legal obligation to assure the provision of basic services. In Finland public telecommunications operators have a general obligation to provide users with sufficient, secure and safe telecommunications under terms that are reasonable and non-discriminatory.

Fig. D1: Call Charges in Finland

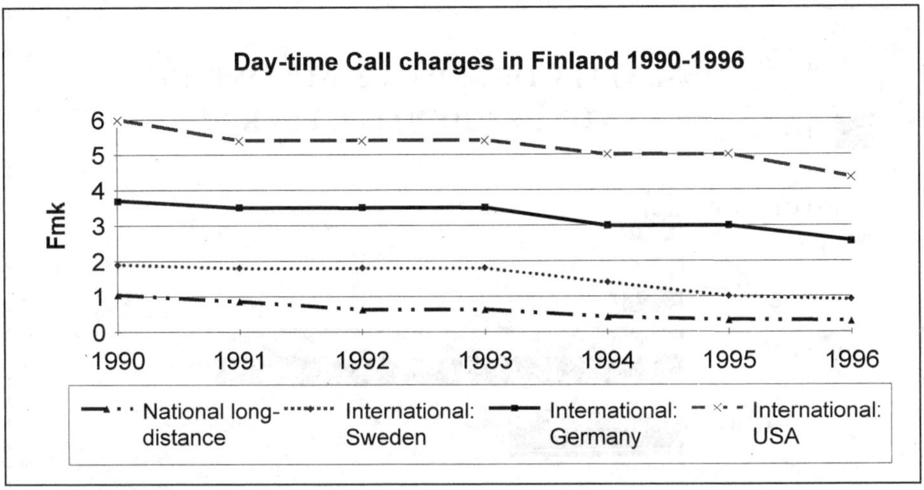

Notes: According to customer surveys carried out in 1994 and 1996, the quality of telephone services seems to have improved. Residential users were more satisfied with the services in 1996 compared to 1994.

Source: MINISTRY OF TRANSPORT AND COMMUNICATION, Telecommunications Statistics, 1990-1996.

In countries where competition is new, more regulation may be necessary. However, if similar regulation is applied when competition already exists, development could, at worst be reversed. The Finnish government aims as far as possible to withdraw sector-specific regulation and to put the sector under normal competition and consumer legislation. For this reason, Finland is pushing for Community legislation that is flexible enough not to lead to a reversal. In an open and competitive market there cannot be strict and detailed regulation on tariffs and quality of service. It is the role of competition itself to set the level of prices and quality. Since August the telecommunications tariffs for Finnish users are, determined freely on the market, and the pricing is steered only by general competition and consumer legislation. However, the European Union's Directives still require us to maintain some specific regulation, for instance, cost-orientation principles regarding public voice-telephony tariffs.

Fig. D2: Quality of Service According to Residential Users

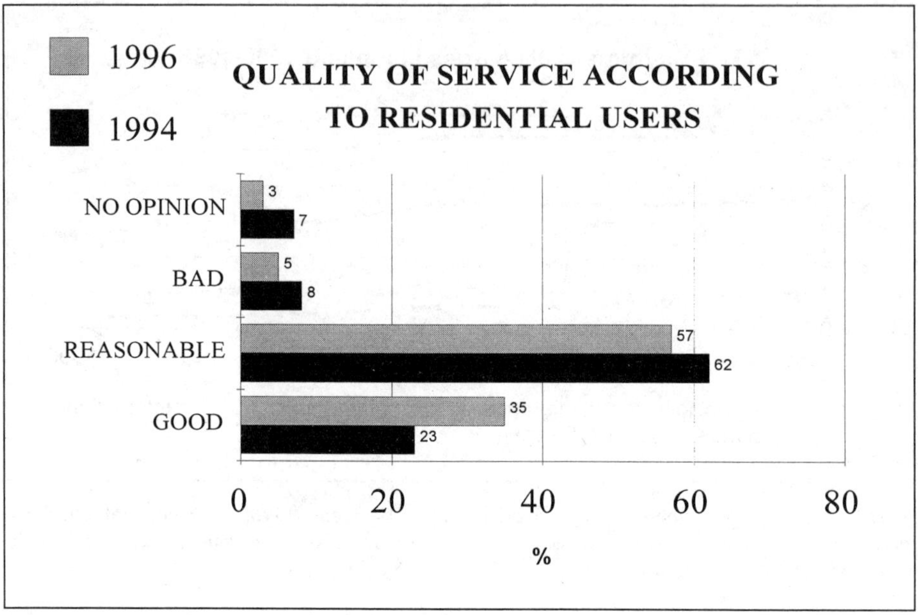

Source: MINISTRY OF TRANSPORT AND COMMUNICATION, Telepalvelut 1994 & 1996.

Interconnection is an area where some special rules are required. Interconnection between telecommunications networks is a necessary condition for effectively functioning services. It is also a key element for a competitive environment. In Finland we have general legal regulations on interconnection and more specific regulations in the form of two ministerial decisions. The basic principle of the Finnish interconnection system is that inter-connection is normally carried out on a commercial basis. Finland has a longtradition of inter-connection negotiations since we have always had several operators.

In Finland the regulator does not continuously scrutinize inter-connection agreements. We believe that the price level can best set through competition and commercial negotiations . In a competitive telecommunications market the "right" tariffs cannot be calculated. According to Finnish telecommunications legislation the fees between operators shall be non-discriminatory and reasonable with regard to costs included for the service.

Ideally the market players should be able to agree upon interconnection tariffs. The regulator becomes involved if an interconnection party or a user makes a complaint. When market players cannot agree between themselves the regulator can mediate in an interconnection dispute and in the worst case deliver a decision. Fortunately we have so far been forced to settle only a few interconnection disputes.

Nowadays we have two main categories of operators in interconnection. Firstly, the traditional network operator, who has rights to construct and maintain a public telecommunications network as well as to operate public telecommunications. Secondly, a new type of market player is the non-network operator or service operator, as we have termed it in Finland. This is an operator, who has switching facilities, but no desire and hence no right to build a network outside its own premises. In other words, one service operator does not have the right to install telecommunications equipment on the land of another, but does have the right to access a network operator's network. The service operator has the facilities to control customer connections. Furthermore, he is supposed to be adding value to the basic service.

Interconnection has become more complex since service operators have entered the field. The network operator must give access to its network, even at a network point other than the normal user network interface, in other words: special network access. This may lead to more interconnection disputes. In Finnish mobile telecommunications there are some quite difficult interconnection negotiations in progress at present. Our third national DCS-1800 operator, Telivo Ltd, is negotiating with the GSM-operators in order to achieve wider territorial coverage for its service. Even though the negotiations have been going on for some months, the parties are not yet prepared to turn to the regulator for mediation. There is still hope for a commercial solution without any regulatory intervention.

Infrastructure competition and the availability of alternative networks are vital elements for achieving full competition in telecommunications. The ideal situation for a new market player offering telecommunications services would be the availability of more than one fixed operator offering interconnection.

Numbering is also an important issue in competition. In Finland every long-distance and international operator has their own access code. This system enables the user to choose the operator on a call-by-call basis. The user can also make an agreement whereby calls will be automatically handled by a particular operator. In such a case the consumer still has the opportunityto override the agreement by dialling another operator's prefix. The user always has the possibility to choose the best offer.

Number portability will be introduced in June 1997. The user will be able to keep his old number even if he changes operator. This is an important step for increased competition in local telecommunications.

Competition in local telecommunications has not been as efficient as in other areas of telecommunications. The bottleneck of local competition is the local loop, connecting the user with the exchange. So far access to the local loop has not been available at a reasonable price for competitors. Alternative networks have been constructed in some cities using mainly radio-based solutions, like DECT and Ionica, but clearly competition has been limited. Only big customers have been able to choose their local telecommunications operator freely. In order to speed up competition, the Finnish Government has given Parliament a proposal for a new Telecommunications Markets Act. The new Act would in particular enhance the possibilities of small and medium-sized undertakings and households to benefit from competition.

The main means provided by the proposed Act for increasing competition in local telecommunications is the obligation imposed on operators to separate the provision of telecommunications networks and telecommunications services from each other financially. This would mean that operators would have to keep separate books on both telecommunications network provision and the services they offer in the network. A network operator with significant market power in local telecommunications services would have to lease subscriber connections to other telecommunications companies so that they would be priced in the same way as in its own service operations. The purpose of this is that the network costs in the user tariffs of the telecommunications service would not depend on whether the services are offered by the telecommunications company owning the network or by its competitor.

The free element or free capacity of a telecommunications network would have to be granted under equal and reasonable terms to all telecommunications companies. For example, the owner of a cable broadcasting network would have to allow the use of the network not only for the distribution of programmes but also for the distribution of telecommunications services. It is believed that this will increase the use of cable broadcasting networks for the provision of telecommunications services.

The new concept in the Telecommunications Markets Act is "significant market power". A telecommunications company with considerable market power could be subjected to more stringent obligations relating to competing operations than those imposed on other telecommunications companies. These obligations would mainly relate to interconnection and the pricing of services sold to other telecommunications companies. This proposal corresponds to the proposed Interconnection Directive in the European Union.

If everything goes as planned, the new Telecommunications Markets Act will enter into force in the Summer of 1997, when the present Telecommunications Act will have been in force for ten years. Hopefully, the proposed Act will achieve its aim and establish full competition in local telecommunications.

References

MINISTRY OF TRANSPORT AND COMMUNICATIONS, Telecommunications Statistics, various issues.

MINISTRY OF TRANSPORT AND COMMUNICATIONS, Telepalvelutaso, various issues.

E: Full Competition in Telecommunications: The US Perspective

Jacqueline Spindler

1. Introduction

I would like to talk a bit about the broad initiatives the FCC is pursuing to implement last year's Telecommunications Act, and how those efforts fit in with the regulatory reforms going on throughout the world.

1.1 Convergence of Technology/Convergence of Regulatory Frameworks

Last night, Dr. Ungerer talked about technological convergence and this morning Chris Moore discussed regulatory convergence. I would now like to discuss this latter kind of convergence, regulatory convergence.

1.2 WTO Agreement

The best evidence of this regulatory convergence came in the recent WTO Agreement, with its market access, foreign investment, and pro-competitive regulatory principles. Most signatories to the agreement have agreed to allow companies market access in their countries for local, long-distance and international services. And most signatories also agreed to allow foreign investors access to their markets.

These two parts of the WTO agreement are in themselves a remarkable achievement - they lift barriers to market access and foreign ownership in virtually all the major basic telecom markets to an extent no one believed possible when these talks began three years ago. But what is truly unique about the WTO agreement is that signatories representing more than 95% of the world's markets have agreed to abide by the regulatory principles of transparency, non-discrimination, and openness to competition. Those signatories who agreed to the Reference paper have guaranteed to assure interconnection at fair prices, to forbid anti-competitive practicing and to mandate transparency of government regulations and licensing. In other words, these countries have agreed to set up rules to ensure that new entrants will be able to compete in practice, not just in theory.

Whatever individual differences in approach may develop, it is clear that the basic principles of non-discrimination, transparency, and encouragement of competition are the essential core of the WTO agreement. These pro-competitive regulatory principles are based upon the experience of those countries that have already invested so much in developing a pro-competitive regulatory framework, not to mention any names...

Of course, the United States' landmark Telecommunications Act of 1996 was one of the key models for these principles, and the world is now watching our implementation process. It hasn't been easy. But perhaps other countries can learn from our experiences - and for them, hopefully, the process will be easier.

1.3 U.S. Implementation of Telecom Act: Lessons for Other Countries

In implementing our Telecom Act we have learned at least three important lessons. Firstly, the marketplace alone cannot guarantee competition where there are incumbent players with market power. Government action is needed to establish fair rules of competition. Mr. Bohla said last night - all o.tel.o really asks is to have fair, clear rules and an effective referee. It is essential to have a truly independent regulatory authority, with rules and procedures that are non-discriminatory and transparent, and that encourage the development of competition. Only then will competitors feel that they have a fair chance to succeed.

Secondly, the Government may need to ensure that public benefits from communications are distributed fairly and efficiently to all citizens. In the United States that means making sure that telephone services reach everyone, from rural and high-cost parts of America, to low income people who need help in gaining access to telephone services, to children in classrooms and public libraries, and to doctors and their patients in rural health care centres.

Thirdly, even as we develop rules to ensure fair competition in the short term, we must plan for competition to replace detailed regulatory rules in the long term. As competition develops, less regulation is needed. So even while we have been implementing the Act, we have simultaneously streamlined and improved our own internal processes by eliminating unnecessary rules and regulations, always working to assure that competitive neutrality - the even-handed treatment of all players - is maintained.

2. The Telecom Act - Key Principles

The three principal goals established by the Telecom Act are: (1) opening local service to competitive entry; (2) reforming our system of universal service support so that universal service is preserved and advanced as the market moves to competition; and (3) promoting increased competition in telecommunications markets that are already open to competition, including the long-distance services market. Thus, our "competition trilogy" is made up of interconnection, universal service, and access charge reform.

3. Rollout of the Trilogy

So much for the easy part - reviewing the general principles. The hard part is turning these principles into something tangible and workable. At what stage is the Commission in its implementation of the Act?

3.1 Interconnection

In August 1996, just six months after the Act was passed, the Commission took its first step in implementing the competition trilogy by establishing rules designed to open the local loop to competition. This is the famous 750-page order. The Commission established uniform national rules on some issues, and the states will establish their own rules on issues that are critical to promoting local telephone competition.

For example, the Commission established some national rules regarding the duty to negotiate interconnection in good faith. The Commission also identified a number of "technically feasible" points at which incumbent LECs must provide interconnection or the physical linking of networks to competitors.

The Commission also required incumbent LECs to allow competitors to lease unbundled parts of the incumbent's network at rates that are just, reasonable, and non-discriminatory. These local exchange carriers are also required to resell retail services at wholesale prices; our experience has been that resale is the first step in the door for many new entrants, and thus the first step towards developing competition in a market. Finally, the Commission provided guidance to the states on pricing methodologies for interconnection, unbundled elements, and transport and termination charges. The order is available on the FCC's website, as is a summary press release about the order.

Some parts of the Commission's order are in litigation in the United States Court of Appeals for the 8th Circuit. The court has issued a stay on certain sections but not on others. We expect the court to rule any day now. It should be noted that the issues before the court have generally to do with questions of federal-state jurisdiction, in particular the FCC's right to set prices for intrastate services. I would emphasise that the fact that this order is in litigation does not mean that it is not effective, or is a failure. Indeed, interconnection agreements with competitive carriers have been negotiated in all 50 U.S. states, and notwithstanding the judicial challenge, a large number of states have adopted the FCC's proxy prices as their own interim prices.

3.2 Universal Service

The second part of the trilogy is universal service reform. Our goal is to remove the link between 'natural monopoly' and universal service, and make universal service compatible with competition. The Commission adopted a Report and Order last week. This order is even longer than the interconnection order! It is also available on our website, along with a summary press release. The website is at "www.fcc.gov".

I would now like to summarise the highlights of the order for you.

As you may know, the Act required that we work with the Federal-state Joint Board to accomplish this reform. The Joint Board submitted its recommendations in November, and these formed the basis of this order. Firstly, the Commission adopted the Joint Board's recommendation that "competitive neutrality" must be the principle for universal service support mechanisms and rules. Competitive neutrality assures that every provider of telecommunications services shares the responsibility for assuring universal service, regardless of what kind of carrier it is or what technology it uses. No one sort of alternative provider, for example, is free of this obligation, and thereby competitively favoured.

Secondly, the Commission listed the services to be supported, and decided that the question of "affordability" merits further study, primarily by the states. The services include single-party voice-grade service with touch-tone, and access to emergency ("911") operators, directory assistance, and interexchange services. The Commission also decided what kinds of carriers should be eligible for support, and how to calculate the cost of providing universal service. In order to be eligible to receive support, a carrier must be a common carrier and must offer and advertise within its service region all of the services listed above. Costs are to be calculated on a forward-looking basis, and the Commission will establish the particulars of this calculation by the end of 1997 - yet another large order!

Thirdly, in regard to existing support programs for low-income consumers, the Commission decided to expand Lifeline to make it available everywhere in the U.S. - in every state, territory, and commonwealth, and to make the contribution and distribution of this support competitively and technologically neutral. The Commission also adopted the Joint Board's recommendations for providing eligible schools and libraries with discounts on all commercially available telecommunications services, including Internet access and Internal connections. Discounts will range from 20% to 90%, with higher discounts for more disadvantaged schools and libraries, and those in high-cost areas. The Commission also established guidelines for universal service support in telecom services for rural health care providers.

Our goal is to assure that the universal service system is efficient and effective, is fully compatible with ever-increasing competition in every aspect of telecom service provision, and does produce truly universal access to telecommunications services at affordable prices.

3.3 Access Reform

Finally, the third part of the trilogy is access charge reform. The Commission adopted a report and order last week. In essence, this is a rate rebalancing process, similar to the investigations going on in many other countries. The Commission is examining how, pursuant to the Telecom Act, we can move, or allow competition to move, rates for origination and termination to cost, thus eliminating implicit subsidies and non-cost-based charges and rate structures; and eventually meeting our goal of deregulation as competition develops.

The existing access charge structure contains implicit subsidies. Some were created to keep local services affordable, and some are a result of how the system is designed.

The current structure was developed at a time when all local service was provided by a monopoly local exchange carrier, and it reflects that origin. By developing a rate structure that is rational and fair, the Commission fosters investment and competition. When hidden subsidies and structural anomalies are removed, rates will fall. By developing a rate structure that treats all parties equally, the Commission provides a level playing field where neither new entrants nor incumbents are favoured.

4. How the Trilogy Principles Apply to Other Countries

4.1 Interconnection

The question now is, how might our trilogy of principles be applied outside the United States? We believe that competition is not about building new networks that duplicating existing infrastructures, but rather about letting new entrants into the market to compete effectively with incumbent operators. Such competition depends on an interconnection regime that gives both new and existing operators the flexibility and opportunity to compete in whatever way they deem most efficient. Again, I refer to Mr. Bohla's metaphor, and say: the referee cannot be effective if neither he nor the players know the rules going into the game.

New entrants should therefore be able to lease separate elements of the incumbent's networks - in other words, the existing network must be "unbundled." The lease price of network elements should be set at a forward-looking economic cost - the price that would exist in a competitive market. Too high a price for unbundled elements means they're not practicably available at all. A new entrant should also be able to resell the incumbent's services by buying them in bulk, at a discount. If the regulator does not put his shoulder to the wheel, the incumbent will always be favoured, and competition will come very slowly and painfully if it comes at all.

4.2 Universal Service

Second, universal service. This is not just a U.S. program, but is a fundamental goal around the world: to make sure that a very high percentage of a country's population has access to telecommunications services.

In the United States we have learned that a universal service policy should promote access for all in ways that are compatible with competition and do not distort the competitive process. Competition will lead to the lowest overall prices and the lowest underlying costs, thus promoting use and reducing the financial burden of universal service support. We have also learned that the best approach to universal service is to take advantage of new technologies, including terrestrial wireless, and satellites. In many cases, these technologies will be the least expensive, most quickly deployed, and most innovative services available.

4.3 Access Reform

Third rate rebalancing: Our goal in the United States is to assure that access charges reflect actual costs. This is a necessary step towards developing real competition. Rate rebalancing must produce rates that reflect costs related to the services provided, so that competition can develop, bringin with it the benefits of increased services and innovation, increased traffic and use, and decreased costs to consumers.

The FCC is also applying these principles to international service in our notice of proposed rulemaking on benchmark settlement rates. In order to help reduce the exorbitant prices American consumers pay for international calls, we have asked for comments on a proposal to lower the high settlement payments U.S. carriers pay to their foreign correspondent carriers to terminate U.S.-originated calls. These settlement rates are the international equivalent of above-cost access charges, but instead of being a few cents a minute over cost, they average more than three times the underlying costs, with many even higher than that. In our Notice, we proposed the reduction of these settlement rates to levels closer to cost-based, over a transition period that will give developing countries additional time to adjust.

This proposal by the FCC has created a lot of controversy, although it relies on principles and agreements already in force - for instance, ITU-T Recommendation D.140, which was adopted more than five years ago, states that ITU member states shall work to implement cost-based settlement rates. The U.S. is trying to do just that - to take a step toward using cost-based settlement rates for international communications. We have been attacked for taking unilateral action, but in fact what we are proposing is, in effect, to take a step to implement an ITU recommendation that applies to, and is agreed upon by, some 190 countries. So, although many vociferously oppose our proposal, I can confirm that the Commission does intend to adopt a final order in that proceeding late this summer. Let me note too that we have received more than 80 comments, and some 30 reply comments, in this notice stage; all are being considered and will be addressed by the Commission. In fact, this is one reason that many of our orders are so long - about 3/4 of any Commission order consists of summaries of comments, and responses to the arguments made. We believe that public awareness and participation are a really important part of developing new rules and policies.

5. "Best Practices" for Other Countries

As mentioned at the beginning of these remarks, there is a growing consensus on the fundamental principles that regulators around the world will be trying to implement in the years to come.

As important as these principles themselves, though, are the procedures regulators follow in developing their new regulatory schemes. The procedural principles that we believe are essential include transparency, public comment and participation, and independence of the regulator from those being regulated.

On these fundamental procedural principles, too, consensus is emerging. But the hard part is activating these procedural principles in developing or modifying regulatory schemes, and defining the role of the regulator. As they say, the devil is in the details. I would like to propose that regulators with experience in implementing pro-competitive rules develop ways of sharing their experience with those who are just starting down this path. This conference is one very effective way to do this. I would note that at the FCC we host a steady stream of visiting foreign regulators who ask us how we have gone about our rate rebalancing and developed our universal service programs, how we make decisions, what problems we have encountered and what advice we can give them. In fact, last year, visitors from 93 countries came to see us and have usefully shared in our experiences. I know our counterparts in other countries host many of the same visitors. The ITU and OECD also provide opportunities for learning and sharing. I believe that it would be helpful if, in one forum or another, independent regulators who have done a lot of work developing rules to encourage competition could come together to compare their approaches, with the aim of providing guidelines or helpful suggestions for countries just starting out. If we can work together to develop a "best practices" model on the difficult implementation issues we all face, we can in fact make all our jobs a lot easier.

F: Market Entry in the Presence of a "Dominant" Network Operator in Telecommunications

Günter Knieps[1]

1. Introduction

The telecommunications sector can be considered an especially fascinating network industry. In spite of the enormous resistance shown by different interest groups in the early eighties, the period of partial entry liberalization will be completed by the end of 1997. The new Telecommunications Law in Germany which was passed in July 1996[2] will allow complete active and potential competition from early 1998. Market entry will then be possible not only in the areas of terminal equipment and value-added network services, but also in the voice telephony market and all other parts of the networks, including cable-based infrastructure. If the new Telecommunications Law is meant to exhaustively promote all possibilities of competition, the role of the market should not be hampered by unnecessary administrative or regulatory intervention. The extent of government regulation in telecommunications markets should therefore be restricted to a minimum and its continuing validity should be periodically reviewed.

Section 2 shows the strong tendency towards over-regulation of the new German Telecommunications Law. The necessity for a symmetric regulatory approach is explained in Section 3, with a focus on monopolistic bottlenecks. Section 4 highlights the dangers of excessive regulation based on the concept of dominant network carriers, with special emphasis on the interconnection of networks and the provision of universal services.

2. Excessive Regulation Due to an Oversized Regulatory Basis

Although the general directive of the new German Telecommunications Law to open all parts of the telecommunications sector to competition can be considered an enormous step forward, the actual law contains a strong tendency towards excessive regulation. In fact, the new Telecommunications Law provides an asymmetric regulatory framework with an intrinsic bias towards the former network monopolist. The view is still widely accepted that asymmetric regulatory intervention is necessary even in liberalized markets, at least for a sufficiently long transition period. Asymmetric regulation is considered necessary as a means of enforcing competition due to the continuing market power of the former network monopolist (PICOT and BURR, 1996, pp. 191ff.; KRUSE, 1996, pp. 77ff.; MONOPOLKOMMISSION, 1996, pp. 26f.) Even following the abolishment of legal entry barriers, the traditional incumbent would still possess a factual monopoly position over its network and the voice telephony services (MESTMÄCKER and WITTE, 1995, p. 12).

The new Telecommunications Law distinguishes on the one hand between a regulatory area in which sector-specific regulatory interventions are considered necessary in order to discipline market power and pursue universal service objectives, and on the other, all other areas, where general competition law applies. The specification of the regulatory basis is not explicitly founded on the differentiation between incumbent versus newcomers. Instead, classification as a dominant firm ("marktbeherrschende Stellung") as laid down in § 22 of German Competition Law (Gesetz gegen Wettbewerbsbeschränkungen/ GWB) is chosen as the central precondition for sector-specific regulation. In order to assess the dominant market position of a firm according to § 22 GWB, a set of criteria, such as relative market power, financial strength, access to input and service markets, etc. may be taken into consideration. In the past, a substantial degree of discretionary freedom has been given to the Federal Bureau of Competition (Bundeskartellamt) in determining whether a firm is classified as dominant. This vagueness is already demonstrated by a different set of criteria for assessing a dominant position ("Vermutungskriterien"), based on market shares, provided that a certain amount of revenue is exceeded. As a consequence, firms may be classified as dominant without possessing actual market power within specific submarkets, resulting in an oversized regulatory basis. For example, the provision of a long-distance telecommunications infrastructure and voice telephone services by a carrier classified as dominant on these markets will be regulated, although active and potential competition is in itself sufficient to discipline market power (see section 3).

The obligation to provide network access holds weight if a dominant carrier provides telecommunications to the public (§ 35 Telekommunikationsgesetz/ TKG). There are different intensities of regulation of dominant carriers' tariffs, depending on the different classifications of licensed services. Whereas all tariffs of dominant carriers have to be free of mark-ups guaranteeing excessive profits, free of predatory deductions, and nondiscriminatory, (§ 24 TKG), the procedural intensity of regulation varies depending on the category of licences the carriers have to apply for. Ex ante approval of tariffs is required for the supply of telecommunications infrastructure and voice telephony (§ 25 (1) TKG). If a carrier is considered dominant in other markets (for example satellite or mobile communications), post regulation of tariffs may take place (§25(2) TKG).

The regulation of telecommunications services on the precondition of a dominant market position is based on § 22 GWB. Nevertheless, in this case the application strongly differs from the usual application of German competition law. According to § 22 GWB, Section 4, competition agencies are typically allowed to intervene against dominant firms if these firms *actually* abuse their dominant market positions. These interventions might therefore be considered as ex post interventions. In contrast, the new Telecommunications Law applies the concept of dominant market position (and not necessarily its abuse) as criterion in order to justify ex ante sector-specific regulatory interventions. This is much too strong a method, involving high costs when applied in such markets where bargaining solutions would achieve more efficient results.

The regulatory approach of the new Telecommunications Law can be illustrated by the following table:

Tab. F1: The Regulatory Approach of the New German Telecommunications Law

	Dominant market position	**No dominant market position**
Voice telephony service and provision of cable-based networks a)	ex ante approval of tariffs; obligatory provision of network access	obligatory private bargaining on interconnetion
All other telecommunications for the public	ex post regulation of tariffs; obligatory provision of network access	obligatory private bargaining on interconnection

Note: a) licences classes 3 and 4

3. The Necessity for a Symmetric Regulatory Approach

Symmetric regulatory conditions should neither advantage nor disadvantage the former network monopolist. On the one hand, all monopoly privileges must be abandoned, on the other hand, all one-sided regulatory obligations (e.g. cross-subsidization of universal services) must end (KNIEPS, 1995, p. 5). "In general terms symmetric regulation means providing all suppliers, incumbents and new entrants alike, with a level playing field on which to compete: the same price signals, the same restrictions, and the same obligations.... But all forms of asymmetric regulation contain an intrinsic bias toward some firms or technologies ..." (SHANKERMAN, 1996, pp. 5f.).

3.1 The Basic Concept of the Disaggregated Regulatory Approach

Even if one accepts criteria like relative market share, financial strength, access to input and service markets etc. as a starting point in evaluating the existence of market power, nevertheless the development of an ex ante regulatory criterion creates a need, for a more clear-cut definition of market power. This is even more important, because "Vermutungskriterien" (conjectures) based on market shares can lead to wrong criteria for government intervention in the telecommunications sector.

Therefore it is important to develop and apply a disaggregated approach to market power regulation. It is necessary to differentiate between those areas in which active and potential competition can work and so-called monopolistic bottleneck areas, where a natural monopoly situation (due to economies of bundling), in combination with irreversible costs, exists. It can be demonstrated that the regulation of market power is only justified in monopolistic bottleneck areas. In all other cases, the existence of active and potential competition will lead to efficient market results.

The pressure of potential competition can itself create an incentive for the active supplier to improve the quality and variety of services as well as to produce more efficiently. These networks are therefore called 'contestable' (BAUMOL, PANZAR and WILLIG, 1982). An essential condition for the functioning of potential competition in order to discipline firms already providing network services, is that the incumbent firms do not have asymmetric cost advantages compared with potential entrants. In contrast, if sunk costs are relevant, consumers who would intrinsically be willing to switch immediately to less costly firms, cannot do this. Market entry therefore cannot be easily expected if sunk costs are sufficiently high and very relevant (KNIEPS and VOGELSANG, 1982, p. 239f.).

Therefore we can conclude that sector-specific ex ante regulatory intervention for disciplining market power can only be justified in non-contestable networks (monopolistic bottleneck areas), i.e. where bundling, in combination with irreversible costs is relevant. Sunk costs are no longer a decision factor for the incumbent monopolist, whereas the potential entrant is confronted with the decision of whether or not to build network infrastructure and thus incur the irreversible costs. The incumbent firms therefore have lower decision-relevant costs than the potential entrants. This creates scope for strategic behaviour by the incumbent firms, so that inefficient production and monopoly profits will not necessarily result in market entry.

The aim of future regulatory policy should, however, not be the global regulation of markets. Instead, only a disaggregated regulation of non-contestable networks is justified. The aim is then to localize market power in monopolistic bottleneck areas and discipline this market power by regulatory intervention. Asymmetry of market power due to monopolistic bottleneck facilities, however, does not by itself require asymmetric regulation. Instead, the symmetry principle requires that all firms have access to local telecommunications networks on terms identical to those of the incumbent (i.e. nondiscriminatory access). The symmetry principle demands that only bottleneck facilities are regulated, irrespective of whether the owner is the incumbent or a newcomer, for example a cable television provider upgrading the traditional local network (see also SHANKERMAN, 1996, p. 5). The basic concept of the disaggregated regulatory approach can be illustrated by table F2.

Tab. F2: The Disaggregated Regulatory Approach

Sub-market	**With sunk costs**	**Without sunk costs**
Natural monopoly a)	(1) regulation of market power (non-contestable networks)	(2) potential competition (contestable networks)
No natural monopoly b)	(3) competition among active providers	(4) competition among active providers

Note: a) bundling advantages; b) bundling advantages exhausted.

3.2 Contestable Telecommunications Markets versus Monopolistic Bottlenecks

The markets for telecommunications services, which are often provided via service networks, provide an important example of contestable networks. Even the market for public telephone services is contestable, because suppliers of value-added services are also prepared to offer telephone services (after legal entry barriers have disappeared). An important condition, however, is the guarantee of number portability. The term "number portability" means the ability of users of telecommunications services to retain, at the same location, existing telecommunications numbers without impairment of quality, reliability, or convenience when switching from one telecommunications carrier to another. Even if the market shares of incumbent firms are large, inefficient suppliers would then be immediately confronted with rapidly decreasing market shares. But contestable sub-areas can also be localized in the area of telecommunications infrastructure. The pressure of potential competition in wireless networks, for example satellite, microwave systems, and mobile communications, is guaranteed as long as symmetric access to complementary inputs, such as rights of way, radio spectrum etc., is ensured. More generally, an important condition for the effectiveness of actual and potential competition is that all (active and potential) suppliers have equal (symmetric) access to the complementary monopolistic bottleneck.

An important example of an area where regulatory intervention is still necessary (at least given the current state of technology) are the local networks. Due to economies of scale with respect to the set-up of a local cable-based network, there is in general only one active provider of a local network. At the same time, the irreversible costs of cable-based networks result in the incumbent firm possessing market power, as its decision-relevant costs are only short-term variable costs, whereas a potential entrant is confronted with the decision of whether to build the network infrastructure thereby incurring irreversible costs. The incumbent firm therefore has lower decision-relevant costs than the potential entrant. However, even in the area of local telecommunications networks, significant potential for competition can be expected in the future, especially due to technological development in mobile communication technologies and cable television networks.

It seems obvious that the criterion of dominant market position based on market shares will lead to a significant overestimation of the need for regulatory intervention in future telecommunications sectors. Competition in the terminal equipment sector, the markets for all telecommunications services as well as all subareas of long distance networks will lead spontaneously to efficient market results. On the other hand, in order to guarantee the functioning of actual and potential competition, it remains necessary that remaining market power in local networks becomes disciplined in an effective way. This is especially true because access to local networks creates a critical input for most of the telecommunications services. Since substantial technological advances in the field of local networks have recently been observed (e.g. radio-based network-access technologies), a gradual disappearance of monopolistic bottlenecks can be expected. As a consequence, the necessity for sector-specific regulation will also gradually disappear.

The disaggregated localization of market power in telecommunications systems is illustrated by the following table:

Tab. F3: Disaggregated Location of Market Power in Telecommunications Systems

	Competitive/ contestable	Non-contestable a)
Terminal equipment	X	—
Telecommunication services b)	X	—
Satellite / mobile networks	X	—
Long distance cable-based networks	X	—
Local cable-based networks	—	X

Notes: a) monopolistic bottlenecks; b) including voice telephone services.

4. The Dangers of an Inadequate Application of Regulatory Rules Based on the Concept of Dominant Network Carriers

The new Telecommunications Law prescribes asymmetric regulatory rules for interconnection and network access. The criterion for the regulation of open-network provision, including the regulation of access charges, is the of a dominant carrier on the relevant market. If the network carrier is not considered to have a dominant market position, market participants are free to find bargaining solutions. As long as public telecommunications are involved, however, private bargaining on interconnection is obligatory.[3]

4.1 Interconnection of Networks

Consider the case where interconnection/access requirements arise among contestable networks. One may think, for example, of a local community operating a mobile radio network and considering one or various opportunities for establishing a long-distance connection by microwaves or the connection of two specialized satellite networks. Other examples are horizontal interconnection among different specialized value added service networks or the (vertical) interconnection of a value-added service network into a microwave long-distance network.

Interconnection among contestable networks, however, does not create a regulatory problem. Potential competition fulfills the function of mitigating market power. Therefore it can be expected that private bargaining of interconnection/access conditions between the different network owners will lead to economically efficient solutions. Strategic behaviour is not relevant, because every bargaining partner can be easily substituted by an alternative (potential) network carrier. Private bargaining solutions on interconnection conditions among contestable network carriers are not only beneficial for the carriers themselves, but in particular improve the market performance of the network services provided to the customers. For example, independent of the market size of the carriers involved, inefficient suppliers of interconnection services are immediately confronted with strongly decreasing market shares, due to the strong pressure of alternative (potential) network service providers. It can be expected that the telecommunications sectors within European countries after the beginning of 1998, having overall free entry into the public switched telephone service as well as the network infrastructure, will provide full opportunities for efficient private bargaining solutions on interconnection/access conditions. Government regulation of such private bargaining processes, however, would disturb the bargaining process and automatically lead to inferior solutions, even if their aim were to improve competition and maximize consumer surplus. Specific regulatory interventions would artificially decrease the scope of bargaining and hence would have the effect of an artificial market barrier reducing entrance of potential network carriers. From this perspective the obligation to bargain in all public (open) networks (§§ 36, 37 TKG) can also be detrimental. The pressure to find joint solutions in a contestable environment may already be creating inefficiencies, because the ex ante freedom of bargaining is hampered.

In contrast to interconnection among contestable networks, the market power involved in non-contestable network infrastructures (monopolistic bottlenecks) crucially disturbs such bargaining processes. The influence of market power in these situations may lead to strategic behaviour which obstructs competition. For example, irreversible costs in local networks may lead to the established firm possessing market power in the provision of interconnection services. Therefore, if a potential competitor plans an entry, the incumbent local network provider could credibly claim to reduce his tariffs on short term variable costs, because his decision-relevant costs are in fact these short term variable costs. The decision-relevant costs of potential local network carriers, however, would be the full costs, including the cable-based investment costs. Examples of the abuse of market power within the bargaining process on interconnection/access conditions may be insufficient network accessquality, or excessive interconnection charges. Since, nevertheless entry cannot automatically be expected, the remaining market power has to be disciplined by regulatory intervention.

Instead of the criteria for a dominant network carrier on the relevant market combined with licensed network area, as laid out in the new German Telecommunications Law, a disaggregated approach is necessary in order to localize the minimum need for regulatory intervention. Hitherto such a fine-tuned disaggregated approach, focusing on monopolistic bottlenecks, has not been the mode of application of the traditional competition law. Moreover, it is not guaranteed that the new regulatory Commission, when applying the new Telecommunications Law as well as the related interconnection and access charges decrees, will apply the criterion of a dominant firm on specific sub-markets where factual market power can be identified rather than applying it to the firm as a whole. It can therefore be expected that the scope of regulatory intervention will be too large.

The new Telecommunications Law also prescribes the regulation of interconnection charges of dominant carriers on relevant markets. This again reflects an asymmetric regulatory approach which strongly differs from the actual minimal regulatory needs. In the US, as well as in European countries, the regulatory need with respect to tariffs for interconnection and access has been significantly overestimated. In this context, the criterion of the dominant carrier again leads to a tendency to over-regulation, since the concept of the dominant carrier typically does not focus only on those areas where actual market power can be localized. For example, the new German Telecommunications Law comprises the possibilities of applying price regulation based on detailed cost-information as well as price-cap regulation (§27 TKG). Although price-cap regulation is expected to be the normal instrument to be applied, the regulatory agency will have a large scope of discretion to evaluate the cost-orientation of a tariff under approval. In particular, it may require detailed information on past and (expected) future revenues, price elasticities, development of individual costs and markups, the justification of price differentiation, the justification of specific allocations of overhead costs, the depreciation methods applied, etc.. Even price-cap regulation may be applied in such a manner that the regulated firms will have the burden of providing detailed cost information, in particular when the initial tariff level and the rate of productivity change is to be determined. The more detailed such price regulation is, the more the competition process is hampered in all contestable areas where regulation is not justified.

Carriers of contestable networks do not possess market power due to the (potential) competition posed by alternative network carriers. Excessive interconnection/access charges which allow monopoly rents would immediately initiate a switch to an alternative network carrier (which also would become available due to free entry with another contestable service network). There is therefore no need for government intervention to discipline the market power of active network carriers with respect to tariff setting, if the underlying networks are contestable.

On the other hand, the question arises whether interconnection tariffs resulting from a competitive bargaining procedure can guarantee the viability of efficient providers of network capacities, as long as they are producing efficiently. Since in contestable natural monopolies fixed costs and related economies of scale are also of significant importance, marginal costs, which are the typical benchmark under competition, cannot be realized, as they would not allow costs to be covered. Even long-run marginal or incremental costs, which include the fixed costs of capacity extensions, are not sufficient to cover the total costs of network provision, due to the importance of economies of scope and related common costs (overhead costs). Price regulation with the aim of achieving interconnection tariffs based on long-run incremental costs (including fixed costs of capacity) would subsequently lead to discrimination against network owners. No firm would voluntarily provide network capacities under such conditions. It is to be expected that the equipment would never have been built, if such regulatory burdens had been known ex ante and could have been taken into account. Thus the task remains to cover the difference between total costs and incremental costs (common costs/overhead costs). In consequence, network providers must have the flexibility to raise interconnection tariffs such that the total cost covering constraint (viability condition) is fulfilled. In particular, they must be free to allocate common costs depending on the relevant demand schedules (including peak-load pricing elements). Ex ante allocations of overhead costs according to fully allocated cost principles, however, would be detrimental (cf. OWEN and BRAEUTIGAM, 1978, pp. 212 - 220). They would be based neither on economically justified cost causality nor take into account demand-side considerations. In consequence, regulators who set interconnection rates on the basis of fully allocated costs would make bypass activities even more inefficient, even when efficient (viable) market solutions exist. Instead, the difference between total costs and incremental costs must be covered by market-derived markups on incremental costs.

Regulation of access/interconnection charges is only justified in non-contestable natural monopoly areas (monopolistic bottlenecks). Market power in such areas (for example local networks without sufficient wireless alternatives) may lead to excessive interconnection tariffs, so that the application of regulatory instruments in order to discipline the market power becomes justified.

The central focus of such a regulatory policy should be to restrict regulatory measures to monopolistic bottleneck areas only. Price or rate of return regulation in complementary contestable networks would contradict the principle of minimalistic regulatory intervention and obstruct the objective of global market opening. Regulation of access tariffs in monopolistic bottlenecks therefore should not lead to the regulation of tariffs in areas where market power cannot be localized (KNIEPS, 1997).

4.2 Universal Services

According to the new Telecommunications Law (§ 19), dominant carriers providing licensed services may be obliged to provide universal services. Such burdens are based on the traditional regulatory concept combining market power regulation with universal service obligations. In contrast to the future when global entry will be allowed, in the past universal service obligations were always combined with legal entry barriers. After the opening of all telecommunications markets a combination of market power regulation and the fulfillment of universal service obligations cannot be recommended. Firstly, the concept of symmetric regulation does not allow the burden of universal services to be imposed on a single carrier (as has been common practice in the past). To the extent that market power in monopolistic bottleneck areas does indeed still exist, this market power should be regulated directly. Secondly, extensive network competition may lead to parallel network offers, so that symmetric universal service obligations would lead to inefficient cost duplications. Thirdly, universal service obligations in exchange for looser market power discipline would be in conflict with the tradition of ex post application of German Competition Law.

Therefore a new instrument should be applied, which is fully compatible with the open telecommunications market that will exist after 1998 - the so-called 'universal service fund' (BLANKART and KNIEPS, 1989, pp. 593f.). The basic idea of a universal service fund is to make the political goal of universal service compatible with the abolishment of all legal entry barriers. Internal subsidization (cross-subsidization), for example between profitable and non-profitable geographical areas due to the aim of uniform tariffs, is then no longer maintainable. Free entry into the profitable part (also called cream-skimming) would make excessive profits unstable, which are necessary to cross-subsidize non-profitable areas. However, the supply of non-profitable services is also possible under full competition, provided they are no longer financed by cross-subsidization, but instead by external subsidies. Under a universal service fund every supplier of subsidized services would have the right to compete for an external subsidy financed out of this fund. Competition for subsidies would lay open the actual burden of the universal service and the minimum cost of traditionally cross-subsidized services. Since the amount of subsidies is sufficient in order to attract tenders, it is no longer necessary to leave the burden of obligation to serve on the shoulder of the traditional network carrier. The required implementation of a fund which is used for the subsidization of universal services raises the question of financing. An external subsidy of socially desired services via the public budgeting is not realistic, due to the increasing scarcity of public finances. Instead, the introduction of a universal services tax to be paid by all suppliers of profitable telecommunications activities (i.e. established carriers and their competitors) seems advisable.

The new Telecommunications Law does indeed allow the possibility of introducing such a universal service fund in combination with the obligation on the part of market-dominating licensed firms to act as service providers. The universal service fund therefore is considered as a complement to the traditional universal service burden of dominant firms. The future will show the actual relation between the different kinds of procedures.

In the meantime, the concept of a universal service fund is favoured on the European level as well as in the US as a competition-compatible alternative. The basic idea is to provide symmetric regulatory conditions for all active and potential providers, so that the objective of an extensive opening of the telecommunications market can be combined with the continuation of the provision of universal services (KNIEPS, 1987; BLANKART and KNIEPS, 1994). Instead of universal service obligations, these services should be provided voluntarily against a minimal amount of subsidy which would be financed out of the universal service fund. If the supply of a universal service does not create a deficit or if subsidies are no longer needed due to technological progress, financing out of this fund will become unnecessary. Since the amount of subsidies would be determined by means of a bidding procedure, the universal service fund (at the given level of socially desired universal services) should have the tendency to shrink. Whereas on the one hand the most efficient provider of a universal service should be found via a competitive bidding procedure, on the other hand symmetric regulatory conditions would require the necessity for all active providers of profitable telecommunications services to contribute to the universal service fund. The criterion of market shares is not adequate for determining which carrier should contribute to this fund by the entry tax.

The setting-up of a universal service fund will lead to a transparent, symmetric, tightly restricted regulatory instrument. The fund should be dissolved immediately if, due to technological progress and altered network conditions under competition, subsidization of universal services is no longer needed. The objective of universal services, in any case, does not demand the establishment of an asymmetric regulatory framework and cannot justify an asymmetric regulation of so-called dominant carriers compared with all other active and potential competitors in the future telecommunications sector after 1998.

Endnotes

[1] I would like to thank J. Merkt and J. Müller for helpful comments. The reader should note that this article has been finished in November 1996 before the new Telecommunications law has been enacted. Moreover, in meantime a revised version of the German Competition Law has been passed.

[2] Telekommunikationsgesetz (TKG) of 25 July 1996, BGBl I No. 39 31 July 1996, P. 1120.

[3] It is interesting to note that the new Telecommunications Law also contains a special form of interconnection regulation, even if no dominant carrier is involved (§§ 36, 37 TKG). Every provider of public telecommunications networks is obliged to bargain on interconnections, if such a demand arises. If bargaining does not prove to be successful, the regulatory agency prescribes

interconnection as obligatory; in addition, the tariffs are then regulated according to the dominant carrier case.

References

BAUMOL, W. J., J. C. PANZAR and R. D. WILLIG (1982), Contestable Markets and the Theory of Industry Structure, New York.

BLANKART, CH. B. and G. KNIEPS (1989), What Can We Learn from Comparative Institutional Analysis? The Case of Telecommunications, Kyklos, Vol. 42, Fasc. 4, pp. 579-598.

BLANKART, CH. B. and G. KNIEPS (1994), Das Konzept der Universaldienste im Bereich der Telekommunikation, Jahrbuch für Neue Politische Ökonomie, Vol. 13, pp. 238-253.

KNIEPS, G. (1987), Zur Problematik der internen Subventionierung in öffentlichen Unternehmen, Finanzarchiv, N.F., Vol. 45, No. 2, pp. 268-283.

KNIEPS, G. (1995), Die Ausgestaltung des zukünftigen Regulierungsrahmens für die Telekommunikation in Deutschland, D.P. Nr. 22, Universität Freiburg: Institut für Verkehrswissenschaft und Regionalpolitik.

KNIEPS, G. (1997), The Concept of Open Network Provision in Large Technical Systems, in: EURAS Yearbook of Standardization (EYS), Vol.1, 1997, pp.357-369.

KNIEPS, G. and VOGELSANG, I. (1982), The Sustainability Concept under Alternative Behavioral Assumptions, Bell Journal of Economics, Vol. 13, No.1, pp. 234-241.

KRUSE, J. (1996/II), Liberalisierung der Telekommunikation in Deutschland, Wirtschaftsdienst, pp. 73-80.

MESTMÄCKER, E.-J. and WITTE, E. (1995), Gutachten zur Zuständigkeit für die Verhaltensaufsicht nach dem dritten und vierten Teil des Referentenentwurfs für ein Telekommunikationsgesetz (TKGE), Hamburg und München, 22. November.

MONOPOLKOMMISSION (1996), Wettbewerbspolitik in Zeiten des Umbruchs, Hauptgutachten 1994/1995, Baden-Baden.

OWEN, B. M. and BRAEUTIGAM, R. (1978), The Regulation Game - Strategic Use of the Administrative Process, Cambridge, Ma.

PICOT, A. and BURR, W. (1996), Regulierung der Deregulierung im Telekommunikationssektor, ZfbF (Schmalenbachs Zeitschrift für betriebswirtschaftliche Forschung), Vol. 48, Heft 2, pp. 173-200.

SHANKERMAN, M. (1996), Symmetric Regulation for Competitive Telecommunications, Information Economics and Policy, Vol. 8, pp. 3-23.

Comments on: Market Entry in the Presence of a "Dominant" Network Operator in Telecommunications

Jürgen Müller

Günter Knieps' main point seems to have been that, while sectoral regulation is complicated, it can be simplified by relying only on certain parts. I would now like to examine just how straightforward his prescription is. One might say that "the proof of the pudding is in the eating", but as Günter Knieps' paper has proven to be quite a heavy pudding, the question remains: is his solution as simple as he would have us believe?

1. Is Market Power Regulation Enough?

His main point is a disaggregated regulatory approach, taking into account only the remaining bottle-necks, which are uncontestable. So far so good. He also says that this approach should be forward looking - essentially examining the remaining pockets of market power caused either by large sunk costs or economies of scale. Looking at this in greater detail, two crucial issues can be identified:

1. The first of these is the degree of remaining market power, which is really an empirical question. Günter has of course not applied an empirical test but one of reason. Were you to apply his test in the real world however, you would encounter problems, and this is what I wish to focus on. In other words, even if we accept this disaggragated approach, how easily can his test be applied? Therefore it is necessary for us to compare his 'ivory tower' approach to the one with which regulators are confronted in the real world, as demonstrated by our colleague from Finland.
2. The second question I would like to raise is related to what we call the double mark-up problem. In other words, if you have a monopoly, the question is, how will this monopoly behave and what will happen in downstream markets? Günter would advise us to look only at those markets where the monopoly has market power. But we know that in the telecommunication market at least, carriers traditionally offer vertical integration, i.e. they are active in a number of markets and often offer point-to-point service. So the question is not really one of whether the dominant carrier's market power is confined only to one place, but whether it can extract the monopoly rent from somewhere else. If that is the case, then what they do in the market in which they are dominant becomes less important, as the regulators are responsible for regulating the whole value chain. The question then becomes one of, if a firm takes out a monopoly profit only once, does it matter

where the exploitation takes place or will the exploitation take place only at the few bottlenecks which Günter wants to regulate? In other words, is it really as simple as Günter Knieps has proposed?

2. Will Contestable Markets be Competitive?

The first questions that arise here are, whether or not entry does take place, and how easy is it? In other words, if we try to implement his sustainability test, we also need to look at the issue of sunk costs. If you take a few simple examples, like Cable TV-networks or other network utilities, we can see that access to other networks is not enough to create a competitive market. If for instance the entrant had access to a Cable TV-network, would that create a competitive market structure? If you compare for example the UK and Germany, you can see that there is quite a difference. The UK Cable TV-network was built up with the intention of having cable networks which also acted as separate telecom providers. As a result, the technologies employed are very different from the ones which we have in Germany, and a competitive structure is emerging. But even if the German government sells the Cable TV-network to an entrant, as he has proposed, theentrant still has to do quite a bit of network-investment to be competitive. In other words, entry costs might be somewhat lower with effective access arrangements for alternative networks, and the related sunk costs may be smaller, but they may still be important, and so a degree of market power remains. If you look at the other alternative networks, such as railroad networks which also have some communication facilities, the same entry problems are evident.

Because Günter's test essentially checks the ease of entry, the next empirical question is, how the ease of entry is influenced by other operating goals, i.e. universal service and universal coverage responsibilities. In theory, where entry is possible, there should be no market power left. But we need also to look at the effect of other regulatory goals, because regulators themselves, by enforcing quite complicated universal service rules, may make entry more difficult. An example to illustrate this point is the problem facing the PCS mobile operators in Germany, like E-plus, who have very high infrastructure obligations. I believe that E-plus now have an obligation to service 98% of the country. If you compare that with the GSM operators of D1 and D2, their infrastructure costs per customer will be two to three times lower at similar penetration rates, because they use a different technology. It is much more expensive for E-plus to achieve that high penetration rate with a low market take-up. Thus a lower required penetration rate would have made E-plus, the third mobile operator, a much more effective competitor.

Therefore, if as a regulator you want to create a level playing field which makes entry easier, you have to bear that in mind and make a trade-off between equity goals (in terms of universal service) and allocational and dynamic efficiency goals (in terms of more competition). The German example of E-plus certainly demonstrates the way in which the regulatory interests are tilted in society. Equity is a much more important political issue than the potential gains from competition.

Thus, in terms of Günter's proposal for symmetric regulation, we need to interpret this much more broadly and look not only at entry regulations, but also at the other regulatory arrangements with which entrants are confronted, in order to determine competitive structures. An example I would like to mention is the fourth mobile license which was recently awarded in Germany. Though entry was open there too, we only had one bidder. Similarly, for the auction planned for the paging service Hermes, there were only three or four applicants for five available licenses. In other words, even though entry into mobile services is possible in Germany, it is clear that certain market segments are not as competitive as Günter would have us believe. One reason for this is that, in addition to the institutional barriers, there may also be strategic barriers to entry created by the carriers themselves. So the story is much more complicated than Günter Knieps claims.

3. Implementing Regulation

The third point lies in the effective implementation of the regulation of the remaining bottlenecks. While Günter and I would both agree that there will be some remaining bottlenecks which will need to be regulated, we would probably disagree on the extent to which they are present. I consider them to be still very important, while Günter does not. In any case, we must reach an agreement on how to regulate them. I would propose two options: one of them is the implementation of the EU's ONP regulation, mentioned briefly by Günter, and the other is interconnection at long-term marginal costs. The crucial question is, what really constitutes long-term marginal costs? Günter, I think, referred to the text book example of the natural monopoly with declining LRMC. But if you look at Deutsche Telekom, which has a large network, I wonder to what extent there are still declining costs. How great are the allocational losses he refers to, when you force them to price access at LRMC?

I would also challenge his assumption that if we regulate here according to this principle, we might make things worse. Even given my distrust for political institutions, I would be surprised if we could not find one or two institutional arrangements which would improve the outcome in the presence of a dominant supplier. But it will be difficult for the "outsider" regulator to really distinguish between scale estimates, due to economies of scale and market power. In other words, what tests of symmetry does he propose, to enable us to make this interconnection regulation really work?

Finally I would like to complement Günter on his idea to model the pricing strategy of the incumbent. This is in essence a good idea. In other words, if you want to regulate, you have to determine what the incentives for the incumbent are. I have already referred to this issue, in my reference to the possibility of extracting monopoly rents at various points in the value added chain. A likely explanation, which he fails to mention, is that monopolies use limited pricing and lock the entrants into the competitive fringe. This may result in a stable structural framework over a longer time period, in which the incumbents continues to dominate. In this case it is really the incumbent who determines the evolution of industry structures and the date when we are able to move from sector specific regulation to general regulation.

4. Is Structural Regulation Necessary?

One issue in this connection, which we have not yet addressed but which I believe to be relevant, is to what extent (using the option to have sectoral restructuring) one should move actively from a state of monopoly to one of a competitive market structure. This point was previously discussed in the paper from Finland. They did already have a telecommunications sector which was advantageously structured for competition because there were a number of players operating even before competition was introduced. The Finns have been fortune in having an effective political institution that exploited that structural option and the resulting benefits from effective competition have been quite large. Italy, Portugal and Denmark, who also had a number of players in the field who could have been used as a potential basis for competition, chose not to take advantage of that market structure, instead, they first structurally rearranged the industry to make the incumbent operator stronger.

If we were to rely solely on Günter Knieps' approach of regulating only the remaining market power area, the evolution to a competitive market structure would take a very long time. We must therefore pursue these two options: active structural reorganisation on the one hand, and the regulation of the remaining monopoly on the other.

G: Electricity Companies and Railway Networks as Newcomers in Telecommunications

Morten Falch

1. Introduction

Whether or not the networks of railway and electricity companies will be able to provide an alternative competitive infrastructure for the provision of telecommunication services, depends both on the existing supply and demand factors shaping the market conditions for telecommunication services and on the type of facilities that railway and electricity companies are able to provide.

This paper analyses the cost structures for the provision of telecommunication services and examines the future role of network infrastructure facilities provided by railway and electricity companies.

Historically, services in the telecom sector have been organised by a monopoly network operator, selling its services on a market. This institutional set-up was based on the fact that a single operator would be able to provide services at lower rates and with wider coverage than a market with a number of competing operators. A single operator is in a better position to plan the construction of the network (technical efficiency) and to avoid duplicating investments and excess capacity. These economies of scale can then be fully utilised to the benefit of all customers. In addition, a single network operator is better able to ensure the compatibility of all parts of the network, and minimise the technical and administrative costs related to network integration and interconnection.

Experiences with this institutional set up have been rather mixed. In practice it has been very difficult to both control tariffs and ensure high productivity. And the pressure to allow new operators into the market has increased, especially given the rapid technological advances and development of new products. Today, government policy and regulatory authorities in almost every country aim to introduce more competition into their telecom industries.

The question now is how much more positive competition can realistically be obtained? A free market alone will not necessarily lead to greater competition, which depends rather on the supply and demand factors shaping market conditions.

In most countries, the point of departure for the creation of a competitive market for telecommunications services is one monopoly service provider equipped with an extensive network infrastructure. As the telecom sector is characterised by very large investment costs, related to the building of network infrastructures, potential competitors are facing substantial economic barriers.

Instead of building up an alternative network infrastructure from scratch, it would be possible to utilise existing networks developed for other purposes, e.g. cable TV networks. Private networks, owned by public utility companies such as railway and electricity companies, are also an option. These networks are often referred to as the third wire.

Many public utility companies, for reasons of cost effectiveness and data security, have established their own internal communication networks. Until recently, these companies have been prevented from selling excess capacity to other customers, but as the market for telecommunications is opening up, this becomes both feasible and attractive. Many public utility companies are considering entering the telecom business once alliances with telecom operators have been established.

We will now briefly examine the facilities potentially offered by railway and electricity companies, and then analyse the cost profile for the provision of telecommunication services by breaking the costs down into various components. Finally, the impact of these facilities on the telecommunication market is discussed.

2. Current Competition from the Network Facilities of Railway and Electricity Companies

Although the incumbent telecommunication operators have had a de facto monopoly on the marketing of telecommunication services, a number of alternative networks have existed since the beginning of telecommunications. These networks have been used for internal communication within large organisations such as the military and public utility companies, who needed a reliable communication infrastructure which was fully controlled by the organisation itself. Later, cost considerations also played a role in this development. Private networks for internal communication are also used by many other types of organisations, but only public utility companies have had the opportunity to use their right of ways to establish extensive cable based networks with wider coverage.

The emergence of still more efficient techniques for the compression of traffic and the introduction of optical fibres have created substantial savings in capacity. This suggests that, if done at the outset, extra capacity can be built into the network at little additional cost. For this reason, utility companies have tended to install more capacity than necessary for their own internal communication. The Danish railway company DSB, for example, employs cables with 12 optical single mode fibres, of which only eight are used for internal communication, leaving four fibres with a total capacity of 120.000 phone lines free[1].

This may sound impressive, however it should be noted that the total cable length of the railway networks is rather limited - especially compared to that operated by the incumbent telecommunication carriers. The European railways have a national coverage, but the density is low compared to other providers of network based utilities. The optical fibre network of the Danish railways (DSB) is at present only 1000 km in total. The Netherlands state railway (NS) operates a network of about the same size.

Until recently it was forbidden to sell this capacity to others, but with the liberalisation of the telecom markets, railway companies can sell this capacity either to a telecom carrier or directly to private customers.

Railway companies have become ideal partners for second telecom carriers who wish to establish their own trunk networks. In this respect, the existing network capacity is not as important as the rights of way connected to the railway lines. However, both coverage and capacity can be extended relatively easily. As long as cables are laid along the tracks, the construction work will be far cheaper than for cables laid virtually anywhere else.

When Britain opened up its telecoms market to a second operator in 1984, Mercury laid much of its fibre along British Rails lines (THE ECONOMIST, 1995, pp.74). MCI - one of the three major US international carriers - has laid much of its fibre optical network alongside those of Amtrack. The US also provides examples of former railway companies that have been acquired by telecom operators solely on the basis of their rights of way. The Danish DSB also plans to lease network capacity to alternative operators and will probably co-operate with Global One - jointly owned by Deutsche Telekom, France Telecom and US Sprint (POLITIKEN NEWSPAPER, 1996).

In some countries, railway companies go a step further and establish their own telecom operating companies. In Canada, the second telecom carrier Unicom is established as a joint venture between the two major railway companies (one public and one privately owned), while in the US, Sprint (another of the three major international carriers) has grown out of the communication division of Southern Pacific Railway (MELODY/MØLLER, 1996). Railway companies have also entered the telecom market in Japan, where regional railway companies are shareholders in Japan Telecom. Having laid cables along their tracks, they have now become a leading competitor to NTT (the former monopoly telecom operator). As railway networks are typically nationalised, the provision of international communication demands an interlinking of national networks. For this reason, 14 European railway organisations have entered into a co-operation with GTS (Global Telesystems Group), an American developer and operator of telecommunication companies in the Eurasian markets, and created Hermes Europe Railtel B.V as a joint venture.

The company plans to become the leading pan-European Carrier by constructing and operating a managed, seamless, pan-European network, and providing high-quality trans-border transmission services for telecommunications carriers across Europe. The Hermes Europe Railtel fibre optic network is built along European railway rights of way. Construction of a fibre optic network began in late

1995. Initial services to 12 cities in five countries will begin in mid-1996, with services being expanded to include another 7 cities in three more countries by the end of the year. By mid-1999, Hermes Europe Railtel plans to connect 55 cities throughout Western and Central Europe. The idea is to act as a carrier for both current and emerging telecom operators (http://www.hitrail.com (1996)).

Electricity companies have not yet entered the telecommunications market on the same scale as the railway companies and the facilities potentially provided by electricity companies are also different. Their networks reach almost every household and are structured in a very similar way to a telecommunication network. The deployment of telecommunication lines along existing regional electricity cables is not economically attractive. Without optical fibres it would also be technically very complicated to combine the deployment of telephone and high voltage cables.

The situation is very different when it comes to the deployment of telecommunication lines along with future electricity cables. Optical fibres can be integrated into the electricity cables at a small additional cost, and it is common today to install optical fibres along with electricity cables - even in the absence of any immediate need for communication facilities. Many electricity companies have already established telecommunication networks along with their cables for internal communication and now plan to sell this excess capacity. For instance the NESA - a Danish electricity company - has established a 150 km optical fibres network in a suburb of Copenhagen, and is planning to extend the network to 450 km within the next few years. The NESA is currently negotiating a lease agreement for this network with the second Danish GSM operator, Sonofon.

In urban areas it should generally be possible to string fibres through the underground ducts provided for electricity cables. In Little Rock, Arkansas, a local electricity company supplies optical fibres that run through their power lines to private homes. This is one of the few examples of a public utility providing communication lines directly to private homes. The existing communication network capacity does not generally reach all the way to the homes of residential customers, and the introduction of optical fibres into customers' homes demands a considerable investment, even if combined with electricity lines. Most electricity companies consider it too expensive and too distant from their core business. In the Arkansas example, the network was built by an electricity company, but the telecom services are managed by Sprint.

Electricity companies may establish telecommunication lines connecting residential customers for other reasons than the provision of telecommunication services. Such lines can also be used to enhance existing power services. Both in the US and in Europe, some electricity companies are urging customers to make savings in energy consumption, so that they can avoid expensive expansion of production capacity. A good way to do this is to control the customers' electrical appliances in order to lower consumption during peak hours. This can only be done by installing a communication line to each customer. This could be a key driver for electricity companies entering the telecom business.

In Germany, two energy conglomerates have been providing cellular phone services for a couple of years. This was the only sector in which competition was allowed. Another reason to embark on cellular services is that the provision of wireless services does not imply investment in a cable based local loop and can be established much more cheaply than fully wired services. In Britain, a number of electricity companies have also entered the telecom market (see Tab. G1).

Tab. G1: Utilities Entering the Telecoms Market

Electricity/energy	
ELSAM	Denmark
NESA	Denmark
RWE Energie	Germany
Veba	Germany
VIAG	Germany
GEB Rotterdam	Holland
Tokyo Electric Power	Japan
Energis	UK
Norweb	UK
Scottish Power	UK
South Wales Electricity	UK
South Western Electricity	UK
Yorkshire Electricity	UK
Duke Power	US
Entergy	US
Pacific Gas and Electric	US
Railway	
Hermes Europe Railtel	European
De Danske Statsbaner SNCF	Denmark France
Deutsche Bundesbahn	Germany
Nederlandse Spoorwogen	Holland
Banverket	Sweden
British Rail	UK
Water supply	
Générale des Eaux	France

Source: THE ECONOMIST (1995), p. 75.

Water companies are further potential suppliers of network infrastructure. The most prominent example is the French Générale des Eaux, which has its own telecompany, Cegetel, which recently has entered into co-operation with British Telecom (COMMUNICATIONS WEEK INTERNATIONAL, 1996, p. 1,37)

3. The Cost Structure of a Telecoms Network

The telecom sector is characterised by very large investment costs. The unique cost and demand structure within the telecom sector has been one of the main reasons for the sector specific regulation of the telecommunication markets. The precise percentage of total costs attributed to investments depends of course on the definition of investments and of telecommunication activities (e.g. whether research, marketing or similar activities are included). Although some sources claim that investments, and investment-related costs make up as much as 90% of the production costs (HEUERMANN, 1984), most estimates based on financial data are between 60 and 75%.

Tab. G2: Wage Shares by Kind of Activity

Industry	Wages as % of Contribution to GDP
Mining and Quarrying	8.9
Agriculture	23.5
Electricity, Gas and Water	29.7
Telecommunication	37.4
Market services (incl. Telecom.)	46.1
Manufacturing	67.1
Construction	78.3
Non Market Services	94.4
Total	62.8

Sources: DANISH BUREAU OF STATISTICS (1995) and calculations based on figures from TELE DENMARK (1994).

Thus, by any standard, the telecommunication sector is comparatively capital intensive. To illustrate this point, Tab. G2 provides a cross sector comparison of wage shares in the Danish economy. The remaining share is almost all attributable to capital expenditures. Tab. G2 demonstrates that primary activities (agriculture, mining and quarrying) are the most capital intensive. In telecommunications and other network based utilities (electricity, gas and water) wage shares are at about 1/3 (and therefore capital shares at about 2/3), while all other industry groups have substantially higher wage shares.

For an assessment of the cost structure's impact on market conditions, more than the level of investments in telecoms is relevant. The type of investment is also important. A notable part of investment is what economists refer to as "sunk costs". These are long-term investments which can be used only for specific economic activities. An example is a fixed access network which provides subscribers with access to the local exchange. This investment only has value for the supply of telecommunication services in this particular local area. Once the investment is made, the operator can only exit this particular market at a considerable cost. Other investments are of shorter duration and/or can be more easily applied to other activities.

Investments in telecom networks can be divided into the following functional elements:

- Terminal equipment
- Access Network
- Switching
- Transmission/Long line
- Others (buildings etc.)

Terminal equipment

Once telephones were, for the vast majority of users, the only type of customer terminal connected to the network. They were all provided by the operator and rent was included in the access charge. It was part of a bundled service. Today a wide range of terminals are connected to the network in addition to telephones (faxes, PC's, PABX's etc.), and customers may now buy their own terminals, either from the network operator or from other suppliers. These terminals are owned by the customers and are not part of the operator's fixed capital. This allows users to become more independent of the operator, but it also reduces the network operator's investment requirements. In most countries, terminal equipment is now unbundled from the telecom network, and for many purposes is not considered part of it.

Access

The local access network connects customers to the national and international networks. The most common form of access is a twisted pair of copper wires from the user's terminal to a local switch. Coaxial cables provide more bandwidth than twisted pairs and are most common in cable TV-networks. Optical fibres are used for certain broadband services, but are mainly used in the interexchange network, where their higher levels of capacity can be used more efficiently. Investments in cables are long term investments, with a lifetime of more than 20 years. Moreover, the investments are very immobile. Once investments are made in the access network in a certain area, profits must be generated through communication services provided to customers located there. It is extremely difficult, if not impossible, to move investments to other, maybe more attractive, markets.

The access network is by far the most expensive part of the network. It covers between one-third and one-half of the investment costs. As access network assets have an above average lifetime, their significant capital outlay is even greater. The main cost components are cables, and construction work related to the laying of cables.

Switching

The switching function is performed at the exchange by automatic, computer controlled equipment (or, in older offices, by electromechanical switches). Next to the access network, switching is the most expensive function. According to an Australian study, 90% of the switching costs are in local exchanges (BUREAU OF TRANSPORT AND COMMUNICATIONS, 1989). Major portions of the investments made in local exchanges, however, can be attributed to long distance communication or special services. The major part of the upgrading of the telecom network involves an upgrading of switching capability, especially with the conversion from analogue to digital technology.

Transmission/Long line

This type of equipment includes cables, radio-links and satellites connecting transit exchanges, as well as transmitters, repeaters, etc. It provides the capacity to provide all kinds of long distance service. Although new technologies have reduced long distance transmission costs dramatically in recent years, they are not really as significant in the total cost picture as access and switching costs.

Detailed cost data that disaggregates network costs among the different parts of the network are quite difficult to obtain and compare. A recent OECD study of national PTOs in the OECD area analysed 1992 expenditures on switching and transmission infrastructure as a percentage of total capital expenditure. Although it showed large variations among PTOs, suggesting different accounting procedures, it revealed that together the PTOs mostly spend between 60 to 80% of their capital expenditure on switching and transmission infrastructure (OECD 1996, p 52). In most OECD countries, the major investments in the access networks were completed long before 1992.

The OECD study also notes that drawing a boundary between switching and transmission functions is becoming increasingly difficult, because both are converging towards software based systems. Some experts suggest that the software cost of developing a telecom exchange could be 80% of the total cost, and the software may need to be upgraded several times over the working life of the exchange.

Tab. G3 summarises the results of four comprehensive studies on network costs made in different countries covering different time periods. The first two studies from Germany and Japan were designed to study long-term investments; the Australian and Canadian studies were made for the purpose of costing services as a guideline for pricing and only provide detailed data for a one year cycle. The categorisation and definition of network components also differs from study to study and comparisons should therefore be made with caution. However, all studies established access and switching as the main cost elements. The variation between figures from Bell Canada and from other operators is primarily due to the fact that certain local switching functions are included in the costs of the access network.

Tab. G3: Network Costs by Network Components in Percentage

	Germany 62-71	**Japan (NTT) 52-90**	**Australia 87-88**	**Bell Canada 1993**
Terminal equipment	7	-	-	-
Access	40	35.5	34.5	50.1
Switching	30	29	25.0	13.9
Transmission/Long line	23	11	11.5	13.8
Other	-	24.5	29	22.2

Notes: Japan: The cost of underground facilities at 19%, have been allocated under access (14.5%) and under transmission/long line (4.5%); Australia: Transmission includes long line equipment; Canada: Calculated on basis of the average investment base. Long line includes all expenses attributed to long distance calls. Access includes terminal equipment.

Sources: HEUERMANN (1984), TADA SAITO (1994), BUREAU OF TRANSPORT AND COMMUNICATIONS (1998) and BIGHAM (1993).

4. The Role of Investment Costs

The most important factors of input to investments in telecommunication networks are electronic equipment, cables and wires. Prices for electronic equipment have decreased rapidly and are expected to continue declining in the future. This affects not only transmission, but more particularly the cost of switching.

Improved cable technology, and in particular the introduction of optical fibres, has reduced cable costs substantially. Prices for copper wire are relatively stable, but new compression techniques are increasing its capacity. Optical fibre cable provides significantly greater capacity, and price reductions now make it competitive with copper cables for the installation of new access networks on greenfield sites in some locations. However, at present it is not economical to replace installed copper cables. In access networks, the laying of cables and wires constitutes as much as 90% of the costs (FALCH, 1993). Thus the cost of the cable itself plays a diminishing role. But in transmission networks, where the increasing capacity of optical fibres can be utilised more advantageously, fibre cable will have a substantial impact. A forecast from Cambridge Strategic Management group estimates that by the year 2000, the raw capacity costs of submarine cables will fall to just 1% of the costs in 1987 (FORGE, 1995).

Although investment goods are becoming cheaper, the level of investment in telecommunication services is growing rapidly and capital costs still constitute a substantial share of the total production cost. The historical development of the cost profile for telecommunication services can be illustrated by US cost data. The FCC has published cost data for US common carriers going back to 1950. Changes in accounting principles complicate comparisons for the years after 1987, but capital related operating expenses (depreciation and amortisation) in 1994 were reported to be 24% of the total operating expenses. Thus it can be seen from Tab. G4 that the proportion of capital related operating expenses has remained fairly constant since the 60's. If the costs of capital and capital related taxes were added, total capital costs would be at least doubled, representing 40 to 60% of the total annual economic costs.

On the other hand, dramatic decreases in traffic related expenditures can be observed. These are due due to the automation of switching functions and the start of the increase in commercial expenses, as more resources are allocated to marketing and advertising. (See Tab. G4.)

Tab. G4: US Common Carrier Operating Expenses in %

	Maintenance	Depreciation and Amortisation	Traffic	Commercial Exports	General Office	Other	Total
1950	29	14	28	12	9	7	100
1960	29	22	19	14	10	7	100
1970	31	24	14	12	9	10	100
1980	32	21	8	15	10	14	100
1987	25	28	5	16	12	13	100

Source: Calculated by data from FEDERAL COMMUNICATIONS COMMISSION (1995).

Tab. G5: Distribution of Costs in a Fibre Optic Network

	Costs in % of Total Costs
Access related costs	71
Distance related costs	13
Capacity related costs	16

Source: STEHMANN (1993).

Technological improvements have changed the balance between services quite dramatically. A study of the cost structure of a fibre-optical network indicated that bandwidth and distance will in future play a smaller role in costs (Tab. G5). Further advances in compression techniques will add to this development. The reason for this is that with optical fibre the cost of cabling is almost independent of capacity needs.

However, these figures should be interpreted with caution: The distribution of costs is estimated on the basis of current services and does not take the network requirements of future services into account. The costs of services demanding more bandwidth are much more sensitive to distance than, for example, the cost of a telephone call. The reason for this is that the capacity of the access link is often under-utilised. A Japanese study by the Ministry of Post and Telecommunication, on the investment costs of a B-ISDN network serving 50 million subscribers, forecast the costs of long line equipment (which must be categorised as distance related costs) as comprising 38% of the total cost (Tab.G6).

Tab. G6: Forecasting of Investments Needed for a B-ISDN Network with 50 mill. Subscribers

Items	Predicted Amount B$	% of Total
Subscriber Line	126	41
Local Switches	63	21
Long Line Facilities	116	38
Total	305	100

Source: TADA SAITO (1994)

This indicates that the demand for new types of services may have a substantial impact on the future cost-profile of network operators.

New services will also affect the cost profile in another way. In some services, the basic network provision itself will only be a minor part of the service delivered. Value added network services and intelligent services will both add new activities and introduce new types of costs to network operators. Some of these costs, such as development costs, will be fixed and independent of usage, but they will not be regular sunk costs, which are tied to the provision of service in a specific geographical area.

There are other implications for the cost structure. Decreasing cost trends for equipment reduce the economic lifetime for installed network capacity. This implies that investments must be depreciated at a faster rate and profitability requirements must be raised. It also increases the exit barrier, as "old equipment" will have less value for alternative uses. Another important factor is the possibility of substituting cables with satellite and cellular technologies. As these new networks compete with cable networks and become part of hybrid networks, the cost profile will continue to change.

5. Changing Demand Conditions

In the OECD area, the increases in revenue of the mid 80's have been followed by more moderate growth rates in the 90's. One explanation for this is the decrease in tariffs brought about by a decline in growth rates in the number of mainlines (Tab. G7). Still, the slowdown indicates that the market may be reaching saturation level in basic telephony services faster than the new value-added services are able to stimulate new growth.

Tab. G7: Growth in Public Telecommunication in the OECD Area

	CAGR 1982-87	CAGR 1987-92
Revenue	7.22	3.44
Mainlines	3.90	2.33

Source: OECD (1995).

Although many new services have been introduced which present impressive growth rates in the number of subscribers, telephony remains by far the most important service. The most important of the new services is mobile telephony, which contributes 5-10% of the total revenue in most OECD countries (1992 figures: OECD, 1995). Only in Sweden and Finland has the revenue exceeded 10%. However, with the present growth rates, mobile services may be expected to play a greater part in the future. Data-services and leased lines represent very small markets compared to telephony services.

Telecom services are offered to two distinct groups of customers with quite different demand profiles: business and residential customers. The distribution between these two groups varies from country to country. In general, the residential sector is most important in countries with a high penetration of telephones. Sweden, for example, has a near universal service with 78% of the lines connected to residential subscribers.

If we examine the money spent internationally on telecommunications, the numbers for the business sector increase. Although Denmark has near universal service with the great majority of lines supplied to residential customers, calculations based on Danish national accounting data indicate that two thirds of the communication revenue originates from business customers.

Tab. G8: Demand Characteristics for Residential and Business Customers

Residential Market	Business Customers
Homogenous market	Heterogeneous market
Many small customers	Both small and large customers
1-2 lines per customer Limited load of traffic per line	Some customers with many lines More traffic per line
Telephony and Cable-TV dominant services	Demand for a wide range of services
Limited use of advanced services	Many customers with special needs

A few decades ago all customers were demanding the same service – namely telephony. Business customers were generating more traffic but the service demand was basically the same. Today many business customers are demanding a wide range of communication services, which only a few residential customers consider to be relevant to them. On the other hand, cable TV is only of limited use for business customers while other infotainment services, primarily directed toward residential customers, are being developed. Therefore, there is a growing segmentation between different user groups in terms of markets, services and interests. The main differences between these two markets are summarised in Tab. G8.

These differences result in different cost and market structures for the different customer groups. For the residential market, the availability of an access network is particularly important. As the load of traffic per connection is relatively low, the needs for capacity have been more stable in residential markets than in business markets. Most residential customers have needed only an ordinary telephone line to meet their demands. Therefore, the need for investments to upgrade the network have been most apparent in business districts.

New operators have tended to concentrate on business customers because of the higher turnover per line (and consequently a higher turnover per investment in infrastructure). There will generally also be a greater demand among business customers for highly profitable services such as international communications.

6. Conditions for Effective Competition

As we have seen from the above cost and demand characteristics, there are a number of barriers to the creation of more competition in the telecommunication sector. The point of departure in national telecommunication markets is one incumbent operator. In theory, other suppliers will enter the market as long as tariffs are high enough to permit them to do so profitably. This will result in competition and a downward pressure on tariffs. This process will continue until tariffs have reached a level where they reflect the efficient cost of production and no more suppliers are attracted. However, it may be very difficult for new suppliers to enter the market due to economies of scale, scope and density, and the need for substantial long-term investments.

These factors affect both newcomers to the market and small companies that may be already present in the market. These factors do not play the same role in all network segments or in all market segments, as cost structures vary from segment to segment.

Both railway and electricity companies are becoming actively engaged in the telecom sector, and this has, particularly in the US, strongly affected the long distance market. It seems that some companies have been able to overcome at least some of the barriers of entry into the market for these services.

Public utility companies can choose either to create their own telecommunication lines or to ally themselves with one of the existing operators. An example of the first option is US Sprint, which was created out of Southern Pacific Railway, at a time before most of the incumbent telecom operators really began to embark on international activities abroad. Today a number of consortia of telecom operators are actively engaged in the search for local partners with their own network facilities and it has become more obviously beneficial to enter into an alliance with a foreign operator. This has two major advantages. Firstly, the provision of technical expertise - operation of a public communication network, with telephony as the dominant service, demands skills quite different to those required for the operation of a network for internal data communication. Secondly, such an alliance can also increase the range of services provided. Public utility networks are most often national based and the provision of international services demands interconnection to other networks. Being part of an international consortium may result in more favourable conditions for interconnection.

Competition in the provision of telecommunication services has tended to concentrate on the markets for long distance and mobile services. The reasons for this are both economic and political. The majority of investments in infrastructure are related to the construction of a wire-based local loop, and it is also the last area where competition is introduced. Another reason is the wide-spread cross-subsidisation between local and long distance services. Historically, many operators have partially financed their universal service obligations through high tariffs for long distance and especially international communications. Technological advances have further promoted this subsidisation, as optical fibres and compression techniques have implied substantial cost reductions - particularly for long distance services. Thus, the long distance and international markets are the most profitable, and the need for infrastructure investment is smaller than with loop services.

In these areas, railway companies are the most obvious partners and they have so far also been the most active. Railway networks connect urban centres and are ideally located for the provision of trunk and long distance services. Although there is excess capacity in the networks built for internal communication, the most important resources provided by the railway companies have been their rights of way along with the railway lines.

This alternative infrastructure has been competitive partly due to a skewed tariff structure. But the market for long distance and international services will become less profitable if cost-based tariff reductions are enforced by more competition. The market will then become less attractive in the future, although international communication is growing at a much faster rate than local communication.

If long distance transmission costs in the year 2000 represent just 1% of the 1987 level, as forecast by Cambridge Strategic Management Group (FORGE, 1995), tariffs for international traffic may be reduced to a level just above the tariffs for local calls. The question then will be, how much revenue will be left to new entrants who do not have their own access networks.

The major share of the costs for wired services are within the local loop, and cost-based tariffs indicate that this may become the major source of revenue. In this market, the railway companies do not have much to offer. Here, the electricity companies and potentially also water companies are in a much better position.
In contrast to railway companies, their networks extend direct to the customer. However, stretching the communication network all the way to the customer will cost at least $450 per customer and for networks supplying interactive services the cost will be as much as $1,100. These costs are substantial also for public utility companies used to dealing with large infrastructure investments. But in areas where power lines or water pipes are being renovated, it is comparatively cheap to employ

communication lines. Furthermore, electricity and water companies both already have direct customer access and expertise in billing. Both qualifications have proven to be important parameters of competition in the markets for telecommunication services.

An alternative to costly investment in a wired local loop is to concentrate on wireless services. These include both mobile and fixed services. A plan to build a wireless-wireline network in Germany has been announced by a consortium formed by the two German energy companies RWE and Viag and British Telecom (COMMUNICATIONS WEEK, 1996). This network will both offer cellular mobile services, cordless telephony and broadband services.

The question is, whether it is possible in this way to provide a completely cost efficient alternative to wired services. Telia has recently abandonned its plans for wired and wireless services. It recognises broadband rather than convergence as the driving force in the market (COMMUNICATIONS WEEK, 1996). A number of operators have announced that they will supply more broadband services through the use of ADSL on the existing copper-wires. The use of existing wires reduces costs to a level where it will be difficult for new entrants to compete, even using either wireless local loop solutions or optical fibres employed in combination with either power lines or water pipes.

7. Conclusion

In the past decade, more competition has been introduced into the telecommunications sector. So far, competition has concentrated on long distance and international services. In this process, railway companies have played an important role, both as suppliers of infrastructure and more importantly, as suppliers of rights of way.

The local loop is the most costly and in the long run probably also the most profitable part of the market. In this market, railway companies do not have much to offer, but electricity companies, with their direct access to customers, are obvious partners. Nevertheless, the establishment of a new infrastructure, able to compete with the existing one owned by the incumbent operator, will be costly.

The key parameter in this competition will be the future development of demand characteristics and the technical capabilities of different infrastructure solutions. If the existing copper-based networks are also able to support future multimedia and other broadband services, the incumbent operators will have a clear advantage. On the other hand, the development of wireless local loop solutions clearly favours the creation of alternative infrastructures. The introduction of optical fibres into the local loop will require substantial investments from both incumbent and emerging telecom operators.

Telecom regulators may be a driving factor in the introduction of alternative networks. The introduction of more competition into the telecom sector is considered to be of vital importance, and new entrants will be supported by the national regulators. It will hardly be acceptable for all new entrants to be driven out of the market, even if the reason is that the incumbent operator is the most cost-efficient.

Endnotes

[1] A more detailed description of the DSB network is provided in MØLLER (1994) chapter 12.

References

BIGHAM, F. G. (1993), A category Costing Approach to Support Telecommunications Service Pricing, Michigan, East Lansing.

BLANK, L. R. (1994), Telecommunication Infrastructure Investments and State Regulatory Reform, USA, A Preliminary Look At the Data: The National Regulatory Research Institute.

BUREAU OF TRANSPORT AND COMMUNICATIONS ECONOMICS (1989), The cost of Telecom's Community Services Obligations, Report 64, Canberra.

COMMUNICATIONS WEEK INTERNATIONAL, London: Various issues, 1995-1996.

DANISH BUREAU OF STATISTICS (1995), Copenhagen: Danish National Accounts Statistics 93.

FALCH, MORTEN (1993), Macroeconomic Technology Assessment, PhD. Thesis at Technical University of Denmark, Lyngby: Technical University of Denmark, pp. 243.

FEDERAL COMMUNICATIONS COMMISSION (1995), Washington DC: Statistics of Communication Common Carriers.

FINANCIAL TIMES (1995), Telecom Markets, London, 12 October, 1995.

FORGE, S. (1995), Re-Engineering the Telecoms Industry. Telecommunications, November 1995, London: International Edition Vol. 29, number 11 pp. 76-79.

HTTP\\WWW.HITRAIL.COM (1996)

HEUERMAN (1984): Gebührenpolitik im Telekommunikationsbereich, Baden-Baden. Quoted from STEHMAN (1995).

MELODY, W. H. and M. DORTE (1996), Rights of Way as a Foundation for Infrastructure Competition, in: MELODY, W. H. (ed.), Telecom Reform, Principles, Policies and Regulatory Practices, Lyngby, Center for Tele-Information Technical University of Denmark.

MØLLER, D. (1994), Methods for Analysis and Design of Heterogenous Telecommunication Networks, Lyngby, Technical University of Denmark.

OECD (1995), Communications Outlook, Paris, OECD.

POLITIKEN NEWSPAPER, 8 October 1996, Copenhagen: Politiken.

SAITO, T. (1994), An Evolving Scenario of Communication Network Towards B-ISDN, in: IVERSEN, V. B. (ed.), Integrated Broadband Communication Networks and Services, Amsterdam,), The cost of Telecom's Community Services Obligations

STEHMAN, O. (1995), Network Competition for European Telecommunications, Oxford, Oxford University Press. pp. 327.

STOLLEMAN, N. C. (1993), Economies of scope in the provision of narrowband and switched broadband services, Telecommunications Policy Jan./Feb. pp. 74-79, Amsterdam, North Holland.

THE ECONOMIST (1995), The Third Wire, London: The Economist January 28th. 1995 pp. 74-75.

TELE DENMARK (1995), Annual Report 1994, Århus, Tele Denmark.

WENDERS, J. T. (1987), The Economics of Telecommunications, Theory and Policy, Cambridge, Mass. North-Holland.

Comments on: Electricity Companies and Railway Networks as Newcomers in Telecommunications

Oliver Lorz

In this paper, Morton Falch raises the following important question: To what extent will electricity and railway companies become new competitors on the telecommunications market? In his analysis, he presents several examples of where these companies are entering or preparing to enter the market. Moreover, they already possess some telecommunications infrastructure - although the size of these alternative networks is at present comparatively small. An overview of existing fibre optic networks in Germany provides additional evidence supporting this analysis (Tab. G9).

Tab. G9: Fibre Optic Networks in Germany

Company	Industry	Network size (km)
Deutsche Telekom AG	telecommunications	87 000
Viag AG/Bayernwerk	electricity	4 000
Deutsche Bahn AG	railways	2 000
RWE	electricity	2 000
Veba AG	electricity/telecom.	1 300
Energieversorgung Schwaben	electricity	1 000
Wintershall AG	natural gas	1 000
Badenwerk	electricity	600
Vereinigte Elektrizitätswerke	electricity	600
Hamburger Elektrizitätswerke	electricity	270

Source: KLODT/ LAASER/ LORZ/ MAURER (1995).

To assess the potential future role of electricity and railway companies in telecommunications, the paper concentrates on cost and demand characteristics of telecommunications services. In this overview, I would like to comment on two aspects not mentioned in the paper, but that may also be essential for the potential success of entry. The first aspect has been brought into the discussion by BAUMOL and SIDAK (1994). It concerns the ability of new entrants in the telecommunications market to conclude *binding contracts* with their customers before investing in telecommunications infrastructure. If such binding contracts are practicable, then new competitors may enter a market even if incumbents in this market have already invested substantial sunk costs.

To illustrate this point, let us suppose that a new competitor plans to connect business customers between the financial centers of London and Frankfurt. This competitor may already possess a long-distance line between these two cities but has to build up a local access network. Without binding contracts with its customers, the potential competitor can expect the incumbent to react to its market entry by lowering its own prices for telecommunication services. The entrant may then be unable to amortize its investments in the local access network with sufficiently high prices. Anticipating the reaction of the incumbent, the potential competitor may refrain from entry. With the possibility of concluding binding contracts with its future customers, the potential entrant can fix prices before investing in the necessary infrastructure. These prices have to be high enough to cover investment costs, but lower than those of the incumbent. Such a contract is profitable for both the potential entrant and its potential customer, and sunk costs do not prevent market entry in this situation. Ex-ante contracting of this kind may lead to some specific problems arising from asymmetric information, time inconsistency on the part of the customers, or possibly high information and transaction costs in negotiating the contracts. However, such market entry does not seem to be completely unrealistic, especially in contracting with large business customers.

The second aspect concerns *network externalities*. Whereas the possibility of binding contracts increases the potential for successful entry by new competitors, network externalities can render such entry more difficult. With positive network externalities, the value of a specific network to its customers depends positively on the size of this network. New customers tmay thus prefer to join the large, existing network of the incumbent to the smaller network of a newcomer, and the mere size of their networks may protect incumbents in telecommunications from new market entrants. The degree to which network externalities serve as entry barriers depends on several technical and demand characteristics, such as the costs of switching from one network to another, the potential technical superiority of one of the competitors, or the specificity of demand for certain connections. It also depends on the strategies employed by the incumbent either to facilitate or to hamper an interconnection between its network and the network of the newcomer.[1] In the latter case, such anti-competitive strategies may justify a regulatory intervention. This regulation, however, will probably not remove all asymmetries between the incumbent and potential newcomers: As long as the regulated firm has an informational advantage compared to the regulatory agency, the firm either earns an information rent on this advantage or faces only incomplete regulatory incentives for an interconnection.[2]

Endnotes

[1] For a discussion of the incentives for interconnection see the surveys of BESEN/FARELL (1994) and KATZ/SHAPIRO (1994).

[2] See LAFFONT, TIROLE (1993) for a general description of this regulatory dilemma.

References

BAUMOL, W.J. and J.G. SIDAK (1994), Toward Competition in Local Telephony, Cambridge, Mass., MIT Press.

BESEN, S.M. and J. FARELL (1994), Choosing how to Compete: Strategies and Tactics in Standardization, Journal of Economic Perspectives, Vol. 8, pp. 117-131.

COMMUNICATIONS WEEK INTERNATIONAL (1996), 7. October 1996.

KATZ, M.L. and C. SHAPIRO (1994), Systems Competition and Network Effects, Journal of Economic Perspectives, Vol. 8, pp. 93-115.

KLODT, H. et al. (1995), Wettbewerb und Regulierung in der Telekommunikation, Tübingen, J.C.B. Mohr (Paul Siebeck).

LAFFONT, J.-J. and J. TIROLE, A Theory of Incentives in Procurement and Regulation, Cambridge, Mass., MIT Press.

POLITIKEN NEWSPAPER, 8. October 1996.

THE ECONOMIST (1995), The Third Wire. January 28.

H: Liberalization of Telecommunications in Central Europe

Jerzy Kubasik

1. Introduction

Until 1989, telecommunication in Central European Countries (CECs) was fully monopolized, along with many other spheres of community and economic life. Telecommunications served three essential purposes:

- as a stimulant of economic development,
- as a medium for interpersonal communication within society, and
- as a factor determining the internal and external security of the State.

Results were unsatisfactory, although the third purpose was given a certain priority.

Since the significance of telecommunications in a modern economy was underestimated, this branch of technology and economy was unable to develop properly, and CECs found themselves among the most backward European countries in this respect. After 1989, the CEC administrations began to realize more fully the strategic importance of telecommunications. It was recognized that closing the telecommunications gap would be necessary in order to eliminate economic backwardness. The economic boom observed in the CECs since the fall of the Soviet regimes requires the adaption of the telecommunications infrastructure to the current demands of the economy and to its development potential. The new governments have recognized that the industrial and service sectors cannot begin to lift themselves out of stagnation until they can attract foreign investment, stimulate technological innovation, and encourage local entrepreneurs.

Reforms in the political and economic systems were followed by rapid changes in telecommunications. Since 1989, telecommunications have been a national priority and the CECs' governments have been embarking on programs and projects to achieve the goals of upgrading, modernizing, and rebuilding the telecommunications networks.

The Czech Republic, Hungary, and Poland are the most developed and market oriented countries in post-communist Central Europe. They are also probably the first ones in this region to join a United Europe as association agreements between them and the European Union have already been signed. The national telecommunications operators who are active in these countries are outstanding companies, in Central and Eastern European terms, of technological potential and economic performance (see Tab. H1). Therefore, their example will provide data for the assessment of telecommunications policies in the countries of this region in the period following the political and economic breakthrough of 1989.

Tab. H1: Main Telecommunications Operators in Central and Eastern European Countries in 1995

Operator	**Turnover** (milion US$)	**Profit** (before tax)	**Main lines** ('000)	**Main lines per employee**
Telekomunikacja Polska	2 124.48	361.00	5 727.6	78.29
SPT Telecom	999.51	265.46	2 480.0	95.03
Matav	941.00	2.12	1 892.9	109.42
HPT Croatia a)	648.47	99.81	1 146.0	58.21
Rostelecom a)	647.08	100.77	...	...
Rom Telecom a)	315.27	15.74	2 805.0	55.93
Telekom Slovenije	307.00	23.00	...	...
Slovak Telecom a)	286.23	113.50	1 118.0	72.75
BTC a)	188.26	46.80	2 487.0	95.54
Lattelekom a)	118.24	6.00	764.0	109.14
Lietuvos Telekomas	111.25	25.00	941.0	94.48
Eesti Telefon	70.84	6.65	411.0	100.54

Note: a) 1994

Source: RZECZPOSPOLITA.

The present paper addresses the following issues:

- the condition of telecommunications in the Czech Republic, Hungary and Poland, and certain political and economic factors in the early stage of the reforms;
- the goals that the countries' administrations have set concerning the reconstruction of telecommunications as a branch of economics and technology;
- the reforms in these countries' telecommunications legislation and the effects of their implementation, in particular with regard to the demonopolization of the market, the emergence of new operators and the privatization of incumbent operators.

2. The Need for Changes

The economies of the CECs are suffering from a severe recession, burdened with the inheritance of former economic policy and practice characterized by:

- neglected infrastructure and services relative to productive sectors,
- infrastructure and services developed on the residual principle and financed through budgetary redistribution,
- production-centered attitude and practice within the infrastructural sector, neglecting relations between service-provider and clients,
- the dominance of monopoly organizations,
- artificially low prices (adjusted to the low level of wages) and the absence of markets and competition,
- extremely underdeveloped telecommunications.

The underdevelopment of telecommunications was partly caused by the centrally controlled reallocation of continually shrinking resources pressured by a distorted structure of incentives. There were, however, highly esteemed investments and demands which needed reliable telecommunications. These demands were mostly fulfilled not by developing the public network, but rather by constructing and building closed private networks.

One of the most important features of the centrally planned economies was the comparatively low value placed on services in the output structure. This neglect of services is particularly visible in the underdevelopment of telecommunication networks illustrated by Fig. H1, where the telephone densities for CECs and OECD countries are compared. In 1989 OECD on average had approximately 43 mainlines per 100 inhabitants, while the average figure for Czechoslovakia, Hungary, and Poland was only about 10 per cent.

The differences in telephone density reflect to some extent the differences in the per capita incomes for the two groups of countries, although it is quite difficult to compare the GDP for countries of such different economic systems. Profits from the telecommunications sectors in CECs were redistributed to other areas of the economy. Although this was also the case of state-owned telecommunications industries in western countries, the problem was deeper in Central Europe where the reinvestment rate for net revenues was exceptionally low. The result of such a policy was the low telephone density noted above as well as the enormous waiting period for a new telephone line, often exceeding 10 years. The official waiting list does not represent all of the unsatisfied demand, as there was certainly a high number of prospective buyers who were not taken into account.

Furthermore, in many of the CECs there exists a large difference between the telecommunication infrastructures in urban and rural areas. Most statistical figures, usually quote only the national average rates. This, however, disguises the fact that penetration varies regionally. In both, Hungary and Poland there are still several thousand villages without a single telephone line. But even in places where some infrastructure exists, due to the obsolete technology still in use in many rural areas, the quality of the services is extremely poor.

A higher telephone penetration and the availability of other telecommunication services is a prerequisite for the overall development of the Central European economies. Thus, all the countries discussed have recently commenced ambitious programs for the modernization and expansion of their telecommunications networks (Tab. H3).

3. Objectives in Restructuring the Telecommunications Sector

For the CECs and their governments it is obviously important to pursue a set of policy objectives in telecommunications which are as far as possible identical with those elsewhere in world, especially in Europe.
In his recent book (SCHENK/KRUSE/MÜLLER, 1997) SCHENK defined a set of telecommunications policy objectives in European countries irrespective of their development level. The so-called *'magic quadrangle'* consists of:

- access to the network for potential users on the waiting list,
- improvement of the quality of network services and of functions offered to users,
- sustainable financing of the network structure (by loans initially and by self-financing in the long term),
- inter-operability with European and worldwide networks on the basis of agreed principles and standards.

The first and most general goal of the telecommunication policy in the CECs will be to close the huge gap between supply and demand for telecommunications as quickly as possible. A massive increase of network capacity is necessary, in parallel with a replacement of large parts of the outdated existing equipment. As this cannot be done in all areas at the same time, it is important to establish the right priorities.

The problem is to establish regional priorities, that is, where to invest first - in urban or rural areas. Penetration rates are highest in conurbations. This is also where demand is growing the fastest and waiting lists are the longest. Capacity in these areas needs urgently to be increased, in order to avoid risks to economic development. But there are rural areas with almost no telecommunications infrastructure.

Fig. H1: Telephone Density in OECD Countries and in Selected CECs, 1989

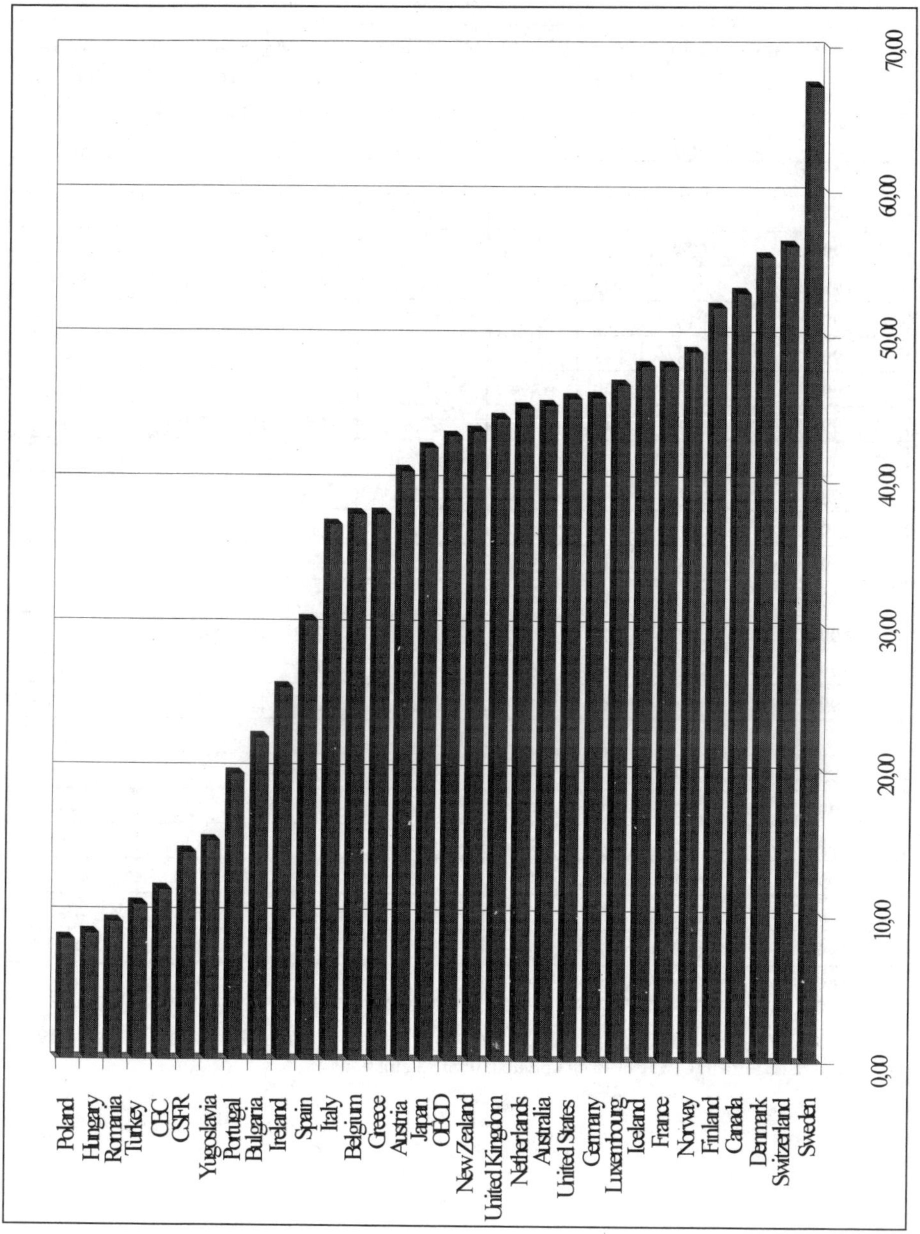

Tab. H2: Development of Telephone Networks in the Czech Republic, Hungary and Poland, 1989-95

Year	Main lines ('000)	New main lines ('000)	Change %	Main lines per 100 inhabitants	Waiting list ('000)	Waiting list as % of main lines	Average waiting time years
Czech Republic							
1989	n.a.	...	...	n.a.	n.a.	...	...
1990	1 624	...	...	15.8	337	20.8	...
1991	1 706	82	5.0	16.7	418	24.5	5.0
1992	1 819	113	6.6	17.7	535	29.4	4.8
1993	1 961	142	7.8	19.0	572	29.8	5.8
1994	2 151	190	9.7	20.7	585	27.8	3.1
1995	2 398	247	11.5	22.8	656	27.4	2.7
Hungary							
1989	916		...	9.2	n.a.		
1990	996	80	8.7	10.0	607	60.9	7.6
1991	1 129	133	13.4	11.3	657	58.2	4.9
1992	1 291	162	14.4	12.5	752	58.3	4.6
1993	1 537	246	19.1	14.6	772	50.2	3.1
1994	1 772	235	15.3	17.2	711	40.1	3.0
1995	2 154	382	21.6	21.1	617	28.6	1.6
Poland							
1989	3 121	169	5.7	8.2	2 349	75.3	13.9
1990	3 293	172	5.4	8.6	2 412	73.2	14.0
1991	3 565	272	8.3	9.3	2 334	65.5	8.6
1992	3 338	373	10.5	10.3	2 411	61.2	6.5
1993	4 417	478	12.2	11.5	2 268	51.3	4.8
1994	5 006	590	13.4	13.0	2 352	47.0	4.0
1995	5 728	722	14.4	14.8	2 247	39.2	3.1

Source: KONTKIEWICZ-CHACHULSKA (1996), SALLAI/SCHMIEDEG/LAJTHA (1996), SCHENK/KRUSE/MÜLLER (1997), updated, own calculations.

Tab. H3: Development Programs for Telecommunications in the Czech Republic, Hungary and Poland

Country	Telecommunications Programs	Development goals	Density goals, % a)
Czech Republic	Telecom project Iaccepted 1991,amended in 1994	- the number of lines doubled between 1995-2000 - modernization completed (digital backbone network built) - demand for telephone lines satisfied in 100% by 1998 - investment: US$ 4-5 billion	39.5
Hungary	The Ten Year Development Program 1990-2000 with I Project 1991-93 and II Project 1994-97	- 3 million fully automated and digital lines built - nation-wide digital backbone network completed in 1993 - density 30/100 in 1997 - SDH transmission - 100% demand for telephone lines satisfied within 6 months by 1997 - investment: US$ 6 billion	40.0
Poland	The Development Strategy of Telecommunications until 2000	- 10 million subscribers by 2000 - digital backbone network completed - new telematic services - improved quality - investment: US$ 6-9 billion	27.0

Note: a) main lines, year 2000

Source: KONTKIEWICZ-CHACHULSKA (1996)

In order to avoid cutting these regions off completely from the economic development of the rest of the country, it is necessary to install some infrastructure here. However, as investment in conurbations costs less and will yield higher revenues than in rural areas, there will be little choice but to concentrate the investment on conurbations.

Priorities must also be established in the field of investment at different levels of the network. While people demand a quick installation of new main lines, the prerequisite for this is an appropriate expansion of the trunk networks. Therefore most CECs prefer a 'from the top down' strategy, developing first the trunk network with the construction of a digital overlay network. As a consequence of this strategy, the number of newly installed main lines can only grow with the progress of the construction of the trunk network.

The paramount problem limiting the pace of infrastructure development is financing. The financing sources which could be mobilized most quickly were loans from financial institutions such as the World Bank, European Bank for Reconstruction and Development, etc. Furthermore, there were supplier credits and loans by several countries to support their own export industry. Domestic loans were not as readily available due to the underdeveloped capital markets, and as far as they were available, interest rates have been extremely high and are only coming down very slowly. Besides loans, some newer financing instruments are gaining importance such as: BOT (build-operate-transfer), and LOT (lease-operate-transfer). There are several variations of these financing instruments, but what they have in common is that the equipment supplied is repaid over longer periods from self-generated revenue.

As soon as the loan repayment begins, self-financing has to take on a more important role. In order to do so, a reasonably high level of tariffs is necessary, contrary to the practice of the former communist states. In fact, while most CECs have failed to reform the tariff structure, some of them, namely Poland and Hungary, have drastically increased the level of their telecommunication tariffs, which are often higher than the European average. Here the CECs face a conflict of objectives. While in most western countries it is one of the most important aims of regulation to prevent monopoly pricing and keep prices at a reasonably low level, tariffs in the CECs need to be high enough to facilitate rapid infrastructure development. The possibility of increasing prices is of course limited.

The inter-operability of the CECs' national telecommunications networks with those of the EU countries is a major prerequisite for the integration of these countries' economies and societies. The means of achieving this goal include the application of universally accepted technological standards, the implementation of pan-European systems of telecommunications networks, harmonizing the telecommunications legislation with the requirements of the EC Green Book of 1987, and, most importantly, the gradual demonopolization and liberalization of the countries' telecommunications markets.

The alterations in telecommunications legislation provide a highly illustrative example of the Central European societies' aspirations to integration. The new regulations have resulted in the emergence of new companies that enhance the range of services on offer, and in some cases replace the incompetent national operator in the provision of the essential telephone services. At the moment, this process is only in its initial stage, and many parties are attempting to check it. Still, it may testify to the advent of competition.

The technical standards of ITU and ETSI have been adopted and made obligatory. In all three countries, only digital technology is used for the installation of new exchanges. Since the COCOM restrictions have been lifted, this technology is readily available in the CECs.

Among new telecommunications networks and services that have appeared in the CECs over the last few years and are compatible with international standards, the most significant are GSM digital cellular telephony, the ERMES paging system, VSAT satellite networks, the ISDN, corporate networks and the Internet.

Privatization of the incumbent operators is effected simultaneously with similar developments in Western Europe, which in the future will enable these companies to operate on the open European market.

4. Networks Developments

Even with the important steps undertaken to improve this situation in the years 1989-1995, the situation of telecommunications in the CECs is still far from satisfactory and further steps are required if the basic mission of telecommunications is to be achieved, i.e. to allow all citizens, all economic agents and all bodies of State and local administration to communicate with each other at any time in a way that matches their needs with the required quality.

As Tab. H2 shows, since the political change, all three countries could significantly increase their telephone penetration. Nevertheless there are notable differences in the network growth. While the initial situation in terms of penetration rate was the highest in the Czech Republic, the growth rates of the networks are the lowest. Hungary, in contrast, has achieved very high growth rates.

Another indication of the success of relative network development in Hungary and Poland in comparison with the Czech Republic can be observed in the development of the relationship between the waiting list and the number of installed main lines. While again the initial situation was best in the Czech Republic, the ratio deteriorated, in contrast to Poland and Hungary where it was improved.

Digital transit exchanges have been put into operation and high performance backbone networks have been completed. The new digital capacity was used to increase the number of main telephone lines as well as to accommodate large customers transferring from the analogue network, providing them with a better service and relieving congestion on the outdated network. The transmission systems employ state-of-the-art SDH technology. New networks are being designed for the needs of national and international traffic and are important part of the Trans-European systems.

Several regional network projects were initiated by different international organizations and investing countries, e.g. Trans-European Telecommunication Network (TET), Trans-European Line (TEL), North-South Line (NSL), Trans-Asia-Europe Optical Fiber System (TAE), etc. The objective of these projects is to establish optical broad-band interconnections between CECs and their neighbors.

CECs are traditionally engaged in international cooperation in the telecommunications domain. They are members of the ITU and took part in the activities of the former CCITT and CCIR. Since the change in political regime, they have become members of several additional European organizations, including CEPT, ETNO, Eutelsat, etc.

For a detailed description of the network developments in the CECs see the bibliography list at the end of this paper.

5. Regulation: Opening Up Competition

To establish the proper legal background for restructuring the telecommunications sector the following steps are necessary:

- separation of regulatory and operational functions;
- separation of postal, telecommunication and broadcasting services into independent state-owned companies;
- liberalization of the telecommunications market;
- privatization of telecommunications.

The first two reforms were implemented by the three countries analyzed in this paper soon after the political change. Other telecommunications reforms in the three CECs share some common patterns. This can be seen in the overview in Tab. H4 and H5.

The time span it took to pass the new telecommunications law varied considerably between the three countries. In addition, there exist substantial differences in the regulatory arrangements. While in all three countries the minister is vested with the responsibility for regulation, in the Czech Republic the ministry of finance has a right to intervene in the case of telecommunications tariffs, and in Poland the ministry has, besides its regulatory function, a conflicting additional right, namely as an owner of the State operator.

In all three countries the ministries are supported by other regulatory authorities, which are responsible for the everyday and more technical regulatory tasks and are subject to ministry directives. Differences between these authorities are more on the level of organizational structure.

As far as the market segments not requiring the building up of a network infrastructure are concerned (e.g. paging, VANs, etc.), liberalization has proceeded quite far.

In the field of telephone networks, the markets have been opened to private investment somewhat more than in most western countries. Here, unlike in western countries, the focus is on local networks.

Tab. H4: General Regulatory Structure in the Czech Republic, Hungary and Poland

Regulation	Czech Republic	Hungary	Poland
New legal framework	Amendment of the Telecommunications Act of 1964, passed 12/03/1992, enforced 24/04/1992; The Main Principles of the State Telecommunications Policy of 08/1994	Telecommunications Act passed 23/11/1992, enforced 01/07/1993	Communications Act passed 23/11/1990,enforced 15/01/1991, amended 12/05/1995
Separation: Regulation,/Operation	24/04/1992	01/01/1989	01/01/1987
Separation: Posts/ Telecommunications	01/01/1993	01/01/1990	01/01/1992
Regulator	Ministry of Economy (Czech Telecommunication Office, Department of Telecommunication Policy); Ministry of Finance (approval of tariffs only)	Ministry of Transport, Communications and Water-Management	Ministry of Post and Telecommunications (functions at the same time as owner of state carrier)
Additional regulatory authorities	Czech Telecommunication Office (within the Ministry of Economy)	Communication Inspectorate (under the Ministry)	State Telecommunications and Postal Inspectorate, State Radiocommunications Agency (both under the Ministry)
Incumbent network operator (market share)	SPT Telecom (95%)	MATÁV (85%)	Telekomunikacja Polska S.A. (TPSA) (~100%)
Legal basis for operation of incumbent network operator	License	License	Telecommunications act
Privatization of incumbent network operator	Since 07/1995: **51%**: National Property Found (state ownership); **27%**: TelSource N.V. (j.v. of PTT Netherlands and Swiss PTT); **16%**: Investment Funds; **3%** private shareholders (voucher privatization),	Since 11/1993: **3%**: EBRD+IFC; **30%**: MagyarCom (j.v. of Ameritech and Deutsche Telekom A.G.); **67%**: State Privatization and Holding Company (state ownership). Since 12/1995: **3%**: EBRD+IFC; **67%**: MagyarCom, **25%**: State Privatization and Holding Company (state ownership).	Now planned for 1997/1998

Source: KONTKIEWICZ-CHACHULSKA (1996), SALLAI/SCHMIEDEG/LAJTHA (1996), SCHENK/KRUSE/MÜLLER (1997).

Tab. H5: Regulation of the Different Market Segments in Telecommunications in the Czech Republic, Hungary and Poland

Regulation	Czech Republic	Hungary	Poland
New legal framework	Amendment of the Telecommunications Act of 1964, passed 12/03/1992, enforced 24/04/1992; The Main Principles of the State Telecommunications Policy of 08/1994	Telecommunications Act passed 23/11/1992, enforced 01/07/1993	Communications Act passed 23/11/1990,enforced 15/01/1991, amended 12/05/1995
Separation: Regulation,/Operation	24/04/1992	01/01/1989	01/01/1987
Separation: Posts/ Telecommunications	01/01/1993	01/01/1990	01/01/1992
Regulator	Ministry of Economy (Czech Telecommunication Office, Department of Telecommunication Policy); Ministry of Finance (approval of tariffs only)	Ministry of Transport, Communications and Water-Management	Ministry of Post and Telecommunications (functions at the same time as owner of state carrier)
Additional regulatory authorities	Czech Telecommunication Office (within the Ministry of Economy)	Communication Inspectorate (under the Ministry)	State Telecommunications and Postal Inspectorate, State Radiocommunications Agency (both under the Ministry)
Incumbent network operator (market share)	SPT Telecom (95%)	MATÁV (85%)	Telekomunikacja Polska S.A. (TPSA) (~100%)
Legal basis for operation of incumbent network operator	License	License	Telecommunications act
Privatization of incumbent network operator	Since 07/1995: **51%**: National Property Found (state ownership); **27%**: TelSource N.V. (j.v. of PTT Netherlands and Swiss PTT); **16%:** Investment Funds; **3%** private shareholders (voucher privatization),	Since 11/1993: **3%:** EBRD+IFC; **30%:** MagyarCom (j.v. of Ameritech and Deutsche Telekom A.G.); **67%:** State Privatization and Holding Company (state ownership). Since 12/1995: **3%**: EBRD+IFC; **67%:** MagyarCom, **25%**: State Privatization and Holding Company (state ownership).	Now planned for 1997/1998

Source: KONTKIEWICZ-CHACHULSKA (1996), SALLAI/SCHMIEDEG/LAJTHA (1996), SCHENK/KRUSE/MÜLLER (1997), updated.

In the field of long distance networks, there are monopolies in all three countries, even if in Poland a second operator would be legally possible.

Private operators in local and regional networks are allowed in Poland and Hungary, but not however, in the Czech Republic, with the exception of some selected local areas where private operators will be admitted as a supplement to SPT TELECOM.

Hungary and Poland have enacted laws providing for licenses in the domain of local telephony, although they differ between the two countries. In both cases the new laws enabled the governments to license independent operators. Effective regulation protecting licensees against discrimination by the public carrier was, however, missing in both countries but for different reasons.

In Poland protection against discrimination was not part of the new law. Thus new licensees were successfully deterred or discriminated against by the public carrier especially concerning fair terms of interconnection. In Hungary exclusive licenses for new entrants were laid out in the law, but the legal provisions for regulation came too late to prevent similar discriminative behavior by the public carrier.

In practice, therefore, the dominance of the monopoly carrier was not challenged until 1994, when in Poland a recommendation was introduced by the minister restricting discrimination, and in Hungary rules protecting new licensees changed the situation for the better. But regulation is still far from constituting a satisfactory framework for the strengthening of competition.

At present only Hungary has given up the exclusive rights of the public carrier over local networks for an eight year period. A number of detailed obligations for independent local operators have been published, such as the 15.5% annual growth of the number of connected mainlines and the stepwise reduction of waiting times.

All three countries have taken some measures to protect their own telecommunications equipment manufacturing industries by tying market access for western companies to investment in the local industry. Thus not all, but most local companies could at least temporarily survive. There are few indications of negative effects. The equipment prices do not seem to be higher than usual compared to international prices. However, the choice of system is limited, which might be a problem for small local carriers

Taking into consideration that telephone networks are open to competition or at least limited competition in all countries, that the equity of public carriers can be sold to strategic investors, and that open network provisions are enacted, one can certainly speak of a liberal approach, going in some important aspects beyond even western European models.

On the other hand it has been observed elsewhere (not only in CECs) that there is a great difference between establishing a liberal law for telecommunications and its practical implementation.

6. Liberalization in Practice: The Example of Poland

Many observers expected the CECs to adopt a course of even more radical liberalization than envisaged in the EC Green Book of 1987 as a basis for economic development, and in order to attain convergence with western countries as early as possible.

This expectation can be confirmed clearly by the example of Poland. The liberalization introduced by the law of 1990 which went far in local networks, pertains to trunk networks with some restrictions (a Polish majority clause for carrier equity), and does not apply to international connections. In other segments of the terrestrial network it is easy to get a license and new carriers and many service providers are already active. The mobile segment is open to limited competition, and the markets for end-user equipment are free. The licensing of several networks implies the need for interconnection between these networks. Another rule of the law pertains to maximum tariff fixing for services of a 'public' nature, but it has not yet been applied.

In terms of concepts, Poland is not behind but rather ahead of some more conservative Western European countries. This does not necessarily mean that the implementation of liberal legal provisions has satisfied initial expectations.

Between 1990 and 1995, out of the 103 operators, 59 started to provide services. Among them, 50 were using private or previously existing telecommunications networks, and only 9 constructed new networks. 44 operators did not provide services. Out of that number, only 7 started to make investments with a view to launching commercial activities. The remaining 37 operators made no investments, and only 22 of them may be expected to satisfy the requirements set out in the licenses. Administrative proceedings were initiated in order to revoke the licenses granted to certain operators. Several operators relinquished their licenses. By the end of 1995, the Minister had revoked 21 licenses.

Operators holding licenses to provide telephone services by means of newly-constructed networks face the following major problems:

- the procurement of funds for investment;
- the imbalanced organization of investments and operation (resulting from the lack of practical experience and standards of operation);
- difficulties with cooperation and with reaching interconnection agreements with the TPSA - Polish Telecom (by July 1995, only 19 operators had concluded agreements with the TPSA, and another 13 agreements were being negotiated).

The last of these is considered to be the main obstacle to the initiation of new operators' activities, and a hindrance to the development of existing operators - and sometimes a threat to their survival. Interconnection and revenue sharing have been the principal subject of the debate over the development of Polish telecommunications over the last few years (KUBASIK, 1996).

7. Privatization of the National Network Operator: Different Methods

Throughout the world, telecommunications is a highly profitable business, and the stock prices of companies operating in this industry continue to rise. Privatization brings about better and more competent management, and reduces the operating costs of privately owned companies. The management is no longer selected as a result of political or personal sympathy. Consequently, only privatized companies can develop competition by improving the quality of services and reducing tariffs. Governments, which usually face a budget deficit and growing public debt, have welcomed the advocates of privatization. The post-Communist countries, in turn, have approached privatization as an opportunity for the implementation of modern technology and the transfer of the funds necessary to modernize their obsolete telephony. The world's leading operators and global alliances are also interested in purchasing stock in other companies.

The first Central European country to undertake privatization was Hungary, where over 30 per cent of MATÁV's stock was sold in 1994. MagyarCom, a joint venture of Ameritech (USA) and Deutsche Telekom (Germany) was selected in the tendering process. MagyarCom paid US$ 875 million. Out of this amount only US$400 million was used to increase the equity of MATÁV. US$335 million was paid to the Hungarian State Holding Company to cover budgetary debt, and US$133 million was paid as a license fee to the telecommunications fund, the foundation of which was stipulated by law. At the moment, the State owns only 25 per cent of this company's stock.

Among the countries that followed in Hungary's footsteps was the Czech Republic. The winner of the contest for strategic partner of SPT Telecom was the consortium TelSource, consisting of PTT Telecom Netherlands and Swiss Telecom. TelSource paid US$1.32 billion for a 27 per cent stake in SPT Telecom. Moreover, the consortium will provide the Czech company with managerial, software and other services worth US$ 131 million. The transaction is the largest direct foreign investment in the country so far. It also holds first place in the European telecommunications market at present time.

The shares of SPT Telecom attracted a large bidding interest in the second wave of voucher privatization and became amongst the highest priced on the domestic stock market. More than a 20 per cent of the company is owned by individual shareholders and investment funds.

Recently the Bulgarian administration has also announced its plan to sell 25-30 per cent of its national telecommunications company's stock.

In Poland, each former Minister of P&T had his own concept for privatizing TPSA - Polish Telecom, although none managed to apply it in practice as Cabinets in Poland were continually changing. The present minister was not really in favor of prompt privatization, and until recently declared that it would begin only at the turn of the century. Recently, in response to the enormous needs of public finances as well as the anticipated privatization of large European telecommunications companies, the date of starting the privatization was set for a less distant future, i.e. the year 1997.

The Minister of P&T is to submit to the government his concept for privatizing the company by the end of 1996. His proposal will be based on three independent analyses conducted by foreign and Polish experts. In the following year, 1997, the company's worth is to be evaluated and the sale of stock is set to begin. The first block of stock would be fairly small (no more than 25 per cent).

The Minister of P&T estimates the TPSA's worth at US$15-20 billion. Some experts claim that the company's value is, in fact, twice as much, quoting the price at which the Czechs managed to sell 27 per cent of the stock in SPT Telecom, even though the Czech market is several times smaller than the Polish.

8. Conclusions

The development of Polish, Czech and Hungarian telecommunications in the years following the political turn-around has exceeded expectations. A number of factors like policy concepts, barriers to political consensus and implementation as well as typical constraints of the transformation phase, in particular the lack of financial resources, are certainly among those which have to be carefully considered in the assessment of telecommunications policy in the three countries.

It can be argued, that the Czech Republic, Hungary and Poland as the larger countries and markets, exhibit differences with regard to the priorities attached by policy makers to telecommunications.

The Czech policy was very close to the minimal variant of policy alluded to in the introduction with only minor priority attributed to this sector and considerable concern over the alignment of tariffs with general economic and social policy. This is also suggested by the stated intentions of the government to preserve a monopoly of the former public carrier until the year 2000.

The Polish approach is markedly different and much more liberal in many respects. But the Polish case gives evidence that this liberal approach did not have an impact large enough to clearly outcompete the Czech Republic in terms of real achievements. This may have to do with the considerable time which is necessary to gather experience and to effectively implement a given policy concept or perhaps with the dynamism of the evolution as long as there is a considerable surplus demand and a certain level of solvent demand.

References

KONTKIEWICZ-CHACHULSKA, H. (1996), Recent Evolution of Telecommunications in the Region of Central Europe, in: WELFENS, P.J.J. and G. YARROW, Telecommunications and Energy in Systematic Transformation. International Dynamics, Deregulation and Adjustment in Network Industries, Heidelberg and New York: Springer.

KONTKIEWICZ-CHACHULSKA, H. and D. PHAN (1996), From Path-Dependent Processes of Structural Change to a Diversity of Market Models in Central European Countries Telecommunications, Proc. of ITS 11th Biennial Conference, Seville (Spain).

KUBASIK, J. (1996), Competition in Polish Telecommunications: Theory, Practice, and Lessons for the Future, Proc. of ITS 11th Biennial Conference, Seville (Spain).

KUBASIK, J. and T. KELLY (1992), Telecommunications Investment and Tariff Policy in Poland, Proc. of OECD/CCEET Workshop 'Improving Conditions for Investment and Growth in Telecommunications for Partners in Transition', Prague, pp. 213-272.

SALLAI, Gy., I. SCHMIDEG and GY. LAJTHA (1996a), Modernization of Telecommunications in Central and Eastern Europe, in: The Froelich/Kent Encyclopedia of Telecommunications, vol. 12., New York, Basel, Hong Kong: Marcel Decker, pp. 1-43.

SALLAI, Gy., I. SCHMIDEG and Gy. LAJTHA (1996b), Telecommunications in Central and Eastern Europe. Similarities, Peculiarities and Trends in the Countries of Transition, in: Telecommunications Policy, Vol. 21. No. 5, pp. 325-340.

SCHENK, K.-E., KRUSE, J. and MÜLLER, J., eds. (1997), Telecommunications take-off in Transition Countries, Avebury.

I: Regulation of the Telecommunication Sector in Russia: Direct Foreign Investments and Options for Competition

Svetlana Petuhova and Alexander Vronetz

1. Introduction

Telecommunications is one of a few domestic branches in Russia which is steadily developing in a difficult period of transition. The State is succeeding in maintaining the integrity of its complex and key position whilst managing this transition. At present this branch is dealing with the problems the country faces in entering the global telecommunication age. The main conditions for achieving this goal are a legal framework and the adoption of an investment policy.

Recent years have been characterized by the intensive development of telecommunications facilities in Russia. New kinds of services have appeared on the Russian market: cellular networks of mobile communication, paging communication, multimedia, video teleconferencing and others. In 1996 approximately 2.0m telephone numbers were introduced (that is more than during any previous period), and networks of cellular communication and paging were organized. A rather prosperous section of the population developed during these years which has access to new forms of communication services including a higher level of service.

As to the extent of communication lines, the primary long-distance public telephone network in Russia is the largest in the world: there are about 200ths km of cable lines and about 120ths km of RRL currently in operation, and only 2% of these are FOL. During the last 4 years the problem of international communications has virtually been resolved. If in 1990 there were only 1ths channels of international communication in the whole former USSR, today there are 50ths such channels (compared to 47ths in Germany and 40ths in France). The creation of seven international sitching centers (4 ISC and 3 international telephone exchanges) with a capacity of 38ths channels is envisaged as part of the planned development of international telecommunications within the Russian territory.

91 automatic exchanges are part of Russia's long-distance telephone network. Some 32% of this total are modern digital. The capacity of trunk exchanges together with those introduced in 1996 will make up some 350ths channels and lines. Digital ATE capacity (Automatic Trunk Exchange) will make up some 200ths, amounting to 57 % of total exchange capacity. By the end of 1996 digital exchanges will be installed in 60 cities. Of the total capacity of Subscriber Concentrator Node (SCN), this amounts to 49 ths channels, 74% of which are

digital. The network does not yet include any OKC-7 equipment yet (this equipment is intended for Common Channel Signaling).

During recent years the network of cross-border telecommunications has been considerably expanded. Murmansk oblast is linked with Norway, Kaliningrad oblast with Poland and Germany, Leningrad oblast with Finland and Denmark, Chita and Amur oblasts and Primorski Krai with China, Chukotsky National Okrug and Magadan oblast with Alaska (USA). Development in these regions is executed predominantly with the use of fiber optic cable and digital transmission systems.

One of the largest remaining problems is that of providing Russian households with personal telephones. Only 44 families in 100 in cities and 20 in rural areas have a telephone set at home. More than 9 m citizens are currently waiting for the installation of a telephone.

The development of telecommunications in Moscow requires special attention. More than three quarters of all domestic financial flows take place in Moscow, where there is a high concentration of joint-ventures operating in Russia and domestic companies, all of which require telecommunications services that are up to European standards. Just during the last two years the number of joint-venture enterprise has increased 2.5 times. Many of these companies want to have their own channels of communication between Russian regions and their parent companies in the West. The strengthening of competition among commercial companies in Moscow and the acceleration of capital circulation increases the need for communication between managers and main offices and between sellers and buyers. This is why on the Moscow telecommunication market, in addition to the usual stable demand for telephony, the demand for reliable and operative data transmission has long been imminent . This demand is being satisfied today with the help of fiber-optic cables laid by private companies.

Further development of the telecommunications branch during the realization of the "Conception for Russian development of the communications complex" in 1996-1997, includes a number of special programs. Firstly, the legal framework and the regulation of the branch is to be improved; secondly, the creation of a more favorable investment climate is being considered. The credits involved are required for the development and realization of new technological projects on a competitive basis.

The main principles of a new policy in the area of communications development are the following: the creation of a legal framework for telecommunications activity in the Russian Federation; reform of the property structure and control system that previously existed in the branch; demonopolization and development of alternative telecommunications services, primarily in the interests of new commercial structures (banks, exchanges, joint ventures, joint-stock companies and others); introduction of a new flexible tariff policy, characterized by liberalization but with some elements of State regulation preserved; development of international cooperation; preferential use for telecommunications development financed by enterprises' retained earnings and their incorporated resources, such as various forms of property and privately owned capital, including foreign; establishment of a State incentive policy for telecommunication development, providing preferential tax and credit systems and in some cases allocation of additional credits from the Federal budget in order to implement especially important programs of national importance.

2. System of Control and Regulation in the Telecommunication Complex

2.1 Legal and Organizational Basis of the Branch

Since 1990 the telecommunications branch has passed through all the stages of a transitional economy. From a completely monopolized system with a four-link, four-level control structure, which was a large post, television, radio broadcasting and space facilitiy, the telecommunications branch has ceased to be a monostructure. Over a period of four years this branch was completely demonopolized on several levels. First - the telecommunication complex is now divided into three components: post, telecommunication, radio broadcasting and television. Second - practically all State enterprises of telecommunication became joint-stock companies; in the public telecommunications system today there exist no state enterprises, but only joint-stock companies. Thus the single type of ownership structure in the telecommunications complex has been replaced by three types, between which new relations have been established, ensuring cooperation, competition and administration. The legal regulation of telecommunications activities within the Russian Federation comprises four levels: international, Federal, regional and the level of local administrations. The legal acts set up and enforced by all these levels constitutes the legal framework.

The creation of a legislative and normative base has been underway since 1992. During this large-scale reorganization, the telecommunications complex of Russia has not lost its systems of control. Systems of licensing, certification and a new normative base were introduced for this purpose, and five new Federal laws have appeared: "On Telecommunication", "On Postal Communication", "On Federal Communication by Courier", "On Ratification of the IVth Additional Protocol for the Charter of the World Post Union", "On Ratification of the Charter and Convention of the International Telecommunication Union".

Fig. I1: Management Structure of Communication in Russia

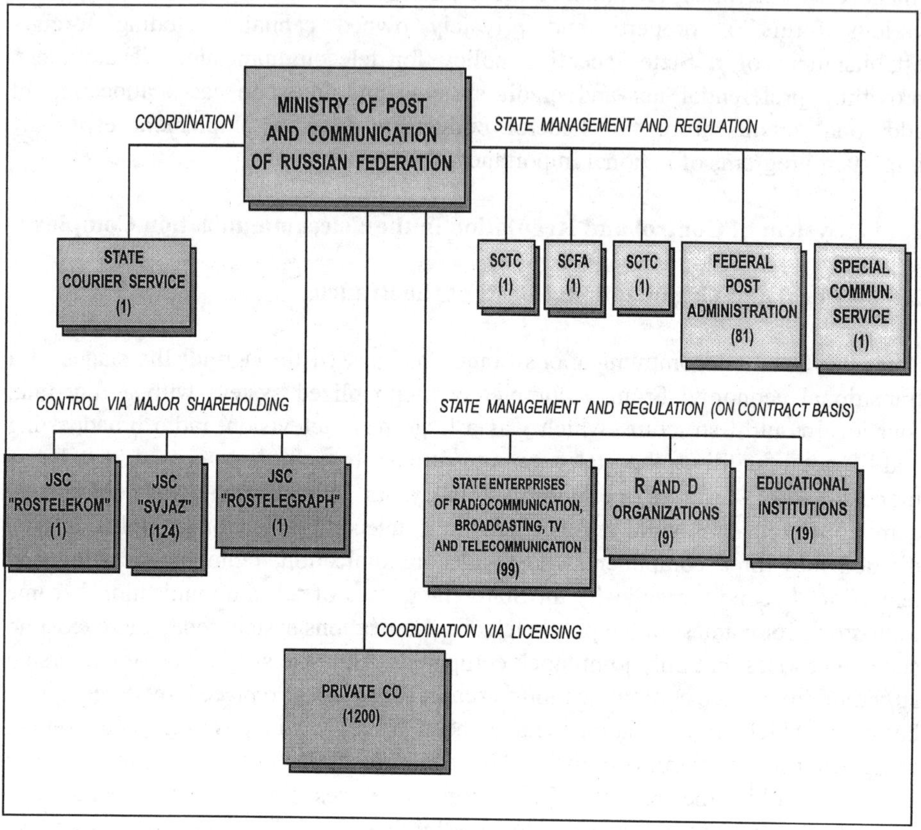

In addition to these laws, more than 30 legal acts have been passed, including the legal basis for the privatization and conversion of telecom enterprises into joint stock companies; the program for the demonopolization of the telecommunications branch; the Russian Federation government's Decree "On Privatization of Telecommunications Enterprises". Rules for granting services for trunk and international telecommunication services, telegraphic communication, wire broadcasting services, local telephone networks, and others, were established by further legal acts.

The function of the Ministry of Communications, which has been transformed from a managing into a regulatory administration, responsible for defining the rules of the game in the Russian telecommunications market, issuing licenses and certificates. New functions of the Ministry are administrative control functions. For this purpose a new structure "Gossvjaznadzor", numbering about 3ths persons and working in all areas of the Russian Federation, was created. "Gossvjaznadzor" has a certain independence with an equal attitude towards operators and manufacturers, irrespective of their departmental subordination and forms of property. The management structure of the telecommunications system is presented in Fig. I1.

Ministry documentation has become obligatory for all owners of communications facilities and particularly for operators, providing services to the public, national economy and all other consumers on Russian territory.

Thus, a new structure, a new hierarchy of property forms and structures of management was created. This structure is compatible with internationally accepted managment frameworks for telecommunication systems, because all measures were conducted on the basis of worldwide experience, with consideration given for a transitive period for Russia in order to accommodate a certain mentality and the geopolitical situation of the State.

The management of activities in the field of communications is carried out by federal bodies of executive authorities, which are incorporated in a uniform system. The basis of this system is comprised of the following:

- At the Federal level - Ministry of Communications of the Russian Federation, including the State Commission for Telecommunications and the Service of State Supervision of Telecommunications; Federal Administration of Postal Communication; Federal Administration of Courier Communication, State Commission on Frequency Allocation, federal ministries and departments, which administer departmental telecommunication networks;
- At the regional level - federal communications bodies.

The legislative base of this branch is the Federal Law "On communications", which has created the legal grounds for the development of a Russian communications complex, having defined optimal conditions for civilized relations between the State and the communications operators, domestic as well as foreign. In particular, it has established the rights and responsibilities of state authorities, enterprises and of users of communications services. It has established measures for branch support from the budget, the order of indemnification for expenses and losses, taxes and other privileges, tariff policy. It regulates the usage of ground and transport, protection and security of communications facilities, rules of frequency allocation etc. All this has allowed a significant increase in the rate of development of the telecoms sector (Tab. I1).

Tab. I1: Rates of Communications Facilities Development

Telecommunication facilities	Years			
	1992	1993	1994	1995
Cable telecommunications lines (km)	2069	3510	3571	2502
Radio relay lines (km)	1500	1998	1743	1597
Trunk telephone exchanges (number of channels)	8910	33484	45578	59715
Urban telephone exchanges (ths of numbers)	705	919.4	1177	1376
Rural telephone exchanges (ths of numbers)	96.5 (64.1)	118.3 (87.94)	115.2 (97.9)	128.6 (128.6)

Source: BULGAK et al. (1995), p. 37-38.

As the sector develops, the normative-legal framework should stimulate the influx of investments by favoring investors in the areas of taxation, export-import tariffs, currency regulation etc.

The Federal Law "On communications" defines the basis of investment activity and conditions for attracting of foreign investments. According to this Law, decisions on state investments at the expense of the federal budget are accepted on the basis of federal state programs. State bodies of the Russian Federation of States and local government bodies determine directions and development of investment programs in the telecoms sector, realized at the expense of appropriate budgets based on plans for the social and economic development of the territories. The natural and juridical participants undertaking development projects and engaged in the provision of telecommunications can be granted, in due order, credits and tax privileges, amongst other benefits. Foreign investments in the area of telecommunications are guaranteed pursuant to the Russian Federation's legislation "On foreign investments".

The transformation of the telecom sector, its qualitative changes and investment policy, find support in the taxation policy. According to the Law "On taxation", part of enterprise profits, directed into investment, is exempted from taxation. According to the Law "On value-added tax", operations connected with securities circulation, that support the impementation of federal programs are exempt from payment of this tax. Enterprises that stimulate the manufacture of modern technologies are exempt for1 year from the payment of VAT, from specific taxation and from customs duty on equipment received from abroad at the expense of joint venture authorized capital.

The licensing of activities in the telecom sector, which began in 1991 after the issue of the Russian Federation government decree "On licensing in the telecommunications branch". The decree establishes state regulation and control over the provision of telecommunications services and ensures equal conditions in the competitive areas, protects customers interests as well as the interests of existing and potential competitors.

Pursuant to the legislation, any juridical person having qualified for a license can be engaged in the supply of telecom services. The issue, change of conditions, extension or termination of licenses are dealt with by the Ministry of Communications. By 1996 the Ministry of Communications had issued more than 1000 licenses for telecommunications, TV, radio broadcasting and postal services.

As of January 1, 1996 a new order of licensing was introduced. Decisions on the issue and withdrawal of the licenses are agreed by a Ministry of Communications License Commission, which is a corporate body comprising anti-monopoly committee experts and representatives of other interested departments. After registration of the license by its owner, an examination of the licensee's networks is carried out by a commission with the participation of "Gossvjaznadzor". Questions regarding the preservation of the license in the case that the licensee does not grant services, or the withdrawal of the license, is decided by the License Commission.

Certification is one of the main levers of State control and regulation. The Ministry of Communication of the Russian Federation began in 1992 to deal with the certification of communications facilities. During the years of operation of these services significant experience was accumulated, leading to the development, accreditation and introduction of a system for certification of telecommunications facilities, which acts on the authority of the Laws "On certification of products and services" and "On communication". This led to the creation of a market for communications equipment, which is represented today by technical facilities of 850 names and which continues to expand.

The Certification Services structure is represented by a central body of certification (Ministry for Communications of the Russian Federation), a body of certification (The Certification Administration), certifying test centers and laboratories (five centers and 21 laboratories). More than 950 certificates for technical communication facilities of different types have already been issued. Once the market was created, market laws and mechanisms began operating, therefore the price of one number of digital ATX decreased from 350 dollars in 1990-1991 to 160-168 dollars in 1995. Certification has become a powerful tool of State administration and regulation, and it facilitated the installation in Russia of 2.0m telephone numbers in 1996. (BULGAK et al., 1995, p. 43).

Cases where equipment is not adapted to the public network and does not satisfy the requirements of Ministry of Communication of the Russian Federation are rare. At the same time the question of State inspection control of certificated equipment has not yet been resolved. The activities of the Ministry for

Communications of the Russian Federation and "Gosstandard" of Russia are not always coordinated to ensure the passage in due order of imported communications equipment through the customs-house.

The new edition of the "Principal Regulations for Certification of Telecommunications Facilities " will provide solutions to the many questions posed by the participants in this interaction process. Due to the recognition of foreign certificates the certification procedure is now more simplified. The term of certification and registration of domestic certificates has been reduced. A new system for extension of certificate validity and a number of other improvements are now being introduced.

2.2 Problems Associated with Demonopolization and Anti-monopoly Policy

In comparison to other industrial sectors the Russian telecommunications sector has become a leading branch interms of development, outpacing such highly profitable branches as oil production and the power industry. The demonopolization of domestic telecom companies was of a certain importance here.

Whereas in advanced industrial countries the demonopolization process concludes once saturation of the market by base services is reached, in Russia these processes occur simultaneously. The danger of impinging on network coordination, the unity of the control system, proportionality of development and the universality of service when liberalizing the services market, requires the creation of definite regulatory documents and strict control of their fulfillment. In so doing the regulatory documents will increasingly meet the requirements of the European Community.

Operating at present on Russian Federation territory on the basis of free competition are the following: Federally owned telecommunications enterprises, subjects of Federal property, municipal property, property of juridical and natural persons (including foreign), acting as telecommunications operators.

The main principles of the Russian Federation's telecom policy are the following: equality of rights of juridical and natural persons actively participating in telecommunications; combining the interests of the Russian Federation and its population; freedom of message transmission over networks and telecommunications facilities; observance of the interests of telecom network users; restriction of monopolistic activity and development of business activity by granting telecommunications services; reliability, survivability and controllability of communications with regard to technological features of the network, based on uniform normative documents and consideration of the recommendations of ITU; solution of nation-wide telecommunications problems in the interest of effective administration, defence and safety, protection of law and order and protection of the population in extreme situations; higher quality and wider range of services;

provision of production priority and introduction of telecom facilities in the Russian Federation pursuant to the national scientific and technological policy; realization of a policy of the largest preference in order to attract investors; finding various sources of telecommunications investments, formation of a priority investment directive; adoption of international practices in telecommunications; assistance in expanding international cooperation, accountability and controlability to Russian Federation State Authority bodies; separation of Federal Executive bodies from economic functions in the area of telecommunications. (MINISTRY OF POST AND TELECOMMUNICATIONS OF THE RUSSIAN FEDERATION, 1994, p. 15-17)

The Ministry of Communication of the Russian Federation together with the State Committee on Anti-monopoly Policy supports and encourages diligent competition in the granting of communications services by the development and application of appropriate normative documents and licenses.

The existing service markets can be classified by their form of transmitted information, by service types, by territorial attributes and structure of the service providers. Service providers are distinguished by the following: State enterprises - economic subjects, subordinate to the Ministry for Communications of the Russian Federation or other ministries and departments; joint-stock companies - economic subjects, based on the creation of State communications enterprises with the controlling block of shares under State ownership; joint-stock societies, partnerships and other participants involved in enterprise activity - private economic participants or those with State participation.

It is rather early to discuss competition between service providers under the current conditions of a sharp defecit in communications services. However the high rate of development in the communications services market in Russia, the increase of providers of quantity services, and the development of alternative facilities and communication networks, promote the development of a competitive environment. This process is developing particularly rapidly in the areas of data transmission, mobile networks for radio telephone communication and international telephone communication. The Federal bodies of Executive Authority encourage and support competition by granting communications services.

State regulation of the market activities of investors is envisioned to restrict competition and prevent the probable gain of a leading market position in the communications services market. The main methods and principles of State regulation are defined by the demonopolization program in the communications sector, which is based on organizational-legal, economic and socio-psychological methods.

The main mechanisms of <u>organizational-legal regulation</u> are the following: legislative and normative documents and acts; a control system and regulation bodies; availability of the network of telecommunications to public use; elimination of obstacles to competition; licensing; certification etc. (MINISTRY OF POST AND TELECOMMUNICATIONS OF THE RUSSIAN FEDERATION, 1993, p. 7)

Economic methods of regulation provide the following: realization of a selective policy and of measures for priority projects ensuring stimulation of development of the coordinated telecommunications system currently operating in the Russian Federation; formation and functioning of new telecom markets; innovative activity in the sector; improvements in tariff policy.

Socio-psychological methods assume: improvement in the monitoring of the sector and greater responsibility for the decrease in quality of supplied communication services; publicity for demonopolization measures and State regulation of activities in the telecom sector.

Operators in any telecommmunications markets across the world, irrespective of the market's level of development or its structure and the operators' degree of market power, are subject to some form of regulation. National legislation on anti-monopoly regulation essentially differs according to the specific conditions of each country. A common factor in the legislation of all countries is the provision of State control over company mergers, prohibition of agreements and business deals between private service providers, and interruption of unfair competition. An exclusive monopoly position held by an enterprise is not necessarily prohibited. Activities interfering with the development of competition in the services market and entailing losses or overlooked profit of other market participants are forbidden.

The anti-monopoly policy is executed on the basis of the acting law on natural monopolies, in accordance with which the State regulation of natural monopolies in the area of telecommunication was created. Under the conditions of the Russian monopoly system this regulation operates according to international practice.

The regulation of natural monopolies could be executed on the basis of profit standardization, or on the basis of modes for "stimulating regulation". The specific characteristics of the Russian telecom sector and of the current stage of market development (non-saturation of the market by telephone communications services, necessity of stimulating investments for the development of networks and telecommunication systems, preservation of the regulatory role of the State over tariff policy) imply that Western models of anti-monopoly regulation need to be studied in detail in order to assess their use in domestic practice.

Pursuant to the existing legislation, three levels of market dominanace have been established: the position of a market participant is considered to be dominant if his market share exceeds 35%. If his market share lies between 35% and 65% the Federal Anti-monopoly Office deems the enterprise as having a leading position in the market. If the share exceeds 65%, the enterprise should present proof to the Anti-monopoly Office that it does not have a dominant position.

In the modern telecom services market the following forms of branch monopoly exist: natural, temporary and long-term monopoly.

Natural monopolies are those where the creation of a competitive environment irrespective of demand is impossible or economically unviable given the existing level of scientific and technological progress.

Temporary monopolies are monopolies with a temporary absence of competition.

Long-term monopoly is a situation where the creation of a competitive environment in the near future (3 years) would be impossible or economically inexpedient, but as obstacles to development of competition are liquidated, alternative services, new kinds of telecommunication and new technologies appear, so that the creation of a competitive environment becomes possible.

Anti-monopoly bodies were created to monitor the situation within the telecommunications markets, and to duly reveal and prohibit abuses of market power. In order to avoid abuse of market power, the licensing term is limited to aperiod of 3-10 years with the possibility of extension.

State regulation of telecom markets that are characterised by a natural monopoly conists of the following: determination of user groups, whom the service provider is obliged to supply; establishment of a minimum level of provision; price control (tariffs) on various telecom services; introduction of a special list of compensatory measures for market investors (for example, tax privileges, credit support, privileged leaseing terms). (Program for Communications Demonopolization, 1995, p. 4)

If a market has one or more dominant enterprises, tax or other privileges are granted for non-dominant participants for a period of up to three years.

3. Economic Indicators of Business Activity within the Telecom Sector

3.1 Privatization, Ownership and Structure of the Telecom Sector

The crisis of the national economy in the early 90s manifested itself in the telecommunications branch through the reduced consumption of telecom services by residential customers, a reduction in enterprises' incomes, a reduction in the production of telecoms equipment and in research and development volumes as well as through the appearance of social tensions.

In order to preserve the provision of essential telecom services under such conditions (required for example for the defence sector and the general functioning of all other branches), the telecom sector of the Russian Federation is undergoing reforms. Thus, privatization of telecom enterprises and the creation of joint-stock companies (open and closed types, joint and small enterprises) has begun.

In Russia there are now about 100 joint-stock companies, which were organized on the basis of former State enterprises. This included “Rostelecom”, which is the operator of trunk and international telecommunications within the Russian territory. Regional joint-stock companies (more than 80) are operating on established algorithms in close interaction with “Rostelecom” and each other.

At the time of privatization the total authorized capital of joint-stock telecom companies amounted to 16 billion roubles or 90% of the aggregate capital subject to privatization. With the creation of these companies more than 16m shares were issued, of which about 6.6m were distributed among workers of the enterprises.

State regulation is carried out by providing Federal bodies with a controlling block of shares in 88 joint-stock telecom companies. Out of the total shares sold at auctions, 85% were bought by legal entities, investment companies and others. Foreign investors have become proprietors of 21.3% of the shares offered in investment competitions. These shares make up 5% of the total authorized capital of the privatized enterprises.

Integration of enterprises based on new organizational principles is becoming the logical conclusion of structural reorganization. Regional operators, formed on the basis of State enterprises, are incorporated in the "Svjazinvest" joint-stock company, the authorized capital of which consists of the consolidation of blocks of shares (38%) of regional joint-stock telecommunications companies fixed in Federal property. Associations of cellular communications operators and associations of documentary telecommunication operators have been created.

The "Svjazinvest" joint-stock company provides for the general coordination of activities under the “Russian National Telephone” program, the main executors of which are regional joint-stock telecommunications companies. The Investment Policy Administration assists in the distribution of budgetary funds, directing them to the executors of the program and also provides interaction with the Presidential Programs Center.

Some enterprises have created joint ventures and purchased shares of other enterprises. Thus, the "Russian Telecommunications Network" joint-stock company has purchased, through investment competition, a block of shares of the "Moscow trunk telephone" joint-stock company. A wide network of private communications companies is now operating on Russian Territory.

During the last five years the property structure of communications networks has changed considerably. More than a thousand new private companies have obtained licenses for providing the population with communications services and are actually operating. The market share of private companies in this branch has grown in Moscow from 0 to 37%, and in Russia as a whole to nearly 42%. The new operators in the market have proceeded from the fact that the obsolete State telephone network is unable to meet growing user demands without the necessary technical and financial resources. Therefore the new private telecommunications companies, organized mainly as joint ventures with foreign capital, have attracted the majority of the investment from abroad for creation of their own communications networks.

Fig. I2: Dynamics of Investment Structure into Russian Federation Communication Industry

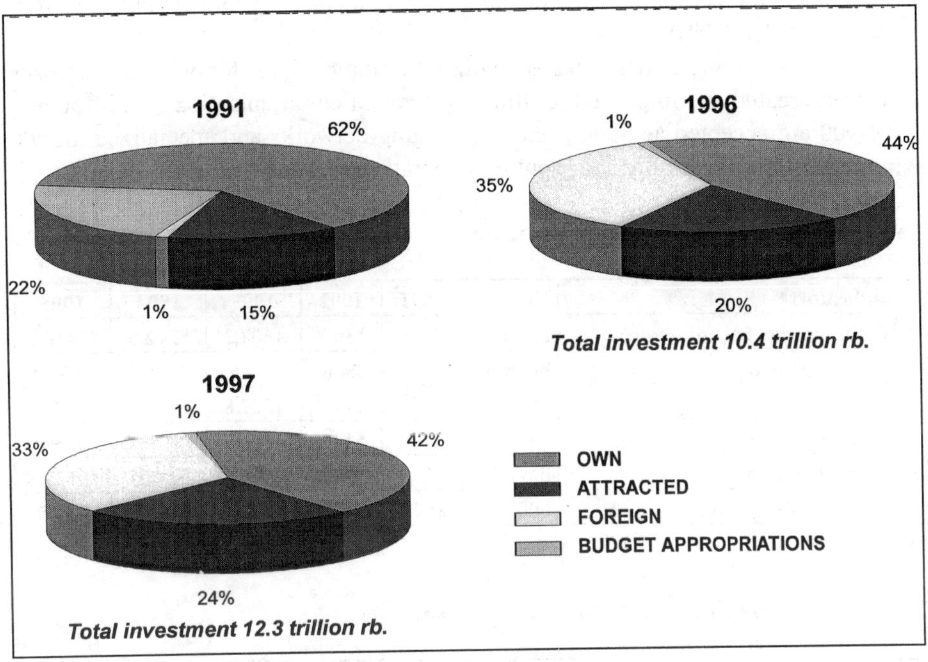

Analysis of the financial position of joint-stock companies and State enterprises of telecommunications in terms of 1996 results, shows that the initial cost of the basic production assets (as of October 1, 1996) with consideration for revaluation in the telecommunications branch, amounts in total to 69,732 billion roubles, including in the case of State enterprises - 13,249 billion roubles (about 19%), joint-stock companies and private enterprises - 56,483 billion roubles (81%). In 1996, 5,810 billion roubles were invested. The joint-stock telecommunications companies have a stable financial position and a good reputation among shareholders and investors.

The position of State enterprises for post, TV and radio broadcasting has worsened considerably. Almost all of these enterprises are unprofitable and require additional State budgetary financing (subsidies).

In 1995-1996 58 digital ATE were put into operation, 29 of these in 1996. The general share of digital ATE will constitute 66%. During the last three years the quantity of international channels has increased by 45 thousand.

During 1995-1996 the number capacity of local telephone networks increased by 35m numbers (1.5m in 1995). Tntroduction of a further 2.0m numbers is planned for the end of 1996. Tables I2 and I3 show the dynamics of change for the main indicators of branch development. (COMMUNICATIONS ADMINISTRATIONS).

In many regions networks of mobile communication for various purposes have been created and improved. Cellular systems of communication NMT-450 and GSM-900 are accepted as State standards. Paging networks and specialized mobile communications are rapidly being put into operation.

Tab. I2: Dynamics of Major Indicators of Branch Development

	Indicators	Units	1991	1992	1993	1994	1995
1	Cross income: Sale of services	bln rub	13.5	136.3	1607.3	8212.6	21416.5
	- population	bln rub	3.8	24.6	319.5	2119.2	6830.4
	- national economy	bln rub	9.7	111.7	1287.8	6093.4	14586.1
2	Fixed assets	bln rub	20.1	514.0	673.0	15559.0	30566.0
3	Production costs	bln rub	10.3	118.1	1386.1	7459.1	19657.8
4	Number of employees	000's	867.0	845.2	824.0	822.9	811.6

Tab. I3: Growth Rates of Major Indicators, %

	Indicators	1992/1991	1993/1992	1994/1993	1995/1994
1	Cross income: Service sales	1008.1	1179.2	511.0	260.0
	- population	642.0	1299.0	663.3	322.3
	- national economy	1152.7	1152.9	473.2	239.4
2	Fixed assets	2559.8	121.4	137.0	196.5
3	Production costs	1146.6	1173.7	538.1	263.5
4	Number of employees	97.5	97.5	99.9	99.0

3.2 Structure and Dynamics of Investment Activity

Investment is an important condition for the development of enterprise activities. Possible sources of investments are the following: State budget; enterprises' retained earnings (profit and depreciation charges on complete restoration); bank credits and financial savings provided by households; loans from local organizations and interested enterprises; private capital from domestic businessmen and foreign capital.

The investment policy for the sector aims develop telecommunication networks with the help of domestic, as well as foreign partners. The attraction of investments is executed in various forms: creation of joint ventures, joint-stock companies, issue of securities, granting of short-term and long-term credits.

For many decades the State budget was the main source of financing. However, in view of the instability of the State economy and a sharp reduction in State investment volumes, financing through the state budget has declined in importance in the telecoms sector. In 1991 the share of budget financing in the total volume of capital investments in the sector constituted more than 22%. In 1994 the share of State budget investments fell to 13%, in 1995 it constituted 1.5% of the total volume of capital investment, and in 1996 it was 0.8%. These funds are directed basically at the development of the following areas: telecommunications facilities in rural regions; space telecommunications systems and broadcasting in the Russian Federation; postal communications; conversions in the field of frequency spectrum allocation to enable better broadcasting services in the Russian Federation; regional and Federal programs and development projects of telecommunication facilities and networks. Therefore, the investment policy in this sector implied the partial withdrawal of the State.

The main forms of institutional financing through large Federal programs and projects are the following: creation of a specialized State investment bank within the sector; creation of a bank consortium together with related industrial sectors; creation of a branch investment fund; creation of a financial and industrial group.

The main advantage of a branch investment bank, which is reponsible for allocating long-term credits of commercial interest, lies in the creation of a unique center for information and regulation in the sector. Such banks are innovation-commercial banks with at least 51% of State participation in the authorized capital and with enterprises and organizations holding shares of common stock. The banks fulfill the following functions: distribution of purpose-oriented investment credits, allocated by the State at concessionary interest rates, for the development of branch infrastructure; distribution of public funds among sub-branches and regions (to finance prospective research and development, reconstruction and technical re-equipment of enterprises); assistance in State securities distribution. For example, the credit policy of "Svjazbank" aims to create a stable resource base and develop a distribution strategy for large credit investments. Hereafter, a large branch structure, i.e. a postal-bank holding enterprise, will be created on the foundations of this bank.

The creation of a bank consortium is envisioned only for the development of programs requiring very large capital investments and the incorporated efforts of several related branches (for example the telecommunications branch, the telecommunications equipment industry and the electronic industry) for the realization of strategically important large-scale projects.

The branch investment fund could be purely State or non-State, uniting on a voluntary basis the enterprises included in the branch. The purpose of its creation is to increase branch stability and the acceleration of its development owing to stabilization of its financial security. Its resources will be created at the expense of deductions from enterprises (established interest from the prime cost of production), of purpose contributions on realization of the joint projects, as well as of incomes generated by its own activity.

A financial and industrial group represents the most flexible and ramificated form of bank, industrial and commercial capital integration. The main purpose of the financial and industrial group is the association of material and financial resources of its participants in order to increase the competitiveness and efficiency of manufacture, to render technical assistance, to accelerate scientific and technological progress and to attract more investments. The creation of the financial and industrial group is one of the main directives within the framework fulfilment of the program for "Reform and development of the Russian economy in 1995-1997" .

In a market economy enterprises retained earnings become an important source of finance. Having adapted to a new ownership system and become joint-stock companies or small enterprises, enterprises invest part of their earned assets, use the credits and try to attract foreign direct investments.

In 1994 the share of enterprise owned resources in the total volume of investments amounted to 49.3%. The volume of enterprise resources directed towards branch development amounted in 1995 to about 3250 billion roubles, in 1996 they will amount to 44%. Over the next years, enterprises' retained earnings will continue to be one of the main sources of investments.

State support plays an essential role in encouraging self-financed investment by exempting such investment from value-added tax - if the investment is directed at upgrading equipment and transmission systems - and by granting preferential custom tariffs on the delivery of equipment.

The specially created joint-stock holding company "Svjazinvest" also plays an important role for investments in regional and local public telecommunications networks. It is currently preparing proposals on a uniform centralized system of financial accounting and crediting of telecommunications enterprises.

Until 1996 bank resources and financial savings of the population did not function as sources of investment because of an unfavourable investment climate and the imperfection of legal regulations. But in light of the new legislation, the share of banks in the total volume of investment in the telecom sector should amount to 10-20 % by 2000.

In order to attract households' savings for investment, about 70% of joint-stock telecommunications companies have issued securities on a sum of 234 billion roubles. They were realized on 178 billion roubles.

The program for "Russian national telephony" has become one of the ways of attracting financial resources from households into investment. Attracting these financial resources through bonds and State privileges, the program can satisfy the demand for the most simple telephone services. Construction of ATX in 64 regions was undertaken wih the help of such financing.

In 1996 about 800ths numbers out of 2.0m were introduced and will be put into operation under the "National telephone" program. The financial resources of local administrations and other borrowed finances constituted nearly 20% of all investment into local networks during 1996.

The financial resources of local administrations are used as a source of investment only in certain cases, when local authorities and enterprise administrations participate in the development and maintenance of telecommunication networks which is in the interest of the general public. The specific share of resources from this source is insignificant and there are no prospects for its growth.

In view of the complicated political situation, private capital is in practice of little significance in the development of telecom infrastructure. Over a 3-year period the increased participation of domestic investors has been only 5 %. Fig. I2 shows the dynamics of the structure of investment into the telecoms branch.

Foreign capital is becoming one of the most important sources of investment for the development of telecommunications networks. Its share has grown from 1% in 1991 to 44% in 1996 and amounts to 520m dollars, with the larger part of these funds given without governmental guarantees. Foreign investments are entering as credits (on a governmental level more than 50% and under commercial agreements 30%) and as direct investments in the development of telecom services (15%). It is expected that in 1996 foreign investment in the branch will amount to 755.5m dollars, that is 38% more than in 1995.

Various forms of credit are used to finance investment projects. These include interstate credits granted for the purchase of equipment (credit lines of "Hermes"), as well as for the realization of complex projects (Great Britain's credit for the joint venture "Comstar"). There are credits from the Russian government credits to operators carrying out projects on "breakdown directions", for example, a project for cellular communication development in Moscow, accomplished by the "Moscow Cellular Communication" joint-stock company. Furthermore, company credits to Russian operators for fulfillment of large projects (joint-stock company "Rostelecom", "Moscow Telephone Exchange", Kemerovo oblast, Kaliningrad oblast, Tyumen oblast), one of the forms of which is the so called "revolving credit". This form of investment credit is also intended for use with the development of leasing in the branch. The volume of credits under State guarantee for purchasing modern technology communications equipment with payment by installments over 10 years is insignificant.

Large-scale projects for the development of trunk and international telecommunications were realized with credits obtained without government warranties. These projects recoup fast and are economically effective and attractive to foreign investors.

However, contributions by foreign investors are now distributed extremely disproportionately among different domestic telecom branches. The largest part is invested in the most profitable forms of telecommunications: international telecommunications ("Rostelecom"), cellular telecommunications ("Vyimpelcom Beeline" or "Moscow Cellular Communication") and the dedicated municipal network services ("Comstar", "Golden-Line", "Sovintel", "Macomnet"). For example, foreign companies compete with each other for international tenders for the right to participate in many projects of "Rostelecom". At the same time all local telephone networks that are members of "Svjazinvest" JSC, including "Moscow Urban Telephone Network" (MUTN), have great difficulties attracting foreign investors.

The inflow of investment can occur through the purchase of shares of privatized telecommunications enterprises. Shares are actively purchased by foreign investors. The most active among these are Cable & Wireless, C.S. First Boston, ULM Enterprises and Kutno Ltd. The shares of privatized telecommunications enterprises are one of the most attractive parts of the securities share market in Russia. Especially in the case of well-organized sales of blocks of shares through specialized auctions carried out by regional property funds with good investment conditions and business plans. The indisputable leaders in the secondary share market are the joint-stock company “Rostelecom”, "Moscow Telephone Exchange", "St. Petersburg network", "Novosibirsk telephone network" and "MMT".

Over the last three years the stated measures have allowed the local telephone network ATX to expand by up to 1.5m numbers annually, 42 digital ATE to be put in operation, more than 30ths km of international and trunk cable communications lines to be laid.

In the near future the branch cannot count upon significant budget grants. Their share in the total volume of investments will be about 1.0%. Large-scale investments by domestic commercial structures based on the income from such investments should also not be counted on.

Starting in 1993, the Moscow telecommunications market began to reach saturation. Competition between many companies for the right to occupy the leading position in different segments of the market became an additional stimulus to accelerated construction of telecommunications networks in Moscow. In 1996 many companies continued laying even temporarily unprofitable lines in order to extend to the maximum their sphere of influence. This year companies which have captured certain market segments by oligopoly, have begun to strengthen their position, reducing service prices by 10% - 20%.

The sources of revenue in Moscow differ from those in the rest of Russia. The "Moscow Urban Telephone Network" (MUTN) obtains the majority of its income not from its own services to organizations and the public, but through its share in the capital stock of 17 joint stock ventures between private firms and foreign companies. In the cases of "Comstar", a joint venture with the British company GPT, and "Telmos", a joint venture with AT&T, MUTN receives 50% of the income, and in the case of "Moscow Cellular Communication" 23%.

In order for foreign investment to become the main source of investment for telecommunications along with retained earnings from enterprises and depreciation, it is necessary to continue the process of privatization and demonopolization of domestic telecom companies. Up to now the Ministry of Post and Telecommunications of the Russian Federation only promoted big foreign businesses which provide up to $500m a year. As to medium and small investors the terms of tenders conducted by the Ministry are in fact unacceptable because of the many different permissions, licenses and extortions required. For all that, the shares of most Russian telecom companies can become liquid on the domestic as well as the foreign market only through the transfer of large blocks of shares between the portfolios of a large number of investors who do not necessarily work in the telecoms branch.

The main sources of financing in 1997 continue to be enterprises' retained earnings, depreciation deductions and foreign investments. Systematic revaluation of the fixed capital cost of telecom equipment and the application of accelerated amortization mechanisms pursuant to government decree promote the increased role of depreciation charges. The Ministry of Communications has the right to supervise depreciation charges as a free part of the income of enterprises, and to control its usage.

The decree of the Russian Federation Government from June 25, 1995, No. 633 "On development of leasing in investment activity" defined new possibilities for financing new telecommunications systems. This form of investment has not yet been applied in the Russian telecommunications market, but it is an alternative to traditional fixed-date and long-term crediting.

In Russia there now exist a series of factors that are conducive to attracting investment into telecommunications. These include:

- High recoupment on investments in telecommunications. According to some estimates 1 dollar of investment results in 4 dollars of income. Thus, the profitability of projects lies between 10% and 50%. The most profitable projects are investments in international telecommunications, bank systems of data transmission, systems of telecommunications for oil and gas companies operating in remote regions, mobile and stationary radio-telephone networks, systems for providing additional communications services to subscribers, as well the creation of dedicated networks in large cities having no outlet for international digital lines.

- Investment recoupment over a period of 4-5 years, especially in the case of new forms of telecommunications. Given that telecommunications networks do not require expenses either on fuel, raw materials or on additional labour and are subject to negligible deterioration as time goes on, the security of income from such investments is rather high. This gives the investor the possibility to obtain a guaranteed income for 10-20 years after the original capital return. But as experience of big Russian-American telecommunications companies shows, investment in communications in Moscow is already recouped within one to two years. Therefore the tempo of development is 3-4 times greater in the capital than in all other regions of Russia. For example, in 1996 the MUTN introduced about 180 ths new telephones in Moscow and Moscow oblast, i.e. three times more than in industrially developed regions of the Volga and Siberia during the same year.
- High degree of liquidity for capital invested in Russian commercial enterprises, in that investors can easily sell their shares should the need arise. The International Bank for Reconstruction and Development, for example, more than once offered "Delta Telecom" and "Sovintel" the opportunity to redeem shares in Russian enterprises.
- Low taxes on services. Russian taxes in the service sector are the lowest by all international standards, especially in comparison with real taxes on profit and turnover in commerce and production. This supports the investor's interest in telecommunications.

The Ministry of Post and Telecommunications of the Russian Federation is now lowering customs barriers in order to assist the adoption of modern foreign technology by domestic telecommunications companies. Despite the fact that the number of permissions, licenses and payments required by the Ministry is as great as previously, continuing saturation of domestic telecommunications with western technology guarantees ever greater compatibility of different units. The rather high level of taxation, the disparity between Russian accounting and western standards, and some other factors prevent the development of telecommunications equipment production within the territory of Russia. But if Russia succeeds in completing tax reform in the next few years, the inflow of foreign investment, including in the telecommunications branch, will be further stimulated.

At the same time, a negative influence on the development of the telecommunications branch is exerted by typical problems facing any business in

Russia (changing legislation, economic instability, tax pressure) as well as excessive monopolization of the branch, which makes the position of any company on the Russian telecommunications market, including foreign, unstable. As a result of this, all profitable sectors of the Russian and primarily of the Moscow telecommunications market are virtually divided among big telecommunications companies. In Moscow the usual mode of stationary telephony services are operated by the oldest monopolist on the market - the "Moscow Urban Telephone Network" (MUTN) JSC. Mobile telephone communication is provided by three leading cellular companies: "Moscow Cellular Communication", "Mobile Telesystems" and "Vyimpelcom Beeline". Translation of computer networks data on-line is facilitated by the extensive fiber-optic lines of the "Macomnet" company and the network of copper cables of the "Golden Line" company. Other companies - "Global One", "Sovam-Teleport", "Sovintel" or "Comstar" - provide services only to a highly prosperous circle of clients.

3.3 Tariff and Pricing Policy in the Telecommunications Branch

Under market conditions the price of telecommunications services depends on the demand for and supply of these services. The tariffs for services should be defined proceeding from conditions of maximum income reception, but in terms of consumer solvency. While many services are not yet satisfactory, the current system of pricing is based upon a combination of State regulation of tariffs on socially important services and on their free formation based on market factors. The current system provides a differential approach to tariffs on the same services for 3 categories of consumers: the public, budget (state-owned) enterprises and for self-supporting (commercial) enterprises.

The differential approach to tariffs is dictated by the low level of solvency of the population; tariffs established for this category of consumer are far below the prime cost of services. The reimbursement of expenses is compensated for by higher tariffs for the other two categories.

The tariff policy in the area of telecommunications, directly connected with privatization, demonopolization and liberalization of pricing processes in Russia, plays an ever more important role in the development of the sector. Today, not only the solvent demand of consumers of telecommunications services and the financial well-being of their providers depend on this policy, but also contributions to the development of telecommunications and replenishing of the State budget, obtaining part of the profit from realization of communications services.

Taking into account the specific features of different regions (geographical situation, territory, size of the network, density of population, telephone density and others) and also features of telecommunication enterprises themselves (structure of services supplied by them) that existed before transition to the market relations, the centralized pricing of telecommunications services and the mechanism for income redistribution have ensured unified tariffs in all Russian territories.

Artificially restrained over several years, tariffs on the services most used and consumed by the public (in particular subscriber payments for a telephone set in urban and rural telephone networks introduced in 1947) were very low and existed at the expense of the income generated by trunk telephone communications, 50% of which was made by leasing of trunk telephone channels (with profitability of more than 1000 %). Insofar as 50% of these channels were leased by the Defence Ministry, KGB, and other budget organizations, the reduced rates of local telephone communication for the population were in the greater part indirectly covered at the expense of budgetary funds (at present the lease of channels makes 6%).

After structural transformation following the issue of new legislative and normative documents, including cancellation of the mechanisim for redistribution of income, telecommunications was compelled to liberalize tariffs, which led to different tariffs for the same telecommunications services in different regions of the country, and even in different areas of one region.

However, the practice of artificial restraints on public tariffs (in conditions where the base level of tariffs for the population and budget organizations was very low) continued almost up to the end of 1994. So by the end of 1994, tariffs for telecommunication services had increased only 1073 times relative to levels in 1991, while the escalation of prices in industry, power engineering and freight transportation was 1122, 2468 and 2197 times respectively. Thus, in real terms the tariffs for a specified category of consumers have decreased even further.

Attempts to reduce losses made within the business sector, which uses only 10% of the telephone networks' capacity, as well as attempts to gain State grants (at a time of budget deficits), were not successful. The situation became critical and the indebtedness of self-supporting enterprises grew. Therefore at the end of 1994, the tariff escalation for self-supporting enterprises was stopped and tariffs for residential consumers started to be raised.

Tariffs for local telephone network services are determined by telecommunications enterprises. In different regions of Russia there is a large difference in the tariff rates for the same services. This is explained by regional differences in the structure of consumers and their solvency, as well as by the subjective approach of administrative bodies responsible for pricing.

The existing system of tariff determination also provides for subsidies on rural telecommunications and wire broadcasting services at the expense of trunk telecommunications services. About 20% of trunk telecommunications profit is directed at subsidizing unprofitable sub-branches.

In 1995 the growth rate of tariffs for telecommunications services for separate consumer categories was slightly greater than the rate of inflation in industry, but on the whole it did not exceed price rises in industry. Thus, in

Decemeber 1996 tariffs on toll calls increased 2.1 times relative to December 1995, public telephone subscriber payments remained at the 1995 level, tariffs for public production services rose 1.4 times and for services as a whole 1.7 times, whereas the industrial price index during the same period increased 1.83 times.

The share of population incomes has increased by up to 32% (before the transition it was 37% in the Russian Federation), which is far lower than in advanced economies, where it is 45-60%. Subscriber payments for telephones by the population compensates only 40% of the maintenance cost. Actually this percentage is lower insofar as costs, especially in connection with depreciation charges, are understated because the backlog in the revaluation of capital assets and norms of depreciation charges that was counted upon recoupment of funds over a period of 30-40 years is less in real terms.

For social and political reasons, the price disproportions will not be adjusted for a certain period of time, as it can result in lowering prosperity, i.e. the alignment of price disproportions and rise in prices (tariffs) would result in social unrest.

The tariffs currently in effect cannot sufficiently compensate for the cost of reconstruction and replacement of telecom networks and their further development. Telephone density is low (18 sets per 100 inhabitants), with large numbers of people waiting for telephones (nearly 10m persons) and there is also the low technical level of telecom networks, 25% of capacity consists of obsolete step-by-step exchanges, more than 50% are crossbar exchanges and only 12% (UTN) and 2.7% (RTN) are exchanges with program control. International telephone communication is digitized by approximately 10%; about 15% of telephone trunk connections are provided with the help of telephone operators. The extent of wear of the main production assets in the telecommunications sector as a whole exceeds 45% and equipment is replaced very slowly: not more than 4-5% is replaced in a year.

In other words, serious reconstruction and replacement of the network, as well as its expansion, are required.

Taking into account, that one number costs about 1000 dollars, fulfillment of the above listed problems requires large capital expenditures. One of the main sources for these capital expenditures is, as mentioned above, telecommunications enterprises' retained earnings, which require an appropriate level of tariffs.

The tariffs for services of international communications are determined in view of ITU recommendations by the Ministry of Communications of the Russian Federation and are uniform for all operators within the territory of Russia. The list of adjustable services with preservation of two-level regulation (Federal and regional) is also determined. The accounts for telecommunications services not included in this list, are made at free- market prices.

Since 1996 the tariff policy has focused on ensuring uniform tariffs for different consumer groups. Tariffs for the public should be increased to cover at least the cost of the services. As the economy stabilizes and the standard of living of the population increases, the tariffs level should provide the necessary minimum profit. Prompt payment for telecoms services is also starting to be enforced. The State administrative body for the regulation of natural monopolies in the communications branch will also be engaged in the regulation of tariffs on separate services.

Whilst telecom operators can only operate subject to a license, which is supplied by the Ministry of Communications of Russia and supervised by "Gossvjasnadzor", tariffs are established independently by private operators, and the accounts are conducted proceeding from the size of the settlement rate, which is stipulated by the special conditions of the license.

The main directives on telecommunications services' ratings found reflection in Decree No. 793 of the Russian Federation Government of August 7, 1996, which aimed at increasing the base level of adjustable tariffs faced by residential customers and budget organizations and adopted a step-by-step approach to achieve uniform tariffs for different consumer categories.

These directives are also incorporated into the telecommunications services' tariff regulation mechanism which has the following aims:

- Establish tariffs with regard to the already formed basic level and to conduct quarterly indexation;
- Calculate indices for each group of consumers individually, proceeding from the achieved basic level of tariffs and the accepted rating conditions;
- In cases of low tariff levels apply an indexation factor in order to ensure step-by-step increases in the basic level of the tariffs (up to cost), approaching them in similarity for different consumer categories and reducing cross-subsidization (granting) of unprofitable services at the expense of high profitability.

Given these aims, the additional accounting of expenditures in sub-branches, dividing them roughly into main services adjustable at Federal and regional levels, will be introduced. Such a division of expenditures according to the kind of service is difficult and currently premature. From January 1, 1996 State statistical reporting by private operators on the international telecommunications services was introduced.

The offered mechanism will allow the current tarrifs to be put in good order, and approach a level at which it will be possible to apply generally accepted methods of pricing and regulation.

The policy of tariff regulation should also provide identity to actions of the regulating bodies of the various States. It should balance the development of regional communication and increase its quality. The State regulation of natural monopolies has three main features: presence of State regulation at the level of local administrations, the necessity of taking the social importance of services into account and the necessity of informing regulatory bodies of the activities of operators with the purpose of timely attraction of additional investments. Unfounded low tariffs for the majority of public services and an accordingly higher degree of cross-subsidizing between separate services and branches of telecommunications exists on the Russian telecommunications market. However it is not permitted to raise tariffs too high where there are operators granting international and local communication; first of all it is necessary to make local telecommunications profitable, i.e. the local operator should also render international services and then create competition for “Rostelecom” at the international level. "Cross-subsidization" (i.e. when the additional profits from one branch are used for the artificial reduction of prices in another) means infringement of the competition mode, because one branch is taxed with high tariffs in comparison with the real cost, while another receives subsidies. In view of the large price disproportions, competition in this area is also limited.

One of the most important indications of pricing system rationality is the balance of the prices structure (tariffs) on separate kinds of services, depending on their consumer properties and value, degree of interchangeability and availability, level of demand satisfaction and the incomes of the consumers, nomenclature and production and realization volume.

The problem of balancing tariffs is topical and timely for the telecommunications branch, granting a multi-nomenclature spectrum of services, conventional, as well as new ones, many of which are interchangeable and mutually supplementary. The degree of satisfaction of public and personal requirements in particular kinds of services, and consequently the opportunity for their further industrial and social development depends on finding the correct solution to this problem.

Special tariff baskets are used for evaluation of the consumption balance of various kinds of telecommunications services and the rationality of their rating system. These tarriff baskets are integrated settlement indexes, which characterize the structure and volume of consumers' expenditure on telephone communications services. They are the sum of lump-sum payment for installation and relatively constant subscriber payment for local telephone communications, as well as payment for trunk and international telephone conversations, which depends on distance and the durations of the channel occupation and are accordingly divided into two groups: fixed payment and payment for use.

Comparison of the tariff baskets for different regions of the country permits not only the evaluation of distinctions in the tariffs for telephone communication services, but also to reveal the unbalance among their separate components, and use of this data for optimization of the tariffs structure (Tab. I4).

Listed in Tab. I4, data of the tariff baskets cost account for the population of some regions of the country testifies to a significant territorial differentiation of the total sum of consumer expenses on payment for telephone communication services: the maximum cost of a basket (Republic of Udmurtia) is about 2.4 times as large as its minimum level (Tula oblast). It means that the identical volume of services to the population of Tula comes out 2.4 times cheaper than to inhabitants of Udmurtia. The lowest cost of the basket of conversations and services was (alongside with Tula oblast) in Nizhni Novgorod and Tambov oblasts - from 8 up to 10 ths roubles a month for the whole complex of telephone services.

But even in those regions, where the basket is rather "heavy" (Republic of Udmurtia, Krasnoyarsk Territory, Republic of Karelia), its "weight" in account for a month (about 17-20 ths roubles) is nevertheless insignificant in the cumulative family budget and certainly does not correspond to that consumer effect which gives telecommunication services to the subscribers.

In the majority of surveyed regions the main part of the cost of tariff baskets is the payment for usage, i.e. payment for trunk and international telephone communication services. For Russia, with its low level of development of local telephone communication networks, the most rational is the tariff basket with a large specific weight of fixed payment, the increase of which will allow in the shorter term the repayment of the expenses of the levied tariffs on the investment for creation of new capacities for UTN and RTN.

But today, because of the influence of the local regulating bodies, the tariffs for local telephone communications services for the population and State budget organizations are so low, that the repayment term of the costs of putting ATX into operation at the expense of amortization is extended for decades.

Thus, analysis of tariff baskets for the population of Russia shows their overly low cost and the unbalance of the constant and the variable components.

Similar disproportions are seen in baskets for the self-supporting organizations. The average cost of a tariff basket for these subscribers is almost 10 times more than the total sum of expenses of the population for payment for telephone communications services (Tab. I5).

Tab. I4: Tariff Baskets for Population

Region (republic, krai, oblast)	Tariff baskets for population in 1994, ths roubles			Specific weight of tariff basket	
	Fixed payment	Payment for usage	Total sum	Fixed payment	Payment for usage
Tula oblast	46.0	55.4	101.4	45.4	54.6
Nizhni Novgorod oblast	62.0	46.1	108.1	57.4	42.6
Tambov oblast	53.0	61.2	114.2	46.7	53.3
Smolensk oblast	39.0	97.4	136.4	28.6	71.4
Republic of North Osetia	45	92.8	137.8	32.7	67.3
Lipetsk oblast	41.0	100.5	141.5	29.0	71.0
Republic of Mordovia	94.5	49.8	144.3	62.4	37.6
Vologda oblast	74.0	85.1	159.1	46.5	53.5
Kaluga oblast	70.1	89.3	159.4	43.9	56.1
Ivanovo oblast	62.0	106.1	168.1	36.9	63.1
Ryazan oblast	55.0	112.7	167.7	32.8	67.2
Sverdlovsk oblast	84.0	92.0	176.0	47.7	52.3
Samara oblast	73.0	120.3	193.3	37.8	62.2
Karachaevo-Cherkesskaya Republic	66.0	130.8	196.8	33.5	66.2
Krasnodar Territory	105.0	95.9	200.9	52.3	47.7
Republic of Karelia	74.0	143.3	217.3	34.0	66.0
Republic of Udmurtia	80.0	158.9	238.9	33.5	66.5
Average meanings	63.0	96.3	159.3	39.5	60.5

If we take into account that the overwhelming majority of urban and rural telephone communication subscribers is the general population, whose contribution to the incomes of trunk telephone communications constitutes up to 32%, it becomes clear why the existing system of services rating does not permit investors to fully realize programs for development of regional telecommunications facilities, and more completely satisfy the existing demand for services.

The current system of rating is characterized by a huge unbalance in tariffs for telephone communication services for the population and for self-supporting enterprises, which has a negative effect on the financial condition of communications operators, as well as on the level of satisfaction of requirements for telecommunications services.

Tab. I5: Tariff Baskets for Self-Supporting Subscribers

Region (republic, oblast)	Tariff baskets for self-supporting subscribers in 1994, ths roubles			Specific weight of tariff basket	
	Fixed payment	**Payment for usage**	**Total sum**	**Fixed payment**	**Payment for usage**
Tula oblast	312.0	482.5	794.5	39.3	60.7
Ivanovo oblast	420.0	464.0	884.0	47.5	52.5
Republic of Mordovia	480.0	501.5	981.5	48.9	51.1
Sverdlovsk oblast	420.0	696.4	1116.4	37.6	62.4
Smolensk oblast	270.0	901.5	1171.5	23.0	77.0
Republic of North Osetia	300.0	940.2	1240.2	24.2	75.8
Tambov oblast	560.0	753.9	1313.9	42.6	57.4
Samara oblast	410.0	1007.4	1417.4	28.9	71.1
Nizhni Novgorod oblast	500.0	928.9	1428.9	35.0	65.0
Republic of Udmurtia	600.0	855.3	1455.3	41.2	58.8
Karachaevo-Cherkesskaya Republic	474.0	1090.3	1564.3	30.0	69.7
Kaluga oblast	444.0	1121.7	1565.7	28.4	71.6
Vologda oblast	500.0	1092.3	1592.3	31.4	68.6
Lipetsk oblast	600.0	1141.7	1741.7	34.4	65.6
Krasnoyarsk Territory	609.6	1196.4	1806.0	33.7	66.3
Republic of Karelia	1100.0	1286.7	2386.7	46.1	53.9
Ryazan oblast	780.0	1908.5	2688.5	29.0	71.0
Average meanings	510.0	948.3	1468.3	34.8	65.2

In OECD countries the difference between costs of tariff baskets for private commercial subscribers also exists. But the baskets for the two groups of users differ in average not more than twice, whereas the tariff basket for self-supporting enterprises in Russia comprises approximately half of the average tariff basket in OECD countries and for the population only one sixth (see Fig. I3).

Analysis of the current tariff baskets permits comparison at regional and international levels between the costs for all telephone services in aggregate, evaluation of tariff structure , and determination of major directions for pricing perfection in the regional, as well as in the branch aspect.

Fig. 13: Comparison of Tariff Baskets in Russia and OECD in 1994

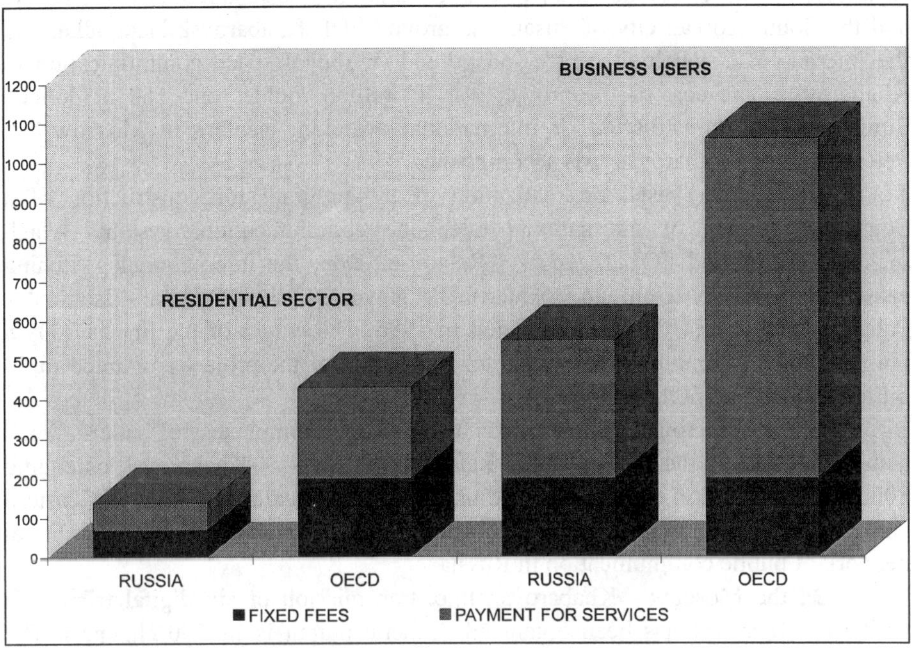

4. Direct Foreign Investments in Development of the Communications Branch

The Russian communications services market has involved foreign partners for a long time, however only with the change of political climate has the foreign capital gained the opportunity to participate in realization of the Russian projects for communications development as a source of investments or as a participant in projects realization. Most of the attention of the foreign partners is involved in highly profitable technologies and realization of projects, directed at development of trunk and international telephone communications systems. Except for large-scale investments into joint large-scale projects, the foreign capital participates in investments in the form of credits for particular local projects. One of the first projects, realized together with foreign investors, was the creation of a modern digital system of international communications Russia-Denmark (Western complex), which was put into operation in April 1993. Expenditure for realization of the project amounted to 500 m roubles and 123 m dollars. The project investors were the joint-stock company "Rostelecom" and the foreign companies Telecom Denmark, Grey Nordik (Denmark) and US West (USA).

In February of 1995 the East complex was opened in Khabarovsk. The basis of the complex is comprised of fiber optic links (FOL) laid at the bottom of the Japanese sea between Nakhodka (Russian Federation), the Japanese city of Naoetsu and the South Korean city of Pusan, the ground FOL Khabarovsk-Nakhodka, and the international switching center and ground station of space communication in Khabarovsk. The cost of the project was 43 billion roubles and 160 m dollars. Simultaneously, construction of international switching centers in Moscow, St. Petersburg and Khabarovsk was accomplished.

The Project based on realization of the program for construction of a Southern complex of international telephone communications systems which includes the ground FOL Moscow - Rostov-on-Don, the international switching center in Rostov-on-Don, underwater FOL Novorossiysk - Odessa - Istanbul - Palermo (Project ITUR) was completed in 1996. The extent of the line is 3539.8 km. The total volume of investments for realization of the project amounted to 70 billion roubles and 50 m dollars.

The connecting link between these three complexes of international communications is the Digital Radio Relay Line Moscow - Khabarovsk extending 8000 km. Its creation has allowed the uniting of all three areas - western, eastern and southern in a uniform network, forming the basis of a prospective digital network of public communication in Russia.

On the Moscow - Khabarovsk line, transmission of six digital tributaries with 155 Mbps rate has been organized. General output is 11 500 channels. The equipment is delivered by a trading house (Japan) and the Siemens company (Germany). In March 1996 International Switching Centers in Samara, Ekaterinburg and Novosibirsk, the construction of which was executed on the basis of electronic switching equipment EWSD from the Siemens company, were put into operation. The capacity of Samara Center equipment is 10,320 channels, including 2160 international channels, in Ekaterinburg it is 3480, in Novosibirsk 7200 and 1620 accordingly. The realization of these projects provides enough international channels for the Russian public communications network.

The profitability of telephone networks averages 30-36%, though some separate telephone networks, located in geographically advantageous conditions and with a large density of population zones, have profitability of up to 50%, because the tariff policy does not permit the exceeding of these limits. In order to create a normal digital telephone network, to modernize and to reconstruct linear structures and telephone exchanges, time and resources are necessary. In the experts evaluation they can be put into civilized order in 7-10 years. The cost of replacement of all telephone structures with modern ones will amount from 200 to 220 billion dollars.

Last year the communications companies and firms managed to input more than 750 m dollars in investments and credits without governmental warranties. A significant volume of the foreign investments are put into quickly and effectively developing networks of mobile communication. The networks of public mobile radio communication in Russia are conditionally divided into Federal and regional networks, allowing operation of a more flexible technical policy. Federal refer networks, uniform for the whole country, guarantee their subscribers a supply of services in all service zones irrespective of territory. The regional networks are called on to solve the problems of communications organization with due attention to local features and they should be organically merged into the regional infrastructure.

By the end of 1996, the number of cellular communication networks subscribers in Russia amounted to 209,400, 88,526 of which are subscribers to communications networks. The networks of mobile communications now cover 60 regions of the country, basically krai and oblast centers and capitals of the Federation States.

The evaluation of the rate of development of cellular communications in Russia is possible with the help of following figures: networks of GSM standard are operating in 11 regions and serve 48,200 subscribers; accordingly for NMT-450 standard - 45 regions and 64,200 subscribers, and for modifications of the AMPS standard - 37 regions and 97,000 subscribers. The growth of the number of cellular subscribers in 1996 in comparison with the end of 1995 looks in percentages as follows: for GSM - 372%, for NMT-450 - 155%, for technology AMPS - 283%.

Interaction with international organizations in the area of public mobile radio telephone communications provides our operators of Federal mobile cellular communication networks of NMT-450 and GSM-900 systems with the opportunity to operate under generally accepted international norms, to use experience of countries that successfully introduced this convenient and commercially profitable service long ago. Due to a uniform policy of organization of these networks, the possibility of "roaming" is provided for customers of NMT or GSM networks, irrespective of their residency, on the territory of any operator country, if this operator is a member of the appropriate international bodies.

In Russia, 5 standards of mobile communications are used in all. Evaluation of the rate of development of cellular communications in Russia is possible with the help of data shown in Fig. I4.

Creation of trunk and paging systems of mobile communication in Russia is progressing in a peculiarly "Russian fashion" - beginning from one fragment of minimal configuration. Further development proceeds with a considerable lagging behind demand. The main object is to minimize primary investment and to "squeeze out maximum from minimum". Transition to the next stage is carried out under serious pressure from the communications services users and conjuncture on the market.

Fig. I4: Mobile Network Subscribers Growth

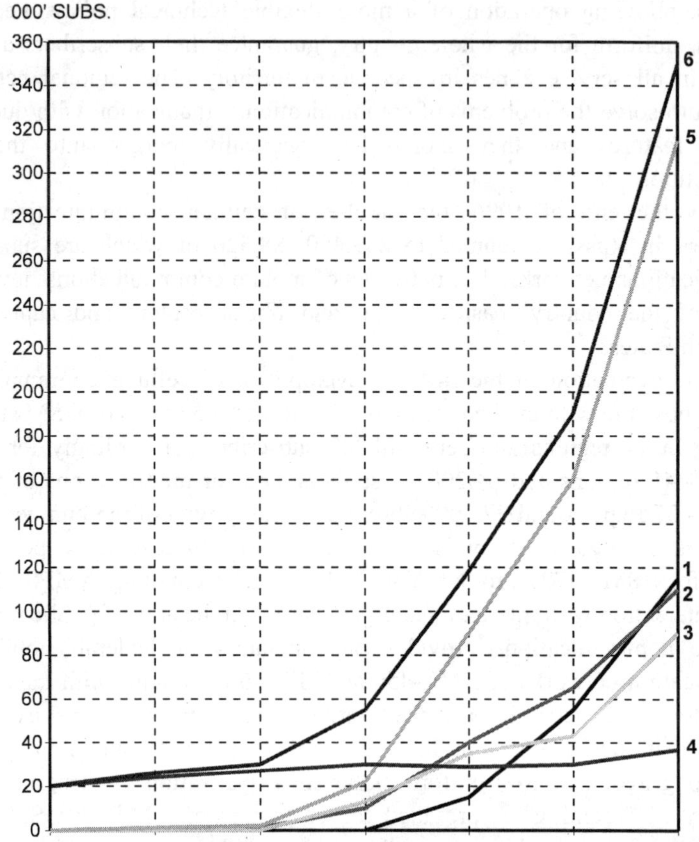

1 Number of subscribers of standard GSM cellular networks
2 Number of subscribers of standard NMT cellular networks
3 Number of subscribers of standard AMPS cellular networks
4 Number of subscribers of "ALTAY" and other types of networks
5 Number of cellular network subscribers
6 Total number of mobile communication networks subscribers

For the systems being considered, the whole infrastructure providing guaranteed radio coverage is formed at best over 3 years. At the end of each year total recoupment of investment is reached with the proviso that the average aggressive marketing policy is used. The basic merit of this approach is that financial resources necessary for creation of trunk and paging are 4-7 times smaller. Therefore not only are the expenses considerably less, but also the risks.

The growth of foreign investment is continuing. The total volume of investments in the first half of 1996 in comparison with the previous year increased by 1.5 times, and by the end of the year by nearly 4 times, therefore a real investment boom is occurring at present. For the time being, the foreign investment into local communications is insufficient. In Russia the home telephone recoupment period is reached on an average in 15 years, and in some regions even 21 years. This sector of our branch is evidently not so attractive to foreign partners yet.

True, at the beginning of 1997 the foreign companies began to show special activity in the so named "small business" sector, participating as communications operators together with the Russian enterprises which received licenses from the Ministry of Communication. Such joint ventures, which were organized and are currently operating in many cities of Russia, are assisting in the development of local communications networks to a considerable extent.

Fig. I5: Changes in Foreign Investment Structure

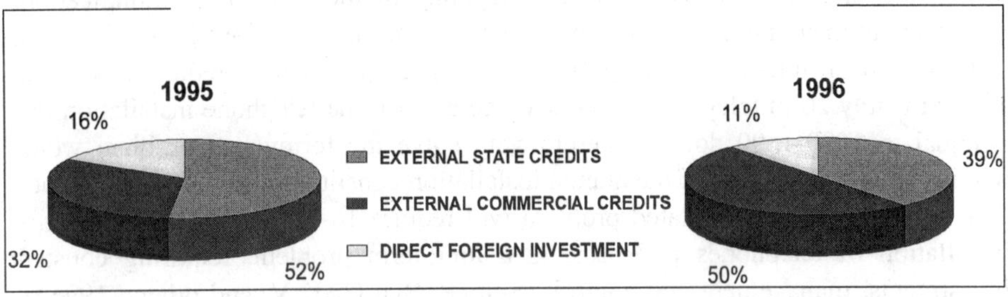

Cooperation with foreign companies supplying equipment on the communications facilities market, is constructed on the basis of choice of the forms of payment for this equipment (barter, delivery on credit with payment at the expense of profit from the equipment usage, leasing, participation of the foreign supplier as a shareholder in activities of the enterprise with authorized contributions to the amount of the prime cost of equipment, preliminary sale to the potential consumers of communications services, who appear due to construction of the given object of communication). Foreign investment structure changes are shown in Fig. I5.

Most actively operating as providers of communications services in the country are the well-known foreign companies - manufacturers of telecommunications equipment such as AT&T, Siemens, Itatel, Alcatel, Motorola, Ericsson, NEC, Samsung and others. One more direction of foreign partners activity is their participation in creation of joint ventures for production of communications facilities on Russian territory (for example, the Russian-Belgian enterprise

"Lenbell" with Alcatel in St. Petersburg, the Russian-Korean enterprise "Samsung-Crosna" in Moscow, the Russian-German enterprise "Izhtel" with Siemens and other companies).

The international communications enterprises can conclude independent operator agreements on the operation of objects and development of services, supplied to customers. Bilateral cooperation raises questions of frequency allocation; licensing of operator activity; coordination of plans of mutual interest; development of international objects of communication; carrying out consultations; exchange of legislative acts and experience.

The normative-legal base for all aspects of bilateral cooperation are the agreements on cooperation at all three levels: inter-governmental, inter-departmental and operators'.

5. Prospects for Telecommunications Development in Russia

The level of communications development in Russia is characterized by a telephone density that is equal to 18 m, in Russia there are serious problems with telephone installation and with the approach of telephony to the level of communications development in countries with advanced economies. There are now 25 m telephones in Russia. If an intermediate stage is aimed for, then it will be required to install approximately 20 m telephones. The average cost of one telephone installation that is equal to 1000-1500 dollars, therefore, to solve the formulated problem would require 30 billion dollars. If the annual installation constitutes 2,0-3,0 m telephones, then solution of the formulated problem will require 10-12 years. This means that installation of telephones in Russia is a long-term problem, requiring constant investments, management and control. (Source: BULGAK V. and others, 1995, p. 127-138. Research Materials, 1996, No. 6, p. 9-12).

In the development of communications in Russia a paradox is springing up, As is characteristic for all countries with an average level of telephone installation, in order to supply communications services to a wide strata of the population there is a need to conduct telephone installation. However the evolutionary character of this process does not allow provision of an accelerated development of communications and especially the fast entry of Russia into the global information infrastructure.

The process of communications development in Russia corresponds to a transitive economic period, when the role of persons, groups and associations concerned with the market economy (so named "business-groups") becomes stronger. For these groups fast and volumetric information, modern communications services and data obtained from powerful computers and complexes, are necessary. The process of supplying such services can be called telecomputerization which is necessary for the division of two concepts, designating processes, occurring simultaneously with each other -telephone installation throughout Russia and telecomputerization of the country.

The process of telephone installation in the country occurs evolutionarily, by a steady process of new telephone installation, which permits supply over telephone channels, telephone and non-telephone services to all possible subscribers under moderate tariffs. Exchange of facsimile messages, data and files between personal computers are intended under non-telephone services.

Fig. I6: Development of Local Telephone Communication in Russia

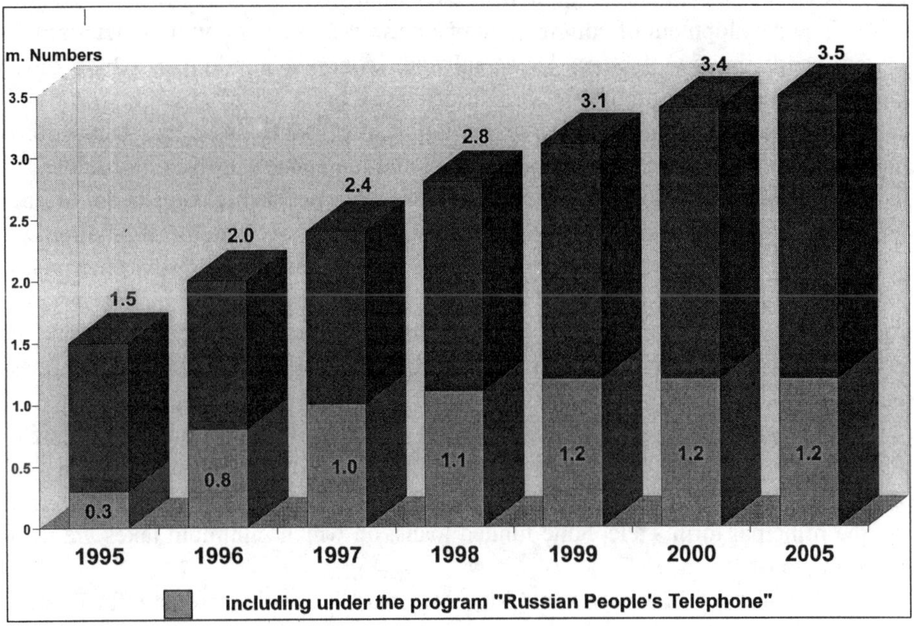

The process of telecomputerization occurs relatively quickly and on account of a narrow circle of subscribers, who under the high tariffs are supplied with services of ISDN, B-ISDN, multimedia etc.

Thus in Russia, development of communications occurs pursuant to the real processes: installation of telephones for all subscribers under moderate tariffs and telecomputerization for business groups under high tariffs.

As far as solving the problem of telephone installation and telecomputerization in large cities is concerned, communications operators in Russia are basically using imported digital exchanges. The problems of telephone installation in small and medium cities are not solved so quickly, primarily because of the shortage of finance .

By 2005, the population of Russia will be approximately 148 m; 69 m of these, that is 47%, will live in the provinces. 30 m or 20 % will be in small towns and settlements, and 39 m or 27% in rural areas. From today's position, the level of telephone density in Russia must be on average 45 telephone sets per 100 inhabitants, therefore the total number of telephones should reach 62 m. It is supposed that from the total number of telephone sets, 52.5 m will be installed in cities and 9.5 m in rural areas (data on development of telephone communications in Russia are shown in Fig. I6). For installation of the telephones in Russian provinces, it is necessary to install and to modernize 28 m numbers.

The development of communications networks in Russia will be determined predominantly by two factors: by social and economic conditions, which have appeared in the country, and by its geopolitical position.

One of the major directions of development of the Russian communications market is the realization of the "Russian national telephone" program, which has a distinct social orientation and should address two problems: expansion of the opportunities for supplying telephone communications services to the population, as well as saving and modernization of working places in domestic industry enterprises under conversion. With this purpose a "Federal Complex Program for Creation of Communications, TV and Radio Broadcasting Facilities" was developed, and it received the status of a Presidential Program in May 1996. This program defines scientific and technology policy and directions of industrial activities.

Lately companies have used three forms of attraction of potential subscribers' money: the contractual form (applied in Voronezh oblast), the form of a certificate, obtained by a citizen who has paid money (in Nizhni Novgorod oblast), and the principal form - telephone funded loans, on which minimum taxes are paid (in Perm oblast).

The situation in Moscow and Moscow oblast is not characteristic for Russia. As a whole the rate of development of the capital's telephone network is much more, than that across Russia, and besides, there is the belief that even further acceleration will take place. Beginning from 1996, the Moscow Urban Telephone Network (MUTN) will direct its main resources not into expansion of the network, but into its reconstruction.

At the base of the new network structure, lies a fiber optical ring (with output of 1 m channels), which will connect the new equipment to be installed (also 1 m channels). The first stage of this program is the "Gold bullet" project, which is being realized by AT&T, "Rostelecom" and Telmos, together with the Moscow Urban Telephone Network. This project, which costs 200 m dollars, assumes the introduction of 400 ths numbers.Problems of radio communication common worldwide, such as compatibility of technologies and standards, are aggravated by our national problems: by necessity of conversion of frequency spectrum and the need to bring it into line with the requirements of the International Radio Regulations. The complexities of maintenance of special purpose communications equipment operation in other frequency bands will remain for a long time yet, and in practice it means significant problems connected not only with competition in the area of cellular network communication because of appearance of new operators using already functioning standards, but also in achievement of the efficient operation of the networks in action.

Production of urban ATX of large capacity and trunk exchanges remains a problem. In order to solve this problem foreign companies, possessing great experience in development and industrial production of such equipment, are attracted and joint ventures are created, such as those with Alcatel Bell, Siemens and others.

Another problem is manufacture of transmission systems for trunk communication lines. Realization of domestic development is leading into serious financial and technical difficulties, which are caused mainly by absence of the necessary component base. In this area interaction with foreign partners is also assumed to be a leading direction.

In the area of space communication, the main efforts are directed at creation of a series of inexpensive, compact ground stations of new generation, operating with the satellites "Express", "Gals", "Mayak" and "Arcos". Work on expansion of the functional possibilities of satellite communications stations - "Koradis" is proceeding. For these stations together with the Bosch company, an effective solid-state transmitter of 16 W power with a low noise level was developed, which has considerably increased the operating characteristics of the station. Such transmitters are delivered to Germany for completing the VSAT stations.

In the area of mobile radio telephone communications, modernization of radial-zonal systems structure based on the "Volemot" radio stations (Voronezh Research Institute of Communications) is carried out; negotiations with the American company QUALCOMM and other companies on cooperation in this area are also underway.

The question of the degree of participation by foreign companies in supplying our country with telecommunications equipment is being constantly discussed in the circles of producers and communications operators. As to our opinion, we believe it is expedient to expand the framework of cooperation with the leading foreign companies primarily in the following directions:

- creation of facilities and systems for public mobile radio communication and primarily to GSM-900 and CDMA standards;
- creation of 155, 622 Mbps and 2.5 Gbps fiber-optic transmission systems of synchronous digital hierarchy;

- manufacture of digital modems for 1.2-64 kbps transmission systems networks;
- creation of ground satellite communications stations, separate assemblies and units for them.

The concept of the development of the "Communications" branch envisages its step-by-step integration into the international communications system. This requires putting the legislation on communications and the technical bases of construction of a mutually coordinated communications network in Russia in conformity with the existing international legislation and tendencies of telecommunication systems development.

Highly developed countries are now in a stage of transition to the post-industrial phase of development - The information society in which the most important role is played by the communications infrastructure. This process has an objective character and it stands out for a series of characteristic tendencies, rendering a decisive effect on prospects of development of the communications industry and stimulating processes in the area of modern information technologies. The following are primarily related to them:

- Formation of the European Union, being a result of centripetal tendencies in the economic development of Europe;
- Evolution of market relations in the direction of creation of more fair conditions of competition on an international scale;
- Granting of non-discriminatory access to various information resources and services of different forms and content.

A number of organizations and institutes determining policy in the area of telecommunications have been formed in Europe. The problem faced by these organizations is the creation of a uniform normative-legal space, taking into account the tendencies, as well as modern achievements in the area of telecommunication technologies (ISDN, ATM, mobile and personal communication, intellectual communications networks and others).

In Russia it has turned out historically, that the international network is constructed upon heterogeneous communications facilities, which include Radio Relay, cable lines and satellite channels. From 1.2 billion toll calls in a year only about 60% are crowned with real connection.

A special place in the development of the Russian communications network is occupied by the valuation of the systems projects of Russian segments of the international systems Iridium and Globalstar, being created by American companies. Usage of these systems will promote the development of Russian telecommunications pursuant to the accepted ideology of a mutually coordinated complex of telecommunications in Russia and its consecutive entrance into the global information structure. However at present there is no normative-legal base in Russia for international cooperation in creation and operation of such global satellite systems of mobile communication. In order to realize the operator functions for supplying services of this system in Russian territory, a Russian company "Iridium-Europe-Asia" has been created by the closed joint-stock company "Zond-Svyaz" and the State Scientific and Production Association named after Chrunichev. Under the “Rostelecom” proposal the question of a joint venture and creation of JSC Rostelecom-Globaltelecom is now being addressed.

Increasing attention is now being given to the problem of international roaming organization. Due to the close cooperation of "Moscow cellular communication" with the independent regional operators, which are actively formatting a uniform "cellular space" of NMT-450 standard within the framework of the Russian Federal cellular network, a system of "National roaming" is being developed. For the purpose of achieving accessibility of mobile telephones, a planned policy of decreasing the prices on all kinds of services is being carried out. Such measures directly influence the growth of the number of subscribers to this network. If in 1992 it was 6,000, by the end of 1996 it was already 209,400. At present there is a rapid development of paging communication.

But there are several restraining factors not only of a technological character, but also due to the imperfect pay-phone system in the country. The owner of a pager, located outside of the telephone service zone, having received a call, has a unique opportunity to establish a bilateral telephone communication, dialing the subscriber number with the help of a pay-phone. However even in Moscow the real quantity of such phones is less than 1%, which is more than twice less than normal.

The perspective of paging network development is bound up with the introduction of two new high-speed protocols - ERMES and FLEX. The FLEX protocol contains a whole family of protocols, providing a wide selection of services such as InFLEXION - a protocol providing voice and message transmission and ReFLEX - a protocol that permits sending from a pager a short radio message confirming reception of information.

One of the problems of increasing the quality of the functioning of the Russian telecommunications complex, is the creation of a securities market for Russian communications companies, with a shares turnover on the international exchanges, which will allow involvement of investment in development of telecommunications by market economy methods. Realization of such work is possible only with participation of the largest international companies, specializing in audit, consulting and other similar services. Such a precedent already exists: in 1996 the "Vympelcom" company appeared on the American securities market with ADR bonds of 3-rd level (the highest in this hierarchy).

Such are some of main directions in realization of particular projects of telecommunications networks and systems creation in Russia.

6. Conclusion

At present, the main avenues of mutually coordinated communications network development in Russia are: automation, optimization and increase of networks operation stability. Taking into account the low provision of telephones and other communications facilities, one of the major directions of development of the telecommunication services in Russia is the quantitative growth of the networks. If we refer to the investment policy, it is aimed at the utmost attraction of investments to the "Communications" complex from domestic, as well as foreign investors. It is accomplished in various forms: joint ventures, joint-stock companies, issue of securities, short-term and long-term credits.

The abundance of operators in the most profitable sectors of the Russian telecommunications market creates a competitive environment. In an effort to regulate the operator's work "Rules for operator work" were issued. Responsibility for fulfilment of these rules, and license issue is placed on "Gossvjaznadzor". The competition among operators is aimed at improvement of the service quality and reduction of its cost.

The in-house communications sector and installation of telephones in the cities and rural areas develops under conditions of state regulation of the natural monopolies according to its legislation. The policy in respect to the natural monopolies is enacted by the Federal Service of Regulation of Natural Monopolies in the Area of Telecommunications, created in April 1996 and by the Anti-monopoly Committee.

With the purpose of increasing investment opportunities for communications enterprises, measures for revaluation of fixed capital based on the increase of norms for depreciation charges for complete restoration networks are being carried out.

The prime problems of development of the communications complex in the country are: perfection and completion of the tariff policy; increase of investments into development of those or other kinds of communication, and primarily, into development of local telephone communication.

In the regions of Russia, the problem of introduction of payment by time is being solved, and such payment will be introduced gradually with due consideration of various factors, such as geographical, as well as psychological.

The Administration of the communications branch of Russia participates in all main measures, being conducted in Europe and worldwide, directed at definition of the prospects for telecommunications development. This activity will allow choice of those technologies, which in view of the interests of domestic subscribers and the condition of the national communications networks, will help Russia to enter the international telecommunications space within the foreseeable future. Besides this, Russia has the opportunity to become the largest country involved in transit telephone communications between Western Europe, Japan, Korea, China and other Eastern countries. But it will require significant investments into the development of fiber-optical communication lines and creation of favorable investments and a competitive environment.

References

ALL-RUSSIAN RESEARCH INSTITUTE OF CONJUNCTURE RUSSIA (1996), Foreign Trade, issue 1-4, Moscow.

BUSINESS FORUM OF MOBILE SYSTEMS (1997), Materials of the International Conference "The Lines of Development and New Technologies of Mobile Communications in Russia and CIS", Moscow.

BULGAK V.B., L. E.VARAKIN, J. K. IVASHKEVICH, V. D. MOSKVITIN, V. G. OSIPOV (1995), Radio and Communication, Concept of the Development of Communications in the Russian Federation.

CENTER OF ECONOMIC CONJUNCTURE IN THE RUSSIAN FEDERATION GOVERNMENT (1997), Russia - 1996: Economic Situation, No. 1, 2, Moscow.

COMMUNICATIONS ADMINISTRATIONS (1995), Statistical Collection on Activities:1993-1995.

DEPARTMENT OF CONSUMER'S MARKET AND SERVICES OF THE RUSSIAN FEDERATION GOVERNMENT (1996), Trade, issue 1-4, Moscow.

EXPERT INSTITUTE "RUSSIA", CENTER ON STUDYING RUSSIA AND EASTERN EUROPE, BIRMINGHAM UNIVERSITY (1996), Analysis of Regional Development Trends in 1992-1995, Moscow.

GOSCOMSTAT OF THE RUSSIAN FEDERATION (1996), Moscow Social and Economic Situation in Russia: January-December 1996.

INTERNATIONAL COMMUNICATION ACADEMY FORUM (1997), Collection of Reports on the "Development of Communications and World. Forecasts, Technologies and Services"; Moscow.

MINISTRY OF POST AND TELECOMMUNICATION OF RUSSIAN FEDERATION (1993), Concept of the Russian Federation Program in the Area of Communication.

MINISTRY OF POST AND TELECOMMUNICATIONS OF THE RUSSIAN FEDERATION (1994), Memorandum on Understanding Main Principles of

Cooperation in Development of Networks and Facilities of Communication on Russian Federation Territory.

MINISTRY OF POST AND TELECOMMUNICATIONS OF THE RUSSIAN FEDERATION (1996), Materials of the Press Office 1995-1996.

MINISTRY OF POST AND TELECOMMUNICATIONS (1996), Materials of the Press Centre of the Russian Federation, Informpress, Moscow.

STATE DUMA (1995), Federal Law "On Communications in the Russian Federation" accepted January 20.

SVJAZINFORM (1995), Program for the Demonopolization of Communications.

Comments on: Regulation of the Telecommunication Sector in Russia: Direct Foreign Investments and Options for Competition

Wolfgang Pfaffenberger

The telecommunication sector in Russia shows a dynamic development which distinguishes it from many other sectors of the economy. What is the role of the market, domestic actors, the role of the state and the role of foreign investors? This paper tries to describe a picture of the situation and the contribution of the various actors. After reading the paper, there are more questions than answers. In the transformation process in Russia, there certainly is a strong difference between formal rules laid down in new legislation and the behaviour of the actors in the newly developing market structures as well as the government agencies.

The paper contains a lot of information on fact and figures about the telecommunication markets, the newly emerging legislation and changes going on in this sector, this information is however organised in a way that makes it a bit difficult for the reader to comprehend the situation and come to conclusions. The reader would like to understand, what the driving forces are, what role formal rules play against informal structures. The questions remaining partly have to do with the way, in which this paper is organised. The headlines of chapters not always describe the content of a certain part of the paper. It would be easier to understand the interaction of regulation, demand driven change and supply conditions, if the paper had been organised in a quite conventional way, by describing the institutional framework laid down in legislation, describing the demand side by using adequate indicators, describing the supply side of the telecommunication markets with its various segments and describing the behaviour of suppliers.

In the paper, the demand side virtually doesn't exist, only from time to time we hear, that there is a shortage of communication equipment. In the former planned economy there was a shortage of everything because prices did not serve as indicators of scarcity. Shortage thus is relative to purchasing power, preferences etc. It would have been interesting to see how the demand and supply situation in Russia compares to others countries relative to GNP and other factors.

The reader would also have taken benefit, if the authors had made clear, from which point of view they are presenting their analysis. Sometimes, one gets the impression, that the paper is written from the point of view of a centrally planed economy, where regulation is not a necessary institutional set up to correct and direct market failures into a desired direction, but a general obligation of the state to be responsible for the development of the sector as a whole.

Whereas market failures are expected particularly in the natural monopoly part of the system, this clear distinction is not made in the paper, so that this general responsibility of the state looms in the background without being explained or defined. The government role could to some extent be derived from network externalities in this sector in a situation where only small fractions of the population can take part in the service of the telecommunication sector. This problem is not dealt with so that the issue remains unclear.

Economists in Russia and economists in the West do not speak the same language, yet there may be misunderstandings just coming from the role, which the authors have defined for themselves. The reader would like to know, what position the authors take, what recommendations they would like to give on particular aspects of development of regulation in Russia what steps they consider adequate in the process of transformation These questions are not dealt with in the paper, however, so that we are left with these questions.

J: Systemic Transformation and Direct Foreign Investment in Russia: Problems and Solution

Ruslan Grinberg

1. Market Reforms and Macroeconomic Stabilization in the Central and Eastern European Countries and Russia: Comparing Intermediate Results

After six years of market reforms in Central and Eastern Europe (CEE), their effectiveness is still subject to constant debate. The social and economic prospects of the region remain rather dim. Predictably, one school of analysts takes a rather negative view of the results of this unprecedented systemic transformation. Others, on the contrary, gravitate towards optimism. Both, however, have serious reasons for their opposing conclusions.

The position of the so called "negativists" is expressed in a concise form in a detailed monograph by A. Amsden, Y. Cohanovich, and L. TAYLOR (AMSDEN/COHANOVICH/TAYLOR, 1994). The authors judge the philosophy and the policies of reforms in all former socialist countries as inadequate in meeting the requirements of political, social, and economic modernization. However it is arguable whether this general assertion is justified. Yet the authors' interpretation of some intermediate results of the six years of the reform seem to be reasonable enough. They state, in particular, that a technological lag between the East and the West continues to expand. Catching up technologically with the West was, in fact, one of the main reasons for dismantling the system of directive planning. The development of market relationships in the CEE countries, has however, never brought about the much-needed re-industrialization, which is to be followed, it is generally believed, by the post-industrial age of information technology. On the contrary, a universal real threat to de-industrialization is emerging everywhere, as proven by a tendency towards a "primitivisation" of export, a decrease in the amount of high-technology equipment in the domestic industry, noticeable cuts to government support for research, culture and education, which private companies fail to compensate for, etc. In order to overcome their previous autarchy, the CEE economies have to specialize to a yet greater extent in primary and semi-finished products, thus throwing themselves back into the position of the West's poor relations - the place they used to occupy in the world economy prior to the 40-year "socialist intermezzo".

The optimists emphasize positive changes evident in the current social and economic situation in the CEE. Most of the CEE economies overcame transitional recession and have seen a pick-up in economic activity for several successive years.

This, as is known, presents a startling contrast with Russia and other CIS countries, where the ruling elites have had to postpone again and again the beginnings of real growth. In the meantime, growth is a reality in CEE countries, though the explanations and prognosis offered by optimists (growth will only accelerate) and pessimists (growth has a weak foundation and will soon cease) differ.

Without going into the details of the argument, we should point out a feature equally important and common to both views. This is steadiness of macroeconomic stabilization as a prerequisite for positive economic dynamics. This seemingly universal rule is in general proven by the official CEE statistics.

The steady decrease in the rate of inflation in the CEE economies speaks for itself. However, the consensus among scholars in transitional economies is confined to this point.

The influence of radical liberalism on transitional economies is still evident both in the explanatory (positivist) and prescriptive (normativist) aspects of the analysis. The radical liberals attribute the tendency of "advanced" economies to overcome high inflation primarily to consistent restrictive monetary policy, and secondly to consistent deregulation of the internal and external economy. Inconsistency in both areas explains the relative failure of Bulgaria and Romania in this respect. Ultimate results depend on the extent of monetary restrictions and state intervention in the process of systemic change. Classifications of transitional economies of various types , which are published from time to time, are all based on just these criteria. It appears that nations less fortunate in terms of macroeconomic stabilization than the Czech Republic, Poland, Hungary, and Slovakia, can still have equally good results. They need only to minimize the role of the government in the economy and tighten control over the increased money supply. Jeffery Sachs, for example, calls on the governments to ensure that reform "stay(s) within the limits of its *primary functions* until better times come for the government and the economy as a whole" (SACHS, 1994, p. 327). In this case he gives this advice to the Russian government but considers it to be universal for both fortunate and "unfortunate" countries. In the range of the government's primary functions he includes only monetary stability, an effective taxation system, and law enforcement, as well as "basic social support for unprotected groups of the population".

A. Aslund also speaks in the same de-etatist logic. He postulates in particular, that "during the period of transition to capitalism the capabilities of the State are limited. Limited to a greater extent than is usually realized..... The State administration is simply incapable of taking reasonable responsible decisions, except for a small number of occasional direct instructions, ensuing from the top leadership. That is why the only recommendation that can be justified is the minimization of the role of the State during the period of transition to capitalism" (ASLUND, 1994, p. 39.).

It is important to underline that the radical liberals' suggestion that the efficiency of the State machinery during a systemic overhaul decreases, can hardly be questioned. Nothing other could be expected after the collapse of the command-based organization of society in general and coordination of the economy in particular. State government designed solely for a command economy becomes poorly suited to the development of a market-type economy. Inadequate statistics, ideological disarray, inadequate training of State officials for work under the new conditions, the fall in their “official” incomes, and universal rampant corruption are the harsh realities facing post communist reformers everywhere. Under such conditions it is difficult for the government to estimate and control the costs connected to its activities.

Campaigning for a minimum governmental role - amid what may be termed as a “lack of system” - is not, however, merely succumbing to these challenges. It jeopardizes the entire process of post-communist economic and political modernization.

Amid systemic transformations, the *laissez-faire* approach alone is unlikely to help these economies. It would not do so even if their macroeconomic conditions had previously been adequate to the market principles of distribution of resources. Here we share the view of institutional structuralists. As known, this school of economic thought places a special emphasis on the role of governments in developing countries that try to catch up with the standards of the developed West through modernization (ADELMAN, 1991, p. 5.). What then can be said of the transitional economies where the behavior of firms, first of all big industrial enterprises - both State - owned and those formally turned into JSC - does not comply with the market rules?

The lessons of the post communist economies showed firstly, that once the command style of economic coordination is abolished, such enterprises immediately get a free rein, unbalanced however by adequate economic responsibility. Such a disproportion inevitably triggers a multitude of anomalies, primarily of inflatory nature. What Poland's ex-Premier Jan Bielecki refers to as paternalist motivation of “social engineering” institutions generates that peculiar type of inflation that monetary and fiscal policies alone could never subdue (BIELECKI, 1992).

Already here in the sphere of macroeconomic stabilization, a new type of government intervention rather than its abolition apparently became necessary. Secondly, soon after the beginning of the transformation, it has become evident that if we rely on *laissez-faire* alone, an inevitable systemic recession is accompanied by shrinkage of not only the “doomed” sectors, but also of potentially viable industries and investments connected with them. Instead of the much-desired restructuring on high-tech Western models, the CEE economies faced the previously mentioned danger of de-industrialization and long term depression in agriculture. It became clear that fending off such a danger implied the right balance between internal and external liberalization on the one hand, and moderate government intervention, on the other. This is taking into account the lack of further coherent theory adequately describing the unprecedented process of transition from a command economy to a market one in general and the role of macroeconomic stabilization in this process, in particular. Nevertheless, glimpses of success in some economies and failure in others warrant a few preliminary generalizations with respect to macroeconomic stability in the transitional systems.

On this point, as has already been mentioned above, there is broad consensus among transitologists which can be confined to the following thesis: "without controlled and managed inflation, successive systemic transformation stands no chance". But as they say "the devil lurks in details", in this case in the selection and application of particular inflation controls, namely such a policy, which results in - the consistent decrease in the price rise - should not obstruct the process of reforms or the revival of general economic activity.

This is how things stand in most of the CEE countries where the main instruments of an anti-inflation policy are firstly virtually identical; secondly, integral in nature and use complementary stabilisors; and thirdly, the application of which is based on the more or less even distribution of the cost of macroeconomic stabilization that thereby makes the whole anti-inflation policy socially acceptable.

The effectiveness of such policies therefore depends not on the degree of the government's monetary austerity, but rather its ability to control money supply in combination with *systematic regulation of some prices, individual incomes and the national currency exchange rate.* This is what orthodox monetarists actually overlook. Meanwhile, this is exactly what is happening in the Czech Republic, Hungary, Poland, Slovakia, and Slovenia. The governments in these countries take care to agree on regulatory measures in each of the four aspects. The result is durable stabilization. Modern literature on transitional economics largely describes the mechanics of monetary and fiscal policies, that is, emphasizes the first of the four aspects discussed above. Such authors either ignore the other three altogether or mention them in passing and treat them as secondary and unnecessary in curtailing runaway inflation. In the meantime, they are all at least *equivalent in importance.*

It is true, however, that the "advanced" countries were initially enthusiastic about a pure monetarism as a tool of macroeconomic stabilization. The Czech Republic, now lauded as all but the model transitional economy, presents an especially good case here. Its government was excessively liberal in agriculture at the very beginning of systemic transformation. No mechanism was provided for the sector to gradually adapt to new economic conditions. The resulting food price rise excessively restricted demand; leading in turn, to fewer orders and cuts in agricultural production. Monopolies in supplies, marketing, and agrotechnology, however, seized the opportunity that price liberalization offered to pass increasing costs on to the few remaining consumers.

The new problems called for a regulation of the food market. The government, to its credit, was quick to adjust its previous policy of non-interference in the free play of market forces. It developed a system of protective measures to regulate demand and supply on the food market. The central instrument of this regulation is the State Market Regulation Foundation. That body approves annual lists of agriculturals to be sold at controlled prices, places orders, processes, stores, transports and markets agricultural produce. Furthermore, the Foundation establishes the size and terms of restocking of supplies of agriculturals,their release on the domestic market, and potential export. It also advises the government on guaranteed price floors for agriculturals and food.

The government regulation of the agricultural market undoubtedly produces undesirable side effects, such as "a freeze" on the structure and volume of production. It also raises barriers to foreign trade. As a result, governments that consistently and permanently intervene in the agricultural sector should always review the extent and forms of regulation. The results of such stabilizatory intervention, however, are quite evident. The Czech market regulation foundation, which deliberately regulates certain agricultural prices, has appreciably slowed growth in the cost of living.

Price intervention is thus rather common in the post-communist economies under systemic transformation. Though prices depend essentially on the market situation, government regulation, though differing in severity, holds back the pressure of inflation. Such regulation protracts the rather harsh consequences of radical liberalization of the economy and foreign trade over a longer period of time. It is important to keep in mind, however, that price controls have almost no effect in isolation. Government intervention in pricing, intended to hold down inflation and yet not block systemic transformations, only works in conjunction with other anti-inflation mechanisms, the first of these - *centralized income regulations.*

It should be stressed that even in long-established, developed market economies there is always a risk that either prices or wages, which may rise for various reasons, may trigger a price-wage race. Such risk is immeasurably greater in transitional economies where civil mechanisms for reconciliation of intrinsically conflicting employer and employee interests are only in the process of formation. In the absence of a strong class of sovereign entrepreneurs and an effective labor market, no one but the government is interested in social concord on restriction of growth in income, beyond the physical ability to dispose of it. Therefore, the durability of macroeconornic stabilization depends, from the very beginning, on government ability and will to strike the right balance between intervention and liberalism in income policy. Moreover, governments must also be able to apply such a new configuration, which is especially important in the Russian context. Therefore, it is not surprising that wherever governments manage to do so, inflation-reducing policies meet with immediate and durable success. Witness the Czech Republic, Hungary, and especially Poland with their rather stiff incomes policies.

Until recently, heavy taxes levied on unwarranted wage rises in those countries effectively held down inflation on both the demand and supply sides.

The fourth and final component of the integral package of macroeconomic stabilization policies is currency regulation in general, and control of the exchange rate in particular. A close look at the currency policies of the governments which have succeeded in macroeconomic stabilization (the Czech Republic, Hungary, Slovakia, and Poland) reveals that they have been positively set on *a fixed exchange rate from the very beginning.* That aim was one of the decisive components of the success of their policies - as well as of all other efforts to reduce inflation, for that matter. The bitter lessons of Bulgaria and Romania, on the other hand, show something different. The concept they adopted - that the fixed rate should follow more or less durable stabilization, with a floating rate until then - does not agree with the essence and philosophy of stabilization, since such a rate itself becomes a potent destabilizing factor.

It follows from the subject discussed above that the obviously effective macroeconomic stabilization in most of the Central and Eastern European economies cannot be related in any way to the consistent application of orthodox monetarism. The governments do control money supply, of course. The degree of restriction varies from tight to neutral. It appears, however, that this alone will not work if the non monetary factors of inflation and the readiness to address them systematically - are not heeded. The response to periodically tight monetary and fiscal policies alone, is soaring failures to pay, rather than a slower price rise. And since such a response is universal, it suggests a type of inflation unique to transitional economies. Characteristic of such inflation are the inertia of the structure of production built under the command economy, under-motivation of producers by the market, their current unchecked over-consumption, loose demand restrictions due to "unenforceability" of payments and, finally, an exceptionally high level of concentration of production, which results in monopoly and monopolist prices. Therefore, awareness and heed of the transformational nature of inflation and, of course, adequate administrative response to that challenge are the decisive factors in the durable slowdown of inflation in the economies discussed. Nevertheless, government declarations usually emphasize the dangers of too soft monetary and fiscal policies.

The CEE reformers succeeded in reducing inflation primarily because they were able to halt two different downward spirals, the most harmful vicious circles in the depreciation of money. One relates to prices and income and the other is created by inflation, which devaluates the national currency, in turn, fueling inflation. The reformist governments displayed their ability to suppress both spirals by applying mechanisms that conflict with the principles of liberalism in form only, since in reality they alone can implement these principles securely and irreversibly. A new quality of government intervention is apparently evident in the case in point. An intervention fearless of condemnation on the part of doctrinal liberals, and well aware of its responsibility for the consistency and security of systemic transformations.

The following conclusions can be derived from analysis of the experience of these countries with a view to its potential application in Russia:

1. all other factors being equal, the rate of transformational inflation is always higher than the normal rate of inflation in the long-established market economies, due to the incomplete process of establishment of new ownership relationships, a greater extent of distributary conflicts, the global nature and duration of changes in the economic structure, and underdeveloped competition and financial market;
2. the slowdown in inflation rates and the pick-up in economic activity show a direct correlation. However, if growth is unstable and short-lived, the possibility of a disruption of macroeconomic stabilization is much more likely;
3. macroeconomic stabilization may durably succeed if systemic transformations are controlled, while stabilization is comprehensive, complementary and socially oriented;
4. whatever policy governments adopt to reduce inflation, they should take care to avoid widening the income gap, swelling the monetary component of inflation, putting public property up for grabs, underestimating administrative price controls for natural monopolies, deliberately easing off intervention to keep down corruption, and instantaneously opening up the economy to the world;
5. overcoming the exchange for domestic use of national currencies for foreign currencies, a line for a fixed exchange rate and the enforcement of a hundred-percent conversion of export proceeds into national currencies are also prerequisites for successful macroeconomic stabilization.

It should be noted that the social „price“ of reforms in Russia has proven to be higher than in the Central and Eastern Europe for the very reason that Russian reformers in the government have seriously begun to implement two immutable but when applied to transitional economies especially arguable dogmas of orthodox monetarism. These are that: “Government intervention always harms efficient allocation of resources” and “Any change in the general price level is the result only of a shift on the supply side.” Russia's ex-COMECON partners did not rush to act with neophyte zeal and learnt to reform and resolve reform-related problems by using mechanisms that, though on the surface conflicting with the abstract concepts of theoretic liberalism, were in fact the only ones to secure real progression towards the civilized market.

Current Russian policy is also showing glimpses of such pragmatism. Suffice to mention the previously reviled fixed exchange rate, the regulation of natural monopolies' prices, currency control, etc. However, all these measures are so far not coordinated. The Russian economic policy clearly lacks cohesion, comprehensiveness and social orientation. This is in fact why it needs considerable adjustment.

2. The Climate of Investment in Russia: Analysis and Conclusions

Even if it is possible to secure more or less steady macroeconomic stabilisation in Russia without following monetary orthodoxy and controlling cost inflationary factors, there is a danger that economic depression will remain, and the country will just "muddle through". This is, strictly speaking, what has been happening up till now, as can be seen in Table J1.

Of course, one of the necessary conditions for economic growth is macroeconomic stability, as reflected in a monthly rate of inflation that does not exceed 1-2%. But this condition, though necessary, is not sufficient. Yet, from 1992 onwards state officials and economists close to government circles repeatedly and categorically stated that after macroecomomic stabilisation was reached, investment would immediately start to flow into Russia, leading to rapid economic growth. This has proven to be an illusion.

Tab. J1: Dynamics of Inflation, Capital Investment and Economic Development

	1992	1993	1994	1995	1996
Inflation rate a) b)	2510	840	265	131	33
Capital investments a)	- 40	- 12	- 26	-13	-17
GDP a)	-19	-12	-15	- 4	-6
Industrial output a)	-18	-14	-21	- 3	-5

Note: a) %, annual changes; b) Consumer prices.

Source: Statistical Yearbook of RF; respective years.

Apart from macroeconomic stabilisation, a number of conditions, which at present are virtually non existent, are necessary for economic growth:

- A fully legitimised system of ownership relations that is considered to be just by the overwhelming majority of society. Numerous well-known occurrences of abuse and corruption during the privatisation process in Russia have tended to undermine the legality of the newly established ownership relations do not allow the society to appraise ownership relationships as just and legal.

- The existence of effective owners for the most enterprises, namely owners who are interested in the normal operation and development of these enterprises.
- A system of resource allocation, whereby resources from inefficient branches are released and moved to more successful industries. In general such a system of allocation should include mechanisms for the bankruptcy of insolvent enterprises, a banking sector that interacts actively with industrial enterprises and/or a well-developed and efficient stock market.

However, there exist a number of factors that block the expansion of investment activities. The most important of these are listed in a concise form and with amazing precision by Dmitry Nikologorsky, an adviser to the Expert Institute of the Russian Union of Industrialists and Entrepreneurs (CAPITAL, 1996). In particular, he considers the following factors as hampering the investment growth (especially private investment):

- Due to the peculiar features of privatization in Russia the majority of shares are owned by the management and labor collectives of enterprises. This category of owners is often not interested in attracting outside investment and using enterprise funds to develop production.
- The absence of a bankruptcy mechanism means that enterprise debts are not seen as real debts.
- The high return on State securities (GKO) implies that investment projects in production are practically uncompetitive. At present attempts are being made to decrease the rate of return on government bonds and certain positive results have been achieved. But given the budgetary problems it is difficult to expect a further drop in the return on bonds in the near future.
- Ownership relations established during the course of privatisation are ambiguous. Privatisation in Russia was generally carried out not on the basis of laws but in accordance with the Presidential Decrees and regulations issued by the Goskomimusshestvo, which in a number of matters contradicted the legal stipulations. Numerous cases of abuse and illegal activities by individuals, state officials and commercial organisations has led to the impression in Russian society that many ownership relations resulting from privatisation are illegal. This is an obstacle to the flow of private investment into privatizaed enterprises.
- The economy lacks mechanisms for attracting savings and small private investments that would be needed to finance industrial development. This is due to the absence of financial organisations capable of accumulating savings and to the the peculiarities of the Russian stock market. The main aim in buying shares on the Russian stock market is not to receive income from ownership but to establish control over share issuers or to sell shares to those who wish to

acquire controlling blocks of shares. Such motives imply a shrinking number of potential share buyers and limit the use the stock market for the generation of investment funds and the development of enterprises.

Under conditions where enterprises and the State have only limited capabilities for investment finance, credits play a vital role in overcoming resource limitations. However, the majority of Russian banks at present do not have sufficient financial resources for large-scale operations, especially those of an investment nature, and the possibilities for their expansion (given the current macroeconomic climate) are very limited. Besides, a number of general economic factors together with organisational shortcomings in the banking system are encouraging banks to favor short-term credits.

Thus, the development of long-term credit arrangements requires State intervention, which should include the following:

- Measures to improve the investment climate through appropriate fiscal, depreciation, customs, pricing policy;
- Measures to stimulate the propensity to save and make long-term saving attractive and hence encourage the flow of savings into the investment sphere;
- Measures to attract credits to the investment sphere by decreasing reserves and taxes on banks, granting state investment credits and introducing State guarantees for banks-investors, etc.;
- The necessity to strengthen enterprises' "propensity to save" demands the introduction of preferential credits (with a negative interest rate) while a restrictive monetary policy continues to be followed. International practice provides many examples of how preferential credits can be organised. State subsidization of interest rate on commercial banks' investment credits has proven to be particularly efficient. However, as State finances in Russia are overstrained, this measure may turn out to be excessively "expensive".

Given the worsening social and economic situation in Russia, there exist an increasing number of policy observers who argue for a Russian type of Keynesian policy approach. Keynesian supporters oppose the current government's policy of total aggregate demand constraints. Instead they argue for an expansion, even if artificial, in aggregate demand, to be stimulated by an increase in government expenditures. Referring to the effectiveness of the famous anti-crisis New Deal of Franklin Roosevelt and the more or less successful implementation of Keynesian recipes in *developed* market economies, the proponents of an expansion in aggregate demand hope to attain a similarly positive effect in Russia. They believe in particular, that an increase in monetary income initiated by the State would stimulate consumer demand, which would in turn lead to a rising production of appropriate goods and services, thus placing the whole economy on a trajectory of dynamic growth. However, given the specific characteristics of the Russian economy, pure Keynesian recommendations are at the least naive. While there is no efficient competition mechanism and ownership relations are underdeveloped and not well defined, the first reaction of enterprises to an artificial expansion in aggregate demand would not be an increase in the use of industrial capacity, but inflation of prices. In fact something of this nature already happened earlier during the reform period. The periodical "pumping up" of monetary demand through non-selective credit expansion has had little effect on industrial dynamics and has always led to the same result - further increases in prices. And if the emergency credit influx has led to outbursts of inflation, it is easy to imagine what might happen to inflation and the exchange rate once artificial aggregate demand expansion becomes an official goal of government economic policy.

What policies should the government, therefore, adopt in order to halt the continued worsening in economic and social conditions and prevent the impending collapse of the economy?

In my opinion, the anti-crisis reformation program should in the first instance avoid the grip of the notorious "monetary-keynesianism" dilemma . It is necessary to finally understand that neither the planned decrease in aggregate demand nor its expansion will lead to a recovery in our economy. Both of these, though being quite legitimate means of fine tuning matured market economies, are absolutely inappropriate for the transitional Russian economy which is in the process of self-destructing. The time has come to give up the almost religious and mystical belief in tested Western recipes that fail to take into account the uniqueness of time and space.

An economic policy aimed at overcoming the crisis in the national economy should be carried out on the basis of a rather prosaic criterion, namely the extent to which it contributes to the development of the real sector of the economy with special emphasis on the domestic manufacturing industry.

Such an approach focuses attention on the most important task at hand, i.e. the need to stop the downward spiral in production and restore production levels to some stable level, thereby creating the pre-requisites for an accelerated recovery.

As to the means of implementing this task under conditions of scarce internal resources and quite doubtful hopes for massive foreign investment, the most important would be a *radical change in the nature of consumption thus far produced in the national income*, namely the decrease as far as possible of non-productive consumption (consumption that is not essential for the developmental needs of production), and an appropriate increase in productive consumption. Such a policy should be consistently pursued both at macroeconomic and microeconomic levels and, of course, not by restoring "top-down" command chains but by influencing the incentives of enterprises regardless of their form of ownership. In other words, the goal should be incorporated into government fiscal policies, taxation and credit policy, labor and wages, structural changes and foreign economic relations, without impeding market transformations.

For example, taking into account the necessity for technical reconstruction of the national economy, as well as the country's extremely limited purchasing power, it is necessary to structure tariffs in a way that hinders a further expansion in consumer goods imports whilst stimulating imports of production means and advanced technologies. Similarly, the approach to privatization of State enterprises should focus on the overall goal of reconstruction. This implies that each case of privatisation is justified only if it leads not only to an increase in profit, but also to an increased use of these profits in further development, namely, the process of its productive consumption. If the opposite of this occurs, privatisation will hinder the accumulation process that will sooner or later inevitably lead to the liquidation of an enterprise, despite its new private status.

By aiming to change the nature of national income consumption, the above mentioned dilemma of the "shrinking-expansion" in aggregate demand should be solved. It is necessary to reduce demand in cases where it is used non-productively, and to stimulate it when its use increases productive consumption. It is important to stress that only through such a differentiated approach to the regulation of monetary demand can the doubly positive effect of a stable increase in production and irreversible monetary stabilisation be achieved.

It is also necessary to bear in mind that it is not possible to apply standard reform programs to the Russian economy, because the economy is actually overdeveloped (though not according to market criteria) rather than underdeveloped. For a long time it was a powerful (if not second in the world) technological center. Fortunately, today Russia still possesses sufficient scientific and technological potential for the development of high technology products. And failure to accept such an advantage by adopting reforms "a la laissez-faire - laisser-passer" and pinning hopes upon the magic of an invisible hand is at the least unreasonable.

It so happens that Russian industry today once again requires catching-up modernisation. And such modernization, as international experience proves, is only possible within the framework of an active and consistent State structural and investment policy.

3. Foreign Direct Investment in Russia

On the whole, in Russia the same characteristics of and motivations for foreign direct investment (FDI) are applicable as in other countries. At the same time it is necessary to emphasize some characteristics that are specific to the Russian case. Firstly, the main funds of FDI have been directed at developing countries and transitional economies with a positive and frequently rather high rate of economic growth. Unfortunately, Russia has not been successful in halting the recession in manufacturing. Secondly, Russian enterprises and their managers have little experience with FDI. Mechanisms and structures for the effective utilisation of FDI in Russia still need to be constructed. Thus, it is necessary to define real spheres and branches for FDI, probable volumes and the State role in maintaining national security and co-ordinating the interests of investors and local enterprises. Similarly, the State still needs to define real opportunities for privatization in attracting FDI and to understand the influence of external State debt on the dynamics of FDI. Thirdly, the general investment climate in Russia at present is less attractive to investors in comparison with the first two groups of countries (these problems will be considered in detail below).

At the same time, Russia posesses a number of advantages for strategic investment. First of all, there are the large deposits of mineral resources and renewable resources, which in terms of world production and consumption offer opportunities for steady development in the long-term. Other advantages include a highly qualified and comparatively cheap labor force, the significant and unexploited technological potential, spare capacity in the military-industrial complex and civil engineering industry, a large prospective domestic market and a favorable geographical position at the junction of two continents.

In the immediate future, Russia is particularly interested in attracting foreign investment in manufacturing. Set against a background of huge external debt amounting to $130 billion, FDI permits the involvement of capital without increasing indebtedness and, once invested, FDI funds are not liquid and cannot be easily used for speculative purposes. The recipients of FDI in Russia are guided by the following reasons: attraction of deficient "live" money, equipment, technologies and administrative experience for existing and new production units as well as modern marketing experience (INFORMATION AGENCY, 1995, pp. 7-16).

Tab. J2: Dynamics of Direct and Portfolio Investment in Russia

	1992	1993	1994	1995	1996
Direct Investment, Million $	1454	1404	671	2017	2500
Portfolio Investment, Million $	196	420	748	90	7500
Total Investment, Million $	1650	1824	1 419	2107	10000

Note: In addition to dollar installments FDI is accomplished also in roubles (reinvestment and so on). In 1995 for example it amounted to 635 billion roubles.

Source: Reference book "Social and economic situation of Russia" for corresponding years. Goscomstat; "Bulletin of Russia Bank", No. 38, August 9, 1996; Balance of Payments. Direct and Portvolio Investment, Вестник российского банка, 20.05.1997, No. 29.

As for foreign investors, first of all their cautious attitude to partnerships with Russian enterprises is noticeable: the size of the investments are insignificant and their fluctuation in time and structure (between direct and portfolio) is great. Secondly, the influx of "other short-term capital" is growing quickly, reflecting investor uncertainty and a desire to increase the degree of their protection. For the recipients, this creates a danger of abrupt fluctuations and fast outflows of funds etc. Thirdly, there is evidence of the reduced gross influx of all kinds of new financial resources on Russia's GDP (from 1992 till 1994 this indicator decreased from 2.1% to 1.6% and 1995 has brought no essential changes).

The quantitative analysis of FDI in terms of volume as well as type can be conducted only with significant speculation, because of the different definitions adopted by various government departments. It is not always possible to differentiate data between data on volumes stated and fixed in the constituent instruments and real investment. In Russia, only contributions into authorized funds of enterprises with foreign participation refer to FDI, and criteria for referring to portfolio investment are generally unclear. Therefore, the estimated total size of both forms of investment differs considerably depending on the source of information used. As of March 31, 1996 one source claimed such investment amounted to $8.7 billion (including $5.91 billion of foreign direct investment), others claimed the amounts were 7.86 and 5.53 respectively. At the end of 1995 estimates were $6 billion (Ministry of Economy) and $4.9 billion (American Chamber of Commerce in Russia) (ДЕЛОВОЙ МИР, 1996a; ЭКОНОМИКА И ЖИЗНЬ, 1996c).

Until recently growth in FDI was primarily at the expense of *small and average* firm operations. This circumstance explains the frequent discrepancy between long-term FDI interests and the tendencies and requirements of the Russian economy, as well as the frequent changes in priorities on the part of the foreign investors.

The above-cited series, though not fully comparable, permits some important conclusions. At present, foreign investors place high priority on stability in the fuel industry, trade and public catering. At the same time we can see that Russia currently has no effective instrument at its disposal capable of influencing the influx of foreign investment in the desired direction. Conclusion of legal discussions "On the agreements on production division", its completion and effective use could change the situation a little, since large projects in the energy sector (ES) provide for accommodation of some 50-70% of the orders for equipment and services among Russian enterprises (ФИНАНСОВЫЕ ИЗВЕСТИЯ, 1995b).

Tab. J3: The Most Attractive Branches for Foreign Investors in the Russian Economy [a)]

1993	1995	1996
Mechanical engineering and metal working	Trade and public catering	Fuel industry
Fuel industry	Finance, credit, insurance, pensions	Trade and public catering
Trade and public catering	Food industry	Finance, credit, insurance
Wood-work and wood-pulp and paper industry	Fuel industry	Food industry
Building material industry	Construction	
	Mechanical engineering and metal working b)	Mechanical engineering and metal working
	Chemical and petrochemical industry	General commerce activity for providing market functioning
	Wood-working and wood-pulp and paper industry	Wood-working and wood-pulp and paper industry
	General commerce activity for providing market functioning	Construction
	Science and scientific service	Transport and communication
		Chemical and petrochemical industry

Note: a) In decreasing order of investment volume; b) Two branches have equal position.

Sources: "Foreign Investment in Russia ...", p. 45, "ДЕЛОВОЙ МИР", May 12, 1996.

The branch structure in many respects defines the regional concentration of FDI. The five five most attractive areas usually include Moscow, Moscow oblast, Tatarstan, Leningrad and Tymen oblasts. Sheer "sorting over" goes further, but the tendency towards the strengthening of positions is gradually becoming evident in the cases of the Khabarovsk and Primorsky Territories (nearness to the Asia-Pacific region), St. Petersburg (large industrial, financial, technological centre, large port), Yamal-Nenetz autonomous okrug (natural resources) and Perm oblast (mechanical engineering, large aeronautical engine factory). According to some economists the shift in the second group of five regions is due not so much to the general problems in Russia, but to the *exhaustion of the absorptional abilities of formerly attractive territories in effective assimilation of FDI under local economic conditions and in methods of interaction with foreign investors.*(ДЕЛОВОЙ МИР, 1996b) This primarily refers to the underdeveloped infrastructure, lack of experience in foreign trade activities, and occasionally, unwillingness on the part of the local administration.

The main form of foreign capital attraction are joint ventures (JV) and enterprises with 100% of foreign partners' capital. In the first quarter of 1996 the total number of such enterprises was 19.4 ths, including 12.4 ths with the participation of distant foreign countries. In comparison with countries of Central and East Europe these indicators look rather modest.

In 1995 the home market realized production worth 44.3 trillion roubles (40% of this in Moscow). 36% of the total volume of production (work and services) was realized in industry, 38% in trade and public catering. Export production made up $5 billion (7% of the general export of Russia). Most of this (93%) consisted of exports to distant foreign countries. Predominant among these exports were fuel and energy resources - they amounted to 51% of total export volume. 44% of exports went to Germany, Great Britain, Italy, USA and Japan. In the same year enterprises with foreign capital participation imported goods worth $3.4 billion.

Two tendencies have engaged our attention: huge JV differentiation in the size of participating foreign capital, and extremely modest results in the activities of Free Economic Zones (FEZ).

The small concentration of JVs is quite justified in the initial period of systematic transformation, but unfortunately there has been no growth even in the later years of transition. In 1995 54% of FDI was directed at only five such enterprises. This shows that the number of projects that are attractive to foreigners and number of investors ready to accept the risk is minimal at present. As a rule, the lion's share of investment is obtained by projects in the energy sector. This situation will probably not change in the foreseeable future, as the bulk of capital will be concentrated on several large oil production projects. One problem facing Russia in overcoming such a tendency is that the excessive concentration on a few beneficiaries could render a destabilizing effect on the economy of the recipient country were friction to develop between participants in an agreement.

The 12 FEZ registered by the beginning of 1996 are at present unfortunately not justified. Only FEZ "Nakhodka" is developing relatively successfully. More than 470 enterprises are operating in its territory. 50% of these are joint-stock companies with 100% participation of foreign capital, 42% are JVs and 8% are subsidiaries of foreign firms. Until the middle of 1995 the total volume of foreign investment generated $380 m in this FEZ, of which $80 m, loans and credits - $300 m. Moreover, investment of $220 m have been attracted for the development of industrial and transport infrastructure. A number of projects amounting to $300 m are in study stage (ДЕЛОВОЙ МИР,1996c). But even here there exists a serious discrepancy between the plans for investment and the actual realization (the Russian-American industrial park as well as Russian-South Korean industrial complex are still waiting to be established). Yet this FEZ has huge opportunities for self-development, because the territory was chosen correctly, the specialization was determined and the mechanisms for the interaction of federal and regional authorities were well-defined. In this context it is appropriate to mention the decree of the president of the Russian Federation president of March 11, 1996, "On some measures for the stimulation of investment activity in the free economic zone "Nakhodka", pursuant to which a specialized zone for export manufacturing is to be created on the basis of Russian-South Korean industrial complex and into which the Korean side is going to invest $700 m. The Russian side provides the ground, infrastructure, labor and the newest technologies, including approbated in space. Not less than 50% of own production will go into exports. The enterprises of the complex are exempted from the profit tax in the territory for 5 years. During the following 5 years the taxation rate will make 50% and then 75%. If the intergovernmental agreement with South Korea is signed and ratified, its status will be higher than the Russian law on FEZ that has been submitted to the Duma (КОММЕРСАНТЪ, 1996a).

The inability of the majority of other FEZ to develop successfully is mainly due to the following miscalculations: a multi-million city or an oblast covering an area of the size of a medium European state were included in FEZ, specialization was eroded and - of special importance- sufficiently detailed evaluations of the potential opportunities for prospective investors were not conducted. Another serious hinderness is the absence of a law on the agreement of tax, tariff and other aspects of activities in FEZ.

In general it is necessary to emphasize, that estimates of Russia's need for foreign investment vary widely but all exceed the currently observed FDI volumes. In one of the preliminary drafts of the Ministry of Economy of Russia the volume of foreign investment realised in 1994 was estimated at $1-1.5 billion, in 1995 at $2-3 billion, and the projections for 1996 were $5-6 billion, 1997 $7-8 billion and 1998-2000 $10-15 billion annually. Up to the end of the century only the energy sector's needs in the foreign capital amount to $10 billion at a minimum. Minister of Economy à. Yasin considers that in the next 15 years of economic reconstruction Russia will require $300-400 billion from abroad (ВОПРОСЫ ЭКОНОМИКИ, 1994; ИЗВЕСТИЯ, 1995, 1996), which amounts to $20-26 billion per year on average. It is necessary to reach an annual level of $10-12 billion by 2000. The All-Russian Research Institute of Forecasting (ВНИКИ) distinguishes between three FDI scenarios for the period 1966-2000. In the pessimistic scenario the volume investment inflows in 2000 will remain at the current annual level of $2.5-3 billion, the 'middle' scenario predicts \$9-10 billion of annual inflows, while the optimistic scenario forecasts \$12-14 billion (БИКИ, 1996).

In conditions of rigid competition in world markets for investment, the problem of attracting investment funds seems to be difficult, but all the same real. In 1995 the share of Russia in the world volume of foreign investment (\$325 billion) was less than one percent and amounted to about 3% of foreign direct investment into developing countries (\$90 billion).

Given the experiences made in other countries and the condition of the Russian economy, it is likely that foreign capital will be attracted first of all by the enterprises in the energy sector (due to provision of prospective needs, reliability of returns at the expense of production imports, attention of the government to large projects, guarantees of the latter etc.). Investors will also be attracted by cheap production factors such as labour; by ecological factors (production with a high load on the environment) and technical know-how (available in conversion enterprises of the military and industrial complex and the aerospace industry). Especially attractive will be operating enterprises and, from the perspective of future sales, the large size of the Russian domestic market will also play a role.

For the massive inflow of FDI in Russia to actually occur it is necessary to formulate a rational policy towards foreign industrial investment, which should replace the often contradictory impulsive actions of administrative structures, legislative bodies, branch ministries and regional authorities. Without such a policy Russia will become "driven" and its inclusion into the world economy will be limited to "the lower floors". The complex program of stimulating domestic and foreign investment (1995) is a step towards regulating the economy's interaction with the external world and towards defining the responsibility for these structures (Ministry of Economy). However, the program does not state clear priorities or even an approximate sequence for solving the various problems. The list of priorities named by the Russian government in 1993 included the production of food-stuffs, medicines and consumer goods, with the basic branches - energy and metallurgy - only being given a secondary importance. In the 1995 program the task of defining priorities is posed again. Such frequent revisions disorient domestic and foreign investors, especially given that in the new version the priorities are actually not formulated at all.[1] The program mentions the necessity of attracting foreign capital in order to create new industries (including export oriented and import substituting industries), modernize and expand productive capacities using the newest technologies and know-how. The program also refers to conversion of the defense industry. Finally, it includes a list of priority industries, sub-industries, productive capacities and regions (including FEZ). This is followed by regional priorities, problems of employment etc. The whole economic complex is practically covered in the document. However, directions for the whole process of investment and priorities for the Russian side as well as priorities for foreign investment are not clear.

Also unsolved remains the problem of management of foreign capital. As is known from advanced market economies, the dominant criterion for the accepting side is the efficiency of operations of a particular economic unit. The public economy effect is realized mainly automatically through saturation of the market, growth of export, taxation system, interest rates, exchange rate etc. The role of the State is limited to the establishment of general rules, development of separate investment programs and projects, privileges and restrictions necessary for economic stability and national security.

The current condition of Russia's economy does not permit the State to focus solely on the problem of providing macroeconomic stability. It must carefully monitor the effect of foreign capital inflow (or absence of it) on macroeconomic indices with the help of economic, legal and, in necessary cases, administrative regulation. Till now the main volume of foreign capital is based on bilateral agreements or comes from international organizations, where the Russian representative is the government or authorized by government bodies. The government is responsible for the solution of the external indebtedness problem, because otherwise it is impossible to count on the essential transfer of capital into the country. The insufficient development of market mechanisms, the existing legal nihilism, the indistinct division of authority between the center and the regions, the continued monopolization of manufacturers - all this prevents the interests of separate enterprises, industries, regions and the country as a whole to coincide or at least point in similar directions. Under these conditions it is dangerous to rely on the principle of laissez faire. The State is simply obliged to care about such things as conformity of branch and regional structures of foreign investment, the problems of structural reorganization of the economy, rational location of productive forces, increases in the FDI contribution to the export potential, increases in the share of finished products in exports, and the effect on the program of conversion and growth in import-substituting manufacturing, participation of foreign investors in privatization on terms of “strategic investment”, protection of domestic producers in the market, as well as for the effect foreign capital transfers may have on the balance of payments.

This is the reason why the State has to develop programs to stimulate foreign direct investment and to adopt incentive measures, including the introduction of some privileges within the framework of the general legislation. It would be desirable to include these in the framework of the national regime (in which norms as a rule are of direct action and do not require numerous subordinate legislation or departmental instructions). However under conditions of rigid competition for foreign investment and the low rating of Russia in world investment markets such an approach will not provide the necessary inflow of capital, as investors show caution despite the potential attractiveness of the country as an object of capital investment (given the fuel and raw material resources). Therefore, it is necessary to provide certain comprehensively calculated privileges for foreign investors who participate in priority projects. The privileges should be limited to designated time periods (determined in the legislative order) with subsequent subordination to the national regime in full volume.

The discussion of this problem, which is rather important for the fate of foreign investment in Russia in the near future, was concluded with a compromise by the government bodies involved. The Commission on perfection of the taxation legislation has advanced an opinion for a national regime, but by granting foreign investors a limited list of privileges. The privileges are distinguished by the type of State regulation (tax, currency, customs) and by the purpose: the general are granted to all enterprises with foreign investment, and the selective to particular enterprises and manufacture of production, which the State regards necessary to stimulate (ЭКОНОМИКА И ЖИЗНЬ, 1996d).

The numerous interrogations, materials of conferences and meetings of the business people, among the reasons, hindering growth of FDI in Russia, designate (in a different sequence) defects of the legislation, obscurity in definition of the property rights, unforeseeable changes of taxation system, level of inflation, political instability, undevelopment of market and investment infrastructure, size of the foreign debt, opacity of the commercial information, recession of manufacture, low yield of the investments, insufficient warranties and insurance etc[2] . The role, which will play the foreign investment, including direct, in economy of Russia, and the character of its integration into the world economy, depends on the decision of these and other problems, connected with them.

4. Regulation and Management of Foreign Investment in Russia

In economic literature, especially foreign, pessimistic estimations of an investment process in Russia prevail. During several years the discussions on these themes have accelerated and acquired inertness that made estimations of the real situation in many respects subjective and unilateral. Really FDI and other kinds of the investment are meeting with many obstacles in Russia, but at the same time a tendency for the benefit of investment cooperation with foreign states is designated.

If, as it was already marked in 1993-1995, among the barriers on the way to the investments, high rates of inflation, political instability and uncertainty in the choice of socioeconomic system were pointed out, at present we can see obvious preconditions for their elimination. Thus, with all actuality of the discussion on convertibility of the macroeconomic stabilization one should highly appreciate the successes of the government in the struggle with high inflation (reduction from 300% to 50-60% per year). The political situation in the country is gradually normalizing, especially after the termination of the military operations in Chechnya and the results of presidential elections. In the questions of property and the choice of a course of development, some corrections are possible but not radical changes. The radical left- and right-wing currents do not enjoy the public support. The public sentiments in the country gain strength for the benefit of the stability strengthening.

From the positions of the foreign investors Russia in the prospect will be transformed into the most perspective partner among the countries with "emerging markets". Already now its share in the total G.D.P. of these countries exceeds 25%. It has an advanced space industry, relatively modern infrastructure, still significant scientific and technical potentials and qualified personnel. Russia distinguishes itself among these countries by possession of natural resources. According to the available estimations they can be appreciated in $10.2 trillion, that is more, than in Brazil (3.3), Southern Africa (1.1), China (0.6) and India (0.4) altogether (ФИНАНСОВЫЕ ИЗВЕСТИЯ,1995a).

At last it is impossible to leave out of one's reckoning the market with almost 150 millions of consumers; the industry with obsolete fixed capital (with a degree of wear close to 50%), which requires updating; an opportunity of obtaining income 2-3 times more than the level of profitability in countries with a stable economy (ФИНАНСОВЫЕ ИЗВЕСТИЯ, 1995d).

Thus in Russia a situation turns out potentially favorable for strategic investment of private domestic, western and east foreign capital. The realization of these opportunities in a decisive degree depends on economic policy, skill to use the market mechanisms in combination with the State possibilities, ability of the government to execute the institutional reforms and to take out the economy of the country from crisis, to give it a progressive motion. Without this it is unreal to count upon revival of the investment process.

Before analyzing the strategic aspect of the foreign investment problem it is expedient to give an estimation of the work conducted during the years of reforms on attraction of the foreign capital into the industrial sphere of the Russian economy.

During the years of open access into Russian economy for foreign capital more than hundred various legal and normative documents were accepted. However these documents are not brought together in a uniform system, they frequently were a product of a compromise of competing political forces, and their acceptance in a number of cases was either late or postponed on an indefinite term at all because of arising disputes. As a result, the current legislation contains many contradictions, it does not provide to the investor due warranties and stable conditions for realization of his business, and as to taxation, the legislation often looks like "interdictory" for the investor. The new laws and normative acts do not always agree with the acting ones, and frequent changes, additions and interpretations raise uncertainty in all participants of the process. High level of enterprise risk leads to the insignificant investment proposal and even to outflow of the capital from the country.

The main legislative acts and normative documents, regulating the activities of foreign investment, are the Law of Russian Federation of July 4, 1991 "On the foreign investment in the Russian Federation", the Law "On the enterprises and business activities" of December 25, 1990, decrees of the Russian government of June 6, 1994, No. 655 "On the State Registration Chamber at the Ministry of Economy of the Russian Federation".

Besides the contents of the Law "On the foreign investment" its *level* and *direct action* were important for foreign investors. Five privileges on tax, currency and customs regulation were given to the enterprises with foreign investment at once, and until now four privileges remain intact (the permission to leave all currency earnings lost force later because of the new normative acts on the currency regulation and control). The common to all economy privileges, half of which is established by the law, (privileges for the enterprises with foreign participation have the legislative basis only on 30%) are granted also to enterprises with foreign participation (ЭКОНОМИКА И ЖИЗНЬ, 1996d). An essential defect of the law about foreign investment is that a number of provisions of the special investment legislation does not agree with the general legislation. Besides the subjects of the Federation (republics of Russia, Moscow, St. Petersburg and others) have began to apply their acts, changing or worsening the position of foreign investors. The absence of warranty about change of the legislation in the form of "grandfather" or "stabilizational" proviso in the law of 1991 was a large defect of this law. After cancellation in 1991-1992 of overwhelming part of privileges for the foreign investors in this area a legal uncertainty was characteristic for a long time, that is a peculiar "time-out". At the same time it should be noted, that in 1991-1993 the remaining privileges were predominantly the norms of direct action.

The Russian President Decree No. 1466 of September 27, 1993 "On perfection of work with foreign investment", containing the "grandfather proviso" could have been an important step in perfection of the legislation about the foreign capital attraction. The Decree prohibited the newly issued normative acts, regulating the conditions of foreign and JV functioning on the Russian territory, to worsen conditions of activities of the enterprises, which were functioning at the moment of these acts coming into force, during 3 years. The Decree did not apply to the normative acts, that provide more concessionary terms of foreign and JV functioning at the Russian territory. As far as the normative acts of the government, the State Committees, ministries and departments, republics of Russia, Moscow and St. Petersburg were canceled, the special proviso was not automatically guaranteed for all foreign investors: they could receive right on it by modification of the particular agreement and concluding an agreement directly with the State. In opinion of the foreign investors, the provisions of the Decree in questions of taxation, especially concerning increase of tax on profits and property of the enterprises, were inconsistent. In item 1 of the Decree the moratorium on application of the norms, worsening conditions, is established and in item 2 the normative acts, able to establish these conditions are listed - the Law or Decree of the President. Meanwhile the taxation authorities consider, that this moratorium is not applicable to the tax legislation, as far as the Decree of December 20, 1993 "On some changes in the taxation and mutual relations of the budgets of various levels", establishing the increased rates and reducing privileges, actually cancels action of the provisions of the Decree of September 27, 1993. Thus, actually the "grandfather proviso" was not realized in full measure. Firstly, it was necessary to define precisely the circle of legislative acts, concerning to which it is introduced, and to explain, what is meant under "newly created acts, regulating condition of functioning"; secondly, the mechanism of the "grandfather proviso" application was not clear and thirdly, in difference from the legislation of other CIS countries, the Decree did not contain proviso of that newly issued normative acts and did not mention that this guarantee applies only to the enterprises with more than 30 % of foreign capital participation. As a result the Ministry of Finance and taxation authorities have defined that the "proviso" is not applied to the taxation regime, that became possible because of inconsistency of the norms of the Decree with the tax legislation.

In 1994 the policy of foreign investment stimulation has again vivified. At the same time essential changes have taken place in this area. In 1994-1995 the privileges had a *selective character*, and 60% of them were privileges of *direct action* (ЭКОНОМИКА И ЖИЗНЬ, 1996d).

The industrial enterprises with foreign capital participation, provided that their share in the authorized capital, paid by the foreign investor, makes not less than 30% and is not less than $10 m in an equivalent sum and registered after January 1, 1994, take an opportunity of the taxation regime, similar to the order of profit tax collection from the small enterprises during the first 5 years. Specifically the taxation mechanism acts in such a manner that such enterprises newly created "during the first two year of operation do not pay the profit tax, if the proceeds from production activities exceed 70% of the gross proceeds from production realization (work, services). In the third and fourth year of operation they pay the profit tax in the amount of 25% and 50% of standard rate accordingly, if the proceeds from production activities makes more than 90% of the gross proceeds from production realization (work, services). When the enterprises with foreign capital participation terminate their activity before expiration of the five-year term, the sum of the profit tax is subject to paying in the Federal budget in full volume for the whole period of their activity". Additional tax privileges for the investors are stipulated by the letter of the State Tax Service of the Russian Federation of June 2, 1994 "On some questions of the foreign investment taxation". According to this document profit, directed, in order of share, on financing capital investment of industrial and non-industrial purpose, as well as on repayment of banks credit, received and used on these purposes is released from taxation.

It is necessary to note also the Russian President Decree of January 25, 1995 “On additional measures for attraction of foreign investment for realization of large-scale projects in branches of material production”. It introduces preferential (cut in half) duties for import into Russia of the firms-investors' finished products at the exception of alcoholic liquor and tobacco products. And these rates can be applied conformably to the investment goods during 5 years, provided that the foreign companies, delivering them, are founders of enterprises, manufacturing similar goods at Russian territory using domestic raw material and labour, and execute direct investment into material production industries in projects, costing not less than $100 m. The foreign participant contribution in the authorized fund of such enterprise should make a sum not less than $10 m.

The Council of Federation has approved the law “On introducing changes and additions in the Russian Federation law “On customs tariff”, that establishes privileges of import duties payment. From duties are exempted: firstly, technology equipment, purchased on account of credits, given by foreign States and International financial organizations pursuant to international agreements with Russia, or under the warrantees of its government; secondly, the technology equipment, having no domestic analogues. In annual calculation the sum of the privileges, by Ministry of Finance estimation will make 1-1.5 trillion roubles (ЭКСПЕРТ, 1996, p. 9).

According to the instruction of the Russian Federation State Tax Service the enterprise with foreign investment and with 100% of foreign capital have the right to tax-free deductions from the currency profit into reserve fund. The sum of such deductions should not exceed 50% of the enterprises taxable profit, and the size - 25% of the total authorized capital. Earlier the President Decree of February 26, 1993 “On creation of international agency on insurance of foreign investment in Russian Federation from commercial risk” and Decree of Russian government of September 29, 1994 No. 1108 “On activization of work on attraction of foreign investment into economy of the Russian Federation” were accepted.

It should be noted, that strengthening of foreign investment legal basis, explaining the subordinate legislation of this time, have improved the investment climate in Russia and made it more attractive for foreign investors. But on March 13, 1995 the law of Russian Federation was accepted “On some questions of granting privileges to the participants of foreign trade activities” No.31- 3, that canceled all earlier given privileges (except of stipulated by the laws “On Customs tariff”, “On value-added tax”, “On excise duties” and by Customs Code of Russian Federation) (ЭКОНОМИКА И ЖИЗНЬ, 1996b). The provisions of the law became retroactive that caused problems with customs warrants by contracts concluded before January

1, 1993 among a number of enterprises. Enterprises with foreign capital participation also suffered from this. By the Decree of the Russian President of January 25, 1995 No. 73 "On additional measures for attraction of foreign investment in branches of material production in the Russian Federation" the foreign investors received a number of privileges, including the privilege on payment of the customs duty. At the same time the later decree of the Russian Federation government No. 751 of July 24, 1995 continues to refer to the Decree No. 73 about sanctions against foreign investors, who received customs privilege, but did not execute their obligations, as well as to other decree No. 1019 of October 12, 1995 and other Presidential Decree No. 1077 "On measures of providing conditions for realization of investment agreements". Such high "fluidity" of the laws and other normative acts puts the foreign investors in a difficult position: it is very difficult for them to understand the hierarchy of the numerous documents of different levels, to find out timely divergence and contradictions, to counteract arbitrarily interpretation of these documents by various departments, really predict the results of their activities when the laws, Decrees and governmental decisions are made to be retroactive. Nevertheless it is appropriately to assume here, that in foreseeable future a certain stability will be introduced by the Taxation Code, as well as by a group of laws, connected directly or indirectly with foreign investments, many of which are already under discussion in the State Duma. So despite of all present defects and deficiencies, discussions and contradictions, in Russia *a system of legislation, that gives to relations with foreign investors civil, contractual character and real equality of the parties, begins to be formed* more and more distinctly.

A special role in development of large-scale and long-term international investment cooperation belongs to the Law "On agreements on production sharing", signed by the President on December 30, 1995. Sharp discussions preceded acceptance of the law, which continue also after its coming into force. This law was basically created for the regulation of the relations between the foreign investor and the State in mineral-raw material branches. On the one hand, the State is a partner of the private investor, on the other - it executes the control of its activity. Otherwise, the law "On production sharing" permits to make certain corrections of the investment mechanism in mineral-raw material branches of economy by wide introduction of the contractual relations between the investor and the State. This is necessary in connection with huge capital-intensity of the investment projects and high price of risk. The volume of the supposed investment only in oil production on the basis of the agreements about production sharing is evaluated in $24 billion, and all such agreements - in $70 billion 8 (ФИНАНСОВЫЕ ИЗВЕСТИЯ, 1996c) .

In opinion of the developers of the law (and it is possible to agree with them), it is a break-through in comparison with investment regimes of bowels of the earth exploitation, established by the laws "On bowels of the earth", "On continental shelf" and "On gas and petroleum". The law fixes legal stability of the concluded agreements *not on limited term but on the whole period of their action.* A more simplified taxation system of the investor accounts with the State is accepted, constructed on rental relations and a system of rental payments with regard to individual features of the deposits. At the same time the formulations of some provisions of the law are not free from contradictions and admit ambiguous interpretation. So, the necessity to negotiate with two proprietors of a natural resource - the government and the executive body of the Federation subject - complicates achievement of the agreement and determination of its conditions, washes away the responsibility, though under the international norms the whole responsibility for fulfillment of such agreements is laid upon the subject of the international law, in this case the Russian Federation. Granting to the Russian legal persons priority on fulfillment of contract work, under other equal conditions, does not entirely agree with international practice. In the world practice the decision is accepted exclusively on the basis of the tender (if there is more than one claimant). Though the taxation system is simplified, the investor should be released from other taxes and payments, including in the Federation subjects budgets, except the agreed fixed rate of the profit tax.

A serious obstacle to FDI inflow can become the continuing sharp discussion about the fate of the law "On the agreements of production sharing". For a long time it can not pass all instances to begin "to work". The recent statements about expediency of reduction of the list of the bowels of the earth and deposits, where the foreign investors can be allowed, hardly probable will become a stimulus for their concentrated attraction to the objects still remained open. At present of 10.5 thousand licenses, given on deposits development, only about 200 were received by JV and 4 - by pure foreign companies. There is apparently a quite reasonable opinion that the present list of deposits opened for foreign investment (250) is rather narrow. At the correct approach, investment of foreign capital into extractive industries can bring benefit not only to these branches, but also to many machine-building industry and enterprises of Military-Industrial Complex, because as it was already marked, up to 50-70% of the orders on the equipment is supposed to place in Russia. The large Russian petroleum companies and regions, where they are located, speak in support of the expansion of the foreign capital participation in development of mineral resources. They are interested in fulfillment of their budgets. Probably, fast acceptance of the bill "On the list of bowels of the earth and deposit sites, the right for using of which can be given on conditions of production sharing", that should introduce clearness and calm the investors, for it will permit the long-suffering Law "On production sharing" to begin acting in full strength. Only after that foreign investors will come to decision about an expedient volume of investment. Unfortunately, around the list of bowels of the earth and deposit sites, disputes begin to flare up, which in case of their prolongation will hamper foreign investment inflow in Russia (КОММЕРСАНТЪ, 1996c; ФИНАНСОВЫЕ ИЗВЕСТИЯ, 1996c).

5. Perfection and Development of Interaction with Foreign Capital

In the domestic and foreign economic literature there is already mentioned a rather steady stereotype, pursuant to which the main obstacles to foreign investment in Russia, especially direct, are political and economic instability, high rates of inflation, imperfection and frequent changes of laws, absence of warranties, criminogenic situation, corruption of bureaucracy, imperfect industrial and commercial infrastructure etc.

All this, in one degree or another, really was and is rendering a restraining influence on inflow of such necessary for Russian economy foreign investment. However, the factors named above are rather symptoms than genuine reason. In my opinion the main obstacle to growth of foreign investment became *the general state of the country economy, system of its administration and regulation, character and rates of reforms being carried out.*

It is clear that investments are the key factor of economic growth. It is clear also that in a country with huge territory, rich natural resources, with almost 150 million population, with rather high degree of higher and trade education, *the decisive role belongs to the domestic capitals.* It is the state of the internal investment process, efficiency of investment in various branches of national economy, that *the volume of foreign capital, ready to investment, as well as the ability of the country to master it successfully* depends in a decisive measure on. The determining role here belongs to the economic policy of the authorities, their skill to choose correct strategy and adhere to it consistently, not reducing this policy to the solution of momentary socioeconomic problems.

Changing of socioeconomic system, disintegration of the Soviet Union, destruction of a uniform public economic complex and inter-republican economic connections have objectively caused the necessity of a comparatively long-term transitional period with distinct statement of the sequence of changes in the economic and social system of the society. "In fact the economic picture in Russia, - notes one of its researchers, - turned out spontaneously: banks, prices, trade basically correspond to the advanced market but the authorities keep the rules of command-administrative system, legislation and the normative acts either do not correspond the existing reality, or in general are absent. Hence - harry and subjectivism at acceptance of the decisions, that is especially evident in discussions of budget questions at the Federal level.., struggle for power and economic privileges" (ФИНАНСОВЫЕ ИЗВЕСТИЯ, 1996b).

Thus, the main link in attraction of the foreign capital becomes the *preparation of a domestic economy for its reception, creation of structures, capable to perceive and to master the strategic investments*. It is especially urgent for FDI, dealing with a specific industrial object, where funds are not only invested, but also participation in management is realized. In this context Russia, in my opinion, will have to undertake the following steps for FDI attraction:

1. To define the scope of industries for FDI attraction. It would be a serious mistake to suppose that it is enough to make up a competent business-plan for obtaining investment outside. Investment into revival of the enterprises with preservation of their level of development, essentially lagging behind the world one, is simply senseless for foreign investor. He will go on it only in the case when he can fill temporarily free niche in the home market and under condition of 100% possession. It is expedient to involve capital from abroad into manufacturing industries for *structural reorganization and achieve the heights of modern technologies*. Taking into account, that the foreign capital is ready to go only in the enterprises, prepared for effective reception of investments, the claimants should pass through a procedure of preparation to investment to prove their viability and to have strategy of development on a period of the order of 5-10 years. Only after this there is a sense to address a foreign investor[3] .

2. Under existing conditions financial and industrial groups, uniting financial establishment (bank); the industrial enterprises and marketing network can become more attractive objects. By its character they remind holding companies in market economy. In Russian G.D.P. their share is 10%. Further development of such groups is braked to by insufficient financing. The external investors are constrained by two factors: absence of effective strategy of development and lack of well organized interaction inside the group. At elimination of these gaps and formation of the numerous group of small-sized enterprises (cluster) around it, these groups will become attractive objects for the foreign investors, ready to participate in the process of structural reorganization.

3. As the most perspective stimulators of attraction of the foreign investment, such organizations as the Russian centre of assistance to the foreign investment attached to the Ministry of Economy of Russia, joint stock company ВНИКИ, domestic and foreign consulting companies, investment bureaus in potential investing countries, must come forward. The process of investment could be revived by special financial funds abroad with participation of Russian capital on a system 50/50 or 25/75. Simultaneously with the fund a managing company is created in Russia, which selects perspective for investment enterprises, carries out their modification according to international standards and together with an authorized Russian bank forms and serves the clusters, enabling to use the investment first of all for structural development. The structure, financial fund abroad, an authorized Russian bank, a managing company in Russia, all this is an effective mechanism of accumulation of large financial resources of the foreign

investment companies. With its help conditions of transition from dot investment to a weighted policy of FDI attraction are created. However it should be recognized, that till now in Russia there is no an effective system for controlling the foreign industrial investments, covering federal and regional levels, as well as interests of the economy as a whole, branches and separate industries, oriented on export and on import replacement of enterprises, financial sphere and real economy. In many respects it is explained by critical situation of the Russian economy and difficulty in such a period to formulate precisely the long-term strategy of economic development, methods of integration into the a world economy and the most adequate to particular conditions forms of interaction with the foreign capital.

4. Alongside with the offered specific measures in items 3-5 an exclusively important role belongs to creation of stimuli for industrial investment inside country, for counteraction to “capital flight abroad”[4].

In the first case a positive role could play measures on reduction still remaining unjustifiably large gap between the profitability of investment into the State securities, issued in order to cover the budget deficit, and investment into the real economy. It is obvious, that the existing legislation and measures of encouragement do not reflect genuine needs of the Russian economy. Therefore first of all it is necessary to change the order of investors in industrial sphere taxation. For example, the profit of the enterprise on received from outside assets should be imposed at the investor, that is the dividends on the shares and/ or interests on the bonds should be deducted from the sum of the taxable profit of the enterprise. It is expedient temporarily to exempt private Russian investors in the corporate securities from paying income tax: their inclusion in production will give incomes, repeatedly exceeding insignificant losses of budget. Reduction of State securities profitability is possible by broadening admission to work with them for a wider circle of investors, first of all foreign ones. This will stimulate business activity as a result of attraction of new investment into real sector of the economy (КОММЕРСАНТЪ, 1996b) .

Return of the “fluent capital” could have render a positive influence upon the general investment climate. It is most frequently offered to allow its legalization together with appeals to its owners to show patriotic feelings. Such an outline is quite acceptable but, taking into account the mentality of “new Russians" and traditions of the proprietors treatment in Russia, it is hardly probable that it will bring the expected results. In our opinion a more effective way can be the association of the exported capitals in the form of JV, funds etc. together with foreign investors, ready to work at the Russian market. The offered method will ensure a more profound warranty of the property preservation and legal immunity to the owners of the repatriated capital till coming out from crisis and achievement of a steady political and economic stabilization in Russia.

5. Some problems of perfection of the legal climate for foreign investment and proposals for its perfection are considered in section V of this paper. The tax legislation causes particular anxiety of real and potential foreign investors. And the main object of criticism becomes not the level of taxation (in general it does not differ from the world practice at all), but unpredictability of tax departments actions, instability and complexity of the taxation regime. For example, retroactivity of some laws, large number and complexity of taxes calculation, unequal interpretation of unclear provisions of laws and subordinate legislation and departmental instructions by regions. Rather often there is lack of agreement between documents of tax, customs, financial and other departments. Just the instability and insufficient transparency of the legal space give raise to uncertainty among investors already working at the Russian market and potential ones (FOREIGN TRADE AND INVESTMENT REVIEW, 1995, p. 15) . At the same time it should be noted, that a customs infrastructure is being adjusted in the country, long-term customs policy begins to be formed, taking into account peculiarities of the transitional period and intention of Russia to enter WTO. Despite some increase of the average weighted rate of the import tariff since July 1, 1995 (from 11.4% to 12.5%), the Russian government decree No. 454 of May 6, 1995 "On confirmation of the rates of the entry duties" designates stages of its sequential reduction up to 80% of the 1995 level from the beginning of 1998 and to 70% from the same level in 2000. Specified will be conditions of importation of the equipment in offset of the contribution of the foreign investor into the authorized capital, equipment for own manufacture etc.

Probably, the State Duma should at the end of 1996 and the first half of 1997 finish acceptance of a package of the laws, stimulating investment, including investment in real economy.

6. Such forms of attraction of the foreign capital as participation in *privatization* of state property are not used in a due measure till now. So far "privatizational channel" could not ensure an essential inflow of foreign capital. Issue of depositary receipts on the shares in the State property is suitable, in difference from the enterprises in their modern situation, for accommodation of the first as well as new issues. Even the announcement of the depositary receipts allocation leads to the growth of share prices of the Russian enterprises. Use of a given mechanism for access of large foreign investors to Russian shares will lead to essential growth of their cost, that will allow the State to sell belonging to it packages of privatized enterprises shares at higher price. In this case however, one must not admit transfer of the main volumes of operations with the most attractive shares to the foreign share markets, as well as conversion of the depositary receipts into the determining factor of formation of share price of the domestic enterprises, especially in the case when the volume of operations with them at the Russian market will exceed the volume of operations with shares themselves (ФИНАНСОВЫЕ ИЗВЕСТИЯ, 1996a).

The new sources of attraction of the foreign capital can arise due to expansion of *leasing* operations. Ministry of Economy with participation of interested departments, commercial banks and leasing companies has developed a project of Federal program of development of leasing in Russia for 1996-2000. The problem is to bring the share of leasing in the investments up to 20% by 2000. In the law on leasing that is being prepared now it is necessary to envisage conditions, which would stimulate foreign companies activity at the Russian market of leasing services (ФИНАНСОВЫЕ ИЗВЕСТИЯ, 1996c, 1996d) .

A certain contribution to FDI attraction can be introduced by the policy of the external indebtedness of Russia settlement. Using part of the debt in offset of the foreign partner's share and reducing the volume of "live money" expands the number of mutually acceptable projects in development of mineral and water resources, forests and in measures of nature protection (ФИНАНСИСТ, 1996, p. 16)

7. Development of a system of commercial investment institutes such as specialized banks, funds and companies should promote growth of FDI in Russia. Such institutes are necessary for formation of a link between the Russian enterprises - emitters of the shares and other securities - and investors, including foreign. In particular such institutes could redeem blocks of shares (in whole or partly) in possession of enterprises, releasing them from not characteristic functions and providing gain in time (besides it is impossible to forget, that the domestic enterprises practically have no experience to work at the foreign financial markets). Creation of investment pools later on will allow to increase the volume of attracted funds owing to foreign investors increase of trust to large, more stable structures, connected with the insurance companies and possessing opportunities to lean on support of federal and regional authorities in necessary cases.

8. Under specific conditions of modern Russia it should be expected, that the process of *portfolio* investment inflow will render strong influence upon the volumes and structure of FDI. Their higher liquidity, less connection with manufacture, especially in the period of crisis, smaller risk at the expense of portfolio investment diversification, permits to state the assumption, that in not so far future their role in the total volume of attracted foreign capital will increase. In some degree they will execute the function of "scout" in relation to FDI, preceding the latter in a number of cases. Therefore it is expediently already now to make active efforts on development of domestic currency and share markets at the federal and regional levels, commercial banks and specialized investment institutes. Realization of this work under aegis of Central bank of Russia will give an opportunity to avoid discrepancies and contradictions between separate links of investment process, that one often had to conflict with at the more earlier stages.

9. Direct and portfolio investment, taken together, make up not more than 10-12% of the total volume of gross inflow of financial resources in Russia from foreign countries and international financial institutes. It is obvious that in this

country a principal policy, directed on outstripping growth of *private* direct and portfolio investment in comparison with the credits, first of all State ones, should be pursued. Massive use of the foreign credits for non-inflational cover of the budget deficit diverts funds from the industrial sphere and is leading to accumulation of external indebtedness that is huge without it. It would be expedient to use a part of borrowed funds for creation of guarantee funds and insurance business development, that would increase inflow of more effective kinds of capital.

10. The destiny of foreign investment in Russia will in many respects be defined by participation of regions in this process: as an example it is possible to cite Tatarstan's initiative that has formulated a package of proposals on accommodation of free money of American banks, investment and insurance funds in the republic. It is offered in particular to invest money into creation of farms on the soils of state reserve on the security of these soils and under government guarantee of petroleum deliveries. Other mechanism is the transfer of state blocks of shares of the largest enterprises of the republic into trust management of the general investor for a period of 5 years and subsequent sale of them to this investor on the securities market. According to estimations, the total volume of USA investment in Tatarstan in case of these projects realization can make up from $4.5 to $6 billion in the nearest 3-4 year (СЕГОДНЯ, 1996)

Endnotes

[1] By the way in the Ministry of Economy also such a point of view was spoken out that the present state of Russian economy does not give an opportunity to pose regional and branch priorities. See for example "Финансовые известия" July 6, 1995a.

[2] See for example "Вестник приватизации и фондового рынка", No. 9, 1995, pp. 24-25; "Complex program of stimulation domestic and foreign investment into economy of the Russian Federation"; Decrees of the Russian President No. 1466 of March 27, 1993 "On improvement of operation with foreign investment" and No. 1928 of September 17, 1994 "On private investment in the Russian Federation" and others.

[3] Some provisions of items 1-3 are taken from the article of the Chairman of the Investors Union R. Yavryan "The country is not ready to investment reception", See "Век", No. 30, 1996; "Финансовые известия", March 28, 1996c

[4] An estimated flow-out of capital from Russia is of the order of $8-10 billion annually that by 3-4 times more than FDI attracted into the country. See "Экономика и жизнь", No. 13, March 1996a.

References

ADELMAN, I. (1991), Long-Term Economic Development, World Development Report, p. 5.

AMSDEN, A., Y. COHANOVICH and L. TAYLOR (1994), The Market Meets Match. Restructuring the Economies of Eastern Europe, Harvard-Univ. Press.

ASLUND, A. (1994), Shokovaya terapiya v Vastochnoi Evrope i Rossu (translation: Shock Therapy in Eastern Europe and Russia), Moscow, p. 39.

BIELECKI, J. (1992), Problems of the Polish Transformation. Communist Economics awl Economic Transformation., vol. 4, no. 3.

DECREES OF THE RUSSIAN PRESIDENT (1993), On improvement of operation with foreign investment, No. 1466, March 27.

DECREES OF THE RUSSIAN PRESIDENT (1994), On private investment in the Russian Federation, No. 1928, September 17, 1994.

SACHS, J. (1994), Rynochnaya ekonomika i Rossiya (translation: Market Economies and Russia), Moscow: VVSMRM., p. 327.

INFORMATION AGENCY (1995),Foreign Investment in Russia: Salient Features and Trends, Second Report, Moscow, pp. 7-16.

ДЕЛОВОЙ МИР (1996a), May 12.

ДЕЛОВОЙ МИР (1996b), July 12.

ДЕЛОВОЙ МИР (1996c), July 19-25.

ЭКОНОМИКА И ЖИЗНЬ (1996a), No. 13, March.

ЭКОНОМИКА И ЖИЗНЬ (1996b), No. 14, April.

ЭКОНОМИКА И ЖИЗНЬ (1996c), No. 23, June.

ЭКОНОМИКА И ЖИЗНЬ (1996d), No. 27, July.

ЭКСПЕРТ (1996), No. 30, August 12, p. 9.

ФИНАНСОВЫЕ ИЗВЕСТИЯ (1995a), July 6.

ФИНАНСОВЫЕ ИЗВЕСТИЯ (1995b), October 6.

ФИНАНСОВЫЕ ИЗВЕСТИЯ (1995c), November 3.

ФИНАНСОВЫЕ ИЗВЕСТИЯ (1995d), December 21.

ФИНАНСОВЫЕ ИЗВЕСТИЯ (1996a), February 2.

ФИНАНСОВЫЕ ИЗВЕСТИЯ (1996b), February 22.

ФИНАНСОВЫЕ ИЗВЕСТИЯ (1996c), March 28.

ФИНАНСОВЫЕ ИЗВЕСТИЯ (1996d), September 12.

ИЗВЕСТИЯ (1995), June 7.

ИЗВЕСТИЯ (1996), July 6.

КОММЕРСАНТЪ (1996a), No. 10, March 26.

КОММЕРСАНТЪ (1996b), No. 22-29, August 6.

КОММЕРСАНТЪ (1996c), No. 31-32, August 28.

СЕГОДНЯ (1996), September 20.

ВОПРОСЫ ЭКОНОМИКИ (1994), 1994, No. 8, P. 6.

ВЕК (1996), No. 30.

ВЕСТНИК ПРИВАТИЗАЦИИ И ФОНДОВОГО РЫНКА (1995), No. 9, pp. 24-25.

Comments on: Systemic Transformation and Direct Foreign Investment in Russia: Problems and Solution

Herbert Brücker

1. Introduction

Ruslan Grinberg presented a valuable paper with detailed information on the legal, administrative and macroeconomic conditions for foreign direct investment in Russia, the structure of FDI and other capital flows to Russia. The paper also made some refreshing policy recommendations and conclusions. While I agree with most aspects of the analysis in the paper, the pithy and to some extent provocative policy statements invite some argument. Most parts of my comment concentrate therefore on these controversial topics as a basis for further discussion. It is organised along six lines: (2) the problems of macroeconomic stabilisation in Russia, (3) the issues associated with institutional reforms in Russia, (4) the economic rationale behind investment in developing and transition countries, (5) the factors motivating foreign investment in transition countries, (6) the role of uncertainty for foreign investment in Russia, and (7) policy recommendations.

2. Why Has Stabilisation Failed in Russia?

Ruslan Grinberg starts his paper with a pithy statement on the key issues of economic reforms and macroeconomic stabilisation. Of course this invites some arguments: firstly, I think it is misleading to distinguish between a *laissez-faire* approach and an *institutional structuralist* approach in the context of macroeconomic stabilisation. The question is not, whether government interferes in macroeconomic stabilisation or not - it interferes in any case - but which policy instruments are to be chosen for stabilisation. Jeffrey Sachs, who is quoted by Ruslan Grinberg and many others as the prime example of a *laissez-faire* view, opted for a fixed exchange rate in the case of Poland. The main problem of monetary stabilisation in transition countries is to break inflationary expectations of former non-convertible currencies. Experience with high inflation countries shows that this can be achieved most rapidly with an exchange rate peg. This is confirmed by the experience of transition countries, in general, and of Russia, in particular: the introduction of the exchange rate peg and the following currency band was the breakthrough for monetary stabilisation in Russia, while the preceding attempts at stabilisation relying solely on interest rate policy and the control of the money supply failed. Thus the late introduction of a currency peg delayed stabilisation which in turn raised the costs of transition. So far I am in total agreement with Ruslan Grinberg. However, in the medium and long run an exchange rate peg may lead to an overvaluation of the currency, large deficits in the current account, and, as a result, speculative attacks against the exchange rate. The devaluation of the Czech Crown in 1997, the large current account deficit in Poland, and the recent currency crisis in Russia are good examples of such risks. But these are problems resulting from the inappropriate management of exchange rate pegs rather than problems associated with a fixed exchange rate regime *per se*. Secondly, from my point of view, price controls might be instruments for structural and competition policies, but are not effective instruments for an anti-inflatory policy. Price controls can at best prevent open inflation, but not inflationary pressure triggered by rising effective demand. The use of price controls is costly: it distorts relative prices and therefore the allocation of resources. Furthermore, I am not convinced by the popular argument that inflation is triggered by monopolistic market structures. Monopolies affect the *level* of prices and generate rents. But they do not affect the *rate* of price changes. Hence, monopolistic market structures are perfectly compatible with stable prices. Price controls in monopoly sectors will therefore affect rents and may improve resource allocation by an adjustment of relative prices among goods and services, but they will have no effect on the rate of inflation. Thirdly, I admit that other nominal anchors beyond exchange rate pegs like wage and employment pacts between governments, employees and employers may help to stabilise expectations and therefore lower inflation. However, such agreements should not be mixed with price controls: they do not interfere in the microeconomic determination of wages and other factor prices. Fourthly, as is recognised by Grinberg, macroeconomic stabilisation has to be embedded in a coherent policy framework. From my point of view, Russia failed to implement a consistent macroeconomic policy mainly for two reasons: it was not able to collect taxes and enforce budget constraints in the public and private sector. Both problems are intertwined. If the government is unable to collect taxes, it is unable to organise its spending accordingly, and if the government does not settle due payments, it is unable to enforce settlement rules in the private sector. Hence, the problem in the case of Russia is not the choice between *laissez-faire* or *structural institutionalist* policy alternatives. The problem is that the Russian government is too weak to enforce the primary functions of the state, which in turn is the precondition for any alternative policy.

3. Was Privatisation and Institutional Reform a Failure?

Many observers including myself have been surprised by the speed of mass privatisation in Russia. However, it is disputed whether privatisation in Russia improved corporate governance. I agree completely with the critical assessment of privatisation by Ruslan Grinberg: mass privatisation failed to create real owners and incentives for investment. In contrast, it provided incentives for the management of enterprises with a high share of employee ownership and other forms of dispersed ownership to extract capital from enterprises. Capital flight is to some extent motivated by corporate governance structures in Russia. I think it is not necessary to provide preferential credit and tax incentives for investment in Russia. In spite of the high level of interest rates for government bonds during long periods of the transition process, there are institutional reasons which prevent investment. The enforcement of payment rules and transparent ownership rights are most important to motivate investment. Credit preferences and other measures cannot compensate for uncertainty created by non-transparent and inconsistent institutional rules.

4. FDI: Is the Glass Half Full or Half Empty?

The analysis of the FDI flows into Russia is embedded in a general analysis of FDI in developing and transition countries. Grinberg's general thesis is that foreign investment cannot be a substitute for domestic investment. I am in full accordance with this view. But I would like to stress a theoretical point in this context and highlight the consequences of modern growth theory for the evaluation of capital flows from developed market economies to transition economies. This should be seen as complementary to the analysis in the paper by Grinberg.

According to the figures of the World Debt Tables quoted by Grinberg, the total volume of net-flows of FDI into developing and transition countries was US$ 90 bn in 1995. In addition, there are good prospects for a further increase in investment flows into developing and transition countries - even if we consider that the quoted forecast of US$ 400 bn in 2020 by De Anne Julius might be too optimistic. From this point of view, the glass is half full. On the other hand, in relation to the population, the size of markets, the factor endowments with labour and natural resources in developing countries, the foreign investment record is poor. [Bitte Ralf wegen dieses Satzes fragen – ich bin mir nicht sicher was der Autor damit meint] In Germany we realised in 1995 FDI of some DM 52 bn direct investment abroad and a net outflow of FDI of DM 39 bn. This amounts to 1.1 per cent of GDP and 5.1 per cent of gross investment. German FDI is concentrated on industrialised instead of developing and transition countries: Some 80 per cent of FDI was invested in OECD countries and only some 9 per cent in transition economies (including China). This direction of FDI is exactly parallel to the direction of German foreign trade. Despite a huge dispute, whether the growth of FDI outflows is an indication for decreasing competitiveness of the German economy, the FDI figures are low by historical standards: At the height of the colonialist period the United Kingdom invested 8 per cent of its GDP and half of its gross investment abroad. The bulk of the UK's FDI was concentrated on developing countries. Despite a tendency of acceleration in the growth of FDI into developing countries, the total level of net capital flows is still low. Considering the absolute FDI levels in relation to the capital demand in transition and developing countries the glass is half empty.

From an economic point of view, the phenomenon of low capital flows from industrialised into developing countries in the post-war era is still a puzzle. Under the assumption of diminishing returns of factors of production the marginal productivity of capital has to be higher in poor countries than in rich ones. Given competitive markets for goods and capital, the higher marginal productivity leads to higher profitability of capital and therefore to flows of savings from rich to poor countries. But contrary to conventional economic wisdom, as Martin Feldstein and Charles Horioka demonstrated empirically, capital accumulation in catch-up countries is financed mainly by domestic savings and not by inflows of foreign capital. In addition, as the Nobel prize-winner of 1995, Robert Lucas, demonstrated, the magnitude of capital flows from rich to poor countries is much lower than we would expect considering actual differences in real income. Assuming a Cobb-Douglas technology and the pricing of the factors of production according to their marginal contribution to national income, the marginal product of capital in India must be 58 times higher than the marginal product of capital in the USA. If we consider differences in the human capital endowments, the marginal productivity of capital in India shrinks to five times the level of USA. But this is still too high to explain low capital inflows based on the imperfections of capital markets.

The radical conclusion of Robert Lucas and other new growth theorists focusing on this phenomenon is that for at least one factor of production, such as human capital or investment in research and development, the law of diminishing returns does not hold. Independent of which specific model is used, spillovers from the given stock of technological knowledge, human capital or physical capital lead to constant returns for the accumulation of the factor involved. This assumption changes the picture for capital flows between rich and poor countries, and for the dynamics of economic development, too: backwardness ceases to be a (major) advantage for growth and capital inflows from developed to developing countries. Growth and capital flows are dependent on the state of accumulation of critical growth factors and the capabilities for the absorption of accumulated knowledge of others. Therefore, contrary to conventional economic wisdom, developed countries with a high stock of modern technology and know-how may have a growth advantage over developing countries. Even if we do not accept the radical proposition of constant returns for at least one factor of production as proposed by new growth theorists, there is ample empirical evidence that factors like knowledge spillovers and increasing returns to scale do at least partly offset the advantage of backwardness. Hence, I agree with one of the key conclusions made by Ruslan Grinberg in his paper, namely that the key factor for economic growth in Russia is domestic investment, which can be complemented but not replaced by FDI.

5. Are Investment Conditions Special in Transition Economies?

According to conventional growth theory, the initial conditions in transition countries for FDI and capital inflows must be very favourable: there is a huge difference in real income between transition economies and the market economies of the EU and other OECD countries. In addition - as Ruslan Grinberg rightly mentioned - the abolition of mandatory planning, the liberalisation of prices and the opening of the economies led to a sharp devaluation of specific assetsthat were irreversibly linked to now obsolete supply and demand conditions. Because of the higher flexibility of human skills, the devaluation of physical assets is much higher than the devaluation of human capital. Under the assumption of diminishing returns, conventional economic theory would therefore expect a much higher marginal product of physical investment in transition countries in comparison to developed market economies.

Taking into account these conditions, the capital inflows from developed market economies are low: according to the figures of the ECE of the UN, FDI stocks per capita amounted at the end of 1995 to US$ 214 in the Central and Eastern European countries (excluding the former USSR), US$ 170 in the Baltics and US$ 28 in the European CIS-Countries - Russia was with US$ 35 slightly above the European-CIS-average. This is hardly what we would expect from the optimistic predictions of conventional economic theory.

The structure of FDI, which is analysed by Ruslan Grinberg in a very informative manner for Russia, supports the view that factors other than high marginal returns of investment play a role in low-income countries. From the empirical evidence provided by Grinberg and others we can draw four major conclusions.

(1) Foreign investment depends largely on the progress and credibility of economic reform. The stability of the legal, institutional and macroeconomic framework is a precondition for most FDI.
(2) The concentration of FDI in some major locations, as a rule the capital city of the country, speaks for the high importance of agglomeration factors like technological spillovers, specialised markets for inputs and labour market pooling. This leads to a herding effect of FDI and an agglomeration of investment at locations with relatively high wages.
(3) For most FDI entry into domestic markets is of high importance. As every investment survey shows, market entry is the leading motive for FDI. The concentration of investment in infrastructure with a stable market and the protectionist behaviour of the foreign car producers in the Czech Republic and Hungary supports this view. If we consider the concentration of FDI in the highly expensive Moscow area, the theory that demand spillovers and increasing returns to scale are a major factor for the direction of FDI might be right.

(4) Among the supply side factors motivating FDI, the exploitation of natural resources is most important. In contrast, cheap labour plays only a minor role. Otherwise we would expect a concentration of FDI in countries with low wages and a large labour force. The non-exploitation of the huge labour force in Russia demonstrates that low labour costs are insufficient to raise the marginal productivity of (foreign) capital and to motivate FDI.

6. Why is Foreign Investment so Low in Russia?

In contrast to most expectations, private capital moved out of and not into Russia for a long phase of the transition period. The Russian balance of payments continuously shows a current account surplus of some US$ 20 bn, which is matched by capital outflows. True, part of the capital outflows is used for foreign debt service charges. But there has been a net outflow of private capital with a volume of between 3 and 6 bn US$. We have to add to these figures an unknown amount of illegal capital flight, which is not covered by the balance of payments. This trend has come to a halt in 1996 and has been reversed in 1997. However, the bulk of foreign investment in Russia is portfolio investment directed at the government budget. The balance of foreign direct investment has been positive in 1996 and 1997, but at a rather low level. It still remains to be seen how the recent currency crisis will affect foreign investment.

I agree with the analysis of the legal and administrative obstacles for investment undertaken in the paper by Ginberg. It is true that legal conditions for investments improved significantly. I also support the view that the huge interest rates for treasury bills are counter-productive for investment. But I would like to add two other important points: firstly, in contrast to the Central European transition economies, there is no clear cut political commitment by all relevant political forces towards economic reform. This raises uncertainty about the relevant economic conditions in the future. Secondly, the major obstacle to macroeconomic stabilisation is the poor tax performance of the Russian budget as mentioned above. The major obstacle to stabilisation is not the budgetary deficit itself, but the inability of the government to enforce tax rules. Without a solution to the tax problem the uncertainty about macroeconomic stabilisation remains high - despite the success in the struggle against inflation. I do admit that there is progress in reducing political and macroeconomic uncertainty, but in relation to other Central and Eastern European countries and other emerging economies uncertainty is still high in Russia. According to new investment theory, uncertainty raises the opportunity cost of investment: in the case of irreversible investments the option value of not-investing and waiting for further information increases with the level of uncertainty. If uncertainty is high the returns to capital that are necessary to trigger investment can easily rise to double or triple the level of returns usually required. That is the major reason why the Russian investment record has been so bad compared to other transformation economies. But there is another side to the coin in this argument: decreasing uncertainty might lead to a sudden upswing in investment. We have seen such an investment hump in 1997. But the recent currency crisis will raise uncertainty and eventually lead to a sudden decline in foreign investment.

7. What Can We Recommend as Policy?

I agree with the general statement, that "the general state of the country's economy, the system of its administration and regulation, the character and rates of reforms being carried out" is the major obstacle to foreign investment. But I do not agree with the policy conclusions elaborated in detail. If I understood the propositions in the Grinberg paper correctly, then in contrast to a *laissez-fair* approach the legal and administrative regulation of FDI, the control of the allocation of funds towards defined sectors and branches is demanded. His catalogue of measures include:

(1) Selection of enterprises for FDI,
(2) Intervention into the enterprise organisation by forming financial-industrial groups, which will build cores of wider clusters of small enterprises,
(3) creation of investment funds with domestic and foreign participation,
(4) tax exemptions and other preferential treatment for FDI.

In the preceding sections of this comment it is argued that increasing returns to scale and positive externalities play an important role for the direction and volume of foreign capital flows. These factors also drive a wedge between social and private returns to investment, which in turn might be a reason for government intervention. But I do not believe that the distortion of incentives and red tape regulation are appropriate measures to internalise positive externalities. I think it is useful to deal with government intervention in a symmetric framework of market and state failure. Government intervention is appropriate if it is reasonable to assume that the costs of state intervention are lower than the costs of market failure. A lot of observers conclude from practical experience and empirical research that the capabilities for state action in Russia are poor. In his paper Grinberg provides additional evidence for that insight. Therefore, the risk of government failure in Russia is even higher than in other countries. Against this background I would like to stress the following points:

Firstly, private investors have advantages relative to government with respect to the selection of enterprises for foreign investments: they have better incentives, because they have to bear the risk of the investment, and they have better information about the future profitability of investments. Therefore, the choice of branches, locations and enterprises should be left to private investors. Market failure might indeed occur due to a lack of information. It is, therefore, helpful to provide additional information through investment agencies but not to intervene in the allocation of funds.

Secondly, private investors have advantages in the determination of the appropriate structure of corporate governance relative to the government. They have better skills, knowledge and incentives to develop an appropriate financial and corporate structure. Hence, the creation of financial-industrial groups will not trigger private investments.

Thirdly, tax exemptions are neither necessary nor helpful in attracting FDI. There is no reason to offer foreigners better investment opportunities than domestic investors. Moreover, since the major obstacle to investment is the high level of uncertainty, tax exemptions will have only minor effects.

In contrast to the proposed measures, an important field for government action might be the resource and the infrastructure sectors. For different reasons there exists market failure in both sectors. Firstly, the exploitation of natural resources generates huge ecological and intergenerational externalities that are not covered by private incentives. It is therefore necessary to develop a contractional and regional framework, which divides resource rents between public and private investors and secures an ecological and sustainable exploitation of resources. Secondly, in most public utilities we face some form of natural monopoly and positive spillovers to the public. It is therefore necessary to regulate prices and the supply to the population and economy in general in order to improve resource allocation.

In addition to those policy areas, the government could adopt a further set of measures to support private investment such as information supply, simplification of administrative, legal and tax rules and the provision of an appropriate infrastructure. Given increasing returns to scale and other factors that support economic agglomeration, we will see a high concentration of FDI in some locations. It is important to concentrate public services - physical infrastructure, transport capabilities, telecommunications, research and development, etc. - in these places. The best the state can do for the support of FDI is to reduce political, legal, institutional and macroeconomic uncertainty on the one hand, and to provide a proper regulation of sectors characterized by market failure and the associated business infrastructure on the other hand. True, this recommendation is not very original, but it is the best lesson we can draw from the experience we have in developed and developing countries.

K: The Role of Foreign Investment in the Russian Internet

Svetlana Petuhova

1. Introduction

The civilized transition to post-industrial (information) society is connected with transition from an extensive information (simple computerization) to intensive one, that is based on computer networks, forming the information space. Such a transition will increase an economic role of the information, will change the structure of the market and the character of market balance formation.

The computer networks are divided into local, corporate, national and international ones.

The local networks permit to unite the capacities of dozens of computers in a uniform system and are used as a rather modern office technology.

The corporate networks cover computer capacities of large corporations, banks and their branches, exchanges with their various platforms, military objects. Such networks already include many servers and communication lines.

The national networks cover appropriate country and contain tens of thousands servers, multi-kilometer telecommunications, including telephone lines. An example of a national network is the network of Great Britain JANET (Joint Akademie Network).

Internet belongs to the international networks.

The networks should be considered as global, beginning from the corporate ones.

The Internet is a world-wide, unique association of interconnected computer networks with universal technology of information exchange. Usage of common protocols TCH/IP (Transmission Control Protocol/Internet Protocol) and uniform address space permits to speak about Internet as a global "meta-net", or as a "network of networks". When working on a computer, connected to the Internet, it is possible to establish communication with any other computer, connected to this network, and to realize exchange of information, using that or another applied service of Internet (WWW, FTP, E-mail and other).

The phenomenon of Internet consists in the absence of a centralized control system. The Internet Society of Operating Coordination (ISOC) - public organization, basing on the contributions of the participants and donation of the sponsors, plays the role of the coordinator. At the same time each State creates legal and organizational machinery for regulation of the Internet usage.

Home computer or the working station of a local network obtains an access to the Internet global network due to an establishment of connection (constant or seance) with a computer of the service-provider (Internet service provider, ISP) - organization, the network of which has constant connection to Internet. The regional service-provider, working with the terminal users, is connected, in its turn, to a larger service-provider -network of national scale, possessing nodes in various cities of country or even in several countries. The national networks receive access to global Internet due to the connection to international service-providers - networks, that are a part of global main-line infrastructure of Internet. In addition, the regional and national service-providers, as a rule, establish communication among themselves and organize traffic exchange between their networks in order to decrease loading of external channels.

All networks have begun wide granting of IP-services (Internet/Protocol) over allocated and switched connections, the main push to which was the explosive growth of popularity of the World Wide Information Web (WWW). (Since 1977 merging of the American network Arpanet with the existing at that time national networks of other countries began. The hyper-network that was formed, access to which had only a narrow circle of specialists, was called Internet).

At present the Internet unites about 100 ths independent computer networks; millions of servers are working in it. Number of users is about 10 m. Therewith the annual traffic makes 300 %. At present the number of documents in it is doubled approximately each two months. Volume of sales of hardware will reach $32 billion, and software - $2.8 billion,. Only in USA advertising expenditures in the Internet in 1996 made more than $350 m, and their growth up to $6 billion is predicted by 2000. In 1996 more than 320 bargains on merge and purchase, touching Internet networks, were carried out in the world, that is almost three times more, than in 1995.

According to information of the American experts, the annual growth of information nodes quantity - electronic hyper-test journals or Web-servers - in USA reaches 100 %. And nontheless not USA are the model of "efficiency" of information resources of the Network usage. The registration data show, that quantity of Internet information objects per soul of the population is much higher in many European countries. For example, there are 18 "souls" per one registered Network address in Finland, 35 in Norway, 69 in Switzerland, 101 in Great Britain, while in USA - 70 and in Russia nearly 3000. These data permit to evaluate the rates of development of information service in the above listed countries.

In the Internet three levels are distinguished at present:

The first level - purely technical, network one. This is a global association of networks, computer communication networks of absolutely different status, but on the basis of uniform protocols and uniform system of addressing. This is tens of thousands of various networks; more than 6 m computers of this mega-network.

The second level - service one. Software, ensuring various network services are inside it: servicing, opportunity to transmit mail, data transfer, usage of a remote terminal mode, search of data bank, usage of the world web, which has brought an opportunity to obtain hyper-text, graphic and audio information, i.e. multimedia. It is important, that all new program service products are becoming the property of all Internet.

The third level is the information space, i.e. the information of different type, different significance, which is transmitted today (conferences; news translation; data banks; exchange, trade and banking transactions; news agencies, electronic scientific journals, guide-books etc.).

The heaviest growth of activity is observed in four sectors of the information market: telecommunication services, hardware maintenance, program products and services, services of information filling of the network.

2. Analysis of the Modern State of the Internet in Russia

The Internet in Russia has repeated the history of Internet in the world. Internet in Russia has emerged from scientific establishments: from the Institute of Space Research, from the Institute of Nuclear Research, Institute of Organic Chemistry and a number of Moscow State University establishments, and then further all this has spread over all Russia. The structure of the Russian Internet segment began to be formed in 1991-1992. (EUnet/Relcom, Sovam Teleport, "Glasnet", FREEnet), therewith the terminal users were granted, basically, only the E-mail services.

The Internet in Russia has been developed intensively practically since 1994. At present there are about 330 organizations-providers in Russia that provide connection to the Network about 50 ths computers of the individual and corporate users, which thus obtain access to 2500 Russian servers. On some estimations, the demand for data transfer services in Russia in the nearest years will increase seven-fold.

On absolute number of information nodes Russia has already come nearer to such State as Holland. The analysis of the inquiries on search of information in the Russian part of Internet shows, that such topics as "Business and economy", "Culture and art", "Science and education" make up to 62 % of all inquiries. The news, multimedia and policy are a subject of interest in 15 % of cases. An extensive subject-matter of sport, resting and various entertainments takes about 22 %.

The distribution of the inquiries to the Russian part of Internet has developed as follows: about 50 % - from the CIS countries, including Russia; up to 30 % - from USA, almost 20 % - from all other countries of the world.

Regional aspect of the Network development in Russia is of interest: in 1996 up to 85 % of all working in a mode of access to information nodes of the world web were the inhabitants of large cities. In summer of 1997 their share decreased to 80 %. The share of Moscovites has fallen from 75 % up to, about, 65 %.

Thus, participation of residents of small cities of Russia is increasing in Internet; the notion of a periphery as of information depth of the country is being washed-out.

The number of E-mail users is annually increasing two times. At the same time 40-50 ths of persons have the opportunity for access to the information resources of the World information web. Their number annually grows four-fold.

Yet since 1995 the Russian Internet was precisely directed to the West; the information to servers was given first of all for foreigners, and the circle of the domestic users was limited basically to computer specialists.

At present "two" Internets have been developed actually. One is a popular, charge-free network, that unites opened for any "visitors" server space. Advertising and general items of information, that does not have commercial character are placed there usually. The "second" Internet network is intended for specialists. Just in it 90 % of all informations is concentrated, the access to which requires registration of the user with appropriate legalization of the agreement of payment.

The situation on the Internet map in Russia varies rather dynamically. The majority of physical surface channels belongs to Rostelecom, which sells them to all interested persons for a rather high price. Any provider can purchase a digital channel (even 2-MB/s) and straight away a new communication appears in the Internet infrastructure. The satellite channels also have their owners, for example Ministry of Defence, which also sells them, frequently through organizations, setting ground equipment of satellite communication. In this connection most interesting is the geography of Russian Rostelecom Internet channels (see the map in the appendix).

The inter-departmental program of creation of a national network of computer telecommunications for science and higher school, realization of which began in 1996 with participation of Ministry of Science and Technologies, Ministry of Education, Russian Fund of Fundamental Research and Russian Academy of Sciences plays an essential role in the development of the Russian Internet infrastructure. This program should connect 32 provincial universities to the Network; it is an original range for development of new data transfer technologies and it is executed together with Soros Fund and is financed from the budget.

Let us notice, that if earlier it was accepted to divide Russian Internet precisely into commercial and scientific-educational parts, assuming that all activities of the latter is financed by the State and/or foreign funds, to conduct such a border today is more difficult. Impossibility of complete centralized financing of current operation and development of scientific-educational networks resulted in development of self-financing principles of activity of many nodes of these networks, directed on the ability to pay its way and reception of extra-budget resources for development of regional infrastructure.

The commercial networks are developing under their business-plans. The number of "primary" commercial providers, having their own channels of communication with the foreign Internet networks is insignificant. At present only in Moscow really operating are more than two dozens of such companies; the largest of them are Sovam Teleport, Demos and Relcom. About 30 % of the market of services on access to Internet falls on the share of each of them. The level of the prices at the largest providers varies from 1.5 to 3 dollars per hour of working in the network. Certainly, each company provides also its own services.

Many other companies, also granting access to the Internet, are "secondary" providers, as far as they take out a booking for a part of a channel from the providers. Non-commercial networks, created for scientific and educational purposes, for example, GlasNet and FREEnet also have access to the Network.

The number of the users is constrained by bad quality of public communication lines and high price. In Moscow it is about 30 times higher, than in USA. For normal communication, including transmission of moving images and audio information, 28-kbps capacity of telephone communication lines is necessary. At Russian lines this parameter is 3-5 times worse. A low general level of the country computerization also has its effect.

In the Russian "Internet large policy" the main acting persons are:

a) EUnet/Relcom

The Russian network EUnet/Relcom is a part of Eunet network - the largest in Europe association of commercial networks, that to the beginning of 1997 united more than 300 ths users. The history of the network began in 1990, when a small narrow-professional network was created and in 1991 its connection to Eunet took place with assignment of an official name EUnet/Relcom (simple Relcom). Management of the network is accomplished by the commercial organization JSC Relcom, which has base nodes in Moscow and St. Petersburg.

On data as of February 1997 the network is represented by 108 nodes in 11 States (former republics of the USSR). The part of the nodes has complete connection to the Internet, and other part performs only E-mail exchange.

The EUnet/Relcom network has two channels of 3 Mbps capacity each: Moscow -Amsterdam and St. Petersburg - Helsinki. In March 1997 work on putting into operation of the second channel Moscow - Amsterdam with 2 Mbps capacity has begun, that will increase the total capacity of the channels up to 6 Mbps. There are no unified blanket rates on all the network as yet, however the tendency to unification of the price policy is strengthening.

b) Demos/Internet

The Demos/Internet network is operated by the Demos company - one of the oldest network companies of Russia, that was standing at the source of the Relcom network. Up to the middle of 1996 the Demos company had a channel in EUnet (256-kbps Amsterdam), and in June 1996 it put into operation a ground channel in USA (Moscow - Boston) with 2 Mbps capacity that has connected the Moscow node Demos directly with the largest American service-provider - MCI Telecommunications Corporation. This channel that is the most high-speed foreign channel of Russian Internet, has fixed the position of Demos/Internet as a large independent Russian IP-network.

All capital equipment of the Demos/Internet network is located in Moscow on several technological sites and in central office of the company, connected by high-speed channels. Here IP-channels of regional providers (nodes of the network in other cities) and of Moscow customers converge, modem pools are located, as well as gateways to other networks and systems. The service-providers' nodes in different cities of Russia, connected to the Demos/Internet network, are numbered in the dozens.

c) Sovam Teleport

Sovam Teleport is a joint venture, created in 1990 by three founders: Institute of Automated Systems (Russia), Cable @ Wireless (Great Britain) and San-Francisco/Moscow Teleport Inc. - at present Global Telesystem Group (USA). Now Sovam Teleport enters in the group of companies Global Telesystems (GTS).

The wide spectrum of telecommunication services granted by the Sovam Teleport company (a set of bank telecommunications, E-mail, access to Internet, connection to remote data bases) is based on the SovamNet network, the digital channels of which connect more than 20 cities on the territory of the former Union and provide several foreign outputs.

The only company in Russia, granting since Autumn 1995 complete access to the Internet and on-line services according to project (electronic issues of the newspapers "Izvestia", "Finansovye Izvestia", "Commersant-Daily", journals "Commersant", "Dengy", financial, commercial, legal and other information), is the Russia-On-Line company. For an initial model there was taken a huge telecommunication and information system of USA - America Online and the project has a complex character. The modem access to the services of the Russia-On-Line company is granted in many cities of Russia and Ukraine (more than 250 lines). Increase of the channels capacity was carried out several times and the regular one (the fifth during one and a half year) took place in March 1997. As a result the company has now three independent international channels with overall capacity of 4 Mbps.

The affiliated company Teleport-TP grants the whole complex of services and is an official communication operator of the international network INTELSAT, as well as one of the founders of European space communication network EUTELSAT. Besides this the Teleport-TP company now develops a satellite communication system over all Russian territory (128 stations) under the name SATELINK. The development of the Internet's project PORTAL that, in its turn, includes a number of satellite technologies of data delivery from the Internet through satellite (DirecPC, NetSat Expres, PES, SCPS), is in full swing.

d) Global One Russia

In 1996 three world largest telecommunication companies - Deutsche Telekom, France Telecom and Sprint united their efforts and created a group of companies - Global One, granting complete complex of modern telecommunication services in many countries of the world. A Russian part of the new world alliance has become an independent group of the companies Global One that unites the Global One company (marketing and sale of communication services) and Global One Network company (communication operator), that have regional representations and partner organizations in more than 60 cities over all territory of the former Union.

e) GlasNet

The GlasNet network (created in 1990) enters the international organization - Association for Progressive Communication (APC). The network has more than 170 direct input modems in Moscow and gateways with a number of Russian networks .25 for reception of requests from more than 250 cities of Russia. One of its features is an opportunity of access to the network from many cities of Russia and CIS through the local input points of other telecommunication networks (Infotel, Rosnet, Russian Sprint, Transinform), that provides roaming for the customers of GlasNet. In the spring of 1997 the GlasNet had two external channels in USA: 512-kbps satellite channel to the CRL network and 256-kbps ground channel to the BBNPlanet network.

f) RosNet

RosNet - commercial public communication network, on the basis of which complex integrated communication, information and telematic services are granted. The owner of the network is the joint-stock company of an open type "Russian Telecommunication Network". The joint venture ROSNET International was formed in 1996 together with the companies AT&T and INTERCON International USA, Inc. (USA). Rosnet's own high-speed channel into the main-line part of American Internet made its appearance in 1996.

At present in Russia there are also several more Federal networks, which play a great role in the Internet development: RUNNet; RUHEP/Radio - MSU; FREEnet; RSSI; RELARN-IP; MSUnet; the projects of the Soros Fund on realization of the large projects on the basis of a basic network in Moscow RMIX-UMOS (Southern Moscow reference network), using the high-speed channel and

FDDI technology (100 Mbps) and uniting 32 Russian universities, for which during the nearest two years centers of free access to the Internet network will be created.

For the Russian businessmen the Investment Promotion Agency Network (IPAnet), created in the Internet with the help of Multilateral Agency on Warranties of the World Bank Investment, is of interest. In this network Russia is officially presented by the Russian Center of Assistance to Foreign Investment (RCAFI) at the Ministry of Economy of Russia, which has an opportunity to place information on the investment projects, as well as general information on business conditions in Russia. Through the RCAFI the Russian companies can become the "second level" members of IPAnet and to place information about themselves independently.

In our country there is a number of specific problems, hindering Internet Network of value use:

- Extremely low level of information culture of the population of the country
- Absence of the unequivocally established legal status of various information objects, by virtue of that unattended their use occurs;
- Unsufficient capacity and low reliability of communication lines and equipment;
- Low level of installation of the telephone in Russia;
- Usage of Russian and other national languages in predominatingly Anglo-Language Internet (the Russian-Language space of Internet is used by 90 % for transfer of E-mail);
- Absence of financial resources for purchase of a computer and connection to the Network in the population ;
- Absence of an opportunity to create main-line telecommunications at the expense of own resources in the State;
- Inconvenience of payments - the credit cards in Russia are of limited occurrence yet, while in the West all accounts between the users and providers are accomplished electronically etc. For all that in Russia growth of demand on the information network services is predicted on 700 % by 2000.

For acceleration of Russia entry in the information association a public organization - Regional Public Center of Internet Technologies (RPCIT) was created; that is an attempt to generate conditions for an effective interaction of the suppliers and consumers of information, for arranging of independent advisory activity and for reducing the gap between quantity and quality of information-network technologies and services.

3. Financing of the Internet Development

The specific character of Russian Internet consists (besides problems with Cyrillic alphabet) in practically complete absence of support from the State. The share of Internet in the gross national product of Russia is 40 times less, than the same parameter in the USA. In order that the Internet Network in Russia should become popular and covering whole regions, significant investments are required. Local providers, especially regional ones, are not able to ensure development of the network at their own expense. Potential source here can and should become the foreign investments.

The main law in Russia is the budget, in which a separate line is, where the Inter-Departmental Program for Science and Higher School is mentioned. Main financing of the Internet State projects in Russia is accomplished through Ministry of Science and Technologies. This Ministry in essence plays a coordinating role. Resources of smaller volumes go through Ministry of Education and the Russian Fund of Fundamental Research.

In 1997 in common with Soros Fund 114 billion RUR were intended for the accepted governmental program on connection of Russian universities to the Internet, but only 6.4 billion RUR have been obtained yet. This is an essential blow to the development of Internet in Russia. In our country there are Inter-Departmental Programs and appropriate Councils, where the problems of main-line Internet infrastructure construction are being solved. To determine the degree of participation of commercial networks in this work is rather difficult. The investments of Soros Fund are being spent on a program agreed with the above mentioned ministries.

The attraction of the domestic investment, as well as foreign one, is accomplished in various forms: joint ventures, joint-stock companies, issue of securities, short-term and long-term credits.

Change of a structure and volume of the foreign investment are presented in Tab. K1.

Tab. K1: Change of Foreign Investment Structure

Foreign investments	1995 (%)	1996 (%)
State credits	52	41
Commercial credits	32	49
Direct investments	16	10

As to the foreign investment, two forms of their attraction are applied in the branch:

- Credits of the partners, which are allocated on the State line, as well as under commercial agreements. When registering credits with the State warranty, certain financial privileges are granted; this form of attraction of foreign investment for Russian telecommunication workers is the most favorable, as independence of the telecommunication network from foreign influence is preserved;
- Direct investment of resources in development of telecommunication services and in the industry for creation on the territory of Russia modern facilities appropriate to world standards of telecommunication. This form has found the heaviest application when creating the mobile means of communication.

Russia involves attention of the foreign investors for many reasons, including as a country of transit communication; moreover its information resources are very attractive. Highly profitable technologies and realization of the projects on development of inter-urban and international telephone communication systems attract the greatest attention of the foreign partners. Beside the scale investments in the large joint projects, the foreign capital participates in investment in a kind of credits under particular local projects. The total sum of foreign investments into development of these networks, making the basis of Internet, has made almost 800 m USD during the last 4 year; the investments of the Russian party have made about 200 billion RUR. One of the first projects, realized together with foreign investors, was the project of creation of a modern digital system of international communication Russia-Denmark (western complex), which commissioning was in April 1993. Costs of the project realization have made 500 m RUR and 123 m USD. The investors of the project were the JSC Rostelecom and foreign companies Telecom Denmark, Gray Nordic (Denmark) and US West (USA).

In February 1995 the East Complex in Khabarovsk was opened. The basis of this complex is a fiber-optics communication line (FOL) laid on the bottom of the Japanese Sea between Nakhodka (Russian Federation) and Japanese city Naoetsu and South Korean city Pusan; the ground FOL Khabarovsk-Nakhodka, international switching center and the ground station of space communication in Khabarovsk. The cost of the project is 43 billion RUR and 160 m USD. Simultaneously international switching centers were constructed in Moscow, St.Petersburg and Khabarovsk.

In 1996 the project of realization the program of construction of a Southern complex of international telephone communication system, including ground FOL Moscow-Rostov-on-Don, international switching center in Rostov-on-Don and an underwater FOL Novorossiysk-Odessa-Istanbul-Palermo (ITUR) was completed.

Construction of an overland part of the fiber-optic communication line Moscow-Rostov-on-Don-Novorossiysk was carried out by the JSC Rostelecom using the equipment and cable of Siemens (Germany) production. Its creation has allowed to unite three sections - western, eastern, and southern in a uniform network, being a basis of the perspective public digital communication network of Russia.

On the line Moscow-Khabarovsk transmission of six digital tributaries of 155 Mbps is organized. The total capacity is 11500 channels. Total volume of the investments for realization of the project has made 70 billion RUR and 500 m USD.

The credits with the State warranty are used for purchase of switching devices for international, inter-urban and local telephone communication, as well as partially for financing of construction of these objects, enabling to provide connection to the Internet. In 1996 the credits of Great Britain under the warranty of the government for the project Comstar made more than 35 m USD, Japan for JSC Rostelecom for RRL Moscow-Khabarovsk - 35 m USD, credit of France - 150 m USD, Spain - 56 m USD.

The direct investment of foreign companies basically directed on creation of joint ventures made in 1996 more than 70 m USD.

In the future the share of the foreign investors credit in the total volume of investments will be saved, but will change on the structure: the credits with the State warranty will be reduced, and the commercial credits will be increased (Norvegian credit, credit of the German Board of Guardians, credit of AT&T). The position of the Department of Communication and Informatics consists in that to go from the budget appropriations as far as possible; the strategy of the problem solution is as follows: at first to develop most profitable kinds of communication - international and inter-urban (this branch has given in the 1995 budget about 2 - 2.5 trillion RUR, while spending - 184 billion RUR) and only then, using the incomes of them, to develop public urban and countryside communication.

In advanced countries the foreign capital "starts up roots" predominatingly in the alternative systems and services. The base networks and traditional services market are considered to be national property. In the USA participation of the foreign capital is authorized only up to 20 %. In Germany in connection with Deutsche Telecom company shareholding organization a number of decrees, prohibiting penetrations of world business giants of telecommunication into the sphere of national operator interests were accepted.

The profitability of telephone networks makes now on the average 30-36 %, though separate telephone networks, located in geographically expedient conditions and with large density of population, have profitability up to 50 %. As estimated by specialists, time of the domestic networks modernization and their transformation into civilized facilities is some 7-10 years. The total cost of all telephone facilities replacement on modern ones will make from 200 to 220 billion USD.

Such well known foreign companies - manufacturers of telecommunication equipment as A &T, Siemens, Italtel, Alcatel, Bell, Motorola, Ericsson, NEC, Samsung and others - are the most active operators of communication in the country. One more direction of the foreign partners activity is their participation in creation of joint ventures for manufacturing communication facilities on the Russian territory (for example, Russian-Belgian enterprise Lenbell with the Alcatel company in St.Petersburg, Russian-Korean enterprise Samsung-Crosna in Moscow, Russian-German enterprise Izhtel with Siemens and other companies).

Rather serious is the problem of compatibility of the equipment, that is caused also by decentralization of management in the branch and absence of a uniform technical policy. During several last years the base operator has acquired much foreign equipment of a different class, systems and manufacturers. The bad compatibility, especially of the software, essentially reduces quality of servicing already now.

4. Prospects of the Russian Internet Development

The boom in the field of information Internet development in Russia will proceed and Russia will increase its share in the World Information web. The economic activity in the Internet at present is comparatively low, because at present there are no generally accepted decisions on protection of the information and intellectual property, ways of payment for the goods and services. The legislation does not regulate such questions, as issue of "electronic" money, conclusion of contracts in the computer networks, measure of the responsibility for their infringement, right of the authors on distribution of electronic copies etc. Already in the near future, probably, these problems will find its solution, that will create essentially new opportunities for the Russian businessmen concerning their outlets to the global markets. However in the meanwhile the domestic businessmen do not display great interest to the business opportunities of Internet. It is explained, probably, by that in Russia usage of "the network space" for the advertising purposes is not expediently, and connection and operation with the Internet requires investments, that do not giving fast return.

Main problems on support and regulation of Internet functioning in Russia are: development and realization of a complex of measures, directed on development of national communication networks; on utmost support of creation program and technical means, enabling to accomplish access to the Internet; on maximal representation in the Internet Network of the information about activity of the Russian bodies of State authorities and bodies of local self-management.

On all the named problems appropriate legislative initiatives and actions are provided in the working plan of the State Duma Committee on information policy and communication on 1997-1999.

Objectively in Russia development of networks of communication pursuant to real processes occurs: installation of the telephone - for all users under moderate tariffs and telecomputerization - for business-groups under high tariffs.

One of the major resources, promoting the development of Internet, are the supporting reference networks. Development of such supporting infrastructures, which will help scientific and educational regional networks, as well as commercial structures, is encouraged within the framework of the Inter-Departmental program.

The second important type of resources are the points of traffic exchange - the Internet-exchange. In Russia there are already two Internet-Exchanges -the Moscow National and the St.Petersburg. Creation of such structures has allowed to optimize traffic exchange between commercial service-providers, that specifies value of such things, if the exchange is not conducted in the narrow-departmental framework.

Finally, the last resource is the address space. The quantity of addresses is limited, i.e. this resource is deficient. The distribution of these resources should be controllable and whenever possible centralized. Now in the world 3 centers exist, which distribute such resources: Internic in USA, Raif in Europe and Apnic in Asia-Pacific ocean region. At present Russia is striving for creation of a fourth network information center, which should be engaged in distribution of such resources. This is just that part, which requires the State support.

Thus and so, except the control of information, control of the Internet infrastructure development is necessary, which provides delivery of this information. Namely here it is important, that the State bodies should define the key points and priorities where it is necessary to invest resources so as to provide that control over the Russian Internet development remained in our State.

In the basis of the new structure of the network lies a fiber-optic ring (having 1 m channels capacity), which will connect the new equipment being installed (also 1 m channels) and will create the possibility of connection to the Internet. The first stage of this program - the project "Gold Bullet" is the project, which is being accomplished by AT&T company, JSC Rostelecom and Telmos together with the Moscow urban telephone network. This project costing 200 m USD, assumes introduction of 400 ths numbers.

Particularly it is possible to give an example about developing the work on expansion of communication channels with Internet at the Demos company. In addition to already existing two channels, leading in USA and having in total 4 Mbps capacity, the company is going to introduce two channels more: one in Europe (it will begin to operate in the end of September) and one in USA (each of 2 Mbps capacity). It is done in connection with that the existing channels are already loaded on 70 %. In addition to that the statistics of the Demos company shows, that 70 % of the traffic falls on the foreign countries and three quarters from them - on the USA.

Besides this, Demos together with the State Enterprise "Space Communication" and Vympel company, has developed the IP Space Link program, that provides users with access to Internet through satellite channels. For this purpose the geostationary satellite Express-2 will be used, the covering zone of which includes the larger part of Russia, countries of CIS, Asia and East Europe. For access to Internet the customers are offered to install ground subscriber's satellite station VSAT Nextar BOD costing 54 ths USD. In this configuration it is possible to order a 512-kbps communication channel. The measures, that were undertaken, are called to solve, if only partly, the problem of connection of regions to Internet.

Manufacture of urban ATX of large capacity and inter-urban stations remains a problem. For its solution foreign companies, having large experience in development and industrial production of such equipment, are involved and joint ventures are created. Acting joint ventures with Alcatel, Bell, Siemens, Italtel companies can be used for this purpose; not long ago the factory of ATX production in Pskov created a joint venture with the Samsung company.

Other problem is the manufacture of transmission systems for long-distance communication lines. The realization of domestic developments runs across serious financial and technical difficulties, caused, mainly, by absence of the necessary components base. In this field it is also assumed to find one's bearing in collaboration with the foreign partners.

In the field of satellite communication the main efforts are directed on creation of a series of inexpensive, compact ground stations of a new generation, operating with satellites Express, Gals, Mayak and Arkos. Work on expansion of functional possibilities of satellite communication stations Koradis is proceeding, for which together with the Bosch company an effective solid-state transmitter of 16 W power with a low level of noise has been developed, that considerably raised the operational characteristics of the station. The transmitter is delivered to Germany to complete the VSAT stations.

The question on the degree of foreign companies participation in providing the country with the telecommunication equipment is constantly discussed in the circles of communication operators and manufacturers.

In our opinion it is expediently to expand the framework of cooperation with the leading foreign companies in such directions, as:

- creation of facilities and systems of mobile public radio communication of and, first of all, in the GSM-900 and CDMA standards;
- creation of fiber-optic systems of synchronous digital hierarchy transmission with 155 and 622 Mbps capacities;
- manufacture of digital modems for data transmission networks with 1.2...64 kbps capacities;

- creation of ground satellite communication stations, separate assemblies and units for them.

Evaluation of the systematic projects development of Russian segments of the Iridium and Goldstar international systems, being created by the American companies, occupies a special place in the development of Internet in Russia. Usage of these systems will speed up its entry into the global information structure.

For the realization of main directions and projects of connection with the Internet in Russia it is necessary to conduct strategic planning of a system of measures on business-processes, business-projects and business-technologies management, bearing in mind the interest of those structures, which develop the Russian industry and economy on the basis of business and diligent competition.

With the purpose of ordering the interaction of the State authority bodies with the international information resources, the Federal Agency has carried out the work on creation of a special Internet domain "Russian Government Internet Network" (RGIN) and a central domain node, which should take over the role of a gateway between computer networks of the State authority bodies of the Russian Federation and the international Internet computer networks.

The main purpose of the network "RGIN" creation is the provision of an effective information support of the operative government measures through an access to all necessary domestic and foreign information resources of Internet, as well as provision of interaction of the State authority bodies, being the members of "RGIN".

At present in Russia development of the Federal Law project, devoted to problems of telecommunication, is being carried out in which, in particular, legal status of the natural and legal persons, granting information and other services with usage of telecommunication networks should be determined. Real judicial protection of the Internet users and providers rights in Russia can not be provided without such a law. The development of Internet in Russia requires introduction of additions and changes in the Federal law, accepted in June 1996 - "On participation in international information exchange".

The problems of legal protection of the person and inviolability of private life should be solved from the point of view of protection of the information about it in telecommunication networks, as far as the rapid development of computer and telecommunication technologies gives huge opportunities of uncontrolled access to the personal information.

The protection of Internet against wrongful actions is especially important in connection with that it enables transnational control of data, material and human resources. But the activities on providing safety of computer information systems should not interfere the development of Internet Network in Russia. The State should provide the safety of the state structures participation in the network functioning, and the non-state organizations should take care of it themselves. These and other questions require an additional analysis of the Russian legislation from the point of view of its completeness and efficiency.

5. Conclusions

The main value of Internet is the huge accumulated and developed by routing protocol global connectivity and service programs - labor product of huge quantity of specialists. The problem of Internet development is that fact, that each new kind of service results in an explosive increase of information quantity, that requires new lines. With the appearance of WWW the traffic has increased thousand times. Therefore many questions are raising about that how to use the available computer space most efficiently.

The further development of Internet in Russia is constrained not only by the state of the technical base, but also by absence of the State policy that determines the role, place and forms of the State authority bodies participation in the Internet.

The swift development of Internet leaves behind the process of an appropriate normative-legal base creation and perfection. Analysis of the domestic legislation shows, that in this area effective regulation is not yet provided. The acceptance of legal acts on protection of the intellectual property in the networks and the international information exchange is extremely necessary.

As far as the holders of main files of information are ministries and departments, the State should determine its policy on formation of national information resources, as well as on usage of Internet, supporting it by an appropriate governmental decisions. The absence of the official suppliers of statistical and other socially useful items of information in the Russian Internet, results in that the authentic information in the network is inaccessible. Without purposeful formation of State and commercial information resources and granting an access to them through the Internet, Russia will not be able to occupy an appropriate to its intellectual potential place in the world information community. The problem of the departmental networks safety should not be transformed into an obstacle on the way of the Internet development, since it uses special software, blocking unauthorized access.

Analysis of on-line commercial companies business shows, that the success of their activity depends not so much on the price policy and quality of the software, which are becoming more and more standard, as from the offered contents. In this area Russian businessmen have not so much foreign competitors, and there is a chance to take dominant positions in the market of the analytical information, news, financial and economic information and granting access to the domestic "electronic" newspapers. The analysis of information business in Russia shows, that gradual saturation of the market by factologic and news information is occurring, but the necessity of analytical materials, especially in regions, remains unsatisfied.

The investment policy should be directed on all possible attraction of the investments to the "Communication" complex both from domestic and foreign investors. This is executed in various forms: joint ventures, joint-stock companies, issue of securities, short-term and long-term credits.

The administration of the Committee on Information Policy and Communication in Russia participates in all main arrangements, carried out in Europe and the world and directed to definition of prospects of telecommunication development. This activity will allow to choose those technologies, which with consideration of the domestic users interests and the state national communication networks will help Russia to enter the international telecommunication space already in the foreseeable future. Moreover, Russia can become the largest country of transit for telephone communication between Western Europe and China and other East countries. But this will require significant investments in the development of fiber optic communication lines and creation of a favorable investment and competitive environment.

References

CHAMBER OF COMMERCE AND INDUSTRY OF THE RUSSIAN FEDERATION (1996), Materials of the conference: The Present and Future of Telecommunication (Russ.), Moscow.

DUMA BULLETIN (1997), No. 10 (Russ), Moscow.

INTELLECTUAL PROPERTY (1997), No. 1-5. (Russ), Moscow.

ROCIT, The Market of Internet in Russia, http/in/WWW.Rocit org/seminars.

SCIENTIFIC PARK (1997), No. 1-5 (Russ.), Moskow.

SHPAGINA, M., Internet as a Facility for People Informatization, (Russ), Moscow, Expert, No. 27, 1997.

SIGALOV, A. (1997), Yellow Pages of Internet, Russian Resources (Russ.), St. Petersburg.

SYSTEMS OF INFORMATION PROVISION OF INNOVATION ACTIVITIES OF THE RUSSIAN FEDERATION (1997), Materials of the Information Analytical Center in Moscow (Russ.).

THE WORLD OF COMMUNICATION AND COMPUTER SCIENCE, 1996 No. 1-12, 1997, No. 1- 6, Moscow.

WORLD TRADE CENTER (1997), Materials of the 8-th International Computer Forum (Russ.), Moscow.

L: Panel Discussion: Competition in European Telecommunications and Market Perspective

Competition in Liberalised Telecommunications Markets

Dimitri Ypsilanti

The fact that competition in the telecommunications industry, both in terms of infrastructure and basic services, has been accepted in principle, does not guarantee that it will occur in practice. Rather, the greatest challenge facing policy makers is to stimulate competition. A large number of regulatory details remain, which need to be implemented (such as interconnection, access charges, numbering allocation, number portability, access to rights of way, licensing, etc.). These are certainly necessary, but are they sufficient?

At present, about 99 per cent of main subscriber lines are still provided by incumbent operators in the OECD area. Competition has mainly occurred in long distance and international services, where it is much easier to achieve rapid market entry and to gain a market share. When competition is introduced into Europe in 1998, it will come in the first instance from existing networks of utility companies and the railways. It also seems likely that there will be a relatively rapid provision of international and Intra-European networks. However, the challenge lies in stimulating local loop competition and in trying to eliminate the bottleneck resulting from the existing monopoly control of the local loop. There are a number of solutions to this, including stimulating fixed wireless technologies for the local loop, allowing new entrants to provide integrated fixed link and mobile services, and encouraging the use of cable television networks. While the latter would theoretically be the quickest way to stimulate local loop competition in most European countries, in practice the incumbent operator tends to be the majority owner of cable television networks. Thus serious consideration should be given to structural solutions which would require incumbent telecommunication operators to relinquish ownership in cable television facilities. This should , for example, apply to Germany and France.

The second important challenge to communication policy will come from the convergence between the broadcasting and telecommunication industries. Existing regulatory structures are based on service specific non-substitutable infrastructures. Convergence requires a single regulatory, administrative and legal structure. However, this can be politically sensitive since it touches on broadcasting policy and therefore on content and culture issues. Other convergence issues relate to vertical integration and raise questions as to whether or not the public telecommunications operator should also be allowed to offer entertainment services.

These issues have already arisen in the United Kingdom and Australia, where incumbent providers wanted to use their existing networks to offer new entertainment services.

It is important that the Eastern European countries and the independent states of the former Soviet Union realise that developments in convergence and broadband may result in them becoming even further behind in their relative network development. The rate of network penetration in the developed economies is not as important as it once was, since most have virtually universal coverage, however the new investments are going into capital deepening, that is, high speed networks. It is therefore important to ensure that the eastern economies make a quantum leap, and this can only occur through competition and foreign investment. The longer they wait, the harder it will become to attract foreign investment for telecommunication, as many new and potentially more profitable opportunities for new communication investment are opening up in OECD economies .

Copyright and Related Rights in the Information Society on a European and International Level

Bert Eichhorn

The use of digital technology allowing for data compression has led to the development of so-called "multimedia"; a medium which typically allows for the interactive and integrated utilisation of various traditional media, such as text, photography, graphics, animation, film and sound. Multimedia distribution platforms include CD-ROM standards, videogames, laser disk and on-line services.

The market in 'on-demand' services is considered to be one of the main areas of growth, with further technological developments to come. 'On-demand' services are unlike broadcast services characterised by the fact that material stored in a digital format is made available to the public or its individual members in such a way that they may access it and request its transmission at a place and a time chosen by them individually.

The rapid development of multimedia has led to growing concerns regarding the adequacy of the current regulatory framework.

The European Commission is discussing the implications of digital technology for copyright and related rights.

EU action in 1999 will focus on reproduction, on-line communications and distribution of protected material, as well as protection against the circumvention of anti-copying devices. A proposal for a directive is discussed at the European Parliament.

On the International level two new Treaties were adopted by the World Intellectual Property Organisation (WIPO) on 20 December 1996 setting international minimum standards in the areas also addressed by the European Commission.

The two Treaties aim to bring international protection of intellectual property rights and anti- piracy methods into line with the requirements of the global Information Society. These Treaties are:

- WIPO *Copyright Treaty:* The Treaty complements the Revised Bern Convention for the Protection of Literary and Artistic Works. It protects authors with respect to distribution, commercial rental, communication to the public and the public availability of their works on-line. Protection is also ensured for computer programmes and databases. Furthermore, the Treaty sets out provisions with regard to technological measures, such as those for the fraudulent circumvention of anti-copying devices.

- WIPO *Performances and Phonograms Treaty:* This Treaty updates the Rome Convention of 1961 and protects performing artists and record producers. Under the new Treaty they will enjoy exclusive rights of reproduction, distribution, commercial rental and the public availability of their performances/recordings on-line. Performers and record producers are also granted royalty rightsfor broadcasting and all forms of communication to the public of recordingspublished for commercial purposes. For the first time, performing artists will also enjoy certain moral rights for both live and pre-recorded performances. As with the Copyright Treaty, the Agreement contains obligations concerning technological measures, rights management, information and enforcement.

With regard to a third Treaty for the protection of databases, negotiations will continue. The WIPO Agreements do not cover audio-visual works. Audio-Visual works are to be addressed by a special protocol.

The two agreements fill existing gaps on international intellectual property protection in the field of new technological applications.

But the work achieved is only a first step towards providing a stable legal framework which will promote international trade in the Information Society, and give consumers access to a wide variety of new products, while at the same time facilitating the fight against piracy in all of its forms.

II. Liberalizing the Energy Sector

M: Vertical Integration in the Electricity Supply Industry: Competition and Investment Issues

Alison Sinclair

1. Why the Interest in Vertical Integration?

Mergers or long-term contracts between firms operating in the same industry but at different stages of supply, such as a manufacturing company and a retailer (e.g. oil companies and petrol stations) or a manufacturing company and a supplier of parts (e.g. car companies and their suppliers), have always been of interest to competition authorities. The potential for anticompetitive behavior following vertical mergers is, however, deemed to be less serious than in the case of horizontal mergers. Nevertheless, in the utilities - electricity, gas, telecommunications and water - the adverse effect of vertical integration on competition could be very important due to the low degree of competition in these sectors in the first place. Thus, natural monopoly characteristics and high sunk costs at one or more stages of supply have traditionally implied high firm concentration and monopolization. This together with state regulation raises the incentive for vertically integrated firms to stifle competition and deter entry in activities which are not naturally monopolistic (YARROW, 1994; VICKERS, 1995).

The ever more widespread desire of governments to introduce competition in the utilities is therefore not only leading to a re-evaluation of the industries' horizontal structure but also their vertical structure. The question is which vertical structure is most amenable for introducing and maintaining competition and, furthermore, whether the benefit from a procompetitive vertical structure outweighs any potential costs.

This paper considers the issue of vertical integration in the context of liberalization in the electricity supply industry (ESI). It is usual to distinguish between four vertical stages of supply or types of activities in the ESI: (1) generation, (2) transmission through high-voltage networks, (3) distribution through lower voltage networks, and (4) supply to the final consumer. The transmission and distribution of electricity being network-based are characterized by falling average costs and high sunk costs, which constitute barriers to exit and entry. Transmission and distribution are therefore natural and non-contestable monopolies, while generation and retail supply are potentially competitive activities. Given these four stages of supply it is possible to think of various vertical structures for the ESI, depending on whether and which of the naturally monopolistic activities are integrated with the potentially competitive ones and whether generators have access to the transmission and distribution networks (vertical integration between generators and retail suppliers). Figure M1 in the appendix illustrates various vertical structures. Basically, governments can choose between three approaches to the vertical links in the ESI: (1) integration, (2) separation, and (3) integration plus network access (also called third party access in the EU and common carriage or free-wheeling - wholesale and retail wheeling - in the US).

Vertical integration. Traditionally, the electricity supply industry in most countries has consisted of vertically integrated and state-owned (sometimes privately owned) monopolies, either at the national or regional level. Since the 1980s, however, a trend towards privatization, removal of the statutory monopoly and vertical de-integration has developed, which has markedly accelerated in recent years - see Table M3 in the appendix for an overview of reforms in the ESI in selected countries.

Vertical separation. Some governments see vertical separation of generation (final supply) from transmission and distribution as a necessary pre-condition for competition in generation (final supply). Separation according to this view allows government regulation to focus on the transmission and distribution stages without encouraging anticompetitive behavior in generation or final supply. Regulation can thus be kept to a minimum. The UK is the most prominent example in this context: having left the vertical structure of the telecommunications and gas sectors untouched at the time of privatization, the government opted for vertical de-integration when privatizing the ESI. In fact the UK government adopted a hybrid model, encompassing separation as well as integration and network access: it separated transmission from generation, but left distribution and final supply integrated and also allowed the integration of generation and final supply via network access. It is notable from Table M3 in the appendix that like the UK an increasing number of countries are choosing to separate at least the transmission network from the other stages of supply (e.g. Norway, Australia, New Zealand, Portugal, Spain, Sweden, California).

Vertical integration and network access. An alternative way of allowing competition in generation and final supply while avoiding costly network duplication is to grant new entrants access to the transmission and distribution networks owned by vertically integrated firms. This alternative is particularly attractive and possibly the only politically feasible way of achieving competition in countries where the ESI is dominated by private or mixed ownership, especially if private ownership has been in place for a considerable period of time.

Before evaluating the above three approaches to vertical integration in the ESI, the paper briefly reviews in section 2 the well-known theoretical arguments for vertical integration from the perspective of the firm. These arguments can apply to any industry and not just the ESI. Section 3 discusses the social welfare implications of integration and analyzes whether there exists a tradeoff between investment efficiency and competition when moving from integration to separation.

The issue of investment efficiency is of particular importance in such a country as Russia due to its geographic size and the need for replacement and new investment.[1] Given the scale of investment needs, privatization without a clear commitment by the government regarding its future approach to competition will either lead to very little investment (as is the case at the moment) or a future problem of stranded assets when competition is finally under consideration (an issue especially under discussion in the US). Section 5 offers some policy prescriptions.

Tab. M1: Takeover/Merger Proposals in the ESI in England/Wales 1995/1996

Announcement date	Target (REC)	Bidder	Successful or not
Dec. 1994	Northern Electric	Trafalgar House (UK construction company)	approved but unsuccessful (due to defense by REC)
31.07.1995	Eastern Electricity	Hanson (UK conglomerate)	successful
25.08.1995	South Western Electricity	Southern Electric International (US utility)	successful
18.09.1995	Manweb	Scottish Power (1 of 2 vertically integrated companies in Scotland)	successful
18.09.1995	Midlands Electricity	PowerGen (1 of 2 dominant generators)	not approved
02.10.1995	Southern Electric	National Power (1 of 2 dominant generators)	not approved
11.10.1995	Norweb	Central & South Western (US utility)	successful
06.11.1995	Seeboard	North West Water (regional water company)	successful
04.12.1995	South Wales Electricity	Welsh Water (regional water company)	successful

Tab. M1 (cont.)

29.101996	Northern Electric	CalEnergy (US independent power producer)	successful
13.11.1996	East Midlands Electricity	Dominion Resources (US utility)	successful
11.1996	London Electricity	Entergy (US utility)	successful

Source: PARKER (1996), p. 229; MMC (1996), appendix 4.5, p. 254; THE ECONOMIST, various issues; FINANCIAL TIMES (1996), p. 17.

Whether the electricity sector in a particular country includes vertically integrated firms or not, the industry structure is likely to change over time following the abolishing of statutory monopolies, as testified by the wave of mergers in 1995 involving British distribution companies (regional electricity companies or RECs) - see Table M1. Though most of the mergers involved foreign electricity companies (US) or non-electricity utilities (water companies) and were approved by the Secretary of Trade and Industry, two proposed but not approved mergers were between domestic generators and distribution companies. Similarly, as privatization of the ESI in eastern European countries progresses, the industry's vertical and horizontal structure will be affected by the increased involvement of foreign electricity companies and globalization trends.[2] Both national and international mergers may affect the state of competition in the domestic electricity market.[3] Thus, as in other industries, competition authorities may repeatedly have to face the decision whether to allow integration at the horizontal level and across different stages of electricity supply.

2. Arguments for Vertical Integration from the Perspective of the Firm

From the perspective of the firm economic theory points to the following four arguments for integration of upstream and downstream activities:[4]

- exploitation of economies of scale and scope
- elimination of vertical externalities
- reduction in transaction costs
- reduction in competition.

The existence of **economies of scale and scope** (together with coordination requirements, see below) have traditionally been the main argument for horizontal but also vertical integration in the electricity supply industry. Given the large fixed costs associated with activities in generation, transmission and distribution, mergers offer the opportunity to economize on at least some of these costs. Thus, economies of scale and scope in the ESI could, for example, be exploited through larger power plants, joint R&D or management units, and information sharing between upstream and downstream activities regarding supply and demand conditions, thereby allowing more efficient load balancing.[5] In its recent evaluation of the proposed mergers between generators and regional distribution companies the competition authority in the UK suggested that increased firm size and expertise at more than one stage of supply would improve the merged companies' ability to compete at an international level.[6] The developments in the England & Wales market also point to a link between horizontal and vertical mergers: third party access to networks and competition for customers (industrial users or households) mean that generators and distribution companies are potential rivals in final supply and hence economies of scale arguments for horizontal mergers also apply to vertical mergers. By taking over a distribution company a generator is buying the expertise of its competitor and taking advantage of economies of scale in downstream activities, such as advertising, customer services and metering costs.

Vertical externalities can occur when a downstream (upstream) firm undertakes actions that affect the demand for the final good without taking into account the effect on the upstream (downstream) firm's profit. The emergence of such externalities requires that both upstream and downstream firms have at least some market power. They can be classified into three categories (see for example TIROLE, 1988, and YARROW, 1991), which may all be relevant for the electricity supply industry:

(i) *Investment in promotional activities that raise final demand.* This, for example, could be advertising, advice on managing energy use or on switching between different energy sources. Because the downstream or upstream firm does not take into account the benefit from promotional activities on other firms' profits it will tend to underinvest in such activities from the point of view of the industry as a whole.

(ii) *Double marginalization.* Assuming both downstream and upstream firms have some market power, both will charge a markup over their respective marginal cost without taking into account that each markup not only reduces demand for their own product but also demand for the good produced by the vertically related firm(s). Thus, the final good's price will be too high and profits below maximum from the perspective of the industry or a vertically integrated firm.

(iii) *Input substitution.* If downstream firms can use inputs in variable proportions and the market for one input is imperfectly competitive while that for another input is more competitive and hence can be bought at a lower price, downstream firms will tend to substitute away from the more expensive input to alternative suppliers. Distribution and final supply companies may, for example, substitute between generators and generating technologies. They could also encourage their customers to switch between energy sources, such as electricity, gas and heating oil or renewable energy sources.

In fact firms can eliminate or at least reduce the vertical externalities described above through other means than vertical mergers. For example upstream firms can use two-part tariffs (with a fixed and a variable component, where the latter varies with the units purchased and equals marginal cost) to avoid the final price distortion due to double marginalization. Firms can also use contracts stipulating the amount of demand promotion to be undertaken by the distribution company or energy service provider. Contracts, however, can suffer from problems of performance measurement and enforceability and hence may entail substantial transaction costs. Reducing transaction costs represents, therefore, a third motive for vertical mergers.

A reduction in transaction costs. MILGROM and ROBERTS (1992) divide transaction costs into:

- coordination costs, associated with the acquisition and provision of information about the availability and price of goods and services
- motivation costs, arising due to incomplete and asymmetric information between transacting parties as well as the impossibility of perfect commitment.

Given the nature of electricity demand and supply - high demand fluctuations between season and time of day coupled with the need for continuous matching of supply and demand to ensure system stability - coordination requirements in the ESI are considerable and constitute another reason why the industry has traditionally been dominated by vertically integrated firms.

Coordination and information sharing would not present a problem for markets if it were possible to write complete contracts, specifying a set of actions and revenue sharing rules for every possible contingency. But because market conditions change over time due to demand fluctuations, technical progress, number of alternative suppliers, government regulation etc. it is impossible to foresee every contingency when designing a contract. This makes contract default and/or costly renegotiation following a change in circumstances more likely. It may, therefore, be advantageous for transacting parties to vertically integrate and to replace external governance structures with internal ones since these offer greater flexibility in responding to external shocks.

Internal governance does not eliminate transaction costs. Coordination and motivation costs will continue to exist between different divisions of the organization, between managers and employees, requiring information sharing and monitoring. In fact although integration saves in negotiation and enforcement costs, thereby reducing transaction costs, at the same time there exists a tendency for transaction costs to rise with integration (WILLIAMSON, 1985). This is because the divisions in an integrated firm will have less high-powered incentives to control costs of production than if they were separate firms having to compete with other suppliers in the market place. Integration may, therefore, entail higher overheads and monitoring costs. Whether transaction costs in the end are higher or lower under integration compared to vertical separation will depend on the characteristics of the market and of the transaction under consideration. WILLIAMSON (1985) suggests that integration is more likely to be preferred to market organization

(i) the higher the asset specificity of the investment associated with the transaction
(ii) the higher the uncertainty about future market conditions
(iii) the more frequently the transaction is to occur.

All three of these factors characterize electricity markets and hence could explain why the sector has usually consisted of vertically integrated utilities.
Asset specificity implies that investment costs are to some degree sunk and thus cannot be recouped, i.e. specific assets cannot easily be used for any other transaction than the one originally envisaged. The traditional example in the electricity supply industry is a utility investing in a generating plant located near a coal mine using generating technology based on coal and possibly on the particular coal mined locally (JOSKOW, 1985). By reducing the bargaining power of the investing party, asset specificity leads to the so-called 'hold-up problem'. Thus, once the generating company or coal mining company has undertaken investment in specific equipment and technology, the other party is in a better bargaining position to renegotiate any existing contracts and increase its share of the investment's return[7] to the detriment of the first party. Anticipating such an outcome, each party is reluctant to undertake specific investment and hence may underinvest generally or reduce the asset specificity of any investment (in spite of possible higher production costs in the future due to less efficient technology). By removing asset ownership from one party and handing it over to the other, vertical integration can lessen the hold-up problem.

High uncertainty about future market conditions, such as competitors' pricing (e.g. pool prices), demand preferences, environmental legislation, number of alternative suppliers, government regulation, raises the likelihood that contract partners will want to renege on their contract at a later date. Full vertical integration offers more flexibility in the face of market uncertainty due to a clearer hierachical structure.

The more frequently two parties interact the greater the benefit from developing a set of rules over time for these transactions. The development of a 'corporate culture' internal to an integrated organization can facilitate this process and hence reduce transaction costs.

A reduction in competition. By integrating forward (backward) an upstream (downstream) firm may aim to foreclose rivals from market outlets (inputs) and hence raise its market share. In fact integration can be the result of a healthy competitive process and not lead to an increase in a firm's market power. Thus, critics of the foreclosure doctrine point out that foreclosing rivals from the upstream or downstream market is not necessarily in the interest of a vertically integrated firm since this could entail an increase in the cost of inputs for the downstream division or a loss in revenue for the upstream division respectively.[8] However, ORDOVER, SALONER and SALOP (1990) have shown that a vertical merger can facilitate collusion at the upstream stage, raising intermediate goods prices and the costs of downstream competitors and thereby leading to higher final goods prices.[9] Similarly, HART and TIROLE (1990) and BOLTON and WHINSTON (1991) have developed models to show that vertical integration and foreclosure may be in the interest of firms. Not surprisingly the ability to foreclose downstream rivals from the supply of inputs (charging a higher price to non-integrated downstream firms and hence raising the own final goods price) will be constrained by the presence of other upstream firms. In the case of the ESI, this implies that the anti-competitive motive for integrating a network-based activity, such as transmission and distribution, with a potentially competitive activity, generation or retail supply, is stronger than for integrating generation and final supply.

The incentive to engage in anticompetitive behavior is also higher if one of the vertically integrated activities is regulated (YARROW, 1994; VICKERS, 1995). Thus, the inability of an integrated firm to earn high profits in one activity encourages it to extract higher profits in the other. By using its market power at one stage of supply to disadvantage actual and potential rivals in the adjacent stage the firm can reduce competition and increase its profits in the unregulated activity. In the ESI this can occur when one or both of the network-based activities (transmission and distribution) are integrated with, respectively, generation and final supply. The ability to disadvantage rivals will be restricted by the form and extent to which the network activity is regulated.

Both the paper by HART and TIROLE and that by BOLTON and WHINSTON also point to the possibility of a 'chain' of vertical mergers assuming an industry structure with several upstream and downstream firms. Thus, one vertical merger may lead other firms to respond with a merger of their own so as to offset the loss in profits. In turn the possibility of a wave of mergers can actually discourage vertical integration from occurring in the first place, depending on the costs and benefits.

To summarize, there exist powerful arguments for firms in the electricity supply industry to vertically integrate, largely resulting from the existence of economies of scale and scope, relationship-specific investment and imperfect competition implying vertical externalities and foreclosure incentives. However, firms can also achieve a number of the benefits with the help of contracts, in particular long-term contracts. The question then is whether a government should enforce vertical separation in the first place and if it does to what extent should it hinder a subsequent 'market process' towards re-integration. The next section, therefore, deals with the social welfare implications of vertical integration and mergers.

3. Social Welfare Implications of Vertical Integration: A Tradeoff Between Competition and Investment Efficiency?

The potential benefits from integration to society as a whole follow directly from the discussion about the private benefits to firms in the previous section - see also Table M2. However, private incentives need not coincide with social welfare considerations.

The obvious cost to the economy is the potential loss in competition leading to higher prices and hence lower consumer welfare as well as lower industrial competitiveness - given that electricity is an essential input of production. In the ESI this reduction in competition may lead to an expansion in regulation from the naturally monopolistic network activities to the adjacent stages, i.e. generation and retail supply. The telecommunications sector and the gas sector in the UK provide examples of vertically integrated firms, where regulation covers final product prices as well as terms of access to the transport network.

Tab. M2: Potential Social Benefits and Costs of Vertical Integration

Benefits	Costs
Exploitation of **economies of scale and scope** leading to higher profits and/or lower prices.	Reduction in **competition** leading to the danger of merger waves, allocative inefficiency (divergence of price and marginal costs of production), productive inefficiency due to reduced market discipline. Anticompetitive behavior at one stage may be encouraged by regulation and reduced profits at the other stage of supply.

Tab. M2 (cont.)

Elimination of **double marginalization** leading to higher profits and lower final goods prices (smaller divergence between marginal cost and final goods prices).	It is not clear whether attempts to avoid **other vertical externalities** are socially beneficial (e.g. demand promotion and its effect on the demand for other goods). Vertical integration aiming to eliminate input substitution would hinder the competitive process, since input substitution reduces the market power monopolistic upstream firms and can lead to lower intermediate goods prices. Nevertheless, to the extent that some market power and price markups will continue to exist due to imperfect substitutability, from society's point of view the inputs will be underused given their relative resource costs.
Reduction in **transaction costs** in terms of lower short-term coordination costs.	Increase in **transaction costs** in terms of overheads and bureaucracy in the integrated firm.
Increased **investment** due to enhanced investment incentives and the reduction of the hold-up problem.	

Given that vertical mergers can occur *for other reasons than* the minimization of production and transaction costs, private and social motives for vertical integration can diverge and a vertical merger that is privately optimal may be socially sub-optimal, due to anticompetitive behavior and higher transaction costs (see also the models by HART and TIROLE, 1990, and BOLTON and WHINSTON, 1991).

It is unclear whether the economies of scale and scope (say in management) and the short-run coordination requirements in the operation of the various stages of supply in the ESI really are substantial enough to warrant vertical integration. Economies of scale in management are in part outweighed by higher overheads and monitoring costs, while the liberalization experience in England and Wales has shown that coordination in operation and system stability is possible even under vertical separation, though it is more complex. Assuming, therefore, that economies of scale and scope and short-run coordination requirements are not that large or different in a vertically integrated monopoly and a de-integrated sector with some competition, the issue of vertical integration in the ESI appears to reduce to a tradeoff between investment efficiency and competition - see Table M2.

Providing appropriate investment incentives is seen as particularly important in countries with underdeveloped or neglected electricity supply industries in need of high replacement investment and as well as new investment requirements, such as the transition economies in eastern Europe and Russia. A tradeoff between investment efficiency and competition would, therefore, suggest that countries with high investment requirements in the electricity supply industry should opt for a vertically integrated structure.

However, the tradeoff is not as simple as that. First, it is not obvious that investment is less efficient under vertical integration than under separation coupled with more competition. Two conflicting pressures need to be taken into account:

(i) Separate ownership and competition implies less coordination in investment plans and an increased danger of underinvestment due to the hold-up problem. Ex ante competition prior to the investment commitment does not reduce the chance of hold-up, so long as the asset specificity and sunk costs associated with the investment are sufficiently high.
(ii) Competition may improve the selection process of investment projects, implying higher return projects and a quicker response to technological change, as well as increase the pressure to control investment costs at the time of implementation (e.g. the costs of constructing new generating stations).[10, 11]

Nevertheless, in spite of the potential positive effect of competition on investment efficiency, the negative effect in terms of reduced coordination in investment plans could be considerable. Thus, the Swedish electricity supply industry shows how a system of several vertically integrated private and public enterprises engaging in limited competition (prior to the 1996 reforms) facilitates the close coordination of long-term investment plans (HJALMARSSON, 1996).

In contrast, the liberalized system in England & Wales, characterized by vertical separation, points to the potential problems that competition can imply for investment incentives. The pricing rule in the electricity spot market (the pool), through which all electricity is traded and dispatched, was designed so as to encourage efficient expansion in generation capacity. To this end it includes a payment to generators for unused capacity, which varies inversely with the amount of excess capacity in the system. With the help of an industry simulation model, BUNN and LARSEN (1994) have investigated the system's tendency for cycles of under- and overcapacity and the effect of strategic 'signaling' of new capacity plans by the two dominant generators aiming to deter new entry. The authors' model shows that, assuming (i) a lead time of at least three years for the construction of a new power plant using combined cycle gas turbine technology (CCGT) and (ii) no foresight or information exchange by the generators, the system will produce substantial cycles in over- and undercapacity. Reserve margins would vary between 8% and 58%, while the target in the British ESI is 21%. The danger of such cycles was already pointed out by the industry regulator OFFER in its assessment of the price system in 1991 (OFFER, 1991, referenced in BUNN and LARSEN, 1994).

However, BUNN and LARSEN'S simulation experiments suggest that the capacity cycles could be reduced if the regulator were to publish 'reliable' information about future excess capacity and smooth the retirement pattern of existing plants. This would imply a more formal process by which the regulator approves construction and retirement plans. The social cost of the remaining tendency towards investment inefficiency may then be small relative to the benefits from vertical separation in terms of increased competition.

But the second reason why there is no simple tradeoff between investment efficiency and competition when moving from vertical integration to separation is that it still is unclear (in theory and practice) whether vertical separation is a necessary condition for competition. Put differently, it is not clear whether the anti-competitive effects of vertical mergers in the electricity supply industry are sufficiently large to require restricting. This ambiguity is reflected in approaches of different governments to electricity liberalization and subsequent merger activity. The UK government, for example, opted in 1989 for the separation between transmission and generation but not between distribution and final supply. California in contrast is preparing to introduce competition and wholesale as well as retail wheeling without breaking up the integrated utilities in terms of ownership - though activities are to be separated in terms of accounting and organization. Thus, utilities will consist of a holding company owning three independent firms: a generation, transmission and distribution company. YARROW (1994, p. 77-79) argues that it is the regulatory framework which is crucial for encouraging entry in generation or retail supply, not vertical separation. Thus, the introduction of third party access to the British transmission network in 1983 (operated by the same state-owned enterprise operating most of the generating facilities) was bound to be ineffective in reducing barriers to entry, given the largely unchanged regulatory regime, originally designed for a vertically integrated monopoly in generation and transmission. In contrast, the new regulatory regime implemented in 1990 allowed competition in the retail electricity market in England & Wales to flourish in recent years in spite of vertical integration between distribution and final supply.

As regards integration between generation and distribution, the Monopolies and Mergers Commission in the UK (MMC) ruled in early 1996 that the two mergers between generators and regional distribution companies would very likely reduce competition in generation, though not in the final supply stage, and "operate against the public interest", but that "the adverse effects of the merger [were not] sufficiently serious to justify prohibition" (MMC, 1996). The MMC recommended, with one dissenting voice among the five-member panel, that the merger be approved by the Secretary of State for Trade and Industry. In the end both mergers were blocked with the justification that they would constitute "significant detriments to competition", even though vertical integration was not "inherently objectionable" (THE ECONOMIST, 27.04.1996).

In conclusion then, integration need not obstruct competition (as long as third party access is granted and enforced), while vertical separation can allow some gains in investment efficiency without producing large capacity cycles (as long as some information exchange and coordination is encouraged through regulation). To obtain a clearer verdict regarding the link between investment efficiency, competition and the electricity's sector vertical structure a detailed empirical analysis is required.

4. Policy Conclusions

Given the above inconclusiveness regarding the optimal structure in the electricity supply industry, one would expect the sector's vertical structure to differ across countries, especially in future years as the trend towards electricity liberalization leads governments to abandon the traditional industry model of an integrated monopoly. Historical accidents, such as the ownership pattern in the ESI, and the need to build political compromises will affect the final vertical structure chosen by any particular government. Globalization and diversification trends will very likely influence the structure subsequently, while the type of regulatory regime will continue to be an important determining factor for the sector's performance. The discussion in the previous sections suggests that (i) the regulation requirement will tend to be lower under vertical separation, (ii) regulation should be directed towards investment coordination as well as the reduction of entry barriers, and (iii) regulatory uncertainty will raise transaction costs and encourage vertical integration.

The remainder of this section will deal with some policy considerations regarding the vertical structure of the ESI in transition economies. In the context of eastern European countries there is some force in the arguments for temporary vertically integrated monopolies under private ownership. Not only can investment plans be coordinated, it may also be easier for governments to attract foreign investors and thereby encourage investment in network expansion/repair, new generating capacity and technological innovation. The government could, for example, attach some investment conditions to the sale of shares and in return promise to restrict entry into the industry and to put in place a looser regulatory regime. The incumbent can then earn the higher profits necessary to finance part of the investments. However, such a move - involving a foreign investor(s) taking over the vertically integrated incumbent and subsequently raising final product prices in a sector of 'national interest and security' - would prove very difficult in political terms, especially given the low prices of electricity paid by households in eastern European countries in the past.[12] Even if the government were to agree to such a deal, foreign investors, anticipating subsequent political pressure on the government to retract its offer and change the regulatory framework, would be wary of accepting the deal or of committing financial resources to particular investment projects too quickly. Thus, even under vertical integration there in effect exists a potential hold-up problem between electricity operators and the government or the regulatory authority, discouraging investment.

This points to three arguments why eastern European governments should consider a vertical breakup of the electricity supply industry:

(1) Even with vertical integration there is a danger that investment incentives are distorted due to uncertainty regarding the regulatory framework. A substantial restructuring of the industry prior to privatization, such as a vertical breakup, could signal the government's commitment to a new regulatory regime.
(2) Privatizing the industry in parts instead of as one vertically integrated company may make it easier to attract strategic investors interested in buying shares in or setting up joint ventures with smaller organizational units. It also would be politically more acceptable, especially since some electricity enterprises could be retained in the public sector (at least for some time).
(3) Political considerations dictating strict regulation of final electricity prices and continued cross-subsidization between different groups of users could mean that introducing competition in final supply is not an option for the government. But assuming some competition is essential to improve efficiency in the ESI (in operation and in investment), the government could encourage competition in the wholesale electricity market by separating generation from transmission.

Appendix: Vertical Integration and Reforms in the Electricity Supply Industry

Fig. M1: Different Types of Vertical Integration in the Electricity Industry

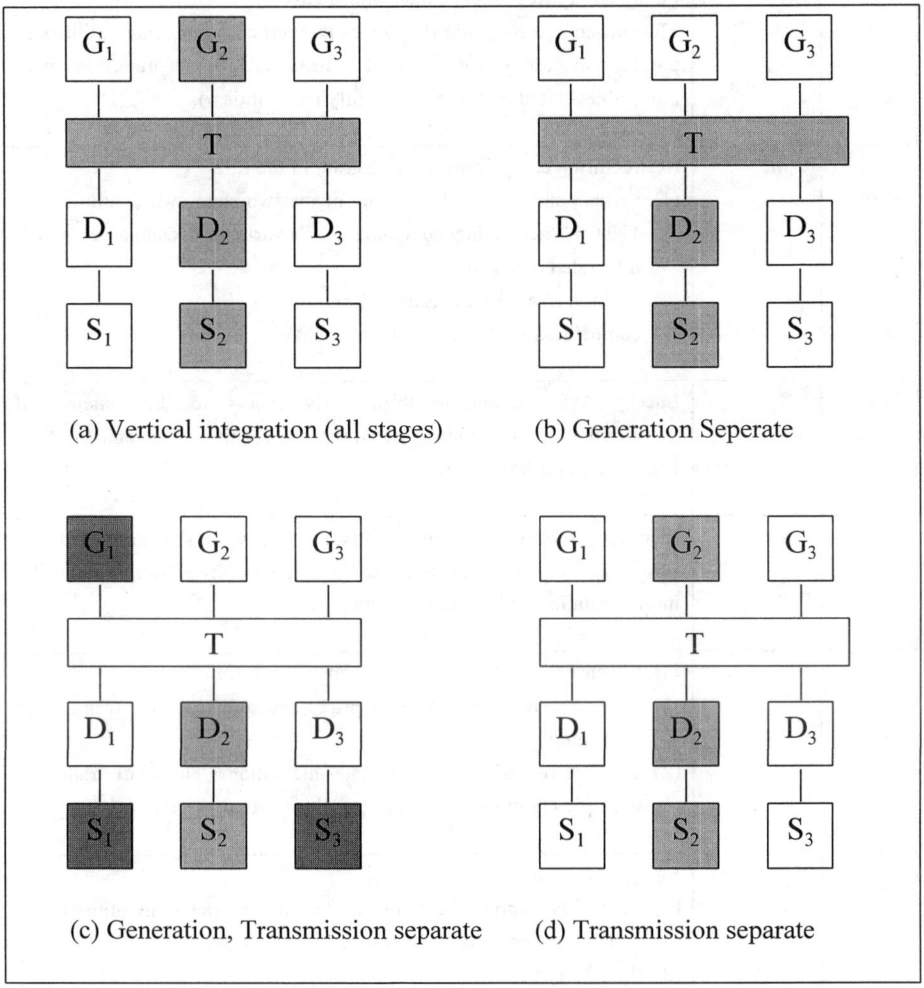

Notes: G = generation, T = transmission, D = distribution, S = final supply. Boxes representing integrated activities have the same shading. The diagrams show more than one company operating in the industry, whether vertically integrated or not. No assumption is made regarding the degree of competition. Competition in the wholesale or retail market requires access to transmission and distribution networks. For example, vertical structure (c) together with access to the transmission and distribution grids describes the ESI-model adopted in the UK, while structure (d) together with access to the transmission and distribution networks illustrates the Norwegian model.

Tab. M3: Recent Reforms in the Electricity Supply Industry of Selected Countries

1978	US	Public Utility Regulatory Policy Act (PURPA) The second section (Title II) obliges the vertically integrated utilities to purchase electricity from non-utility firms using cogeneration or small renewables-based technology ('qualifying facilities').
1978-1989	Chile	Restructuring and privatization program of the ESI (1) vertical and horizontal breakup of the two state-owned utilities (by 1992 11 generating companies, 21 distribution companies and 2 integrated companies) (2) creation of a National Energy Commission (3) competition for large customers (>2MW).
1983	UK	Energy Act, introducing third party access to the state-owned transmission and distribution networks and requiring the regional Area Boards to publish their tariffs.
1989	UK	Electricity Act, determining the privatization, vertical separation of the ESI and the establishment of a separate regulatory authority, implementation taking place in 1990.
1990	EU	Price Transparency Directive and Transit Directive (1) utilities have to publish their prices and terms of sale to industrial consumers (2) member countries must facilitate international electricity trade, for example involving transit through third countries.
1991	Norway	Energy Act comes into effect (1) vertical breakup of the dominant state-owned electricity utility into a generating company and a transmission company (2) third party access (3) competition for all customers based on bilateral trading.

Tab. M3 (cont.)

	Australia	Industry Commission's report on the ESI, proposing (1) corporatization of all state-owned enterprises (2) vertical separation of generation, transmission and distribution (3) horizontal breakup of generation (4) unification of transmission networks into a national grid (5) common carrier system in transmission and distribution (6) privatization.
1992	Hungary	Creation of a two-tier joint stock company with regional distribution companies separated from the transmission grid, which is operated by the holding company. Distribution companies to be sold except for a golden share remaining in state hands.
	EU	Commission draft directive, setting down a framework for introducing an internal market in electricity and gas (1) abolishing special national rules for building new capacity in generation and transmission (2) administrative - management and accounting - separation of generation, transmission and distribution in vertically integrated utilities. (3) third party access to transmission and distribution networks. [proposal subsequently withdrawn and modified]
	US	Energy Policy Act, which provides the Federal Energy Regulatory Commission (FERC) with the authority to enforce more open access for independent power producers to transmission networks.
	New Zealand	Energy Companies Act, corporatizing all distribution enterprises or 'power boards'
	Argentina	Privatization and introduction of competition for large and medium-sized customers (>0.1 MW).
1993	Australia	Commitment at federal and state level to introduce competition in generation from July 1995, separating transmission from generation and distribution.

Tab. M3 (cont.)

	EU	Commission's amended draft directive, setting down a modified framework for introducing an internal market in electricity, including (1) bidding system for building new capacity in generation and transmission (2) accounting separation of the different stages of supply in vertically integrated utilities (3) negotiated third party access
1994	California	California Public Utility Commission's preliminary decision to introduce a common carrier system, gradually allowing consumers to choose their supplier.
	New Zealand	Separation of the transmission grid from the main state-owned electricity generator.
	Portugal	Vertical break up of state-owned monopoly (though still owned by one holding company) into one generation company, a transmission grid company, 4 regional distribution companies and 10 service companies. Large-scale generating companies sell electricity to transmission company (no third party access). From 1997 small independent power producers will be able to sell directly to consumers.
1994	Spain	Electricity Act (1) creating a Commission of the National Electricity System (2) generation and distribution accounting to be separated in vertically integrated companies (3) legal separation after 2000 (transmission grid already operated by separate state-owned company) (4) competition to be introduced through bidding system (5) independent system to be created (similar to Portugal), allowing new producers to sell directly to consumers via third party access to the transmission grid.

Tab. M3 (cont.)

1995	Finland	Electricity Market Act comes into effect (3) abolishing the need for special permits to build new capacity (3) third party access (3) allowing users with consumption exceeding 500 kW to choose freely between suppliers (3) free choice of suppliers for all consumers by 1st January 1997. The dominant state-owned electricity firm continues to be vertically integrated, operating generating facilities and one of two transmission grids. In October establishment of a national grid company to start operating the two joined transmission networks in late 1996/early 1997.
	California	State public utility commission's decision to introduce competition (including retail wheeling) by implementing a pool system, according to which all electricity trade has to take place through the pool and customers are free to choose between suppliers (largest industrial users from 1998 and all others from 2003).
	Hungary	Privatization of the 5 regional gas distribution companies (sale of majority stakes) and of 8 out of 14 regional electricity distribution companies (sale of minority stakes).
1996	Sweden	Liberalization of the ESI according to the same principles as the 1991 reforms in Norway, with a view to creating a Nordic electricity market including a spot market: (3) third party access to the transmission grid since 1995 (operated by separate state-owned enterprise) subject to capacity constraints (3) third party access to the distribution networks (3) elimination of regional franchise areas in 2000, though free choice possible earlier if customer notifies utility 6 months in advance and pays for meter installation.
1996	US	FERC issues Order 888 aimed at introducing competition in the wholesale electricity market: (3) transmission to be separated from other activities in vertically integrated companies (3) non-discriminatory tariffs (3) mechanism for compensating utilities for stranded investment costs.

Tab. M3 (cont.)

	EU	Council of Ministers agrees on how to liberalize the ESI: (1) generators allowed to build power stations in any member country (2) generation, transmission and distribution activities to be separated in accounting terms (3) competition to be introduced in each member state in 3 stages, initially covering 22.5% of the market, 28.5% after 3 years and 32% after 2006 (4) member states can open their market using either negotiated third party access or the single buyer model (5) public service clause, allowing states to restrict competition on the grounds of environmental protection or security of supply.

Sources: CROSS (1996), FINANCIAL TIMES (1996b), IEA (1994, 1996a, b), KUMKAR (1995, 1996a, b), SPILLER and MARTORELL (1996).

Endnotes

[1] According to the International Energy Agency (IEA, 1995) 40 GW out of the 212 GW total capacity in Russia will be in need of replacement by the year 2000.

[2] As in the telecommunications sector the introduction of competition to domestic electricity markets (together with privatisation) is expected to encourage international takeovers and alliances. See also GRAACK (1996) for an analysis of the internationalisation trend in telecommunications.

[3] To the extent that foreign involvement will be allowed in electricity markets as statutory monopolies are abolished, competition could move from the national to the international level, i.e. occur between market players interacting in more than one market. Such multimarket contact will affect the companies' incentives to engage in vigorous competition (see for example TIROLE, 1988).

[4] PERRY (1989) provides an in-depth survey of the literature on vertical integration. See also YARROW (1991) and WATERSON (1993).

[5] See for example the view expressed by WADDAMS in MMC (1996), p. 230.

[6] See the Monopolies and Mergers Commission's report on the merger between PowerGen and Midlands Electricity (MMC, 1996, pp. 41, 167 and 179). In contrast, the industry regulator, i.e. the Director General of Electricity Supply, thought the international performance of the two companies did not depend on a merger and could be achieved through joint ventures (MMC, 1996, p. 155).

[7] The share of 'appropriable quasi-rents', as KLEIN, CRAWFORD and ALCHIAN call it, is a more accurate expression. This is the return from putting the relationship-specific asset to its originally intended use rather than its next best use, given that the investment has been made already (PERRY, 1989, p. 213). For a simple numerical example of quasi-rents see BESANKO et al. (1996, p. 115).

[8] See BOLTON and WHINSTON (1991).

[9] This result does among other things depend on the assumption of Bertrand competition and does not carry through under Counot competition. See HART and TIROLE (1990) and the comment by Carlton for criticism of the ORDOVER, SALONER and SALOP model.

[10] These effects can to some extent be secured by replacing public with private ownership, assuming there is sufficient pressure from shareholders and the stock market and assuming government regulation leaves sufficient incentive for long-term cost reductions.

[11] YARROW (1994) argues that higher investment efficiency should be the main efficiency gain from the reduction in the barriers to entry and hence competition in the British electricity supply industry.

[12] Household electricity prices in eastern European countries have been low even in the 1990s, both in comparison to other countries and relative to prices faced by industrial users, though they are being adjusted.

References

BESANKO, D., D. DRANOVE. and M. SHANLEY (1996), The Economics of Strategy, New York: John Wiley & Sons.

BOLTON, P. and M. D. WHINSTON (1991), The 'Foreclosure' Effects of Vertical Mergers, in: Journal of Institutional and Theoretical Economics, Vol. 147, pp. 207-226.

BUNN, D.W. and E. R. LARSEN (1994), Assessment of the uncertainty in future UK electricity investment using an industry simulation model, in: Utilities Policy, Vol. 4, pp. 229-236.

CROSS, E.D. (1996), Electric Utility Regulation in the European Union: A Country by Country Guide, Chicester: Wiley & Sons.

FINANCIAL TIMES (1996), 9.12.1996.

FINANCIAL TIMES (1996b) 22.06.1996.

GRAACK, C. (1996), Telecom operators in the European Union: Internationalization strategies and network alliances, in: Telecommunications Policy, Vol. 20, No. 5, pp. 341-355.

HART, O.D. and J. TIROLE. (1990), Vertical Integration and Market Foreclosure, in: Brookings Papers on Economic Activity, pp 205-276.

HJALMARSSON, L. (1996), From club-regulation to market competition in the Scandinavian electricity supply industry, in: GILBERT, R.J. and KHAN, E.P. (eds.), International Comparisons of Electricity Regulation, Cambridge: Cambridge University Press.

IEA-International Energy Agency (1994), Electricity Supply Industry: Structure, Ownership and Regulation in OECD Countries, Paris: OECD.

IEA (1995), Energy Policies of the Russian Federation, Paris: OECD.

IEA (1996a), The Role of IEA Governments in Energy, Paris: OECD.

IEA (1996b), Energy Policies of IEA Countries. 1996 Review, Paris: OECD.

JOSKOW, P.L. (1985), Vertical Integration and Long-Term Contracts: The Case of Coal-Burning Electric Generating Plants, in: Journal of Law, Economics, and Organization, Vol. 33, pp. 32-80.

KUMKAR, L. (1995), Widerstände und Spannungen auf dem Weg zum europäischen Binnenmarkt für Elektrizität, in: Weltwirtschaft, No. 4, pp. 444-470.

KUMKAR, L. (1996a), Wettbewerb im Stromsektor der USA I: Re-regulierung der Großhandelsebene, Kiel Working Paper No. 738, Kiel Institute of World Economics.

KUMKAR, L. (1996b), "Wettbewerb im Stromsektor der USA I: Re-regulierung der Großhandelsebene," Kiel Working Paper No. 739, Kiel Institute of World Economics.

MILGROM, P. and J. ROBERTS (1992), Economics, Organization and Management, London: Prentice-Hall International.

MMC - Monopolies and Mergers Commission (1996), PowerGen plc and Midlands Electricity plc: A report on the proposed merger, Cm 3231, London: HMSO.

ORDOVER, J.A., G. SALONER and S. C. SALOP (1990), Equilibrium Vertical Foreclosure, in: American Economic Review, Vol. 80, pp. 127-142.

PARKER, M. (1996), Competition: the Continuing Issues, in: SURREY, J. (ed.), The British Electricity Experiment, London: Earthscan.

PERRY, M.K. (1989), Vertical Integration: Determinants and Effects, in: SCHMALENSEE, R. and R. D. WILLIG, eds., Handbook of Industrial Organization, Vol. 1, Amsterdam: North-Holland.

SPILLER, P.T. and L. V. MARTORELL (1996), How should it be done? Electricity regulation in Argentina, Brazil, Uruguay, and Chile, in: GILBERT, R.J. and E. P. KHAN, eds., International Comparisons of Electricity Regulation, Cambridge: Cambridge University Press.

TIROLE, J. (1988), The Theory of Industrial Organization, Cambridge: MIT Press.

WATERSON, M. (1993), Vertical Integration and Vertical Restraints, Oxford Review of Economic Policy, Vol. 9, pp. 41-57.

WILLIAMSON, O. (1985), The Economic Institutions of Capitalism, New York: Free Press.

VICKERS, J. (1995), Competition and Regulation in Vertically Related Markets, Review of Economic Studies, Vol. 62, pp. 1-17.

VICKERS, J. and G. YARROW (1988), Privatization: An Economic Analysis, Cambridge (Mass.): MIT Press.

YARROW, G. (1991), Vertical Supply Arrangements: Issues and Applications int the Energy Industries, in: Oxford Review of Economic Policy, Vol. 7, pp. 35-53.

YARROW, G. (1994), Privatization, Restructuring, and Regulatory Reform in Electricity Supply, in: BISHOP, M., J. KAY and C. MAYER, eds., Privatization and Economic Performance, Oxford: Oxford University Press.

Comments on: Vertical Integration in the Electricity Supply Industry: Competition and Investment Issues

Peter Palinkas

In this very interesting paper concerning vertical integration in the electricity supply industry and consequences for competition and investment, the author draws three main conclusions:

- the regulation requirement will tend to be lower with vertical separation
- regulation should be directed towards investment coordination as well as reduction of entry barriers and
- regulatory uncertainty will raise transaction costs and encourage vertical integration.

The author explains that governments can choose between three approaches to vertical links in the context of liberalization in the electricity supply industry (ESI):

- integration
- separation
- and integration plus network access (also called Third Party Access in the EU).

The EU-Directive 96/92/EC of 19 December 1996 (OJ L 27 of 30 January 1997, pp. 20-29) on common rules for the internal market in electricity allowed Member States to choose between two competing systems (see Box I and Box II):

- the so-called single-buyer (SB) system (single buyer shall mean any legal person who, within the system where he is established, is responsible for the unified management of the transmission system and/or for centralized electricity purchasing and selling).
- the Third Party Access (TPA) system. The TPA-system opens the way for the negotiated access of third parties to grids, i.e. limited opportunity for end-users to negotiate directly with producers or suppliers of electricity. This is intended to enable large (mainly industrial) consumers, for whose competitiveness energy prices are very important to seek more favourable sources of supply.

BOX I

The Internal Market in Energy as Part of the European Union's Internal Market Concept

Free trade in goods, services and capital and freedom of movement of persons are cornerstones of the European Union. The EEC Treaty is based on the principle of competition which may not be obstructed, either by subsidy or discriminatory rules. The comparative advantages of the individual Member States will thus be given the fullest play, which will in the final analysis be for everybody's benefit.

Energy, as a good or a service, falls within the sphere of the EEC-Treaty. A strict interpretation of the articles dealing with competition would therefore mean that any consumer, large or small, could buy gas or electricity wherever he wanted.

However, hardly any other market segment is so regulated and subject to such government supervision as the energy market. This is partly due to factors in the distant past associated with energy's strategic role in the traditional nation state. With the exception of the United Kingdom, all the EU Member States have guaranteed their public utilities supply areas, usually demarcated, which in some cases cover the whole national territory. In France GdF (Gaz de France) and EdF (Electricité de France) even had the exclusive right to import and export gas and electricity.

Like the transport, telecommunications and postal sectors, energy has been the subject of extensive liberalization measures for some years.

BOX II

The Internal Market in Energy: The Commission's '3-Stage Concept'

In the run-up to the completion of the European internal market the Commission announced its intention in 1989 - on the basis of an own-initiative report of the European Parliament (EP) (Linkohr-Report, Doc. A2-0158/89) - to open up the electricity and gas markets in most respects. On 21 February 1992 the Commission submitted proposals for two directives designed to bring about general liberalization of the electricity markets and - in parallel - the gas markets. The Commission proposals thus conformed to the strategy of progressively completing the EU internal market in electricity and gas, which the Commission believes should proceed in three stages.

First stage:
The first stage comprises the implementation of the three directives already adopted: the directives on the transit of electricity and natural gas[1] and the 'price transparency' directive of June 1990[2]. The two transit directives were intended as a first step towards opening up the electricity and gas transmission grids, although this was confined to large interconnected energy supply undertakings; two energy supply undertakings were not to be prevented from engaging in transfrontier trade in energy. Transit between large high-voltage grids (electricity) and between large high-pressure transmission grids (natural gas) is thus to be encouraged.

Second stage:
In the second stage the electricity and gas markets will be liberalized and other operators admitted, with existing structures respected. The following fundamental aspects of these proposals should be emphasized:

- freedom to produce electricity or gas and to build electricity lines and gas pipelines,
- general abolition of exclusive rights,
- separation of the management and accounting of production, transmission and distribution operations in the case of vertically integrated undertakings ('unbundling'),
- access for large industrial and distribution companies to the grid (third party access - TPA).

BOX II (cont.)

Third stage:

The Commission's original idea was to have a third stage - defined in the light of experience acquired during the second - entering into force on 1 January 1996. Due to the late adaptation of the electricity and gas directives (adaptation in 1996 in the case of electricity and 1998 in the case of gas) the third stage is postponed.

The Commission will review in the light of experience gained in due time the possibility of a future opening of the market which would be effective nine years after entry into force of the Directive (taking into account the coexistence of the two systems (Single Buyer and Third Party Access).

The author explains that "some governments see vertical separation of generation (final supply) from transmission and distribution as a necessary precondition for competition in generation. Separation, according to this view, allows government regulation to focus on the transmission and distribution stages without encouraging anticompetitive behaviour in generation of final supply".

This is exactly the EU-approach to electricity regulation, where unbundling and transparency of accounts of vertically-integrated electricity undertakings is one of the cornerstones (see: Article 14, paragraph 3 of the electricity directive of 19 December 1996):

"Integrated electricity undertakings shall, in their internal accounting, keep separate accounts for their generation, transmission and distribution activities, and, where appropriate, consolidated accounts for other non-electricity activities, as they would be required to do if the activities in question were carried out by separate undertakings, with a view to avoiding discrimination, cross-subsidization and distortion of competition. They shall have included a balance sheet and a profit and loss account for each activity in notes to their accounts".

An explanatory statement to this regulation states (see recitals 30-33):

- whereas, in order to ensure transparency and non-discrimination the transmission function of vertically integrated undertakings should be operated independently from the other activities;
- whereas a single buyer must operate separately from the generation and distribution activities of vertically integrated undertakings; whereas the flow of information between the single buyer activities and these generation and distribution activities needs to be restricted;

- whereas the accounts of all integrated electricity undertakings should provide for maximum transparency, in particular to identify possible abuses of a dominant position, consisting for example in abnormally high or low tariffs or in discriminatory practices relating to equivalent transactions;
- whereas, to this end, the accounts must be separate for each activity;
- whereas it is also necessary to provide for access by the competent authorities to the internal accounts of undertakings with due regard for confidentiality."

It is obvious, as the above extracts from the respective electricity directive reveal, that the EU-policy concerning the deregulation of electricity and creating an internal electricity market with more inherent competition was fully in line with the author's recommendations, i.e. looking for reduced vertical integration in order to enhance competition in the electricity supply industry.

This interesting paper on liberalizing the energy sector is, therefore, not only impressive from an academic or intellectual point of view but also highly important for the present and forthcoming political debate in the EU on liberalizing the energy market.

Endnotes

[1] Council Directive 90/547/EEC of 29 October 1990, OJ L 313, 13.11.1990, and Council Directive 91/296/EEC of 31 May 1991, OJ L 147, 12.6.1990.

[2] Council Directive 90/377/EEC of 29 June 1990, OJ L 185, 17.7.1990.

References

EUROPEAN COMMISSION (1990), Official Journal, Council Directive 90/547/EEC of 29 October 1990, OJ L 313, 13.11.1990, Council Directive 91/296/EEC of 31 May 1991, OJ L 147, 12.6.1991, Council Directive 90/377/EEC of 29 June 1990, OJ L 185, 17.7.1990.

N: Privatization and Modernization of the Electricity Sector in the CEE Transition Countries

Zdenek Hruby

1. Introduction

According to the European Bank for Reconstruction and Development (EBRD), a total of 6 billion US dollars of foreign investment flowed into the transition countries' major infrastructure companies between 1990 and early 1996. These investments were primarily in the telecommunication industry and, to a lesser extent, the electricity and gas sectors. This represents 20% of the cumulative flow of direct foreign investment for the period. International commercial banks have also become more active in the region, although in 1995, twice as much lending money flowed into the infrastructures of Latin American countries (a region with a population of about 450 million compared to 400 million in the EBRD's countries of operations.)

As each country has taken a different approach to the restructuring of its energy sector, any evaluation of the investment opportunities in Central and Eastern Europe (CEE) requires a careful review of each country's specific situation.

Although there are considerable differences among transition countries, centrally planned economies generally have an underdeveloped infrastructure. The different levels of foreign investment into the telecommunications and energy sectors are reflected in the telecommunication and transport situation, particularly road transport and electricity. While telecommunication and transport infrastructures need to develop further, in order to meet the growing demands of a market economy, the electricity sector must adapt to a decreasing demand caused by the decline of industrial and economic output. This decline is mainly due to major restructuring work, such as the contraction of heavy industry. While the industrial consumption of electric energy has declined substantially, household consumption rose between 1989 and 1994, despite a drop in disposable incomes over the period. Reasons for this increase in residential electricity consumption include the improved access of households to electrical appliances and, in some cases, a switch from coal and oil to electricity for heating, caused by an increase in primary energy prices compared to electricity tariffs.

The way in which electricity is generated needs to respond to increased environmental concerns. The most significant contributors to air pollution in the region are electric power plants, while the safety and reliability of nuclear power plants remains controversial.

Compared to other infrastructures, electric power has been a priority for centrally planned economies, both for material production and household consumption. Ideologically there is much support, but little attention has been paid to costs, with the result that in transition economies, electricity intensity per unit of output remains high, well above the levels in developed countries. In 1994, the electricity intensity as measured by the consumption of electric energy per unit of GNP at PPP exchange rates, was twice as high in CEE as in the EU. The electricity intensity in the FSU was even greater, exceeding that of the USA and Canada by a factor of two. The electricity intensity in the USA and Canada is about 50% greater than that in the EU, reflecting differences in the cost of primary energy (including transport costs) and in energy taxation.

Tariffs remain generally low, with tariff structures out of line with cost structures. Residential tariffs are below those for industrial users. Electricity costs are naturally lower for big industrial users than for residential customers. While tariffs have been raised from the very low levels found under central planning, especially in the countries of central Europe and the Baltic region, they do not yet accurately reflect service costs or the financial constraints on governments.

Tab. N1: Energy Intensity Improvements

	1971-1992 % p.a.	1992-2010 % p.a.	
		CC	ES
OECD	1.3	1.2	1.6
FSU/CEE	-0.1	1.2	2.0
ROW	-1.1	1.5	1.7
World	0.8	1.6	2.0

Notes: FSU: Former Soviet Union; CEE: Central Eastern Europe; ROW: Rest of the World.

Source: IEA (1995).

2. Energy Supply and Demand

World energy intensity improved by 0.8% per annum in PPP[1] terms between 1971 and 1992. For the 1992-2010 period, the OECD will be the only region in the world where energy intensities will continue to follow the historic trend. In other regions, improvements in energy intensity can be expected to be much higher, both in terms of Capacity Constrains (CC)[2] and Energy Savings (ES).[3] World-wide energy intensity is projected to improve by 1.6 % annually in the CC, and by 2% in the ES. Energy intensity in CEE improved by 1.1% annually between 1980 and 1989. In the

FSU, it improved by 1.2% annually during the same period. From 1989 to 1992, however, energy intensity deteriorated, concurrent with the collapse in economic activity. In the FSU/CEE there is great scope for improving energy intensity: the industrial sector is oriented towards energy intensive industries and intensity could be improved in the residential/commercial sector by the introduction of individual metering and higher energy prices. In CEE, annual energy intensity is projected to improve by 2.1% in terms of CC and by 2.8% in ES. The corresponding estimates for the FSU are 1.2% and 2%, respectively.

Tab. N2: World Electricity and Heat Demand and Generation

	1992	2010	
		CC	ES
Demand, Mtoe	1048	1747	1588
Generation, MWh per capita	2.3	2.9	2.6

Source: IEA (1995).

The international demand for electricity and heat is projected to increase at an annual average rate of 2.9% in the case of CC and 2.6% in the case of ES between 1992 and 2010. During this period, an average growth rate of 1.6% in CC and 0.8% in ES per annum has been recorded in the FSU/CEE countries. The increase in annual world electricity generation is projected to amount to around 8000 TWh in CC and 6000 TWh in ES. World electricity generation per capita is expected to increase from 2.3 MWh per capita in terms of CC and 2.6 MWh per capita in terms of ES. The share of FSU/CEE is difficult to estimate, primarily because of the uncertainties surrounding the future of nuclear plants in this region.

Most CEE countries have extremely limited domestic fossil fuel resources. Those with reserves contributing significantly to domestic electricity generation include Poland (surplus coal for export), Romania (enough gas to cover most internal needs in the short run), the Czech Republic (some lignite) and Hungary (some brown coal, lignite and gas). Russia is still the major source of oil and gas for the region. All CEE countries are attempting to reduce their dependence on Russian fuel imports. This will be difficult for many reasons, including the following:

- Russian supplies are usually cheaper than alternatives.
- The region's infrastructure (especially for gas) is geared primarily towards receiving Russian supplies. Adapting it to alternative sources would require significant investment.
- An expected contraction in fossil fuel production in most CEE countries, in addition to strict new environmental legislation in some of them (e.g. Hungary,

the Czech Republic and Slovakia) implies a reduction in the role of domestically produced solids fuels.

3. Power Sector

Most CEE countries rely on nuclear power to a large extent. Bulgaria, Hungary and Slovakia already depend on nuclear power for more than 35% of their needs, whilst in the Czech Republic and Romania, nuclear power is becoming increasingly important. Poland is the exception, having initiated a program, without then generating any nuclear power. Such a high dependence on nuclear power raises questions about:

- the safety of existing facilities
- plans for future additions to nuclear capacities
- the potential for displacing existing nuclear facilities with conventional generation

Tab. N3: Nuclear Plants in CEE, 1992

	Total Nuclear Capacity a)	RBMK, VVER 440/230s b)	Total Nuclear Generation c)	RBMK, VVER 440/230s d)
Bulgaria	31	15	32	13
Czech Rep.	15	0	23	0
Hungary	23	0	45	0
Slovakia	26	13	51	13

Notes: a) as per cent of Installed Capacity; b) as per cent of Installed Capacity; c) as per cent of Total Generation; d) as per cent of Total Gen.

Source: IEA (1994).

The share of nuclear power plants within total generating capacity, as well as nuclear energy's share of the total electricity generation for CEE is shown in Table N3. Also shown is the percentage of high risk nuclear reactors in terms of capacity and generation. Those reactors commonly placed in the high risk category by western experts are RBMK and the VVER 440/230. For the most part, safety issues involving improvements or decommissioning are linked to aid (both current and future) on the part of Western governments. The closure of relatively unsafe facilities (for example, Bohunice 1 and 2 in Slovakia, and Kozloduy 1 and 2 in Bulgaria) may be entirely contingent on the completion of modern nuclear units (Belene, and Kozloduy 5 and 6, respectively). Right across the region there is little potential for the displacement of nuclear capacity by conventional generation. There are several reasons for this low potential, including a lack of incentives to switch, a shortage of capital for the construction of alternative facilities, the absence of domestic, preferably clean, energy sources, and the need to control thermal emissions. The best opportunities for displacement may be found in Slovakia and Bulgaria (maybe as much as 1.5 GW).

Another condition prevalent in the region is the ageing of thermal generation facilities. Most facilities in CEE are between 20 and 25 years old, and some have far exceeded their useful life. Many thermal plants, especially in Bulgaria and Romania, have been inadequately maintained and their performance rates poorly. The electric power systems are inefficient also in that they use larger amounts of primary energy per kWh of electric energy output than the power supply systems in developed market economies. The overall thermal efficiency of coal- or lignite-fired power stations in the transition economies is usually below 30% and in many cases does not exceed the 20- 25% range. This does not compare well with an EU thermal efficiency rating of about 35% for modern coal-fired plants and up to 50% for gas-fired combined cycle plants. Furthermore, the technical transmission and distribution losses in the power supply systems of transition economies are often in the order of 10% of net generation and sometimes as high as 15-20%, whereas in western Europe they are usually between 4-9%.

For the above mentioned reasons, the amount of electricity generated in nuclear plants exceeds their capacity.

Tab. N4: Production of Electricity by Primary Energy Source, 1994

Countries	**Total production** GWh	**Thermal** %	**Nuclear** %	**Hydro** %
Bulgaria	38 133	56	40	4
Czech Republic	58 705	75	22	3
Hungary	33 486	58	42	0
Poland	135 347	97	0	3
Romania	55 136	76	0	24
Slovak Repub.	24 740	32	49	19
Slovenia	12 681	37	36	27
CEE	375 363	74	16	10
EU	2 267 240	51	35	14
USA	3 473 616	72	20	8

Source: IEA (1996).

4. The Environment

In 1990, sulphur dioxide emissions from power plants exceeded EU levels on a per capita basis by a factor of nine in Bulgaria and six in the Czech Republic. In these countries, local coal is the primary energy source for power generation, which accounts for the bulk of total sulphur dioxide emissions from all sources.

The need to modernise varies considerably among these countries. Modernisation is primarily seen as a means to mitigate environmental damage and achieve better energy efficiency. Some governments, such as in the Czech Republic and Poland, have embarked on programs for the installation of flue-gas desulphurisation equipment and circulating fluidised-bed combustion units to replace older, dirtier, pulverised coal-burning units. The facilities in Bulgaria, Romania, and Slovakia are generally considered to be most in need of future rehabilitation efforts.

Limited access to capital is a constraint for most CEE countries, and this in turn affects the extent and scheduling of the various types of power generation investments (upgrades and new plants) that are being contemplated. Borrowing ability is most limited in Bulgaria, Romania and to a lesser degree, Slovakia. Poland and Hungary fare better, and the Czech Republic has the strongest access to capital.

Tab. N5: Emissions of Sulphur Dioxide in Selected Countries, 1990

Countries	**SO_2 from power plants**		**Power plants as % of total SO_2**
	1000 tonnes	kg/capita	%
Bulgaria	1 453	173	72
Czech Republic	1 163	113	62
Hungary	430	42	48
Poland	1 589	41	49
Romania	903	40	69
Slovak Republic	243	33	65
EU	8 600	23	50

Source: EUROPEAN COMMISSION (1996) and IEA (1996).

5. Tariffs

Electricity tariffs should be set at levels which aim to ensure the financial viability of power utilities and to encourage efficient use. Financial viability requires an adequate return on invested capital, with depreciation based on appropriately valued assets. Efficiency in distribution demands that tariffs reflect supply costs, including the external costs associated with electricity generation. It is important to recognise that households are more costly to supply than large industrial consumers per unit of electricity. Reasons for this include the higher distribution costs to households and the fact that they contribute much of the peak-load demand, which is normally supplied by the generation capacity with the highest marginal costs.

Power rates vary significantly across CEE according to the progress that has been made in transition. In most advanced industrialised countries, power utilities are financially profitable, although it is questionable whether electricity tariffs fully reflect costs, including those associated with pollution and decommissioning of nuclear power plants. In the EU, electricity tariffs average 7 cents per kWh for large industrial users and 15 cents per kWh for households. These tariffs include indirect taxes. The comparable tariffs in the USA and Canada are 4 cents per kWh and 7 cents per kWh respectively. In other words, industrial tariff rates are between 45 and 55% of those for households in industrialised economies. Although the economic costs of primary energy in CEE are similar to those faced by EU utilities, in 1994 the average tariff level in CEE was approximately 50% of the average level in the EU:

- Industrial rates are the lowest in Slovakia and Bulgaria (between 2.5 and 3 cents per kWh), while in Poland they are nearer 4 cents, over 5 cents in the Czech Republic and up to 6 cents in Hungary and Romania.
- Residential rates are very low in Slovakia and Bulgaria (below 2 cents/kWh), around 3 cents/kWh in the Czech Republic (where there is the most cross-subsidisation) and between 4 and 5 cents in Poland, Hungary and Romania. While Hungary and Romania are quite heavily subsidised, Poland has reformed its tariffs: it is the only country in the region where residential rates are actually higher than industrial rates.

No government in the region has yet completed a reform of its price-setting mechanism, though all plan to raise electricity tariffs to cost-covering levels in the medium term. Many have already done so for industrial tariffs, though in some countries (e.g. Bulgaria and Romania) such rises have often been overtaken by inflation.

Many utilities, if not most in the region, are unable to cover costs based on tariffs and to generate adequate funds for necessary investments. As it is unrealistic to continue to place this burden on the state budget, price reforms are essential. The present situation is not only inconsistent with the goal of improving demand-side efficiency, the low tariff levels are also an obstacle to mobilising private finance for electricity investments. While increased tariffs would initially represent an additional expenditure for enterprises and households, these steps would make measures aimed at energy efficiency more attractive, easing the long-term impact on real incomes.

6. Electricity Privatization and Investment Opportunities: Countries Overview

Former East Germany

- Completed 1994
- VEAG and majority stakes in regional distributors sold to German 'Big 8'
- LAUBAG sold to RWE/VIAG/VEBA
- MIBRAG sold to PowerGen/NRG/Morrisson Knudson
- ENRON/MEAG acquired 120 MW plant
- Municipalities/communes own large minority stakes in distributors
- Municipalities want to distribute - and in some cases generate - their own power

Baltics

- Political support for privatisation
- Investment opportunities in plant upgrades and distribution
- Interconnection/export opportunities to neighbouring countries
- Development of BALTEL network
- Corporatisation planned or completed
- Price formula/regulatory framework under review
- Price subsidies being phased out

Poland

- Restructured -1992: 40 gencos, gridco and 33 distributors
- Competitive framework planned
- Regulatory framework is in progress
- Political support for privatisation
- But lack of general privatisation strategy
- Opportunities in equipment upgrades in generation due to:
  - (a) Modernisation (Patnów II)
  - (b) Obsolete equipment
  - (c) Environmental improvements
  - (d) Integration into UCPTE

Slovakia

- Restructured - 1993: One main generator (SEP) and 3 distribution companies
- Priorities:
  - (a) Increase profitability
  - (b) Complete Mochovce and Gabèíkovo
  - (c) Refurbish and modernise other plants
  - (d) Environmental improvements
- No immediate privatisation plans
- Investment opportunities in plant upgrades, interconnections

Czech Republic

- CEZ made USD 600 m profit in 1993
- Price formula/regulatory framework still outstanding
- Political support for privatisation (not unanimous), do not need the money
- Elections due June 1996
- Privatisation imminent
- Restructuring - 1990: 8 distribution companies separated from generation/ transmission company (CEZ)
- Priorities: Temelin, environmental, UCPTE
- 30% of CEZ sold to public/investment funds via voucher privatisation 1992. CEZ No. 210 in F500 by market capitalisation in 1994
- Ownership of distribution companies clarified (20% available for strategic investors?)

Hungary

- Restructuring and corporatisation - 1992:
  - (a) Non-core businesses sold out
  - (b) Coal mines/coal fire power plants merged
  - (c)Share ownership - SPA, MVM and AVRt
  - (d) Reduce reliance on imports
- Attempt by SPA to sell-off minority stakes in 6 regional distribution companies 1993:
  - (a) 11 bids received, but cancelled by pressure from AVRt
  - (b) No regulatory framework
  - (c) Low bid prices
  - (d) Shareholding transfers to AVRt
- Act on "Production, Transportation and Supply of Electric Energy" - 1994
- Hungarian Energy Office established

- Government decree - 1994: Outlines privatisation conception and rime schedule
- New Privatisation Law - 1995: APVRt established
- Government decree modified - 1995:
  - (a) MVMRt own Paks, OVIT
  - (b) Percentage shareholding to be tendered to strategic investors
  - (c) Government to own 1 golden share
- By 1997 majority shareholding could be obtained in power generation and supply companies
- Government decree - August 1995:
  - (a) In effect till 1 January 1997
  - (b) Price increases to be implemented, after 1997 price must contain 8% return on equity
  - (c) Pricing formula complicated

Bulgaria

- Privatisation unclear
- Restructuring in early steps, state monopoly
- Priority: Completion of modern nuclear plants and elimination of outdated ones
- Projects for the improvement of conventional plants
- Lack of capital/ low power rates

Romania

- Support for potential promotion of independent producers
- State monopoly
- Restructuring (disaggregation) is delayed by high costs for large refurbishment programme
- Projects for improvements of conventional plants
- Lack of capital

7. Summary of Regional Deregulation and Privatization Trends

Although demonopolisation is a general goal, each country faces a set of choices, depending on the degree of deregulation it aims to achieve:

- It may only involve the corporatisation of monopoly functions within a holding company.

- It may call for further unbundling, involving a division of the power sector between a generation-transmission entity (GenTran) and separate distribution companies (Distco's).
- It may consist of a further split including separate generation companies (Genco's), a Grid company or Gridco, and separate Distco's.
- Ultimately, in addition to these, a Power Pool Company (Poolco) may be set up to perform an independent dispatching function.

To date, Bulgaria, Romania and Slovakia have not shown the intent, nor developed the necessary legislation for deregulating their power monopolies. Hungary is poised to shift to the Gridco/Genco/Distco stage as a result of recent tenders for seven Genco's and six Distco's. Hungary will retain its state utility, MVM, in a reduced form, to provide baseload nuclear power and transmission/grid services. The Czech Republic may be poised for a shift as well, but is still awaiting enabling legislation before changing from its current GenTran/Distco structure. At this point, the focus in the Czech Republic is more on further privatisation rather than power sector reform. Finally, Poland has to date restructured its sector the most.

By comparison, the situation in regard to open access and power contracting is rather different:

- Open access is strongly encouraged in Poland, while it is moderately favoured in Hungary and disregarded in the Czech Republic.
- Hungary seems to favour long-term power contracts, while Poland would appear to favour spot sales (perhaps around 20%). The situation in the Czech Republic is still unclear on that point.

Different approaches to privatisation are available to CEE countries:

- One approach is to aim at a shared ownership between the state and municipal or regional governments, achieved by a direct transfer or shares, usually 15 to 20%.
- A more involved approach calls for the federal government to create partial privatisation, again usually 15-20%, by floating a portion of its majority stake or issue vouchers to the public. Voucher privatisation is often criticised for its inability to bring in fresh capital to advance the restructuring and modernisation programs.
- A further privatisation of the government stake might involve a strategic partner for each company, usually a foreign participant with capital to invest.
- Finally, full privatisation would occur when the governments (both central and local) sell significant portions of their residual shares to the public or to private partners.

Here too there is a big difference between CEE countries. The monopolies of Bulgaria, Romania and Slovakia are state-owned. Hungary currently has shared ownership, but takes on strategic partners through the Genco and Distco sales. The Czech Republic has partially privatised through voucher programs. Generally, private sector participation in power sectors tends to lag behind the pattern seen in CEE economies overall.

8. Capacity Construction and Rehabilitation

Nuclear

- The Czech Republic plans to finish the 2x1000MW Temelin plant, whose first unit is already near completion.
- Romania expects to complete Unit 1 of a 5x700 CANDU-6 plant at Cernavoda. Completion of Unit 2 would require an additional USD 1 billion. Romania has halted work on Units 3,4 and 5, which are unlikely to be needed this century.
- Slovakia plans to complete two units of a VVER 440/213 nuclear plant at Mochovce, though Units 3 and 4 may be delayed. Upgrading of Units 1 and 2 in Bohunice.
- Bulgaria upgrades Units 1-4 (4x400 MW VVER/230 reactors) of Kozloduy nuclear plant.

Thermal

- Bulgaria may build up to 1000 MW of replacement capacity, after decommissioning a planned 1090 MW. To be completed with a MECU 40 from the EBRD and MECU 45 from the EIB. Conversion of major CHP station into combined cycle.
- Hungary plans to replace 4600-5000 MW, mainly with combined cycle. After completion, other units are (optionally) planned. Conversion of district heating plants.
- Poland plans to build some 5000 MW of new capacity, with another optional 10000 MW by 2010. A new, hard coal-fired plant is currently under construction near Opole. Restoration of 4000 MW coal-fired capacity.
- Romania has some 1400 MW of new plants in various stages of construction, but only 630 MW are scheduled for completion. Estimated costs about USD 2.2 billion.
- The Czech republic is requiring all plants with capacities over 300 MW to reduce emissions. This means approximately 7400 MW (much of it lignite-burning) would have to be retrofitted, at an estimated cost of USD 2.6 billion.

- Slovakia retrofits thermal plants to meet stricter environmental legislation, at an estimated cost of USD 700 million.

Hydro

- Bulgaria probably completed two units of pumped storage.
- Romania has 1420 of capacity in various stages of construction, but only 364 MW are scheduled for completion.
- Slovakia plans to commission a new 50 MW at Cunovo, at a cost of USD 30 millions. Doubtful Gabcikovo/Nagymaros project with Hungary.

Both power sector deregulation and privatisation can create opportunities for activities outside of monopolies - independent power (IP). Greenfield and privatisation paths are being followed in the region. 39 IP projects with a total capacity of over 9 GW have been identified in the region between 1995 and 2004, out of a total forecast of 23 GW of plants capacity additions. This implies a 40% IP contribution. There are only two operating projects (with a combined 96 MW) that have been privatised and there are no operating greenfield projects as yet. The vast majority of market initiatives (37) is under way:

- 27 greenfield projects with a combined capacity of 3.4 GW. Few of them have made significant progress to date. Most of them involve plant expansions rather than clear greenfield projects. In addition, this number does not include awarded or pending bids, since there have been no competitive offers for new capacity in the region as yet
- 3 privatisation projects involving privatised plants where additional capacity is planned or under development. Seven pending offers (or tenders) for privatised generating assets reflect a total capacity of 5.2 GW

Hungary dominates CEE's IP activity with over 70% of combined activity. Poland comes second, with about 10% capacity, and only with greenfield. The Czech Republic is third, with similar capacity in both greenfield and privatisation, but only 5% capacity. Slovakia has 4% of the capacity, in greenfield projects only. Bulgaria and Romania have not announced any IP projects.

9. Summary of CEE's Available Investment Needs in Power Sector

- Bulgaria is currently planning to invest USD 128 million into new capacities and up to 3900 MW re-powering at an average of USD 375 per kW.
- Czech Republic (CEZ's investment programme) plans to invest USD 6.5 billion between 1993 and 2000, of which the completion of the Temelin

nuclear plant represents the largest part. 5-10% represent hydro, 5-10% thermal conversion, 30% FGD installations, and about 4% high voltage systems.

- Hungary: USD 2.7-3 billion by 2000, USD 5.9-7 billion by 2005
- Poland: Total estimate by the year 2000 is about USD 15 billion.
- Romania (RENEL's investment programme): 1993-2000 USD 2.2 billion
- Slovakia (SEP's investment programme): USD 340 million for upgrading of Bohunice 3 and 4; USD 250-270 million for upgrading of Bohunice 1 and 2; ? for nuclear plant in Mochovce; USD 700 million for retrofitting of thermal plants; USD 30 million for hydro.

Energy exports from FSU/CEE

Supply of EU by FSU/CEE's energy will continue in the long term. Direct exports[4] include Russian oil, natural gas, Polish coal, Czech or Ukrainian electricity. There are, of course, many indirect exports through energy intensive products such as cement, aluminium, steel, paper.

- Exports of natural gas from Russia are increasing and are mostly directed at the European market, a third going to CEE and two thirds to western Europe. The largest expansion scheme is a pipeline to Frankfurt/Oder in Germany, via Belarus and Poland, however the first phase is unlikely to be completed before 1997. Even if construction remains on schedule, CEE will remain largely dependent on gas transit via the Ukraine through the end of the decade.
- Oil production in Russia has decreased over the past few years, and the problems associated with it are well known. Nevertheless, the relative export shares, mostly to Europe, have risen. Out of 123 mil. tonnes of exports in 1994, 34 mil. were destined for other FSU countries and 89 mil. tonnes to western Europe and CEE. Romania and the Ukraine are the only significant regional producers outside Russia, though neither is able to supply all its own domestic needs.
- Although oil and natural gas exports from Russia are the most dominant in FSU/CEE exports, there are others. The growth in Polish coal exports, mostly to Germany (30% of total German imports) is way ahead of other FSU/CEE exporters, FSU countries and the Czech Republic. 80% of Polish exports are destined for the EU.
- After a considerable fall in industrial output in CEE in the first half of the 90's, there are, or will be, possibilities for electricity exports from conventional plants in the Czech Republic, as well as from nuclear plants in the Czech Republic and the Ukraine. Their capacity is estimated at 600 MW. However, such estimates are ceteris paribus. We must recognise not only the need for major reconstruction of classical, as well as nuclear plants, but also the environmental opposition to it in these countries, and the problems which may

arise from further development and investment in new nuclear plants. Thus, while electricity exports are potentially possible, they are not very probable.

Endnotes

[1] Purchasing Power Parity.

[2] According to IEA methodology, Capacity Constraints case means trends in past behaviour are assumed to continue to dominate future energy consumption patterns.

[3] According to IEA methodology, Energy Savings case means additional energy efficiency improvements are assumed to be greater than those suggested by past behaviour.

[4] These exports are encouraged also by differences between domestic and world prices. E.g. domestic prices of both oil and natural gas were at below 40% of world prices in Russia 1995.

References

EBRD (1996), Transition Report - Infrastructure and savings, London.

HILL, R (1996), Seven years after the fall of the Berlin Wall difficult tasks at the heart of transition remain to be tackled, says EBRD's 1996 Transition Report, EBRD, London,.

HRUBY, Z. (1994), Energy Sector Study: Czech and Slovak Federal Republic, ESRC East-West Programme Working Paper No. 1, Heriott-Watt University, Edinburgh.

JASINSKI, P. (1994), Competition in the Electricity Supply Industry, RPRC Working Paper No. 4, Hertford College, Oxford.

JASINSKI, P. (1994), Regulation and systemic transformation, RPRC Working Paper No.2, Hertford College, Oxford.

MEINECKE, H.U. (1995), CEE What Are the Opportunities? Paper presented at The Fourth Annual Independent Energy Forum, NRG, Berlin.

MIT (1993), Energy in the Czech Republic, Prague.

MIT (1995), Energy Policy in the Czech Republic, Draft, Prague.

OECD/IEA (1994), Electricity in European Economies in Transition, Paris.

OECD/IEA (1995), World Energy Outlook, Paris.

PLANECON Reports. Different Issues. Washington D.C., 1992-1993.

VALENTINY, P. (1994), Energy Regulation in Hungary, ESRC East-West Programme Working Paper No. 3, Heriot-Watt University, Edinburgh.

VALENTINY, P., UNGVARI, G. (1995), Evolving Regulatory Schemes in Hungarian Energy Industries, Paper presented at Regulation network Meeting, Berlin.

WEISHEIMER, M. (1995), Zum längerfristigen Einfluß von Mittel- und Osteuropa auf die deutschen Energiemärkte, WiW 11/1995, IWH Halle.

YOUNG, M.A. (1995), CEE: Where Are the Opportunities? Paper presented at The Fourth Annual Independent Energy Forum, Price Waterhouse, Berlin.

O: Russian Electricity Industry: Towards Market Economics

Vladimir Voloshin

1. Structure of the Electricity Industry and Degree of Internationalisation in Russia

The power industry is one of the main branches of the national economy, it provides consumers with the most technological and ecological kind of energy. It forms the base of the fuel-energy complex (FEC) - the most important sector of the Russian economy, in which the interests of the largest industrial and financial groups are involved. These groups have significant impact on the economic life of the country.

The power industry combines the generation, transmission and distribution of electric energy, it includes electric and cogeneration power stations, power networks, dispatching offices and service infrastructure (repair and construction enterprises, scientific and design organisations and so on). In contrast to other countries, in Russia the electric supply is closely connected with district heating. The reason is, first of all, the extensive development of cogeneration power stations (CgPS) in Russia, which generate electric power, steam and hot water simultaneously.

The structure of the power industry as a research subject is the sum of separate parts and connections which form the electric power complex. The different compositions of structures are formed dependent on the common features at the base of these parts and connections.. The main compositions under consideration in this work are branch and regional structures, and inter-branch proportions. One important composition is the organisational structure of the branch. The reform of this structure has a significant value for the effective functioning of the power industry during the transition to market economics.

1.1 Branch and Regional Structure of the Power Industry

The availability of fuel-energy resources is one of the most important factors determining the development and structure of the power industry. Russia has significant and varied fuel resources. On Russian territory (about 10% of the Earth's dry land and 2,6% of its population), more than 33% of the world's explored gas reserves, 13% - oil, 23% - coal and 14% - uranium are concentrated (SHAFRANIK, Yu 1995, p.85). Moreover, in Russia there is a large hydroenergetic potential, corresponding to a yearly electric power generation of 850 billion kWh, or total electric power generation at all power stations in the country. (SHAFRANIK, Yu 1995, p.105). This situation allows the development of all branches of the fuel-energy complex. In 1996 301,2 million tons of oil (including gas condensate), 601,4 billion m^3 of gas and 242,5 million tons of coal was produced. .(GOCKOMSTAT of RUSSIA,1997).

The availability of these complex resources provides the means of forming the power industry based on the use of different kinds of energy. The Russian power industry is based on three different technical, economical and ecological systems - thermal, nuclear and hydraulic power stations. The total generation of the geothermal, solar and tidal energy is very small, although these energy sources could play an important role in the energy supply tosome regions.

From '70s to the mid'80s, there was a tendency for preferred development of the nuclear power stations, and construction of economical hydroelectric stations and large thermal power stations for low-cost fuels. In the electric power generation structure, the role of nuclear stations was increasing, whereas that of thermal power stations was decreasing and that of hydraulic power stations was remaining practically unchanged.

After the accident at the Chernobyl nuclear power plant, the program of nuclear power development radically changed. The competitiveness of the nuclear power plants has decreased in comparison with the thermal and hydraulic power stations due to the necessity of increasing their safety and reliability. The priorities of the development of different power industries branches have changed. Nuclear power has ceased to be the most dynamic branch of the power industry.

The early '90s became a new turning point in the development of the power industry in Russia. The transition towards market principles in the economy demanded radical changes in all systems of economic relations. In conditions of deep economic crisis embracing all of Russia, the generation of electric power in 1995 dropped by 22% in comparison with 1990 and amounted to 845 billion kWh, including Condensation and Congeneration Thermal Power Stations (TPS) - 67,4%, HPS - 20,9% and NPP - 11,3% (Tab. O1).

Tab. O1: Structure of Electricity Production in Russia in 1995 by Types of Power Stations

Station type	**Production of electricity,** billion kWh	**Share in production of electricity, %**
NPP	99.3	11.7
HPS	176.6	20.9
TPS	569.3	67.4
Total	845.2	100.0

Source: Goskomstat (1996).

The total capacity of the power stations in Russia at the beginning of 1996 amounted to 204,6 million kW, including 192,1 million kW in the United Power grid of Russia. 10,4% of capacity is due to the nuclear power plants, 21,5% - hydroelectric and 68,1% - thermal power stations (Tab. O2).

Tab. O2: Structure of the Installed Capacity of Power Stations in Russia at the Beginning of 1996

Type of power station	**Capacity,** million kW	**Share in installed capacity,** %
NPP	21,3	10,4
HPS	43,9	21,5
TPS	139,4	68,1
including TPS	73,3	35,8
CPS	66,1	32,3
Total	204,6	100

Notes: NPP=Nuclear Power Plants; HPS=Hydroelectric Power Stations; TPS=Thermal Power Stations; CPS=Condensation Power Stations

Source: Goskomsstat (1996).

The main technological form of organisation in the Russian power industry is the United Power Grid (UPG). The system consists of six parallel working Regional Power Grids (RPG) - the North-West, Center, Middle Volga, Ural (including the Tumen power system), North Caucasus, Siberia. The seventh Regional Power Grid - is weakly integrated into the United Power Grid.

UPG of Russia is part of the UPG of the former USSR, which formerly included the regional power grids of Kazakhstan, Ukraine, Transcaucasus and Middle Asia. RPG of the North-West included the power system of the Baltic Sea region. After the disintegration of the USSR some regions were connected to the power systems of other CIS countries, and others to the UPG of Russia. The presence of this additional load influences the balance of capacity and consumption of the Russian RPG as an obligatory export, at least for the next few years.

The grid system of the Russian UPG is formed by 220-330-500-750-1150 kV transmission lines of a total length of more than 148 thousand km. The share of the seven regional power systems in the total installed capacity of power stations in Russia, is about 95%. In its turn, the regional power grids consist of 72 single-area power systems - the basis of AO "Energo". The shares of the different RPG in production and consumption of UPG's electricity are identified in (Tab. O3).

Tab. O3: The Share of the Different RPG in Production and Consumption of Electricity in Russia

Region	Number of single-area power systems	Share in consumption of electric energy in 1995, %	Share in production of electric energy in 1995, %
North-West	10	7	9
Center	19	29	25
Middle Volga	9	10	15
Ural	8	26	18
Siberia	10	20	22
Far East	7	3	6
North Caucasus	9	5	5
Total	72	100	100

Source: KAPITAL-STRATEGIYA (1996).

The dispatching system is based on the hierarchic principle and is characterized by a multi-level structure. Three dispatching levels can be connected to base ones - Central Dispatching Office of UPG (CDO of Russia's UPG), United Dispatching Offices of RPG (UDO of RPG), and Central Dispatching Offices of regional power systems. Below them are local offices of the distribution grids and offices of power stations.

The CDO of Russia's UPG controls most of the UPG operation as a whole. This includes the inter-system flows of electric power, the main connections in UPG, export of electric power, operation of blocks (having an important role in providing reliability and efficiency of electric supply). The UDO of RPG controls the intra-system flows in regional systems. The CDO coordinates the operation of the power stations on the boundaries of regional systems.

The operation of power stations in Russia's UPG makes it possible to:

- increase the reliability of the electricity supply by means of the mutual redundancy of capacities;
- economize fuel and improve the ecological situation;
- decrease the necessary redundancy capacities of power stations;
- decrease the installed capacities of power stations due to time disagreement over passing of load maximums;
- increase the capacity of units and power stations.

The reliable energy supply to consumers within all territories of the country is provided at relatively low cost to the electrical power reserves (3-5%). An essentially identical level of energy supply reliability is provided by the electric power industry of the developed countries, but the electrical power reserves are around 30- 40%. This means the operation of the Russian United Power Grid provides enormous investment savings, which are commensurable with expenditures on the construction of 50 Mwt electric power (THE STATE PROGRAM of MEASURES for PROVISION of ENERGY SECURITY of RF, 1996, p.3).

The territorial structure of power in the industry depends mainly on the location of fuel-energy resources and consumers of electrical energy. Before the construction of high-power transmission lines for long-distance energy transmission, the power stations were built near energy consumers. For power production local or imported fuels were used. The production and consumption of electrical energy concurred regionally. The dependence of power station location on the disposition of the main consumers is clear . In the European part of the country, including the Urals, where the main electric energy consumers are located, about 70% of the total capacity of power stations is concentrated. The united energy systems, located in industrial developed regions, provide the maximum volume of electrical energy.

After the construction of long-distance transmission lines, the fairly strong dependence between the location of power stations and consumers diminished. The inter-regional connections for “import” and “export” of electrical energy rose. From Povolzhie, where the large hydroelectric stations operate, the excess electrical energy is transmitted to central regions of theEuropean part of thecountry and to the Urals. In some cases it became profitable to construct the TPS in fuel-producing regions and transmit the electrical energy to other regions. In many cases the technical progress in electricity transmission makes its long-distance transmission more profitable in comparison with fuel transport. Moreover, the long-distance transmission of electricity allows the involvement in economic turnover of the energy resources remote from main energy consumption regions. This is particularly important because these resourses are located very irregularly throughout the country, mainly in remote and hard to reach regions. About 80% of explored reserves of oil and gas, and 50% of coal are found in Western Siberia. The expected oil and natural gas reserves of Timano-Pechora basin, Eastern Siberia and offshore from the Arctic Sea amount to between 50% and 80% of total expected reserves (VNIIKTEP,1993, p.87).

The main reserves of water power are concentrated in Siberia and the Far East. The economic potential of water power in these regions, i.e. economically proven potential in relation to the present ratio of prices for equipment, materials and manpower, is more than 700 billion kWh. The usage level by operating power stations under construction, in terms of HPS is about 20%. In the European part of the country, including the Urals where power potential is considerably less, the same indicator is about 50% (Tab. O4).

The level of hydro-resources utilised in Russia is considerably lower than that in industrially developed countries. France, Switzerland, Austria, and Portugal have developed more than 90% of economic hydro-energy potential. Between 65% and 90% of potential has been developed in Japan, Sweden, and Germany; and 45% to 65% in USA, Canada, Italy, and Brazil.

The nuclear power plants are the most maneuverable to locate.Nuclear fuel is transported with relatively lesser cost in comparison with other fuels, because of its high energy capacity and the small quantity necessary for NPP operation. The energy from usage of 1 kg of uranium - 235 is equivalent to the energy created from burning 2.5 thousands tons of high- quality coal. This is why the location of NPP does not rely on the location of nuclear fuel resources (KHRUSHCHEV,K,1986,p.201).

Tab. O4: Hydroelectric Potential of Russia

Economic region	**Economic hydroelectric potential,** billion kWh	**Developed potential of HPS in operation and under construction,** billion kWh	**Level of hydro-resources used**
West Siberia	77	1.7	2
East Siberia	350	116.6	33
Far East	294	19.0	6
Total Russian Fed.	**852**	**199.8**	**23.4**

Source: SHAFRANIK (1995).

The location of different types of power stations is determined by the relative efficiency of their operation in a particular region.The economic advantages of nuclear plant location in zones of high electrical energy demand, led to orientation of the nuclear power sources in the European part of the country which has a high population density. While moving from the European part of the country to the Urals, the efficiency of the NPP is decreased, the efficiency of the TPS is increased. The zone of effective application of the NPP narrowed after the Chernobyl accident, because of the increase in construction costs in connection with the toughening of demands of NPP location (ENERGY INSTITUTE, 1994, p.136).

The nuclear power plants play an important role in the power systems of the North-West, Centre and Middle Volga regions. The RPG of the Ural and Central regions covers more than half of all the capacity of the TPS in Russia. The thermal power stations in the European part of the country use mainly oil and gas fuel. In the Siberian and Far Eastern RPG, coal and hydraulic energy are used for production of electrical power (Fig. O1).

Fig. O1: The Distribution of Power Station Capacities by Regions and Types of Fuel

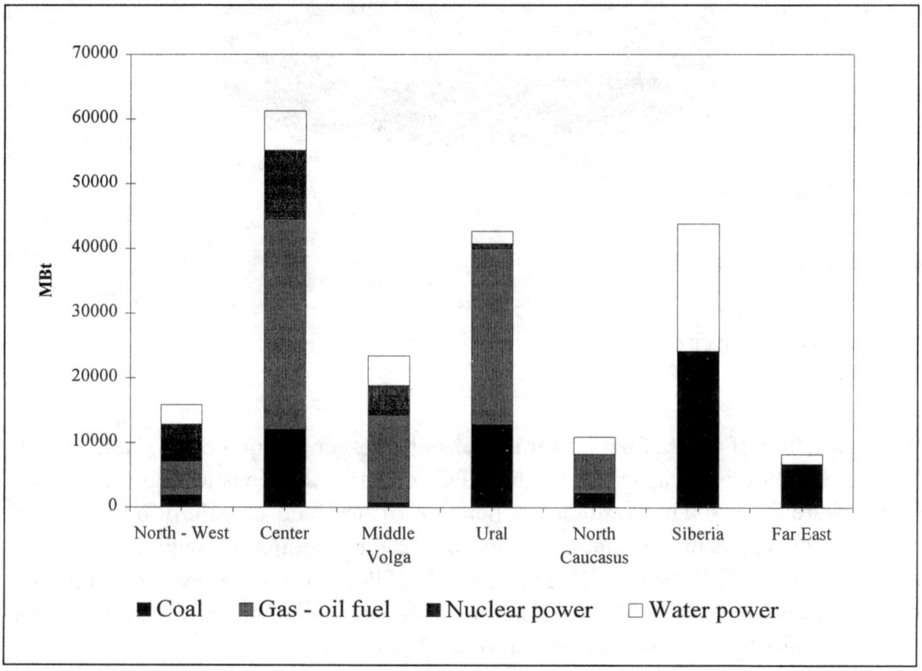

Source: KAPITAL – STRATEGIYA (1996).

1.2 Intra-branch Proportions

The thermal power stations are the base of the power industry. The reason for this is connected, on the one hand, with the relatively developed fuel industry, and, on the other hand, with special features of the thermal power stations. Such stations, unlike hydraulic power stations, can generate electrical energy without seasonal fluctuations. The TPS are constructed quickly with smaller labour input and material resources. In the structure of fuels, used by TPS in 1995, the figure for natural gas was 63%, coal - 24% and fuel oil - 10% (Fig. O2).

Fig. O2: Structure of TPS Fuels in 1995

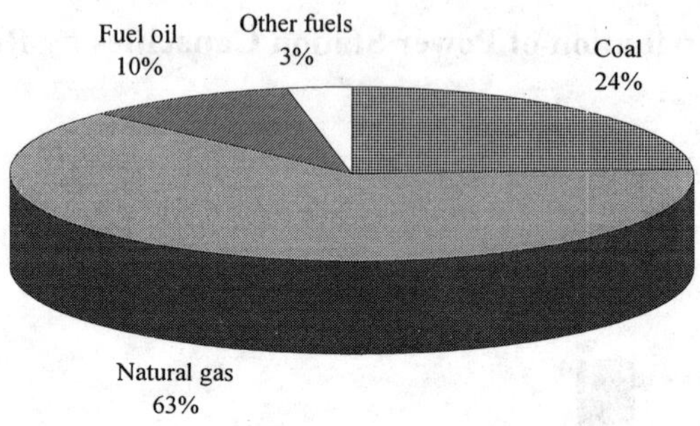

Source: GOSKOMSTAT (1996).

In the structure of the thermal power stations, the co-generation power stations share (CgPS) 35,8% of all capacities of the UPG, and the condensation power stations (CPS) share 32,3%. The combined generation of heat and electricity by the CgPS allows their efficiency to increase up to 70% as compared with the 30-35% maximum of the CPS (ENERGY INSTITUTE,1994, p.65). As a result of combined heat-and-power generation ten million tons of fuel are economized. Accordingly the ecological situation in large towns improves significantly.

The capacity of the power-generating units, installed in the power stations, has grown. The construction of power stations with 500 and 800 MW power-generating units instead of 300 MW allows (under comparable conditions) the reduction by 1.5 times of the specific number of operating staff, and the consumption of material resources also decreases substantially by 1 kW of the installed capacity (ENERGOATOMIZDAT,1984,p.38).

Further increasing the unit capacity of the power-generating units does not significantly improve the economic efficiency of the CPS.. This is explained, in the first instance by heat cycle properties (where futher increase of the steam parameters gives no substantial benefits), and, secondly, by the design characteristics of the power-generating units. This is why before the appearance of new quality technical decisions the increase of the equipment capacities shows no economic effect.

The mode of electricity consumption in the European part of the country in particular, largely influences the capacities structure of the thermal power stations. It is well known that the operation of the TPS and NPP within the variable of the electric load curve is unsuitable due to technical reasons. The thermal and nuclear power stations are intended mainly for operation of the basic load. HPS are used mostly for providing the peak and semi-peak loads and for controlling the frequency and voltage of the electric current, that is, for increasing the power supply quality to the consumers.

The choice of optimal ratio between different types of power stations allows a rational provision of electric power to consumers. This task is comparatively simple in regions with relatively large resources of hydraulic power, such as the Caucasus, and the eastern part of the country. In contrast, in the main power systems of the European part of the country (where there is a high irregularity of electricity consumption,and hydraulic resources are restrained) the problem under consideration is particularly important.. An interim solution has been the application of gas turbine and steam-gas units, which due to manouverability are used for supplying peak loads.

The second position in production of electrical power falls to the HPS. These stations have always played an important role in providing electricity to consumers. The rational combination of the HPS, TPS and NPP ensures the reliable and effective operation of the power systems. As a result of the application of renewable resources, the HPS has replaced organic fuels in electricity production technology. In 1995 HPS provided a saving of about 50 million tons of coal-equivalent fuel. Hydraulic power stations are characterized by ease of control and high efficiency (more than 80%). The required staff of the HPS is 15-20 times less than the TPS.

The development of hydro-power engineering followed in in the footsteps of constuction of the large HPS and increased the unit capacity of the power-generating units. The 4000, 4320, 4500, 6000 6400 MW power-generating units operate on the Angara and Yenisey rivers. The capacity of the Ust-Ilim HPS is 4320 MW, Krasnoyarsk HPS - 6000 MW, and the Sayano-Shushensk HPS - 6400 MW. In order to more fully exploit the hydraulic power, chains of HPS are consructed on the rivers (GOSCOMSTAT of RUSSIA,1996).

The complex use of water resources is the main feature of hydraulic power development. In addition to electricity production, conditions for navigation, irrigation and flood protection were created. At the same time the construction and exploitation of water storage basins produced some undesirable effects - the flooding of vast useful territories, new barriers to fish migration, a worsening of conditions in their habitats, decrease of the flow of running water, and so on. As a result, economical intercommunications and connections between ecological elements (formed on the planet over many centuries) were destroyed.

the accumulation of energy. These plants are intended to cover the variable part of the load curve, for frequency and voltage control. In charge mode the PSP use NPP and TPS energy.

The interest in exploiting local renewable energy resources through construction of small hydroelectric stations on the small rivers in Russia has resurged. Formerly such stations were spread quite widely throughout Russia. By the early 1960s there were about 5000 small hydroelectric stations in the country, which provided electrical energy to a significant numberof rural areas. After the connection of rural consumers to large stations, the small stations were closed. The unit cost of electrical energy production on the small rivers was substantially more than in large power stations. In addition, the large stations provided electrical energy based on preferential tariffs. Presently the situation has altered as a result of the abrupt increase of tariffs for electricity, fuels and transport costs. It would be advisable to construct small hydroelectric stations in decentralized energy supply regions. The technical potential of the small hydroelectric stations in Russia is estimated at 60 billion kWh.

Before the accident at the Chernobyl APP the role of nuclear energy in the formation of the country's rational energy balance was constantly increasing. The development of atomic power was based mainly on the application of two types of power reactor - water-moderated with 440 and 1000 MW (WMPR-440, WMPR-1000) capacity, and uranium-graphite with 1000 MW (UGPR-1000) capacity. These reactors are related to so called thermal (slow) reactors.

The availability of two types of nuclear reactors allowed a fairly rapid increase in nuclear power capacities, because uranium-graphite reactors did not require construction of special machine manufacturing enterprises. However, the reduction of NPP construction costs was based on the use of design types and unification of equipment, design and construction decisions. It was thought that the best means of acheiving this would be the use of one type of reactor for all NPP. It was conceived that two types of reactors would be used in the first stage of nuclear power development, then, from the beginning of the 1990s the manufacture and application of uranium-graphite reactors would be terminated. (IEMSS,1988p.87) After the accident at Chernobyl NPP (where the uranium-graphite reactors are installed) the NPP program of construction involving this type of reactor was halted.

It was anticipated in the 1970s that the new direction in the use of nuclear fuel would be the supply of centralized heat from nuclear heat supply power plants (NHSPP) and nuclear heat-and-power plants (NHPP). It was anticipated that the use of nuclear energy for heat supply would provide the opportunity to economize on a significant volume of organic fuels. However,after the Chernobyl accident all activity in this sphere was stopped, and the first block of NHSPP in Voronezh was not put into operation, although it was ready for start-up.

Parallel with application of the thermal (slow) nuclear reactors, experience of industrial exploitation of fast reactors of 600 MW (FNR-600) was accumulated. If nuclear power develops on the base of thermal (slow) reactors only, then prospectively (by the middle to end of next century), an NPP fuel deficit could arise. Fast reactors provide a solution to this problem, because they are able to reproduce nuclear fuel in enlarging quantities. The energy efficiency of 1 kg uranium increases more than 100-times. In this case the uranium reserves would be sufficient for many centuries, and it would be economically possible to develop much poorer uranium fields.

Safety provisions for NPP operation is the main problem of nuclear power. The power-generating units currently in operation were placed on stream at different times, they were constructed using different designs and varying degrees of fill safety requirements.. From this viewpoint the power-generating units currently in operation can be divided into two groups:

1. Power-generating units with first generation (about 13 million kW) reactors UGPR and WMPR-440;
2. Power-generating units with second generation reactors WMPR-1000, WMPR-440 and FNR-600(about 8 million kW).

The reactors of the first group require premature removal from service. Another means of increasing their safety is technical modernization. This will enable operation up to the end of the design operation term (30 years). The reactors of the second group largely conform to safety requirements and their operation can be continued up to end of the design operation term (VOLOSHIN,V, 1994, p.7).

1.3 The Main Problems of the Power Industry Development

Presently the Russian power industry faces the need to solve some important problems. Some of these are the result of the rigid centralized planned economy, others - the result of errors and objective difficulties in the transition to the market economy. The efficiency in solving these problems will determine in many respects the prospects and structure of the development of the power industry

One of the central problems of the power industry, connected with the total state of the national economy, is the low efficiency of electrical power usage. The consumption of electrical power per unit of GDP in Russia is double that in many industrially developed countries. The high power-intensive GDP is explained primarily by the low technical level of the economy and its highly energy-intensive structure.The resource-intensive cost model of economic development has formed in Russia over decades. The result is the low efficiency of fuel and energy usage.

Savings of a large volume of energy and the provision of economic growth can be made without additional energy sources.

Throughout the economic fall of the 1990s, power production has declined more slowly than the reduction of the GDP. Whilst the GDP in 1995 decreased by more than one half in comparison with 1990, electricityproduction declined by only 22%. This led to the growth of power-intensity in the economy. The high power-intensity of GDP is combined with comparatively low per capita power consumption. In Russia in 1995, per capita power consumption was 5,7 thousand kWh of electrical power produced, - that is, half as much as in the USA.(GOSCOMSTAT of RUSSIA,1996).

In theory, the transition to the energy-saving model of economic development, economic restructuring and technical progress, creation of adequate mechanisms for saving energy, permit the increased efficiency in electric power usage. Presently however, the objective conditions for realizing energy-saving potential do not exist. Owing to high inflation and credit rates enterprises don't yet have the tools for industry innovation and the implementation of special measures for energy-saving. Large-scale structural conversions in the economy require large investments and a signicant time period.

The transformation to a market economy destroyed the State system of administering the national economy. At the same time the mechanisms for economizing energy (inefficient, but active) were broken. The expected self-regulation of energy efficiency as a result of the new economic conditions (in particular, of the change in property form and the significant growth of fuels costs) did not eventuate.

The growth of electric power consumption in the public utilities sector will counteract the drop in the power-intensity of the GDP. This sector uses 2-3 times more electrical energy in Russia, than in industrially developed countries. This situation is linked with the low number of the population with household appliances and the low number of houses equipped with services and utilities. Technical progress has a contradictory effect on the dynamics of electricity consumption. On one hand it promotes the reduction of electricity consumption costs in the production of products, but on the other hand the growth of power availability per individual, and per capita electricity consumption are the objective rule of social development.

The age, state and high degree of wear on operating equipment in the branch are major problems for the power industry. The condition of equipment threatens the reliability and quality of the nation's electricity supply. The problem is complicated by the fact that investment cycles in branches of the power industry are lengthy and capital-intensive.

The limited terms of equipment operation in the thermal power stations (which have been prolonged several times) are variable from 30 to 45 years. At the

The limited terms of equipment operation in the thermal power stations (which have been prolonged several times) are variable from 30 to 45 years. At the beginning of 1996 about 13 million kW of equipment, used beyond its service life, was in operation, out of a total of 139 million kW. By 2000 the amount of such equipment will be 40 million kW, and by 2010 - 80 million kW. This is 58% of the TPS capacity, installed at the beginning of 1996 (Fig. O3). Most of this ageing equipment is concentrated in the European part of the country. More than half of the "ageing" TPS equipment in these regions of the country uses gas-fuel oil fuels.

Fig. O3: The Dynamics of Worked-out Equipment

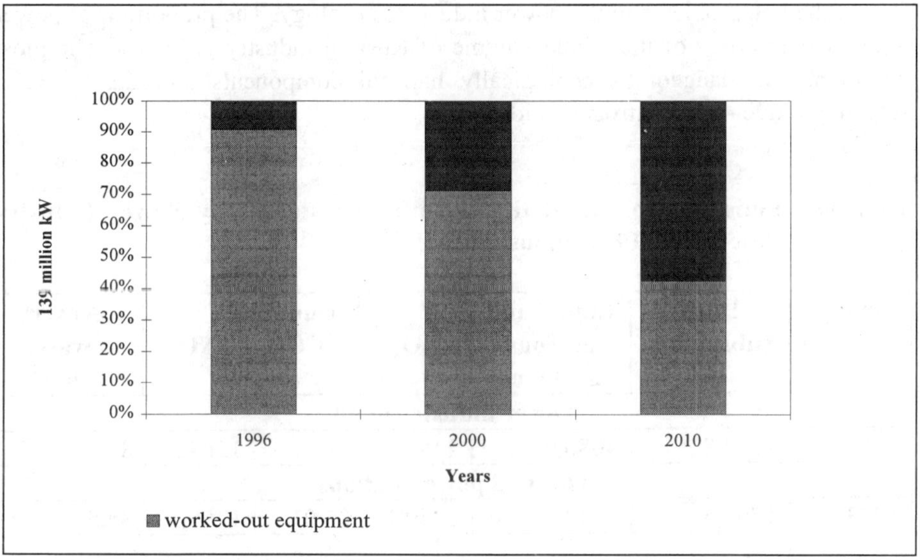

Source: SHAFRANIK (1995).

In the hydraulic power industry the capacity of HPS with a 30-year operation term to 2000 will approach 10 million kW (Tab. O5). The service life of HPS equipment in the recent past was 25-30 years, but it was then prolonged and for some types of equipment amounted 40 years

In the nuclear power industry the design service life of the nuclear power-generating units is 30 years. The operating capacity of power stations by 2000 will decrease by 1,5 times and amount to about 14 million kW. The premature withdrawal from operation of the NPP of first generation reactors of WMPR and UGPR types, further complicates the situation because they do not meet safety requirements.

Tab. O5: Number of HPS with 30 Years Service Life

Date of the resource working off	Number of HPS	Number of the power-generating units	Installed capacity, million kW
01.01.1996	8	29	1.2
01.01.2000	17	108	9.8

Source: ENERGY INSTITUTE (1994).

One of the key problems in the power industry is ecology. The proportion of power industry enterprises of the whole volume of Russian industry is 26.6%. The most important and dangeorous ecologically harmful components are: dust - 31%, sulphur dioxide - 42%, nitrogen oxides -
23,5%

Tab. O6: Emissions to Air of the Harmful Substances by Power Industry Enterprises 1994 (thousand t)

Total	Hard substances	Liquid and gaseous substances	Including SO_2	CO	NO	Recovery of waste, % total
Power industry at all						
5898,8	1812,8	4086,0	2489,4	190,7	1384,2	84,4
Thermal power stations						
5343,4	1705,6	3637,8	2269,1	83,01	1266,6	85,5

Source: SHAFRANIK (1995).

The energy industry is the one of the main sources of water pollution. The enterprises of this industry are one of the main water consumers in the country, but they do not always clean the output water. The significant amount of this water is used for cooling in thermal and nuclear power stations. The great part of the water is directed for ash disposal in the thermal stations, which use solid fuel. The hydrotechnical structures influence the level of ground water, this often leads to salinization and bogging of the soil and to decreasing its productivity.

Significant areas are alienated as a result of using territories for warehousing of power stations' wastes. The waste, in volume about 1,2 billion tons, is accumulated in the ash dumps of thermal power stations. The ash dumps cover about 20 thousand hectares in territories which were formerly high-productivity agricultural lands.

The future influence of the hotbed effect on the power energy structure will grow, and as a result of this effect, the average temperature near the Earth's surface will increase. Carbon dioxide has the greatest influence on the thermal balance of the planet. The increased hotbed effect, in some estimations, 45%, is connected with the increase of carbon dioxide concentration (VOFBERG,D,1989, p.7). The power industry is the main source of increased carbon dioxide concentration in the atmosphere. One way to decrease the effluents of carbon dioxide is to improve the structure of the energy balance, in order to decrease the amount of fuels characterized by the largest content of carbon (coal, shales), and also to increase the amount of fuels with a low content of this substance (natural gas). The level of nuclear and hydraulic power in the energy balance along with alternative sources of energy must also be increased.

In any event, all power stations have a harmful effect on the environment. Under normal conditions of exploitation, the NPP have the smallest harmful effect in comparison with the TPS and HPS. The operation of the TPS involves creation of significant waste effluents. The HPS also have an adverse effect on the environment. Non-traditional energy sources sources (wind-operated, solar and geothermal power stations, for example). cause the smallest amount of damage to the environment. However, the current role of these sources of electrical energy production is minor, and it is not expected to grow significantly

The most complicated problem in the power industry is the financial one. The transition to the principles of a market economy have sharply affected sources of financing.. Opportunities for financing through the traditional source - the State budget have decreased sharply. The State can no longer fulfil the necessary financial requirements, thus aggravating the overall problems of financing in the sector, and leaving the most imperative problems unsolved, namely,equipment repair and maintenance, remuneration of labour and fuel.

Non-payment is among the major reasons for financial shortages in the country. Revenues from electrical power supplies are part of the mainstream of financial flow to the Russian Joint Stock Company of the Power Industry and Electrification (RAO "UPG of Russia") and the Regional Jpint Stock Company of the Power Industry and Electrification (AO "Energo") which integrate domestic thermal and hydro plants. However, the upward trend towards overdue payments is visible. Consumers paid only slightly more than 65% of electricity bills in 1995, the industry debt totalled 30% and railways owed 17% of their overall power consumption. Agriculture is the greatest debtor, 91%, although they enjoy half the level of power tariffs placed on industry. The cumulative power-sector debt jumped from Rb16 trillion to Rb42 trillion (or nearly $9 billion) in 1995, with the highest debt rate (a factor of 3.7) being reported for enterprises and organisations funded by the federal budget (FINANSOVYE IZVESTIYA,22 MARCH 1996).

The CIS countries owed Russia a total of $0.7 billion in 1996, Kazakhstan is the largest debtor with overdue payment presently some $400 million. Consumer non-payment added to the overall fuel debt in the energy sectors. Total debt reached Rb2 trillion (about $0.4 billion) for coal, Rb1.4 trillion ($0.3 billion) for residual oil and Rb15.8 trillion ($3.3 billion) for gas.

The energy financing problem is closely interrelated with the investment crisis. Severe investment shortcomings lead to lowered plant capacity and removal from service, additionally hampered by hazardous wear on facilities. Energy plant start-ups in Russia dropped from 5.03 million kW in 1988 to as little as 1.35 million kW in 1995. Only Rb16.2 trillion ($3.5 billion) investment was made in 1995 and some Rb600 billion ($130 million) was required for the recovery of destroyed energy facilities in the Chechen republic FINANSOVYE IZVESTIYA, 22 MARCH 1996).

The present taxation policy is one reason for this investment breakdown. The enormous tax burden undermines the investment ability of the power tariff - one of the primary investment resources. Capital flow to the power sector, from foreign sources in particular, is hampered by the unfavourable investment climate in the country.

The main reasons for the present financial and investment recession originated beyond the power sector and are the outcome of the macroeconomic policy. These issues should therefore be handled in line with the overall economic environment in the country. However, much will depend on the adoption of the market economy within the power sector. The persisting problems could be handled at minimum cost through adequate methods and areas of industry reform,such as restructuring, rearrangement of ownership rights, the building a competitive power industry market environment.

1.4 Future Opportunities

The future of the Russian electricity industry is greatly dependent on the overall economic environment in the country and Russia's ability to overcome the recession. The rate of economic transition, combined with power conservation, scope and price profile, will define power consumption and the resultant industry framework.

Numerous outlooks exist providing different assessments of Russia's prospects for economic recovery. To our mind, the gross domestic product (GDP) could reach an all-time low of about 60% of the pre-crisis level by 1997. Industrial resumption is most likely in 1999 and 2000, followed by an economic growth period where the pre-crisis GDP level could be attained by 2010 (Fig. O4).The present economic restructuring and the employment of resource-saving technologies are both focused on better fuel and energy performance. Provided the market mechanisms suit these transformations, one can expect lower power content in GDP as a result of economic resumption.

Fig. O4: GDP Profile Outlook

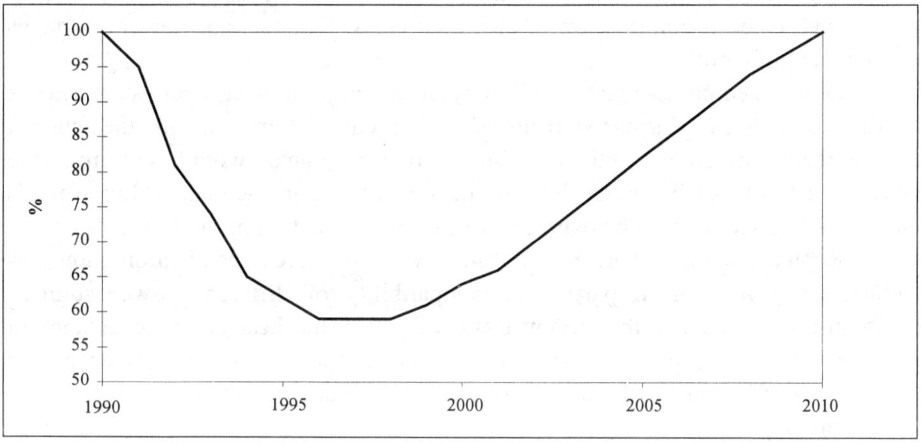

Source: MEZHGOSTATKOM CIS (1996).

Power consumption predictions assume that electricity prices will increase 1.6 - 1.8-fold from 1995 to 2010. This growth is attributed, not to the fuel-component of costs, but rather to higher salaries, more expensive consumables and added investment in facility upgrades and new construction as well as re-assessment of basic assets among existing facilities.

According to the expected economic recovery rates, power price profile and power conservation opportunities, the indigenous electricity consumption could reach some 1,100 billion kWh by 2010 or become equal to the 1990 level. The total capacity of power plants will remain virtually unchanged from 1995. Power exports are assumed to be a fraction of the total, or around 30 billion kWh by 2010, and thus are unlikely to impact the power sector structurally.

Given a high degree of wear on energy equipment, early upgrades of existing plants will be required to meet the expected electricity demand. Wide-scale decommissioning of obsolete plants which were built extensively in the second half of the 1950s and during the 1960s is presently under way.

Under unfavourable financial conditions, inexpensive and fast-returning projects would help eliminate rapidly growing capacity shortages. Such projects primarily include finalizing the construction of thermal, hydro and nuclear power stations that are currently more than 70 - 80% completed, as well as new transmission lines that could use the present excessive capacity to shave shortages in a number of regions using a “bubble” present elsewhere. Other possibilities include nuclear plant revamps aimed at enhancing operating safety - otherwise they would have to be decommissioned, at higher costs, thus making power shortages worse in a number of grids.

Downsized power plants could become essential in meeting consumer needs in the short term, during start-up capital accumulation and in the current unfavourable investment climate. Small power plants would require little investment and involve smaller risks. In the longer term, an adequate influx of funds into the power sectorcould be expected to foster construction of larger plants.

Replacement of obsolete plants and new startups are dependent on numerous factors, the following in particular: compatibility of different power sources, environmental pressures, the current status of power and heat grids, acceptance of innovative power equipment. Eventually, all such factors would be driven by the economic performance of the analysed power supply options and by new investment opportunities.

The comparative performance of upgrades versus new construction projects in Russia has been studied within the framework of a 1993-1994 joint Russian-American project envisaged by the Chernomyrdin-Gore commission .(JOINT RUSSIAN - US STUDY, 1994).The essential conclusions are as follows.

- Combined heat and power plants (CgPS) will have comparable performance with condensate power plants (CPS), applied to both upgrades and grass-roots level. Upgrade of facilities in all categories is more beneficial than construction of new plants of similar type. In some cases, construction of new TPS (gas-fired in particular) would be more preferable than CPS revamps. Gas-fired CgPS are more economical than plants that fire coal.
- Replacement of steam turbines by steam/gas units and gas turbines is the most viable option for CCP upgrade projects. Gas-fired CHPs are more efficient compared to other types of CHP or nuclear plants.
- Third-generation nuclear plants perform better than coal-fired CCPs and, moreover, meet stringent environmental requirements in all European regions of Russia and the Far East. They are nearly equal in performance to coal-fired CCPs in the Urals. In Siberia, nuclear plants presently fail to compete with the performance of Kansk-Achinsk or Eastern Siberian coal-fired CCPs. In future, it will be viable to build small-sized hydro plants on plains rivers and combined mid-power plants in mountain areas of the European part of Russia. Hydro-

plant construction in Siberia and the Far East could be justified since huge hydraulic reserves are present there. It would therefore be viable to complete existing facilities and embark on new smaller sized hydro plant projects.

- A Power industry development forecast through 2010 could be made based on the above mentioned factors and predictions based on the expected Russian capacity. The role of different power plants is expected to be virtually unchanged. Thermal plants will dominate the power industry. Similarly to 1995, thermal hydro and nuclear plants will account for 68%, 22% and 10% respectively, with the previous thermal-to-condensing plant ratios being unaltered (Fig. O5).

Fig. O5: The Possible Structure of Power Stations in Russia in 2010

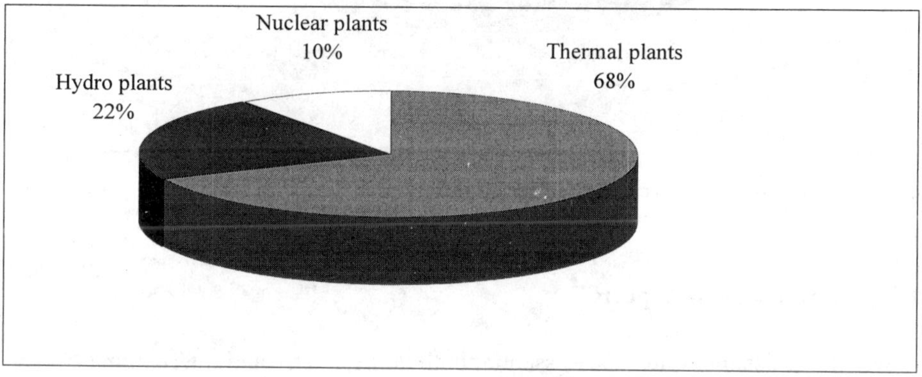

Source: JOINT RUSSIAN-US STUDY OF ENERGY DEVELOPMENT ALTERNATIVE (1994).

However, structural changes are expected in the fuel consumption mix. As residual oil diminishes with expanded and improved oil conversion at refineries between 1996 and 2010, the figure for gas is likely to increase from 63% to 67% of overall thermal plant capacity. Coal is expected to rise from 24% to 26% and residual oil will possibly drop from 10% to 4% (Fig. O6). Substantial growth is expected for innovative gas turbines and steam/gas units employed by thermal plants.

The Unified Power Grid will continue to be the mainstream of Russia's power development. Power shortages are expected in the Urals and Northern Caucasus with a capacity generating "bubble" in Siberia, the Mid-Volga and northwestern regions. The situation demands construction of power transmission lines from the middle Volga to central regions and the Northern Caucasus as well as capacity expansions for. Siberian-Ural lines to match .inter-system cross-flows. The construction of high-capacity power links between the Unified Power Grid of Siberia and the Far East is unlikely in the foreseeable future.

Fig. O6: Thermal Plant Fuel Outlook to 2010

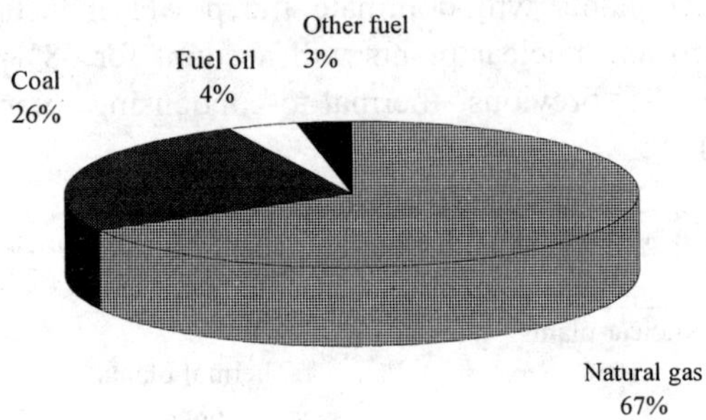

Source: JOINT RUSSIAN-US STUDY OF ENERGY DEVELOPMENT ALTERNATIVES (1994).

1.5 International Aspects

Power transmission systems are essential both domestically and internationally. The Unified Power Grid of the former Soviet Union could be a solid foundation for co-operation between the CIS, and Baltic states and a general European power system integration. However the breakdown of the USSR and a general national separation trend have resulted in the establishment of national, rather than unified, power systems. This has undermined the UPG of the FSU and has disintegrated its generally imbalanced plants. A number of regions such as Kaliningrad, Pskov, Omsk and Northern Caucasus, have found themselves dependent on transit supplies from within the CIS.

The power systems of Kazakhstan, Uzbekistan and Belarus are the most tightly linked with Russia. Power supplies to these countries in 1994 were some 27.6 billion kW including 15.6 billions for Kazakhstan. In turn, Russia received 14.5 billion kWh from these countries including 8.7 billion kWh from Kazakhstan , as can be seen from Tab. O7

Russia and Kazakhstan have the most common energy supply interests. Russian plants feed numerous neighbouring regions of Kazakhstan. Conversely, a number of Russian regions such as Kurgan, Tyumen, Kemerovo and Omsk have been traditional consumers of Kazakh power supplies.

Tab. O7: Power Flows within the CIS (Billion kWh) in 1994

	Russian exports	Russian imports
Ukraine	6.5	5.1
Belarus	5.5	0.7
Kazakhstan	15.6	8.7
Other	5.3	4.2
Total	**32.9**	**18.7**

Source: SHAFRANIK (1995).

The UPG of Russia is operating in connection with numerous power systems in the CIS such as Ukraine, Trans-Caucasian Republics, Kazakhstan, Belarus and Baltic States. Closer co-operation in this area is supposed to improve power availability in the CIS countries. It has been agreed in particular that RAO "UPG of Russia" has a controlling block of shares (5%) in AO Kirgizenergo. RAO "UPG of Russia" is planning ventures with companies that manage power systems in Georgia, Belarus and other CIS countries.

Fig. O7: Electricity Export from Russia

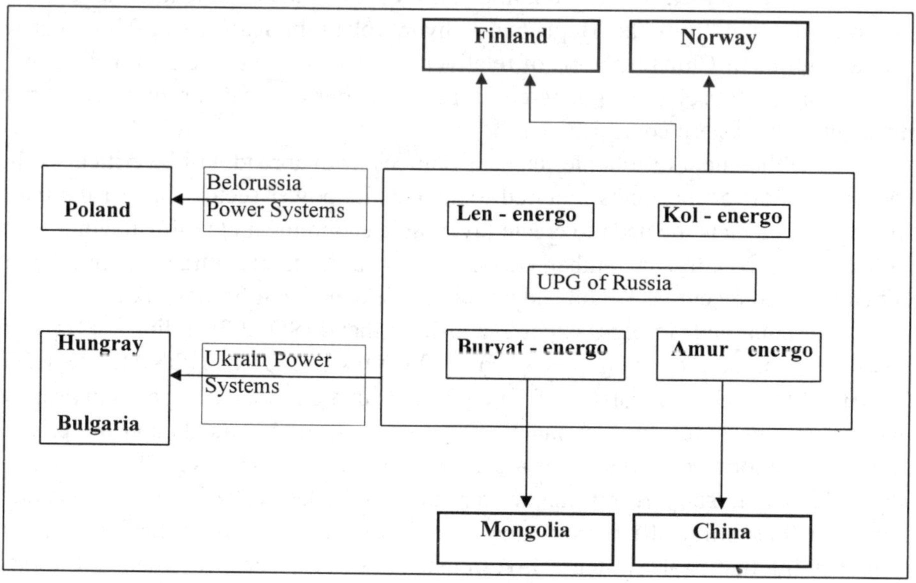

Source: MANAGEMENT OF THE POWER INDUSTRY OF RUSSIA (1995).

Power systems involved in the Central Supervisory Control Department headquartered in Prague (formerly the Mir Power System) are using power grids in Belarus and Ukraine in line with the UPG of Russia. Belarus is transmitting power to Poland, and Ukraine transfers power to Bulgaria and Hungary. Russia exports electricity to Finland, Norway, Mongolia and China (Fig. O7). Nearly 5 billion kWh of power was exported by Russia to remote countries in 1994.

Establishment of the European power energy market could be an important area of Russia's cooperation with other European countries since this would fall in line with the objectives of the European Energy Charter Treaty. This could be backed by the inter-state power transmission line grid that was built within the former Comecon system. An 1,800 km long and 4 million kW capacity international DC transmission East-West project is planned to meet this particular goal. The 1,800-km line will run from the Smolensk regional power plant to deliver 4 million kW power to Borken, Germany. The project has been spurred on by Preussen Electra (Germany), RAO "UPG of Russia", the Polish Electric Grid Company and the Belarus intopenergo (THE MOSCOW INTERNATIONAL ENERGY CLUB, 1995, p.87).

The Baltic and Black Sea regions could be promising regional power systems. Expanded links to northern Europe have also been assessed as viable. The St. Petersburg-Vyborg-Finland power transmission line has been in operation for around 15 years so far. Power supplies from Russia to the Far East are equally important both politically and economically. It could be also viable to build a power transmission line from the Boguchansk hydro plant in Russia via Mongolia to central regions of China. Exports of relatively inexpensive electric power generated by the Angara-Enisei river plants could be profitable and will promote economic links with Far Eastern countries.

Establishment of reliable financial sources from abroad will be critical as the country is short of the funds required to support its power sector. One of the main issues in this area is the need to create favourable economic and political conditions. Note that the country has embarked on creating a relatively attractive investment climate only in recent years and had no initial adequate legal framework .

Russian and foreign experts consider that USD 2-3 billion of foreign investment can be effectively used (THE MOSCOW INTERNATIONAL ENERGY CLUB, 1995, p.83). The raising of foreign funds in a non-loan manner is invisaged, mainly through direct investments coming from both governments and the private sector. These forms of investments are believed to be more beneficial than credits.

Financial support for major facilities could be realized via consortiums involving foreign and Russian strategic investors and using opportunities coming from the International Strategic Investment Association and International Credit Bank Alliance. This approach would cut all kinds of risks that are typically present in Russia. Dedicated investment studies are being carried out for the following facilities - Krasnodar and Urengoi thermal plants, Beloporozhskaya hydro plant and a 750 kV power line - following "The Investment Strategy for the Russian Energy" programme that is focused on building power plants and grids with foreign involvement.

Cooperation with foreign power companies and financial institutions involves the following mainstream areas:

- manufacture of high-performance power equipment and control systems in Russia;
- raising available foreign funds for the Russian power industry;
- investigation and employment of international experience in power privatization, and the transfer of government property rights;
- a multilateral approach to defining Russia's position and role in power development strategy for Europe and other regions neighbouring the Russian Federation.

In line with wide-scale foreign involvement, Russia has established a number of joint ventures including SP Inturbo, a deal with Siemens involving the Leningrad Mechanical Plant, and focused on gas turbines rated to 150 MW; SP ABB, - Nevsky Zavod for the manufacture of gas turbines in the 100 MW capacity range and other projects. The Northwestern Thermal Plant project is underway in St. Petersburg as part of a German - Finnish consortium. A number of contracts involving new construction and facility upgrades have been signed with AO Nizhnovenergo, Kubanenergo and Lenenergo. Work is continuing with the International Bank for Reconstruction and Development (IBRD) and the EBRD on the upgrade of Lenenergo's TETS-2 plant and construction of the Krasnodar thermal plant by AO Kubanenergo . (THE MOSCOW INTERNATIONAL ENERGY CLUB,1995,p.86).

The Russian government signed an agreement with the EBRD in 1995 to finance safety improvements in the operation of nuclear plants. A non-return subsidy, detailing related grant conditions was fixed at around $100 million. The Russian government has assumed the obligations of co-ordinating with the EBRD over its power generation conditions at nuclear plants in need of more upgrades, negotiating a design concept for enhancement of the Russian nuclear power industry, and taking into account the bank's recommendations concerning an energy tariff policy.

We believe, however, that such arrangements should be treated conservatively since their future implementation may involve potential losses for the country. A sum of $100 million is far from being adequate for nuclear plant modernisation. This amount is assumed to be insufficient for even a single upgrade, while Russia is running a total of nine such plants. We also anticipate a potential danger of becoming dependent on western nuclear technologies if these funds are used to pay for the services of foreign firms . Finally, Russia could find herself too reliant on spare part supplies from other countries,becoming doomed to continuous in-situ revisions where western engineers gain access to Russian nuclear technologies to say nothing of being directly involved in the domestic nuclear strategy.

One option involving mainstream international co-operation could be the recovery of Russia's former position on energy construction markets in developing and former socialist countries. Russia has substantial experience in this area. As of 1 January 1990, Russia had a list of some 400 power facilities under commission. Numerous new energy projects had been discussed and/or planned. However, after the breakup of the USSR and due to other reasons, Russia failed to retain its world energy construction markets, although favourable development trends could be observed there. According to current estimates, the developing countries are expected to invest around $1 trillion in developing their power sectors by the turn of the century.(THE MOSCOW INTERNATIONAL ENERGY CLUB, 1995, p.148).

2. Towards Competition, Privatisation and Direct Foreign Investment

2.1 Natural Monopolies and Competition

The electric power industry features a high degree of natural monopolism due to the involvement of specific technical and economic reasons. Competition in this industry is not economically viable for all power flow segments where the so-called natural monopolism would be more typical for power transmission services. Were a competitive environment in this area achieved, capital expenses for electricity transmission would be far greater than at present. The monopolistic option offers a higher power supply performance than a plurality of competing companies. A natural monopoly is known to be sustainable when the nation-wide, cumulative economic benefits favour a single company rather than a number of competitors on the market.

On the one hand, technological aspects of the power industry suppose a high degree of natural monopolism and thus require introduction of centralized control. Many experts agree that substantial performance gains could be reached if the sector were decentralised where possible, i.e. where market-driven competition and pricing are present (JASINSKY, P, 1994, p.2; PFAFFENBERGER, W. and WELFENS, P. and OTHERS,1996, p.28). Historically, different approaches have been used for removing contradictions between technological and management performance requirements.

The power sector has passed through a number of development stages, from small stand-alone power plants to large integrated systems (called complexes). Technological, economic and regulatory operating conditions vary from sector to sector.. Accordingly, concepts for monopolists application areas have changed over time. During the early stages of industry development both power plants and transmission lines were built with the aim of entering new power markets and squeezing existing competitors, although the situation changed dramatically later. Due to high capital-intensiveness, high power generation and transmission costs, construction of new generating facilities - to compete with existing plants - was not conceivable, with some minor exceptions.

To avoid unjustified capital expenses, special regulations have been introduced worldwide to ban competition in natural monopoly areas, where a nation would not benefit from competition. "The Natural Monopoly" law entered 19 August 1995 was essential in terms of shaping a legislative framework for the federal policy with regard to natural monopolies. The law identifies the following inherently monopolistic areas: pipeline transmission of liquid fuel and natural gas, railway shipments, and some others.

Similarly to any other monopolistic entity, a natural monopoly would be unable to eliminate a number of known operating dangers such as:

- supplier domination which helps energy companies resolve their problems at the expense of consumers;
- imposing on consumers the economic consequences resultant from an energy company's inadequate actions;
- price and other kinds of discrimination against some consumer groups;
- attempts to "save" on quality and reliability of power supplies;
- a danger of a gradual monopolist's degradation due to lack of competition and poorer incentives for efficiency improvements;
- economic power of a monopolist supported by legislative opportunities can open the way to corruption, "shadow" economy and criminal business.

These dangers necessitate establishment of a third-party supervision body that would replace the competition mechanism in all natural monopoly-related economic areas. International experience reveals that governmental regulatory control could be a viable monitoring method. Alternatively, it is necessary to expand market-driven operating elements where appropriate.

Over the last decade, dominating economic doctrines have been changed in many countries. Neo-liberal economic concepts were found most viable - they emphasise market operating principles as most appropriate for all economic sectors. These efforts foster competition and minimise governmental role in management of the economy.

The liberalisation trend has also impacted on the power sector which has progressed a from a competitive free market in the late 19th - early 20th century to tight control in mid-20th century followed by a slow backward move to competition. The power sectors of industrially developed countries are expanding their market operations. A number of factors apply here. They are as follows.

1. Mainstream trends in power sector technology tended to damage the competitive environment in power markets over past decades. Growth of the installed capacity of individual plants was accompanied by better performance and smaller funds requirements for power generation in relative terms. However, this was accompanied by higher plant costs and longer construction periods and thus hampered introduction of market mechanisms. The case is similar regarding power transmission area. Higher transmission line voltages reduce power losses but lead to higher grid construction costs and longer schedules. The latest technical innovations have resulted in breaking up the tight relationship that existed between power plant installed capacity and facility performance. This could be exemplified by integration gasification combined cycle (IGCC) and gas-turbine units that combine high efficiency at relatively small capacity with low capital requirements and short construction periods. This is essential for designing new generating units, power plant construction and thus shaping a competitive environment.
2. Electricity consumption growth rates were notably lower during the 1980s as a result of the total electrification of industrial plants, households and public services in industrially developed countries. This imposes heavy limitations on new large-scale generating units and power plant construction and thus undermines the potential savings involved in larger facilities. Moreover, the previous investment policy generally assumed an accelerated power demand, resulting in overcapacity and inadequate utilisation of existing power generating potential. In the 1990s, power consumption also dropped in Russia, followed by build-up of a plant capacity "bubble". However, this recession was caused by country-specific reasons. In Russia, it was primarily the deep economic recession .
3. Competition benefits from a wider scope of power conservation. These measures could be assessed as an additional power supply opportunity which would undermine the monopolistic positions of large energy companies. Energy savings are critical in an environment of high fuel prices, added investment risks and lower revenues from new facility construction. Remarkably high potential benefits are known to be linked to power conservation in Russia.
4. An information gap is typical for power markets. Price information reaches power buyers with substantial delays and faintly reflects actual power supplier costs, although strong daily variations exist in electricity generation costs. As a result, consumers would normally pay power prices that have an insignificant relation to suppliers' expenses, and this hampers an overall market performance.

Information management improvements could relieve this information gap problem and thus enhance market opportunities for the sector.

The factors mentioned above are believed to facilitate the market-driven approach to handling power management problems. Contradictions between technological and management performance requirements and, hence, centralised and decentralised management schemes, could be resolved by wider use of market mechanisms.

2.2 International Experience with Building Electric Power and Capacity Wholesale Markets

One of the principal areas of enhancement of market-driven management is the establishment of power and capacity wholesale markets. A number of basic models exist in this area (EDELMAN,V. (1992), p.18; SOROKIN.I. (1992) p.12; SOBOLEVSKY,Y. (1995) p.15)

A Co-Operative Intersystem Swapping Model (Fig. O8) is the most widely used in numerous countries (USA, Canada, Japan, Germany and other). Large, vertically-integrated energy companies appear to be virtually exclusive market players following this model. They comprise "natural monopolies" within the specified service area (region, state or province). Inter-system power swapping (or trade) between such energy companies does not suppose direct consumer involvement. The process centres on co-operation and is focused on cutting overall company costs involved in power supply to consumers. Benefits are reaped in the form of savings from bilaterally reserved power and other system-related effects, development plan co-ordination etc.

Unlike traditional commodity markets, the wholesale market built around the "co-operative inter-system swapping" principle creates competition, rather than a typical fight for consumers, in an indirect manner - sale agreements between power companies avoid consumers' preferences impacting directly. A power company with a monopolistic position in a particular region will directly sell electricity to consumers or distributors. In terms of routine operations, power trade is in the form of joint supervisory control over energy cross-flows. This control is essentially built around some sort of competitive rule simulation. The mechanism involves on-line identification of opportunities for buying cheaperal electric power from neighbouring power systems or preferences in selling own power.

The baseline idea for alternative wholesale power and capacity market-building models is promotion of competition mechanisms through breaking up the monopolism of large vertically-integrated companies. Each concept differs in the extent of competitive involvement. Authors of these models believe that greater competition would improve an overall power sector performance, cut electricity tariffs and enhance service quality.

Fig. O8: Model of Organization of Market Based on Principles of "Intersystem Exchanges on Basis of Cooperation"

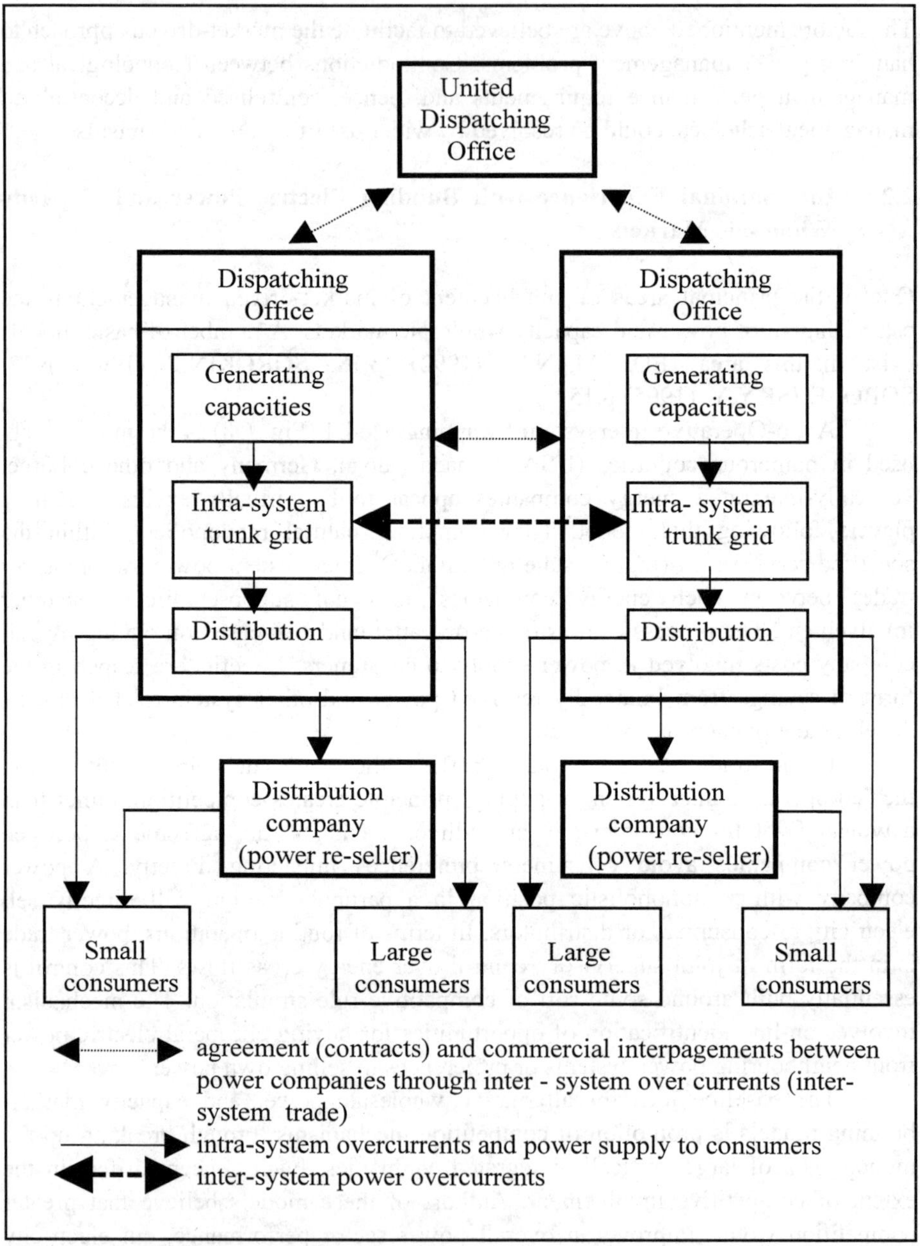

Source: SOBOLEVSKY (1995).

Opposed to competitive market models, the wholesale power market based on "co-operative inter-system swapping" would not require sophisticated economic behaviour rules for the electrical companies in question. However, the implementation of a competitive wholesale market model would require a complex economic calculation system for market players to be initially developed and mutually agreed.

A network company (NC) should be created concurrently, to serve a regional or country-wide trunk grid. NCs are supposed to enhance horizontal links within the system.

This network company will be a reseller, i.e. aquiring power from generators and forwarding it to suppliers and distributors. NC would be sole buyers of a generator and a single seller to suppliers and distributors. This predefines the monopolistic position of NCs on the wholesale power market and thus limits competitive factors.

Applied to Russia, the monopolistic elements inherent in the "networked reseller" principle have been greatly exacerbated by establishment of RAO “UPG of Russia”, a power industry holding company. Apart from an overall networked United Power Grid (or “UPG in Russia”), the company incorporates all the major, and the most efficient, power plants. As a result, RAO “UPG of Russia” rather than being a net "reseller" on the wholesale market, plays the role of a company interested in selling its own products (electric power). This imbalanced accumulation of monopolistic functions within a single company could cause serious conflicts on the maturing wholesale power market. Substantial problems also emerge in the sphere of anti-monopoly regulation.

There has been no wide acceptance of the "networked reseller company" model abroad. Some positive actions in this area have been undertaken in Spain and the Netherlands. However, this model is frequently assessed as a transition to a more radical concept of competition on the wholesale power market. This new model centres on a networked company - a transmission company - rather than a monopolist that accumulates all the processes involved in wholesale acquisition and resale of electrical power. This gives another name to the model: "a networked transmission company model". It was employed during privatization of the British national power industry.

Fig. O9: Model of Organization of Market Based on Principles of "Grid Reseller Company"

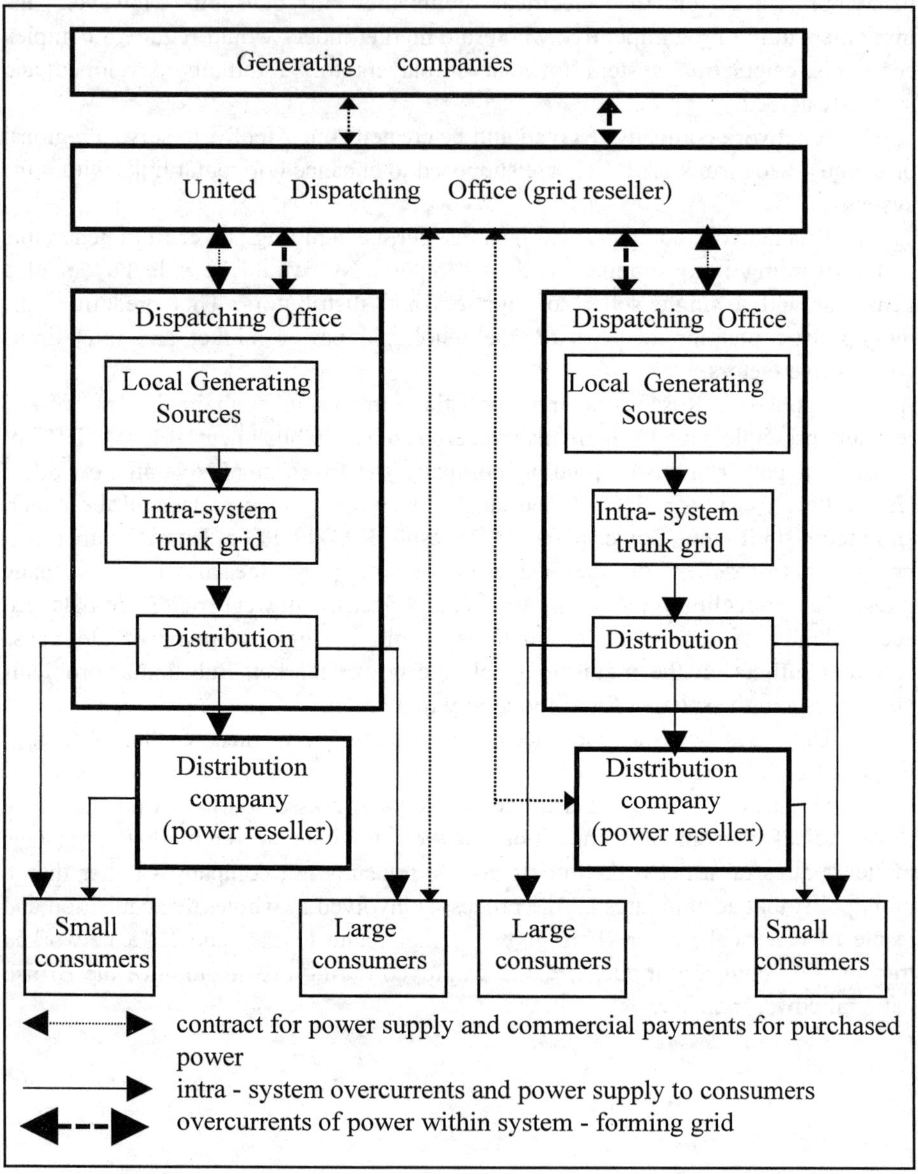

Source: SOBOLEVSKY (1995).

A Networked Reseller Company Model (Fig. O9) has been chosen as a foundation for development of a restructuring and shareholdings programme for the power sector of Russia. The model envisages vertical disintegration of regional energy companies along with formation of independent enterprises that would enter the wholesale power market. Such enterprises include power generators, suppliers and distributors.
A networked transmission company assumes direct power delivery agreements between generators and wholesale buyers. Other principal functions of such a company involve:

- maintaining a supply-demand balance on the wholesale power market and supervisory control functions;
- creating conditions that promote high specs of generated power;
- routine maintenance and development of a trunk power grid.

At present, no unambiguous conclusions could be drawn with regard to the economic performance of "alternative" wholesale power market concepts. Experience with implementation of these concepts is greatly limited so far, both abroad and in Russia, and thus the issue requires additional study. The ambiguous status of this issue could be exemplified by a continued discussion, in Russia and other countries, on the most preferable power reform options. Numerous analysts have noted that the background idea - power generation improvements through implementation of some sort of "alternative" model - would inevitably affect other performance components of overall power generation, transmission and distribution framework. Performance loss risks, a far greater complexity of power regulatory control schemes and erosion of "co-operative" principles in power industry interrelations - all these factors combine to contradict with optimistic assessments made by supporters of "alternative" wholesale power market models.

2.3 Key Problems in Reforming the Russian Power Industry

Before the beginning of market reforms the power sector was property of the State. There was a rigid system of State control. The main means of control were 72 regional industrial associations with juridical status. All the power stations of UPG of Russia, energy construction and equipment repairing enterprises and some other organizations worked within the frame of these associations which produced, transmitted and distributed electricity. Later on the basis of these industrial energy associations - the AO "Energo" was established.

Control of the power sector before the commencement of market reforms had a number of important peculiarities. Among them:

- centralized planning of electricity production and distribution to the consumers according to the quota system;
- State regulation of tariffs which were stabilized for a long period;
- guaranteed minimum profits for enterprises and confiscation by the State of the remainder of the profits;
- budget financing of power sector.

The system of control in the power sector based on State property and rigid control was to a high extent a response to the technological organization of this sector. This provided the reliable qualitative (requiring parameters on frequency, voltage and so on) energy supply for the consumers. However, because of the lack of market incentives, according to the opinion of many specialists, the efficiency of the work of this branch was not high enough. This was due to a number of essential shortcomings. Among them were the following:

- the lack of connection between the financing of enterprises and the results of their work;
- the guaranteed minimum of profits didn't provide the necessary incentives for their effective operation;
- the cost type method of forming tariffs;
- redistribution of revenues between effective and non-effective enterprises.

The market reforms in the Russian power sector have two main objectives:

- the provision of a high level of reliability and quality of energy supply;
- the increase of the operational efficiency of the power sector within the conditions of intensification of environmental activities in this branch.

In order to achieve them it is necessary to:

- reform the property relations and organizational structure of the sector;
- demonopolize and form the capacity and electricity market;
- establish an efficient system of market capacity and electricity regulation;
- change the pricing and financing mechanisms.

The reforms in property relations are closely connected with the changes in the organizational structure of the sector. During the transition towards the market principles of economic management it will be necessary to restrict vertical property relations and production, transmission and distribution control without breaking the functional integrity and unity of the power system. The redistribution of property rights should stimulate (through the competitive market of shares and bonds) the formation of attractive conditions for investments.

Demonopolization of the power sector is one of the central tasks of the power sector reformation. The decision to undertake this task is linked with the organization of competitive markets for the production and purchase-sale of electricity. At the same time it is necessary to highlight the natural monopolies in the power sector (federal and regional networks, dispatching)and to create conditions for their regulation.

The achievement of the main objectives of these market reforms cannot be undertaken without access to financial sources. Today the main financial source - the State budget - has been practically removed, and new financial sources are still being established. In order to expand financial sources and to increase the volume of the power sector's own sources, which should be used for capital construction purposes, it is necessary to solve one of the most important problems - that of non-payments. Access to financial sources will depend to a high extent on the capability of the power sector to meet the requirements of investors and on the general investment climate in Russia.

For the implementation of reforms in the Russian power sector a transition period is required. Numerous political, general economic and industrial factors will influence thelength and efficiency of the reforms. The dynamics of changes in the power sector should be acceptable from the social point of view and the economic-legislative environment should correspond to proposed transformations. The problem of reforms in the power sector could become a subject of sharp political discussions.

Reforms in the power sector would be limited by the following circumstances. The first of them:

- non-stability of the political and economic situation in Russia;
- imperfect actual legislation;
- the lack of a mature credit-banking system;
- non sufficient coordination of the activities of federal and regional authorities;
- inertia in the power sector (due to lengthy period, required to improve the structure);
- non-sufficient preparation of power sector personnel for the new conditions of power sector operation and development.

2.4 Privatization and Transfer of Government Rights for Property

After the introduction of market reforms, the power industry management and branch organizational structure began to change. Decrees NN 922, 923 and 1334 of the RF President dated 1992 initiated the beginning of the privatization and transfer of government rights over the property of the Russian power industry. Decree N 922 fixed a special order for the privatization of power enterprises, into joint stock companies with consideration for the special conditions for exploitation of the united power and gas systems in Russia and the exceptional importance of the fuel-energy complex for population activity in the country.This order was determined in accordance with special Decrees of the RF President. At the same time shareholding of the other branches was taking place in accordance with Decree N 721 of the RF President, published 1.07.1992. The Decrees NN 923 and 1334 determined the organization of the management of the Russian power industry in situations of government property privatization. In December 1992 the Russian joint company for power and electrification RAO "UPG of Russia" was established as a holding organization, controlling a series of power industry enterprises. At the same time the joint stock companies - AO "Energo" began formation based on 72 power industry regional production associations.

In accordance with Decrees NN 923 and 1334 the following authorized capital of the RAO "UPG of Russia" was transferred as a government contribution :

- the controlling block of shares all large thermal power stations (with capacity 1000 MW and more - 29 stations with total capacity 59,8 million kW);
- the controlling block of shares in all large hydraulic stations (with capacity 300 MW and more - 22 stations with total capacity 33,9 million kW);
- the main system-forming transmission lines, making up the United Power Grid of Russia;
- the dispatching system (Central Dispatching Offices - CDO, and United Dispatching Offices - UDO);
- scientific-research, design, construction and others branch organizations (about 400 enterprises);
- 49% of shares of AO "Energo" for a term of 3 years (afterwards the term was prolonged further by 3 years).

Fig. O10: Formation of Authorized Capital of RAO "UPG of Russia"

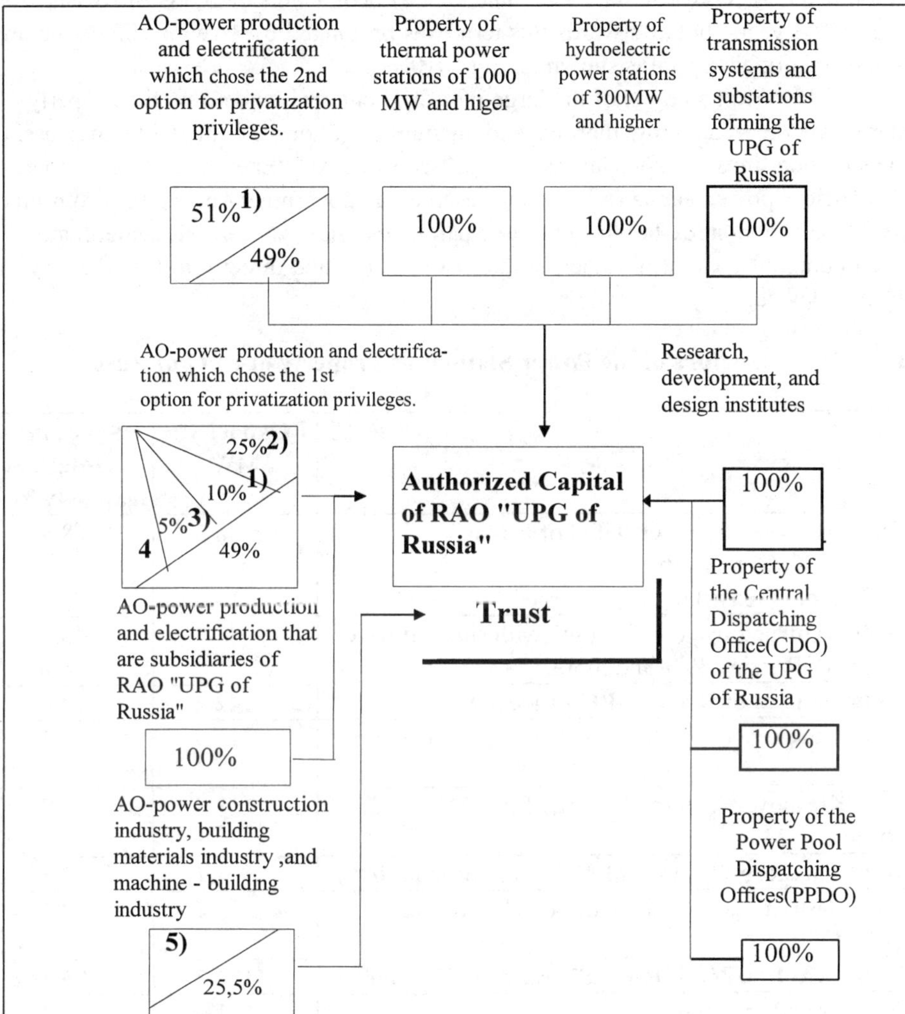

1 - Shares of the authorized caital of the AO sold to the members of the work collective at par value
2 - Shares of the authorized caital of the AO presented to members of the work collective free of cost
3 - Shares of the authorized caital of the AO, sold to the management of the AO at par value
4 - sale of shares to outside
5 - shares solid locally

Source: MANAGEMENT OF THE POWER INDUSTRY OF RUSSIA (1995).

CDO and UDO were being transferred to stock companies and became the property of the PAO "UPG of Russia". The State kept 51% of shares of "UPG of Russia" for a term of 3 years, but afterwards this term was prolonged by 3 years). The structure of the authorized capital is shown on Fig. O10.

The power stations of the large industrial enterprises became the property of these. All the remaining thermal and hydraulic stations of the UPG of Russia, transmission lines and substations were passed to 72 AO "Energo" as their property. The nuclear power plants (NPP) were reserved as government property. From nine NPP, eight (non-stock-holding) became part of the State concern "Rosenergoatom". The Leningradskaya NPP (stock-holding) was submitted directly to the Ministry of nuclear power.

Tab. O8: Structure of the Power Stations as Property of UPG of Russia

	Capacity, MW	**Share in total capacity,%**
Stations owned by PAO "UPG of Russia" • (51...100%) • including leased to AO "Energo"	58.9 15.8	28.8 7.7
Stations owned by AO "Energo" with share of RAO "UPG of Russia" 49% and more	83.3	40.8
Total control of RAO "UPG of Russia"	**142.2**	**69.6**
AO "Irkutskenergo", share of RAO "UPG of Russia" (0%)	12.9	6.3
AO "Krasnoyarskenergo", share of RAO "UPG of Russia" (- 33%)	8.0	3.9
AO "Tatenergo", share of "UPG of Russia" (0%)	**7.1**	**3.5**
AO "Bashkirenergo", share of "UPG of Russia" (- 15%)	5.1	2.5
Total RAO "UPG of Russia" and AO "Energo"	**175.3**	**85.8**
Nuclear power plants	21.3	10.4
Stations, owned by enterprises	7.8	3.8
Grand total	**204.4**	**100**

Source: THE RUSSIAN POWER INDUSTRY (1996).

Actually the property structure of the power industry differs from that, provided in the Decrees (Tab. O8). This is accounted for by the following reasons:

- AO "Tatenergo" and "Bashkirenergo" didn't transfer the corresponding stations and 49% of shares to RAO "UPG of Russia" out of considerations for State sovereignty;
- some AO "Energo" performed the shareholding and privatization before the Decrees came into force; resulting in the shares remaining the property of the local administration;
- the series of large stations, transferred to the PAO 'UPG of Russia", was subsequently leased to the corresponding AO "Energo".

Concurrently with the process of privatization and the redistribution of property rights a new power industry management structure has been forming (Fig. O11).

The State released itself from the functions of direct economy management and transferred them to enterprise level. The significance of the vertical connections was limited, but the role of the horizontal ones increased. The central position in the system of power industry management was taken up by the PAO "UPG of Russia". Fig 12. Important functions were placed on this organization, including:

- Ensuring reliable functioning and development of the United Power Grid of Russia (UPG of Russia);
- boosting the efficiency of UPG operation;
- performing the centralized operational-technological management.
- organization and development of the competitive wholesale market for electricity and capacity;
- carrying out the unified scientific-technical policy and boosting the attracted capital, including the foreign investment.

The existing structure of the Russian power industry must be considered transferred from planned to market economy. This structure provides the maintenance of the United Power Grid of Russia in conditions for the development of market principles in the economy, formation of the wholesale and retail market for electricity and capacity. The prospects of changing the power industry structure are connected with boosting branch competition, whilst the high degree of functional integration in the United Power Grid of Russia is maintained.

Fig. O11: Management of the Power Industry of Russia

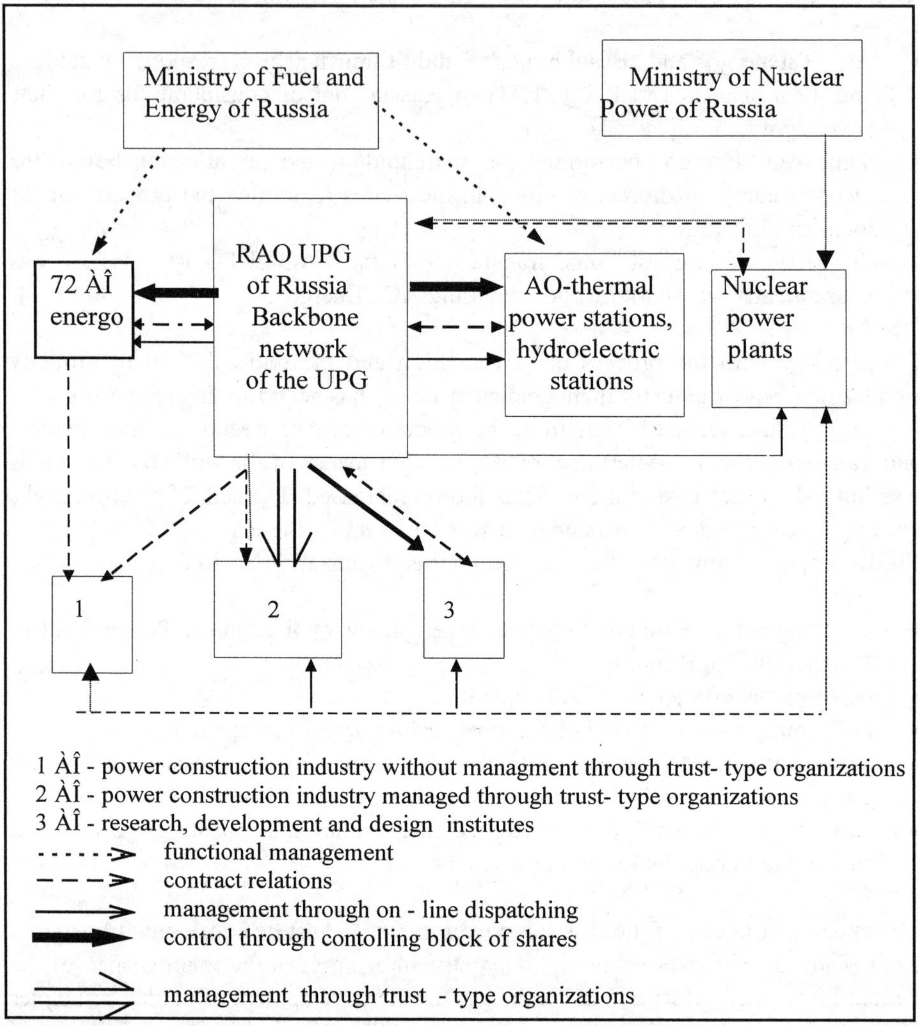

Source: MANAGEMENT OF THE POWER INDUSTRY OF RUSSIA (1995).

2.5 Building Competitive Power Markets

Change of forms of ownership became an important stage in the formation of the electricity and power market, making it possible at the same time to retain control of the national power production system. The main principles of the development of the federal wholesale market of electricial energy and power were confirmed by the Government Act N 793 from 12.07.1996 "With reference to the federal (All - Russian) wholesale electrical energy (power) market ".

Power is being delivered to the wholesale electricity and power market by 25 major power stations using traditional technologies (TPS and HPS), which were transferred to RAO "UPG of Russia", 9 NPS (with the exception of Bilibinskaja NPS, which is not connected with "UPG"), as well as power-abundant AO "Energo".(MANAGEMENT of the POWER INDUSTRY of RUSSIA, 1995,p.16). Participants in the wholesale market are major power plants producing relatively cheap energy. About 30% of all the electrical power produced in Russia is delivered to this market. The buyers of electrical power in the wholesale market are major industrial users and are energy-deficient AO "Energo".

"UPG of Russia" acts as the wholesale market operator. The participants in the wholesale market are linked with high-voltage interconnection networks. These are incorporated into RAO "UPG of Russia" and are assigned to federal networks. The network voltage is, as a rule, 330 kW and higher. Direct and operating control over federal networks is implemented by RAO "UPG of Russia". Interconnection networks are incorporated in RAO "UPG of Russia", they connect participants in the retail power market. Those are assigned to regional networks. Technically, federal and regional networks perform the same function - the transmission of power. However, they are considered separately as they belong to different structures: RAO "UPG of Russia" and AO "Energo".

Nowadays RAO acts as both the owner of a number of power stations, transferred to RAO temporarily, and the wholesale market operator. This retards the development of the competitive environment. The increase of competition will be possible in the case where independent producers are created based on the stations which are now incorporated in RAO "UPG of Russia". It should be mentioned that RAO "UPG of Russia", as a holding company, controls the activity of AO "Energo", which contradicts their economic independence. However, this makes it possible for the State to control the power generation industry. The State is known to possess the controlling block of shares of RAO "UPG of Russia".

The restriction of the independence of subjects of economic activity in the first stages of market transformations is in our opinion justified. Transition to market relations in the power generation industry is a complex and lasting process requiring State regulation. The established structure of ownership makes it possible for the State to control the situation in the industry effectively enough. In the future, minimizing the role of the State as the main owner in the power industry is being contemplated to encourage competition. The State's block of shares in the capital of RAO "UPG of Russia" is due to be sold off. The State is going to perform the basic regulatory functions not through RAO "UPG of Russia" but through the federal and regional power commissions which are in the development stage now and cannot yet provide for an effective control over the industry.

There are a number of projects for the reformation of the power generation industry. Most of them suggest the following:

- organizing the State licensing of various kinds of activity in the power generation field, including the interconnecting transmission of power, the performance of central control functions, the production of power to be sold in the market, etc.;
- implementation of the transition to contractual relations by the subjects of wholesale markets. To encourage some other competitive generation sources AO "Energo" to enter the market, to stimulate the emergence of new independent power producers;
- shifting from wholesale market price control based on average costs to competitive pricing based on marginal prices;
- transforming the structure of ownership in the electrical power generation industry. Eliminating the sectorial holding structure and minimizing the role of the State as the main owner in the industry;
- implementing State control over the power generation industry only through the State regulatory system.

In the course of strengthening and developing the wholesale market the functions of RAO "UPG of Russia" and the structure of RAO's property will change. It is envisaged that RAO "UPG of Russia" will sell its shares in the capital of all the generating subsidiaries (AO "Energo", AO-stations) to encourage competition in the power generation industry, while retaining the functions of an all-Russian network company and the function of direct process control.

The two most thoroughly developed projects for the reformation of the Russian power generation industry were prepared by foreign consulting companies with the participation of Russian specialists. One of the projects was developed by KMPG and PHB with the assistance of "London Economics Ltd.", the other was developed by Hagler Bailly Consulting, Inc. (KPMG 1994; HAGLER BAILLY CONSULTING, 1995.)

The Hagler Bailly project suggests formation of a wholesale market for producers and users of electrical power. According to the project, utilization of the power stations can not be optimal unless power producers and users have free access to the wholesale market. The more effective power stations (e.g. those belonging to AO "Energo") are often underloaded whereas the less effective ones operate at full capacity.

The scheme envisages daily submission of applications by both producers and users to RAO "UPG of Russia". The applications contain information on the likely amount of power offered, on demand and price. The market operator arranges the applications in accordance with the increase of prices till demand and supply are in balance. In this way, the users are served primarily by the most effective power stations, i.e. those stations who produce the cheapest power. Then comes the turn of the less effective ones. In the market prices are forming which reflect marginal costs, and the competition of power producers stimulates the decrease in production costs. The aim is to balance demand and supply for the time of day and for regions. Use of such a pricing mechanism is expected to lead to the most effective resources allocation in the power production industry, when the most effective stations are utilized first.

Apart from implementing the direct control function, the wholesale market operator - RAO "UPG of Russia" will grant licenses to participants in the market and control their activities, elaborate a strategy of development for the industry, and render analytical and informational services (e.g. information on regional prices on an hourly basis, long-range forecasts). According to the plan, RAO "UPG of Russia" will be responsible for the safety and stability of the functioning of the market. Therefore, it is intended to for RAO "UPG of Russia" to maintain ownership of not only the direct control system and federal networks, but also, a number of HPS as a reserve to cover peak demand.

As the wholesale market operator, RAO "UPG of Russia" will charge the participants in the market rent. The intention is to form several competitive companies on the basis of RAO "UPG of Russia"-owned power stations. RAO "UPG of Russia" will operate the federal network and implement direct control and service.

The project for the reformation of the Russian power production industry, developed by Haggler Baily, reflects the interests of RAO "UPG of Russia", which is expressed in overly favorative rights granted to this company. In turn, the KMPG and PHB project protects the interests of AO "Energo" and FEC. This project provides for the transfer of the authority of RAO "UPG of Russia" to grant licenses and control participant activities in the wholesale market to FEC. The elaboration of the strategy of development of the industry should be assigned to FEC, as well. The project suggests making the wholesale market more effective as the first step, concentrating only afterwards on the compulsory movement of the power stations to the market. As for the subjects of wholesale markets, those could be integrated with AO "Energo", incorporating all the generation stations in the region in question. Acting as a whole, the region will sell abundant power or buy deficient power. Such a decentralized system will lead to relatively high prices in the wholesale market, as the abundant regions will consume all cheap power domestically. However, it will stimulate the saving of power and the construction of new power stations in power-deficient regions.

Despite a few differences, the projects have much in common in essence. Besides, both projects have potentiality for compromises. The allocation of property and functions amongst RAO "UPG of Russia", AO "Energo" and regulatory bodies will be determined largely by the balance of authorities between the bodies and subjects of the federation.

A number of important changes could take place in the retail market too. The retail market includes the power stations incorporated into AO "Energo" and the users of their power, particularly major end users who can sign direct contracts in the wholesale market. In the role of the retail market, operators act corresponding AO "Energo". To encourage competition, it is contemplated that AO "Energo" will cease to own their power stations in the future. The basic functions of AO "Energo" will be the following: direct control, management and allocation within regional power systems.

It is likely that a need will arise to develop and adopt AO "Energo" rules for major users to sign contracts for the purchase of power in the wholesale market directly and pay AO "Energo" for using their regional networks. It will be necessary to work out a tariff for the use of regional networks and to determine terms and procedure for the transmission service (permission to use local networks to transmit power) for major users.

As the development of informational technologies widens, AO "Energo" will receive more accurate information on wholesale market prices. Using more the accurate price indications of the wholesale market (value of electrical power as a function of the time of day, demand for electrical power), AO "Energo" will be able to develop and apply a more precise tariff system for their customers aiming at a more effective use of power.

2.6 Wholesale and Retail Markets Regulation

To regulate the Russian electrical power market federal and regional economic commissions have been set up (FEC and REC). [13,14] They implement their functions on two levels: federal and regional. One level is associated with the wholesale power market and the other is associated with the retail power market.

The FEC was set up in 1972 in accordance with Decision No 483 of the Council of Ministers. The staff of the commission included representatives of State bodies and private business. The president of RAO "UPG of Russia" is a member of the commission.

Basic functions of the FEC are as follows:

- to regulate tariffs in wholesale electrical power markets;
- to set payment for electrical power transmission services;

- to develop a method for the calculation of retail tariffs used by regional companies;
- to act as the supreme arbitrator while settling disputes on the regional level.

The REC were set up in 1993, the total number being 74. They are located in each of the 72 areas served by AO "Energo", as well as in Moscow and St. Petersburg. The staff of the commissions includ representatives of local authorities, power distribution companies and retail users. The basic function of these commissions is to control the retail power market in the subject area and to protect the users' interests from the monopoly of power generation companies. (SUMMARY of the REGULATION on the ELECTRIC and THERMAL ENERGY in1995,1996, p.23).

The establishment of the energy commissions was aimed at exercising an effective state control in the fields of activity which show signs of a natural monopoly. However, in reality the aims have not been achieved yet for a number of reasons. One of the basic reasons is that the appropriate institutional environment has not been formed. In the absence of this environment the activity of the natural monopolies does not fall under effective State control.

Another reason is that federal and regional electrical power commissions are not independent from the natural monopolies. Representatives of the natural monopolies are members of the electrical power commissions. This makes it possible for power monopolies to impose their own "rules of the game", to tariff all justified and unjustified expenses. In the end, it is the customer who has to cover the expenses associated with "problems" and faults of the natural monopolies.

One more reason is that there exists no mechanism for the realization of FEC and REC decisions. The electricity commissions have none of the required authority to assure the execution of their decisions.

To assure an effective State regulation of the activities of the natural monopolies, it is necessary to form the appropriate institutional environment, which is lacking now. This applies primarily to the formation of legislation to specify the functioning of the regulatory bodies. The regulatory bodies should be made independent from the natural monopolies. It is necessary to clearly specify and allocate functions among the FEC and REC on the one hand, and federal and local authorities and the subjects of the federation on the other hand. It is necessary to legalize the principles used as the basis for the functioning of the electrical power commissions. The work of the commissions should be opened to the social organizations and to the public. It would be expedient to vest electrical power commissions with authority to fix by law the procedures for the settling of disputes on both regional and federal levels.

To eliminate the dictate of the natural monopolies, it is necessary to legally fix the principles for the functioning of the wholesale and the retail markets, the structure of the markets, the rules for forming tariffs. It would be expedient to extend the principles of the functioning and pricing in the wholesale electrical power market throughout the country and to substitute them for the regional laws. This would authorize FEC to solve a great number of problems concerning the development of the wholesale market.

One of the main goals of forming the institutional environment is to create conditions for the financial and investment activities of the natural monopolies to become "transparent", i.e. opened to the regulatory bodies and to public inspections. To accomplish this, it is necessary to differentiate distinctly between the monopolistic and the competitive activities, to change the accounting system of the power generation companies, and to correct the structure of the information coming to the regulative bodies.

The latter is important, as the effective functioning of the electric power commissions is impossible without a developed information bank. It should contain:

- information on prices, finance, technology, concerning the work of the power company to be regulated;
- data reflecting all the important aspects of the supply of electrical power to various groups of users in the region;
- information on the socio-economic status of the region, including problems concerning industrial and budgetary policy.

The accounting system should be organized in such a way that separate accounts will be kept of each type of activity. Such a differentiation in the accounting system will help the regulatory bodies to watch expenditure in all the stages of the process flow, to create "transparent" relations between the subjects of the market, control bodies and the State.

As the basic regulation means a license system can be used which will authorize the licensees to act in the appropriate fields,the licenses will specify conditions to be met by those who wish to obtain permission for the continuation of activity. In cases where the conditions are not met, the power enterprise will lose the right to be rendered the licensed service in the future. There will be a special regulative body to make sure that the license conditions are met. It is necessary to legally establish the rules and procedures of licensing to specify legal conceptions concerning the order of access of power enterprises and legal personnel to the electrical power market.

It is expedient to concentrate the regulating activity primarily on problems concerning pricing, quality, and the increase of competition in the industry. To do this the following is required:

- control of profits derived by monopolies from the rendering of products and services;

- control of special prices of monopolistic products or services established for certain groups of citizens. The prices should be set based on costs and should not be of discriminatory type;
- regulation of the quality of monopolistic services, which must be as high as in a competitive market;
- encouragement, where possible, for the creation of a competitive environment.

The more competitive the market is, the less regulation will be needed. Such fields of activity as the transmission of electrical power over federal and regional networks, and direct control, will function under strong regulation as they fall into the category of natural monopolies. Electrical power producers will work under more competitive market conditions. Therefore they will not be subjected to strong regulation though they will have to meet license conditions.

2.7 Financing

The sources of Russian power industry financing include:

- internal funds of enterprises;
- branch investment funds;
- budgetary funds;
- other sources (commercial banks and large national companies, internal capital markets).

The budgetary financing of the power industry sharply decreased in the '90s. If at the end of the '80s the share of State centralized investments was over 75%, then in 1995 the share of federal budget in the total power industry capital investments constituted 2.2% in the electric power industry and 13.5% in the nuclear power industry (Tab. O9).

Under the conditions of transfer to the market economy decentralization of the investment process began. The role of the internal funds of enterprises in financing of investment projects began to increase. In 1995 the percentage of internal funds in the structure of capital investments of the electric power industry was 42.5%, and in the nuclear power industry - 86.5%.

Tab. O9: Structure of Power Industry Financing by Types of Sources in 1995 (%)

	Internal funds of enterprises	Branch investment funds	Federal budget	Other sources	Total
Electric power industry (total), including:	42.5	54.2	2.2	1.1	100
• hydro-and thermal power industries	40.2	57.0	1.7	1.1	100
• nuclear power industry	86.5	-	13.5	-	100

Source: MINISTRY OF ECONOMICS (1996).

Financing using the internal funds of enterprises is attributed to profit and amortization. The hard taxation policy reduces the share of profit, which is directed for investments. The possibilities for investment are limited because of the delay in revaluation of the cost of capital assets and the sum of their depreciation charges. The situation has become aggravated because of non-payments for delivered electrical energy.

The main source of financing in the hydro- and thermal power industries is branch investment funds. At the same time the nuclear power industry, which is State-owned, is lacking in this source of financing. Compared with other branches of the power industry, the nuclear power industry has more State budgetary support.

In the 1990s there has been a sharp drop in capital investments in the Russian electrical power industry. The 1994 level of capital investments dropped to 40.6% compared with 1990 (in comparable prices). This resulted in drastically reducing the on stream position of energy capacities in Russia.

The main reasons for the investment crises include:

- non-payment ;
- enormous tax burdens;
- high inflation, rates that hamper long-term production cost predictions;
- substantial creditors interests and their short-term preferences;
- no consistent econonomic climate;
- a hardly predictable economic and political situation

The overcoming of the investment crisis is connected with the creation of a favourable situation in the country. The elimination of non-payments,and reduction in inflation rates and rates of refunding by the Central Bank of Russia contribute to the reduction of credit resource prices and reorientation of these resources into the investment sphere. The annual revaluation of enterprises capital assets allows significant enlargement of the financial base of investment. The accelerated amortization contributes to attraction and fast turnover of the capital. The reform of the tax legislation will enable the reduction of the taxation load on enterprises and will allow the transfer of additional assets to investment.

The capital markets, which are still being formed at the present time, could prospectively be the significant source of electric power industry financing. Voucher privatization has been exchanged for sale for ready cash. The realization of electric power company shares will provide for financial resources by attracting assets of the population and of different organizations and banks. The government continues to hold the controlling block of shares in the Russian Joint Stock Company of the Power Industry and Electrification (UPG of Russia). In turn, the UPG of Russia has the controlling blocks of shares in the 72 regional joint stock companies "Energo" (JSC "Energo").

The shares of the UPG of Russia and large JSC "Energo", for example, JSC "Mosenergo" and JSC "Irkutskenergo", are quoted as the highest. The power company shares attract the attention of the investors, first of all, not by the possibility obtaining revenues, but by the possibility of acquisition of quite effective basic production assets on the basis of underestimated prices. The shares of all Russian electric power companies are considerably underestimated in comparison with shares of analogous companies in industrial and developing countries. This situation is due to various reasons. Among them: political and economic instability in the country, the absence of an appropriate legislative base, and the undeveloped state of the share market.

The expansion of financial possibilities for investment is connected with the establishment of the effective share market. The application of the procedure of evaluation of companies, adopted in international practice, and the bringing of Russian standards into conformity with those worldwide, promote the formation of such a market.

The commercial banks will prospectively become a major source of financing. There are about 2,000 licensed commercial banks in Russia. Among them more than 200 are characterized by their level of capitalization, which has grown nearer to world standards. Some banks have experience in short-term financing of the electrical power industry. The Electrobank was originally established for financing electricity industry investment. The JSC "Mosenergo" conducts banking transactions through the intermediary of the Moscow industrial bank, which granted credits for investment in the technical maintenance of electric power stations. After overcoming the non-payments crisis and with the beginning of the economic growth in the country, the commercial banks are showing interest in financing the electricity industry.

The large domestic companies, having strong connections with the electrical power industry, could be another significant source of financing. The formation of unions with other partners, such as RAO "Gasprom", which provides gas to the electric power stations and earns currency by the export of it, could be profitable for both parties. Similar unions are useful between electric power companies and large industrial electric power consumers, for example, producers of aluminium and steel. The principle of share partnership of government-commercial financing will be promotion of the attraction of non-state investors' capital. At the same time the State will take the part of garantor for project realization.

Additional financing of electricity could be realized through sale of government shares in the electric power companies, and transfer of recovered assets to UPG of Russia and JSC "Energo". Tax exemptions on investing assets could be another means of State support for electric power industry development.

The financing of the Russian electricity industry will prospectively be realized mainly from internal sources. The reason for this is that the industry is oriented mainly on internal market. However the role of foreign investors will be significant also, and it will be increased as the investment situation improves. A system of investment insurance must be created for protection of capital, using principles adopted in international practice. The improvement of the existing normative-legal base of investment is suggested respecting the insurance of private property rights, deposit right, leasing operations and development of a market for registered stocks.

2.8 Pricing

Between 1990 and 1995 prices of electricity industry products increased 6,4 thousand times. The growth of prices of electric power were less than the price growth of industrial products, which increased 8,4 thousand times in the same period (Tab. O10). Taking into account the fall of the rouble exchange rate, the average electricity tariff level in Russia was 0.04 \$/kWh. This level corresponded to the average level of tariffs in Canada and was 2.2 times less than in Germany and 1.5 times less than in France (Fig. O12).

Fig. O12: Level of Tariffs for Electricity in Russia and Several Developed Countries

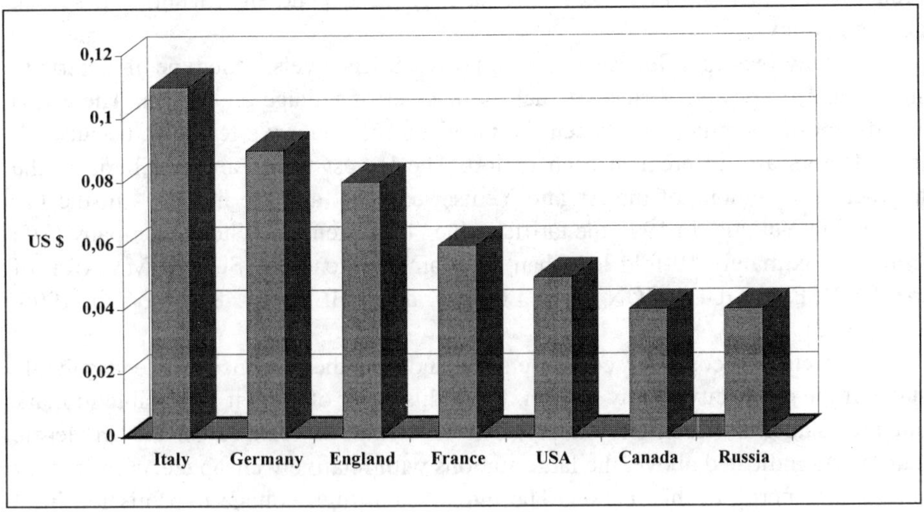

Source: THE STATE DUMA (1996b).

Tab. O10: Energy Pricing in Russia Relative to the 1990 Growth Rate Ratio

	1991/ 1990	1992/ 1990	1993/ 1990	1994/ 1990	1995/ 1990	March 1996/ 1990
Price index of industrial products	2.4	49.2	487.1	2484.1	8446.0	9206.1
Price index of fuel industry products	2.2	75.2	1181.3	5433.8	17931.6	19366.2
Price index of fuel for FEC	2.0	42.4	402.8	2054.3	7395.4	7913.1
Price index of electrical power industry products	1.8	48.2	492.0	2214.2	6421.2	6999.1

Source: THE STATE DUMA (1996).

The tariffs were based on the necessity for reimbursement of expenses for generation, transmission and distribution of electricity, and on providing the economically justified profit rate. The tariff levels depend significantly on special taxation policy.

Many factors influence electrical power tariffs levels, - the type of electricity station and its power, variety of fuel used, level of voltage and so on. There is a significant differentiation between the tariffs in the country's territory, because all these factors are different in each region. The lowest tariffs are in Siberia at the hydroelectric stations of the Angaro-Yenisei cascade, and the highest - in the Far East and in Yakutia. In 1995 the tariffs in the "Irkutskenergo" Stock Company (SC) were approximately 10-fold less than in "Kamchatskenergo" SC. (SUMMARY of the TARIFF REGULATION on ELECTRIC and THERMAL ENERGY in 1995, 1996, p.12).

Electricity costs for consumers depends on their connection to a suitable stage of the electricity supply system. From this point of view it is possible to mark out four stages of electricity supply. The first stage is realized on the wholesale market. As indicated above, the large stations with relatively cheap electrical energy supply the energy to this market. The inter-system high-voltage transmission lines with voltage, as a rule, of 330 kV and higher, connect participants in the wholesale market. The energy transmission costs of participants of this market are also relatively low. As a result, the energy cost of this market is not more than one third of the energy cost for household users. (KUSHNAREV,F and PLATONOV,V, 1996, p.4). However, only very large energy consumers can enter the wholesale market (steelworks with electrical melting processes, electrified rail roads and so on).

The second stage of electricity consumption is realized at the level of high-voltage inter-system power networks, to which the large industrial consumers of the region are connected. At this stage the electrical power is transmitted by transmission lines with a voltage of 110-220 kV. In this case the energy cost is one third greater than the cost on the wholesale market.

The third stage of electrical energy consumption is realized at the level of networks with an average voltage of 6-35 kV. A large number of industrial and non-industrial consumers, and wholesale electric power resellers are also connected up to these networks. The cost of energy at this level is almost twice as much the wholesale market cost.

The fourth stage of electrical energy consumption is realized at the low voltage level of distribution networks with a voltage of 0.4 kV. The low voltage networks are largely the property of wholesale speculative purchasers. The urban and rural electrical networks, and also low voltage networks of large enterprises are such speculative purchasers. The total length of low voltage distribution networks is tens times greater than the length of high voltage networks. The service of low voltage networks is the most expensive, and the cost of electrical energy for household consumers is approximately three times more than the cost of wholesale market energy.

In international practice the tariffs are established in such a way that they accelerate the process of transition from the first stage of energy consumption to the fourth one. Formation of tariffs according to cost allows consumers to obtain undistorted information about real expenditures in the energy system. This is reflected in the stimulation of the operational efficiency of the energy consuming enterprises. At the same time conditions are created for a reliable and undiscriminating energy supply for all consumers.

The market economy proposes that electrical power tariffs are formed according to the real cost of generation, transmission and distribution of electrical power. However, in Russia this condition of tariff formation isn't accomplished. The substantial disadvantage of the active system of tariff formation is the conservation of a preferential group of consumers. The population and agriculture are among these. They buy the electrical energy at a substantially lower price than the real unit cost. However according to the Federal Law "Regarding government regulation of tariffs on electrical and thermal energy" the electric power industry is permitted self-financing. This means that underpayment by the population and agriculture are transferred to tariffs for industry. As a result the "transferred" tariff system formed in Russia. With this system the industrial consumers pay the highest price for electrical energy, and the population and agriculture - the lowest. If in 1990 the average electrical power tariff for population was 1.9 times higher than the average tariff for industry, in September 1996 the former was 29% of the latter.

It should be mentioned that in the great majority of countries tariffs for the population, as a rule, are 1.5-3 times higher, than the tariffs for industry. (REGARDING CONCEPTION of the CREATION and PRINCIPLES of FUNCTIONING of the FEDERAL WHOLESALE MARKET of ELECTRICAL ENERGY , 1996, p.10).

The "transferred" tariff system negatively influences on the economic position of predominantly large enterprises with high power-intensity, having a high share of electric energy in total production costs. As a result the competitiveness of products from enterprises with high power-intensity decreases, and these enterprises work in conditions of equipment underutilization or interrupt their operation; thus crisis processes are developed.

The introduction of preferential tariffs for all population is based on the necessity of providing social protection for the public. However the final imeffectiveness of using of understated price for some goods as an instrument of social policy is widely known. Under these conditions it is necessary to provide address support to the poorer part of the population at the expense of the high-paid one.

Some actions were undertaken to eliminate the discrepancy between tariffs for population and industry. The Government Act N 1024 from 09.09.1994 stipulates payment by the population of all real charges for electrical energy. The Decree of the President of RF N1451 from 17.10.1996 recommends to the regional energy commissions to proceed from the real value of generation and transmission of electric energy in the process of tariff formation. However the regional energy commissions, actually subordinated to the governors, abstain from implementing this unpopular decision. They prefer to shift underpayments by the population onto tariffs for industry. The regional energy policy is farmed out to the local administrations, which interpret it taking into consideration their own political popularity or filling their budgets.

The first consideration is expressed in unwarrantedly underrated tariffs for population and agriculture, and second, in unwillingness to let local industrial consumers onto the cheaper wholesale market. For local administration this means not only loss of the budget receipts, but also the necessity to increase tariffs for remaining consumers.

The development of the electrical energy and power wholesale market promotes the reduction of electrical energy tariffs.For this purpose it is necessary to remove all electrical power stations from the wholesale market which are enumerated in the Decree N 923 from 15.08.1992 of the President of the RF. At the same time it is appropriate to create conditions for other electrical power stations and large energy-intensive consumers to enter this market. As a result, the consumers can avoid the energy resellers and pay directly to the electrical power stations. Otherwise the nuclear power plants, which do not belong to RAO "UPG of Russia" and which are paid according to remaining principle, find themselves in a worse situation. The Government Act published in November 1996 dealt with changing payment principles. According to this Act many industrial consumers of energy from nuclear power plants will pay directly to these stations. The development of the wholesale market for electrical energy and power will allow the decrease in number of energy resellers and limit the possibilities of tariffs "transferring".

In conclusion it should be mentioned that the elimination of dicrepancies in electricity pricing is the important condition for the effective functioning of the electrical power industry. It is necessary to bring the tariffs for different groups of consumers into correspondence with their real value and costs for generation, transmission and distribution of power. It is important to abolish the donations to the public and other groups of consumers on account of industrial enterprises and to define the mechanism of addressing support for poor people. Electrical power tariffs must provide self-financing for electrical power industry enterprises, reflect the real costs of fuel and growth of depreciation charges and taxes.

References

REGARDING CONCEPTION of the CREATION and PRINCIPLES of FUNCTIONS of the FEDERAL (ALL-RUSSIAN) WHOLESALE MARKET of the ELECTRICAL ENERGY (1996), Moscow, RAO "UPG of Russia".

ALL - RUSSIAN CONFERENCE of POWER ENGINEERING SPECIALISTS (1996), December 18, Moscow, RAO "UPG of Russia".

EDELMAN V.(1992), The development of the organizational conception of the electrical power wholesale market. Moscow.

ENERGOATOMIZDAT (1984),Current Energy Problems. Moscow.

ENERGY INSTITUITE (1994), Power and Electrification Development in Russia. Moscow.

FINANSOVYE IZVESTIYA, 22.03.1996, No. 21.

GOSKOMSTAT of RUSSIA (1996),Output of Major Power Industry Products in January - December 1995. Moscow.

GOSKOMSTAT of RUSSIA (1997), Output of Major Energy Products in January - December 1995. Moscow.

HAGLER BAILLY CONSULTING (1995), The Questions of Reforming of the Organizational Structure of the Electric Power Industry and Bodies of Regulation. Hagler Bailly Consulting, Inc. Arlington.

IMESS (1988), COMECON Countries:Cooperation Opportunies for Fuel and Energy Industries, Moscow, USSR Aced.Sc.

JASINSKI, P. (1994),Competition in the Electricity Supply Industry, Regulatory Policy Research Centre, Hertford Colledge and Campion Hall, Oxford University.

JOINT RUSSIAN - US STUDY of ENERGY DEVELOPMENT ALTERNATIVES (1994), Development and Investment Scenarios for the Power Industry of Russia, Moscow.

KAPITAL-STRATEGIYA (1996), The Russian Power Industry. Problems and Energy Equity Market Trends. Moscow.

KHRUSHEV, A. (1986), The USSR Industry Geography, Moscow.

KPMG MANAGEMENT CONSULTING (1994), The Russian Electric Power Industry: Change of Structure and Adaptation to the Market Economy, Hayes and Bartlett Ltd.

KUSHNAREV, F. and V. PLATONOV (1996), The Energy Crisis: Reasons and Ways of Elimination. Rostov-na-Donu.

MANAGEMENT of the POWER INDUSTRY of RUSSIA (1995), Moscow ,RAO "UPG of Russia".

MEZHGOSTATKOM CIS (1996), Community Independet States in 1995, Moscow.

MINISTRY OF ECONOMICS (1996), Problem of Development of Russian Electricity Industry, Moscow.

PFAFFENBERGER, W., P. J. J. WELFENS, P. OPITZ, Z. HRUBY and A. SINCLAIR (1996), The process of Economic Transformation in Eastern Europe: The Strategic Role of the Energy Sector, University of Potsdam.

SHAFRANIK, Yu. (1995), Ed., The New Energy Policy of Russia, Moscow, Energomashizdat.

SOBOLEVSKY, V. (1995), The Tariffs Policy in the Russian Electrical Power Industry, Moscow.

SOROKIN, I. (1992), The Development of Organizational Conception of the Electrical Power Wholesale Market.

SUMMARY of the TARIFFS REGULATION on ELECTRIC and THERMAL ENERGY in 1995 (1996), Moscow, RAO "UPG of Russia".

THE MOSCOW INTENATIONAL ENERGY CLUB (1995), Russia - Europe. The Energy Security Strategy, Moscow.

THE STATE DUMA (1996), The federal Meeting of RF., The Parliament Hearings. on Energy Supply to Enterprises and Population of Russian Federation and Preparation of the Energy Supply Enterprises to Winter Moscow, May 21.

THE STATE DUMA (1996b), The federal Meeting of RF: The Parliament Hearings. The Strategy of Development of the Electrical Power Industry in the Country in the Context of Average Term Program of the Social-economical Development of the Russian Federation in 1996-2000 and Sources of Financing of this Program. Moscow, December 3.

VNIIKTEP (1993), Recovery of Mineral Resources, Moscow.

VOLFBERG, D. (1989), CO_2 and Climate Changes. Impacts on the Energy Policy of the USSR and European COMECON Countries. Report for UNE EC.

VOLOSHIN, V. (1994), The Nuclear Industry in Russia and the CIS. Headlines of The Nuclear Industry - Into the 21st Century, The Financial Times Conference, London.

Comments on: Russian Electricity Industry: Towards Market Economics

Misha Belkindas

Dr. Voloshin presents an in depth analysis of Russian Electric industry. This is a well prepared and well written paper, which helped me learn a lot about Russian Electricity System.

This study deals with a very important and timely issue: Russian electric energy system, its problems and possible solutions. As very well known, energy is the blood veins of an economy and without it the economy of a country cannot function, and it can be obtained from two types of sources: renewable (water, wind, solar) and non-renewable (fossil based). Declining reserves of non-renewable energy sources forced countries to find better ways, and the share of electricity in the total energy consumption has drastically increased over the last century across the world. Further, with the growing environmental awareness not only in industrialized countries but also in developing and transition countries, it is expected that electricity will keep replacing fossil based energy resources wherever possible. It is also a major tool to improve the living standards of people by introducing more and more equipment in people's daily life. In that sense, generation, distribution and administration of electric energy occupies a special place in policy makers' as well as general public's agenda.

To some degree, industrialized western democracies have solved their electric energy and related problems such as production, distribution, management, and pricing by either privatizing or heavily regulating. However, many developing and most of the transition countries are far from solving this problem. Hence, this study may provide a valuable guidance for other transition countries with similar problems.

Reforming or restructuring such large scale, integrated and complex, in some cases monopolistic enterprises is very difficult in transition economies because of two distinct characteristics: during the planed economy period there was very tight control and strictly state ownership, during the transition period there is minimal control and very loose state ownership. This leaves such enterprises in a chaotic environment and force them to fight on two fronts. First, they need to fight against the problems originated within the enterprise such as old equipment and technology, financial troubles and old fashioned management methods. Second, perhaps more dangerous one, they need to deal with surrounding economic and social environment which is beyond their control or influence, which can be called demand side of the issue. In addition, the lack of required capital accumulation or the concentration of available capital in the hands of very few groups or individuals may make it difficult to properly privatize, to split up natural monopolies and later on, to reform and restructure them. These environmental or exogenous factors can worsen the internal problems of these enterprises.

Dr. Voloshin has provided valuable information about what happened in Russian electric industry in terms of above discussed issues. However, He has not given us a clear picture of alternative solutions to make system work better. A comparative study, even within Russia for different time periods, would be a good approach to understand problems of the industry and their solutions. Such a comparison within the transition countries with similar experiences, or outside the transition economies would make this study more robust.

It would also be very valuable to put the issues of the electricity sector in a macroeconomic prospective, i.e., contribution of the sector to growth of the economy and improvement in the living standards of the population.

P: Restructuring Infrastructure in Transition Economies[1]

José Carbajo and Steven Fries

1. Introduction

The provision of telecommunications, electricity and transport, in centrally planned economies, was distinguished from that in market economies in at least three ways. Firstly, some services, such as electric power and rail freight transport, were abundantly supplied to enterprises as part of a strategy of directed growth. With the focus on expanding material inputs, certain infrastructure services were supplied to industry with little regard for their production costs, including their environmental impact. Secondly, with an ideological bias in favour of material production and a neglect of services, there was relatively little investment in telecommunications, despite its potential for raising productivity and output. Thirdly, vital infrastructure services, such as electricity and urban transportation, were provided to households for free, or for a nominal charge, as part of an approach to income allocation in which basic consumer goods and services were supplied at prices well below cost.

The provision of telecommunications, electricity and transport services in the transition economies must now adapt to recognise costs, meet new market demands, and to address environmental concerns. Tariff levels and structures must adjust to reflect the costs of production and the fiscal constraints of governments and to guide new investment decisions throughout the economy. The levels of service provision must also adapt. In some infrastructure sectors, such as railways and electric power, market adjustment involves lower service levels, albeit of greater reliability and higher environmental standards. Other sectors, such as telecommunications and road transportation, must respond to expanding demands. Achieving higher environmental and safety standards is also an important part of restructuring infrastructure. Under central planning, some infrastructure sectors played a central role in the process of environmental degradation, both through their own production and in their encouragement of wasteful use of resources, particularly electricity.

The restructuring of infrastructure is thus a major challenge in the transition to a market economy. Meeting this challenge is particularly difficult, however, because the policies on which governments typically rely to induce enterprise restructuring - hard budget constraints, privatisation and product market competition - can be problematic when applied to infrastructure. For example, hardening budget constraints may require the liberalisation of tariff levels and structures to allow the elimination of production subsidies, but the impact on income distribution can create strong political opposition. Effective privatisation requires complementary measures to introduce either product market competition or effective regulation, but there is little experience in the transition economies with regulatory instruments and institutions.

Thus the purpose of this paper is to characterise the infrastructure restructuring challenge in the transition economies and to examine carefully the government policies that can effectively promote this restructuring. The remainder of the paper is organised as follows. Section 2 assesses the prevailing imbalance in markets for infrastructure services in terms of inherited supply capacities (i.e., the capital stock put in place under central planning), changing patterns of demand for infrastructure services, and tariff levels and structures compared with market economies. Section 3 examines the pressures and incentives for a commercial approach to infrastructure and the potential it creates for its restructuring, including increased investment and access to private finance and greater operational efficiency. Section 4 considers the role of government in supporting a more commercial approach to infrastructure, a role that involves establishing boundaries between competition and regulation in infrastructure and providing effective regulation where competition is not possible. Section 5 contains a summary and draws some conclusions.

2. Challenges in Restructuring Infrastructure

This section characterises the restructuring challenges in telecommunications, energy and transport in the transition economies. It compares measures of both the level of service provision and the level and structure of tariffs to appropriate benchmarks from market economies. The section also examines environmental and safety issues.

2.1 Telecommunications

Supply networks

With a bias towards material production and a neglect of services, central planning placed a low priority on the provision of public telecommunications services.[2] Hierarchical network structures reflected concerns for security and bureaucratic control of the economy, with relatively limited access to telecommunications by both enterprises and households. Much of the technology was antiquated (analogue rather than digital) and unreliable.

Fig. P1: Telecommunications Network Penetration Rates, 1994

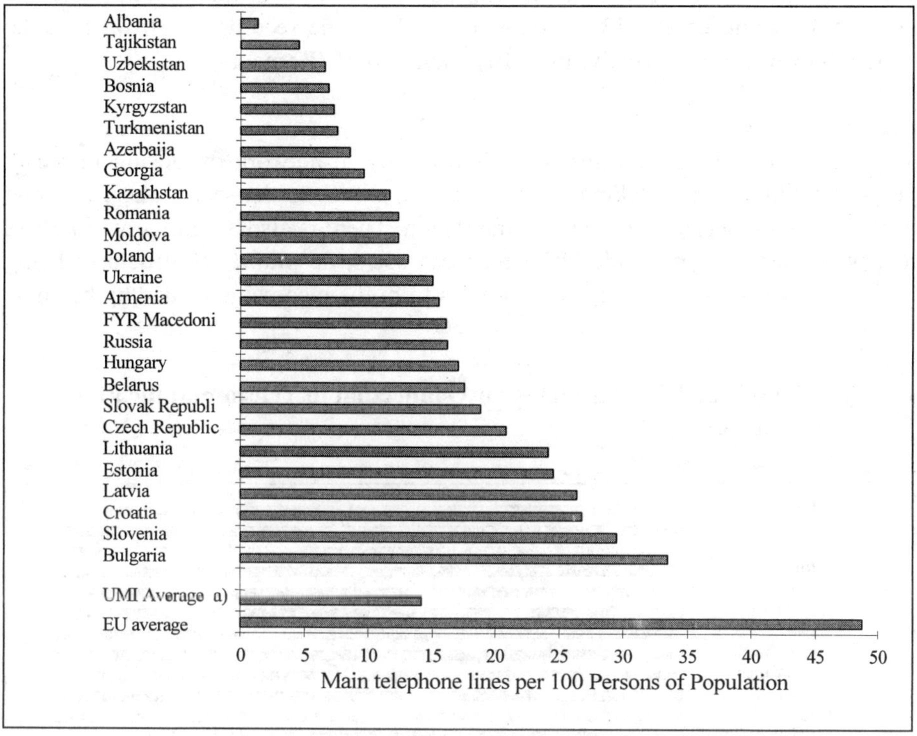

Note: a) UMI = Countries of upper and middle income

Source: INTERNATIONAL TELECOMMUNICATIONS UNION/OECD (1994a).

The size of a country's telephone network is typically measured by the number of telephone lines relative to the size of the population, the so-called network penetration rate. Figure P1 shows that the network penetration rates in transition economies are on average similar to those in upper middle-income developing countries with comparable per capita income levels. However, the rates are only between one-quarter and one-half of those in the European Union. Low penetration levels persist despite a belated effort under central planning to place a higher priority on telecommunications services as awareness of their importance to enterprise productivity increased.

In terms of quality, inherited telephone networks are burdened with a high percentage of outmoded equipment and high fault rates. The information on faults per number of main lines, a standard measure of service quality, is incomplete for the region. For those countries where data is available, the average is 45 faults per 100 main lines in 1994, compared with an average rate of 34 for upper-income developing countries and 13 for those in the EU. The recorded fault rates in the region, however, range widely, from 10 (Latvia) to 95 (Romania).

Unmet demands

While some countries have invested significantly in network expansion in recent years, particularly those taking a commercial approach to the sector, there are long waiting lists for services in much of the region. There is also a definite willingness to pay for services, particularly by business users, despite tariff structures being designed to cross-subsidise household users from the income generated by business users.

Fig. P2: Average Waiting Times for Connection to Telecommunications Services, 1994

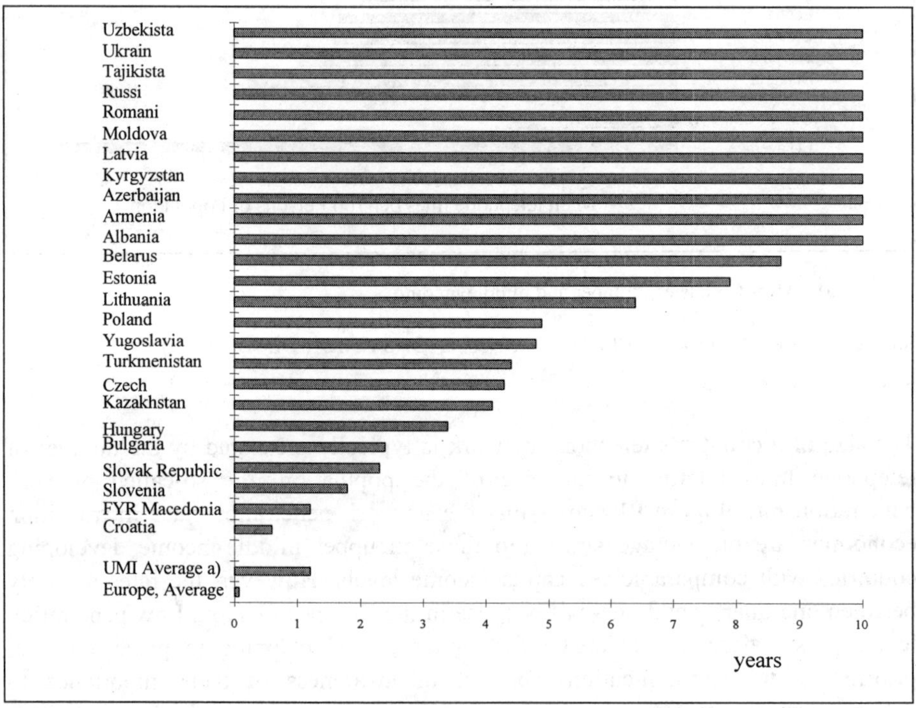

Note: UMI = Countries of upper and middle income

Source: INTERNATIONAL TELECOMMUNICATIONS UNION/OECD (1994a)

Official waiting lists show that between 1 and 8 per cent of the population of transition countries are on a waiting list for network access, but the demand for telephone connections is probably considerably higher. The average expected waiting time for services is three years, compared with an average of one year in upper middle-income developing countries and less than one month in the EU (see Figure P2). With such long waiting times in transition economies, there may well be a significant number of discouraged potential subscribers who have not yet joined the queue for services.

The development of cellular networks in transition economies provides one example of customers' willingness to pay for quick access to reliable services. This willingness is particularly true of business and high-income households. In some countries, the cellular network penetration rates have reached west European levels, despite the fact that charges for cellular services are substantially above those for fixed services and those for cellular services in the EU. Surveys of business users in the region confirm this willingness to pay for quick access to reliable services (INTERNATIONAL TELECOMMUNICATIONS UNION, 1994b).

Tariffs

The tariff structure under central planning consisted of subsidised but limited services for households (local calls were largely un-metered and free) while high charges were levied on enterprises for long-distance and international services. However, this tariff structure does not reflect the cost of services, for which the distance of a telephone call is not the dominant factor. The major component of service costs is the connection to the network itself.

While detailed data on long-distance and international tariffs is not available, average monthly subscription charges for households and businesses provide some indication of tariff levels and structures. Figure P3 shows average monthly subscription charges for both household and business consumers for countries in the region grouped by their stages of transition.[3] A comparison across these stages reveals how tariff levels and structures have evolved during the transition. As a rule, those countries at more advanced stages of transition have adjusted tariff structures to allow for more balanced charges between households and businesses and have raised the overall level of tariffs. An exception is the very high tariffs levied on business users in countries at intermediate stages of transition. Nevertheless, tariff levels in countries at advanced stages of transition remain below the average for household and business users in both upper middle-income developing countries and those in the EU.

Fig. P3: Average Telecommunications Tariffs by Countries Stages of Transition, 1994

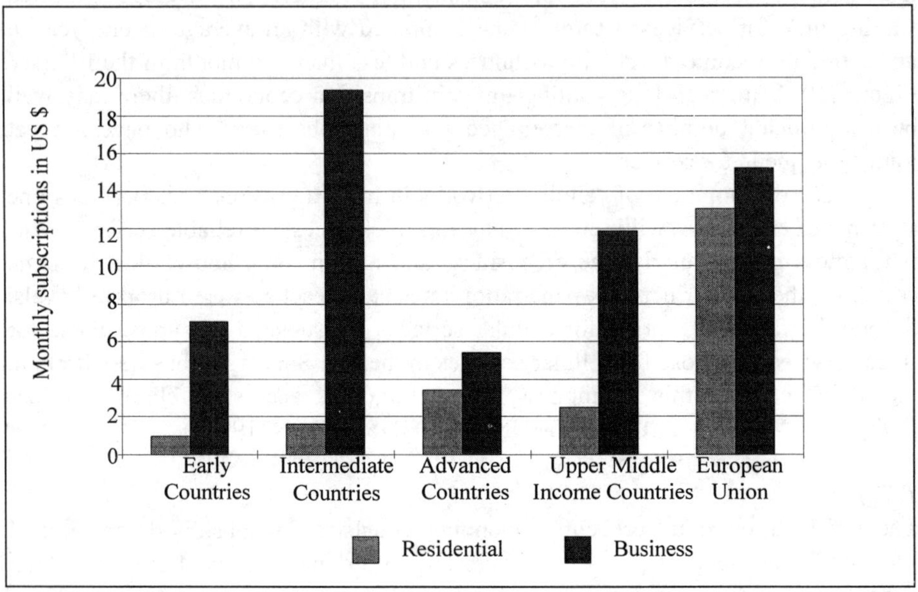

Source: INTERNATIONAL TELECOMMUNICATIONS UNION/OECD (1994A). EBRD Transition Report (1996).

2.2 Electric Power

Generation and supply networks

The installed generation capacities in the countries of eastern Europe, the Baltics and the CIS were designed to meet electric energy requirements prior to the transition. Since demand has declined in most transition economies since 1989, the installed capacity now exceeds present requirements in the region as a whole and in most individual countries. However, many thermal plants in transition economies are comparatively old and often not well maintained. In addition, the coal and lignite used in these plants are often below the quality for which the boilers of existing power plants were designed. As a result, the effective capacity of power plants is often below their design levels.

In 1994 the electricity intensity of output, as measured by the consumption of electric energy per unit of GNP at purchasing-power-parity (PPP) exchange rates, was twice as high in eastern Europe and the Baltics as in the EU (see Figure P4). The electricity intensity in the CIS was even greater, exceeding that in northern

America by a factor of two.[4] The electricity intensity in northern America is about 50% greater than that in the EU, reflecting differences in costs of primary energy (including transport costs) and in energy taxation.

In the EU, industry typically accounts for between one-third and one-half of the total electricity demand, with households and small-scale commercial users each accounting for about half of the remainder. In transition economies, particularly in the CIS, industry's share of electricity consumption was typically higher at the beginning of the transition period. In 1990, for instance, industry accounted for 60% of electric energy demand in Russia (INTERNATIONAL ENERGY AGENCY, 1995) and 65% of the demand in the Ukraine (INTERNATIONAL ENERGY AGENCY, 1996), reflecting the priority attached to abundant supply of power for material production. Much of the high energy intensity of the transition economies can be attributed, therefore, to industry. However, variations in electricity intensity among the transition economies are significant. These differences reflect in part endowments of primary energy resources and installed capacity for nuclear power generation.

While central planning encouraged wasteful consumption of electricity, the electric power systems in the region are also inefficient in the sense that they use larger amounts of primary energy per kilowatt hours (kWh) of electric energy output than do the power supply systems in industrialised market economies. The overall thermal efficiency of coal- or lignite-fired power stations in the transition economies is usually below 30% and in many cases only in the 20 to 25% range. This compares with thermal efficiencies of about 35% for modern coal-fired plants in the EU and up to 50% for gas-fired combined cycle plants. Furthermore, technical transmission and distribution losses in power supply systems of transition economies are often in the order of 10% of net generation and sometimes as high as 15-20%, whereas in western Europe they are usually between 4 and 9%.

Changing demands

Since 1989, electricity consumption has fallen by over 30% in the Baltics, and by 22% and 16% in the CIS and eastern Europe respectively (see Figure P5). The fall in energy consumption matches the decline in real GDP in eastern Europe. However, in the Baltics and CIS, recorded GDP has fallen by much more than electricity consumption. This may reflect in part the difficulties of measuring output in the former Soviet Union, where statistical coverage of the new private sector is often weak.

Fig. P4: Electricity Intensity of Output, 1994

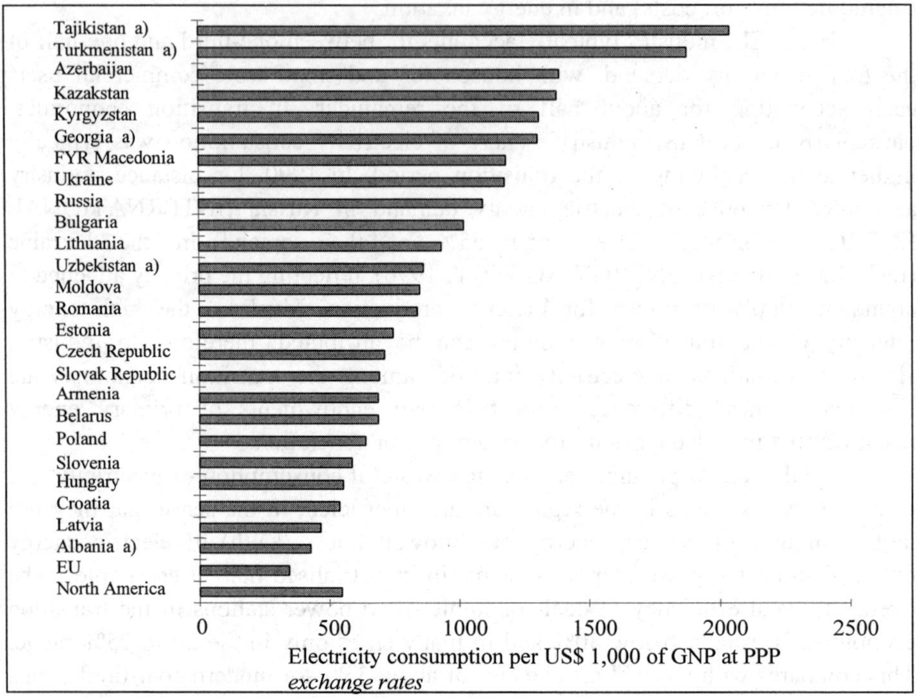

Note: a) 1993

Sources: INTERNATIONAL ENERGY AGENCY and WORLD BANK, various sources.

While industrial consumption of electric energy has declined substantially in the region, households in transition economies consumed more electric energy in 1994 than in 1989, despite the fall in disposable incomes over the period. The reasons for the increase in residential electricity consumption include the improved access of households to electrical appliances and in some cases a switch from coal and oil to electricity for heating – for example, in cases where primary energy prices have increased relative to effective electricity tariffs.

Fig. P5: Change in Electricity Consumption, 1989-94

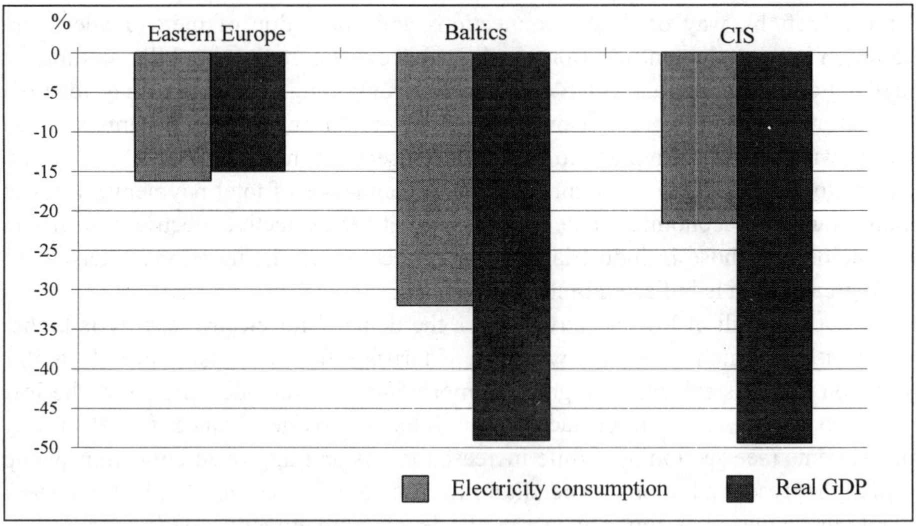

Source: INTERNATIONAL ENERGY AGENCY and EBRD

Tariffs

Electricity tariffs should be set at a level which aims to ensure the financial viability of power utilities and to encourage efficient use. In most advanced industrialised countries, power utilities are typically financially profitable, although it is questionable whether electricity tariffs fully reflect costs, including those associated with pollution and decommissioning of nuclear power plants. In the EU, electricity tariffs average 7 US cents per kWh for large industrial users and 15 US cents per kWh for households. These tariff rates include indirect taxes. The comparable tariffs in northern America are 4 US cents per kWh and 7 US cents per kWh respectively.

In the transition economies, the level and structure of electricity tariffs tends to vary with progress in transition. Those countries at early and intermediate stages of transition (primarily CIS countries) still have tariff structures which are inverted, in the sense that charges to industrial users are above those for households. In addition, their tariff levels are low in relation to both those in the EU and the United States (see Figure P6). Those countries at advanced stages of transition (primarily in eastern Europe and the Baltics) have begun to re-balance their tariff structures between households and enterprises and to raise their levels.

Not all electricity consumption in the region, however, is actually billed and paid for on time. Moreover, non-cash payments in the form of barter transactions or give-and-take fuel contracts account in some countries for a large proportion of billed electricity resulting in low levels of cash receipts. "Non-technical" losses, largely theft by way of illegal connections and corruption of meter readers, are common in several countries. Some utilities have difficulty issuing bills on time for metered consumption, and often customers are unwilling or unable to pay for their consumption once bills are received. Mechanisms for enforcing payments are also weak, with an unwillingness to disconnect users for non-payment. As a result, arrears to power utilities account for a significant share of total payment arrears in many transition economies. The discrepancy between effective electricity tariffs in the region and those in industrialised market economies is, therefore, likely to be even greater than is indicated in the above chart.

As a result of low effective tariffs, the demand for electric energy is higher in transition economies than it would be if tariffs reflected costs.[5] Not only is this situation inconsistent with the goal of improving demand-side efficiency, the low tariff levels are also an obstacle to mobilising private finance for electricity investments (see section 3). While increased tariffs and improved collection would initially represent additional expenditure for enterprises and households, these steps would make measures aimed at energy efficiency more attractive, easing the longer-term impact on real incomes.

With low and inverted tariffs and weak collection efforts, reflecting in part past use of electricity as a mechanism for distributing benefits and resources under central planning, it is important to recognise that the untargeted subsidisation of electricity can be a regressive measure. This adverse effect arises to the extent that higher-income households consume more electricity than do lower-income households, not only on a per capita basis but also as a proportion of income (FREUND and WALLICH, 1996). A more progressive measure would be the provision of a basic or life-line service for households at subsidised tariffs rates to help ease the impact of cost-reflective tariffs on those who are unable to afford them. One way to fund such a subsidy would be to charge progressively higher tariffs for those who consume greater amounts of electricity.

Environment

At the start of transition, the power sector contributed substantially to the poor air quality in a number of countries in the region. In 1990, sulphur dioxide emissions from power plants exceeded EU levels on a per capita basis by a factor of nine in Bulgaria, seven in Estonia and six in the area of what is now the Czech Republic (see Table P1). In these three countries local coal, or oil shale in the case of Estonia, is the primary energy source for power generation, and power generation accounts for the bulk of total sulphur dioxide emissions from all sources.

Fig. P6: Electricity Tariffs by Countries' Stages of Transition, 1994

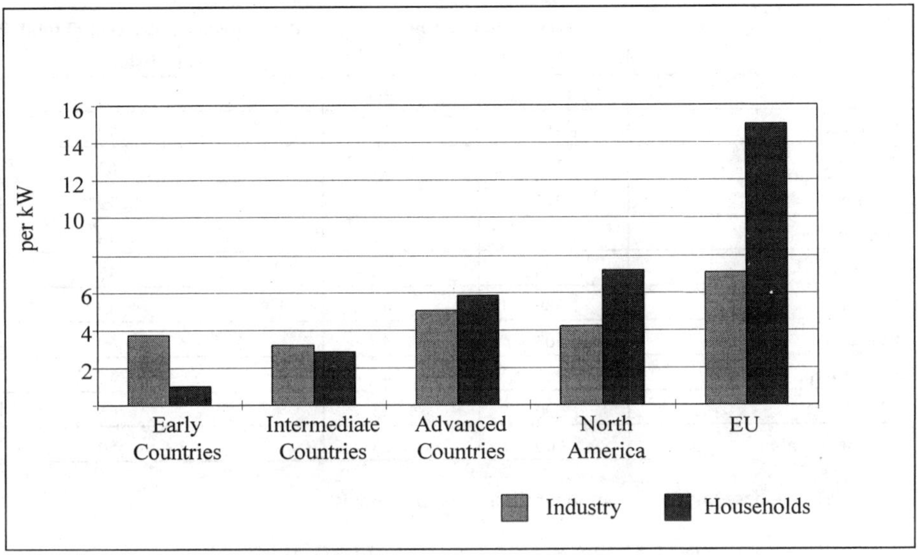

Notes: Average of countries for which data are available; Early Countries: Belaurus; Intermediate Countries: Albania, Bulgaria, Kazakstan, Romanmia, Russia, Ukraine

Sources: INTERNATIONAL ENERGY AGENCY.

It is difficult to assess the change in air quality in the transition due to a lack of consistent emission data, particularly of sulphur dioxide, since 1990. Indications are, however, that any improvements to date are limited primarily to the effects of reduced thermal power generation. Strict environmental standards have so far tended to be enforced only for new power plant investments. However, where stricter environmental legislation applies also to existing plants, it is likely to be the driving force behind major power sector investments over the coming years, as for example in the Czech Republic and Poland.

Tab. P1: Emissions of Sulphur Dioxide in Selected Countries, 1990

	SO_2 from power plants		Power plants as per cent of total SO_2 emissions
	1000 tonnes	kg/capita	
Bulgaria	1 453	173	72
Czech Rep.	1 163	113	62
Estonia	217	141	79
Hungary	430	42	48
Lithuania	105	28	47
Poland	1 589	41	49
Romania	903	40	69
Slovak Rep.	243	46	45
Ukraine a)	1 690	33	65
European Union	8 600	23	50

Note: a) Includes emissions from fuel refining and processing.

Sources: INTERNATIONAL ENERGY AGENCY (1996). EBRD (1996)

2.3 Transportation

Road and rail networks

Transport networks in the region tend to have relatively well-developed railways, but only limited road systems. The intensive use of railways under central planning reflected the emphasis on primary and heavy industries, which created transport requirements for bulk commodities. Moreover, industrial production and location decisions gave inadequate weight to transport costs, establishing overly centralised and vertically integrated production facilities and thereby generating an artificially high transport requirement. The capacity and cost advantages of railways over long distances and for bulk cargoes meant that this transport mode was well suited to the freight requirements of central planning. In most countries in the region, railways also provided a high share of passenger transport, not only for long-distance traffic but also for commuter and regional travel. Alternatives were in short supply. Low car ownership, limited bus services and poor roads all added to rail use.

The densities of transport networks are typically measured in relation to a country's population or to its land area. Figure P7 provides the densities of railways and roads in the region in relation to population. Two broad features stand out. First, the rail densities are high compared with those in the EU and United States. For example, the Russian rail network density in relation to population is about 50 per cent greater than that in the United States; although, if the densities were calculated in relation to land area, they would be broadly similar. Many countries in eastern Europe and the Baltics also have relatively high rail densities, and their land sizes are roughly comparable to those in the EU. Second, the road densities in relation to the population of most countries in the region are substantially less than those in the EU and the United States.

The quality of the transport networks reflects a number of factors, including their initial design. For example, in the Baltics the major trunk roads run east to west rather than north to south. The trunk roads in the former Soviet Union were also designed for lower vehicle weights than in the EU, although this is consistent with the traffic tasks which they had to perform in the past. With respect to railways, design standards are less exacting than those in the EU. However, most rail lines have adequate speeds and are of a sufficient standard for the majority of rail freight services currently provided. Partly as a result of the greater use of rail for bulk freight, passenger speeds are generally lower than on main lines in the EU, offering less competition to emerging road coach and medium-distance airline services.

Another important dimension to the quality of infrastructure is maintenance and renewal. Here, piecemeal evidence points to considerable neglect. In Russia, the extent of rail track subject to speed restrictions, for example, has doubled since 1988 to stand at 20% of the network (EBRD, 1993a), while about 25% of tracks in eastern Europe are estimated to be in unsatisfactory technical condition (FOREIGN INVESTMENT ADVISORY SERVICE, 1996). The latter often serve as major trunk routes for new trading patterns. However, many secondary and branch rail lines with low traffic were probably maintained to excessively high economic standards in the past. With respect to trunk roads, an estimated 38% of the system in Russia requires upgrading or reconstruction, and an additional 25% is in need of resurfacing (EBRD, 1993b).

Changing demands

High volumes of freight transport in relation to output characterise transport activities inherited from central planning, with the sector being heavily dominated by rail. In 1988 freight intensity of output in the former Soviet Union (measured in terms of tonne-kilometres of domestic freight per dollar of GDP at purchasing power parity exchange rates) was nearly five times that in the United States (EBRD, 1993c). Freight intensity in eastern European countries was similar to that of the United States, but well above the EU. The freight intensity of EU output is about one-third of that in the United States.

Fig. P7: Rail Network Densities 1993

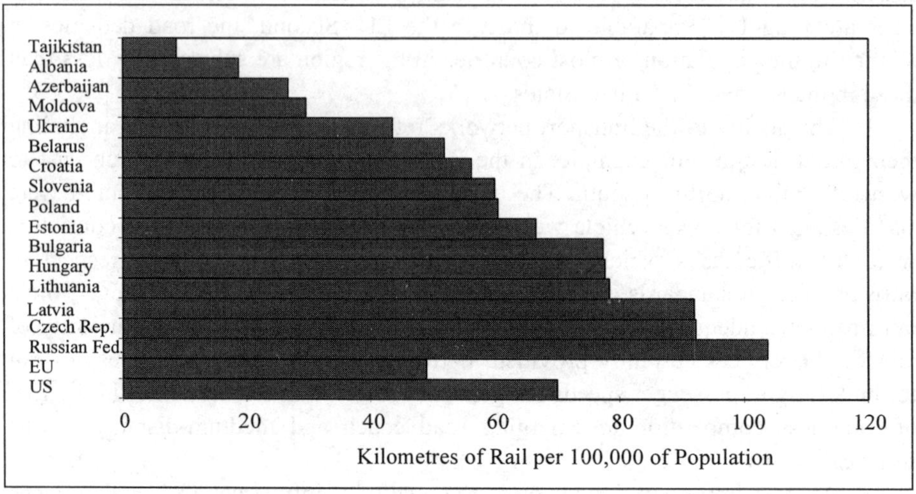

Source: INTERNATIONAL ROAD TRANSPORT UNION (1996).

During the transition, the demand for transport services has changed dramatically. There has been a sharp reduction in overall freight volumes, especially on the railways. Between 1989 and 1994, rail freight volumes declined by about 50% in eastern Europe, the Baltics and the CIS (see Figure P8). This decline is greater than the fall in real output in these economies, particularly in eastern Europe, pointing to a reduction in the freight intensity of output. However, the trends in road haulage in the region are more diverse. In eastern Europe, road haulage fell by 5% from 1989 to 1994, indicating that the proportion of freight carried by road transport has increased. However, in the Baltics road haulage has declined by more than rail. Only very limited data on road haulage in the CIS are available, and these figures point to substantial declines in the initial years of transition.[6]

Even if railways successfully restructure, road transport can be expected to carry an increasing share of total freight traffic for three main reasons. Firstly, the shift in composition of output away from lower-value bulk commodities towards higher valued products and the location of new production facilities, which take account of transport costs, will lead to a fall in the transport intensity of output. Secondly, with the shift towards higher-value products, road haulage will become more competitive for freight transport in terms of costs and services compared with rail. Thirdly, the road haulage sector will be operating in the private sector and will tend to be more responsive to customer demands. This outlook presents an infrastructure challenge both for road infrastructure providers and competing rail networks.

Fig. P7 (cont.)

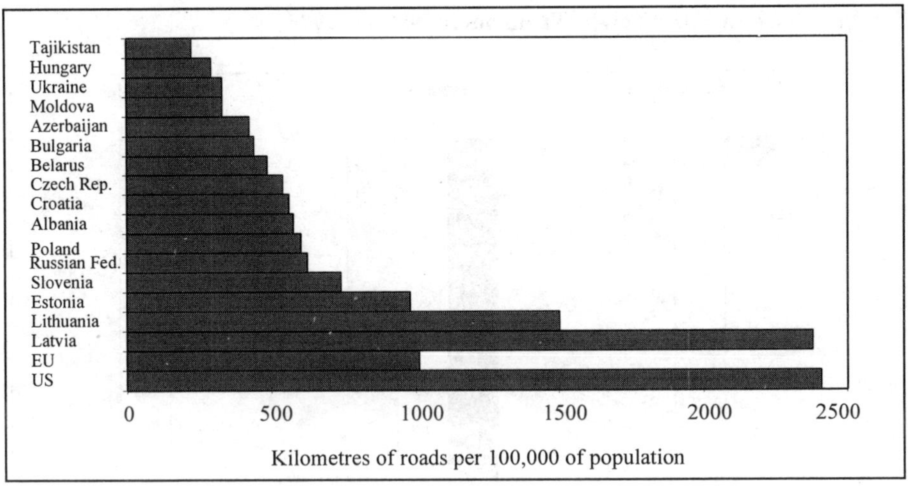

Source: INTERNATIONAL ROAD TRANSPORT UNION (1996).

Changes in the scale and nature of the demand of passenger travel also determine infrastructure needs. There has been a sharp increase in automobile registrations in the region, albeit from low levels. Personal mobility, measured by annual kilometres travelled per capita, was significantly lower in the centrally planned economies than in the EU. In eastern Europe and the Baltics, the number of registered vehicles is now between 20 and 30% above its pre-transition levels. Limited data from the CIS points to increases in registered vehicles ranging from 15 to 30%.[7] As living standards increase, it can be expected that car ownership will increase sharply. In urban areas in particular this will create environmental pressures and tend to have a damaging effect on surface-based public transport unless policies are pursued to protect it.

Cost-reflective tariffs and prices

Historically, most railway systems in the region had higher rates of operating cost recovery than their counterpart public railways in the EU, mainly due to the much higher freight traffic intensities arising out of centrally planned production. Despite recent traffic reductions, rail freight still returns a margin above operating costs in many countries in the region, but there is increasing difficulty in earning sufficient revenue to fund the renewal of infrastructure. This shortfall is partly due to higher costs, but also to governments requiring, or encouraging, freight services to support passenger services in an effort to cushion the impact of falling household incomes, while not impacting on the government budget. The result is a significantly inverted structure of railway tariffs.

Fig. P8: Change in Freight Transport: 1989 vs. 1994

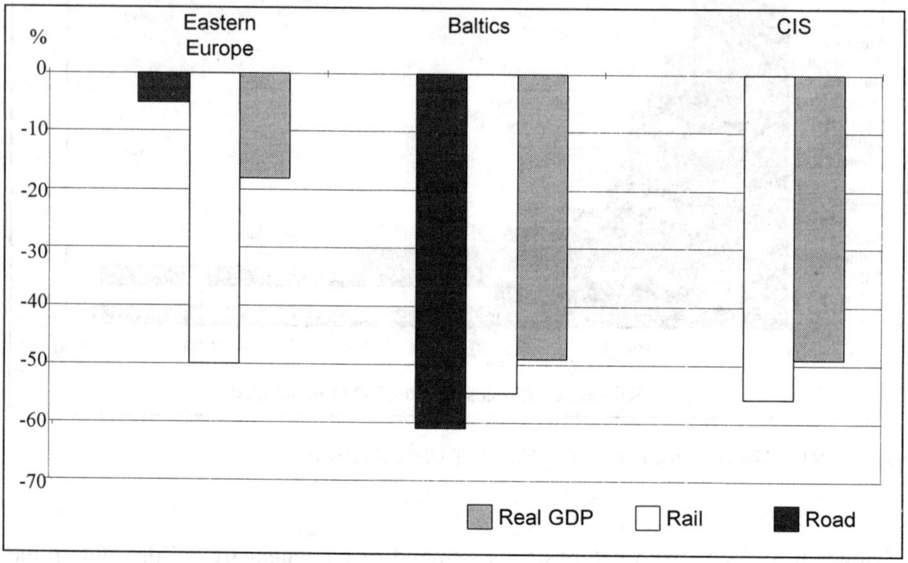

Sources: WORLD BANK, Railway Database, ECMT (1996a) and EBRD.

In the EU, passengers' fares are about 55% higher than freight rates. In the advanced transition economies, this tariff structure is inverted, with passengers' fares about 55% below those for freight in 1993 (THOMPSON and FRASER, 1996). The inversion in tariffs is even greater for those countries at intermediate and early stages of transition (see Figure P9). These cross-subsidies threaten to overprice freight and prompt a shift to road transport, thereby reducing the resources needed for railway renewal and improvement. An alternative approach can be found in EU transportation policies, which prescribe that loss-making services should be operated under contractual arrangements, including financial compensation from the relevant authorities (municipalities for urban services, regional governments for rural services, and central governments for intercity services).

Safety and the environment

While there are safety challenges for all modes of transport in the region, the largest existing and potential problem, in terms of people at risk, relates to road use. The number of annual deaths in the transition economies, caused by traffic-related accidents, compares unfavourably with that in the EU. In eastern Europe, the number of deaths relative to the number of registered vehicles exceeded that in the EU by a factor of three in 1994 (ECMT, 1996b). A similar difference exists for the number of traffic-related deaths in terms of distance travelled. Fatality rates on Russian roads are between four and five times higher than those in western Europe and the United States (WORLD BANK, 1993). With the increased registration of passenger cars and the projected expansion in road haulage, there is a need to improve safety in the design of both vehicles and roads as well as improve drivers' awareness of road safety.

Fig. P9: Ratio of Average Passenger Fares to Average Freight Rates [a], according to Countries' Stages of Transition, 1993

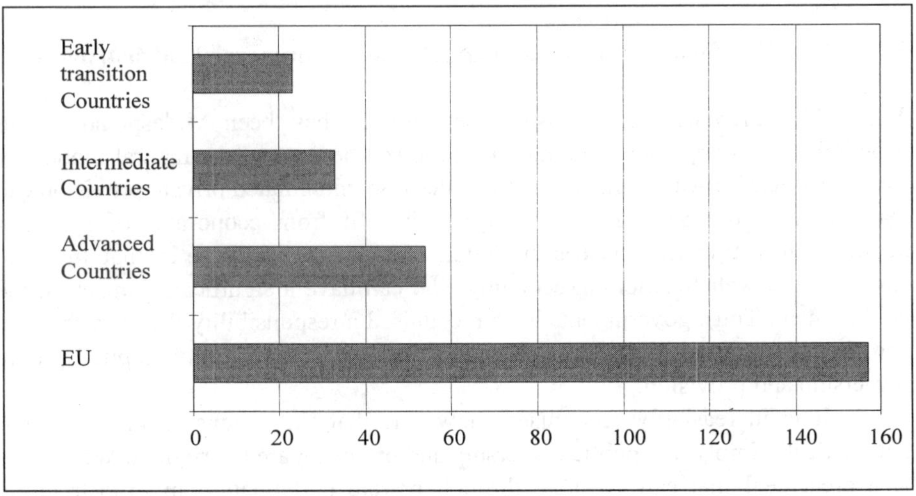

Note: a) (total passenger revenue/passenger km) to (total freight revenue/tonne-km) in per cent

Source: WORLD BANK, Railway Database.

The rapid growth in the size and use of vehicles, the average age of vehicles, and the vehicle technology in use have focused attention on the environmental impact from road transport. Air pollution from motor vehicles is now a growing concern in some cities, such as Warsaw, Budapest and Prague. Authorities in a number of eastern European countries have set emission standards for new vehicles that comply with EU standards, but the main problem remains the control of emissions from vehicles already in use, which form the majority of vehicle ownership. Engine retrofitting and the development of well-targeted vehicle inspection and maintenance programmes are cost-effective ways to address this problem.

2.4 Summary

The evidence presented in this section shows that infrastructure capacities in transition economies diverge widely from market demands and concerns for the environment and safety. As a result, infrastructure must be substantially restructured, requiring new investment, more effective management and greater efficiency. Tariff levels and structures also continue to be heavily influenced by the use of infrastructure as a way of distributing income and resources under central planning, which encourages inefficient use of services, distorts investment decisions throughout the economies and impairs the financial viability of infrastructure enterprises.

3. Tariff Reform and Restructuring through Commercial Infrastructure

The public provision of infrastructure services has been widespread in all economies. This approach is commonly followed because of the natural monopoly aspects associated with infrastructure and because unregulated private provision can lead to monopoly pricing or a failure to benefit from economies of scale. In addition, infrastructure services are often regarded as strategic in that they are essential to a well functioning economy, and can have a significant impact on the environment. Thus, governments have recognised a responsibility for infrastructure and, in many cases, it has been assumed that this responsibility implied public ownership and provision.

It is increasingly recognised, however, that these considerations do not automatically imply that public ownership and provision are the right answer. There is a great deal that can be done through private participation in infrastructure, particularly where there is scope for competition among, or effective regulation of, service providers. Where private participation is not considered possible, governments are taking an increasingly commercial approach to publicly provided services. Here, commercial infrastructure refers to both private participation in infrastructure (new entry and privatisation) and the commercialisation of state-owned utilities.

A commercial infrastructure can help overcome the legacies of central planning in infrastructure in at least two ways. The first is to provide some insulation from arbitrary political influence. The sheltering of infrastructure from excessive political intervention can be instrumental in achieving and sustaining tariffs which reflect the costs of production and the fiscal constraints of governments. Such tariffs also help to unlock access to private finance for needed infrastructure investments, as many governments have sharply cut back public investment due to the fiscal strains associated with transition. The second is to promote restructuring by selecting the most capable service providers and strengthening their incentives. The selection of managers for infrastructure enterprises under central planning was influenced not only by the distorted priorities of the old system, but also by the way in which bureaucracies operate.

3.1 Political Influence, Tariff Reform and Access to Finance

Evidence of the distorted tariff levels and structures and of ineffective tariff collection presented in the preceding section reveals an important aspect of an uncommercial approach to infrastructure in the region. It is not easy for governments to overturn the legacy of using infrastructure distributing benefits to households and allocating resources to enterprises. A new approach involves charging customers with higher tariffs and more determined collection.

Initial steps towards mitigating political pressures can involve the commercialisation of infrastructure enterprises. Commercialisation refers to reforms in the oversight of, and incentives within, state-owned enterprises. These changes include legal incorporation and exposure of state enterprises to commercial laws and bankruptcy; selection of an agent with clear responsibility and accountability for representing the state as owner; transparent procedures for selecting enterprise managers; and managerial incentives and performance measures. However, even with such reforms, the government still retains considerable discretionary control over the state-owned infrastructure enterprises.

A further instrument for reducing political pressures is to introduce private participation, thereby adding a clear and consistent voice for cost recovery and efficiency in tariffs (WILLIG, 1994; NEWBURY, 1994). Moreover, even though government may retain a regulatory role in setting infrastructure tariffs, a private service provider would be relatively insulated from political influence compared to a state enterprise. This insulation arises from the fact that, in order to attract private investment in infrastructure assets, governments must first put in place institutions to protect private rights, including credible regulation (see section 4 below). Private ownership then serves to insulate the infrastructure enterprises from political influence beyond the contractual terms of the regulations. It is the respect of private property and contracts that serves to insulate private, albeit publicly regulated, infrastructure enterprises from arbitrary political influence.

A more commercial approach to infrastructure, founded upon the principles of tariff levels and structures which reflect the costs of production and the fiscal constraints of governments and of financial autonomy for infrastructure enterprises, can also help to unlock access to new sources of investment finance. Infrastructure enterprises which are financially viable can often attract private finance. Recent innovations in international capital markets have helped to foster the recent world-wide expansion in the private financing of infrastructure, particularly the rapid development since the late 1980s of project finance. Expanding access to private finance is particularly important in the transition economies because of the severe fiscal strains associated with the transition.

When faced with extreme fiscal pressures, governments often defer capital expenditures, and those in transition economies have proved no exception. However, some caution is required when interpreting trends in government capital expenditures. Under central planning, the government budget provided much of the funding for investment in both infrastructure and in fixed assets by enterprises. Nevertheless, even allowing the inevitable shift of some investment spending away from government to enterprises, public investment in the region continues to fall even in the most recent years and stands at quite a low level. In most countries in the region, public investment in 1995 amounted to less than 3% of GDP.

3.2 Commercialisation, Private Participation and Restructuring

Government policies typically used to promote enterprise restructuring in the transition economies include: the strengthening of objectives and incentives within enterprises; the introduction of market selection of producers through privatisation and market entry and exit; and the intensification of product market competition to reduce organisational slack. With respect to infrastructure enterprises, their commercialisation aims primarily at introducing market-oriented performance goals and strong incentive structures and, in some cases, market selection of managers. Private participation infrastructure, either through selective new entry into market niches or through the privatisation of dominant services providers, tends to introduce a stronger mechanism for market selection. Competition in the provision of infrastructure services is closely bound up with the issue of effective regulation, and this is the focus of section 4.

Commercialisation

Governments in many transition economies have used a number of instruments to promote commercial qualities in their infrastructure enterprises, and these measures have been extensively surveyed in a recent study (PANNIER, 1996). The most fundamental step is corporatisation, the legal separation of public utilities from government through incorporation. This change serves to establish clear boundaries between a public utility and government, thereby separating ownership from enterprise management. In transition economies, these two roles were often blurred under the structures inherited from the old regime, preventing the establishment of clear responsibilities and systems for accountability for both managers and those within government who performed an ownership role. Corporatisation can also involve subjecting state enterprises to the disciplines of commercial law and bankruptcy, although this is not always the case in transition economies.

With separation of ownership from management in state enterprises, a government must select an agent to represent it as the owner of these enterprises. This responsibility can reside with particular government ministries, or a separate agency can be established to perform the task. In transition economies, leaving the ownership role with the branch ministries that formerly operated infrastructure enterprises runs the risk of leaving unchanged long-established relationships between ministries and the state enterprises which they formerly operated. Several transition economies – including Hungary, Poland and Russia – have established a separate government agency or ministry to represent the state as the owner of enterprises. However, branch ministries in the transition economies have often maintained considerable influence over the state enterprises that they formerly operated.

Improving the management of infrastructure enterprises typically requires the selection of capable managers and the introduction of managerial incentive contracts based on performance standards. Under central planning, the selection of enterprise managers was neither competitive nor transparent, and a number of governments in the region have recently begun to adopt more open procedures. However, incumbent managers in some cases have been able to use their inside knowledge and personal connections to maintain their positions. Where managers are selected on the basis of fair competition, available evidence suggests that significant gains in performance can be realised (MCMILLAN, 1996). Until recently, performance evaluation and incentives were largely absent in transition economies. Their effective implementation requires the development of quantitative and qualitative assessments of managerial performance and the setting of targets that are sufficiently demanding. There is not yet a sufficient track record to gauge their effectiveness in the region.

Available evidence from developing countries on performance-related contracts for public-sector managers, however, reveals that they are often ineffective. A comprehensive survey of government enterprises in developing countries found that the implementation of reforms based on performance contracts with public-sector managers had little impact on enterprise performance, including profitability, labour productivity and total factor productivity (WORLD BANK,1996b, Chapter 2). Factors behind these disappointing results include the inability of governments to overcome the information advantage of inside managers in negotiating performance contracts, the weakness of rewards and the absence of penalties for poor performance, and the frequent breach of contract terms by governments, including the regulation of infrastructure tariffs according to fair and consistent rules. This latter finding is particularly significant for infrastructure in transition economies, where attainment of socially efficient tariff structures is a priority.

Selective private entry

Selective private entry into infrastructure can take the form either of new operators serving market niches where competitive provision is possible or of concessions to operate public infrastructure assets. The latter approach allows for competition for the right to serve a market where competition in that market is not possible. There are several advantages to expanding private participation in infrastructure in these ways. While these approaches usually require supportive measures to reduce the scope of public utility monopolies, they typically do not require the creation of regulatory institutions or the break-up of dominant utilities; yet they allow for increased competition. The regulatory conditions that are required are usually written into the licensing agreements or concession contracts. The use of contracts and the courts, at least as a transitory arrangement, allows for a more rapid implementation compared with comprehensive regulatory reform.

Scope for competition in the market is created by limiting the extent of the monopoly granted to integrated utilities to those parts that are truly natural monopolies and by allowing competition elsewhere (common examples of the latter are cellular telephony and independent power generation). While those services that are provided competitively do not necessarily require price regulation, they are usually delivered to consumers through existing infrastructure networks; and determining the terms and conditions for accessing these networks can be a difficult issue to resolve. Two basic requirements are that competing service providers have access to the networks on equivalent terms and that consumers are free to choose among competitors.

Competition for the market is created through bidding for concessions to operate infrastructure assets for a fixed period. This bidding can help to reveal information about the potential efficiency of alternative private contractors and operators. However, this approach to competition can foster at least three types of problems. First, the terms of concession are limited to those events that can be reasonably foreseen, and unexpected circumstances can lead to the renegotiation of the concession. Second, the private concession holder may not have an incentive to maintain infrastructure assets, particularly near the end of the concession period. Third, some types of concessions (e.g., operating concessions or leases) do not obligate the concession holder to make investments, thereby limiting some of the benefits from private participation.

In transition economies, selective private entry into infrastructure has been most prevalent in the telecommunications sector (see Figure P10). These projects have focused on cellular telephony, specialised networks for data transmission and other business services, and, to a lesser extent, long-distance and international services. These infrastructure services are in relatively short supply and their production technology allows competitive provision. In power there are relatively fewer projects involving selective private entry, in part because existing capacity in many of the countries was already large. In the transport sector, there are a small number of airport and port projects.

Fig. P10: Selective Private Entry in Infrastructure Sectors: Number of Projects [a)]

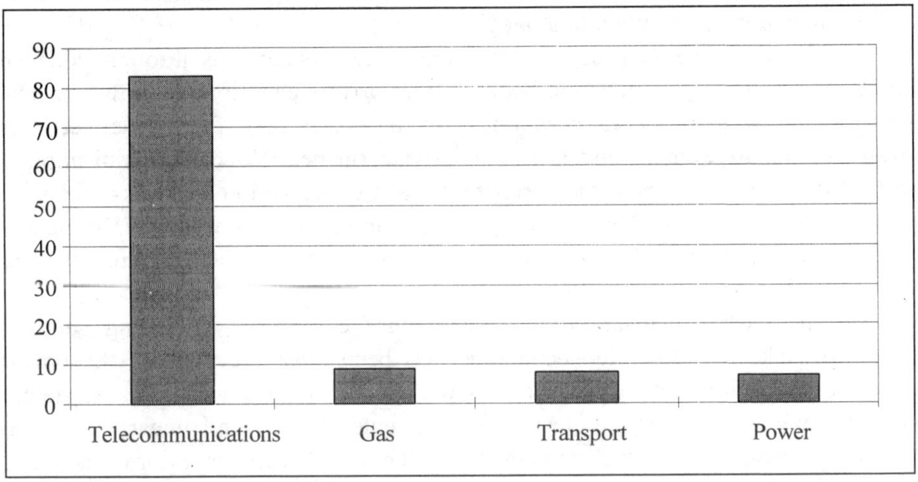

Note: a) Projects with awarded contracts or in operation.

Sources: EBRD and WORLD BANK, Private Infrastructure Database.

Privatisation

Privatisation of infrastructure enterprises can extend the benefits from private participation beyond selective areas of infrastructure to include much of the sector. However, successful privatisation can require two types of institutional change, which may take considerable time to implement. First, infrastructure enterprises themselves may require restructuring to create scope for competition or to enhance their commercial viability. Second, where monopolies are being privatised, effective regulatory institutions must be developed. Private investors must be assured that the approach to setting infrastructure tariffs is transparent and that the institutions responsible for regulation are robust enough to balance fairly the inevitable pressures from governments, consumers and producers.

Some attempts to sell dominant infrastructure enterprises in Hungary and Russia to strategic investors have failed partly because investors lacked confidence in nascent regulatory arrangements. In Kazakstan, electricity sales have been quickly achieved, but at low prices. Building the necessary regulatory institutions takes time and there can be beneficial interchanges between potential private investors and government over their design (EBRD, 1996, Ch. 5).

One form of infrastructure privatisation which has also proceeded quickly is privatisation through vouchers in the Czech Republic and Russia. These countries have distributed minority stakes in major telephone, electric power and gas utilities as part of their mass privatisation programmes. In the Czech Republic, however, this initial distribution has been followed by the cash sale of additional shares in the dominant telephone provider to strategic investors.

The complete privatisation of infrastructure enterprises through vouchers could well compromise potential benefits from private participation, however. Due to resulting weaknesses in corporate governance, it may fail to deliver deep restructuring, investment and access to private finance. Voucher privatisation of infrastructure enterprises in the absence of effective regulation also risks creating a constituency in favour of monopoly provision and may require the government to compensate shareholders for interference with property rights acquired through voucher schemes.

The cash privatisation of infrastructure enterprises, including sales of minority stakes, in transition economies has been most prevalent in the power, telecommunications and gas sectors (see Figure P11). Hungary, Kazakstan and Poland have privatised major electricity or gas enterprises, with Hungary separating electricity generators, transmission grids and regional distributors prior to their cash sale. Given the apparently adequate capacity in the electric power sector, privatisation is likely to be the more prevalent form of private participation compared to selective private entry (e.g., in the form of independent power producers). Estonia, Hungary, Kazakstan and Latvia have sold at least minority stakes in dominant telecommunications enterprises to strategic investors. The Czech Republic has also sold a minority stake in its dominant telecommunications operator to a group of strategic investors, following the partial voucher privatisation.

Fig. P11: Cash Privatisations in Infrastructure Sectors: Number of Privatised Enterprises

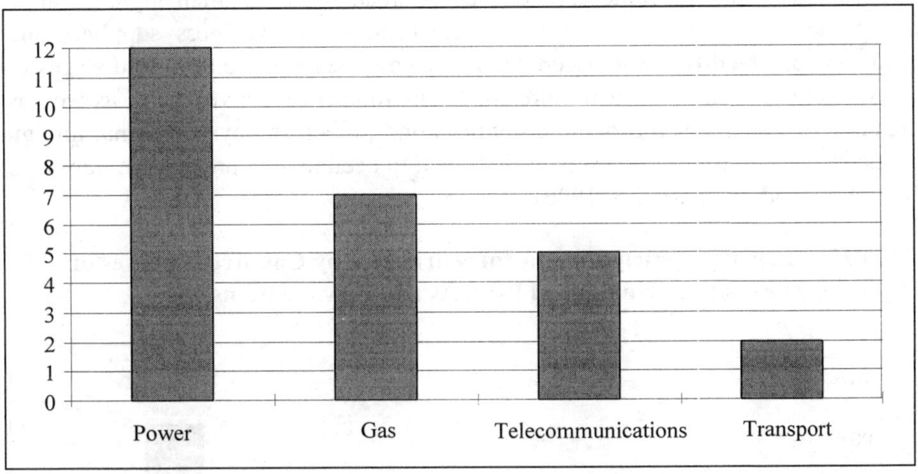

Sources: EBRD and WORLD BANK, Private Infrastructure Database

Total cash investments by strategic investors in major infrastructure privatisations in the region amount to US$ 6 billion. This represents 20 per cent of cumulative foreign direct investment in transition economies from 1990 to 1995.

3.3 Private Participation and Progress in Transition

Like other forms of private investment, private participation in infrastructure requires a supportive environment. The relevant features of this environment go beyond issues of competition and effective regulation. In transition economies, the development of this environment is measured in part by indicators of progress in transition. Investors in privatisations of infrastructure enterprises, as well as those in infrastructure projects involving selective private entry, will typically require a sound legal framework for private transactions and share ownership, access to finance and material inputs, a stable macroeconomic environment, and a credible regulatory framework and reliable tax regime which will allow an assessment and limitation of risks and a market return on the investment. Satisfying these needs requires progress in transition.

The EBRD's transition indicators embody many of the key factors determining the extent to which an effective environment for the private sector has been established (EBRD,1996, Chapter 2).

In the early stages of transition, when major structural reforms have yet to be undertaken, or even in the intermediate stages when many of the consequences of reforms have yet to become apparent, commercial risks are often high. Relative prices can remain volatile and the creditworthiness of business suppliers and customers can be difficult to ascertain. Those countries at more advanced stages of transition tend to have a much more stable environment for investment, as well as greater progress in macroeconomic stabilisation.[8] In fact, surveys show that foreign investors' perceptions of investment risks tend to decline with progress in transition (LANKES and VENABLES, 1996).

Fig. P12: Private Participation in Infrastructure by Countries' Stages of Transition: Number of Projects and Privatizations

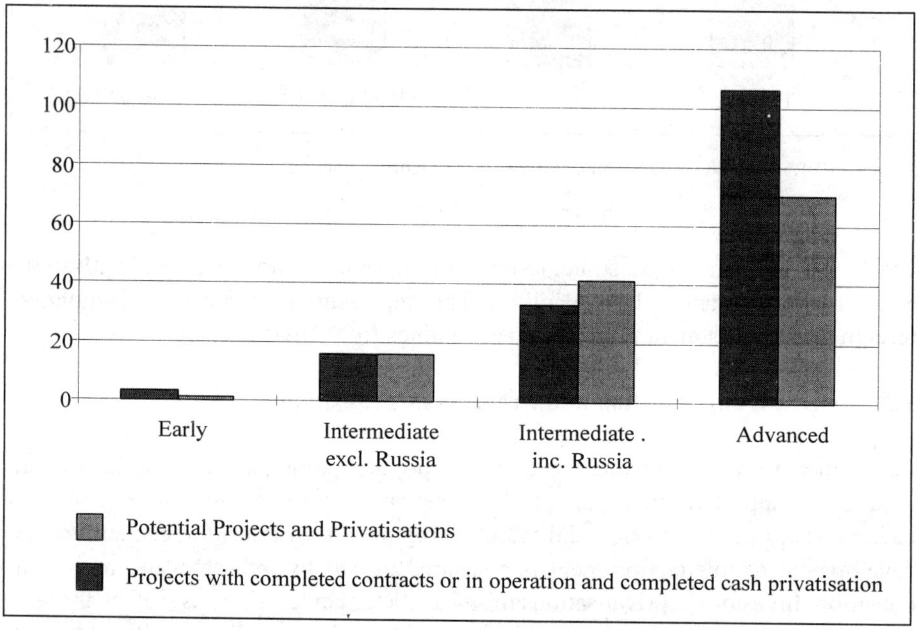

Source: EBRD and WORLD BANK, Private Infrastructure Database.

In transition economies, private participation in infrastructure exhibits a very positive relationship with progress in transition (see Fig. P12). This correlation holds true for both cash privatisation of infrastructure enterprises and for selective private entry. The positive correlation exists for potential projects as well as those that are already operational, reinforcing the point that progress in transition contributes to and facilitates private participation in infrastructure. The strength of the relationship also highlights the particular importance of a stable environment for private investment in infrastructure, where many investments are large and irreversible.

3.4 Summary

The priorities in infrastructure in the transition economies are threefold. The first is to move toward tariff levels and structures that reflect the costs of production and the fiscal constraints of governments, that encourage more efficient use of these services and that guide investment decisions throughout the economy in an appropriate manner. Secondly, the expansion of access to private finance, through the financial autonomy of infrastructure enterprises, is a priority due to the severe fiscal constraints and sharp cut backs in public investment associated with transition. The third priority is to promote restructuring by strengthening incentives for infrastructure enterprise managers and by allowing increased market selection of service providers. A more commercial approach to infrastructure, particularly in greater private participation, is a key instrument for achieving these objectives. Considerable progress in transition appears to be necessary however, for the increased private participation in infrastructure.

4. Competition and Regulation

An important complementary policy to commercial infrastructure is the introduction of effective regulation or competitive provision of infrastructure services. Effective regulation or competition provision can enhance the effectiveness of a more commercial approach to infrastructure and these policies in their own right can add a further impetus to the restructuring of infrastructure.

A fundamental task in the regulation of infrastructure is to determine the boundaries between regulation and competition. In the past, infrastructure used to be considered a natural monopoly but it is now seen as a sector where competition can play a significant role (WORLD BANK, 1994). This development owes something to changing technologies. More importantly though, it is possible to restructure the industries concerned so that there is at least a functional separation and even a separation of ownership between activities, according to their potential for allowing competition.

The introduction of competition wherever possible is desirable because it avoids the high costs imposed by regulation. These costs arise because regulation requires considerable economic and sectoral expertise, which is scarce, and because of the uncertainty that state intervention brings to private investors whose confidence in the future is critical to providing the capital requirements of transition (EBRD, 1996, Ch. 4). Competition in infrastructure can also promote better operational and financial performance by service providers via competitive pricing combined with the threat of bankruptcy for loss-making firms or *via* competitive market entry and exit. Finally, competition can reveal information about the comparative performance of firms operating in the same sector which can be used to improve incentives within both public and private firms.

The scope of competition and necessary regulation, however, depends on the state of technology and the provision of alternative services, both of which are constantly changing. This difficulty in foreseeing the potential problems for a system of regulation points to the need for flexibility in responding to unforeseen developments. But flexibility also has a cost. Investors need to be reassured that the profitability of their investment will not be compromised by future regulatory decisions that might lower prices or increase standards to court political popularity, exploiting the fact that capital investments, once "sunk", cannot move elsewhere. Typically, investment in infrastructure is extremely capital intensive, has a long lead time and subsequent operating life, and once made cannot change either its function or its location. The "sunk" nature of investment in infrastructure makes it particularly vulnerable to fears about adverse regulatory decisions in the future.

Given the need for both flexibility and credibility, the most challenging task for regulation is not one of deciding what to do at any given moment, but of deciding who should have the power to make decisions. Infrastructure regulation is in an important sense a task of constitution making rather then merely policy making. This distinction is particularly important in transition economies where there have been major changes in political regimes and there has not been time to develop the regulatory institutions and predictability that investors require.

This section of the chapter examines the main issues concerning regulation and competition in infrastructure. It is organised according to infrastructure sector, with telecommunications followed by electric power and transport.

4.1 Telecommunications

Challenges

The evidence in section 2 indicates that the overwhelming priority in telecommunications is investment in new capacity and improvement in the quality of existing capacity. Given fiscal constraints, the bulk of this investment must come from the private sector, and much of the private finance of infrastructure in the transition economies has so far flowed into this sector. There is ample evidence that the willingness of users to pay for new telecommunications capacity will continue to exceed the costs of providing this capacity for the foreseeable future. However, there is at present a significant imbalance between the low tariffs for local calls and the high tariffs for trunk and international calls, which may bias new investment towards long-distance traffic at the expense of local networks.

Therefore the challenge for regulation in this sector centres on investment. Most importantly, a framework must be established in which investors are confident that they will recoup the costs of the sizeable investments required, together with enough of a profit to compensate for the risks involved. In facing this challenge, a number of crucial policy issues for the sector need to be resolved. Firstly, in which parts of the sector is competition desirable? Secondly, what is an appropriate pace for market liberalisation? Thirdly, what is the appropriate regulatory structure in a situation where a degree of monopoly power remains?

Scope for competition

In market economies there has been increasing competition in many parts of the telecommunications sector. The manufacture of equipment is a potentially competitive activity like any other, and in the transition economies this activity has long been separated from the telecommunications operators. The provision of enhanced services and cellular telephony to the final customer can be undertaken by rival operators, provided access to the physical transmission network can be assured on appropriate terms. Competition in cellular telephony has already been introduced in 11 transition economies (see Table P2). Although the fixed network has long been considered a natural monopoly, even this structure is changing, for a number of reasons. First, local radio links (which are not subject to significant scale economies) may soon be sufficiently low-priced to replace fixed links. Second, the falling cost of fibre-optic transmission, as well as the fact that telecommunications services can be bundled with other services, such as cable television or electricity distribution, means that the cost disadvantages of duplicating parts of the main network may be small compared to the overall value of the services provided and to the potential benefits from competition.

In the transition economies, competition in the core telecommunications services (local, domestic long-distance and international services) remains limited. In the great majority of countries, there is still a monopoly telecommunications operator, usually a government enterprise that is both owned and regulated by a government department or ministry. Partial privatisation of the state operator has taken place in five countries (the Czech Republic, Estonia, Kazakstan, Latvia and the Russian Federation) and majority private ownership has been achieved in only one (Hungary). However, this privatisation has only in a few cases been accompanied by general liberalisation, although this is sometimes promised for the future. The move towards liberalisation is most extensive in local services. In Poland, Hungary, Kyrgyzstan, the Russian Federation and the Ukraine, local authorities have legally opened local networks to competition. Poland, the Russian Federation and the Ukraine have also legally opened long-distance telephony to competition, but only the Ukraine has allowed private entry in long-distance and international services through an operating concession.

Tab. P2: Telecommunications Sector

Services legally open to private entry (number of private entrants)	
Cellular telephony:	Albania (1), Belarus (1), Bulgaria (2), Croatia (2), Czech Republic (3), Estonia (3), FYR Macedonia (1), Hungary (3), Kazakstan (1), Latvia (2), Lithuania (3), Poland (3), Romania (1), Russian Federation (9), Slovak Republic (1), Slovenia (2), Ukraine (2) and Uzbekistan (1)
International long- distance services:	Ukraine (1)
Domestic long- distance services:	Poland, Russian Federation and Ukraine (1)
Local services:	Hungary (16),[a] Kyrgyzstan, Poland (14), Russian Federation and Ukraine
Privatisation of dominant operator (share of private ownership)	
	Czech Republic (49 per cent), Estonia (49 per cent), Hungary (67 per cent), Kazakstan (49 per cent), Latvia (49 per cent) and Russian Federation (49 per cent)
Regulatory institutions	
Separate telecoms department within ministry:	Czech Republic[b] and Slovak Republic[c]
Separate telecoms authority:	Hungary and Latvia (for tariffs)[d]
Anti-monopoly office:	Poland[e]

Notes: a) Of the 54 local telephone companies, concessions to operate 16 of these companies have been awarded to consortia that do not include the dominant Hungarian telephone operator, MATAV. b) Ministry of Communications retains authority for licensing new service providers. Authority for resolving disputes over the terms of inter-connection with the fixed network remains unclear. c) Telecommunications office within the Ministry of Transportation, Posts and Telecommunications is responsible for monitoring service quality, while the Ministry itself is the licensing authority. The Ministry of Finance sets tariffs. d) Telecommunications office within the Ministry of Economy proposes tariffs and issues licences for private networks and services, but final decision on tariffs rests with the Ministry of Finance. e) The Telecommunications Law established an independent Tariff Council to set tariffs, while the Ministry of Transport and Communications is responsible for overall telecommunications policy, radio frequency management, mobile licensing and relations with international telecommunications organisations.

Sources: EBRD (1996) and WORLD BANK.

Pace of liberalisation

While it is undoubtedly easier to introduce competition in areas of new technology, such as cellular telephony, where there are fewer entrenched interests at stake, in the rest of the sector difficult questions arise about the appropriate pace at which competition should be introduced. There are at least two reasons why phased competition is desirable. It allows both for an initial period of monopoly profit as an incentive to investors and for a period of learning and adaptation to new conditions. In Hungary, for example, under the terms of the sale of the 30 per cent stake in MATAV (the state operator) to a Deutsche Telekom/Ameritech consortium in 1993, MATAV will enjoy a monopoly position for eight years. Similarly in Estonia, the partially privatised operator Esti Telefon was granted an eight-year exclusive right to provide long-distance services. By contrast, the partial privatisation of the Latvian operator Lattelekom in January 1994 involved a monopoly right for a period of 20 years (subject to some limited rights of competition in enhanced services and the establishment of private networks). The comparison with Estonia and Hungary suggests that such a lengthy period may be an unnecessarily long time to wait for the benefits of liberalisation. With only a distant prospect of competition, there may be limited incentives to invest now in new capacity and service improvements.

International evidence on the value of phased competition for fixed-link telephony is difficult to assess conclusively, but it seems most appropriate where the requirement for network investment is high, as in most transition economies. However, even where phased competition in the market is appropriate, it is desirable to ensure that there is competition for the market – for example, through the award of licences by competitive tender. The main difficulty with phased competition, lies in ensuring that the timetable for liberalisation is credible. Granting monopoly or duopoly rights creates interest groups with a powerful incentive to resist further liberalisation.

Effective regulation

For those activities that remain monopolies, the structure of regulation is of great importance. Only Hungary, Latvia and Poland have seen the establishment of independent regulatory powers. In the great majority of transition economies, price regulation is still carried out by a government ministry, sometimes the same ministry that is responsible for the ownership and management of the sector's assets. The fact that such a ministry is also subject to considerable political pressure has contributed to maintaining tariffs for local services below cost-recovery levels. In the Russian Federation, the effectiveness of regulation is further hampered by the fragmented organisation of the telecommunications system and its control (ARMSTRONG and VICKERS, 1996).

In Poland the responsibility for price regulation lies in the hands of the Anti-Monopoly Office (AMO). This approach has to some extent avoided the difficulties of excessive protection of state-owned firms witnessed elsewhere. Indeed, the AMO has ruled against the state-owned operator on several occasions. However, in its implementation, a number of issues emerge. First, the Ministry of Communications issues permits for new service providers, but remains the owner of the dominant operator. Second, the legal framework for the terms of access to the fixed network remains unclear. Third, despite the AMO's efforts, the tariff structure still discourages investors from entering the market for local services, where licensing is more liberal.

There are also more general issues raised by relying on AMOs to regulate telecommunications tariffs. While it is beneficial to have regulation carried out independently of a Ministry of Communications, assigning the responsibility to a general competition authority tends to confuse the task of creating competition and regulating prices in its absence. Many transition economies need to establish the principle that competition policy is not merely price control in disguise, and allowing competition authorities to retain price control makes the establishment of that principle more difficult. Also, there is no good argument for the pooling of expertise, since the nature of the training and skill required to regulate telecommunications is very different from that of more general anti-trust policy.

In Hungary, an attempt has been made to overcome regulatory uncertainty by making use of the provisions of contract law. The concession granted to MATAV in 1993 offers an eight-year monopoly in the supply of long-distance and international services, in 29 of the country's 54 local districts. This monopoly is conditional on performance targets with respect to the rate of growth of installed exchange lines. It is also conditional on a price-cap formula that allows retail prices to rise by 7.5 per cent per annum in real terms, and this is reviewed every four years (by the Minister for Transport, Telecommunications and Water Management). Although the terms of this review are potentially politically charged, the fact that it must take place after four years represents a constructive attempt to use the greater certainty of contract law to mitigate the vagaries of regulatory politics in the interests of creating greater certainty for investment. In some transition economies, contract law is as uncertain as regulatory politics, but the solution seems well-adapted to circumstances in Hungary.

4.2 Electric Power

Challenges

The immediate challenge is to provide electricity tariffs that reflect costs and to enforce payment by electricity users. These measures would lead to a long-term decline in the electricity intensity of the transition economies from the current high levels documented in section 2. It would be wrong to conclude, however, that the region's power generation capacity is likely to adequately meet power needs in the medium term, particularly where there is a strong recovery in economic output. This is due to the fact that much of the current capacity is in very poor condition, due to years of inadequate maintenance, and many generating units will have to be closed, and many more upgraded and fitted with pollution control mechanisms. Moreover, there is significant scope for improved efficiency in the management of existing assets in the sector. In many ways, the need to encourage investment in existing and new assets in the sector raises similar issues for electricity as for telecommunications.

Tariff reform is thus necessary to ensure adequate incentives for investments that use the most appropriate form of energy and that encourage investment in existing and new assets. Users of electricity must make current investment decisions in the knowledge that the tariffs they will face will reflect the true costs of electricity production to the economy, particularly since the prices of tradable forms of energy (oil and gas) have reached international levels in much of the region. Tariff reform is also necessary to raise the returns and reduce the risks of investment in the electric power sector itself, given that tariffs in this sector have been historically low. Furthermore, there is a need for credible environmental regulation of electricity, and tariffs must reflect the costs of regulated environmental standards.

There is also significant potential for the restructuring of the electric power sector so as to allow greater competition. Electricity generation (which is potentially competitive) can be separated from high-voltage transmission (which is a natural monopoly). This in turn can be separated from local distribution, where there are elements of natural monopoly alongside the potential for limited competition.

Tariff reform

The electricity users with the greatest medium-term potential for investment in energy-saving techniques are companies, and the establishment of cost-reflective tariffs is therefore a matter of urgency for them. However, in most countries the discrepancy between prices and costs is greatest for households, with their low average income limiting the scope for closing the gap quickly. Some progress has been made in raising tariffs in recent years (usually because of fiscal pressures), although there remains a considerable way to go, particularly in the countries at early and intermediate stages of transition (EBRD, 1996, Chapter 3). Households are responsible for much of the peak energy demand (which is supplied by generating units with the highest marginal costs and often with the most polluting plant). It is uncertain how sensitive household demand is to prices, but there may be substantial efficiency gains to be made from better management of this demand. Given the legacy of low tariffs in transition economies, as well as the potential importance of electricity in household budgets, the challenge is to find ways of structuring tariffs so that they are perceived as both fair and efficient.

The perception of fairness is important, particularly given the poor payment records of both households and enterprises, and the widespread theft in some countries. Raising household electricity tariffs to cover costs fully would have a significant impact on the real incomes of households (unlike with telecommunication charges). While there is evidence that this impact is not generally regressive, some poorer households would be severely affected. It is important, therefore, to ensure that other tax-and-benefit policies are implemented in order to minimise the impact on poorer households.

Factors other than the overall income distribution may also affect the perceived legitimacy of electricity charges, and therefore the willingness of customers to pay. If large and well-connected state-owned enterprises fail to pay their bills and are not cut off (as has happened in a number of countries, including the Russian Federation and the Ukraine), there will be severe resentment if smaller enterprises or households are penalised for non-payment. This suggests that policies to improve payment need to be introduced broadly and systematically so that any burden is perceived as being distributed equally.

As emphasised in section 3, privatisation in the electricity supply industry can play an instrumental role in establishing credible economic tariffs (NEWBERRY, 1996a).

Hungary provides a good example of such a process at work, in that the government's efforts to privatise electricity distribution companies in 1992-93 failed to meet its expectations of sales values, because investors lacked confidence in the future regulation of tariffs. These problems were addressed by establishing a more credible tariff policy, including the separate energy regulatory authority, and eight electricity companies successfully privatised in early 1996. In contrast, the inclusion of 30 per cent of the main vertically integrated company in the Czech voucher privatisation scheme and of 49 per cent of the Russian companies in similar schemes has involved no such pressure for improved regulation.

Effective price regulation

As with telecommunications, an important task is to separate regulation from the state's responsibilities of owning and managing assets in the electricity sector. There has been a variety of approaches adopted by transition economies, as Table P3 indicates. In some countries, prices are regulated by a branch of government that is separate from the energy ministries, although in such circumstances it is important to ensure that environmental and safety issues are not neglected. In Hungary and the Russian Federation, a separate regulatory authority for energy as a whole has been established. It is too early to tell how effectively these agencies will be able to function, since it is unclear whether they will be able to operate with real autonomy. For example, the Federal Energy Commission in the Russian Federation is the successor to an earlier body that was widely criticised for having few powers and no real independence, since it was composed mainly of industry representatives. It has now been restructured to allow consumer representation and has been granted enhanced powers to gather information, but the effectiveness of these changes has yet to be tested.

The energy sector could be regulated as a whole, rather than through separate regulators for electricity, gas and other energy forms. The case for an integrated approach may be strongest in those parts of the former Soviet Union where natural gas is in plentiful supply but where international trade in gas is limited by security concerns in importing countries and the inadequacy of pipeline facilities. The choice of techniques and the location of plants in electricity generation should be made on the basis of coherent long-term decisions about the prices not only of electricity but also of different kinds of fuel. Again, this task could be made easier by an integrated approach to regulation for the sector as a whole. A single regulatory agency could however be particularly vulnerable to special interest groups, especially in resource-rich countries.

The environment and nuclear safety

Environmental regulation by an energy ministry which continues to own the assets of, or be closely identified with the interests of the industry is certainly undesirable. Such regulation is expensive and will tend to be resisted within the industry itself. The alternatives are regulation by either a general environmental agency or by whichever agency is charged with regulating other aspects of electricity. The advantage of the former is that it enables an integrated and coherent approach to overall environmental regulation. It also ensures that the political difficulties faced by the industry in raising tariffs do not provide an incentive for lax enforcement of environmental standards.

The regulation of nuclear safety poses particularly difficult problems, since it is often the most dangerous plants that provide cheap, base-load power and which the national authorities are therefore most reluctant to shut down. Since nuclear safety has significant cross-border implications, the effectiveness of this regulation is an entirely proper matter for international concern and negotiation.

Tab. P3: Electricity Sector

Comprehensive unbundling (number of enterprises)	
Generation:	Armenia (5), Hungary (8), Poland (35), Slovenia Ukraine (6)
Distribution:	Armenia (53), Belarus (6), Czech Republic (8), Hungary (6), Poland (33), Russian Federation (72), Slovak Republic (3), Ukraine (27)
Independent power generators	
(number of projects)	Hungary (3), Czech Republic (1)
Privatisations[a] (number of privatised enterprises)	
Integrated utilities:[b]	Czech Republic (1),[c] Kazakstan (1)[d], Russian Federation (1)[e]
Generators:	Hungary (3), Kazakstan (1), Poland (1)
Distributors:	Czech Republic (8),[f] Hungary (6), Russian Federation (27)[g]
Regulatory institutions	
Separate department within ministry:	Armenia,[h] Belarus, Bulgaria[i], Georgia Lithuania,[j] Ukraine[k]
Separate energy authority:	Hungary, Russian Federation
Anti-monopoly office:	Kazakstan, Kyrgyzstan

Notes: a) Including partial divestiture. b) Including regional integrated utilities. c) CEZ (Czech Power Company) (high-voltage transmission and some generation) partially privatised using vouchers. d) Regional integrated utility, Almaty. e) RAO EES Rossii (Russian Joint Stock Company for Electric Power and Electrification) (high-voltage transmission and some generation) partially privatised using vouchers and through direct sales to insiders. f) Partially privatised using vouchers. g) Partially privatised to insiders, with the remaining shares owned by the integrated utility, RAO EES Rossii (high-voltage transmission and some generation). h) State Committee on Prices deals with tariff issues; an independent regulatory authority is to be established. i) Committee on Energy, which reports to Council of Ministers. j) Establishing an Independent Regulatory Agency. As an interim step the government has established an Energy Pricing Council, which submits proposals to the Cabinet. k) An independent regulatory authority is to be created as part of the 1995 reorganisation of the Ministry of Power.

Sources: EBRD (1996)and WORLD BANK, various sources.

Scope for competition

There has been significant restructuring in the electricity sector even without privatisation, with considerable separation of distribution companies both from each other and from the grid, and some separation of generation as well (see Table P3). In some countries, such as the Russian Federation, this restructuring involves basically the creation of regional monopolies (distribution, vertical integration of regional transmission and generation, and the national grid provides the means for trade between these monopolies; the grid also has large shareholdings in the regional companies). Since the distribution companies may be able to pass on their costs of generation to the customer, the presence of the grid provides no real incentive to generate electricity efficiently.

Elsewhere, there is potentially a more competitive structure in which generation, transmission and distribution are fully separated in order to break up both generation and distribution into separate operating companies. Armenia has five generating companies, Hungary eight, Poland 35 and the Ukraine six. It can be argued that at least the larger countries (the Czech Republic, Hungary, Poland, Romania, the Russian Federation and the Ukraine) should eventually be able to privatise a sufficient number of separate generation companies to ensure reasonable competition (a minimum of five companies is an appropriate rule of thumb; NEWBERY, 1996a). However, the short-term prospects for competition in the market for power generation is limited by the sector's lack of financial viability, given the current tariff levels and structures.

In the meantime, the unbundling of the electricity sector provides scope for competition in the right to supply the market, through bidding for long-term contracts, provided access by private suppliers to the grid can be ensured on non-discriminatory terms (BACON, 1995; BESANT-JONES, 1996). This approach relies on long-term "take-or-pay" contracts with independent power producers, which ensure vigorous competition for contracts, but which provide weaker incentives for efficiency improvements after contracts have been signed. Although distribution cannot be a competitive activity, except for the supply of retail services to certain large customers, the separation of distribution companies from each other at least provides for accounting transparency and consequently makes it easier for price regulation to be based on comparative cost or "benchmark" information.

4.3 Transport

Challenges

In transport, considerations of overall system capacity are less significant than the geographical and functional mismatch between the components and quality of transport infrastructure and likely future demand. As trade patterns in transition economies reorient themselves towards existing market economies, there is a need for new and expanded westward links, by road, rail, sea and air. Rail use (relative to GDP) is still very high in comparison with industrialised market economies, but has declined sharply in the transition. The changing market share in favour of road transport reflects the more diversified composition of production in the transition. In addition, transport networks are often in poor condition and not as effectively managed as they could be. Major investments are required in maintenance and in upgrading the quality of existing infrastructure in line with market demands, and more effective management is required.

To find the right balance between competition and regulation in the transport sector, it is necessary to examine the scope for competition, the type of regulation needed and the role that governments should play.

The scope for competition in transport depends largely on the specific characteristics of individual modes of transport and on the existence of alternative modes which can provide competitive services in the same markets. The distinction between competition within the market and competition for the market is particularly important in this sector. Competition in the market can take place between firms in the same mode of transport – intra-modal competition – or between firms in different modes (road or rail, for example) competing in the market for the same service, namely transport between two points. Competition for the market takes place when different firms compete for the right to provide a service for a given period of time (urban bus franchise) or to build and operate infrastructure under a concession agreement (toll motorway concession). Transport modes differ regarding the potential scope for each type of competition, and the extent of institutional and financial restructuring that needs to be undertaken first.

Government strategic planning and regulation have important roles in transport infrastructure investment. These roles reflect the influence of transportation on many aspects of economic activity and social life and its impact on land use and the environment. These considerations mean that uncoordinated and unregulated private investment cannot be expected to respond adequately to the needs of the economy and society as a whole.

Competition within the market

Competition within the market is usually more feasible and desirable for the supply of transport services than that of transport infrastructure. Certain services, such as road haulage, inter-city coach services and air transport, can be opened up fairly fully to competition, and experience in market economies provides valuable lessons. In transition economies there has been extensive privatisation and liberalisation of road haulage, often as part of a process of the divesting of services by large vertically integrated enterprises. Hungary and Poland, for example, liberalised and privatised their road haulage services from existing local public enterprises and own-account fleets. Because of the large number of these privatised service enterprises, as well as the lack of significant economies of scale in such activities, this has resulted in *de facto* liberalisation of haulage markets. In some countries however there are still significant obstacles to entry. These include difficulties in obtaining operating licences, or preferential contracting policies by state authorities. There has been less progress in liberalisation of inter-city bus transport.

Although the deregulation of road haulage, inter-city bus services and air transport in market economies has not been problem-free, existing evidence strongly suggests that general restrictions on entry into these markets serve no useful purpose, and that the amount of institutional restructuring required prior to open competition is minimal (MORRISON and WINSTON, 1986; MCGOWAN and SEABRIGHT, 1989; THOMPSON and WHITFIELD, 1995).

Introducing competition among train-operating companies is more complex. It can require a large amount of enterprise restructuring, regulatory frameworks for gaining fair access to tracks, mechanisms for allocating capacity, and new contractual frameworks between infrastructure owners and operators to ensure safe and reliable services. There are basically three ways in which railways can be restructured, and each creates different potentials for competition. The first is to put the railway infrastructure under the direct managerial responsibility of the main passenger or freight operator which uses it and to charge other operators which might also use it for access. The second is to establish infrastructure as a separate internal business within an integrated railway and then to create an internal market with the freight and passenger division. The third approach is to establish the infrastructure business as a separate corporation, so that commercial relationships with freight and passenger operating companies are formalised in legal contracts.

Each of these approaches aims at creating scope for competition by unbundling vertically integrated railways, and each has advantages and disadvantages which vary with the particular circumstances of the railway. EU directives require the second approach, and they may be strengthened in due course to require the third. However, EU countries, with the exception of Great Britain, have not embraced the notion of competition among railway operators.

Most countries in transition have recognised the need to adapt their railways to the market economy. Some are in the planning stages of reform, and a few have begun the process of vertical unbundling. The latter countries include Bulgaria, the Czech Republic, Hungary, Poland, Romania, the Russian Federation, and Slovenia (see Table P4). In comparison with railway restructuring in western Europe and other industrialised countries, the envisaged pace of change is very rapid, given the extensive use of railways under central planning and the sharp decline in demands for their services in the transition. These plans must recognize the impact of strong competition from other modes of transport, but there remains the need to continually re-appraise productivity targets, equipment utilisation and unit cost levels.

Tab. P4: Transport Sector

Functional separation of state railways:[a]	Bulgaria, Czech Republic, Hungary, Poland, Romania, Russian Federation[b] and Slovenia
Concessions for ports and airports: (number of projects)	Hungary (1), Kazakstan (1) and Turkmenistan (2)
Motorway concessions: (number of projects)	Hungary (2), Poland (bidding stage) and Romania (bidding stage)
Regulatory institutions: (separate motorways authority)	Hungary, Poland, Romania

Notes: a)The functional separation of railways involves establishing separate operating units within the state railway along functional lines, typically, freight haulage, passenger services and infrastructure (tracks, signalling, stations). b)Commitment under the 1995 Statement of Modernisation Strategy and Commercialisation Principles for Russian Railways.

Sources: EBRD (1996) and WORLD BANK.

The fact that the vertical unbundling of infrastructure and service operations can create scope for competition within the market, applies to other modes of transport as well. For example, the joint operation and management of airport and airline services in transition economies is a practice inherited from the integrated structures of the past, and is a system which hampers competition. There are no financial or practical reasons for maintaining airports and airline operations together. Moreover, there is ample scope for introducing competition in airline services and to a lesser extent in airport management. After the US experience with deregulation, the scope for introducing viable competition in the provision of commercial aviation services is no longer in doubt. Airports represent a case where ownership of infrastructure can be successfully separated from the running of airport services, such as runway maintenance or baggage handling, with the possible exception of air traffic control.

Competition for the market

Competition for the market can provide for private participation and efficiency gains in many areas of transport infrastructure provision and management, such as road and rail track maintenance, the construction and operation of toll motorways, airport terminals and port berths. Through competitive bidding for the right to provide and/or manage a given infrastructure facility or support service for a period of time, or to undertake a particular investment, it is possible to achieve significant cost reductions and service quality improvements. In the Russian Federation, for instance, competitive bidding for road maintenance works was introduced in 1994, leading to increased competition in the selection of contractors and to a reduction in costs per unit of lane-kilometre of road upgrading work being contracted (BOUSQUET and QUEIROZ, 1996). Likewise, open tendering for major road works is becoming common practice in Romania as part of the restructuring of the road sector, including the construction industry and the Ministry of Transport.

Concessions to build and operate parts of the transport infrastructure can also attract private participation and new investment into the sector. Toll motorway concessions have been granted in Hungary and are at the bidding stage in Poland and Romania (see Table P4). In principle, the use of tolls means that such concessions can involve 100 per cent private finance. However, traffic flows in most road corridors in the region are not yet sufficient to bear the full cost of upgrading to high-standard, dual-carriageways. Nevertheless, motorways typically have social rates of return well in excess of their private rates of return because of their contribution to reducing congestion and accidents and creating new land use opportunities, although in some circumstances they may impose significant environmental costs of their own. Where private rates of return are inadequate to make the project independently viable, this suggests that public-private partnerships, in which the state contributes a subsidy in recognition of the social benefits thereby created, may make an important contribution to mobilising investment finance in this sector.

Concessions for other elements of the transport infrastructure (airports and ports) can work in similar ways to those discussed for toll motorways. Four such concessions are in operation in the transition economies.

Regulation

The nature of necessary regulation depends very much on the nature of prevailing and potential competition. When inter-modal competition is strong and there are no artificial barriers to entry into the market, there appears to be little reason for price regulation. While the safety aspects of road and air transport usually need specialised regulatory expertise, evidence from market economies suggests that, provided the conditions for granting licences to operators are reasonably clear and non-discriminatory, and that an appropriate safety regime is properly enforced, regulation of the general process of competition in the provision of these services can be left to competition agencies.

Even in the presence of strong inter-modal competition, however, the relationship between modes of transport is complex and will require some co-ordination as well as competition. For example, the development of airports requires a consideration of road and rail links; the scope for seaports to handle container traffic depends on the quality of rail links as well as on the presence of inland container terminals. For these reasons, decisions about the location of infrastructure investment requires regulatory supervision by local and/or national planning authorities. However, since these decisions usually have significant consequences for the profitability of existing service operators, such authorities can come under strong pressure to favour established operators against new entrants. A strong presumption in favour of competition and rights of new entrants is therefore appropriate.

When there is competition for the market, a certain amount of regulation is necessary to monitor compliance with the concession agreements signed between the public authorities and the private concessionaires. In addition, it is necessary to have an arbitration authority, which need not be a specialised one, to resolve disputes that may arise between the parties in cases of non-compliance. It is essential to ensure the independence of these regulatory bodies as well as to limit their proliferation. In Hungary, Poland and Romania, independent authorities have been established to oversee the toll motorway concession (see Table P4).

Government credibility and consistency is vital if private participation in transport infrastructure investment is to be encouraged. The cancellation of toll road projects, after the private sector has committed significant resources to the projects, has occurred in some countries in the region, and such reversals will undoubtedly make it difficult to attract investment in similar projects in future.

Government will continue to play an active role in some transport sub-sectors, due to the inherent obstacles to efficient resource allocation posed by the fact that prices faced by alternative competing modes do not reflect true social costs. This is the case in urban transport, where basic economic principles suggest that pricing may require government subsidies to operators to support public transport, which is needed to reduce urban congestion and pollution levels. The degree of subsidy required will also depend on the complementary policies adopted with respect to taxation of private transport. For example, if congestion pricing could be adopted for roads, private car transport would become significantly more expensive, and public transport could compete without the need for large subsidies. Although market economies have been slow to consider the adoption of congestion pricing for roads, this is no reason for transition economies not to learn from earlier experiences.

5. Summary and Conclusions

Infrastructure in the transition economies requires substantial restructuring. Section 2 of this chapter characterises the restructuring requirements in the telecommunications, electric power and transport sectors in the region.

The supply of telecommunication services in transition economies is scarce and poor in quality. The network densities are low compared with those in the EU, the waiting times for access to services are long, and there is a high frequency of line faults. Tariff structures fall relatively heavily on businesses and more lightly on households, and the overall level of tariffs remains low in most countries. There is a substantial need for investment in this sector, in order to expand capacity and improve service quality. Annual investment in telecommunications, in upper-middle income developing countries with similar network densities as those in transition economies, averages about 4 per cent of GDP (compared with about 1 per cent in the EU).

The main legacies in the power sector are high electricity intensities of output, existing overcapacities of supply facilities (albeit needing maintenance and renewal), poor environmental performance and, in some countries, nuclear safety concerns. The inadequate levels, structure and collection of tariffs hinder demand-side efficiency and make investment in existing and new assets in the electric power sector unattractive. Cash-strapped utility companies are often primarily concerned with the immediate need to purchase fuel to meet demand and have insufficient funds with which to improve operating and environmental performance and, in some cases, nuclear safety.

In the transport sector, there is a functional mismatch between the inherited components of the transport infrastructure and market demands. Given the shift in composition of output, toward higher value-added products, and the increased demand for personal transport, there is likely to be a shift towards greater reliance on road services. In fact, there has already been a sharp decline in demand for freight services, which in eastern Europe has fallen particularly heavily on the railways. However, the current structure of railway tariffs (and fuel taxes) runs the risk of encouraging an excessive substitution of road for rail-based services, and this should be realigned. Estimates of annual investment requirements in eastern European road and railway rehabilitation and development range between 2 and 3 per cent of the eastern European GDP over the next decade (NEWBERY, 1996a)

In view of these major challenges, it is imperative to ask what government policies can bring about the necessary tariff reforms and restructuring of infrastructure. For enterprises in general, governments typically rely on hard budget constraints, privatisation and product market competition to induce restructuring. But each of these policies can become problematic when applied to an infrastructure sector. Sections 3 and 4 of this chapter sought to identify ways in which these problems could be overcome.

A more commercial approach to infrastructure, including greater private participation, is an effective means for facilitating tariff reform and expanding access to private finance for investment, which have the effect of hardening the budget constraints of infrastructure enterprises. In particular, by creating a constituency for their attainment, private participation in infrastructure can promote the establishment of cost-reflective tariffs and financial autonomy of infrastructure enterprises.

The commercialisation of infrastructure enterprises, selective private entry and privatisation, moreover, are measures which aim to change the objectives of infrastructure service providers the constraints under which they operate, and the composition of service providers through market selection. While experience with commercialisation of infrastructure remains limited in terms of duration, experience in developing countries suggests that greater private involvement may be required. Selective private entry into infrastructure has been most extensive in the telecommunications sector, where there is both insufficient capacity and scope for competitive service provision. In contrast, privatisation has most frequent in the power sector, where existing capacity is adequate but where tariff reform and improvements in operational performance are required.

The privatisation of existing infrastructure enterprises has proceeded more slowly than selective private entry. This form of private participation can require two types of institutional change: the restructuring of enterprises before their privatisation, and the creation of effective regulatory institutions. Nevertheless, considerable progress in transition, as measured by the EBRD's transition indicators, appears necessary for both selective private entry and privatisation.

Policies which are complementary to commercial infrastructure are the introduction of competition in service provisions where possible and of effective regulation where it is not.

Although the particular regulatory challenges vary across the sectors, two common themes emerge. First, competition for the right to supply the market is possible and important – in particular where competition in the market is either impossible or unlikely to be achieved in the short term. Competition in the market can be quickly achieved in some activities, as with cellular telephony and road haulage, although the scope for competitive provision in telecommunications extends well beyond cellular services. Electricity generation, airports, ports and toll motorways are services where competition for the market has the potential to increase efficiency and encourage private investment in infrastructure in transition economies and thus to promote its restructuring.

Second, independent yet accountable regulatory institutions are needed to oversee competition for the market, to guard against the abuse of monopoly power and to take into account the environmental impacts of infrastructure, such as pollution and urban congestion. There is no recent history with independent regulatory institutions in transition economies, and only limited progress has so far been made in the establishment of regulatory institutions that are separate from the government ministries which oversee infrastructure sectors. Given the time required to establish effective institutions, the initial steps towards their creation should not be delayed.

Endnotes

[1] This paper draws extensively from chapters 3 to 5 of the *Transition Report 1996: Infrastructure and Savings*, a product of the Office of the Chief Economist at EBRD. The views expressed in the paper are not necessarily those of the EBRD. Comments and information from Egbert Jöhrens, Christof Rülh, and Paul Seabright are gratefully acknowledged. An earlier version of the paper was presented at the international conference "Competition in Network Industries: Telecommunications, Energy and Transportation in Europe and Russia" organised by the European Institute for International Economic Relations and held in Potsdam on 21-23 November 1996.

[2] See INTERNATIONAL TELECOMMUNICATIONS UNION/OECD (1992, 1994a) and CAMPBELL (1995) for analyses of telecommunications in transition economies.

[3] See EBRD (1996), Chapter 2 for a discussion of measuring stages of transition and the classification of countries.

[4] Northern America refers to Canada and the United States

[5] The impact of the low tariffs on demand depends on the price elasticity of demand, which is smaller in the short term than in the long term, when power consumers can adjust the number and type of electrical appliances, production processes and even the location of electricity-intensive industries. Price elasticities within transition countries are difficult to estimate, as the price effects are particularly difficult to distinguish from structural changes in the demand pattern caused by other factors

[6] It is instructive to compare this experience with EU railways, which have faced decades of increasing competition from road haulage and of declining heavy industries. Rail freight transport measured in tonne-kilometres in the EU has declined by about 22 per cent over the last 25 years, while the railways' share of the freight market share has halved to about 15 per cent. The loss of rail freight traffic in eastern Europe, the Baltics and the CIS has had the effect, therefore, of compressing decades of gradual market-driven change in the EU into a few years. The organisation, management structures and operating methods of the railways in the region, however, are very similar to those in the EU 20 years ago. Railways in eastern Europe and the Baltics need to reform at a faster rate and more successfully than EU railways in order to secure an effective long-term role in freight transport.

[7] Information provided by DRI/McGraw-Hill from their database.

[8] WORLD BANK (1996a), Chapter 2, argues that progress in transition is necessary for control of fiscal and quasi-fiscal deficits and macroeconomic stabilisation

References

ARMSTRONG, M. ,S. COWAN and J. VICKERS (1994), Regulatory Reform: Economic Analysis and the British Experience, MIT Press, Cambridge, Mass.

CAMPBELL, R. (1995), Soviet and Post-Soviet Telecommunications: An Industry Under Reform, Westview Press, Boulder Co.

References

ARMSTRONG, M. ,S. COWAN and J. VICKERS (1994), Regulatory Reform: Economic Analysis and the British Experience, MIT Press, Cambridge, Mass.

CAMPBELL, R. (1995), Soviet and Post-Soviet Telecommunications: An Industry Under Reform, Westview Press, Boulder Co.

BACON, R. (1995), Competitive Contracting for Privately Generated Power, Private Sector, No.3, pp.23-26.

BOUSQUET, F. and C. QUEIROZ (1996), Road Management in Russia, World Bank Internal Discussion Paper, Europe and Central Asia Region, February.

EBRD (1993a), Railway Sector Survey of Russia, Belarus, Ukraine and Kazakstan, January.

EBRD (1993b), Roads and Road Transport Study. Russia, Belarus, Ukraine and Kazakstan, January.

EBRD (1993c), Transport Sector: Issues and Options, March.

EBRD (1996), Transition Report.

ECMT (1996a), Trends in the Transport Sector 1970-1994, March.

ECMT (1996b), Trends in the Transport Sector in the ECMT Countries in Transition, March.

FOREIGN INVESTMENT ADVISORY SERVICE (1996), Infrastructure services in central and eastern Europe: The current situation, World Bank Background Paper for Vienna Roundtable.

FREUND, C. and C. WALLICH (1996), The welfare effects of raising household energy prices in Poland, The Energy Journal, 17, pp. 53-77.

GASPARD, M. (1996), Transport infrastructure financing in central and eastern Europe, European Commission (DGVII) Working Paper, April.

INTERNATIONAL ENERGY AGENCY (OECD/IEA) (1995), Energy Policies of the Russian Federation, 1995 Survey, OECD, Paris.

INTERNATIONAL ENERGY AGENCY (OECD/IEA) (1996), Energy Policies of Ukraine, 1996 Survey, OECD, Paris.

INTERNATIONAL TELECOMMUNICATIONS UNION/OECD (1992), Telecommunications Indicators of the Former Soviet Union, ITU, Geneva.

INTERNATIONAL TELECOMMUNICATIONS UNION/OECD (1994a), Telecommunications Indicators for Economies in Transition, ITU, Geneva.

INTERNATIONAL TELECOMMUNICATIONS UNION (1994b), Demand for Business-oriented New Telecommunications Services in Central and Eastern European Countries ITU, Geneva.

LANKES, H.P. and A. VENABLES (1996), Foreign direct investment in Eastern Europe and the former Soviet Union, EBRD Policy Studies to Promote Private Sector Development.

McMILLAN, J. (1996), Restructuring enterprises in central and eastern Europe, EBRD Policy Studies to Promote Private Sector Development.

McGOWAN, F. and P. SEABRIGHT (1989), Deregulating European Airlines, Economic Policy, No. 9, pp. 283-344.

MORRISON, S. and C. WINSTON (1986), The Economic Effects of Airline Deregulation, The Brookings Institution, Washington, DC.

NEWBERY, D. (1996), Guidelines for Private Sector Involvement in the Electricity Supply Industry of Eastern Europe, EBRD Policy Studies to Promote Private Sector Development.

PANNIER, D. (ed.) (1996), Corporate governance of public enterprises in transitional economies, World Bank Technical Paper No.323.

THOMPSON, D. and A. WHITFIELD (1995), Express Coaching: Privatisation, Incumbent Advantage and the Competitive Process, in Bishop et al. (1995).

THOMPSON, L. and J. FRASER (1996), Command legacy will take time to overcome, Rail Business Report, Railway Gazette Yearbook 1996, pp. 5-14.

WORLD BANK (1993), Transport Strategies for the Russian Federation. Studies of Economies in Transformation, Washington, DC.

WORLD BANK (1994), World Development Report, Oxford University Press, Oxford.

WORLD BANK (1996a), World Development Report, Oxford University Press, Oxford.

WORLD BANK (1996b), Bureaucrats in Business: The Economics and Politics of Government Ownership, Oxford University Press, Oxford.

Comments on: Restructuring Infrastructure in Transition Economies

Paul J.J. Welfens

The paper by Carbajo and Fries gives a broad overview about the restructuring of telecommunications, electricity and transportation in postsocialist economies of Eastern Europe. The authors at first look at the inherited infrastructure and supply-side shortages relevant for the new market economy framework. They also focus on the pressures and the rationale for a commercial approach in the building and provision of infrastructure. Finally they adopt a two-pronged approach to changes in infrastructure development by taking into account the role of competition and regulation. As the authors show telecoms penetration rates were not only very low in eastern Europe compared to the EU average but the high recorded fault rates imply a much lower availability of network services than penetration rates might suggest. Moreover, there were long waiting times in all socialist economies. One may argue that such long waiting lines create an ideal opportunity to introduce network competition already in the first transition stage. As is well known both the Czech Republic and Hungary opted for mainting a temporary monopoly in the fixed link segment.

The authors emphasize that very high subcription tariffs are levied on business users in countries at intermediate stages of transition. It is unclear how this could be explained; one might assume that with little progress made on the road to the market economy and hence low growth in telephony services the monopolistic operator fully exploits the low price elasticity for telephone subscription of business customers. Once the transition process and economic development take off the optimal strategy for the monopolistic fixed link operator is to reduce subscription rates in order to generate additional telephone revenues from increasing telecommunications.

While excess demand was typical for telephony high supply capacities were available in electricity generation. With prices fixed at low rates the electricity intensity of output was high in socialist times. As adjustment and structural change take their time it is not surprising that the electricity consumption per unit of output is declining only gradually. The authors rightly emphasize variations in electricity intensity among the transition economies. Since industrial output has been falling strongly one should expect a transitory excess supply of electricity until high growth rates of income generate additional demand. Falling output figures in Russia have contributed to a high excess supply in generation and poor prospects for foreign investors in power generation equipment. Arrears to power utilities are a major problem in many transforming economies as is pointed out by the authors.

The discrepancy between effective electricity tariffs in eastern Europe and those of EU countries therefore are even greater than indicated by the high rates for firms and the low rates for households. For political reasons prices for households were kept low in the command economies. It certainly will be difficult to achieve a fast price rebalancing and to eliminate the collection problems in electricity. An interesting aspect emphasized by the authors is that low and inverted tariffs might ultimately have a regressive effect as higher-income households consume relatively more electricity than low-income households. It indeed will be difficult to cope with collection problem as long as government itself does not pay wages regularly. Massive collection lags also point to the erosion of the rule of law. In capital intensive industries non-collection will seriously undermine the generators´ ability for reinvestment and new investment so that negative effects on the labor market and aggregate income development may be expected. Accepting foreign investment in the electricity sector might help to reduce collection problems as firms and households will anticipate that foreign investors are more likely to cut off electricity to non-paying users than nationally owned power generators.

In the field of transportation the problems are somewhat different from those in telecommunications and energy. The main problem with transition is the massive rise of private car ownership and the contradictions between poor road networks and rapidly increased traffic. Low road densities in combination with poor road quality will raise the private and social costs of mobility. Major investments in the road network are required in the context of transformation and economic opening up where an important aspect is that with the integration into the world economy the east-west links and in some countries the north-south links become quite important. High traffic risks and long transportation times are equivalent to a tariff on east-west trade. To the extent that trade is an engine of economic growth it therefore is quite important that adequate modernization and expansion in the road network will take place.

The authors rightly emphasize that for various reasons railways transport is likely to reduce, while road transportation will increase. Rapid restructuring and privatization of the railway system might, however, be a suitable remedy to slow-down the fall of market share of the railway system. In a market economy speed is quite important in transportation. Without a modern ligistics system the railways system can neither optimize its network use nor increase the productivity of its rolling stock. It would take bold decisions to privatize the railway network - or at least part of it - in transforming economies. Looking for a strategic private investor could be an interesting policy option. As regards passenger prices in railway subsidies there used to cross-subsidization in favor of passenger traffic. However, it should be possible to switch to reduced cross subsidization once that two-part tariffs are applied. Fixed costs can be recovered more easily if frequent users have to pay a fixed fee plus a reduced variable rate. Railway operators certainly can increase capacity utilization by offering better services and by introducing differentiated prices for peak hours and non-peak hours for commuters. Additional differentiation for the weekend and late night trips could also be introduced. While the authors argue that tariff reform is a very difficult field for political reasons one could argue that strong price differentiation is the key for success. More price differentiation seems to feasible but more doubtful is that government will come up with sufficient investment funds to modernize the railway system quickly. At the same time truck operators from Western Europe will invade eastern Europe, where entrepreneurs in turn will imitate Western organization schemes. Poorly paid truck drivers from eastern Europe will become increasingly active as workers in the EU. This also reinforces the tendency for rising East-West traffic. Severe fiscal strains have occured in many countries - as emphasized by the authors - but there is still room to undertake more public investment in the Czech Republic, Slovenia and Poland. The alternative is, of course, to rely on public private partnership or to fully rely on private investors which will recover investment costs from private users. France successfully adopted such an approach in the 1960s and 1970s. Indeed operators from France could become major operators in Eastern Europe once major projects are adopted. The authors point in their analysis of options to improve the productivity effect of modern infrastructure to introducing managerial incentive contracts based on performance measures. However, the authors also emphasize that performance-related contracts for public-sector managers are often ineffective. This result from surveys in developing countries underlines the opportunities that could stem from selective private operator market entry.

As regards regulation the authors point out that selling infrastructure enterprises to foreign investors sometimes failed because of insufficient confidence in nacscent regulatory schemes. This indeed point to the two challenges in transformation. Establishing stable governments and reliable regulatory authorities which base their decisions on clear principles. At the same time one can only warn against mass privatization schemes which distribute minority stakes to workers. Rather workers should be entitled to obtain shares from infrastructure funds because otherwise the direct ownership is likely to undermine restructuring efforts and to delay closure of inefficient plants.

As regards regulation and competition the high share of sunk costs in many investment projects creates a typical hold-up problem for the investors. In countries with a weak rule of law one will therefore find underinvestment of private firms in infrastructure. It is up to the government to establish credible rules. It might be wise to follow in an environment of unstable political regimes the Polish example and allocate (in telecommunications) the competence for price regulation to the Anti-Monopoly Office. In telecommunications technological progress supports the introduction of competition. In electricity competition depends less on technology but clearly more on vertical disintegration of the industry. Few countries are likely to follow the bold Polish example which in turn was influence by the British model. One may add that international organizations - especially the EBRD and the EU - have a high responsibility for competition in eastern Europe to the extent that their involvement in financing schemes should facilitate to introduce market elements in the infrastructure sector. While we still see remarkable differences in approaches to infrastructure policies in Eastern Europe the quest for mobile real capital is likely to spread best-practice approaches across transforming economies. For all transforming economies the lessons to learn are hard and the inconveniences of transition are likely to last at least for one more decade. Improving the infrastructure will ultimately spur private sector development and help to intensify competition in goods markets as well as to link eastern Europe and western Europe. The authors give an excellent overview on the situation in transforming economies and remind us of the many hidded reform options in infrastructure policies in the whole of Europe.

Q: Lessons from Restructuring the Energy Sector in East Germany

Georg Erdmann

1. Introduction

The process of restructuring the East German energy sector since 1990 offers an opportunity to study the complex interactions between the overall economic order, in particular the regulations for the energy sector, and the performance of the energy industry. At a first glance, the success story seems to be convincing, particularly if the East German situation is compared to the other countries of the former Comecon block. However, the ambient political decisions concerning the electricity market liberalization on the one hand and the protection of certain ancient structures on the other create a burden for the restructuring process that becomes more and more visible.

2. Change in the East German Energy Sector

Within the short period of 10 years practically the whole Bast German *capital stock* in the energy supply industries will have been renewed and upgraded. Through overall investments in the energy industry of up to 10 bil. DM per year no sector is exempted from this progress. Looking ahead into the year 2000, 80 to 90 percent of all filling stations will be younger than 10 years. A new 4.8 bil. DM oil refinery is already producing close to the city of Halle. The high pressure gas pipeline system is linked with the western grid and will significantly be extended. In the year 2000 about 80 percent of the electricity generation capacity will have been retrofitted or completely rebuilt. The investments are reported to reach 20 bil. DM. In addition the same amount of money will have been invested in lignite extraction that is the major feedstock for the Bast German power plants. Municipal and industrial producers also contribute to the renovation of the energy sector by building new combined heat and power plants and distribution networks. Though district heating is modernized at a slower rate, 7 bil. DM will have been invested into this sector by the year 2000.

Once all these investments are accomplished, a sharp drop in the investment volumes has to be expected. It is unlikely that - as today - one third of all German energy investments will be undertaken in Bast Germany, where only 20 percent of the German population lives and less than 15 percent of the German gross domestic product is generated.

The investments have and will have a strong impact on both the primary energy and final energy structure. While in 1990 significant differences between the Bast and West German structures did exist, small structural differences remain today. In no more than five years most structural differences in the *primary energy shares* disappeared (Fig. Q1). The major remaining difference refers to nuclear energy that had been shut down in Bast Germany due to security issues but had not been in the west.

Fig. Q1: Primary Energy Supply Structure in Germany

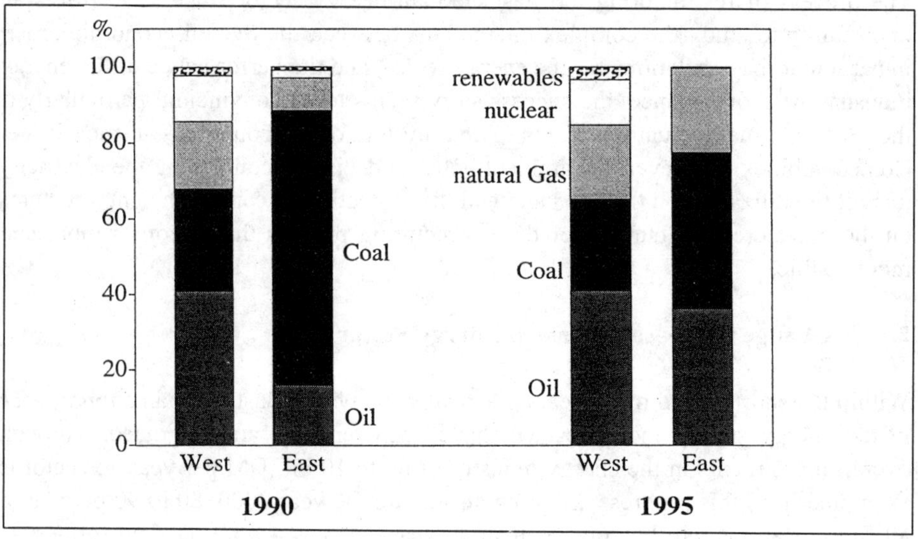

Source: DEUTSCHES INSTITUT FÜR WIRTSCHAFTSFORSCHUNG (1997)

The *final energy* shares are also converging towards western structures (Fig. Q2). In 1995 district heating and coal are more important in the east than in the west but the coal share will continue to decline with the modernization of the building stock.

Fig. Q2: Final Energy Consumption Structure in Germany

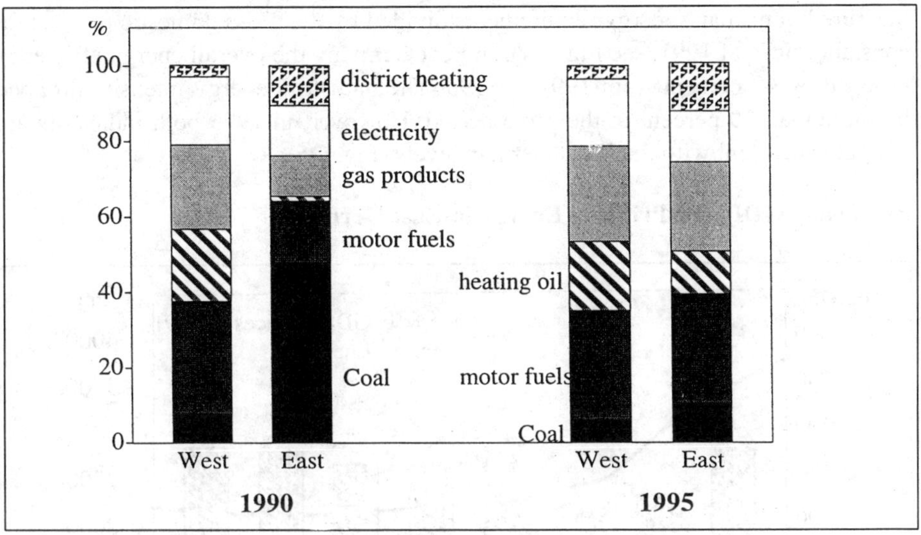

Source: DEUTSCHES INSTITUT FÜR WIRTSCHAFTSFORSCHUNG (1997)

Fig. Q3: Per-capita Primary Energy Consumption

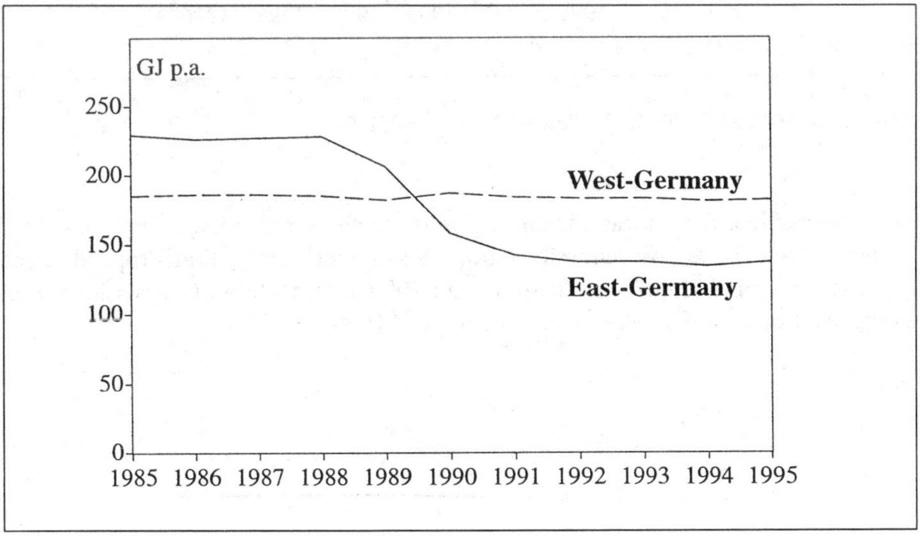

Source: BUNDESMINISTERIUM FÜR WIRTSCHAFT (1997)

The particular speed of the transition in the energy sector is reflected by the improvements of the energy demand per capita (Fig. Q3) and the energy efficiency measured in primary energy requirements divided by the gross domestic product (at constant prices of 1991, see Fig. Q4). In East Germany the overall energy efficiency dropped by 40 percent from 1991 to 1995. The industrial energy intensity dropped by more than 50 percent in the same period. However, in 1995 both indicators are not yet equivalent with the West German levels (Fig. Q5).

Fig. Q4: GDP and Primary Energy in East Germany

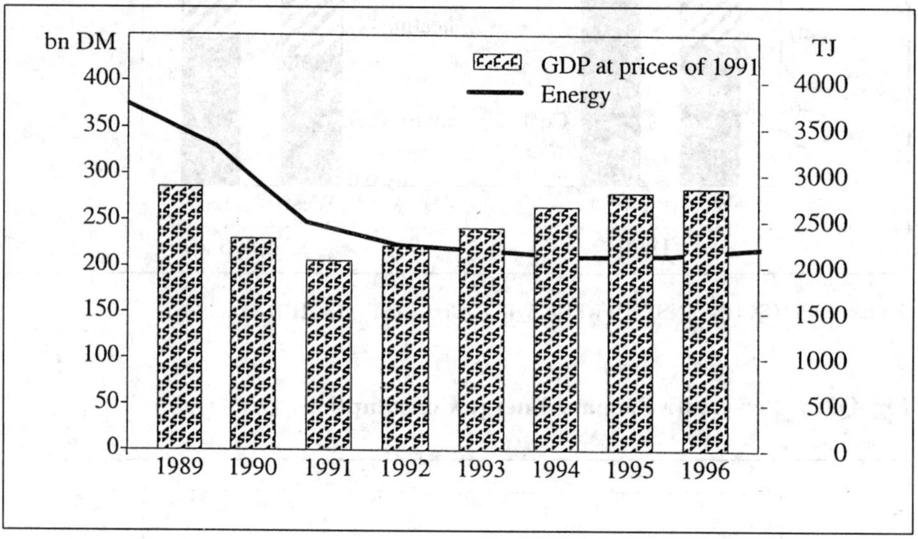

Source: BUNDESMINISTERIUM FÜR WIRTSCHAFT (1997)

A positive side effect of the transformation is the sharp reduction of environmental emissions and risks. Air emissions from fossil fuel combustion dropped to 65 percent (NO_X) and 45 percent (SO_X) of their 1990 values while $C0_2$-emissions came down to 54 percent compared to the situation of 1990.

Fig. Q5: Energy Efficiency in Germany

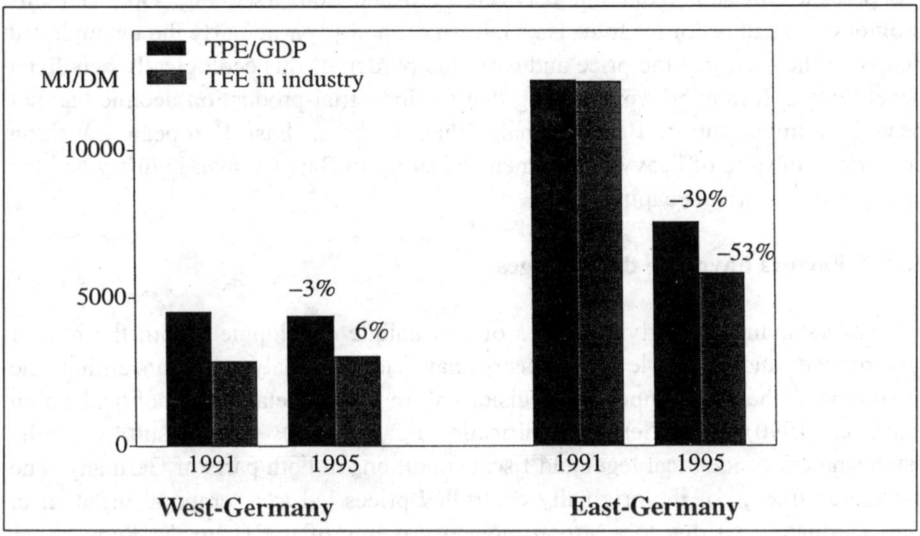

Note: 1991 Prices

Source: BUNDESMINISTERIUM FÜR WIRTSCHAFT (1997)

Fig. Q6: Annual CO_2-Emissions in Germany

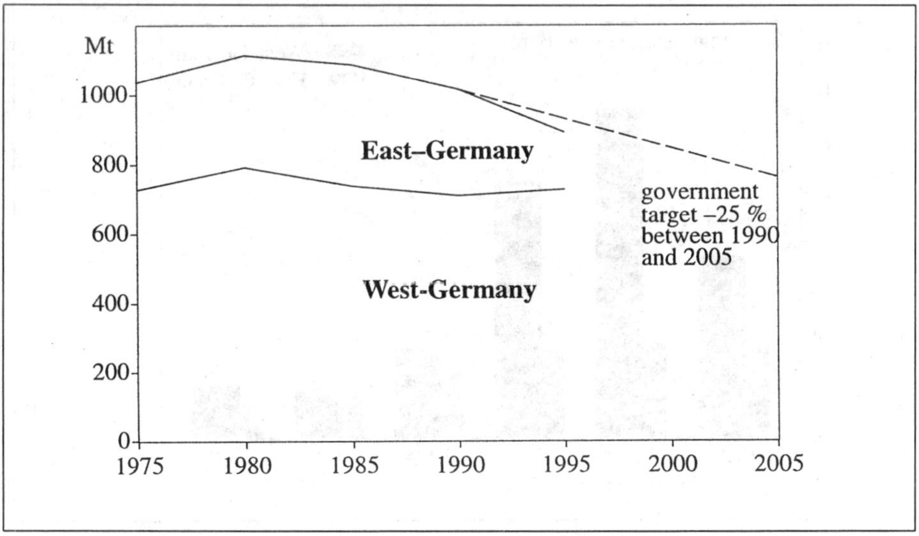

Source: BUNDESMINISTERIUM FÜR WIRTSCHAFT (1997)

This development has contributed to the federal government $C0_2$ reduction target (25 percent emission reduction between 1990 and 2005 (see Fig. Q6). But this progress was and is not for free. The German economy, particularly the unemployed people in the east, pay the price and carry the burden of this ecologically beneficial development. It may be worth noting that the industrial production decline had not been less important in Bast Germany than in other East European transition countries - in spite of heavy government subsidies to Bast German industry and the large inflow of private capital.

3. Factors Favoring the Changes

For understanding the driving forces of this unique development both the role of government and the role of industry have to be analyzed. Concerning the government, the most important decisions were the monetary and political union (summer 1990) and German unification (fall 1990). The result was the establishment of identical legal and fiscal conditions in both parts of Germany. The associated freeing of the originally controlled prices led to a temporal inflation in Bast Germany, but due to a strong monetary policy of the *Deutsche Bundesbank* (implying an increase in unemployment) the inflation was stopped within three years (see Figures Q7 and Q8).

Fig. Q7: Consumer Price Increase in Germany

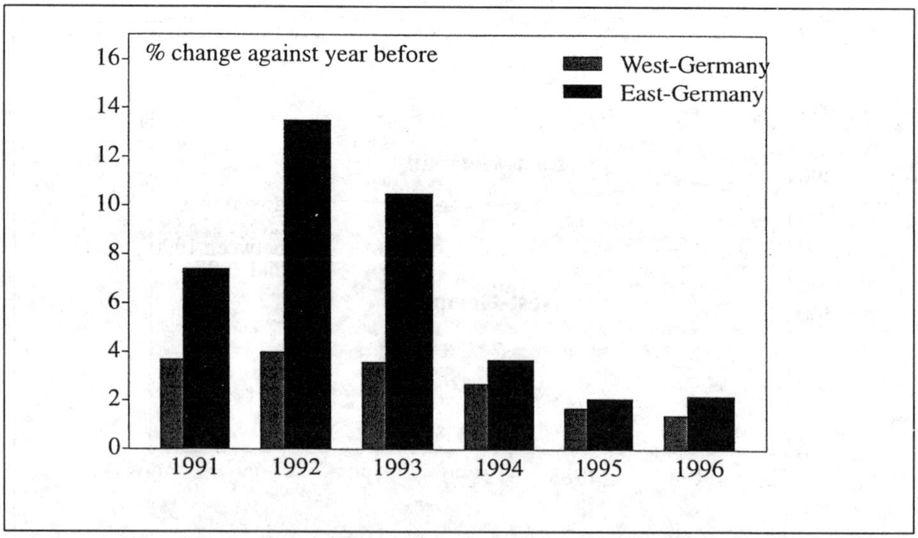

Source: BUNDESMINISTERIUM FÜR WIRTSCHAFT (1997)

Fig. Q8: Energy Price Indices in East Germany 1994

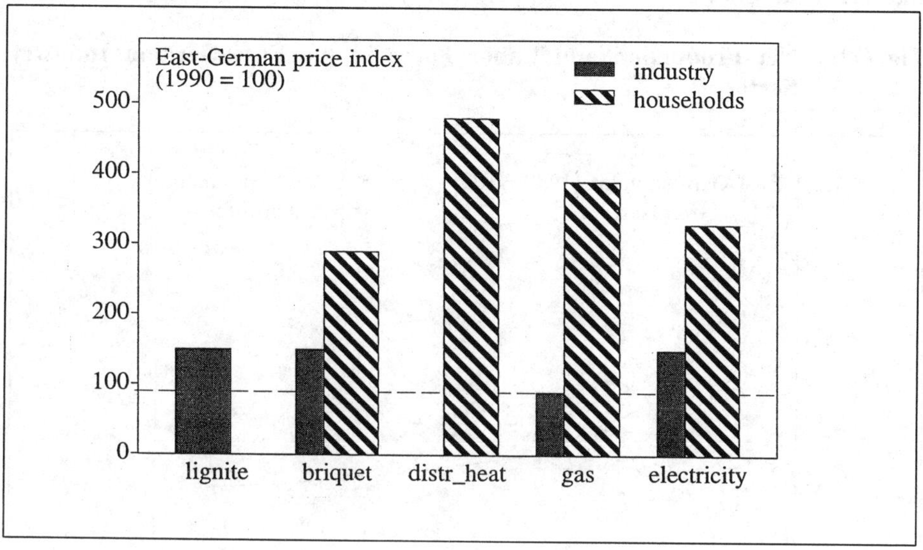

Source: WEISSHEIMER (1995), p. 285.

Another important aspect was - and still is - the large transfer of funds from West to East Germany. It allowed the fast modernization of public infrastructure, the private real estate sector and the rapid shift to western car and household equipment standards. According to estimates published by RWI (1996), public transfers from West to Bast Germany accounted for 7% of West German GDP (1991-1995) and has been financed through

- 43 % higher taxes and social contributions
- 15 % reduction of other government expenditures
- 42% public deficits

The federal government is not yet going to develop strategies about how to gradually reduce these transfers after the year 2003.

A third governmental driving force to mention is the privatization policy of the *Treuhandanstalt* which took over the whole nationalized East German economy in 1990. The key strategic decisions for privatization were (1) rapid sales with substantial prior restructuring; (2) the establishment of a private industrial management (which implied the transformation of many production facilities into subsidiaries of western companies); and (3) the protection of so-called *industrial cores* by compelling the new owners to sustain production capacities in compensation for a low selling price of these facilities (and low cash incomes for the *Treuhandanstalt)*.

Fig. Q9: Net Production and Labor Force in the East German Industry Sector

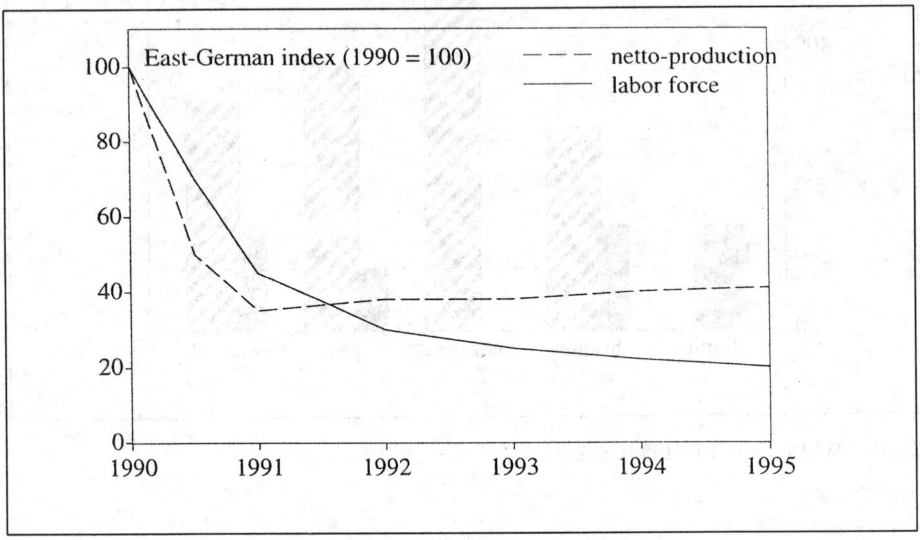

Source: BUNDESMINISTERIUM FÜR WIRTSCHAFT (1997)

Concerning the driving forces from the private sector, the supply of private capital and private investors should first be mentioned. Practically at no time was there a lack of private investors in the Bast German energy sector, and this was due to

- the expectation of controlling promising energy markets as privileged suppliers (and avoiding the emergence of potential competitors from Bast Germany in the western part of the country);
- significant tax incentives *(50* percent depreciation allowances which reduced both the corporate and the private income tax bills); and
- direct investment subsidies (10 percent of the investment volume on average) and financial support by subsidized credits and guarantees (20 to 30 percent of the investment volume on average).

However, the rate-of-return of many of these private investments is challenged by a sharp decline of the industrial production and the associated decline in purchasing power and in energy demand, particularly electricity demand. Between 1989 and

1992 the electricity sales in Bast Germany declined from 88 TWh to 52 TWh (-41 percent). Thus obsolete energy supply capacities were able to be removed without any supply shortages, but the capacity utilization of the new investments is still comparatively low.

4. Unresolved Issues and Problems

The weak performance of the recovery policy leads to the unresolved issues and problems of the Bast German energy markets. One of the striking facts in Bast Germany is that, in spite of rather favorite political and financial conditions, economic growth is rather weak. According to many experts the main reason for it is the spread between the wages and the labor productivity (Fig. Q10). The productivity gap was larger in 1991 than today, but the West German figures are by far not yet reached.

Fig. Q 10: Wages and Productivity in the Industry Sector of East Germany

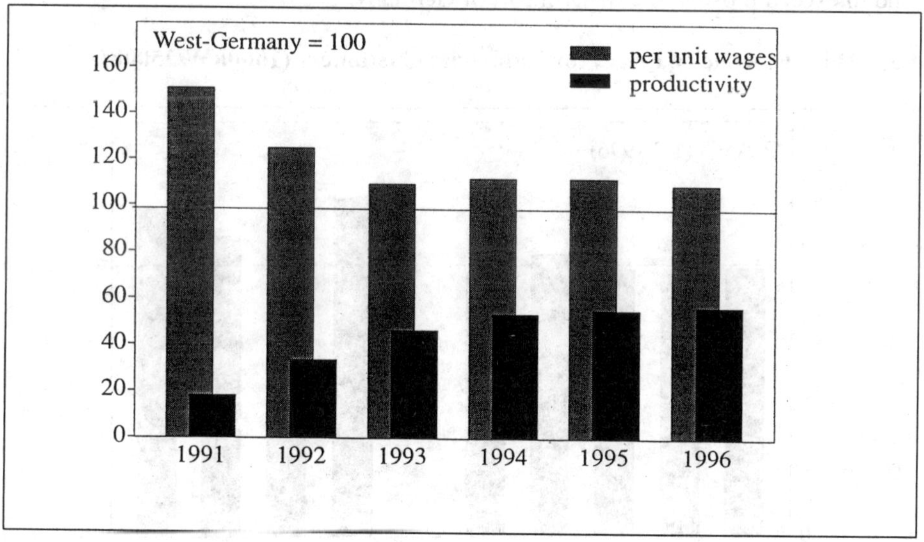

Note: Nominal figures

Source: DEUTSCHES INSTITUT FÜR WIRTSCHAFTSFORSCHUNG (1997)

To reduce the unemployment rates below 20 percent, a lot of measures were taken - starting from early retirement programs and schooling to construction and wage subsidy programs. But when in 1998 some of these programs expired another reduction of employment was the consequence. Thanks to the still functioning social security system this development has not yet had major implications on energy markets.

A second problem is the introduction of competition in the electricity sector. By restructuring the Bast German electricity industry the market was organized according to the West German pattern - one state-wide power and grid company (VEAG AG), about a dozen regional distributors, and a larger number of communal distribution companies. But one exception was made in order to protect the lignite industry as one of the industrial cores of Bast Germany. The regional and communal distribution companies had and still have to buy at least 70% of their electricity sale volumes to final customers from the VEAG AG. To make things even worse a price supplement of about 0.02 DM/kWh was commanded, which later was eliminated through market forces. Still electricity prices in Bast Germany tend to exceed those in the western part of Germany.

Fig. Q11: Electricity Prices for Industrial Customers (1000kW/2500h/a)

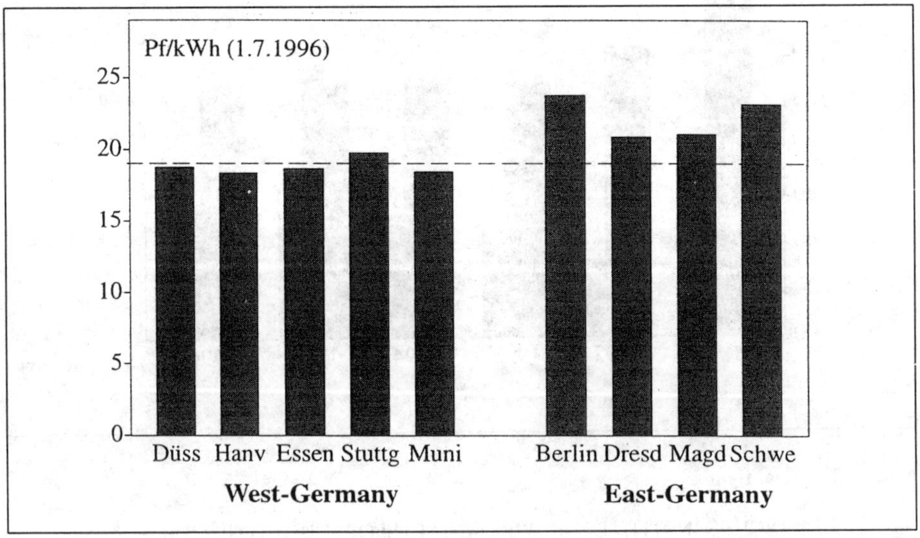

Due to the massive, not yet depreciated investments in power and distribution capacities, electricity in East Germany cannot be sold at prices offered by West German utilities which can benefit from a pool of new, high cost and old, low cost capacities. But the relatively high electricity prices made East Germany into a paradise for power investments into autogeneration and combined heat and power capacities. Both independent power producers and public utilities went into this business. lt took some time until the VEAG AG started to understand this market rule and reduced the electricity prices - between 1993 and 1997 by 12 percent on average (Stotz 1998, p.84). But the price cuts came too late and were too soft for avoiding the ongoing buildup of massive overcapacities in the power sector.

With the recent introduction of competition in the German electricity sector these overcapacities are an invitation to customers, particularly to large ones, to successfully bargain for further rate reductions. The new federal energy law realized the dilemma of the East German utilities that are caught by the requirements of freeing of market forces and the desired protection of the lignite industry. According to an exception from market liberalization by the year 2003, the East German grid owners are allowed to refuse third party power transmissions if this is proved to be necessary for lignite fed power generation.

There are several dilemmas associated with an extensive use of this legal preference through the East German utilities:

- With the prospect of a free market after 2003 (or perhaps *2005),* today's major concern should be customer relations. lt would probably suffer if a utility would give too much weight to the actual protection of its power.
- The utilities cannot avoid reducing their prices down to competitive levels because that would be a misuse of monopolistic power.
- It is not evident how to legally prove that a certain third party power transmission through the East German grid is challenging the lignite industry and thus can be rejected.

Thus it might turn out very soon that the temporal protection might not be helpful for a sustainable development of the Bast German lignite power industry. Experience shows that in changing markets, size and monopolistic power are usually not any more a strong success criteria but rather the speed to which the new market chances are taken. It is a challenge for the Bast German power industry to adapt to two major system changes within only one decade, but it seems that it hasn't yet learned how to quickly adapt to such kinds of challenges.

References

BUNDESMINISTERIUM FÜR WIRTSCHAFT (1997), Energiedaten 1997. Nationale und internationale Entwicklung. Bonn: BMWi.

DEUTSCHES INSTITUT FÜR WIRTSCHAFTSFORSCHUNG (1997),

Gesamtwirtschaftliche und unternehmerische Anpassungsfortschritte in Ostdeutschland. Wochenbericht 3/97. Berlin: DIW. pp. 553-562.

MEYE, J. (1993), Energieversorgung aus der Sicht der Praxis. In: Technische Universität Berlin (Bd.) Energiekonzeption und Energiepolitik in Berlin/Brandenburg - Schlüsselaussagen und Orientierungshilfen. Unterlagen zur Tagung "Genshagen 1". Berlin, pp.43-53.

SCHLEMMERMEIER, B. (1998), Marktverhalten der VEAG (Vortragsmanuskript). Berlin.

STOTZ, J. (1998), Restructuring the Electricity Supply in a Competitive Environment: The Experience in East Germany. In: Gesellschaft für Energiewissenschaft und Energiepolitik (Bd.) Electricity Markets - What's New? Berlin, pp. 79-87.

VBAG (VEREINIGTE ENERGIEWERKE AG) (1998) Portrait und Unternehmenskonzept des ostdeutschen Verbundunternehmens. Berlin.

WEISSHEIMER, M. (1995), Preise und Preisaufsicht im Ergebnis der Systemtransformation. Erfahrungen der neuen Bundesländer. Energiewirtschaftliche Tagesfragen 45 (5).

III. Changes in the Transportation Sector

R: The Regulation of the Privatised Railways in Britain

George Yarrow

1. Introduction

There has been a distinct trend in the complexity of the structural and regulatory reforms that have accompanied the privatisations of major network industries in the United Kingdom. British Telecom (1984) and British Gas (1986) were transferred to the private sector without major restructuring (although British Gas had been stripped of its offshore oil interests in 1983). The privatisation of the water industry (1989) saw the removal of some environmental protection functions from the water authorities before they were sold, and the separation of monopoly and environmental regulation (which had earlier been implicitly bundled). Electricity privatisation (1990 and 1991) was the first major privatisation in which there was substantial industrial restructuring prior to flotation: the major generation and transmission corporation, the Central Electricity Generating Board was split into a transmission company and three generating companies, one of which was specialised in nuclear generation and was retained in the public sector.

In all the industries, however, there has been a steady drive toward unbundling of different business activities, and an associated tendency for co-ordination of activities to rely more and more on contractual relationships and less and less on administrative resource allocation procedures. In the language of Oliver Williamson, there has been a shift from hierarchies to markets. And, where the unbundling occurred before privatisation, government was itself compelled to put in place an in initial contractual framework. Thus, in the electricity, distribution companies and generating companies were sold with supply contracts already in place.

This is also the case in railways, and the privatisation of British Rail was the most complex of all the policy exercises. The degree of fragmentation imposed on the previously monolithic state-owned enterprise (SOE) was much greater than in any other case, including electricity. Moreover, having broken up the SOE, the government was faced by the huge task of establishing contractual structures that would enable efficient co-ordination among the various parts.

Although much larger than the enterprises with which the current study is concerned, British railways case is of particular significance for several reasons:

- The new industrial and regulatory structure incorporates both classic regulated monopoly and franchise competition for operating rights.
- Vertical separation was imposed, among other things to reduce asset handover

problems.

- There are two separate types of agency involved in regulation, once concerned with regulation of access to the infrastructure and the other with franchise contracts for operating companies.
- Many of the franchises are for loss making operations, and hence the arrangements have provided for subsidisation of many routes.
- Subsidies have been provided via the competitive bidding process for franchises.
- The form of the privatisation illustrates the conflict between the promotion of competition via open access to infrastructure facilities and via competitive franchise bidding for monopolistic market positions.

The measures taken, therefore, provide a number of illustrations of the kinds of options that are available when restructuring and re-organizing public utilities, including at a local and regional level. More than in any other example of privatisation, the rail case illustrates the practical ways in which both competition and efficient use of subsidies can be promoted in what had been a loss-making industry.

2. General Background

The first major re-organisation of the SOE, the British Railways Board (BRB), was completed on April 1st 1992. It changed BRB from an organisation based on six geographic regions to a business management structure based upon the rail products offered (inter-city traffic, London commuter traffic, freight, etc.), with each business unit trading internally.

Government proposals for privatisation were published in a 1992 White Paper, entitled "New Opportunities for the Railways". The paving legislation for privatisation, the Railways Act, was passed in November 1993.

2.1 The Reorganisation in Broad Outline

The government decided to privatise the industry without any attempt to substantially reduce the size of the network. Since, with current cost and demand structures, the network as a whole was loss making at prevailing prices and would be likely to remain so at any other set of prices, this fact has had a major influence on the new structure of the industry. In brief the plan was to:

- vertically separate network infrastructure from rail operations;
- convert basic infrastructure activities (track, signalling, etc.) into a privately owned, regulated, monopoly;

- franchise, rather than sell, geographically based, passenger operating companies, so that on loss making routes companies can bid for subsidies in a competitive tendering process;
- sell rolling stock separately, in the form of three companies whose business is to lease it to operators; and
- split the other operations of British Rail (see below) into a relatively large number of separate companies operating in competitive markets.

2.2 New Bodies

As already stated, British Rail has been split into a number of new companies. The three major sets of institutions that are of interest here are:

Railtrack

Railtrack owns and operates the track, signalling and other associated infrastructure as well as owning most of the stations and light maintenance depots. A key aspect of restructuring is that the ownership of a facility such as a station does not necessarily imply that the same company operates the facility (although Railtrack does operate fourteen mainline stations). Railtrack grants and charges for access to the network, operates the central timetable and signalling network, and is responsible for the planning of train services to ensure co-ordination of services. The company is required by the Treasury to earn a rate of return on capital which was set at 5% in 1994/95 and was planned to rise by 1% a year until it reached 8%. Later regulatory decisions have indicated that this initial rate of return, calculated on a replacement cost basis, was rather generous.

ROSCOs (Rolling stock companies)

Three ROSCOs were created to own or lease the vast majority of rolling stock previously owned or leased by British Rail. Each ROSCO was allocated between 3,000 and 4,200 vehicles and was made responsible for securing finance for any new rolling stock and heavy maintenance. The ROSCOs were sold in November 1995 for £1.8 billion (the government was also to receive an £800 million cash dividend from the companies).

Train Operating Companies (TOCs)

The 25 TOCs are responsible for the operation of passenger services in their area (and also for operation of some stations and light maintenance depots). They were wholly owned subsidiaries of British Rail until they were franchised. TOCs gain access to track by means of regulated agreements with Railtrack. They also enter into leasing agreements from the ROSCOs for their rolling stock requirements.

3. The Regulatory Structure

The loss making characteristic of the rail network, coupled with the vertical separation of infrastructure and operations, has led to the development of a system of regulation that is unique in the UK privatisation programme. More specifically, two new regulatory agencies have been created for the industry.

3.1 The Rail Regulator

The main functions of the Rail Regulator under the Railways Act are to:

- Grant licenses to operators of railway assets (with the consent of the Secretary of State or in accordance with a general authority issued by the Secretary of State).
- Supervise the granting of rights of access to track, station and depots.
- Promote competition using powers which give him the functions of the Director General of Fair Trading with regard to railways.
- Act as a guardian of the users interest (which includes responsibility for determining whether any proposed closure of facilities or services should be allowed).
- Investigate breaches of license agreements and closure restrictions, and to enforce compliance.

The legislation specifies that the Regulator should exercise his functions in a manner best calculated to:

- protect users interests (particularly disabled passengers);
- promote the use and development of the railway network;
- promote efficiency and competition;
- promote measures designed to facilitate through journeys.

He is also required to:

- impose the minimum restrictions possible;
- allow those providing railway services a reasonable degree of assurance to make plans for their businesses;
- where he believes a potential monopoly situation exists in non-franchise operations, to regulate price and quality of service;
- regulate the price and quality of railway facilities to those who provide passenger or goods series;

- consider general safety and the effects of the railway industry on the environment;
- until the 31st December 1996, take into account any guidance given by the Secretary of State;
- always have regard to the position of the Franchising Director (see below) and of the holders of network licenses in attempts to finance any proposed or current activities.

Restrictions on the powers of the Regulator in the exercise of the general authority given by the Secretary of State include:

- he can not impose public service requirements;
- subject to certain exceptions or, unless the Secretary of State approves, licenses must not contain provisions which:
- allow conditions of the license to be modified or cease,
- regulate the level of passenger fares or level or quality of service of stations with regard to franchises or certain agreements;
- relate to anti competitive practises.

The licenses must include conditions for insurance, the environment, through ticketing, supply of timetable information to Railtrack, agreements with the British Transport police, protection of disabled peoples interests, and must allow the Regulator to revoke a license given a serious breach of the Railways (Safety Case) Regulations (except in the case of depot licenses) and must contain no other reference to safety.

Guidance given by the Secretary of State in the initial period has required that the Regulator should:

- exercise his functions in a way which facilitates privatisation and franchising;
- discuss with the Franchising Director requests for moderation of competition, and discuss with Railtrack and consult with the Franchising Director in respect of Railtrack's proposals for contracts with open access operators;
- ensure that terms of access are based on the agreed templates unless where not doing so would help conformance to other parts of the Secretary of State's guidance;
- ensure that payments to Railtrack should be sufficient for Railtrack to cover its reasonable costs and to meet its rate of return "under the government's financing regime".

Under the same guidance the Regulator has been required not to:

- grant access which would seriously prejudice the franchising programme;
- require or approve any access agreement relating to BR's freight only depots;
- grant rights of access to track, stations and depots in such a way as to prevent their transfer to the private sector or closure where their is insufficient market demand.

Licenses

Licenses are required for the operation of certain railway assets. There are four types: network, train operator (of which there are two categories, passenger and non-passenger), station and depot. In granting a license the Regulator must be concerned with his duties in the Railway Act and must require assurances about the suitability of the applicant to operate railway assets (in particular, with regard to train and station licenses, that the Health and Safety Executive (HSE) has accepted an operator's safety case).

Franchise operators generally do not require network operators' licenses. The three forms of license TOCs require contain conditions relating to insurance, claims allocation and handling, compliance with railway group standards, environmental protection, the British transport police, provision of information to the regulator, payment of fees and change of control. Depot and station licenses include provisions relating to non-discriminatory access, emergency access and accounting separation from other operations. Station and passenger licenses have conditions of consumer protection. Passenger and non passenger licenses have conditions regarding inspections and exclusionary behaviour. Passenger licenses include requirements that network benefits are protected (eg. through ticketing and timetable requirements) and that prohibit predatory pricing.

The Franchise Director negotiates access agreements for TOCs before the franchising process begins. Hence, when franchises are acquired the necessary licenses are already be in place. However, the change of ownership of a TOC constitutes a change of control and require the regulator's approval.

A change of control is one of the events that may require a revocation of a license. The Regulator treats any change of control as if the new owner is applying for a license. In the case of franchising, the Franchise Director is required to consult with the regulator on whom should be given an invitation to tender, and during the tendering process the Regulator investigates the suitability of those seeking the franchise.

Safety

The responsibility for safety in the new system lies with the body controlling the activity in question; For example, the TOCs are responsible for train safety. To ensure the safety of the system as a whole Railtrack is expected to impose safety requirements before granting access and to inspect them in accordance with HSE regulations. It is intended that existing safety standards develop and change through time, and this process too is the responsibility of Railtrack.

3.2 The Franchising Director

The franchising director's main function under the Railways Act is to designate services as eligible for franchising, to award the franchise, and to ensure franchise assets are maintained and that there is no disruption to service at the end of the franchise period. (Initially all of British Rail's timetable services were made eligible for franchising.) He is required to do this in the manner calculated best to fulfil the objectives given by the Secretary of State and in accordance with any instructions and guidelines - instructions require specific action, guidance sets out general principles - given to him by the Secretary of State.

The principal objectives initially set by the Secretary of State were to ensure that railway passenger services are provided under franchise agreements as soon as reasonably practicable and to secure an overall improvement in the quality of passenger and station services. More specific objectives are to encourage efficiency, promote the cost effective development of and investment in the network, and promote the awarding of initial franchises to companies with a large proportion of qualifying railway staff. He is required to allow maximum scope for initiative of franchise operators, to impose minimum possible burdens, and allow them to plan the future of their businesses with the a reasonable degree of assurance.

The Director is instructed to include the following in a franchising agreement:

- provisions to the effect that franchisees will participate in local concessionary fare schemes as long as no net cost falls on the franchisee or the franchising directors budget;
- conditions on through ticketing and inter availability of tickets;
- each franchise must publish a passengers' charter;
- the franchisee must keep relevant local authorities informed of planned significant changes to services.

The following guidance has been given by the Secretary of State:

- the length of an agreement is to be determined on a case by case arrangement to allow maximum flexibility (although, in practice, seven years quickly became the norm);
- service patterns should not be allowed to ossify - the agreement should leave scope for franchisees to change patterns to better meet demands;
- performance standards should maintain or improve on existing standards;
- the Franchising Director should take into account BR's position when evaluating its bids for franchises;
- disruption should be avoided at the end of the franchise period;
- the Secretary of State should be consulted before the Director makes any significant commitments with regard to the development of a leasing market in rolling stock.

The Director also has the powers to enforce the agreed terms of franchise agreements and to impose financial penalties on franchise operators. More generally, and in extreme circumstances with the consent of the Secretary of State, he can go to the courts to request a Railway Administration Order, the major purpose of which is to allow the Franchising Director to maintain passenger services and to transfer, as a going concern to other companies, parts of the business.

The Franchising Director has a secondary concern in respect of regulation of fares charged by franchise operators and in ensuring the participation of franchise operators in certain discount fare agreements. The Franchising Director must consult the Regulator on the inclusion of provisions requiring the charging of reasonable fares in a franchise agreement. He is also concerned with the issue of the possible closure of both franchised and non franchised passenger services. In the main this is just an interest in being informed, but in some circumstances the Director may ensure the provision of services which would otherwise be discontinued. (He has powers to: enter into agreements with BRB to secure provision of certain services not provided under a franchise agreement; form and finance companies; and acquire and dispose of certain property rights or assets.)

3.3 Moderation of Competition

The Regulator's current position is that while competition between train operators will have substantial benefits in the long run it should initially be moderated, since the railway industry undergoing a process of major restructuring and it is not clear what the effects of unrestricted competition would be (a secondary argument is that franchising has introduced significant competition anyway, in the form of competitive bidding for the rights to operate a particular service and to receive public subsidies for doing so).

One of the key issues in the debate on the role of competition has been the conflict between franchising and open access. Franchising requires bids to provide designated levels of service over certain routes and, where necessary, to receive public subsidies for so doing. It has been argued, therefore, that open access would allow (non-franchisee) new entrants to cherry-pick profitable routes within a franchise area, leaving the franchisee with insufficient revenues to finance its commitments under the original contract. Franchise competition - which is based on rivalry for monopoly rights - therefore sits uneasily alongside open access provisions which foreshadow the elimination of monopoly positions.

In the event, no significant competition will be allowed on any route prior to March 31 1999, and substantial protection will remain until March 31 2002, by which time a review of the position will have been conducted (the Regulator plans to review competition and access charges in 2001). Meanwhile it is the Regulator's task to moderate competition, and this is achieved via the requirement that regulatory approval be given to access agreements between Railtrack and train operators.

4. Interactions Among the Companies in the Restructured Industry

As noted at the outset, the privatisation of British Rail represented a deliberate attempt to replace co-ordination through internal organisation by co-ordination through contracts. The new commercial relationships among the various companies, expressed in large measure in the relevant contracts, are therefore perhaps the most interesting aspect of the reforms. We summarise the more important relationships in what follows.

4.1 The Franchise Agreements

Successful bidders for the passenger rail franchises (the franchisees), acquired the share capital of the TOCs which operate the passenger rail services (the franchise operator). While each of the franchises can differ, the Franchising Director ensures that there are certain common elements. Initially the Franchise Director negotiated draft access contracts with Railtrack for each franchise, so that bidders for each franchise knew that hey would have access to the track they require to maintain at least the minimum standards specified in their franchise agreement.

Passenger Service Requirements (PSRs)

Typically the core service pattern includes the minimum number of trains on each service, first and last train times, weekend services, through services, stations to be served, frequency, and maximum journey times. For certain services load factor conditions and capacity requirements can also be set. To meet load factor standards the operator is required to operate more than the minimum level of services. Specified connections may also be required.

If demand is estimated to change significantly, and the operator would therefore likely be required to increase capacity to meet load factor regulations, there are provisions for the cost to be first shared with, and then be solely payable by, the Franchising Director (above specified limits). Once a service is timetabled the operator is obliged to supply it regardless of whether it is part of the PSR.

There are limits on the number of cancellations or failures to comply with load factor or minimum capacity requirements that are allowable in a time period once any force majeure has been taken into account. Failure to comply with PSR standards can result in a "call in", breach of the agreement, or default. (Sustained call ins can lead to a breach, a breach of an obligation after notice has been served to remedy the breach can lead to a default, a default can lead to a financial penalty or termination of the agreement.)

Either party may propose a modification to the PSR which, if agreed, is be implemented. Disputes are resolved through the Railway Industry Dispute Resolution Rules. (Complaints against the Franchising Director are dealt with by the courts.) The Franchising Director is entitled to reject any PSR change which would result in either an increased level of payments by the public or a reduced level of service.

The Franchising Director may impose additional requirements upon the franchisee providing these do not require a greater than specified percentage increase in train mileage or in expenditure on capacity, and the relevant limits are to be set out in the initial franchise agreement. Similarly, a franchisee is allowed to retain a certain set proportion of any net gain that a new plan proposed by a franchisee will cause.

Prices

The prices charged by TOCs for unrestricted standard class fares for short journeys, unrestricted standard class return fares, saver fares, and certain standard class season tickets are regulated. In certain commuter markets (at present London, Cardiff and Edinburgh) where it is felt that rail has particular market power a stringent approach was taken, as it was in areas where the local Passenger Transport Executive (PTE) plans to cease funding passenger rail services in its area (as Greater Manchester PTE plans to from April 1 1996). For the three years from 1 January 1996, prices are not be permitted to rise at a rate in excess of increases in the retail prices index (RPI), and for the four years following the increases shall not exceed RPI-1. Price control is exercised by reference to tariff baskets containing all relevant fares, weighted roughly according to the income derived from each. Within tariff baskets individual fares may be increased by up to 2% above the RPI. Improvements or deteriorations in quality of service can lead to a further increase or decrease of up to 2% in the allowed price changes.

Financial Regime

The level of financial support provided by government to a particular operating company is determined during the competitive tendering process, though there is also be an incentive system for payments depending upon quality of service. The principal element is a fixed, annual payment, which is agreed (bid) in advance for every year of the franchise agreement. In areas where OPRAF (the regulatory body for franchising) believes that, in the medium term, the operator has monopoly power or, where it is believed that the cost of providing passenger services is disproportionate to the revenues gained from the passengers, this arrangement can be modified so that a payment from OPRAF to the franchisee or vice versa is made depending upon quality of service. This provision is separate from: load factor payments; modifications in RPI-X price changes associated with changes in quality of service; and the performance regime which operates between Railtrack and the TOCs as part of the track access agreement.

Franchise Reviews are intended to protect franchisees against unexpected change, and they can be called by the Franchising Director or franchise operator after: the Regulator's access charging review; moderation of competition review; and any change in the fare regulation regime of the Franchising Director. They allow the Franchising Director to reduce uncertainty for franchisees caused by events outside their control, require them to pass on any benefits from a change to the access agreements or from force majeure, and allow agreements to be renegotiated if the viability of the franchise is in question. The basic regime prescribes that, if the franchise operator is materially affected (to the extent of 0.5% of the sum of the franchise operator' passenger receipts and franchise payments/subsidies), then the outcome of the review would leave the operator no better or worse off than if the review had not occurred. If the franchise operator gains from the access review the same criteria shall be used. Similar terms apply to allow a proportion of the increased costs attributable to a change in law to be passed on to the Franchise Director.

Performance and season ticket bonds will be required from the franchise operator, although it was intended that, overall, there would be minimal requirements for capital to operate a franchise. This both encouraged bidders for the first franchises and offset any possible asset handover problems.

Each franchise operator had, as part of the bidding process, to submit a passenger's charter which was at least as favourable to customers in terms of compensation for poor service as the previous BR charter. Various other customer related obligations such as provisions of timetables at stations, customer satisfaction surveys and the like are required, as well as certain station standards.

Inter-Operator Agreements
It is a condition of franchises that franchise operators participate in a number of schemes designed to maintain certain network benefits, such as arrangement for through fares, various railcard schemes. and other ATOC schemes. (The Franchising Director has been instructed to this end by the Secretary of State, provided only that participation in the schemes results in no new cost falling on the Director's budget)

Continuity of Service
Tenders for franchises are for a minimum of seven years, though the Franchising Director invited bid for longer periods. To ensure continuity when a franchise changes control the Franchising Director designates certain assets as primary franchise assets which will normally stay with the franchise and be transferred to the new operator. These include assets such as outstanding fares and rights in certain specialist equipment. They will be transferred, at the end of the franchise period, at a value calculated using standard accounting techniques. No value will be assigned to contracts, fares other than season tickets, or goodwill.

Competition
Exclusionary behaviour by the franchisee where the franchisee competes with other services supported by the Franchising Director is not allowed. Bidding for more than one franchise was allowed, though the Franchising Director required separate accounts for the franchises and bids could have been disqualified if it had been felt that competition would be materially reduced. The Director General of Fair Trading (DGFT) may also consider such a bid (on merger grounds), as may the Rail Regulator (on merger grounds, exercising the DGFT's powers in respect of railways, or on the basis of those provisions in track access agreements relating to competition).

4.2 Dealings between Railtrack and TOCs

These dealings are subject to regulated access agreements. The Regulator initially published draft model contracts, and once entered into these agreements can not be amended unless approved by the Regulator.

TOCs usually hold the leases (from Railtrack, the landlord or "facility owner") on the stations and light maintenance depots that they use the most intensively, except for fourteen large mainline stations for which Railtrack is not only the landlord but also the facility operator. For stations and depots that they do not operate the TOCs gain access via regulated agreements with the TOC which operates the facility. They must also enter into a collateral agreement with the landlord to allow direct enforcement of obligations under the station access conditions (a set of rules which are station specific and are included in all station leases, collateral agreements and access agreements). A similar regime applies to light maintenance depots.

4.2.1 General Principles

The Regulator has published criteria for the approval of passenger track access agreements. Generally he seeks to be satisfied that an agreement does not unduly limit competition or come into conflict with an existing agreement, and that it is sufficiently flexible not to require continual referral to the Regulator for approval of amendments. For franchise operators there are certain rights and obligations which are central to its business that are identified as protected rights and which restrict the Regulator's ability to modify track access agreements.

Track access agreements are required to be consistent with the Regulator's policies relating to the moderation of competition and the maintenance of performance. They must also ensure that there is no undue discrimination among operators and no undue constraints on new train companies competing in the market.

Some of the complexities of the contractual structure are illustrated by a number of major, current areas of concern with regard to timetable rights:

- whether there are inbuilt provisions which unduly limit available network capacity;
- whether the agreement specifies the rights unambiguously;
- the cumulative effect on Railtrack's ability to vary timetable bids of operators on the granting of access to other operators;
- the impact of rights to additional train slots on capacity available for other train operators; and
- Railtrack's ability to maintain the network.

Charges

The Regulator has sought to achieve greater transparency and greater variability (to reflect costs) of Railtrack's charges. He required an 8% reduction in access charges in 1995/96 compared with 1994/95 and, from 1996/97, the target is an annual real reduction of 2% in individual track access charges in line with the expected reduction in Railtrack's costs.

The Long Term Charge for station access is subject to an RPI-2% price cap for the five years from 1996/97. It is intended that any variations in income from

Railtrack's projections should be shared between Railtrack and the train operators. There is expected to be a further review of charges in the year 2000 (to be implemented in 2001).

4.2.2 Access Agreements

Track Access Agreements

Railtrack grants the train operator the right to use specified routes on the network, and sets out the permitted rolling stock and the train movements that are permissible using that rolling stock.

The duration of an agreement is normally of a fixed term of up to seven years. Where the operator's trains are subject to a franchise agreement the track access agreement can be amended to run for the same duration as the franchise agreement. It also contains collateral contracts which are essential to the operation of the services, such as access to independent stations and an agreement under which the train operator becomes party to certain industry wide agreements. Also included are the restrictions Railtrack can impose on a train operator to maintain its function of managing the network.

The principal formula for calculation of charges that Railtrack levies has, to date, been made up of the following components:

- a fixed annual charge;
- a variable track use charge based on vehicle miles travelled;
- a variable traction electricity charge;
- an adjustment designed to reflect benefits or costs Railtrack incurs as a result of a change of law (and, in general, acts of the Regulator do not count for this purpose);
- an adjustment designed to reflect the financial consequences for Railtrack of managing or dealing in property (eg. operators benefit if Railtrack makes large profits from property disposals).

There is also a performance regime to provide incentives for punctuality and reliability. This requires Railtrack (where feasible) to attribute responsibility for delays and lateness. Compensation is payable from Railtrack to the train operators or vice-versa depending upon the details of the performance regime.

Station Access

Railtrack is responsible for repairs to the structure of stations, some maintenance, and some other obligations of a landlord, while the facility operator is responsible for routine maintenance, certain repairs, and the provision of services to users.

A station access agreement (a bilateral contract between the station facility owner and a user which includes the station access conditions) generally lasts for a fixed term of up to seven years. There are two contract review mechanisms: the first provides that, in the first 12 months of the agreement, both parties, in consultation with the Franchising Director, to conduct reviews of the agreement; the second allows the Regulator to modify the station access agreement as a consequence of a change to the station access conditions.

Charges payable for the use of a station by a passenger train operator comprise:

- a share of the long term charge (a contribution towards Railtrack's costs of repairing and maintaining the structure of the station);
- charges for common services, which are allocated in proportion to the passenger departures attributable to each user from that station; and
- negotiated charges for services exclusive to one operator.

The station access conditions may be changed in two ways: the first is via the Regulator following consultation and in accordance with his duties; the second is by a vote of the station facilities operator (SFO) and the passenger operators who use the station, where votes are weighted according to the numbers of their passenger that depart from the station. Railtrack can not vote, but it can object, and any appeal would go to the Regulator. Similar arrangements apply to changes to the arrangements for the supply of the common services provided at each station. Non-franchise operators can enter into similar access agreements but are not permitted to vote on proposals to amend the station access conditions.

Station Leases

Station leases are of a duration equal to the duration of the franchise. The rent charged to the operator has three components:

- a long term charge;
- a property rent; and
- 50% of actual receipts of the SFO for car boot sales, markets, and fairs held in the station car park under arrangements which existed before April 1 1994

Depots

Access to light maintenance depots is broadly the same as access to stations. Railtrack's depots are leased to TOCs or to BR. The initial access agreements included both regulated services (eg. light maintenance) and unregulated services (eg. interior cleaning).

The depot facility owner (DPO) rent to Railtrack comprises:

- a charge for depot land and buildings; and
- a charge for plant and equipment at the depot.

Depot users' charges comprise:

- a charge in return for an agreed minimum level of depot services;
- a charge in return for depot services above the agreed minimum level but not above an agreed maximum;
- a charge in return for depot services where no minimum has been specified;

4.3 Dealings between ROSCOs and TOCs

Each ROSCO has entered into a master lease with the companies that use its stock, intended to last for the duration of the first franchise period (most TOCs lease stock from at least two ROSCOs). The initial leases were made up of a capital element which was fixed for the duration of the lease and a non-capital element comprising heavy maintenance charges and overhead charges. It changes each year by an amounted determined by the increase in the producer price index less 3% (PPI-3). The level of rental may also vary if the assumed level of mileage varies and results in changed maintenance costs.

Each TOC has responsibility for light maintenance and certain repairs while the ROSCO is responsible for heavy maintenance which it procures from heavy maintenance depots.

4.4 Direct Agreements Between the Franchising Director and ROSCOs

These contracts with the ROSCOS contain the following provisions:

- In certain circumstances the Franchising Director has the right to tender for stock which the ROSCO intends to dispose of.
- If a ROSCO intends to terminate a contract due to default by a TOC the ROSCO must give the Franchising Director warning. If the Director so wishes, he can postpone the termination (and compensate the ROSCO). If the lease is terminated, the Franchising Director has the right to take a new lease on the same terms for all of the rolling stock. If the Franchising Director terminates a franchise he can require that the ROSCO terminate any outstanding leases (again subject to compensation).
- The ROSCO must provide certain information to the Franchising Director to facilitate the franchising process.

5. Preservation of Network Benefits

Agreements on fare setting, through ticketing, and inter-availability
There are two basic types of fare:

- Permanent fares which may be created by passenger operators three times a year in the fare setting round. The operators notify the RSP of their proposed fares, and these proposed fares are then disclosed to other operators who may, if they so wish, respond by informing the RSP of amendments to their proposed fares.
- Temporary fares which are not part of the fares setting round and can be notified to the RSP at any time. They may not last for more than seventeen weeks and must not replace a fare with the same or substantially similar rights and restrictions. A temporary promotional fare may be retailed only by those passenger operators who are required or authorised to do so by the creator of the ticket.

On any particular flow two categories of fare may be created:

- a "dedicated" fare, which is a fare created by a single passenger operator and is valid on its trains only; and
- a jointly agreed fare, which is a fare created by more than one passenger operator and which allows a passenger the benefit of a through journey using the trains of more than one passenger operator and/or a choice between the trains of different operators on the same flow.

Certain flows are deemed to be "compulsory inter-availability flows", and on these the agreement with the Director specifies a lead operator (usually the operator with the greatest commercial interest in or understanding of the flow). The lead operator may create through- and inter-available fares which other TOCs on the flow must honour. This does not apply to tickets with an advance purchase train-specific requirement or to special fares. Competitors may create their own dedicated or jointly agreed fares, while the lead operator is only permitted to create certain jointly agreed and dedicated fares in limited categories. The aim here is to prevent the lead operator from marginalising its inter-available fares. (Open access operators can choose on an all or nothing basis to be bound to compulsory inter-availability.)

Other Flows
On flows where there is no compulsory inter-availability there is no lead operator. Any operator that operates over more than 50% of the route mileage on the flow (called a "major flow operator") can create through fares for the whole flow (it is a

requirement that for the part of the journey for which the TOC is responsible its customers must travel on its trains). Again it is not possible to bind other operators to honour advance purchase, train-specific fares or special fares.

Retailing and Income Allocation
There is an obligation for lead retailers at stations to sell tickets impartially at least 51% of its open ticket windows. Non-lead operators have no obligation to sell tickets impartially. Commission to retailers is based on nationally agreed scales. For dedicated fares all income goes to the creator minus any retail commission. For jointly agreed fares the income is split as specified in the agreement. For inter-available fares created by a lead operator the principle is that income should be allocated according to the number of passenger miles travelled on each operator's trains.

Provision of Train Services
Many TOCs rely on arrangements with other TOCs to provide train crews. This is beneficial in the light of the geographic distribution of rail routes, the location of train crew depots, and HSE standards relating to hours worked. These arrangements are governed by bilateral agreements between the supplier and the customer which have been agreed centrally.

6. The Position in the Freight Business

In issuing licenses to freight operators, the Regulator must have regard to his general duties, and in particular to the various safety issues. Other requirements are broadly similar to those relating to passenger operators' licenses.

In respect of access, there is a general regime of negotiated charges designed to cover common costs of freight whilst not pricing any freight off the market which could cover its avoidable costs. Thus the Regulator has stated that: "no user who is able to pay at least the direct costs imposed on the network should be denied the opportunity of moving traffic by rail rather than road".

Although there exists regulatory protection for freight operators, it is widely believed that for the vast majority of freight traffic Railtrack is close to being a price taker (rather than a price maker). This is a consequence of the ease with which most freight can be switched from rail to road and the small market share of total freight accounted for by rail. In other words, it is assumed that, at or around current levels of charges, Railtrack faces a highly elastic demand for its services from freight operators.

In respect of freight traffic, the Regulator initially required Railtrack:

- to change the basis on which it sets its minimum charge (and a mechanism has been set up by which the Regulator is able individually to review proposed charges if they are felt to be excessive);
- not significantly to distort competition among freight operators as a result of its access charges; and
- to give operators more information about its overall freight costs and revenues.

Freight operators generally pay a standard charge per visit to a station on an assumed number of visits. Increased visits may lead to an increased charge.

In order to support freight of goods by rail, a new grant/subsidy has been put in place to contribute towards increased track access charges which operators have been required to pay. There is also a "freight facilities" grant scheme that provides assistance for capital expenditure on rail-related equipment.

Since 1 April 1994 new freight operators have been able to negotiate access rights and charges with Railtrack and to offer services in competition with BR 's freight operations. Individual customers can also negotiate directly with the component parts of the restructured industry for services, for example directly with Railtrack for access and with the TOCs for train services.

7. In Conclusion

The structural reform of the rail system that accompanied privatisation is the most comprehensive of the whole privatisation programme in Britain. Around 100 new companies were created out of British Rail. Of these, perhaps about 50 could be described as significant players in the new environment.

The motivation for the reforms was to promote a more efficient rail network by de-politicising decision making, introducing the profit motive, and promoting competition. The view underlying the reforms was that new technologies and management methods have considerably increased the potential efficiency of a decentralised, contract-based industrial structure, and that the relationships among the various component parts of the industry are sufficiently stable to prevent contract-based co-ordination being undermined by costly litigation.

S: Russian Railway and Transportation

Lev Resnikov

Railway transport of Russia is traditionally a leading transport branch, ensuring communication between the enterprises and citizens of various regions of the country and thus its economic, political and cultural unity. In spite of significant reduction of transportation of freight and passengers by railway transport during the years of reform, it continues to hold a leading position among other types of common carriers, providing at present 78% of freight turnover and 40% of passenger transportation. This circumstance explains the attention which is given to railway transport operation by the bodies of State administration and public opinion of the country as well as the sharpness of discussions and disputes being carried out on problems of its reforming in the transitive period and being experienced by the country now.

At present the main document which determines the strategy of development and transformation in the branch is the document entitled "Main Directions of Development and Social and Economic Policy of Railway Transport over a Period through 2005" that was authorized by the All-Russian Convention of railway workers that took place in Moscow on May 17-18, 1997. This document was maintained by the branch governing body.

The Decree of the President of Russia, B.N. Yeltsin, in which the government was entrusted to accept measures toward realization of this document, authorized by the Convention, was proclaimed at the Convention. The speech of the chairman of the government, V.S. Chernomyrdin, that took place at the Convention fully corresponded to the key provisions of the "Main Directions" document.

The question of the ways for railway transport to adapt to the market reforms being carried out in the country was formulated from the very beginning of their carrying out. An important moment in finding an answer to this problem was the law "On Federal Railway Transport of the Russian Federation" accepted in 1995 under the initiative of the government. This law has consolidated railways as State property and thus has excluded the possibility of their privatization. During acceptance of this law the specified position was supported by all 84 subjects of the Russian Federation, by the Federation Council and State Duma.

The supporters of the State status of railways consider that legislative consolidation of the railways as State property assists to avoid rupture of the railway bed among separate regions, that in conditions of immense Russian expanses would inevitably have catastrophic consequences. Preservation of the unified management of the transportation process, providing of complete technological coordination of the railway transport functioning, conducting of a uniform tariff policy and mutual settlement of accounts, and progress in foreign economic activities are also connected with the State status of railways.

Maintenance of a rather stable and relatively high level of its employee material security during all the years of the reform is also directly related to the State status of railway transport. In particular, absence of the threat of unemployment of the railways, the provision of social warranties and privileges for employees and members of their families as stipulated by the branch tariff agreement, and maintenance of the wages in this branch at the level of the first dozen of basic branches of the national economy are borne in mind.

It should be especially emphasized that the supporters of the railways consolidation as State property by no means excludes the necessity of deep reformation of railway transport as an economic system, reasoning from the requirements of the market. They consider conversion of railways into full-fledged subjects of the market, struggling for the volumes of transport services through free-market prices, as one of the major purposes of such reformation. But referring to the peculiarities of the country, its economy, as well as to the fact that at present the State is not ready to have railways free from centralized management, the supporters of the State status of the railway transport offer an algorithm of its reformation such that railway transport, not losing the State status as a whole, will smoothly evolve from one state to another, gradually transforming its economic mechanism into a mechanism of a market type.

During the course of the specified transformation it is supposed to realize deep qualitative changes of organizational, institutional and economic order that in turn will allow change of the intra-branch economic relations, as well as relations of the branch with the State and the users of the services.

In the organization-administration sphere it is planned, in particular, to realize the so called "straightening" of the branch management system first to three, and then to two links. At present a four-link railway transport management system is functioning: the Ministry of Communications - the railway - the railway department - the railway line enterprise. This system, based on the territorial and branch principle, was formed back in 1958 when it replaced the previous system that was based exclusively on the branch principle. (Though the territorial railway departments appeared as long ago as 1946, at that time they functioned as railway line divisions).

Today when the requirements of operative manageability of the technological and economic processes in the branch have sharply increased and the volumes of transportation have significantly fallen with simultaneous increase of their structure mobility, such a system of management is recognized as inflexible and cumbersome. It is considered that in these conditions integration of the railways, abolition of their departments and transition to the branch principle of their management depict the imminent transformation of the administrative system.

The main sense of the named transformations is to develop a branch management system such that each division would ultimately bear responsibility not only for technical activity and decisions but also for the final economic (commercial) result. It is supposed that these requirements will be better met by a direct management system: Ministry of Communications - regional (integrated) railway - railway line enterprise and subsequently Ministry of Communications - regional integrated railway. It is a three- or two-link railway transport management system instead of the four-link one that exists at present.

For adaptation of railway transport to the market relations environment, while preserving the State status, a broad complex of measures are provided for changing and debugging the mechanisms of cooperation of railways with the subjects of the market as well as relations of railways with the State and the regions. This is to advance alongside with perfection of the organizational structure of management.

The solution of the problem of increasing the market efficiency of railways is based first of all on cardinal change in relations with the users of transport services. With this purpose in mind new technologies of transportation process and, in particular, a proprietary system of transport servicing uniform for all railways ensuring progressive forms of interrelations with clientele are being introduced. Operative formation of the transportation orders and contractual relations with the customers are widespread now.

Moreover, cooperation of railways with banks is being expanded everywhere. Bank affiliates were opened in railway departments and are servicing the expanding circle of railway enterprises while introducing the bank-customer system.

During the period of 1991-1996 a uniform insurance system was created consisting of a branch-wide insurance company JASO having affiliates at all railways and railway insurance companies established with its participation. Financial means of the latter allow them to accept responsibility for significant risks and really participate in protection of the branch enterprises' property interests. The financial means of the insurance companies' fund of precautionary measures are used in financing the insurance companies' measures for providing safety of railway traffic, freight safety of railway traffic, and freight safety. A significant part of the profit from the insurance activity is directed to financing of the branch public health services and solution of the branch social problems.

The further development of the branch insurance system is connected with solution of two main problems: attraction of additional financial means for providing development and financial stability of the branch in market conditions and reduction of the branch losses at the account of insurance. Solution of these problems is supposed to occur by way of broadening of insured objects, expansion of the offered services sphere, and growth of the insurance sums on the basis of a compulsory and voluntary insurance combination.

The emphasis in the change and debugging of the intra-branch economic relations is made first of all on transformations in the sphere of labor and wages organization. Among these transformations are the following ones:

- Transition from centralized management of wages to the collective and contractual form of payment regulation and creation of contractual form models for managers and specialists;
- Introduction of normative formation of financial means for remuneration of labor;
- Development of regional regulation of the wages by means of interaction with the local (territorial) authorities;
- Perfection of the premium system, stimulating creation of an anti-expenditure mechanism; introduction of resource-saving technologies; and keeping personnel according to the normative number of regular staff;
- Improvement of organization and rating of work using computers;
- Within the framework of the system, formation of social partnership of the new forms of the collective and contractual relations that provide perfection of remuneration of labor and social welfare, warranties of employment and the order of payments of privileges and compensations, extra charges and surcharges on the basis of cooperation with trade unions;
- Development and realization of the program of employment for the railway.

In improving the intra-branch relations of railway transport, at least as much attention is being given to reduction of the transportation expenditures and decreasing of production costs. The following measures are determined here as primary ones:

- Rigid limiting of expenses depending on the character and volumes of work and rate setting of fuel and raw material consumption by the operations elements;
- Introduction of resource-saving and information technologies;
- Laying-up or realization of excessive capacities and liquidation of unprofitable railway lines with the heaviest volume of work (the extent of such lines is rather large and consists of about 9-9.5 thousand km);
- Bringing the number of workers into accord with the volume of the work carried out taking into consideration that more than 25 % of the operational expenses falls on remuneration of labor.

The new tariff policy being carried out by the State since 1996 is exclusively important for the railway transport, that is preserving the State status. Here we are dealing, in particular, with introduction of differentiated tariffs by the sorts of freight, of establishing special tariffs for remote regions, and of granting privileges for foodstuffs freight.

It is especially necessary to note the government activity on regulation (as a rule restraining or reduction) of tariffs on freight traffic. By this measure significant economy of financial means in industries using railway transport is attained, and existence of a considerable number of industrial enterprises is supported.

As to the losses of railway transport, related to the above mentioned lowering of the tariffs, their indemnification is realized (should be realized) by means of granting partial tax exemption, increasing of budgetary funds for investment in railways, and temporary subsiding of passenger transportation for remote regions.

Speaking about the present strict tariff regulation of railway transport, it is necessary to take into account that despite preservation of its State status, this is nevertheless considered only to be a temporary measure connected with monopolism. It is considered, that subsequently, with the development of competition from other kinds of transport, it will be possible to conduct a step-by-step policy of freight tariffs liberalization.

In the adaptation of railway transport to market reforms a highly important place is occupied today by the debugging of the mechanism of its interrelations with regions. In this connection the contract form of relations between enterprises and local authorities is considered to be especially of interest as is the establishment of new partnership relations between the Ministry of Communications, as a Federal government body, and government relations between railway transport and the territories. Today these relations are regulated by the "General Agreement on Interaction of the Ministry of Communications and Executive Power Organs of Russian Federation Subjects on Improvement of Transportation Services of Regions and Providing of Steady Railway Transport Enterprises Operation" signed in 1995 with direct participation of the chairman of the government.

Acting pursuant to the "Law on Railway Transport" and the "Main Directions", the government today is striving also to develop the mechanism of investing in objects of railway transport having nation-wide and regional significance. One of the purposes of this mechanism is seen precisely in defining the measure of all budget levels participating in the development of railways.

In summarizing the multilateral experience of functioning and transformation of railway transport, nations of railway transport, and the preserving of the State status under conditions of market relations being consolidated in the country, this experience should not be qualified as completely without problems. The opponents of the model accepted today of railway transport adaptation to the market are pointing out that sooner or later the solution of this problem all the same will make the withdrawal from the - in its essence - administrative type of management inevitable; this type of management was rather effective in the past but cannot completely meet the requirements of the developing market economy. In their opinion, this already today requires radical change of the existing system of railway transport management; moreover, it requires such a change which in turn can be successfully carried out only with intrusion into the existing property relations.

However not all opponents of the present model of the railway transport reformation are associating such an intrusion with privatization and transformation of the State property into private property and therefore with liquidation of the State status of railway transport and its replacement by private status.

Thus, an alternative has been put forward based upon a dismembered share form of State property in contrast to the present model of the railway transport reformation with its characteristic, non-dismembered monolithic form of State property. Differently speaking, the question is about transformation of the property status of railway transport of the country (and first of all of the railways networks) into joint-stock property of the newly created uniform national railway company. Their shares in the authorized capital of this company will have Federation, territories and municipalities components. It is emphasized that the relationship between the named shares could be, for example, as follows: Federal - 60 %; territorial - 30 %; and municipal - 10%.

Thus in this case the question actually is not about privatization and transformation of State property into the private property but rather about a peculiar restructuring of State property itself by means of joint-stocks and its transformation from being non-dismembered and monolithic into being dismembered among State property of different levels - Federal, regional and municipal.

Supporters of the specified transformation of the property relations at the railway transport consider that such transformation will provide a number of appreciable advantages which will allow essential improved management of the railway complex. Among the primary advantages named using this scheme are a more clear-cut personification of the State property subjects, division of proprietor function and function of management, as well as change of the forms of state property management, which will completely correspond to the requirements of the market economy and will allow the involvement of market means and methods of economic managing to a maximum degree. As to the advantages of the specified model of the property transformation we refer also to the transition into its above-described share form, that will allow, on the one hand, better taking into account of local interests, and on the other hand, avoiding the division of the railways network among territories and thereby ensuring unity of the country transport complex.

In distinction to formation of trust-type or administrative-type management of railway transport that was used by the Ministry of Communications and that is now of the past, among the variants of transformations being considered, it is offered actually to pass on to the combine model or administrative model of its management, including in it such components as industrial or operative management, personnel management or control of the staff, innovation and financial management, and marketing etc. In the combine model of railway transport management the main purpose will consist, in the opinion of its supporters, in orientation of the national railway company to the requirements of demand in the market of transportation services and to multiplication of its assets owing to profitable and economic operation.

Alongside the national joint-stock railway company the share principle of property is offered to be used also when organizing territorial railway companies, ensuring local transportation. It is supposed that when the efforts of the railway and the territory will be united that this company will become that personified organ, which can represent itself as a direct subject of property of station buildings and structures, platforms and electric trains, other property, frequently remaining today in a certain degree without a proprietor.

It is planned that the main founders of the territorial railway company should be the railway, the city and the territory. Attraction of private individuals is not excluded here. The structure of the authorized capital of such a company could, for example, in the opinion of its planners, include 60 % railway capital, 10 % oblast capital, 10 % city capital, and 20 % of other establishments' capital. It is considered that the territorial railway company, created on such foundations, will strive for avoidance of unprofitableness, inasmuch as this could result in stoppage of the local traffic. In turn it will obligate the railway to approach the tariffs establishment and the local authorities towards establishing privileges for the population more weightily.

Alongside the above discussed alternative to the present variant of railway transport reformation is a variant offered by experts of the European Bank for Reconstruction and Development (EBRD) of June 1997. It is also being actively discussed today. This variant provides conversion of the Ministry of Communications into a purely political body and creation of a State holding company "Russian Railways" as an economic structure. Within the framework of such a holding it is provided to create 40 to 50 completely self-supporting commercial companies. Therewith it is planned that the infrastructure objects (railway tracks, bridges, electric power lines) will be in the management of regional companies for freight traffic, and the passenger and 91 interregional freight companies should be obliged to pay for using these objects.

The supporters of preserving the present railway transport status consider acceptance of the EBRD project not only as not improving its operation but on the contrary causing a number of negative consequences. Among such consequences the following ones are usually named in particular:

- Occurrence of official post costs connected with conclusion of bargains between various companies (the so called transnational costs);
- An increase of payment for using "infrastructure objects above prime cost";
- An increase of empty runs when the parking of freight cars is divided.

The general conclusion is reduced to the idea that in the end, all this will cause the increase of the transport services tariffs and will adversely affect the customers.

Among the positions which are alternatives to the present course of the railway transport reforms is the position of the Ministry of Transport of the Russian Federation which also deserves attention. When this ministry was established, its main task was formulated by the government of the Russian Federation as "pursuance of a state policy in the field of air, sea, river, automobile, urban electric transport and road facilities, directed to satisfaction of the state requirements, enterprises needs...and citizens in transportation."

As to railway transport, its management was not imposed upon the Ministry of Transport functions, but it was entrusted with an independent body – the Ministry of Communications.

The crux of the Ministry of Transport proposals consists in merging the Ministry of Communications with the Ministry of Transport. In regard to the functional part of the Ministry of Communications, it is offered to transform it into a state transport company; it is considered that in so doing functions of administrative and economic management of railway transport will be divided. In such a scheme the Ministry of Communications as an administrative body would be abolished.

The critics of the Ministry of Transport position usually refer to extremely unsatisfactory, as a whole, results of transport activities already subordinated to this ministry and already reformed under its prescriptions. They refer, in particular, to unsatisfactory results of the functioning of hundreds of thousands of new isolated and privatized truck fleets, hundreds of airlines, and dozens of sea and river transport companies. Domestic motor transport enterprises are not competitive and 75 % of export-import motor transportation is accomplished now by European companies. As to the Russian airlines, even their own existence is ensured today to a large extent only at the expense of restrictions of the foreign competitors' flights in Russia. The merchant marine fleet of Russia has practically ceased to function; many ships have turned out to be in the property of off-shore companies.

From all this it is concluded that realization of the reform models offered by the Ministry of Transport not only will not improve and reduce the costs of services, but on the contrary will create a threat of manageability loss that could in its turn have catastrophic consequences for the country; this conclusion is reached by taking into account special features of this kind of transport and the role which the ministry plays in the national economy.

The practical measures of the economic reforms and structural reconstruction of railway transport are inseparably linked with the investment policy and financing of its infrastructure.

The problem of the branch development financing can be solved in the first place by means of Federal support; secondly it can be solved by interaction of transport branch enterprises at the regional level, bearing in mind that it is functioning as a single whole manufacturing-technology complex with a centralized system of administration; and thirdly this can be accomplished by means of cooperation within the CIS framework. This includes cooperation on the part of the Council on Railway Transport on the basis of the Program of State Support of Railways adopted by all States as well as interaction with distant foreign countries and attraction of foreign investments.

In conditions of market relations the problem of railway transport financing at the Federal level passes from the plane of State budgetary subsidizing into the sphere of financial support within the framework of the general regional and budgetary policy. The regions' role of railways financing is increasing and in its turn requires strengthening of Federal and local organs' interaction and the solution of problems of effective distribution and redistribution of financial and material resources for railway infrastructure development.

A complex of measures on expansion of the sphere of railways participation at the regional transportation markets is envisaged as the main direction of the branch development up to 2005 (compensation of the increased expenses at the main lines of regional importance by means of measures of economic nature; conclusion of agreements on tariff discounts on transportation of the local industry production at the expense of tax exemptions provision; and increase of transportation volumes in regions at the expense of non-public investments into highly effective projects on production and processing of local natural resources).

An investment fund "Baminvest", created by the Ministry of Communications and Administration of the Eastern regions of Russia, can serve as an example of the latter. Its task is the completion of the Baikal-Amur main line building and development of the economy adjacent to the BAM territories by means of financing projects on production and processing of local natural resources, in so doing creating conditions for increase of the main line traffic growth.

Western companies are giving ever more attention to the problems of Russian railway infrastructure development. During the last two years the inflow of foreign investments in Russia is increasing rather briskly. In 1995 the volume of foreign investments increased in comparison to the previous year by a factor of 2.7 and in 1996 in comparison to 1995 by a factor of 2.3. The inflow of capital creating investments, i.e. in capital investment, general overhaul, non-material assets (patents, licenses, program products, research and development works) and in reserves of the circulating assets, has the greatest significance for Russia.

In 1995 126 million U.S. dollars were invested into the development of railway transport; in 1996 this figure was $ 93 million; and during the first half of 1997 $ 112 million was invested. More than 32 % represents direct investment; some 3 % represents portfolio investment and 65 % others. The greatest attention to the Russian railways is paid by Germany, Sweden, Spain and Italy. In 1996 a cooperative agreement was concluded between the Novocherkassk electric locomotive works and Asea Brown Bovery (ABB) that envisages the development and manufacturing of a DC electric locomotive on the basis of electronic power equipment of ABB Technomasio - an Italian enterprise of the corporation. With construction being in 1997, the participants are supposed to subsequently establish a joint venture in Russia for production of such electric locomotives after termination of the new locomotive testing.

With their investments within the framework of this joint venture, established in Russia for manufacturing modem ABB signaling systems, Swedish companies are taking part in railways modernization. The Swedish share in the joint venture makes up 60 % with the Russian share being 40 %. The first system was assembled at the Losynoostrovsky works in the beginning of 1997; it was installed at the Gorkovskaya railway with the following one being scheduled for installation at the Kulbyshev railway towards the end of 1997. Priorities of investments into the track facilities are defined by the need for railway track strengthening and the acquisition of a considerable credit from the European Bank for Reconstruction and Development for purchasing a number of track engineering facilities. In combination with domestic machinery, these facilities provide the latest technology of railway track works.

The signing of an agreement with Germany about the allocation of DM 500 million for preparation of the production of passenger cars for Russian railways is underway. This sum represents a part of the preferential credit package of DM 7 billion granted to Russia by Germany. The main part of the DM 500 million fund (DM 350 million) will be invested into development of Tver carriage works; the rest is intended for cooperating plants. The carriage works in Tver that is specialized in production of long distance train passenger cars has not obtained investment for modernization and reconstruction of production capacities in more than twenty years.

An important direction for the effective use of investments is cooperation with Spanish companies in the solution of the above discussed critical problem of replenishment of the dilapidating passenger cars fleet by means of its radical modernization on the basis of Spanish technology. Technically bringing the passenger cars up to date and repairing and modernizing them to the level of Western standards will cost 2.5-3 wines cheaper.

Modernization of the passenger car fleet will be accomplished by the "Recon" Joint Venture with authorized capital of US$ 1 million established by

Oktyabrskaya Railway and the Ministry of Transport and Social Work of Spain – the Spanish railways "R-I-N-F-I". A new enterprise being counted on for modernization of 150-200 cars yearly is supposed to be built in Tosno. Creation of a number of joint ventures for production of components and equipment necessary for passenger cars modernization is also planned.

As to the problems of railway transportation tariff policy that have a structural character, it is important to do the following: to provide its balance and to solve the problem of subsidizing unprofitable passenger transportation (now it is accomplished at the expense of freight transport); to provide tariff differentiation on kinds of production being transported; to establish special tariffs for remote regions (the matter is that high railway tariffs, in spite of discounts, are increasingly reducing, for example, the attractiveness of the Trans-Siberian Railway as a transport bridge between Europe and Pacific Ocean region countries); and to provide unity of a tariff system within the CIS framework, etc. In the process of economic reforms, the banking system, insurance activities, financial and industrial groups and other constituents of market forms of effective operation of the whole infrastructure of the railway transport are to be developed.

T: Intramodal Competition and the Reform of the German Railway System: Problems, Policy Options and Results

Andreas Brenck

1. Introduction

The railroad industry belongs traditionally to the most heavily regulated sectors. In Europe and Japan the railways have been nationalized, in other countries like the USA the railway industry has been regulated. But in the last 20 years the picture has changed dramatically; privatization and deregulation are now common features of the railway industry.

The reasons for this change are quite clear: The railways in the industrialized countries have experienced massive losses of market shares; the european and the japanese public enterprises have produced massive financial deficits, that - at least partially - created additional burden for the federal budgets; scientific research showed theoretically and empirically the inefficiency of many regulatory policies. While the reasons for these reforms are quite clear, the question in what way the regulatory regimes should be reformed is still controversial. A central point of discussion in reforming the railway industry is the necessity and the possibility to install intramodal competition, that is competition between different railway operators on the same market. Those who support the idea of implementing intramodal competition have different expectations on its effects:

1. Some expect intramodal competition to replace regulation where the railway industry possesses market power.
2. Even if regulation can't be replaced, intramodal competition may be helpful to improve regulation. The lack of knowledge concerning cost and demand conditions of an industry is one of the most serious regulatory problems. The theory of yardstick regulation has shown the possibility to use competitors' performance as a benchmark.
3. The previous arguments have been rather static - and this is true for most of the literature on intramodal competition. Especially the austrian and the evolutionary theory stress that it is a failure to equate competition and the optimal use of already existing knowledge. Instead these theories focus on the competitive process as a trial and error-process (the generation of new price-quality-combinations or new production technologies, the selection of inferior innovations through consumers' choice, the diffusion of succesfull innovations). Entry (as some kind of innovation) has - according to this view - a value in itself.

This paper will concentrate on the german railway reform and the possibility to introduce intramodal competition. It first describes some central features of the railway industry. It then considers the problems of railways and options to solve them. The new organisational arrangements realized in Germany will then be described in more detail. The last two sections are devoted to the theoretical discussion, whether intramodel competition will arise respectively how intramodal competition can be introduced.

2. Some Characteristics of the Railway System

Two characteristics of railway services distinguish the railways at least gradually from other network industries: Rail operators act on several distincted markets and they do face stiff intermodal competition in most markets.

Looking for example at freight transportation, there is not one transport market but a number of markets with specific characteristics, those at the two extremes being that for bulk products of low unit value and a low logistical requirement profile, and that for costly goods where the volume carried is small but the market value high and the quality requirements for the transport are more important than its price. Between these two extremes lies a range of markets, often requiring specialised carriers. All these factors reflect a radical change in production structures which may in future lead to the more general use of just-in-time-systems whereby a greater number of smaller consignments are carried over longer dinstances and the predominant requirements will be speed and punctuality. Quality of service criteria are in fact at present assuming greater importance than the price of transport alone. Accordingly, competition is based on quality of service and no longer essentially on price.

Concerning freight transportation (but the same is true for passenger transportation), it was - and still is - quite difficult for the railways to adapt to the new emphasis on quality requirements in the choice of mode since the flows are more numerous, smaller in volume and diversidied, while the main requirements are speed and punctual delivery. The railways naturally focused on the markets in which they have the greatest commercial advantages, namely long-haul transport of bulk consignments, but these segments become economically less and less important. Some experts even consider railways to be an outmoded means of transport without real possibilities to be competitive in a modern society with other demands on transport efficiency and quality.

„Now there is little doubt that rail operators do face stiff competition in most markets“ (NASH, 1997). Sometimes it is argued, that rail operators possess markt power in markets for commuter services (due to the limited road capacity) and some bulk commodities (due to cost advantages or safety regulation).

Another aspect that deserves some attention is the partial dominance of public demand for rail services. There seems to be „a general public will to maintain railway services and, indeed, a desire that railways should be used more, particularly by freight" (BRADSHAW, 1997). Many of these services are not financially viable without public subsidies.

The cost characteristics of railway systems have been investigated especially for the United States; but some studies for european railways show similar results, so that it is not too obscur to apply the results. Some widely accepted stylized facts of railway systems are:

- Vertically integrated railway firms exhibit at best sligthly increasing economies of firm size.
- Rail operations exhibit economies of density (decreasing average costs with increasing utilization of a given network), though the size of these economies is controversial. Simulations show, that these economies are not mainly achieved by a better utilisation of fixed track but by larger trains and better utilisation of the equipment and crews. These economies are greater if service levels (e.g. number of trains per time unit) are held constant (KEATON, 1990).
- Between 50 and 80 per cent of infrastructure costs are fixed in the short run. Anecdotical evidence suggests that even in the longer run economies of scale exist (moving from single track to double track, for example, involves a less than double cost increase but often quadruples capacity) (NASH and PRESTON,1993).
- No clear results exist concerning economies of scope between different services (passenger and freight services) and especially between rail operation and network provision. The advocates of separated ownership (e.g. LAASER, 1991; EWERS, 1995) give some intuitive reasoning on this point, arguing that - even if such economies exist - they should be of negligible size.

3. Restructuring the Railway System: Necessity and Options

Until 1994 the german national rail carrier, the former Deutsche Bundesbahn, was part of the public administration. It showed the typical characteristics of european railway enterprises (RODI, 1996):

- A declining position in the transport markets. Its share of person transportation declined from 13% in 1963 to 6% in 1993; its share of goods transportation from 38% in 1963 to less than 20% in 1993.
- Permanent, high deficits (1963: 1 billion DM; 1993: 9,5 billion DM) that had to be financed by external borrowing. These deficits occured although the DB received massive public subsidies (since 1978 ca. 13 billion DM per year).

- Low productivity. Several international comparisons show, that the productive efficiency of the Deutsche Bundesbahn was below average compared to OECD railways.

The most obvious reasons for this disastrous development are - as outlined in the last section - changing demand patterns and technical restrictions of the railway system - compared to its competitors. But these market developments are just one side of the coin. Now, there is a wide agreement, that the public ownership was one of the main reasons for the inadequate adjustment. Several empirical and theoretical studies have shown that public enterprises are not inevitably inefficient, but that inefficiency can be expected when

- no clear and operational enterprise objectives have been defined,
- the public enterprise instead has to reach several, often inconsistent goals,
- the political system intervenes in strategic and operational planning,
- the public enterprises are protected through regulation or subsidies from competition (GROSSEKETTLER, 1988).

The efficiency of a public enterprise hinges on how the hierarchical principal agent-problem is solved (HELM and THOMPSON, 1991): the ultimate principals are the electorate; the ministers are chosen from their agents (the elected politicians), and these in turn, together with civil servants, attempt to control the public enterprise managers. Under the conditions named above the resulting lack of transparency over costs and the delineation of powers makes an effective control over political actors and managers almost impossible and allows these actors consequently to realize their own goals.

The central options to reform the railway industry are: the privatization of the railway enterprise as a whole without or with further regulatory interventions and the separation of operations from infrastructure. The first option is appropriate when the railway system possesses no market power; in this case, to find the optimal industry structure should be left to the market. The second option should be considered when the market power is of real concern and when intramodal competition is generally possible (as the cost studies indicate) but suppressed by discrimination of a vertically integrated carrier. The separation of operations from infrastructure is an alternative to the second option; by eliminating the integrated carrier it can facilitate the operation of services by a variety of operators over the same route, but economies of scope may be lost.

Tab. T1 shows, that Japan, Great Britain, Sweden and Germany have realized different options and that additionally the horizontal separation of operations and / or infrastructure is used to facilitate competition (especially when there are considerable barriers to entry) or yardstick regulation. Looking at the realized options, one has to record, that the optimal structure of the railway structure is up to now indetermined.

Tab. T1: Reorganization of the Railway Industry in four Countries

	Japan	Great Britain	Sweden	Germany
Year[a)]	**1987**	**1994**	**1988**	**1994**
Vertical separation?	yes, separation of freight division; passenger transport and infrastructure remain integrated	yes, separation of freight, passenger and infrastructure	yes, separation of operations from infrastructure	no (but divisionalization of F, P, I; from 1999 on: organizational separation)
Horizontal separation?	F: national monopoly; P+I: 6 regional monopolies plus three shinkansen companies	F: no P: 13 enterprises, regional monopolies I: no	no (but decentralisation of responsibility for regional passenger transport)	no (but decentralisation of responsibility for regional passenger transport)
Property rights/ remaining regulation?	F: PO P+I: PO; yardstick and access charge regulation (based on avoidable costs) F+P+I: Privatization announced	F: PE (franchise bidding); free entry P: PE (franchise bidding); price / quality regulation I: PE; price cap regulation	F+P: PO; restricted free access (passenger services on behalf of public authorities only) I: PO; access charge regulation	PO; free access to infrastructure, access charge oversight
Main Form of competition (without intermodal competition)?	F: none P+I: yardstick competition	F: actual and potential competition P and I: franchise competition	F+P: franchise competition for contracts to run subsidized regional services	F+P: eventually potential competition P: franchise competition for regional services

Notes: F: freight services; P: passenger services; I: infrastructure; PO: Public Ownership, PE: Private Enterprises; a) Year of implementation

4. The Railway Reform in Germany

The reform of the german railway system is of immense complexity. Several laws, including even the german constitution, had to be changed in 1993, new institutions were set up, and the organization of the railways, with its more than 375.000 employees (1993), was totally restructered. In what follows, only a few aspects of the reform can be discussed (for more comprehensive surveys see BOWERS, 1996; RODI, 1996; WISSENSCHAFTLICHER BEIRAT BEIM BUNDESMINISTER FÜR VERKEHR, 1997).
The legislative changes that came into force in 1994 hat three main targets:

1. Denationalization / Privatization
2. Financial Cleansing
3. Deregulation.

Ad 1.: The central target of the reform was to establish a clear-cut dividing line between commercial tasks and governmental functions. Accordingly, the responsibility for the development and financing of the infrastructure and the regional public transport, two activities that are judged to be of public concern, have been separated from the DB AG. Additionally, and presumably even more important, the formal privatization reduces at least formally the possibility of political interventions.

A dramatical change has taken place concerning regional or local public transport. Until 1993, the Deutsche Bundesbahn was almost never able to shut down unprofitable services or routes due to the strong position of the german states (Länder). Today, the duty of the DB AG to perform unprofitable services is at least formally abolished. If the Länder want the DB AG to perform such services, they have to buy them from the DB AG (so called Bestellprinzip). To compensate the Länder for the inceasing expenditures, they receive 12 billion DM per year from the federal government until 2002. (This dowry was of crucial importance for receiving the necessary approval of the reform from the Länder.) The Länder have the right to organize their local affairs by comprehensive transport planning and are free to use bus systems or other rail providers than the DB AG; so, it can be expected that a competition for the market will emerge in the future.

The development of the infrastructure and its financing remains with the government. The network development is part of the process of multimode transport planning by the Federal Ministry of Transport. Where the investments are at the commercial instigation of the DB AG it has to pay at least the depreciation on the investment and the costs of maintenance and operation of the network; otherwise the payments will be negotiated between the DB AG and the Federal Ministry of

Transport. Additionally, the DB AG has the possibility to realize (and to finance) infrastructure investments on its own.

Privatization: The Deutsche Bundesbahn (after it has been merged with the former east german railway, the Deutsche Reichsbahn, DR) has been transferred into the Deutsche Bahn AG (DB AG), a public limited company (Aktiengesellschaft, AG) with the federal government as the only shareholder (formal privatization). The services of the DB AG have been split up into four divisions (see Figure 2). Until 1999 the DB AG has to be transferred into a holding company, and every division will become a public limited company (a wholly-owned subsidiary of the holding company). The government will still be the only shareholder.

Whether this kind of privatization is an effective measure to reduce the political influence on the railways is questionable. On the one hand, the German Stock Corporation Law clarifies and widens the authority of the management - at least compared to the situation of the special assets of the Federal Government. On the other hand, the government has - as the only shareholder - still any possibility to influence strategic and even operational decisions of the DB AG; and in the past, the government has always used the possibility of direct interventions into the corporate policy of its companies. So, the assessment of the privatization depends mainly on the question, whether a material privatization will follow.

Whether there will be an additional third phase of the reform is still unclear. According to the law (Gesetz über die Gründung einer Deutsche Bahn Aktiengesellschaft), the government has the right - but not the duty - to sell shares of the holding and the transport AG's to the public. The selling of shares of the infrastructure AG will require another legislative change, and the federal government will have to keep a share of at least 50,1%.

The newly founded Federal Railway Office will assume regulatory responsibility for the railways. The regulatory oversight includes especially the fixing of technical standards for the use of the infrastructure and the control of negotiations between the DB AG and other rail operators that wish to use the network.

Ad 2.: The debt of the DB and DR, 70 billion DM, and their assets, as long as they are not directly required for the provision of railway services (especially land holdings with an estimated value of 40 billion DM), have been transferred to the newly founded Federal Railway Authority (Bundeseisenbahnvermögen). Public transfers and sales of land holdings will be used to repay the debt.

In addition, this agency took over the excess staff, who cannot be made redundant since they have lifetime contracts and conditions of service as Beamte (government employees). The Federal Railway Agency will direct these employees to other governmental jobs or to jobs on the railway where they are required. In the last case the Federal Railway Authority continues to pay the employees, and receives payments from the DB AG equivalent to the gross income of comparable employees newly hired by the DB AG (BOWERS, 1996).

Last but not least, the value of the fixed assets has been reduced dramatically. Compared to the consolidated balance sheet of 1993, the fixed assets of the DB AG amounted to 25%. As a result, the depreciation expense the DB AG has to earn reduces considerably.

Ad 3.: A central feature of the german railway reform that distinguishes it at least gradually from others is its empasis on intramodal competition. Consequently, the DB AG is (according to the german railway law) obliged to grant non-discriminatory access to (1) all german public railway operators, (2) german private railway enterprises, as long as they open their network to the DB AG, (3) international groups from EU member states that offer international services, (4) railway enterprises from member states of the EU or the EFTA, as long as they open their network to the DB AG. These regulations are a considerable extension of the European Commissions directive 91/440.

To meet these requirements the DB AG has already established a pricing system for the use of its infrastructure. Basically, the access prices reflect the average costs of a specific railway line but also include discounts and surcharges according to train specific characteristics (weight, speed, required punctuality). Rebates are available for customers who operate high overall train-kilometres per year, and those who order slots for several years in advance. The allocative inefficiency of the realized pricing system (average costs instead of marginal costs or Ramsey Prices, no peak load pricing), the lack of incentives to reduce costs and the use of bulk discounts, that favours the DB AG, have been critizised and led to a revision (RODI, 1996). Up to now considerable market entries have not taken place.

Fig. T1: Reorganization of the German Railway System

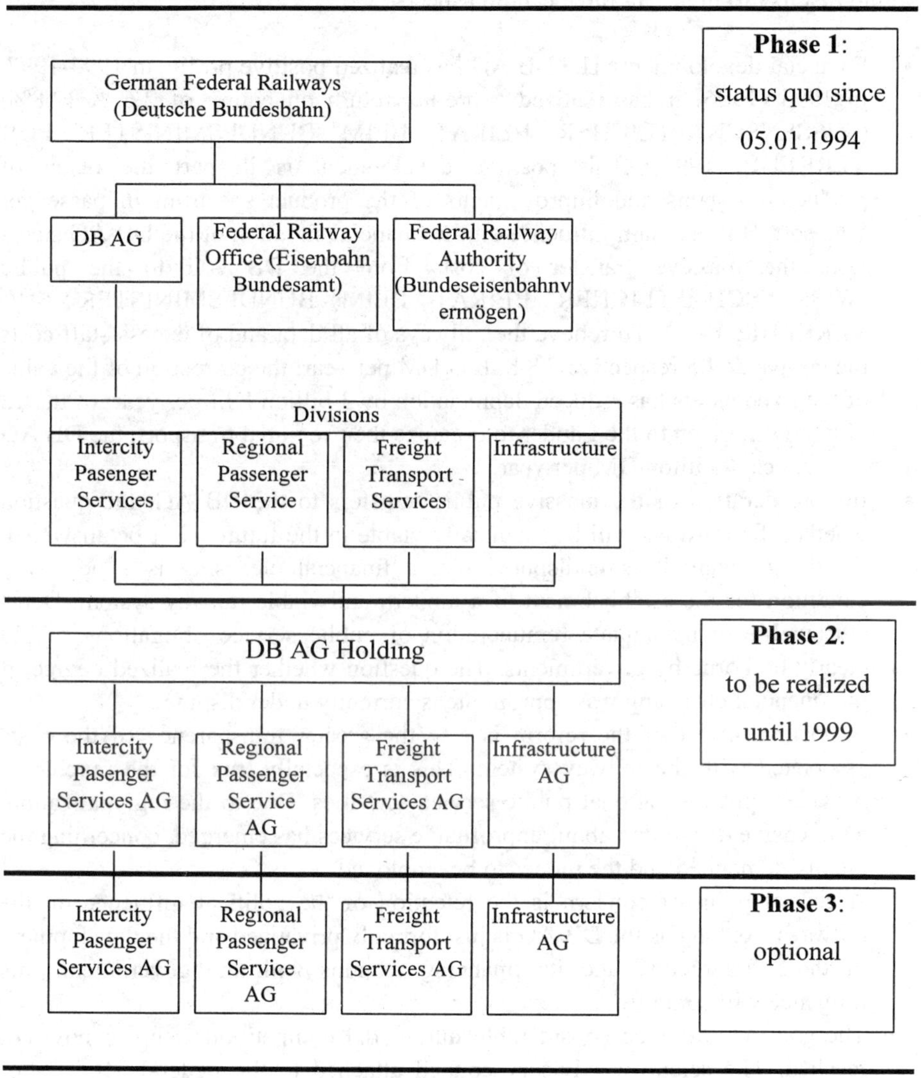

Notes: The suppression of the Federal Railway Office and the Federal Railway Authority in Phase 2 and 3 is due to space limitations, they will continue to exist.

To assess the success and failures of the reform is almost impossible. Here, I would just like to highlight three central aspects:

- Financial development: The DB AG has realized positive profits in 1994-1997. In 1995 (1996) it has realized a pre-tax return on equity of 2,6 % (2,8%) (WISSENSCHAFTLICHER BEIRAT BEIM BUNDESMINISTER FÜR VERKEHR, 1997). This positive development is in part the result of productivity gains and improvements of the product spectrum in passenger transport. But the main influence on the financial situation of the DB AG stems from the massive transfer of costs from the DB AG to the public (WISSENSCHAFTLICHER BEIRAT BEIM BUNDESMINISTER FÜR VERKEHR, 1997): To relieve the railways of all debt and of excess staff costs the tax-payer 4,5 respective 7,8 billion DM per year; the correction of the value of the fixed assets has reduced depreciation by 3 billion DM per year; of the 12 billion DM, given to the Länder to organize their regional transport, the DB AG receives ca. 8 billion DM per year.
- In consideration of the massive public transfers to the DB AG, the question whether the railways will be financially viable in the future can't be answered. But in germany it is undisputed that a financial cleansing is a necessary condition for the establishment of a modern and viable railway system. Debts attributable to inadequate remuneration of public service obligations should clearly be borne by governments. The question whether the realized degree of the financial cleansing was appropriate is currently under dispute.
- A positive effect of the reform is also the greater transparency of the costs associated with the railway system. This is especially true for the purchaser-provider split for regional public service activities. Due to the regionalization, an intensive discussion about unprofitable services has emerged, concerning the quality demanded and the modes to be employed.
- A central point of concern is the retention of the political influence on the railways. As long as the DB AG is just formally privatized and the development of the infrastructure and its financing remains with the government, this influence will continue.
- The goal to introduce considerable intramodal competition is up to now not reached. The scientific advisory council attached to the Federal Ministry of Transport sees the main obstacle in the incentive and the possibility of a vertically integrated railway enterprise to discriminate against actual and potential competitors. Appropriately, the council demands the separation of operations from infrastructure.

The next two sections comprise a closer inspection of the hypothesis of the scientific advisory council, that vertical separation is a necessary prerequisite for intramodal competition. Section 5 takes a look at the incentive of an integrated enterprise to discriminate, while section 6 investigates the possibility of a conduct regulation to avoid discrimination.

5. Intramodal Competition and the Need for Access Regulation

Assume that some Firm M has an unregulated monopoly over the network services that are an essential input for production of a final good (let's call them upstream and downstream market respectively). The central questions to be answered are: (1) Does M have an incentive to extend its monopoly to the downstream market, for example by means of prohibitive network access charges? (2) If some kind of restrictive behavior occurs, how is it to be judged in terms of social welfare?

The answers to these questions are still highly controversial in economic theory. The clearest statement stems from the Chicago School of Antitrust Analysis: (1) Any monopoly profit from an industry can be extracted just once. (2) The upstream monopoly will and can realize this profit by pricing arrangements and eventually by vertical restraints or vertical integration. It will choose the most efficient means. (3) The chosen vertical arrangements will always lead to a higher social welfare. Productive efficiency and the monopoly price ensure the highest possible profit; so the monopolist will avoid every action that raises costs or leads to a price increase. Especially the monopolist will

- withdraw from the downstrean market and realize an open access if other firms have cost advantages. It can extract the - now higher - monopoly profit using nonlinear prices (the firms in the downstream market will have to pay marginal costs plus a fixed fee);
- avoid the problems of double marginalization or distorted input choices by using non-linear prices;
- internalize horizontal external effects in the downstream market (for example by establishing exclusive territories, TIROLE, 1992).

The problem is - according to this view - not the vertical relationship but the upstream monopoly position of firm M. „If endowed with full information and commitment power, and enough instruments of control, a monopolist in one activity would have nothing to gain from inefficiency in a vertically related activity because maximizing profit would entail maximizing efficiency" (ARMSTRONG/COWAN/VICKERS, 1993, 147).

The analysis of the Chicago School has been proven to be oversimplified. Several authors have identified situations in which vertical foreclosure is profitable for the monopoly but suppresses social welfare (for a review see ARMSTRONG/COWAN/VICKERS, 1993, or TIROLE 1992). Vertical foreclosure may be profitable for the upstream monopoly - even if it lowers productive efficiency – if

- positive bargaining costs and / or sunk costs in the downstream market exist that put the non-integrated downstream firms on a strategic disadvantage compared to internal divisions of the monopoly;
- the vertical integration raises barriers to entry in the upstream market.

Even more important than these considerations are the problems that arise if we deal with a vertically integrated monopoly that is a public enterprise or a regulated private monopoly. In both cases the objectives of the regulatory agency, the form of regulation it employs and its information status have to be taken into account.
In the case of a public enterprise, the assumption, that the monopoly maximizes its profits (or social welfare), has to be questioned. Due to the double agency problem (the government is not just the principal of the rail management but acts as the electorate's agent; VOGELSANG, 1990, 49) it seems more appropriate to assume, that the regulator uses the enterprise to achieve objectives that belong to environmental, technology or regional policy.

A good example for the way in which governments objectives could influence intramodal competition is the current policy towards the german magnetic levitation system ‚the Transrapid, a technology that is heavily subsidized and promoted by the german government. To export this technology, so the official argument goes, it is necessary to prove its technical maturity by establishing a regular service within Germany. For this reason a route, connecting Hamburg and Berlin, will be build. The DB AG binded itself by contract to refrain from using high speed trains on this connection to avoid any competition to the Transrapid. Consequently the danish rail announced an interest in offering a high speed train on this connection. To hinder this entry is in the interest of the DB AG and its owner.

Can foreclosure be expected when the upstream monopoly is regulated? Without an access price regulation three aspects have to be highlighted:

1. Entry often conveys informations to the regulator about cost structures and demand. So, irrespective of the chosen regulatory regime, inefficient foreclosure seems to be likely, if the monopoly expects the regulator to use these informations for tightening the regulatory constraint (see e.g. LAFFONT and TIROLE, 1996).
2. Under a cost based regulation (e.g. rate of return regulation) the maximum profit achievable for the regulated firm depends on its costs (e.g. invested capital). „Consequently, the firm has an incentive to take actions to increase its capital stock even if such actions are not otherwise profitable or efficient“ (ORDOVER and SALONER, 1989).

3. Under a price cap-regulation things differ. Assume that there exists a price cap for some final services. In this case, the regulated utility has no direct incentive to exclude entry. Since the monopoly is the residual profit claimant under price cap regulation it will allow entry as long as it can extract the industry profit through charging (non-linear) access prices.

Where did our discussion get us? We have considered the case of a vertically integrated monopoly to see whether there is a need for access regulation. Three results can be drawn:

1. The only role intramodal competition can play in this setting is to enhance productive efficiency. The upstream monopoly will prevent the realization of allocative efficiency.
2. In a wide variety of settings, the upstream monopoly will not restrain entry as long as it improves productive efficiency. The necessary conditions for this statement to hold are: The upstream monopolist (1) maximizes his profits and (2) is free to choose the appropriate instruments (including vertical restraints), (3) bargaining between the monopoly and downstream firms is costless, (4) entry in the downstream market is not associated with sunk costs, (5) the upstream monopoly is not contested.
3. Public ownership and conduct regulation can be severe obstacles to efficiency improving entries.

For the future of the railway system these results are of some interest. Some economists argue, that due to strong intermodal competition the railway system does not possess market power; in this case, allocative efficiency could be left to the intermodal competition. Consequently the appropriate policy should be a further liberalization of the railways because public ownership and regulation are the main obstacles to efficient vertical relationships.

6. Intramodal Competition and Access Regulation

Controversely to the view taken in the foregoing chapter, intramodal competition is more often seen as a means to reduce market power of a network utility. To realize this aim, a totally different public policy is needed: Here, to regulate the public utility is a necessary condition for realizing efficiency.

The regulation of access charges serves to avoid (1) monopolistic pricing of the network service and (2) the exclusion of competing final product suppliers by the monopoly, while at the same time (3) allowing the monopoly to recover efficiently the fixed costs of the network (throughout this chapter we rule out public lump sum transfers to the network operator, thus the monopoly has to cover its fixed costs) (LAFFONT and TIROLE, 1996, 229; ARMSTRONG, DOYLE and VICKERS, 1996, 131). Numerous ways to calculate „optimal" access charges have been discussed and realized. In what follows we will discuss cost based approaches, the Efficient Component Pricing Rule and the Global Price Cap respectively.

For entrants and some regulators a cost based regulation seems to be some kind of natural solution. According to this view the access charge should be set e.g. by the formulae: Optimal access charge = long run incremental costs of access + mark up.

A mark up is included to cover deficits that would result if the network exhibits economies of scale. The question is how to determine the mark up because, as is well known, every way to allocate joint costs is arbitrary. The most simple solution is to allocate joint costs proportionally to network use.

At a first view the cost based regulation seems to reach all the stated aims in a forward manner and it seems to be relatively easy to realize (e.g. no information on demand and competition in the downstream market is necessary). But cost based regulations have well-known disadvantages (LAFFONT and TIROLE, 1996; RODI, 1996):

1. No incentive to minimize the network costs is implemented. But in industries like the railway system, network costs constitute the major part of total costs. So even if entry occurs, the productive efficiency of the industry may not improve sufficiently.
2. Allocative efficiency is not reached even if the downstream markets are - due to intramodal competition - perfectly competitive. Average cost pricing always leads to a loss in social surplus compared to marginal cost or Ramsey pricing.
3. Cost based access charges establish a strong incentive for the monopoly to discriminate competing final product suppliers, especially by using non-price instruments. Incremental costs plus mark ups do not reflect the monopoly's opportunity costs (profit reduction in the final product market), so non-price discrimination can be a profit maximizing strategy. Especially in the railway industry, numerous possibilities to discriminate exist (e.g. careless handling of trains, uneven treatment in case of delays).
4. The formulae doesn't account for congestion costs. With limited capacity, network users affect each others use of the network due to the fact that congestion externalities appear. Efficiency requires the access charge to reflect the costs a user imposes on others (LERZ, 1996).
4. To determine long-run incremental costs is a rather difficult task.

To overcome some of the problems that characterise cost based regulation, BAUMOL (1983) offered another fomulae, the Principle of Parity or, as it is now called, the „Efficient Component Pricing Rule" (ECPR): Optimal access charge = Long run incremental costs of access + Opportunity cost of providing access.

Here, the opportunity cost is defined to be the reduction in the monopoly's profit per unit of access caused by the provision of access. To see this more clearly we can express the ECPR by the following formulae: Optimal access charge = M's final price - M's incremental cost in the downstream market.

The logic of this formulae goes as follows: As long as the monopolists just breaks even, the difference between its final product price and its incremental costs in the downstream market is nothing but the necessary contribution to network costs, „including opportunity costs, congestion costs, common costs, cost of use of capital facilities valued at replacement cost and a rate of return equal to the current cost of capital" (BAUMOL, 1983, 353). Without this charge, the monopoly won't be able to cover its costs.

The ECPR has at least three properties that make it very attractive: (1) It seems to be relatively easy to implement, because (using the second formulation) you don't have to care about network costs. All you need is the final product price and incremental costs in the downstream market. BAUMOL (1983), discussing the application of the formulae to railway systems, was of cause fully aware of the problems associated with these informational requirements, but his conclusion, that these requirements are easier to meet than to estimate incremental network costs, can hardly be questioned. (2) The ECPR ensures, that the monopolist has no incentive to foreclose it's rivals through non-price methods. The access charge compensates him by definition exactly for his reduction in profit. (3) Only entrants, who are more efficient than the monopoly, have an incentive to enter. Entrants have to charge the monopoly's network costs plus its profit but less than the monopolists' price if they are to make profit. Obviously, this can only be reached if the entrant is more efficient in the downstream market.

Despite these favorable characteristics the ECPR-formulae has to be critizised for at least two reasons:

1. Competition will not lead to allocative efficiency, if the monopolist initially has market power (ECONOMIDES and WHITE, 1995). The necessity for an entrant to earn the monopolists' opportunity cost (it's profit) will protect the market power against the competitive erosion of prices. To put it differently: The ECPR is a partial rule that has to be complemented by a regulation of final prices.
2. The estimation of opportunity costs requires the regulator to take the competition in the downstream market into account. BAUMOL (1983) examined in his original contribution only the case, where an entrant replaced the monopolists' service. But in many cases competition with differentiated products seems to be more relevant. In this case the estimation of opportunity

costs requires the knowledge of cross price elasticities. ARMSTRONG, DOYLE and VICKERS (1996) showed that efficient access charges usually deviate from ECPR-charges.

Having reached this point, it's only natural - as LAFFONT and TIROLE (1996) have done - to regard access charges as an integrated part of firm regulation. To reach their proposal they use the usual two way argument:

In a first step, the optimal, welfare maximising, prices of the monopoly for all of it's services are determined. This results of cause in Ramsey-Pricing. Access to the network is treated here as just another final good provided by the monopoly. So, the inverse-elasticity rule also applies to access charges (the difference between access charge and direct costs of access depends on the inverse elasticity of demand for access and the shadow price of the budget constraint).

In a second step it is argued that an optimal global price cap regulation (global, because access is treated as a final good) will induce the firm to select the proper Ramsey structure. To reach this well-known result, the weights of the prices have to be determined exogenously (the regulated firm has no ability to influence the weights) and they have to be proportinal to the optimal (Ramsey-efficient) quantities of the associated goods (e.g. VICKERS and YARROW, 1988).

The advantages and disadvantages of price cap regulation have been discussed extensively (e.g. BEESLEY and LITTLECHILD, 1989, LISTON, 1993). But some aspects still deserve to be highlighted:

1. With a properly implemented global price cap regulation it is difficult to see any incentive to foreclose rivals through non-price methods. „Intuitively, under a global price cap, the regulated firm can elect to earn most of its income through interconnection and it then has no incentive to reduce its demand for access" (LAFFONT and TIROLE, 1996).
2. A price cap regulation that meets LAFFONT and TIROLEs requirements is very difficult to implement. The establishment of efficient weights of the prices assumes implicitly that Ramsey-prices and -quantities are already known.
3. The efficiency of a price cap regulation depends on the way it is practiced. The central idea behind the price cap regulation is to establish a price ceiling in relation to the level of costs which the firm is expected to achieve if it performs efficiently over the review period (HELM and THOMPSON, 1991). In practice, price caps partly relate to actual profits and this reduces the incentives for the regulated firm to introduce profit-enhancing cost savings or investments because increased profits may lead to a tighter price ceiling in the next review period. „It is difficult to be enthusiastic about price caps: like all aspects of regulation they are unsatisfactory devices" (ROBINSON, 1996).

What lessons have to be learned from the ongoing debate over access charge regulation? The first and most important one seems to be: To reach overall efficiency simply by relying on access charges means to demand too much from this instrument. Or as LAFFONT and TIROLE (1996) put it: „A discussion of an access rule without reference to the rest of the regulatory environment has limited interest. The quality of an access pricing rule depends on the determination of prices for the final products". Thus, if the railways possess market power, a „simple" access charge regulation will not suffice.

7. Conclusions

The necessity to free railways from political interventions, to enable them to pursue commercial targets and to abandon unprofitable services is now widely accepted. The establishment of intramodal competition could also help to improve the efficiency of the railway system by allowing different, presumably specialized rail operators to discover and to create profitable market segments.

The measures that have been taken to reach these goals differ markedly from country to country. Up to now, the german reform focuses on the commerzialisation of the railways within the framework of public ownership, financial cleansing, and on the realization of intramodal competition. While the necessity of a financial cleansing is not debated, many observer question the suitability of a formal privatization and whether intramodal competition will emerge as long as the DB AG is a vertically integrated monopoly.

The review of the literature has shown, that a vertically integrated carrier will have an incentive to discriminate potential entrants under many circumstances, especially when the carrier is a regulated or publicly owned enterprise. If these obstacles can be removed, it can be expected that entry is accomodated by the carrier as long as the entrant increases productive efficiency while the erosion of monopolistic positions of the DB AG cannot be expected. To enhance allocative efficiency the regulation of access will be necessary, but the discussion has shown that access regulation will not be sufficient.

So, the question what role intramodal is to play and the analysis of alternative arrangements, especially the separation of operations from infrastructure, will have to stay on the political agenda.

References

ARMSTRONG, M., S. COWAN and J. VICKERS (1993), Regulatory Reform: Economic Analysis and British Experience. Cambridge and London: MIT Press.

ARMSTRONG, M., C. DOYLE and J. VICKERS (1996), The Access Pricing Problem: A Synthesis. Journal of Industrial Economics, 44, pp. 131-150.

BAUMOL, W. J. (1983), Some Subtle Pricing Issues in Railroad Regulation. International Journal of Transport Economics, 10, pp. 341-355.

BEESLEY, M. E. and S. C. LITTLECHILD (1989), The Regulation of Privatized Monopolies in the United Kingdom. Rand Journal of Economics, 20, pp. 454-472.

BOWERS, P. H. (1996), Railway Reform in Germany. Journal of Transport Economics and Policy, 30, pp. 95-102.

BRADSHAW, W. P. (1997), Competition in the Rail Industry. Oxford Review of Economic Policy, 13, pp. 93-103.

BRENCK, A. (1993), Privatisierungsmodelle für die Deutsche Bundesbahn, in: ALLEMEYER, W. et. al., Privatisierung des Schienenverkehrs. Göttingen: Vandenhoeck & Ruprecht, pp. 37-184.

ECONOMIDES, I. and L. J. WHITE (1995), Access and Interconnection Pricing: How Efficient is the „Efficient Component Pricing Rule"? Antitrust Bulletin, pp. 557-579.

EWERS, H.-J. (1995), Wettbewerbskontrolle: Zugangsbedingungen bei den europäischen Schienennetzen, in: Deutsche Verkehrswissenschaftliche Gesellschaft, ed., Europäische Verkehrspolitik nach Maastricht. Bergisch-Gladbach: DVWG, pp. 160-165.

GROSSEKETTLER, H. (1988), Deregulierung und Privatisierung. Modeströmung, überfällige Korrektur oder ordnungspolitische Daueraufgabe? Volkswirtschaftliche Diskussionsbeiträge der Westfälischen Wilhelms-Universität Münster, 108, Münster.

HELM, D. and D. THOMPSON (1991), Privatised Transport Infrastructure and Incentives to Invest. Journal of Transport Economics and Policy, 25, pp. 231-246.

KEATON, M. H. (1990). Economies of Density and Service Levels on U.S. Railroads: An Experimental Analysis. Logistics and Transportation Review, 26, pp. 211-227.

LAASER, C. F. (1991), Wettbewerb im Verkehrswesen. Tübingen: Mohr.

LAFFONT, J.-J. and J. TIROLE (1996), Creating Competition through Interconnection: Theory and Practice. Journal of Regulatory Economics, 10, pp. 227-256.

LERZ, S. (1996), Congestion Theory and Railway Traffic. Capelle: Ridderprint.

LISTON, C. (1993), Price-Cap Versus Rate-of-Return Regulation. Journal of Regulatory Economics, 5, pp. 25-48.

NASH, C. (1997). United Kingdom, in: EUROPEAN CONFERENCE OF MINISTERS OF TRANSPORT, The Separation of Operations from Infrastructure in the Provision of Railway Services, Paris: OECD, pp. 53-89.

NASH, C. and J. PRESTON (1993), The Policy Debate in Great Britain, in:: European Conference of Ministers of Transport, ed., Privatisation of Railways. Paris: CEMT, pp. 81-119.

ORDOVER, J. A. and G. SALONER (1989), Predation, Monopolization, and Antitrust, in: Schmalensee, R. and Willig, R. D., ed., Handbook of Industrial Organization. Volume I, Amsterdam: Elsevier, pp. 537-596.

ROBINSON, C. (1996), Profit, Discovery and the Role of Entry: The Case of Electricity, in: SAYER, S. et.al., Regulating Utilities: A Time for a Change?, Trowbridge: Redwood, pp. 109-144.

RODI, H. (1996), Effizienz im Schienenverkehr. Göttingen: Vandenhoeck & Ruprecht.

SWIFT, J. (1996), Comment (to HELM, 1996), in: SAYER, S. et.al., Regulating Utilities: A Time for a Change?, Trowbridge: Redwood, pp. 184-187.

TIROLE, J. (1992), The Theory of Industrial Organization, Cambridge: MIT Press.

VICKERS, J. and G. YARROW (1988), Privatization: An Economic Analysis, London: MIT Press.

VOGELSANG, I. (1990), Public Enterprice in Monopolistic and Oligopolistic Industries. Chur: Harwood Academic Publishers.

WISSENSCHAFTLICHER BEIRAT BEIM BUNDESMINISTER FÜR VERKEHR (1997), Bahnstrukturreform in Deutschland - Empfehlungen zur weiteren Entwicklung. Internationales Verkehrswesen, 49, pp. 626-633.

U: Material Intensity of Transportation and Implications for Sustainable Mobility in Europe

Hartmut Stiller

1. Introduction

In general transport is regarded today as one of the ecologically most critical sectors of our economy. However, up to now studies focused mainly on the emissions caused by the various transport modes (VIA 1990; HÖPFNER et al. 1993; HASSEL et al. 1995, MAILBACH et al. 1995), whereas the material intensity has been rather neglected. Therefore, in the following paper the material intensity of transportation will be analysed. In the beginning, the concept of material intensity analysis and its methodology will be introduced. Thereafter, results for the material intensity of infrastructure, vehicles and their use for various transport categories will be presented. Finally, the implications for a more sustainable mobility will be discussed.

2. Material Intensity as a Screening Indicator for Environmental Impact Potential

Today it is increasingly being accepted that the resource intensity of the conventional western lifestyle is unsustainable. Human-induced material flows often exceed those by nature, thereby shifting ecological equilibria with unknown consequences and risking to overload ecological carrying capacities. In order to bring the precautionary principle into operation, a reduction of human induced global material flows by half is needed to restablize the interaction of anthroposphere and ecosphere (SCHMIDT-BLEEK, 1994). If our wealth is not to be reduced, this can only be achieved by increasing resource productivity. However, the current consumption of natural resources is unequally distributed globally, and the per capita consumption of industrial countries cannot be adopted by the world population without ecological collapse. Thus, an increase in resource productivity by a factor of ten is a necessary precondition for sustainability (Factor 10 Club, 1995). A factor four can already be reached wich technology that is currently available (VON WEIZSÄCKER, LOVINS, LOVINS, 1995).

If the ecosphere as a whole is endangered by human activities, operational indicators are needed which show at least approximately the environmental impact potential of those activities. Because of the enormous complexity of nature this will only be possible to a limited extent. Looking for a small set of indicators, parameters should be applied that are provisionally in accordance with the precautionary principle. These parameters have to be independent of specific known environmental impacts. If they were based on effects that already happen, this would imply that we know today the total environmental impact of material flows, or we can at least assume that the unknown impact is proportional to the known impact. Experience tells us that this assumption is obsolete.

Therefore it is suggested to at least supplement the information on specific known impacts which would lead to re-action measures with information on general impact potential leading to pre-active improvement measures. A global environmental impact potential can be indicated by the life-cycle-wide input of materials, energy and space. This information may be sufficient to distinguish between product alternatives. (SCHMIDT-BLEEK, 1994; BRINGEZU et al., 1995).

Highly sophisticated approaches of life-cycle-analysis (LCA) depending on 10 to 100 specific environmental impacts and their harmonized evaluation will probably not be applied to the millions of products which today´s economy offers on the market. Against this background, material intensity analysis (MAIA), as a part of basic resource intensity analysis, can serve as a screening tool that provides a first approximation of the order of magnitude of the environmental impact potential of goods and services. If additional information, e.g. on eco-toxic impacts, shall be considered, a comprehensive full scale LCA may be performed at the next step (BRINGEZU, STILLER, SCHMIDT-BLEEK, 1996).

3. Indicating Environmental Impact Potential of Material Flows

Practically all human activities are associated with material flows which are linked to the extraction of primary materials and - as a consequence - to the release of emissions and waste.

The magnitude of the input to the anthroposphere determines the final volume of its output. Whereas the different input and output flows have different (and in most cases unknown) impacts, the main categories can be defined in such a way that increasing numbers will indicate a rising pressure and a decreasing number will reflect a falling pressure on the environment. The classification of material flows may also be orientated towards sustainability criteria, e.g. the rate of natural regeneration. Thus, the first approximation is a distinction between abiotic (=non renewable) and biotic (=renewable) resources. In the case of water, we account for any volume extracted or actively drained off from natural reservoirs or water flows. Air is quantified as an input if it is chemically or physically transformed. Whereas material flows themselfes do not necessarily lead to a chemical transformation of the material, chemical reactions potentially mobilize the whole volume of the material processed, which can be indicated by the volume of air reacting.

Altogether, a system approach leads to 5 categories of material flows which have to be distinguished (SCHMIDT-BLEEK, 1996):

1. abiotic raw materials
2. biotic raw materials
3. soil
4. water
5. air

These material flows are calculated on a "cradle to grave" basis for products. The material vector which is not part of the weight of the product itself is called the environmental rucksack. Materials like stone or gravel only have a rather small rucksack, whereas materials like gold or tin have a large one due to the enormous material flows during their production.

Consequently, energy carriers are also accounted in mass units because first, the environmental impact is in most cases caused by substances and not by the energy itself, and second, a quantitative comparison of energy carriers and other materials is only possible on the basis of non-energetic units (MANSTEIN 1995).

In the case of transport, abiotic raw materials, water and air are of principal interest. However, as water supply varies considerably depending on local conditions, a life-cycle-wide calculation of water consumption must be interpreted carefully.

4. Methodology

4.1 Service Unit and Target Question

As in life-cycle-analysis, the MAIA calculations are performed on a cradle to grave basis. Input of primary materials can be related to the service unit (functional unit) of a product, resulting in the MIPS (Material Input per Service Unit). The first step of a material intensity analysis is the definition of the target questions, based on the principal interest in the material intensity of the product and service of concern (SCHMIDT-BLEEK, 1996). This definition is of crucial importance for the final results. A single act of transport under specific conditions can lead to completely different results compared to a broad system comparison of several alternative transport modes.

In practice the definition of the service unit is not that easy as each good generally provides a whole bundle of services. Additional services of a good are often the reason for differences in material intensity, but they also restrict the implementation of more resource effective solutions. In the case of freight transport the transport of one ton of freight over a distance of one kilometer (t-km) seems to be the principal service unit, although for example the velocity of transport is an important additional service which restricts substitution by the most resource effective option to a certain extent.

Moreover, system analysis reveals that each act of transport not only moves a product from A to B but is also connected with the transfer of goods. In the following, therefore distance dependent material flows have been separated from handling activities which will be accounted for in t/t transfered.

In this paper first the actual material intensity of different transport modes in Germany will be compared. In a second step a more detailed classification shall allow a calculation of the material intensity of transport chains for basic materials and consumer goods. The problem now lies in the fact that ,on the one hand, millions of different transport services have to be categorized down to a few easy to handle numbers but, on the other hand, that differences in the material intensity due to scale effects or specific local and regional conditions like industrial structure or population density, should not be neglected to leave room for further optimisation. Therefore, waterways for example have been distinguished in Rhine as the by far most intensivily used German waterway, rivers and channels as artificially created waterways (STILLER, 1995b).

In other cases different parts of a network serve slightly different services. Whereas highways serve mainly long distance traffic, local roads have to provide final distribution and give access to other network units. The differentiation between highways, national, regional, country and local roads takes these functional differences into account.

However, it should be mentioned that availability of appropriate statistical data is one of the pre-conditions for classification. There might be cases in which a local road is comparable to national roads, but it is a feature of any classification that in a specific case average values do not necessarily reflect the real situation.

For vehicles the problems are quite similar. Scale effects and load optimization but also the transported goods are the principal factors for differences in their material intensity. Again, available statistics significantly influence the final classification as not only the total number of vehicles but also the total services provided need to be documented (see HEUSCH, BOESEFELDT 1994; BMV 1994; DB 1992).

Thus, for categorizing ocean-going ships world fleet statistics have been used where a classification of different types of ships reflecting the main categories of goods transported can be found (Lloyd´s Register 1992). For trucks a classification according to the total vehicle´s size has been choosen, using statistical data of the German vehicle federal agency and vehicle specific traffic accounting in some former projects initiated by the German Traffic Ministry.

4.2 Allocation

In the case of several target outputs of processes, MAIA in general foresees an allocation due to mass units. However, firm specific allocation parameters for the distribution of the "material overhead" are allowed. As in the case of economic joint products and the distribution of fixed costs of production, there exists a certain degree of arbitrariness (PREIMESBERGER, 1994).

Of the several cases of transport with joint services, most important is the allocation of the material input to personal and freight transport by roads and railroads. This is performed by dividing the material input according to gross-ton-kilometers based on the weight of persons, freight and vehicles transported each year on the infrastructure. For reconstruction of roads, however, the contribution to the observed damages is taken as allocation principle (STILLER, 1993).

Some additional services of infrastructure like the use of channels for leisure purposes have been disregarded as the infrastructure was not originally built for this purpose. But in most cases material input for other services has not been accounted for, e.g. ploting roads in urban areas has been considered to be a general settlement service not directly directed to road transport.

A specific allocation problem occurs in the case of infrastructure networks as these are not a single product but rather a developing network changing its size and structure over the lifetime of its components. In general, material intensity analysis requires a look at the whole life-cycle of a product. However, a road, or more extreme one km of a road, in general can only deliver a service if it is part of a network.[1] Therefore, balancing infrastructure has to consider the whole infrastructure networks although these are continously changing units. Thus, inputs for the construction are linear depreciated according to the expected lifetime of the parts of an infrastructure network, but then those values are related to the total transport services provided by the network during a reference year, e.g. 1992. This implies that inefficient use of an existing network yields to high MIPS-values. At the same time, development over time of infrastructure networks limits a temporal comparison of their efficiency.

Material intensity calculation is always based on those networks for which the total provided services are known. A consequence of such methodology is that some changes in infrastructure only lead to minor changes in their material intensity. This reflects the fact that infrastructure networks can not be changed abruptly and have to be developed rather smoothly.

Finally, it must be mentioned that as these calculations are made using the actual performance of transport systems and based on broad average values, it is not possible to just take the results for the impact assessment of concrete planning decisions. In this case specific calculations can lead to results different from the values presented below.

4.3 Lifetime of Infrastructures and Vehicles

The problem experienced when estimating the lifetime of durable goods like vehicles and especially infrastructure in general is that no data exists which is based on experiences about sold products nowadays. Thus, values based on old, similar products and economic depreciation times are the only sources available for plausible estimations. One might assume that the average age of vehicles in the market is a good estimate for the total lifetime. However, as markets change over time the statistical lifetime of vehicles laid up seems to be the better estimate. As it is not only a question of time but also of frequency of use, the lifetime of trucks has been combined with a km-dependent depreciation.

Instead of these experience-based lifetime values one might think of using economic depreciation times. This would have the advantage that no additional estimates would be required. However, as economic estimates in general are shorter than real lifetime, e.g.to get taxation advantages, unrealistically high values for the material intensity in the first years would be the consequence, which violates the polluter pays principle if material balances shall also be kept over time. On the other hand, if the estimated lifetime is really too short in a specific case, one could see the further use as using a waste product with no additional material input required.

Thus, in this study the lifetime of vehicles has been calculated according to the statistical data for vehicles laid up or scrapped. For infrastructure, however, such data are not available. Because of the much longer total lifetime, values depend much more on new technological developments or changes of demand in the economy and society and less on equipment being specifically worn out. Moreover, parts of the infrastructure form a network which is developing over time. A network consists of main connections and less intensively used parts down to the final distribution. In general, local connections seem to have a shorter lifetime compared to key lines as one can see from the German railway network, where a lot of local lines have been closed down over the last 40 years. However, as enlargement and reconstruction of infrastructure is continually taking place e.g. to provide higher velocities especially on key connections resulting in a de facto renewing, and as lifetime varies considerably, no distinction will be made between the lifetime of different parts of infrastructure. Thus, calculations here are based on the mean lifetime values for economic infrastructure depreciation calculated by the DIW (ENDERLEIN, KUHNERT (1992), 62,93,99).

When durable goods and infrastructures are analyzed, the future use of specific recycling technologies is uncertain. Therefore allocation in material intensity analysis is based on the actual input of primary or secondary materials in processes.

The implications of such an accounting in infrastructure can be seen for example, in the reconstruction of highways where even if all waste material is reused, additional virgin material is required to get the same pavement quality. Thus, an input orientated accounting avoids that an increase in the stock in the technoshere is regarded as environmentally neutral.

5. Results

1. A comparison of the different freight transport systems in Germany 1992 shows that from the view of a material intensity analysis, transport should the provided best by ocean-going ships, followed by inland navigation, trains and finally by trucks. Fig.U1-U3 show that in each category sea transport is the most efficient transport mode. It is followed by waterway navigation, which only due to the high water losses of channels has the highest water consumption. The current German railway system has nearly the same input of abiotic resources as road transport, but significantly less air und water consumption. Thus, in general the well-known ranking from other emission-based studies is supported by a material intensity analysis, but partly for other reasons.
2. For each transport system the bulk of abiotic resources is used for infrastructure, whereas the vehicle´s use dominates the air consumption (and CO_2 emissions). The high contribution of infrastructure to the total material input is characteristic for the ecological impact of infrastructure. Neglecting the infrastructure would yield to an ecological misallocation.

The presented figures are based on the actual level of services provided by the different transport systems. Whereas the German road infrastructure network is used in a relatively efficient way, the efficiency of the German railway system is rather low. Enhancing the maximum number of trains on key lines from the current 12 trains per hour to the technically feasible 50 trains would increase resource productivity sharply (see also SCHALLABÖCK, HESSE, 1995). The second reason for the rather high material intensity of railway infrastructure is the smaller slope and larger curve of railway lines which result in large earth movements during railway construction. This part of the material intensity indicates the large change of landscape due to infrastructure construction.

Similar effects are hidden behind the average value for inland vessels. Whereas the Rhine river is used in a very efficient way (Fig. U1-U3), channels, and to a smaller extent canalizing of other rivers, require huge material movements for their construction. Navigation on channels is calculated to have borne a rucksack of 1310 g/t-km of abiotic materials in 1990 (STILLER, 1995b). Again a potential increase in transport volume would reduce these figures dramatically.

Fig. U1: Material Intensity of Transport Systems - Germany 1992: Abiotic Materials

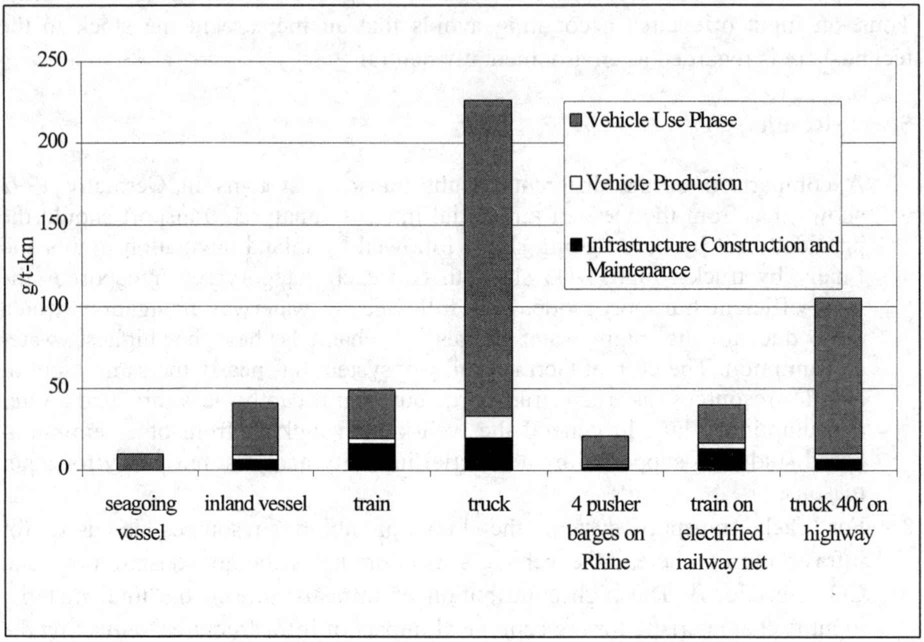

Fig. U2: Material Intensity of Transport Systems - Germany 1992: Air

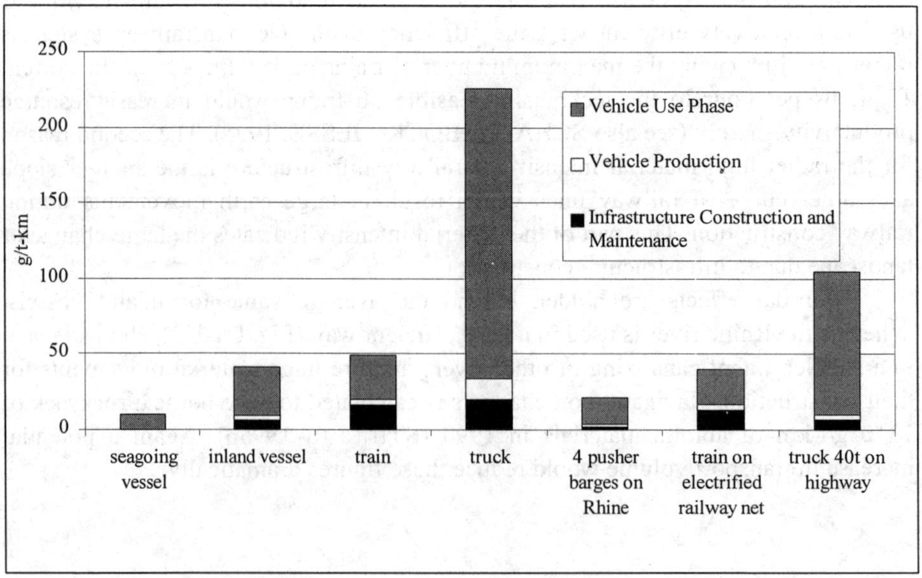

3. There are large scale effects in infrastructure efficiency which are revealed by a detailed analysis. Yet the three addititional transport modes in Fig. U1 indicate that the transport on main lines has a significantly smaller material intensity per ton-kilometer compared to the final distribution of goods on local roads. As a more detailed example Fig. U4 shows the abiotic raw materials calculated for the transport of one t-km via different types of German roads. It reveals that transport via local roads requires ten times more abiotic resources compared to long distance transport. Of course, if goods are transported over hundreds of kilometers, the absolute contribution of long distance transport to the total material intensity of goods and services remains dominant. But, in total, highways contribute only 15% to the whole annual material consumption of road infrastructure. Similarly, material intensity of trucks and ocean-going hips declines with increasing vehicle´s size by a factor of 5-7 (Fig. U3; STILLER, 1995,1996).

Fig. U3: Material Intensity of Transport Systems - Germany 1992: Water

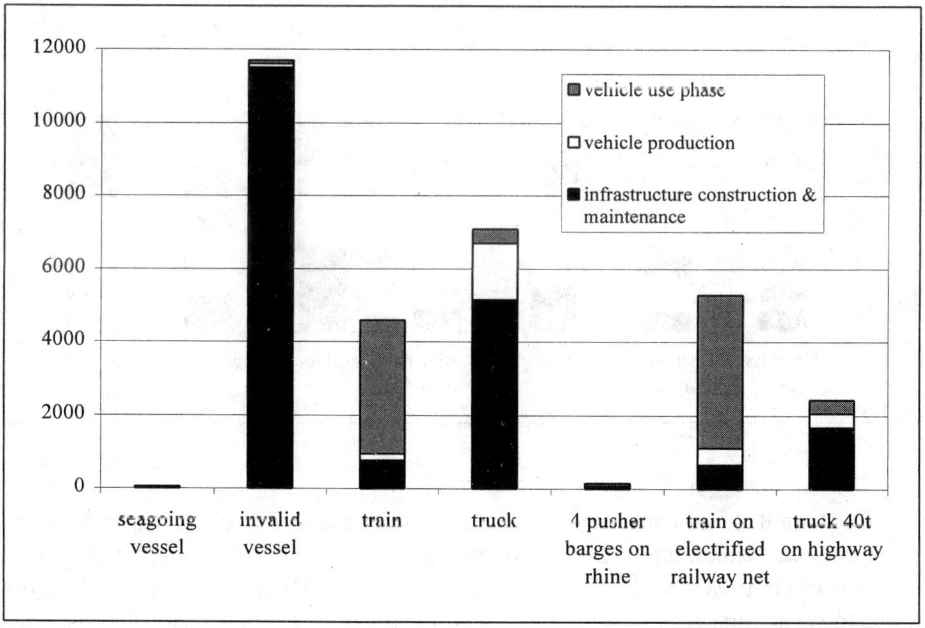

Therefore, micro-distribution has to be given more attention. Not only highways but also all local roads are connected with huge material consumption. A spacial-structure and urban sprawl, which in the statistical extreme leads to the separate settlement of each German citizen 66m away form his neighbour is more unecological than most cities. Finally, the scale effects lead to overlapping in the material intensity of different transport modes for some applications. Especially for small traffic and transport volume, the use of generally less ecological transport modes can have an ecological advantage.

Fig. U4: Material Intensity of Road Infrastructure - Germany 1992: Abiotic Raw Material

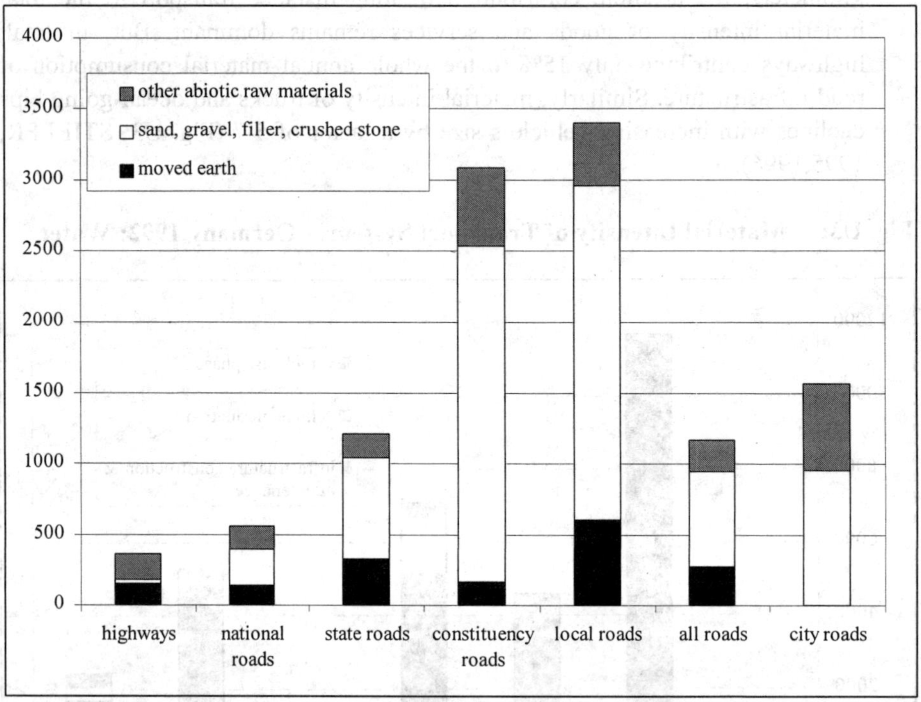

4. Each unit of transport is associated with loading, handling and unloading processes which have to be accounted in t/t. Unfortunately, as these processes are often linked with storage processes, their calculation is rather difficult. However, first results show that, in counterbalance to the previously described scale effects, the material intensity of the transfer of goods increases with the size of the transport units. Whereas material input for sea transport is rather low, for each handling in west European harbours nearly 500 kg/t of abiotic raw materials are moved. For a typical 8000 km sea crossing transport this would result in a MI of 60 g/-tkm, ten times more than the MI of the ocean-going ship use. Transfer installations of inland navigation and rail yield similar

absolute contributions to the material intensity . These figures have to be taken into account by the ecological optimisation of transport chains.

Tab. U1: Estimation of the Material Intensity of Transfer Installations, Germany 1991-92

Estimate of the Material Intensity of Handling Installations kg/t transfer of goods					
		abiotic raw materials		**water**	**air**
		all	dredging		
freight stations		>5		19	1,1
inland harbours		20	16	12	>0,7
sea harbours	all	491	486	27	>0,7
	crude oil	844	843	9	>0,2
	containers	430	425	29	>0,7
	bulk materials	430	425	27	>0,6

Source: STILLER(1995a,b); own calculations.

Tab. U2: Long-term Marginal Material Intensity in % of the Total

	Highways (% of total)	**all roads** (% of total)
abiotic ressources	27	51
water	70	66
air	87	82

Source: STILLER (1995a,b); own calculations.

5. The marginal material intensity of existing infrastructure is, of course, smaller than for new construction. However, it is far away from being zero in the long run. New paving, repairing of bridges etc. are is calculated to consume between 27 and more than 50% of the material input required for primary construction (Tab. U2).[2] Similarly, continous harbour and waterway dredging for (inland) navigation and renewal of rails and ballast lead to significant material flows which follow the already constructed infrastructure. Thus, it cannot be argued that exisiting infrastructure can be neglected for decision making.

6. Implications for Sustainable Mobility

The presented results indicate that, albeit necessary, raising gasoline taxes alone will not solve the ecological problems connected with transport as they would mainly yield only a slightly decrease in the air consumption in the material intensity. Rather we have to think about how it can be achieved that supply and demand, that the decision-making process of investors and users take more into consideration the large material flows in infrastructure.

Material efficiency of infrastructure networks significantly depends on the transport volume of the network. Today the highway network is used rather efficiently, while the bulk of the German railways are not intensively used. On the other hand, the German railway company has up to now failed to improve rail management on its key connections, thus restricting their use.

Similarly, the MIPS analysis for waterways reveals large differences in the ecological efficiency on various subsegments. Transport volume is rather small, especially on the upper parts of some rivers which have been canalized with enormous efforts. In these cases investment didn´t recognize the limited demand, leading to ecological as well as economical inefficiencies.

High, unsustainble material intensity is the consequence of such developments. From the point of view of existing infrastructures this has to be welcomed as increasing transport volume ceteris paribus is not very ecological. However, infrastructures are investments connected with large material flows. If the above mentioned dematerialisation takes place by a factor of ten, transport volume would be reduced dramatically which would even increase inefficiency in infrastructure use. The question arises whether these developments are inevitably a consequence of structural development or a consequence of wrong incentives. It seems to be necessary that at least those developments should be considered in the decision-making process on future infrastructure investment.

WELFENS et al. (1996) have shown that automotive traffic is granted so-called shadow subsidies, e.g. for parking. This is one of the counterproductive incentives which should be abolished. If free parking in city centers did not exist and all parking spaces would cost more or less the same, there wouldn´t be any incentive for visitors to look around for the cheapest parking place causing a lot of traffic. Also, incentives to use public transport and sharing initiatives would be encouraged.

Further, the actual financing of infrastructure, which neglects the demand side or does not calculate it realistically for political reasons, should be revised. It should be investigated whether financing and operation which are more orientated towards market calculation, would yield economical and ecological advantages.

Apart from railroads transport infrastructure in general is supplied by the state. As a result, there is motivation to neglect the real demand for political reasons. As German regional and local infrastructure in general is financied by money coming from various state levels, for local authorities infrastructure seems to be cheaper than it really is (see also KNOFLACHER, 1990; WINK 1996). A good example of this effect are also the structural funds of the European Union which grant financial aid to infrastructure projects for political reasons as the idea of economic cohesion in the European Union. Today in peripheral regions of the European Union infrastructure projects can be visited which would never have been constructed if they had been paid for by local money alone. In would seem to be better if those who decide on and have the benefit of an infrastructure were also the ones who pay for it, and in those cases where a combined interest of various state acteurs exist, if the contribution of the higher regional administrative body would be reduced.

This also implies a reformulation of the funding criteria because funding is often linked to an appropiate (large) dimension of new infrastructure. However, it must be mentioned that the demand for larger roads also results from the increasing speed of vehicles.

Privatisation of infrastructure networks, however, only makes sense if real competition can be organized. Otherwise a state monopoly is to be preferred. Competition can be organized on long distance infrastructure in the form of competing transport modes, but for local infrastructure in general only by temporary limited monopolies. Here operating companies, which after a call for tender receive a licence for 5 to 10 years for operation and maintenance, could be a model for putting such ideas into operation. However, for such long-term investments like infrastructure, where specific local features and regulations play a big role, it has to be checked if markets like those for goods can be organized. There is some evidence that in the case of full privatisation the high sunk costs in infrastructure investment would create large barriers for new competitors to enter the market (KNIEPS, 1991,12).

Results for infrastructure networks show that not only the micro-distribution of goods but also passengers contribute to a large extent to the total material flows of transport infrastructure. Thus, it has to be discussed whether those parts of infrastructure could not be much smaller than in the past: smaller dimensions would imply smaller vehicles in freight transport, but also reduced speed in urban areas.

However, one of the driving forces for oversizing of infrastructure is the high handling costs which act as an incentive for not changing between different transport modes. Thus, these costs are reducing the competition between the transport modes like rail and road, and result in an obstacle to using of the most material productive transport mode. Furthermore, they create a strong demand for oversized local infrastructure to allow the use of large, and according to the actual shadow subsidized prices, cheaper vehicles. Thus, it is ecologically desirable to develop material and cost efficient handling processes.

Besides a more efficient supply of infrastructure, a more adequate charging of their users has to be discussed. Costs of infrastructure including the ecological costs should be addressed as closed as possible to those using it (BAUM 1991, 17), recognizing the polluter pays principle although there always remains a large degree of latitude. However, traffic density for a lot of roads does not seem to require a time dependent road pricing as it would be the most accurate way for cities and highways. If road pricing is not introduced, e.g. for international reasons, it should then at least be considered whether the tax on vehicles should be raised on a local level to relink tax payment and the demand for infrastructure supply (KÅGESON 1993, 151).

Finally, it has to be examined whether or not a regional structural policy which tries to compensate for the specific disadvantages of life in cities, on the one side, or in the countryside, on the other side, by granting shadow subsidies does in effect lead to unecological structures and an unsustainable high level of mobility.

Endnotes

[1] Exceptions are e.g. specific infrastructures to give large mines access to the international transport networks.

[2] Results for highways are smaller because of the larger portion of moved earth for route location

References

BAUM, H. (1991), Infrastrukturpolitik als Mittel zur Steuerung des Verkehrsträgerwettbewerbs, in: Zeitschrift für Verkehrswissenschaft, 62nd Volume, Issue 1, p. 6-19.

BRINGEZU, S. et.al. (1995), Indicating environmental pressure for national economies and industrial sectors on the basis of integrated economic and environmental accounting. Paper presented at the Scientific Workshop on Indicators of Sustainable Development, organized by SCOPE et al., Wuppertal, November 15-17.

BRINGEZU, S., H. STILLER. and F. SCHMIDT-BLEEK (1996), Material Intensity Analysis - a screeing step for LCA, in: Proceedings of the 2nd International Conference on EcoBalance, Tsukuba.

BUNDESMINISTER FÜR VERKEHR BMV,ed., (1994), Verkehr in Zahlen.

DEUTSCHE BAHN (DB) AG (1991), Geschäftsbericht, Berlin.

DEUTSCHE BAHN (DB) AG (1992), Geschäftsbericht, Berlin.

ENDERLEIN, H. and U. KUHNERT (1990), Berechnung der Kosten und der Ausgaben für die Wege des Eisenbahn-, Straßen-, Binnenschiffs- und Luftverkehrs in der Bundesrepublik Deutschland für das Jahr 1987, DIW, Beiträge zur Strukturforschung , Issue 119, Berlin.

ENDERLEIN, H. and U. KUHNERT (1992), Ermittlung des Ersatzinvestitionsbedarfs für die Bundesverkehrswege, DIW, Beiträge zur Strukturforschung , Issue 134, Berlin.

FACTOR 10 CLUB (1994), Carnoules Declaration, Wuppertal.

HASSEL, D. et al (1995), Abgas-Emissionsfaktoren von Nutzfahrzeugen in der Bundesrepublik Deutschland für das Bezugsjahr 1990. Final report of the TÜV Rhineland, ed., Berlin.

HEUSCH, H. and J. BOESEFELDT (1994), Nutzfahrzeug-Jahresfahrleistungen 1990 (1986) auf den Straßen der Bundesrepublik Deutschland, Aachen.

HÖPFNER, U. et al. (1993), Motorisierter Verkehr in Deutschland 1988 und 2005, Studie des Institut für Energie- und Umweltforschung IFEU, Heidelberg, on behalf of the German Federal Environmental Agency, Berlin.

KÅGESON, P. (1993), Getting the Prices Right. A European Scheme for Making Transport Pay its True Costs. European Federation for Transport and Environment (T&E), Stockholm.

KNIEPS, G. (1991), Möglichkeiten und Grenzen einer Privatisierung im Verkehr, in: Privatisierung im Verkehr, Schriftreihe der Deutschen Verkehrswissenschaftlichen Gesellschaft e.V. B145, Bergisch Gladbach.

KNOFLACHER, H. (1990), Finanzstrukturen im Verkehrswesen und ihre Auswirkungen, in: Beiträge zur Verkehrsplanung 1/1990, Institut für Verkehrsplanung und Verkehrstechnik, Technische Universität Wien.

MAILBACH, M., D. PETER and B. SEILER (1995), Ökoinventare Transporte. Grundlagen für den ökologischen Vergleich von Transportsystemen und den Einbezug von Transportsystemen in Ökobilanzen, von INFRAS, Zürich.

MANSTEIN, C. (1996), Das Elektrizitätsmodul im MIPS-Konzept, Materialintensitätsanalyse der bundesdeutschen Stromversorgung (Öffentliches Netz) im Jahr 1991, Wuppertal Papers No. 51, Wuppertal.

PREIMESBERGER, C. (1994), Die Materialintensität pro Dienstleistungseinheit als ökologische Schadschöpfungseinheit der betrieblichen Stoffflußwirtschaft. Diplomarbeit, Linz/Halstatt.

SCHALLABÖCK, K. O. and M. HESSE (1995), Konzept für eine Neue Bahn, Wuppertal.

SCHMIDT-BLEEK, F. (1994), Wieviel Umwelt braucht der Mensch ? MIPS - Das Maß für ökologisches Wirtschaften, Basel, Boston, Berlin: Birkhäuser Verlag.

SCHMIDT-BLEEK, F., ed. (1996), MAIA - Einführung in die Materialintensitätsanalyse nach dem MIPS-Konzept, Wuppertal.

STILLER, H. (1993), Material consumption in transport infrastructure, in: Fresenius Environmental Bulletin, Vol. 2, No 8, Basel, pp. 467-472.

STILLER, H. (1995a), Materialintensitätsanalysen von Transportleistungen (1), Seeschifffahrt, Wuppertal Papers No. 40, Wuppertal.

STILLER, H. (1995b), Materialintensitätsanalysen von Transportleistungen (2), Binnenschifffahrt, Wuppertal Papers No. 41, Wuppertal.

STILLER, H. (1995c), Bilanzierung von Stoffströmen in der Schiffahrt, in: Das Schiff in Leichtbauweise, 16. Duisburger Kolloquim Schiffstechnik / Meerestechnik, p. 207-208, Duisburg.

STILLER, H. (1996), Materialintensitätsanaylse von Transportleistungen - Neue Prioritäten für Instrumente ?, in: KÖHN, J. and WELFENS, M. J., eds., Neue Ansätze in der Umweltökonomie, Marburg.

VERKEHRSWISSENSCHAFTLICHES INSTITUT der RWTH Aachen VIA (1990), Spezifischer Energieeinsatz im Verkehr, Ermittlung und Vergleich der spezifischen Energieverbräuche, Aachen.

VON WEIZSÄCKER, E.U., A. LOVINS and A. H. LOVINS (1995), Faktor 4, Springer Verlag, München.

WELFENS, M. J. et al. (1995), Schattensubventionen im Bereich des Automobilverkehrs, in: KÖHN, J. and WELFENS, M.J. (eds.), Neue Ansätze in der Umweltökonomie, Marburg 1996.

WINK, R. (1996), Verkehrsinfrastrukturpolitik in der Marktwirtschaft, Schriftenreihe des RWI, Volume 59, Essen.

Comments on: Material Intensity of Transportation and Implications for Sustainable Mobility in Europe

Rainer Hillebrand

Hartmut Stiller's paper deals with the material intensity of transport. Some often neglected, but very important issues of the environmental dimension of transport are raised. These aspects are becoming ever more significant as the process of economic globalization leads to longer transportation hauls and a rising number of transport processes and, therefore, increasing transport-induced environmental problems. Though the broadening of the view on the environmental effects of transport is commendable the link between Stiller's line of arguments and the suggested policy recommendations remains rather unclear. Let me critically outline the approach and then briefly refer to the neoclassical approach of environmental economics.

The Material Input Analysis of Transport

The environmental harmfulness of transport is often reduced to the emissions - in particular air pollution - caused by the various transport modes during the process of moving a good from location A to B. In fact, this is not the whole story. In order to change location, goods usually have to be stored, loaded and handled. Moreover, the movement itself requires adequate infrastructure and transport means which need to be constructed and maintained. Seen from this "cradle to grave" perspective transport leads to more material flows than the usually discussed emission of air pollutants. Five main categories of material flows can be distinguished: abiotic raw materials, biotic raw materials, soil, water and air. According to Stiller abiotic raw materials, water and air are of prime interest in the case of transport (but one should not forget the soil consumption by transport infrastructure, especially the reduction in natural living space).

Material intensity analysis faces the challenge of assigning specific material consumption to a transport service unit, i.e. - in economic terms - to determine an input/output relation. The first problem arises with the definition of a service unit. This definition should not be restricted to the volume of freight being transported and handled (measured for example in tons) because a service unit also depends on the way the transport is carried out, above all on the velocity, flexibility, frequency and reliability of the transport activity. This multi-dimensionality of the service unit leads to "millions of different transport services" which have to be reduced to "a few easy to handle numbers" for the application in material intensity analysis. But due to the standardization of the service unit and its confinement to purely physical terms (instead of valuation with prices) the material intensity indicator can no longer be used as a criterion for an individual's case-specific decision. It thus only serves as "a screening tool that provides a first approximation of the order of magnitude to the environmental impact potential" of transport services.

On the material input side further problems occur. Infrastructure and vehicles are not specifically built for a single transport act, but serve different needs at the same time and the same need at different times. As a consequence overheads have to be allocated to the single act of transport. This is problematic for several reasons: (a) The future use of infrastructure and vehicles has to be estimated, both with respect to lifetime and future utilization intensity, in order to be able to calculate the share which has to be allocated and charged to the act of transport in question. (b) The material input of providing a certain piece of infrastructure differs according to local and regional conditions like industrial structure, population or topography. Thus, on the one hand, a deep classification has to be made in order to avoid meaningless averages, on the other hand, the availability of statistical data restricts the possible grades of classification. (c) The material input for construction and maintenance of single roads or channels is accompanied by external net effects due to the net character of infrastructure. Though Stiller deals with these problems he again only does so with reference to physical units. The outcome of the material intensity analysis is eventually measured in g (material input) per t-km (service output).

In his paper Stiller basically faces the shortcomings of the material intensity analysis. Nevertheless he comes to the following main findings: According to the ranking of material intensities for Germany in 1992, "transport should be provided best by ocean-going ships, followed by inland navigation, trains and finally trucks". Stiller emphasizes that the neglect of transport infrastructure's and vehicles' material input during construction and use leads to an ecological misallocation (though it has to be mentioned that the purely emission-oriented studies come to the same ranking of transport means in terms of ecological harmfulness but for different reasons). Stiller's conclusion is that a rise in gasoline taxes alone will not solve the environmental problems of transport. Rather additional actions have to be taken: subsidies such as free parking in cities should be abolished, infrastructure supplied in accordance with demand (best accomplished through privatization) and/or systems of road pricing need to be introduced.

There should be no doubt: Stiller's suggestions on how to solve the environmental problems of transport cannot be argued with. Rather unclear remains the role played by material intensity analysis in justifying these steps (GAWEL, 1996). Though no valuation quantities are calculated during the analysis the conclusion refers to price instruments. This throws up a number of questions: Who needs the information revealed by the analysis and what for? What does the pure information on volumes of air used or abiotic raw material transfered tell us about the environmental harmfulness of material flows? How can g/t-km of air compare to g/t-km of abiotic raw material without valuation at some kind of prices? Should any decisions concerning the expansion of the infrastructure be derived from material intensity analysis given the restrictive assumptions? Does an entrepreneur or a household take into account the material intensity of different transport systems when choosing between such systems? And if so where does he obtain the adequate information from for his specific case when statistics only offer highly aggregated data? As long as these questions cannot be answered satisfactorily there exists no need for a material intensity analysis except for providing a very first general assessment of the link between transport and the environment.

A Neoclassical Approach

Instead of the aggregation approach underlying material intensity analysis the neoclassical solution to the environmental effects of transport focuses on the decision faced by the individual economic agent. It is based on the assumption that the individual maximizes his or her welfare under a given set of rules and conditions. The task therefore is to change these rules and conditions adequately. If the rules, for example, take into account fees for parking, using roads, airports or stores as well as charges for emitting air pollutants - i.e. the internalization of all external costs (MACKENZIE, DOWER, CHEN, 1992) - the environmental rucksack of alternative transport services will automatically be included in individual decisions: Goods that have been transported by trucks in a more pollutive way will then *ceteris paribus* be more expensive than those transported by ocean-going ships (though transport by ships, vessels or trains does usually require additional road transport for final distribution.). Accordingly individuals will consume more of the cheaper good, thereby diminishing environment-intensive consumption and increasing the market share of environment-efficient consumption. Individuals' maximization processes which take into account the scarcity of environmental resources will therefore result in sustainable mobility.

Thus, the challenge, which increasing transport processes compel us to face, is to implement adequate instruments that reflect the price of using scarce resources rather than to calculate material intensities.

References

GAWEL, E. (1996), Neoklassische Umweltökonomie in der Krise?, in: KÖHN, J. and WELFENS, M.J., eds., Neue Ansätze in der Umweltökonomie, Marburg: Metropolis, pp. 45-87.

MACKENZIE, J. J., R. C. DOWER and D. D. T. CHEN (1992), The Going Rate: What it Really Costs to Drive, World Resources Institute, June 1992.

V: The Transport Multimodal - European Transport Network

Daniel Höltgen

1. Introduction

Let me first of all thank you for the invitation to speak today at such an important - and I think *necessary* - conference on the subject of international infrastructure. The issues we are discussing today are in many cases global problems, which we are approaching from a European and pan-European perspective. I therefore welcome this conference as an opportunity to contribute to an informed debate on infrastructure decision-making and to consider *which types of infrastructure* in particular need to be developed to ensure economic integration and, in the case of transport, an efficient and sustainable transport system.

As you know, the free movement of people, goods and capital has from the outset been regarded as one of the main objectives of the European Community. For many years, the primary role of Community transport policy has therefore been to *remove the technical and institutional barriers* that exist between the Member States. In essence, the aim was to create a *common transport market*.

2. Trans-European Networks (TENs)

However, it has become more and more evident that a common transport market is not alone sufficient in providing free mobility in a region as large and diverse as the European Union, now representing 15 countries with a total population of some 370 million. The citizens of Europe, and its growing trade cannot move freely without the proper means to do so. This is why the European Union has gone a step further, and engaged upon a *major infrastructure programme* for *Trans-European Networks* (TENs). I must emphasise that this really marks a *new era in transport planning*, which has traditionally been a national domain. TENs are intended to meet the increasing demand for fast, reliable and safe transport while at the same time contributing to *economic and social cohesion* among the Member States.

But TENs are not only designed to bring people and markets closer together. They must be seen as a pre-condition for the functioning of the Single European Market under conditions that are sustainable in the long-term. If we believe our forecasters, the volume of passenger and goods traffic in Europe will continue to grow, and perhaps even *double*, in the next two decades. In freight transport, much of this growth will take place on Europe's already congested roads.

The railways, on the other hand, might well continue their decline to a market share of *only 5% of all goods traffic* by the year 2010.

This *business-as-usual scenario* is perhaps rather pessimistic, but I think we have to face the realities and plan methods for dealing with the current traffic trends. Today, all parties concerned are agreed that the continuing growth of traffic, in particular of road transport, is causing serious environmental and social problems which are detrimental to our personal welfare and also to the economy as a whole. Furthermore, increasing congestion and subsequent delays are posing a real threat to Europe's competitiveness. Transport policy clearly needs to address these problems - the question is *how* and with *what measures*.

3. Towards a Multimodal Approach

At the Commission, we believe the current situation cannot be resolved with a conventional *unimodal* approach which treats each mode individually and without connection. Our proposals for the TENs therefore seek to develop an *integrated network* which should benefit the use of less environmentally harmful transport modes and facilitate the *interchange between different modes*. In short, we believe TENs need to *prioritise multimodal infrastructure*.

However, all of you will agree that we are still a long way from achieving a truly integrated, multimodal and *trans*-European network. In fact, the reality is rather a *patchwork* than a network. And despite all attempts and declarations, intermodal transport is still the exception rather than the rule.

Of course, some countries are more advanced than others, but in general, the Union still has to overcome long traditions of national and sectoral planning. To a certain extent, these traditions are already outdated following the development of increasingly global logistics chains and the introduction of worldwide Information and Telecommunications Systems, which are set to revolutionize transport as we know it today. It is clear that we are only just now starting to develop the organisational and institutional tools for creating our European network and the information systems which complement it.

This brings me to the main *institutional and political aspects of developing multimodal transport infrastructure in the European Union.*

Since many of you will have more experience of decision-making at national and regional levels, I will keep to the principle of subsidiarity and focus on the problems we are facing at the Union level.

4. Institutional Development of TENs

Allow me to summarize the main steps and elements in the TENs programme as it has developed over the last few years.

The Maastricht Treaty on European Union in 1992 formally gave the Community a mandate to contribute to the establishment of trans-European networks in the fields of transport, telecommunications and energy infrastructure. Article 129b of the Treaty stipulates that the Union should promote:

- the *interconnection* and *interoperability* of national networks;
- the rights to *access* these networks;
- the development of *projects of common interest*, taking into account the need to connect island, landlocked and peripheral regions with the central regions of the Community.

The aim is not, therefore, to develop new infrastructure as such - this remains the reponsibility of the Member States - but to *interconnect* and *harmonize* national networks, and to *overcome technical and institutional bottlenecks*. In order to achieve these aims, the Treaty entrusts the Union with five main tasks:

- firstly, to establish *guidelines* covering the objectives, priorities and broad outline of measures necessary to identify *projects of common interest*; these are key links specified on maps for rail, road, inland waterways and airport networks;
- secondly, to take any measures that may be necessary to ensure the *interoperability* of networks, especially in the field of *technical standardization*;
- thirdly, to support - and I must emphasise *support, not replace* - the financial efforts of Member States towards projects of common interest, in particular through feasibility studies, loan guarantees and interest-rate subsidies.
- fourthly, to co-ordinate developments among Member States: this, I think, is the real challenge for the Member States set out in Article 129c of the Treaty which states that Member States, in liason with the Commission, shall *co-ordinate their national policies* towards achieving the trans-European networks. This clearly implies a *common effort*, but at the same time it indicates that the main responsibility for building the network remains with the Member States.
- and finally, to co-operate with the so-called "third countries", which means working together closely with Central and Eastern Europe, the Mediterranian region and, of course, Switzerland in the context of the European Economic Area.

5. Financing TENs

Regarding this last point, it may be useful to add a few words on financing. A number of important sources of funding have been identified at the EU level. The European Investment Bank has already loaned some 6.4 billion ECUs for the TENs. In addition, the European Investment Fund was set up in 1994 to provide loan guarantees to projects on a commercial basis.

The Cohesion and Regional Development Funds support certain infrastructure projects in the less prosperous regions of the Union.

Then, there is the specific part of the EU budget dedicated to the Trans-European Network - which offers some 1.8 billion ECUs for the period 1995-1999.

Undoubtedly, these EU funds represent a significant contribution. But they will never even begin to match the overall cost of completing the transport TENs, currently estimated in the region of *400 billion* ECUs. But we must realise that the main financial burden will remain with the Member States.

This of course also means increased involvement of the *private sector* and in particular of *private-public partnerships*. One of the key issues here will be the *allocation of risks and rewards* between the different parties involved. Furthermore, new methods of infrastructure financing will require new kinds of *pricing* which have to be transparent and, above all, *fair*. The Commission has recently published a Green Paper on *fair and efficient* transport pricing - which I shall return to in a moment.

To summarize, the Union's role in the TENs is therefore to act as a *catalyst and problem-solver*; the Union *proposes* the network, it *encourages* the Member States to implement projects and it *tries to find new financial and regulatory solutions* - using its own budget for "leverage".

6. Sustainable Mobility

Another element in the plans for TENs - though it is sometimes forgotten - is the concept of *sustainable mobility*. In the same year as Maastricht, the Commission devoted much attention to this in its White Paper on the future development of the Common Transport Policy. *Sustainable mobility* is an *ambitious* concept for maintaining the level of mobility necessary for economic growth, while at the same time trying to limit the negative effects of transport. In this context, multimodal TENs can be seen as *the physical basis* for achieving sustainable mobility throughout the Union.

7. Priority Projects

In 1993, the White Paper on growth, competitiveness and employment focused the spotlight on the *economic role of TENs* and proposed that their implementation should be *accelerated*. However, in view of the many problems that have to be resolved to speed-up the development of the whole network, the Commission proposed to concentrate on a small number of *priority projects*. As a result of these proposals, the European Council decided to create a special Group of Personal Representatives of the Heads of State, chaired by the then Vice-President of the Commission, Henning

Christophersen. The group's task was to move the TENs forward and indentify the priority projects.

In December 1994, the Essen European Council endorsed the famous *list of 14 priority projects*. These priority projects were selected on the basis of three main criteria:

- their large scale;
- their *maturity* - implying that they could be launched within two years;
- their economic viability and attractiveness to private investors.

Now we know the choice of projects has been criticised by some as political horse-trading - and I could imagine that some of you share these reservations. I would agree that the methodology for evaluating TENs has to be improved. But please bear in mind that we are only just now starting to develop the necessary evaluation tools and criteria. Nevertheless, we have clear goals. I should point out that roughly 80% of the planned investment into the priority projects is allocated to rail, a further 9% to rail/road links and *only about 10% is proposed for new roads*. So there is definitely a *priority* to support alternatives to road transport - and hence, to foster sustainable mobility.

As regards the progress on the priority projects, some are already well on track, such as the Öresund fixed link project between Denmark and Sweden and the introduction of the new TGV-*Thalys* services (although not necessarily with regard to the rapid construction of infrastructure), and the *PBKAL high-speed rail line* to Amsterdam. Other projects unfortunately, have been delayed due to problems of planning and financing. The most common problems seem to be:

- planning procedures lasting up to seven years or even longer;
- lack of communication between the various parties involved;
- the difficulty in attracting private finance;
- and, most importantly, Member States have different ideas about *priorities*.

I think these problems demonstrate that there is a real necessity for co-ordination and co-operation at the European level - a task the Commission is committed to fulfilling.

8. The Co-Decision Procedure

However, TENs are not only subject to intense co-ordination and co-operation between the Member States and the Commission. According to the Maastricht Treaty, the TEN Guidelines have to be decided through *co-decision* between the European Parliament and the Council. As you may know, this has turned out to be a somewhat lengthy and complicated procedure. Finally, on 23 July 1996, the European

Parliament and the Council adopted Decision No. 1692 on Community guidelines for the development of the trans-European transport network. This gives the Community a legal basis for the development of the TENs. On the other hand, it is clear that the guidelines are by nature *indicative* and *do not represent a detailed set of binding rules*. This of course also applies to the priority projects and the environmental question.

The guidelines must be seen as providing a *basic framework* for the establishment of the Trans-European Network and the various aspects which have to be considered in its development. The guidelines do not, I think, determine the precise nature and implementation of the network. In any case, a detailed *revision* of the guidelines has to be undertaken in the next few years - this not a final decision.

9. Multimodal Nodes and Terminals

Let me add that the TENs revision will also cover *multimodal transport infrastructure* - an area in which there is still a lot of work to be done. Let me give you one example.

Apart from the road, rail and waterway networks, the guidelines also outline a *European network for combined transport*. As you know, a crucial element in combined transport are the *nodes*, that is to say the *terminals* which function as *interfaces* between different transportation modes and operators. However, while the Community has been able to establish the key *links* of the network, it has not been able to designate exactly those nodes of which the network is to consist. One reason for this is that the planning of terminals is considered to be subject to subsidiarity. Another reason is that the role of different types of terminals for trans-European traffic has not been fully established yet. To a certain extent, this also applies to seaports, although here there is also a *major issue of competition* - between different ports and different Member States.

Well aware of the political sensitivity of these issues, the Commission is currently examining various options regarding multimodal connection points and I hope to have the first results on combined transport terminals later this summer.

The PACT Programme for Combined Transport

At this point, I would also like to mention that we are currently undertaking an evaluation of our PACT programme.

The programme for Pilot Actions for Combined Transport runs out this year. As many of you will know, this programme aims to enhance the quality of combined transport operations by supporting innovative projects on certain pilot axes. We hope to continue this support in the future, as we are convinced the programme is a small, but effective contribution to the development of multimodal transport.

10. Internalisation of External Costs

Finally, my summary of institutional aspects of TENs infrastructure would not be complete without mentioning the continued efforts of the Community as regards our Common Transport Policy. I would like - only very briefly - to touch upon two current topics: the *internalisation of external costs* and the *Citizens' Network*.

In its Green Paper entitled *Towards Fair and Efficient Pricing*, the Commission has taken up the issue of negative transport externalities which are not yet adequately reflected in user prices. As I indicated at the beginning of my speech, the external costs vary between different modes and increase with the level of congestion. The paper therefore discusses various options for charging for congestion, including road pricing. Of course we realise that such measures will affect different regions and different parts of the population in different ways. Any charging system will therefore have to be *flexible* and take these variations into account. As a result of internalising external costs, however, we should see a clear priority on multimodal infrastructure, which, in turn, should help us take a further step towards sustainable mobility.

Let me add that the Commission is very keen to receive the views of transport users and decision-makers on this "hot issue".

11. The Citizens' Network

Giving priority to multimodal infrastructure is an equally important aspect of the Citizens' Network, which was also presented in a Green Paper at the end of last year. Although public transport remains subject to subsidiarity, we have to realise that many, if not most, traffic problems occur in the area of local and regional transport. Even the best long-distance TENs make little sense if they are not properly interconnected at the local level. This is why the Commission has ventured to propose a policy for integrated urban and regional networks. Our proposals for the Citizens' Network are focused on three main areas:

- information exchange and promotion of best practice among public transport operators, such as the implementation of new through-ticketing and integrated reservation systems;
- extension of public procurement legislation to ensure that public transport tenders are open to EU-wide competition;
- and last but not least, improved funding possibilities for public transport, notably in the area of research & development.

A central aim in the Citizens' Network is therefore to promote projects with a high degree of interconnectivity and intermodality. Major airports, for example, need today to be connected with high-speed rail services.

12. Conclusion

In conclusion, despite the complex institutional procedures and sometimes slow progress, it is important that the Community continues to deliver the political visions for a truly integrated European transport system.

Turning this vision into reality will require a strong financial and political commitment from all of us - in Brussels as well as from the Member States and regions - from the public sector as well as from the private sector. I think there is now a broad consensus that investment in infrastructure is vital to securing employment and prosperity in Europe. Furthermore, it is evident that multimodal infrastructure must play an increasing role in Europe's transport system. In parallel to creating this multimodal infrastructure, however, we need policies that will encourage people and companies to use it. Here, we are still some way from a consenus, but it is already clear that we are heading for a new, pragmatic approach without the national and sectoral constraints of the past.

Trans-European Networks and Fiscal Federalism: The Rationale of European Infrastructure Policy

Claus-Friedrich Laaser

1. Introduction

Trans-European Networks (TENs) in transport, telecommunications, and energy which serve the end of linking together European Union's member states more closely, completing the Single Market, and thereby fostering economic growth all over Europe are a fascinating notion of European integration. Daniel Höltgen from the European Commission has provided in his paper impressive insights into the options and chances of TENs in transport and the actions already taken by the Commission. The purpose of this paper is to present some general reflections on the underlying economic policy rational for infrastructure policy on EU level, in particular to raise again the old - and ugly - question of subsidiarity, or: what may be the European Unions's proper role as supra-national and quasi-federal layer[1] in infrastructure policy in terms of fiscal federalism? This perspective seems justified just because TENs are such a fascinating vision of deepening European integration. For infrastructure policy on European level - at least to the extent as it is envisaged by the TEN initiative - is a new feature of common economic policy and may absorb substantial financial resources in the future.[2] So a careful examination of policy options is called for.

To some extent raising the question of subsidiarity may be outdated. This refers at least to the legal basis, as it is provided by Art. 129b-d of the Maastricht Treaty, where the Union layer already has been granted with the competence of taking actions towards forming and completing Trans-European Networks (TENs) in transport, telecommunications, and energy by (i) providing connections of the national networks of the member states, (ii) easing the access to these networks, both for service providers and end-users of these services, (iii) guaranteeing the (technical) interoperability of the networks, and (iv) helping to enhance the connections of peripheral and insular regions of the Union with the economic centers and core regions. But even if the legal basis has been prepared already, the actual actions taken and planned by the Commission may still be questioned, and this may also be justified by the fact that the Maastricht treaty is not very precise in its definitions and bestowes the Commission with a wide range of economic policy discretion.

2. The Main Characteristics of TENs

What TENs in transport are, and which services they are to render to the integrated European economy, has been comprehensively put forward by Dr. Höltgen in his paper. Of course questions of TEN transport networks play a prominent role in his paper not only because transport issues are the topic of this session, but also because the European Commission can point at various initiatives towards TENs mainly in the transport sector. However, also in telecommunication and energy the Commission has launched several important initiatives (but not all of them finished), if you interpret "infrastructure policy" in a wider sense.

When discussing infrastructure policy, we have to consider various "hardware" and "software" provision tasks in the three network industries that arise when linking European Union's member states' networks more closely with each other. These functions are mutually interrelated. Infrastructure (and infrastructure policy) can be thought upon in a broader or in a narrower sense. Basically one can distinguish between (i) the *provision of infrastructure facilities* themselves including planning, projecting, designing, building, maintaining, and financing on the hardware side - this would be infrastructure (policy) in the narrower sense -, (ii) the complementray task of *(de-) regulating service markets* and formulating *economically rational user-regimes* for the networks on the software side - this would include some kind of institutional infrastructure -, and (iii) finding appropriate *technical and virtual standards, norms, and interfaces* between various network facilities and components, a task where both hard- and software characteristics can be found in. All three components taken together can be thought of as infrastructure and correspondingly infrastructure policy in a wider sense.

In all three network industries addressed by the TEN initiatives the policy mix of these three tasks is different, due to (a) different technical characteristics of the industries, (b) institutional settings in the past and (c) different provisions in the legal foundation of the EC treaty. In the *transport sector* in Europe you have in the case of roads, air transport, and inland shipping a public provision of infrastructure facilities based on the common carrier principle (but in most cases without direct user-cost financing) with meanwhile mostly deregulated carriers on the service side. The deregulation of transport service markets as a consequence of the Single Market Program has stressed the institutional infrastructure policy side in transport. In rail transport you find after the Commisions' directive 91/440 an attempt of introducing the common carrier principle by dividing up rail network provision and rail transport, which has resulted so far, for example, in the German Railway Reform of 1994.[3] Rail networks, however, are still provided mainly by public entities and largely payed for by the tax-payer, but the institutional setting has changed. The institutional question is how to formulate rational user-cost and access regimes to enhance the competitive position of European railways.

In *telecommunications* the provision of hardware infrastructure still lies with the (partly former) public network monopolies which, however, now are going to be exposed to private network competition at least in 1998, when the last markets are opened up and the last service and network monopolies are abolished and the Single Communications Market will be completed with some minor exceptions. A separation of networks and services may (but not necessarily will) become one of several options of future market formation. The future hardware provision itself is not regarded as the future core problem in this industry. This can be regarded as one of the findings of the report of the Bangemann group, who concludes that the ends of infrastructure provision are best served by formulating an efficient regulatory regime, by drawing a welfare-enhancing border-line between the state regulator and private suppliers, and by defining appropriate interfaces (TURNER, 1995b, p. 506). So the emphasis of infrastructure policy in telecommunications lies on the software side.

In the *energy sector* the regulatory task is the most urgent one, too. The Single Energy Market cannot claim to be completed yet in this sector. On the hardware side public or private monopolies in most member states are providing the infrastructure facilities on own acccount, feeling that capital costs can be borne by end-users. Here, however, the very envisaged deregulation and completion of the common carrier principle might create infrastructure problems not known so far, at least according to branch offcials.

Summing up, one can state that hardware problems of TENs - planning, providing and financing infrastructure facilities - at least at the moment arise only in transportation because of a lack of private supply, due to obstacles in raising direct user-costs which would pay for capital amortisation in the long run, but of course the paradigm is changing here, too. Software related tasks - regulating competition and user regimes on the one hand and defining suitable norms and interfaces on the other hand -, however, we find in all three industries.

To be precise: The recent deregulation of transport markets and formulating user-regimes for the member states' railways has been performed already by the Commission on the legal foundation of the Common Transport Policy as given by the old EC-treaty and the Single Market Program of 1985. The same comes true for telecommunication, where deregulating national monopolies is deducted from the Single Market Program, too, in this case motivated by industrial policy considerations. In the energy sector the current discussion on future regulatory guidelines is also based on the aim of completing the Single Energy Market. Concerning infrastructure (hardware) provision in transport, however, the Maastricht Treaty has bestowed on the Union level a new quality of competences.

3. What Fiscal Federalism Tells on the Assignment of Economic Policy Tasks to Various Federal Layers

Of course Dr. Höltgen is representing here the very institution that is promoting the idea of the TENs, the European Commission. It's only natural that his paper stresses the positive impacts of the TENs and the Commissions' competence for preparing the basis of the Union's task to provide border-crossing infrastructure facities. The task of this paper may be to provide some opposing thoughts in order to animate the discussion, though - to put forward this in advance - in principle I do not question an EU competence for infrastructure policy in general, but oppose to the "how", the depth, and the policy-mix of this competence.

Just to rule out a potential misunderstanding: If I'm going to question the Union's competence for providing infrastructure facilities partly and to shed some doubts on the instruments being employed, this does not mean that I would not sympathise with the idea of infrastructure facilities being able to perform their task as complementary means of facilitating and enhancing trade and the spatial division of labour. Just the opposite comes true: no region and no country will be able to join the international division of labour and to reap the fruits of trade and specialisation if it cannot dispose of an efficient transport, communications, and energy infrastructure which facilitates the exchange of goods, services and information.

To quote Fredéric Bastiat, the 19th century French advocate of free trade and a liberally designed market economy: "We have learned that impediments to transport have the same consequences than protective tariffs and vice versa. One can state that a tariff increase has the same implications as a rutty road, potholes amidst the road or even a canyon - or in one word, as an serious obstacle to transport that substantially widens the differential between production costs and pro loco market prices. It is thus indisputable that swamps, canyons, landslips and so on are effective and important protective tariff barriers." (BASTIAT, 1880, pp. 145, own translation). Or to take as a somewhat more actual example the Aschauer debate on the role of public infrastructure for economic growth: The findings of ASCHAUER (1989) of a high correlation between the stock of public infrastructure and productivity growth were from the side of his opponents questioned on the one hand mainly because of methodological, econometrical, and empirical reasons and on the other hand because of doubts in the effectiveness of extra public spending for infrastructure in well-developend industrial countries, but not because of doubts in the basic character of infrastructure as prerequisite for economic development.[4]

So it seems quite clear that free trade, the spatial division of labour and effective competition in the European Single Market needs a complementary and effciently functioning infrastructure - it's no question at all. And it is totally comprehensible that after opening up markets institutionally by the Single Market Program of 1985 the EU - with the Maastricht Treaty of 1992 and the initiatives follwing the White Paper on "Growth, Competitiveness, and Employment" of 1993 (KOM, 1993) - has concentrated her efforts on the complementary infrastructure, on which the exchange of goods, services, and information takes place (TURNER, 1995a, p. 37).

But what we have to ask ourselves is another question, namely for the economic rational of the EU's competence and, in particular, its proper role and instruments in infrastructure policy, or, in general, for the aims and instruments of infrastructure policy on various federal layers in the framework of fiscal federalism. This question has to be asked just because we are so convinced that an effciently functioning infrastructure lies in the core interest of every single member state and forms a kind of "basic need" of successful economic development and growth. In this setting one should think that no one in any single member state should doubt in the necessity of providing infrastructure facilities and linking them together with the other member states, each one providing the facilities within its own territory. So, where's the problem with European infrastructure policy on member states' level and why should the EU as quasi-federal level be involved?

Of course we can find several problems with decentralised infrastructure policy,[5] and the theory of fiscal federalism (either the traditional one with the benevolent Pigovian social welfare maximizer in the background, or the enhanced one which includes political economy and second best arguments[6]) provides an overall justification for an involvement of the federal (or supra-national) level in one or another respect.[7] My reasoning, however, is directed towards stressing the Unions's software competences while questioning the hardware components in the Maastricht Treaty in Art. 129 b-d and the White Paper on "Growth, Competitiveness, and Employment" (KOM, 1993).

The traditional theory of fiscal federalism tells us that the decentralisation theorem which is the normal outcome following from the famous subsidiarity principle (OATES, 1972) is not applicaple if we face border-crossing non-pecuniary externalities between regions or countries, public goods with a high transmission range (going at least beyond national borders), or production costs economies of scale and/or scope that can only be exploited at the central level (See e.g. KLODT/STEHN et al., 1992, pp. 8; LAASER/SOLTWEDEL et al., 1993, pp. 6; LAASER/STEHN, 1996, pp. 63). Second best arguments for central provision would, for example, apply if substantial externalities between various economic policy measures could be found at the central layer, or if serious lock-in-situations or information asymmetries that cannot be tackled directly, were existing. The political economy would, for example, argue in favour of a centralisation of economic policy if the resistence of influential local or national pressure groups had to be overcome (PERSSON, ROLAND and TABELLINI, 1996, p. 4ff.).

4. Applying Fiscal Federalism to Infrastructure Policy

If we look at the characteristics of three network industries, of course we find something from this catalogue of arguments in favour of centralisation, in the first place border-crossing externalities, if infrastructure facilities are not financed by user-costs but by national tax-payers. In this case others can share in the benefits without contributing to the costs. Next, we find network externalities that are a predominant feature of transport, communications, and energy networks (WELFENS, 1995, p. 8). But what follows from this for the policy instruments to be adopted? Or to put the question in another way, which kind of centralisation should be pursued? Is a central planning, providing and financing or co-financing of "hardware" facilities, infrastructure links, roads, rails, fiber-optic cables called for? Or more of a special kind of "software" which could help to smooth hardware provision obstacles between member states if border-crossing network-bypasses are concerned, i.e. rules for the establishment and working of associations of common interest and purpose between the very member states which are directly concerned of the border-crossing infrastructure links?[8]

Taking the different characteristics of the three network industries as granted and applying the criteria of fiscal federalism to them, a clear pro for EU's action can be devoted to the EU competence of *regulating the market order for the user regimes for the infrastructure* and *deregulating service markets*, because here the task lies in formulating and enforcing rules, let me say, in defining the playing rules, which we can look upon as a central task. The referee function may indeed be a task which has to be performed centrally, otherwise one could forget about free exchange of goods, services, persons and capital (the four freedoms of European integration).

A bit less clear cut is the case if we take *norms, standards and interfaces within networks*. Of course, common interfaces facilitate transactions between networks. They help to internalise network externalities and to lower transaction costs. But do we or does anyone at the green table know the actual best interfaces or the most progressive ones to come? Whether there is a central obligation for providing compatibility will highly depend on market structures, competitive positions and market development phases (BLANKART and KNIEPS, 1994). Optimisation of norms and interfaces can only be brought upon on existing knowledge. In early market phases an ex-ante harmonisation of norms - formulating compatible norms - may be harmful and cost pushing, because the dynamic competition for the best solution is hindered. In later phases of the product cycle of the network infrastructure, however, uncompatible norms may be more costly, because competition in or between networks or parts of them is impeded (See also KLODT et al., 1996, pp.121).

Least convincing to me is the case of *hardware infrastructure provision* at the central (European) level, as far as we understand it as performing the very task of planning, providing and financing concrete extra infrastructure capacities (road and rail links, inland waterways and so on). As far as only a very rough "global" network link planning would be concerned, this might still be covered by the internalisation argument. But planning links in details as the guidelines do or co-financing actual infrastructure projects from EU structural and cohesion funds would go too much into the direction of execution of infrastructure plans. And in this respect I distrust very much to Dr. Höltgen's reasoning that the European Commission would only provide information and software, but would not engage in planning and providing. The reason for this distrust is that evaluating and choosing projects for co-financing means actively intervening into the very planning process.

One should not forget that we cannot employ the argument of cost minimisation for this central planning, because any planning action for executing infrastructure plans has to be done twice, nationally and on EU level. Remember that one of the criteria for projects to be included in the EU's co-financing schemes is the completion of the national planning process (WINK, 1996, pp. 305). Thus, also costs for this have to be incurred twice.

Furthermore, subsidiarity means that member states normally should be more capable of identifying their future infrastructure needs and future network bottlenecks than any far away situated central institution. Border-crossing network externalities that are not accounted for in national cost-benefit analyses and that plead in favour of a unified European infrastructure network are an economic problem from the theoretical point of view, but they can normally be internalised in bi- or trilateral agreements between the very concerned member states. Network externalities are most prominent in new networks or in the transition phase between old and new networks, but less in "aged" and already advanced network industries, where they may arise only at local bottlenecks. It is hard to believe that all 15 member states should be involved if a highway link or a transnational high speed rail system[9] is to be planned and built (VAUBEL, 1994). Not the least, the existence of border-crossing externalities does not mean automatically, that the whole task of provision of an entire public service (encompassing all functions needed for this) has to be transferred to the next higher federal layer, but that the task can also be provided by an association of common interest being founded for the very purpose. The rules for agreement, performance, sanctions in case of dissence and the standing orders, of course, are to be provided by the central referee. But this would normally be sufficient to solve even lock-ins and information asymmetries between the concerned member states. Subsidiarity not only applies to the entire task, but also to the means the state can dispose of in doing his job.

There is to me one case concievable, however, where a central infrastructure hardware planning and provision may be called for, namely if free trade and free movement and competition that have been introduced by the Single Market Program would be impeded by a local or national reluctant infrastructure policy (or better: refusal of providing capacities) in order to influence administratively the modal split (PAQUÉ/SOLTWEDEL et al., 1993, pp.60).

5. Some Practical Problems with TEN-Policy

If I turn to some more practical problems of TEN transport infrastructure policy, just let me touch two interrelated issues. If you look at the Maastricht Treaty and the White Paper, there may be a trade-off between internalising border-crossing externalities and regional policy objects. TENs are intended to serve the locational quality not only of Europe as a whole compared with the rest of the world, so to say in global competition, but also of peripheral and insular areas within the Union compared with the economic centers of the Union. Of course both locations - central and peripheral ones and thus the whole EU - can gain in locational quality, if transport networks are enhanced and - admittedly - even the centers will gain if the connections to the periphery are improved.[10] But a trade-off arises if the budget constraint enters the stage: With the same sum of publicly collected and spended money you can either enhance central links - the hub -, as would be called for by the existence of substantial border-crossing externalities and also in terms of global competitiveness of the EU, or you can upgrade center-periphery links - the spoke-rays -, as follows from the aim of cohesion and regional policy. Any EURO you spend for cohesion may be lacking for purposes of enhancing global competitiveness and internalising substantial externalities on links between central locations in Europe, which form the economic rational for TENs at all (WINK, 1996, pp. 302, 306).

Consequently, this trade-off has left its footprints in practical TEN transport infrastructure policy. If internalising network externalities were the main purpose of TENs and EU infrastructure policy, the European Commission's guidelines and infrastructure schemes as well as the list of priority projects for the various transport modes would contain mainly projects enhancing the links between central European regions. From the envisaged infrastructure plans this may at best come true with respect to high speed rail links. But in general, of course, cohesion is the dominant aim, and so the lists contains both kinds of projects, i.e. hub-links, but also links joining the various peripheral regions to the more central regions. Furthermore, due to institutional reasons in the decision making process[11] mainly secondary projects with regional or local impact are included, so that the infrastructure plan reads like a shopping list for all the member states, not only the less wealthy ones. In some respect this reminds me of the youngest (fourth) daughter of a colleague of mine: The first word the little girl was able to speak was not "Mama" or "Papa", but "Me too!".

6. Conclusions

To conclude: Infrastructure is indeed an important locational factor and crucial for economic development. Thus TENs in general are a good thing, but I would prefer a somewhat revised policy-mix with more weight on the software side (internalising and further deregulating), but less weight on the hardware provision side. Even in hardware provision for Trans-European infrastructure-links the central (European) task should lie more on software aspects, i.e. providing and enforcing rules for planning, building and financing by the very member states concerned. The case for an European infrastructure provision competence would be much stronger, however, if one could detect tendencies in member states to use reluctancy in infrastructure provision as a tool of re-regulation transport markets via infrastructure policy thus impairing free mobility of goods and services in the Single Market.

There remains, however, still another so far not mentioned uncomfortable feeling with the EU's TEN initiative, that may follow from granting the infrastructure competence to the EU layer: The competence to plan and provide TEN-links by the EU might lead to an EU right of borrowing or a right to raise central taxes, as has already been discussed in this respect. I would feel uncomfortable with this, because this kind of fiscal sovereignity might only lead to higher public expenditures in the EU in the long run due to (i) less tax competition at the central layer, (ii) more mixed financing by more co-financing programs by the EU and (iii) further centralisation tencencies in other policy areas (based on higher fiscal means at disposal) which might be much less jusitified on public good and subsidiarity grounds than the TENs themselves (LAASER/SOLTWEDEL et al., 1993). By this the trade and competition facilitating and thus welfare enhancing effect of TENs might in the long run be overcompensated by a higher public expenditure quota in the EU

Endnotes

[1] Keep in mind the discussion on whether the EU, at least with the Maastricht treaty, has already gained a status of partial sovereignity of its own or whether it must still be looked upon as a pure association of common interest of the completely sovereign member states, in other words: a kind of club for special purposes (cf. for this discussion GRIMM, 1995). In the first case the EU would be a true federal layer, in the second not. But anyway, the theory of fiscal federalism can be applied to evaluating the pros and cons of the Union's task in any case.

[2] The European Commission' forecast of financial funds needed to link and upgrade TENs in transport amounts to 200 bill. ECU up to the year 2000 and 400 bill. ECU up to 2010. Even if the

Communities' share in financing would not exceed 10 p.c. as it is envisaged this would be a substantial amount. Cf. ERDMENGER (1996, p. 13).

[3] For an assessment of the German railway reform cf. LAASER (1994) and BOSS/LAASER/SCHATZ et al. (1996, ch. B.).

[4] For an appraisal of the Aschauer debate cf. MUNNEL (1993), PFÄHLER/HOFMANN/ LEHMANN-GRUBE (1996), PFÄHLER/HOFMANN/BÖNTE (1996).

[5] For supra-national coordination requirements in infrastructure policy cf. WELFENS (1995; 1996).

[6] For this distinction see PERSSON/ROLAND/TABELLINI (1996, pp. 2).

[7] For a general discussion of an allocation of economic policy tasks to the EU and the member states see CEPR (1993; 1995; 1996) and KLODT/STEHN et al. (1992); LAASER/SOLTWEDEL et al. (1993).

[8] This could be described as an attempt to construct a more "perfect mapping" of the public task (cf. BRETON, 1965) above the member states', but below the Union's level.

[9] With respect to rail transport, one should remind the fact that any problems arising from neglecting border-crossing externalities in rail traffic operation are the result of the old regime of state-owned national railway companies. The more the privatisation and demonopolisation of European railways will progress the less these problems may occur.

[10] Concerning the gains and losses,however, we have to take into account the well-known problem of infrastructure policy for peripheral regions that a better connection of a region with the center may also lead to an economic emptying of the location in terms of domestic product. See for example VICKERMANN (1996).

[11] Criteria for selection of projects are for example the project being included in the member states' national infrastructure plan, a completed planning process and compatibility with the national infrastructure plan. Furthermore, including projects into the lists is connected with financial support from structural and cohesion funds thus producing incentives for member states to apply for inclusion of expensive infrastructure projects of pure national character (see WINK, 1996, p. 306).

References

ASCHAUER, D. A. (1989), Is Public Expenditure Productive? Journal of Monetary Economics, Vol. 23, 177-200.

BASTIAT, F. (1880), Gegenseitigkeit, in BRAUN-WIESBADEN, K. (Hrsg.), Friedrich Bastiat - Eine Auswahl aus seinen Werken, Berlin: F. A. Herbig, 145-149.

BLANKART, Ch. B., G. KNIEPS (1994), Market-Oriented Network Provision, Institut für Verkehrswissenschaft und Regionalpolitik, Albert-Ludwigs-Universität Freiburg/Breisgau, Diskussionsbeiträge, 9, Freiburg i. Br.

BOSS, A., C.-F. LAASER, K.-W. SCHATZ, E. BODE, H. BÖHME, E.-J. HORN, A. ROSENSCHON, B. SANDER, R. SCHMIDT, H. SICHELSCHMIDT, J. STEHN (1996), Deregulierung in Deutschland: eine empirische Analyse, Kieler Studien, 275, Tübingen: Mohr.

BRETON, A. (1970), Public Goods and the Stability of Federalism, Kyklos, Vol. 23, 882-902.

CENTRE FOR ECONOMIC POLICY RESEARCH (CEPR) (1992), Is Bigger Better? The Economics of EC Enlargement, Monitoring European Integration, 3, London: CEPR.

CENTRE FOR ECONOMIC POLICY RESEARCH (CEPR) (1993), Making Sense of Subsidiarity: How much Centralization for Europe? Monitoring European Integration, 4, London: CEPR.

CENTRE FOR ECONOMIC POLICY RESEARCH (CEPR) (1995), Flexible Integration: Towards a More Effective and Democratic Europe, Monitoring European Integration, 6, London: CEPR.

ERDMENGER, J. (1996), Transeuropäische Netze im Bereich Verkehr, EUREG Europäische Zeitschrift für Regionalentwicklung, No. 3, 6-15.

GRIMM, D. (1995), Braucht Europa eine Verfassung? Carl-Friedrich von Siemens-Stiftung, Themen, 60, München: Carl-Friedrich von Siemens-Striftung.

KOMMISSION DER EUROPÄISCHEN GEMEINSCHAFTEN (KOM) (1993), Weißbuch Wachstum, Wettbewerbsfähigkeit, Beschäftigung, Brüssel: EU.

KLODT, H., C.-F. LAASER, J.-O. LORZ, R. MAURER (1995), Wettbewerb und Regulierung in der Telekommunikation, Kieler Studien, 272, Tübingen: Mohr.

KLODT, H., J. STEHN, C.-F. LAASER, R. MAURER, A. D. NEU, R. SOLTWEDEL (1992), Die Strukturpolitik der EG, Kieler Studien, 249, Tubingen: Mohr.

LAASER, C.-F. (1994), Die Bahnstrukturreform - Richtige Weichenstellung oder Fahrt aufs Abstellgleis? Institut für Weltwirtschaft an der Universität Kiel, Kieler Diskussionsbeiträge, 239, Kiel: IfW.

LAASER, C.-F., R. SOLTWEDEL, A. BOSS, H. KLODT, H. LEHMENT, J.-V. SCHRADER, J. STEHN (1993), Europäische Integration und nationale Wirtschaftspolitik, Kieler Studien, 255, Tübingen: Mohr.

LAASER, C.-F., J. STEHN (1996), Marktwirtschaft und Subsidiarität: Die föderative Arbeitsteilung auf dem Prüfstand, Zeitschrift für Wirtschaftspolitik, Vol. 45, Nr. 1, 58-91.

MUNNELL, A. H. (1993), An Assessment of Trends in and Economic Impacts of Infrastructure Investment, in ORGANISATION FOR ECONOMIC CO-OPERATION AND DEVELOPMENT (OECD), ed., Infrastructure Policies for the 1990s, Paris: OECD, 21-54.

OATES, W. E. (1972), Fiscal Federalism, New York: Harcourt Brace Jovanovich.

PAQUÉ, K.-H., R. SOLTWEDEL et al. (1993), Challenges Ahead - Long-Term Perspectives of the German Economy, Institut für Weltwirtschaft an der Universität Kiel, Kieler Diskussionsbeiträge 202/203. Kiel: IfW.

PERSSON, T., G. ROLAND, G. TABELLINI (1996), European Integration and Theory of Fiscal Federalism, in: Siebert, Horst (1997), Quo Vadis, Europe?, Thübingen: Mohr.

PFÄHLER, W., U. HOFMANN, U. LEHMANN-GRUBE (1995), Infrastruktur und Wirtschaftsentwicklung. Kritische Bestandsaufnahme, Erweiterungen und Fallstudien, in OBERHAUSER, A., Finanzierungsprobleme der deutschen Einheit III. Ausbau der Infrastruktur und kommunaler Finanzausgleich. Schriften des Vereins für Socialpolitik, N.F., 229/III, Berlin: Duncker & Humblot, 71-188.

PFÄHLER, W., U. HOFMANN, W. BÖNTE (1996), Does Extra Public Capital Matter? An Appraisal of Empirical Literature, Finanzarchiv, N.F. 53: 68-112.

TURNER, C. (1995a), The Financing of Trans-European Networks: Are the Member States Committed? European Business Journal, Vol. 7, No. 2, 37-42.

TURNER, C. (1995b), Trans-European Networks and the Common Information Area: The Development of a European Strategy, Telecommunications Policy, Vol. 19, No. 6, 501-508.

VAUBEL, R., (1994), EU/Transeuropäische Netze und Subsidiarität, Kollektiv ersetzt Bilateralismus, Handelsblatt, Nr. 238 vom 9./10.12.

VICKERMAN, R. W. (1996), Restructuring of Transport Networks, EUREG Europäische Zeitschrift für Regionalentwicklung, No. 3, 16-26.

WELFENS, P. J. J. (1995), Koordinationserfordernisse der EU-Infrastrukturpolitik, Europäisches Institut für internationale Wirtschaftsbeziehungen, Universität Postdam, Diskussionsbeiträge, 9, Potsdam: EIIW.

WELFENS, P. J. J. (1996), Koordinationserfordernisse der EU Infrastrukturpolitik, in KARL, H. (Hrsg.), Die Koordination der Finanz- Währungs- und Strukturpolitik in der EU, Institut für Europäische Integrationsforschung e.V.

Bonn, Bonner Schriften zur Integration Europas, Bd 7, Bonn: Europa-Union Verlag.

WINK, R. (1996), Transeuropäische Verkehrsnetze: Für Wachstum oder für regionale Umverteilung? Wirtschaftsdienst, Vol. 76, No. VI, 301-308.

W: Panel Discussion: Transportation and Electricity Networks: Financing Infrastructure Investments in Europe and Russia

Financing Transportation and Electricity Networks in Europe and Russia

Christoph Schalast

1. From the point of view of a lawyer, any foreign or national investment in Networks in Russia, the CIS or other reforming countries in Middle and Eastern Europe can only be effective for both investor and country if the following basic preconditions are fulfilled:

- modern and easily comprehensible regulations for the energy sector, the transportation sector, and other sectors, and the most important neighboring legal fields such as competition law.
- implementation of these regulations by local and regional authorities and the courts
- knowledge of the regulations in force and professional advice
- legal security and certainty.

I will concentrate my speech here on the Energy Sector. The comments are based on a study, which I carried out in the Spring of 1996 for the General Directorate of Research of the European Parliament (European Parliament, 1996).

2. Before 1990 most of the former communist countries had no special legal rules relating to the energy sector. This sector was more or less integrated into the planned economy system and had the principal task of supplying the energy required by industry and private consumers at the lowest possible prices.

Generally speaking, energy sector law is characterised by an assortment of specific structural problems. First energy law cannot be interpreted in isolation from other important neighboring laws. The energy sector is part of the system of rules which make up the economic constitution of a society, that is, the main regulations in the fields of civil law, company law and competition law. For foreign investors, regulations in the field of investment law and tax law are of great importance. In addition many of the rules of public law, such as the responsibilities of local authorities, and public highway laws (rights of way and concessions) are of great importance. The essential concern in energy sector law is, however, political in nature, namely the degree of influence of the State or the State authorities over the sector. The question of deregulation of the energy sector is the subject of a heated debate not only in the Western countries. In the European Union today many different models compete with one another.

In addition, the legal and shareholder structures of companies active in the area of energy generation, distribution and sales are of great importance. In this matter, the restitution- and privatization regulations in the reforming countries must be taken into particular account.

The countries of Central- and Eastern Europe are, generally speaking, interested in investment in the energy sector. In addition the Visegrad Countries are particularly active in seeking membership of the European Union. Therefore, these countries are obliged in the reform process to align their legal systems as far as possible with Community law. The European Energy Charter Treaty is very helpful in this process, because it has for the first time, created binding obligations in international law for an energy sector framework between the member states. The Energy Charter rests on four main principles:

- each state has sovereignty over its own natural resources
- non-discrimination among signatory states
- the principle of market-based price setting
- the fundamental principle of minimization of environmental burdens.

3. As already pointed out, energy sector law reform needs legal security and certainty to create the necessary conditions for foreign investment. On the other hand however, energy law reform must decide on special legal issues such as the influence of the State in the sector, the assignment of the energy sector to public or private law, competitive elements and the emphasis given to environmental considerations. All these are difficult and not easily comprehensible questions for outsiders of the respective legal systems. This returns us to the opening points of my presentation and the necessary legal and administrative basic conditions for investment in the sector.

References

EUROPEAN PARLIAMENT (1996), Ed., East-West Energy Cooperation, Energy and Research Series W-22.

Project Finance in the Energy Sector of the Transition Economies

Matthias Rußwurm

The development of efficient infrastructure is a crucial element in a country's economic transition. Private sector productivity is largely determined by the quality and quantity of infrastructure services. Following the relatively rapid progress caused by low wages and the reallocation of resources in recent years, Eastern and Central European businesses need better telecommunication, energy and transportation services if they are to continue increasing their productivity and remain competitive. This applies above all to regional commercial centres which are important in a country's development.

In the energy sector, capital expenditure has been significantly reduced in the 1990s. Consequently, thermal and nuclear power plants are often not well-maintained, inefficient and comparatively old. Environmental and safety problems will continue to arise. Against this background, Cambridge Energy Research Associates (DEESE, 1996, p.3), a leading research house, predicts that Eastern Europe and the Former Soviet Union (FSU) will require approximately 40 GW of new capacity by 2005, although the installed capacity already exceeds present requirements in the region. Assuming total costs of private power plants at around US $ 1,100 per kW, the investment requirements add up to US $ 44 billion over the next decade. This is half of what is estimated for Western Europe and equals the amount for Latin America.

At the same time, the Transition Economies lack the internal sources of capital to finance the above capital intensive investments. According to the Transition Report 1996 of the EBRD (EBRD, 1996, p.3), their savings rate has fallen from approximately 30% in 1989 to 18% at present. Specifically, there are no long term funds available for private investors in most of these countries. Governmental capital expenditure has sharply diminished due to extreme fiscal pressures. Despite increasing efforts to mobilise household savings and to improve tax raising efficiency, substantial international capital inflows are necessary to meet the investment requirements in the foreseeable future.

International project finance is one method used to fill the gap between the need for infrastructure investment, such as new power plants, and the shortage of domestic capital. In this context, project finance is defined as the risk allocation between the various parties involved in a project that provides lenders with the necessary comfort to finance a specific asset with only limited recourse to the sponsors but based primarily on the future cash flow of the asset itself. Basically, risk diversification across various assets in corporate finance is replaced by risk allocation between various parties in project finance.

What does this approach - involving a special purpose project company as the borrower - offer in comparison with utilities or governments in these transition economies borrowing on a corporate or sovereign basis in the international capital markets?

In financial terms, the project finance approach can provide the following advantages:

First of all, project finance can mobilise large amounts of long term debt that are not available in the domestic market (due to lack of capacity) and would otherwise not be available in the international markets either. The reason for the latter is that lenders may have difficulties assessing the balance sheet of the utility, and that the country itself is not yet able to tap the international capital markets for very long maturities without credit support from other parties. Although the syndicated loan market currently offers very favourable financing terms, most Eastern European countries still find it very difficult to achieve debt funding maturities for longer than 5 years. Power plants, on the other hand, require redemption periods of at least 10 to 12 years. The project bears a refinancing risk if long term assets are financed by short term funds. Traditional risk coverage for up to 12 years from export credit agencies is often not available for the required amounts.

Secondly, a project company borrowing large amounts of long term debt can reduce the cash contribution of the utility or government (financial leverage) thus freeing financial resources for other purposes such as investments in the electricity grid and helping to cope with fiscal problems that prevail more or less throughout the transition economies. Although additional credit enhancement from the utility and government, in particularly undertakings regarding the power purchase, is usually necessary to secure financing, the type of contracts typical in project finance (for example lump sum turn-key construction contracts) limit the exposure of the utility and/or government (risk transfer).

In addition to these financial advantages, project finance demands a very commercial approach when building and operating the power plant. Through competitive bidding the more rigorous selection of plants leads to greater cost-consciousness, market-orientation and realistic pricing of electricity. This is a good starting point for further liberalisation of the power market, which generally involves some kind of vertical disintegration, by means of ownership separation between generation and transmission (creating a wholesale electricity market at the grid level) or by so-called unbundling (maintaining separate financial accounts between generation, transmission and distribution entities within the utility) to create a basis for pass-through fees allowing third-party-access and head-to-head competition for end-users. Furthermore, project finance is a way to choose the best qualified investor for an individual project and to facilitate a transfer of know-how. This applies to brownfield investments in particular.

Altogether, the project finance approach supports the governments and utilities in pursuing a tariff-driven policy, maintaining competitive tariffs despite spikes in fixed cost structures which unavoidably occur when new power plants are commissioned. This objective is supported by identifying risks and advising on their allocation as well as by considering an increasing range of financing options in addition to syndicated loans and export finance facilities.

After having mainly gained project finance experience in telecommunications so far, project finance in the power sector of the transition economies has substantial growth potential. Apart from the pure investment needs, this is fostered by the macroeconomic stability and legal frameworks reflected in the encouraging debt ratings a number of countries have recently gained. As power projects generally earn no foreign exchange and rely heavily on contractual agreements, such issues are of immense importance for investors. At the same time the liberalisation under way in the EC countries will push the international utilities to look for business opportunities in the emerging power markets of the transition economies.

References

EBRD (1996), Transition Report, EBRD London, 80.

Statement on: Transportation Network Financing

Claus-Friedrich Laaser

As far current and future infrastructure investments in Russia, and in all other economies in transition, are concerned, I believe that the raising of funds for maintaining, upgrading and adding to transport network facilities is an even more difficult task than for the two other network industries discussed in this conference.Investment in transport infrastructure, financed by the international capital market or the foreign tax payer need a functioning and stable market economy - encompassing the prevalence of the rule of law, democratic decision making and effectively enforced contracts – as prerequisite.

The reason for this dependency on a stable framework is that depreciation periods for transport infrastructure are quite long, investments are associated with low costs, the pay-off may occur only in the long run, and in most cases can be reaped only in diverted form - namely by the indirect rentability of growing economic activity and increasing tax returns in the future, unless a user-pay scheme is employed. Generally 'hit and run' transport infrastructure investments, allowing for a rapid covering of capital costs and a low risk pay-off after a few years are unlikely. 'Hit and run' investments, however, are the only ones a country can expect to attract if its progress towards a functioning market economy is slow, the rule of law is not fully guaranteed, and an atmosphere of insecurity prevails.

It should be stressed that this kind of institutional infrastructure is crucial to attracting any foreign investment in industry and infrastructure. A country failing to provide a proper institutional framework may become a capital trap for foreign investors, who are forced to take great risks. This is particularly true for infrastructure, due to its above-mentioned characteristics. Hence the transition economies will need to create proper institutional frameworks if they wish to attract large-scale infrastructure investment, whether private or public, the latter provided by tax payers from the West. In this context one should also consider the fiscal drag and the aggravating scarcity of public funds in nearly all Western countries. Even if Western countries, motivated by genuine self-interest, invest in the stable and expanding economic development of reform countries, the Western tax-payer cannot be responsible for the entire task of financing.

If the transition economies are able to fulfil these basic institutional prerequisites, they will encourage investor confidence in an emerging stable economy. Even the transport industry infrastructure is open to major private investors, who could use the new models of 'public-private-partnership' developed in the West in the transition economies (either in financing alone or in conjunction with the operation of infrastructure facilities on a user-pay-system).

Some progress is visible in infrastructure policy already. Let me refer here to an example from my current research. In a report we recently prepared at the Institute, on the current state of the reform process and structural developments in the three Baltic countries Estonia, Latvia, and Lithuania (SCHRADER and LAASER, 1997), we concluded that Estonia had not only caught up with the Visegrad countries in terms of the institutional framework of its market economy , but is now moving towards privatising companies in the infrastructure sector, while Latvia and Lithuania pursue a more traditional infrastructure policy. In Estonia, the national telecommunication provider has already been partly privatised (49% of its shares.) According to the Estonian Privatisation Agency, the privatisation of the transport sector will cover port management and even parts of the national railway system. Foreign investment is welcomed in the recently completed industrial 'big privatisation' push. Estonia is thereby not only attracting urgently needed capital for the upgrading and maintenance of its infrastructure , an area in which, like Latvia and Lithuania, its Soviet heritage is apparent, but it is also managing to import foreign expertise and much-needed know-how. Furthermore, new options for a 'public-private-partnership' in infrastructure can be employed.

References

SCHRADER, K., C.-F. LAASER (1997), Der Transformationsprozeß in den baltischen Staaten: Ordnungspolitische Fortschritte und strukturelle Anpassungsprozesse, Institut für Weltwirtschaft an der Universität Kiel, Kieler Arbeitspapiere, 783, Kiel.

LIST OF CONTRIBUTORS

Dr. Martin Andersson,
Finnish Ministry of Transport and Communications, Helsinki, Finland

Dr. Misha Belkindas,
World Bank, Washington, D.C., USA

Dr. Andreas Brenck,
Technical University, Berlin, Germany

Prof. Dr. Horst Brezinski,
TU Bergakademie Freiberg, Germany

Dr. Herbert Brücker,
DIW, Berlin, Germany

Dr. José Carbajo,
EBRD, London, Great Britain

Dr. Bert Eichhorn,
Eichhorn & Partner, Cologne, Germany

Prof. Dr. Georg Erdmann,
Technical University, Berlin, Germany

Dr. Dieter Elixmann,
WIK, Bad Honnef, Germany

Prof. Dr. Morten Falch,
Technical University, Lyngby, Denmark

Dr. Steven Fries,
EBRD, London, Great Britain

Dr. Cornelius Graack,
University of Potsdam, EIIW, Germany

Prof. Dr. Ruslan Grinberg,
Russian Academy of Sciences, Moskow, Russia

Rainer Hillebrand,
University of Potsdam, EIIW, Germany

Dr. Daniel Höltgen,
European Commission, DG XIII, Brussels, Belgium

Dr. Zdenek Hruby,
Charles University, Prague, Czech Republic

Dr. Piotr Jasinski,
Oxford Economic Consulting Ltd, Great Britain

Prof. Dr. Günter Knieps,
Albert-Ludwigs-Universität, Freiburg i.Br., Germany

Prof. Dr. Jerzy Kubasik,
Technical University of Posnan, Poland

Dr. Claus-Friedrich Laaser,
IfW, Kiel, Germany

Dr. Oliver Lorz,
IfW, Kiel, Germany

Dr. Jürgen Müller,
DIW, Berlin, Germany

Dr. Peter Palinkas,
European Parliament, DG IV,
Luxembourg

Dr. Svetlana Petuhova,
Russian Akademie of Sciences,
Moscow, Russia

Prof. Dr. Wolfgang Pfaffenberger,
University of Oldenburg,
Bremer Energie Institut, Germany

Dr. Lev Resnikov,
Akademie of Sciences, Moscow,
Russia

Dr. Matthias Rußwurm,
Deutsche Morgan Grenfell, London,
Great Britain

Prof. Dr. Pieter Ruys,
Tilburg University, Netherlands

Prof. Dr. Christoph Schalast,
RAe Schalast Claus Schwertfeger,
Frankfurt amm Main, Germany

Alison Sinclair, M.A.,
University of Potsdam,
Germany

Jaqueline Spindler,
FCC, Washington, D.C., USA

Dr. Hartmut Stiller,
Wuppertal Institut für Klima,
Umwelt, Energie, Germany

Dr. Vladimir Voloshin,
Russian Academy of Sciences,
Moscow, Russia

Dr. Alexander Vronetz,
Russian Akademie of Sciences,
Moscow, Russia

Prof. Dr. Paul J. J. Welfens,
University of Potsdam, EIIW,
Germany

Prof. Dr. George Yarrow,
Hertford College, Oxford, Great
Britain

Dr. Dimitri Ypsilanti,
OECD, Paris, France